SL 1Day

FO **NS**
OF **NG**

THIRD EDITION
THIRD EDITION
3 EDITION
EDITION
THIRD EDITION

FOUNDATIONS OF MARKETING

Third edition

David Jobber and John Fahy

 **McGraw-Hill**
Higher Education

London Boston Burr Ridge, IL Dubuque, IA Madison, WI New York San Francisco St. Louis
Bangkok Bogotá Caracas Kuala Lumpur Lisbon Madrid Mexico City Milan Montreal
New Delhi Santiago Seoul Singapore Sydney Taipei Toronto

Foundations of Marketing, third edition
David Jobber and John Fahy
ISBN-13 978-0-07-712190-7
ISBN-10 0-07-712190-2

McGraw-Hill
Higher Education

Published by McGraw-Hill Education
Shoppenhangers Road
Maidenhead
Berkshire
SL6 2QL
Telephone: 44 (0) 1628 502 500
Fax: 44 (0) 1628 770 224
Website: www.mcgraw-hill.co.uk

British Library Cataloguing in Publication Data
A catalogue record for this book is available from the British Library

Library of Congress Cataloging-in-Publication Data
The Library of Congress data for this book has been applied for from the Library
of Congress

Commissioning Editor: Catriona Watson/Rachel Gear
Development Editor: Karen Harlow
Marketing Manager: Alice Duijser
Senior Production Editor: James Bishop

Text design by Graphicraft, Hong Kong
Cover design by Adam Renvoize
Printed and bound in Italy by Rotolito, Lombarda

ISBN-13 978-0-07-712190-7
ISBN-10 0-07-712190-2

Dedication

For Mary Jobber

David Jobber

To Theresa, The screen door slams . . .

John Fahy

The authors

David Jobber is an internationally recognized marketing academic. He is Professor of Marketing at the University of Bradford School of Management. He holds an Honours Degree in Economics from the University of Manchester, a Master's Degree from the University of Warwick and a Doctorate from the University of Bradford.

Before joining the faculty at the Bradford Management Centre, David worked for the TI Group in marketing and sales, and was Senior Lecturer in Marketing at the University of Huddersfield. He has wide experience of teaching core marketing courses at undergraduate, postgraduate and post-experience levels. His specialisms are industrial marketing, sales management and marketing research. He has a proven, ratings-based record of teaching achievements at all levels. His competence in teaching is reflected in visiting appointments at the universities of Aston, Lancaster, Loughborough and Warwick in the UK, and the University of Wellington, New Zealand. He has taught marketing to executives of such international companies as BP, Croda International, Allied Domecq, the BBC, Bass, Royal & Sun Alliance, Rolls-Royce and Rio Tinto.

Supporting his teaching is a record of achievement in academic research. David has over 150 publications in the marketing area in such journals as the *International Journal of Research in Marketing, MIS Quarterly, Strategic Management Journal, Journal of International Business Studies, Journal of Management, Journal of Business Research, Journal of Product Inno-* *vation Management* and the *Journal of Personal Selling and Sales Management*. David has served on the editorial boards of *the International Journal of Research in Marketing, Journal of Personal Selling and Sales Management, European Journal of Marketing* and the *Journal of Marketing Management*. David has acted as Special Adviser to the Research Assessment Exercise panel that rates research output from business and management schools throughout the UK. In 2008, he received the Academy of Marketing's Life Achievement award for distinguished and extraordinary services to marketing.

John Fahy is an internationally recognized academic and one of Ireland's leading marketing thinkers. He is currently Professor of Marketing at the University of Limerick. Prior to this he lectured at Trinity College, Dublin; he holds a Master's Degree from Texas A&M University and a Doctorate from Trinity College.

His research interests are in the areas of marketing strategy, global competition and neuro-marketing. He is the author of three books and over 70 articles in journals including the *Journal of Marketing, Journal of International Business Studies, Journal of Business Research, Journal of Market-Focused Management, European Journal of Marketing, International Business Review* and *Sloan Management Review*. He is the winner of several major international research awards, such as the AMA Services Marketing Paper of the Year Award and the Chartered Institute of Marketing Best Paper Award at the Academy of Marketing Annual Conference. He is also a distinguished case study author and the winner of several case competitions.

He has a distinguished teaching record at all levels including undergraduate, postgraduate and executive, where he specializes in marketing strategy. He also has extensive international experience having held visiting appointments at Senshu University, Japan, Texas A&M University, USA, and Monash University, Australia. He retains close links with industry through consulting assignments and his involvement in executive training programmes, and is regularly invited to speak on business issues.

Brief table of contents

Detailed table of contents

Case list

Vignette list

Marketing Spotlights

Marketing in Action

Preface to the third edition

It has been three years since the last edition of *Foundations of Marketing*; in some ways, so much has changed since then and, in other ways, very little has changed. We have seen the rise of China and India as economic superpowers; Web 2.0 with its social networks and user-generated content was scarcely getting a mention three years ago; and concerns surrounding climate change and sustainability have begun to dominate mainstream debate. The study of marketing has also continued to move on, with themes like consumption, relationships, measurement and technology issues dominating much of what has been written in the past three years.

In other ways, very little has changed. The core concepts of marketing remain the same. The ever evolving customer is still the centre of the marketing universe. No customers means no business. The job of the chief marketing officer (CMO), or whatever designation she has, is still to manage that relationship with the organization's customers. She must understand them, interact with them, and deliver to them the kinds of products and services that meet their needs and wants.

And the exciting thing about marketing is that this relationship between the organization and the customer is always changing and evolving. What we are now seeing is an unprecedented level of power moving to the customer. Marketing is not something that is done *to* customers any more. Customers can avoid interruptive marketing messages like television advertising by simply zapping them. They can quickly find information about products and services through online contact with friends or on shopping websites. The customer is a much more active rather than passive entity. But what this means is that the core idea of marketing, namely the delivery of value to customers, is more important now than it has ever been. Because it is only through the delivery of value in an ever faster-moving and more competitive environment that profit-driven and not-for-profit organizations will survive and prosper.

The third edition

This edition builds on many of the popular features that made the second edition such as success, and includes several exciting new initiatives.

The overall ethos of the book remains the same. Marketing is a real-life activity that everyone engages in on a daily basis, and the book aims to capture that through the inclusion of many examples, vignettes and cases that the modern student can relate to. The structure of the book remains the same, with the logical framework of the marketing plan broadly used to guide the sequence of content. The book retains the popular pedagogical features of the second edition, including the Learning Outcomes and Marketing Spotlights at the beginning of each chapter, Marketing in Action vignettes giving examples of marketing practice throughout the chapter, as well as Summaries, Key Terms and Suggested Reading sections at the end of each chapter to aid revision and further study.

But there are some important new features in this edition. These are now discussed below.

Ethical Debates

For some time now, ethical issues have been important in marketing, and have been featured in previous editions of this book. But in many ways the issue of ethics has tended to be treated as a special case. Companies engage in corporate social responsibility (CSR) programmes and that takes care of their ethical obligations, while some additional pages in a textbook take care of the author's need to discuss ethics in marketing. But when we look at issues in society such as the rise in materialism, obesity among children, people queuing to buy US$5000 handbags while much of the world lives in poverty, it becomes clear that ethics is not a special case but central to marketing. In recent times, the practice of marketing has been the subject of trenchant criticism and has been accused of creating many of society's current ills. Therefore students and practitioners need to know where they stand on these issues.

Ethics are defined as the moral principles and values that govern actions, so therefore one cannot be absolutist about them. Different people will interpret situations using their own frames of reference and will have different opinions. Therefore the discussion of ethics in this book is structured in terms of debates. In total, there are seven Ethical Debates, located throughout the book at appropriate junctures. They are longer than other vignettes, and try to capture both sides of the argument. Like any good debate, they are designed to promote discussion and further inquiry so that readers can make up their own minds.

Technology Focus

Technology has always influenced the practice of marketing. The development of the car created out-of-town shopping centres, the development of television revolutionized how firms communicated with customers. In recent years new technologies, such as mobile telephones, the internet, digital television, and so on, have had a profound effect on business.

Previous editions of the book included e-marketing vignettes to reflect the importance of these technologies and to describe how they were impacting upon businesses. This edition takes a different approach. Information technologies like the internet are now so mainstream in business that treating them separately is redundant. Therefore, in this edition, technology companies and examples of how technology is being used to alter the practice of marketing are integrated into the Marketing in Action vignettes. Whether the piece concerns a technology issue or a non-technology issue does not matter. The purpose of the vignette is to illustrate the practice of marketing and to allow the reader to consider the theoretical implications.

But this in no way downplays the level of attention we pay to technology issues. And because technological changes have the power to radically alter the practice of marketing, we have included five Technology Focus pieces throughout the book. These are extended, detailed and thought-provoking reviews of how technology is currently influencing and will continue to influence the practice of marketing in the future. Taken together with the discussion of internet marketing in Chapter 10, these pieces could enable the educator to develop some stimulating and contemporary classes on e-marketing. They offer readers an opportunity to speculate on the directions that marketing may take. Some, such as the issue of data privacy, are very controversial. For example, current technology enables the creation of sophisticated databases, which assist in the development and management of customer relationships, but it also means that customers' behaviour is accurately recorded and monitored—often without their knowledge or consent. This is clearly an important issue for both organizations and their customers.

Marketing practice

A core concern at a foundational level, is how marketing is practised. What have companies done, how have they done it and has it worked? Like the previous editions, this one provides insights into the world of marketing through a wide variety of Marketing in Action exhibits in each chapter. In all, there are close to 50 such vignettes in the book. The organizations featured are large (e.g. Sony), small (e.g. Tyrell's Potato Chips and Think Nordic ASA), geographically dispersed (e.g. Lenovo and Icelandic Water Holdings), technologically driven (e.g. Last.fm), both product- and service-orientated (e.g. Nintendo Wii and Holiday Inn), and profit- and not-for-profit-orientated (e.g. Google and ActionAid). Each Marketing in Action vignette opens with a study guide to help the reader make the connections between the theoretical concepts being discussed in the chapter and the actual examples being used to illustrate them.

Case studies are also an essential aspect of the study of marketing. In this edition, there are eleven new case studies and one, LEGO, which has been retained and updated since the last edition because of some very interesting changes that have taken place at that organization. The subjects of the cases are many and varied and include famous organizations and brands (e.g. Nike and Sony PlayStation), rising stars (e.g. YouTube and innocent drinks) and rapidly growing new industries (e.g. gambling—Paddy Power —and spa treatments—Inchydoney Lodge and Spa). A great deal can be learned from studying the experiences of these kinds of organizations.

New themes

Finally, the book introduces the reader to many important new themes in marketing. For example, in this edition, the Marketing Spotlight feature has been used in some instances to briefly examine important new conceptual domains such as experiential marketing, multichannel marketing and neuro-marketing. Other spotlights focus on the groundbreaking initiatives coming from practice, such as Radiohead's 'name your price' strategy for the launch of one of their albums, or the booming global businesses of counterfeiting. All these subject areas are indicative of the new directions in which the field is heading.

Consequently, each of the chapters has been rewritten to update core material and, where appropriate, to introduce new material. For example, the emerging field of marketing metrics promises to change the way marketing activity is measured and controlled, and this is discussed in Chapter 12. Similarly, buzz marketing is a rapidly growing form of direct communications and is examined in Chapter 10. Other core themes, such as internet marketing, mobile marketing, product placement and many others, have been extensively revised and updated.

Guided tour

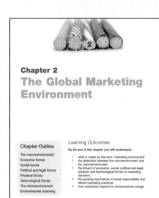

Chapter Outline and Learning Outcomes

The topics covered and a set of outcomes are included at the start of each chapter, summarizing what to expect from each chapter.

Marketing Spotlight

A lively vignette begins each chapter to introduce the main topic and show how marketing works in real life.

Key Terms

These are highlighted throughout the chapter, with definition recaps at the end of each chapter for quick and easy revision.

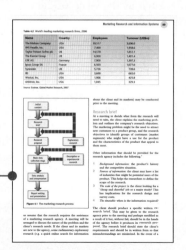

Adverts, figures and tables

We've included a hand-selected array of contemporary adverts to show marketing in action. Key concepts and models are illustrated using figures, tables and charts.

Marketing in Action vignettes

In each chapter you'll find these fun and useful examples of marketing in action, which show how the issues covered in the chapter affect real-life companies and products.

Ethical Debate and Technology Focus boxes

Seven Ethical Debate boxes are located throughout the chapters, designed to highlight ethical issues and provoke further discussion and interest. Similarly, five Technology Focus boxes take a detailed look at how technology continues to influence marketing.

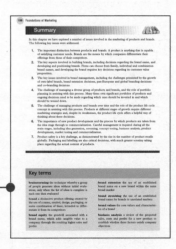

End-of-chapter material

The chapter Summary reinforces main topics to make sure you have acquired a solid understanding. Study questions allow you to apply your new knowledge. Suggested reading and References direct you towards the best sources for further research.

Case studies

Every chapter has its own case study, directly relating to the issues discussed and designed to bring the theories to life. See page xiii for a full list of companies and issues covered. Questions are included for class work, assignments and revision.

Technology to enhance learning and teaching

Visit www.mcgraw-hill.co.uk/textbooks/jobber today

Online Learning Centre (OLC)

After completing each chapter, log on to the supporting Online Learning Centre website. Take advantage of the study tools offered to reinforce the material you have read in the text, and to develop your knowledge of marketing in a fun and effective way.

Resources for students include:

- *New case studies*
- *Self-test questions*
- *Internet exercises*
- *Glossary*
- *Ad Insight videos*

Also available for lecturers:

- *Lecturers' manual*
- *Testbank in EZTest format*
- *Animated PowerPoint Slides*
- *New case studies*
- *Image bank*
- *Lecturer videos*

Test Bank available in McGraw-Hill EZ Test Online

A test bank of hundreds of questions is available to lecturers adopting this book for their module. A range of questions is provided for each chapter, including multiple-choice, true or false, and short-answer or essay questions. The questions are identified by type, difficulty and topic to help you to select questions that best suit your needs and are accessible through an easy-to-use online testing tool: **McGraw-Hill EZ Test Online**.

McGraw-Hill EZ Test Online is accessible to busy academics virtually anywhere—in their office, at home or while travelling—and eliminates the need for software installation. Lecturers can choose from question banks associated with their adopted textbook or easily create their own questions. They also have access to hundreds of banks and thousands of questions created for other McGraw-Hill titles. Multiple versions of tests can be saved for delivery on paper or online through WebCT, Blackboard and other course management systems. When created and delivered though EZ Test Online, students' tests can be immediately marked, saving lecturers time and providing prompt results to students.

To register for this FREE resource, visit www.eztestonline.com

Videos

Ad Insight

On the student centre of the OLC you will find a wealth of TV advertising campaigns, many of which are linked to topics in the book. Look out for the Ad Insight icon in the text to refer you to watch the relevant clip and put your marketing skills into practice by answering the accompanying questions.

Exclusive suite of Video Cases for Lecturers

We are excited to offer an exclusive set of new video cases to lecturers adopting this text. Each video illustrates a number of core marketing concepts linked to the book to help students see how marketing works in the real world.

What do the videos cover?

The videos offer students insights into how different organizations have successfully harnessed the elements of the marketing mix, including discussions about new product development, pricing, promotion, packaging, market research, relationship and digital marketing. The videos feature interviews with business leaders and marketing professionals, researched and conducted by Professor John Fahy to ensure seamless integration with the content of the new edition of this text.

How can I use them?

To ensure maximum flexibility for teaching purposes, the videos have been edited to focus on key topics so that short extracts can be easily integrated into a lecture presentation or be delivered in a tutorial setting to spark class discussion. To ensure painless preparation for teaching, each video is accompanied by PowerPoint slides, teaching notes and discussion questions.

This fantastic video resource will add real value to lectures, providing attention-grabbing content that helps students to make the connection between theory and practice.

Some highlights of the video package include:

- An interview with **Paddy Power**, founder of the eponymous bookmaker, reveals the story behind their ground-breaking and often controversial marketing campaigns
- A first-hand account of how a young student entrepreneur set up the thriving **SuperJam** brand, taking his homemade preserves from the kitchen table to the supermarket

The Super Fruit Spreads

- The Marketing Director of **Burnt Sugar**, luxury toffee confectioners, explains how his company has used innovative online forums, events and other customer feedback to develop and promote their products.

Look out for more new videos in the coming months!

How do I get the videos?

The full suite of videos is exclusively available to lecturers adopting this textbook. If you are interested in this resource, please contact your McGraw-Hill representative or visit www.mcgraw-hill.co.uk/textbooks/jobber to click through to request a demonstration.

Custom Publishing Solutions: Let us help make our content your solution

At McGraw-Hill Education our aim is to help lecturers to find the most suitable content for their needs delivered to their students in the most appropriate way. Our Custom Publishing Solutions offer the ideal combination of content delivered in the way which best suits lecturer and students.

Our custom publishing programme offers lecturers the opportunity select just the chapters or sections of material they wish to deliver to their students from a database called Primis at www.primisonline.com

Primis contains over two million pages of content from:

- textbooks
- professional books
- case books—Harvard Articles, Insead, Ivey, Darden, Thunderbird and *BusinessWeek*
- Taking Sides—debate materials.

Across the following imprints:

- McGraw-Hill Education
- Open University Press
- Harvard Business School Press
- US and European material.

There is also the option to include additional material authored by lecturers in the custom product—this does not necessarily have to be in English.

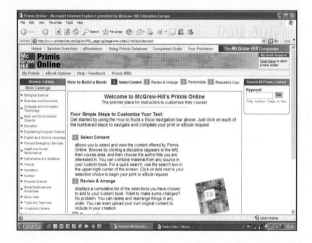

We will take care of everything from start to finish in the process of developing and delivering a custom product to ensure that lecturers and students receive exactly the material needed in the most suitable way.

With a Custom Publishing Solution, students enjoy the best selection of material deemed to be the most suitable for learning everything they need for their courses—something of real value to support their learning. Teachers are able to use exactly the material they want, in the way they want, to support their teaching on the course.

Please contact your local McGraw-Hill representative with any questions, or alternatively contact Warren Eels e: warren_eels@mcgraw-hill.com

Make the grade!

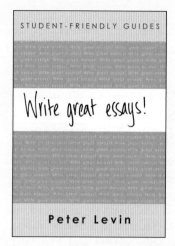
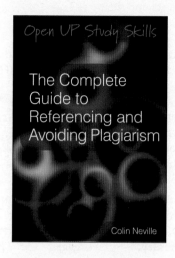
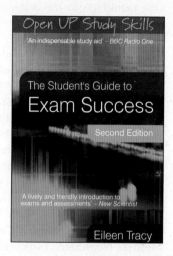

Acknowledgements

Our thanks go to the following reviewers for their comments at various stages in the text's development:

Glyn Atwal, Esc Rennes School of Business
Andrea Beetles, Cardiff University
Noel Dennis, University of Teesside
Barry Emery, University of Northampton
Ruth Gosnay, Leeds Metropolitan University
Wendy Hein, Dublin City University
Even Lanseng, BI Oslo, Norway
Mohammad Latifi, Uppsala University, Sweden
Kiefer Lee, Sheffield Hallam University
Gert Matthias Warn, HRS, Denmark
Erwin de Meij, Erasmus University, Rotterdam
Mehran Noghabai, Linkoping University, Sweden
Connie Nolan, Canterbury Christ Church University
Loïc Plé, IESEG, France
Mike Redwood, University of Bath
Vicky Roberts, Staffordshire University
Usha Sundaram, Coventry University
Amy Tiwsakul, University of Surrey
Angela Vickerstaff, Nottingham Trent University
Philip Warwick, University of York
Teck Yong Eng, Kings College London

We would also like to thank the following for contributing case studies:

Glyn Atwal, Esc Rennes
Conor Carroll, University of Limerick
Helen Goworek, Nottingham Trent University
Rose Leahy, Cork Institute of Technology
Loïc Plé, IESEG, France

As well as the **ICFAI** for granting permission to reprint two further case studies.

Picture acknowledgments

The authors and publishers would like to extend thanks to the following for the reproduction of company advertising and/or logos:

Exhibits

1.1: Thanks to Matthew Packer; 1.2: Thanks to Nielsen Media Research UK; 1.3: Thanks to Polaroid, BBH, Noelle Pickford and Dave Stewart; 1.4: Thanks to Levi; 1.5: Thanks to Saatchi & Saatchi; 2.1: Thanks to Nielsen Media Research UK; 2.2: Thanks to Nielsen Media Research UK; 2.3: Thanks to Hunky Dorys; 2.4: Thanks to Toyota Motor Europe; 2.5: Thanks to Nielsen Media Research UK; 3.1: Thanks to Philips Electronics UK Limited; 3.2: Thanks to Bang & Olufsen; 3.3: Thanks to Sony Europe. 'Sony', 'like.no.other' and 'BRAVIA' are registered trademark or trademark of Sony Corporation; 3.4: Thanks to Lifestyle mortgages; 3.5: Thanks to ABN-AMRO and Doremus and Company Limited; 4.1: Thanks to iStockphoto; 4.2: Thanks to Matthew Packer; 4.3: Thanks to Matthew Packer; 4.4: Thanks to Mars and Freud Communications; 5.1: Thanks to Toyota (GB) PLC and Tim Simmons; 5.2: Thanks to Nielsen Media Research UK; 5.3: Thanks to HSBC Global Banking and Markets, photo copyright Michael Kenna; 5.5: Thanks to the Coca-Cola Company; 6.1: Thanks to Matthew Packer, Apple Inc. and Hoover; 6.2: Thanks to Matthew Packer; 6.3: Thanks to Nielsen Media Research UK; 6.4: Thanks to Green and Black's and Brave; 6.5: Thanks to iStockphoto; 7.1: Thanks to Nielsen Media Research UK; 7.2: Thanks to Alamy Stock Photography; 7.3: Thanks to TripAdvisor; 7.4: Thanks to Scandinavian Airlines International; 7.5: Thanks to Macmillan Cancer Support; 8.1: Thanks to Nielsen Media Research UK; 8.2: Thanks to TKMaxx; 8.3: Thanks to CD Wow!; 8.4: Thanks to Orange and GolinHarris, Photographer – John Short, Set Stylist – Chrissie Macdonald; 8.5: Thanks to Nielsen Media Research UK; 9.1: Thanks to Nielsen Media Research UK; 9.2: Thanks to Paddy Power; 9.3: Thanks to Boots; 9.4: Thanks to Dyson; 9.5: Thanks to Getty Images; 9.6: Thanks to OMEGA; 10.1: Thanks to Kompass Data Ireland; 10.2: Thanks to FILTER Talent; 10.3: Thanks to La Redoute; 10.4: Thanks to Bebo; 10.5: Thanks to Alamy Stock Photography; 10.6: Thanks to iStockPhoto; 11.1: Thanks to Alamy Stock Photography; 11.2: Thanks to Patek Philippe; 11.3: Thanks to Nielsen Media Research UK;

11.4: Thanks to Nielsen Media Research UK; 11.5: Thanks to Getty Images; 11.6: Thanks to Nielsen Media Research UK; 12.1: Thanks to Gibson Guitars; 12.2: Thanks to British Airways and M & C Saatchi; 12.3: Thanks to Jo Malone; 12.4: Thanks to Nielsen Media Research UK; 12.5: Thanks to Matthew Packer.

Chapter Spotlight Images

1: Thanks to Apple Inc.; 2: Thanks to Alamy Stock Photography; 3: Thanks to iStockphoto; 4: Thanks to Getty Images; 5: Thanks to Boffi; 6: Thanks to Nespresso; 7: Thanks to Vapiano; 8: Thanks to Getty Images; 9: Thanks to Marks and Spencer; 10: Thanks to Corbis; 11: Thanks to the GAME Group Plc; 12: Thanks to Matthew Packer.

Case Images

Case 1: Thanks to YouTube; Case 2: Thanks to innocent Drinks; Case 3: Thanks to Oasis; Case 6: Thanks to Gorenje Group; Case 9: Thanks to Nike; Case 12: Thanks to the LEGO Group.

Every effort has been made to trace and acknowledge ownership of copyright and to clear permission for material reproduced in this book. The publishers will be pleased to make suitable arrangements to clear permission with any copyright holders whom it has not been possible to contact.

Chapter 1
The Nature of Marketing

Chapter Outline

What is marketing?

Creating and delivering customer value

The marketing mix

Marketing and business performance

The scope of marketing

Planning marketing activity

Learning Outcomes

By the end of this chapter you will understand:

1   what marketing is and how it has evolved
2   the nature of customer satisfaction and value
3   the relationship between adopting a marketing philosophy and business performance
4   the scope of marketing
5   the role and importance of marketing planning.

The success of iPod

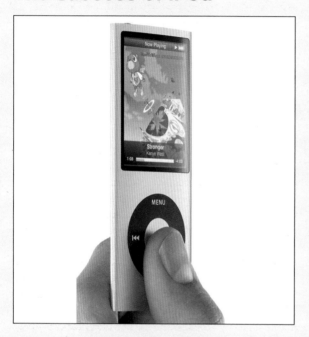

The activities of companies both reflect and shape the world that we live in. For example, some argue that the invention of the motor car has defined the way we live today because it allowed personal mobility on a scale that had never been seen before. It contributed to the growth of city suburbs, to increased recreation and to an upsurge in consumer credit. It gave us shopping malls, theme parks, motels, a fast-food industry and a generation of road movies.

Not all inventions have such a long-lasting impact, but almost every year some new product or service comes along that captures the imagination of the marketplace and succeeds on an unprecedented scale. One such launch has been Apple's portable digital music player, the iPod. When it was brought on to the market in 2001, Apple was a struggling company as, over the years, its share of the computer market had been eroded by Microsoft. So it launched the iPod as an upmarket accessory to its personal computers in the hope of boosting sales of the latter. Instead it was the iPod that became the star of the show. Already, 100 million of them have been sold—so many that it has become the dominant manufacturer in the sector by a wide margin, with its market share in the USA reaching a high of 92 per cent. Such is its popularity that 'iPod' has become the generic name for this type of device in the same way as 'Walkman' did for personal cassette/CD players.

The iPod caught the wave of change in how consumers enjoy their music. MP3 players are seen as superior to more traditional formats such as cassette and CD. They are capable of storing a great deal more music and also allow users to bypass traditional record shops and download songs from various online suppliers. And they fit seamlessly into modern lifestyles characterized by long commuting times, outdoor activities, and the dominance of the personal computer as both a work and recreation device. Capitalizing on these market trends, the iPod has become a phenomenon. More than 70 per cent of US cars have iPod connectivity and there are now more than 4000 accessories for the device, ranging from cases to speaker systems.

Apple stole a march on its competitors due to the superior design of the iPod with its sleek appearance, ease of use and functionality, its excellent storage capability and its adaptability. And with the launch of the iTunes online music store, holding over five million songs, 350 television shows and over 400 movies, sales of the device were boosted hugely as it became easy and legal for consumers to download music and film. The premium pricing of the iPod helped Apple generate a net income increase of 300 per cent in 2004 and its stock price has risen over 2000 per cent since 2003.

The success of the iPod to date demonstrates the power of innovation and market awareness. Companies need to be sensitive to the subtle changes that take place every day in the marketplace. Sony dominated the first wave of portable music players with its hugely successful Walkman but has ceded the advantage to Apple this time around. Being able to anticipate the next need, and deliver a response to it, is the challenge facing the marketer, and that is what this book is about.[1]

In the exciting world of business, there are new successes and failures every day. For example, towards the end of the 1990s, there were many predictions that the future was online and that a new wave of e-businesses was about to obliterate many of the more established enterprises. Thousands of new companies were started, billions of euros of investors' money was spent and the vast majority of these start-ups have already disappeared. At the same time, there are many young and old businesses that continue to thrive and grow. Unlike their fellow dotcoms, companies like Yahoo! and Google have enjoyed a meteoric rise in the past decade. Venerable brands like Coca-Cola, Virgin, IKEA and Nokia continue to command big shares of their markets, though others—such as Sony and Volkswagen—struggle. And everywhere around the world there are small, local enterprises that thrive on the support of local customers.

At the heart of all of this change is marketing. Companies succeed and fail for many reasons but very often marketing is central to the outcome. The reason for this is that the focus of marketing is on customers and their changing needs. If you don't have customers, you don't have a business. Successful companies are those that succeed not only in getting customers but also in keeping them through being constantly aware of their changing needs. The goal of marketing is long-term customer satisfaction, not short-term deception or gimmicks. This theme is reinforced by the writings of top management consultant Peter Drucker, who stated:[2]

> Because the purpose of business is to create and keep customers, it has only two central functions—marketing and innovation. The basic function of marketing is to attract and retain customers at a profit.

What does this statement tell us? First, it places marketing in a central role for business success since it is concerned with the creation and retention of customers. The failure of many products, particularly those in sectors like information technology, is often attributed to a lack of attention to customer needs. Second, it is a reality of commercial life that it is much more expensive to attract new customers than to retain existing ones. Indeed, the costs of attracting new customers have been found to be up to six times higher than the costs of retaining existing ones.[3] Consequently, marketing-orientated companies recognize the importance of building relationships with customers by providing satisfaction and attracting new customers by creating added value. Grönroos stressed the importance of relationship building in his definition of marketing, in which he describes the objective of marketing as to establish, develop and commercialize long-term customer relationships so that the objectives of the parties involved are met.[4] Third, since most markets are characterized by strong competition, the statement also suggests the need to monitor and understand competitors, since it is to rivals that customers will turn if their needs are not being met. The rest of this chapter will examine some of these ideas in more detail, and provide an introduction to how marketing can create **customer value** and satisfaction.

What is marketing?

The marketing concept

The modern **marketing concept** can be expressed as 'the achievement of corporate goals through meeting and exceeding customer needs better than the competition'. For example, the mantra at Procter & Gamble, one of the world's leading consumer products companies, is that it must win at the first and second moments of truth—that is, in the shop where the consumer decides which brand to select and in the home when he/she uses it. Three conditions must be met before the marketing concept can be applied. First, company activities should be focused on providing **customer satisfaction** rather than, for example, simply producing products. This is often not an easy condition to meet. For example, the once booming 'lads' magazine market in the UK is now a study in sectoral decline. Leading titles like *FHM*, *Loaded*, *Maxim* and *Arena* lost almost one-third of their circulation in the second half of 2007[5] (see Exhibit 1.1).

Exhibit 1.1 Not too long ago, 'lads' magazines were one of the fastest-growing segments of the print media; in recent years, sales have fallen dramatically, illustrating the speed with which market demand can rise and fall

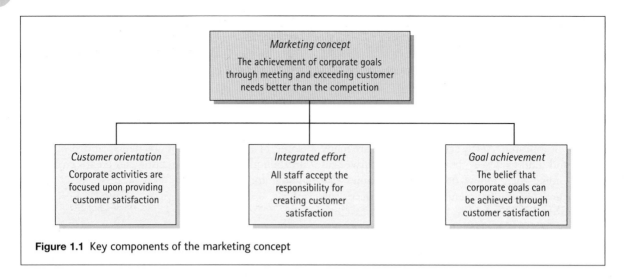

Figure 1.1 Key components of the marketing concept

Smash Hits, the once popular magazine aimed at teenage girls, closed down in 2006, no longer effectively meeting the needs of its customers. Second, the achievement of customer satisfaction relies on integrated effort. The responsibility for the implementation of the concept lies not just within the marketing department but should run right through production, finance, research and development, engineering, and other departments. The fact that marketing is the responsibility of everyone in the organization provides significant challenges for the management of companies. Finally, for integrated effort to come about, management must believe that corporate goals can be achieved through satisfied customers (see Figure 1.1). Some companies are quicker and better at recognizing the importance of the marketing concept than others. For example, Nike was a late entrant into the running shoe business dominated by brands such as Reebok and Puma, but it has established itself as the world's leading sportswear company, through the delivery of powerful brand values.

In essence, the marketing concept is a philosophy of business that puts the customer and customer satisfaction at the centre of things. For example, through implementation of the marketing concept, the Body Shop grew rapidly from a small cosmetics retailer in the south of England to a well-known global brand. Senior management were committed to an alternative approach to the marketing of cosmetics, and all activities within the company were focused around meeting customer needs. Companies like the Body Shop also exemplify what has become known as the 'societal marketing concept', which holds that companies should deliver customer satisfaction in a way that improves both the consumer's and society's well-being. We will examine this issue in greater detail in the next chapter.

The development of marketing

The origins of modern marketing can be traced to the Industrial Revolutions that took place in Britain around 1750 and in the USA and Germany around 1830.[6] Advances in production and distribution, and the migration of rural masses to urban areas created the potential for large-scale markets. As businesspeople sought to exploit these markets, the institutions of marketing such as advertising media and distribution channels began to grow and develop. Marketing as a field of study began in the early part of the twentieth century, growing out of courses that examined issues relating to distribution.[7] The focus of marketing courses in the 1950s and 1960s was on 'how to do it', with an emphasis on the techniques of marketing.[8] In more recent times, attention has been paid to the philosophy of marketing as a way of doing business, and to the nature and impact of marketing on stakeholders and society in general.

Despite this long tradition, there is no guarantee that all companies will adopt a **marketing orientation**. Many firms today are characterized by an inward-looking stance, where their focus is on existing products or the internal operations of the company. Figure 1.2 illustrates **production orientation** in its crudest form. The focus is on current production capabilities. The purpose of the organization is to manufacture products and sell them aggressively to customers. Airbus's decision to launch its wide-body, long-haul jet, the A380 superjumbo, has been criticized as being production orientated, with sceptics arguing that 90 per cent of the aircraft required in the marketplace for the next 20 years will be in 200-seat to 400-seat category compared with the 550-plus-seat A380. Market results appear to bear this prediction out. Airbus sold just 21 A380s in the first six months of 2006, compared with 96 orders for its

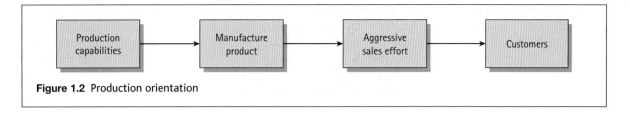

Figure 1.2 Production orientation

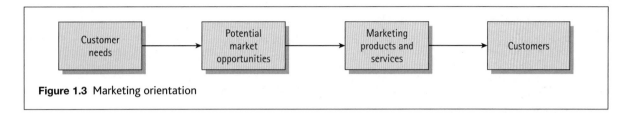

Figure 1.3 Marketing orientation

A320 aircraft.[9] Similarly, a report on the funds management industry in the UK found that, in general, the sector was characterized by a lack of customer focus and a lack of effective market segmentation, with the result that many products being offered were unsuitable and potential sales were being lost.[10]

Companies that are marketing orientated focus on customers' needs. Change is recognized as endemic, and adaptation considered necessary for survival. For example, dry cleaning used to be a big industry but changing consumer behaviour patterns mean that it is now less attractive. Research has found that 46 per cent of people in the UK never use a dry cleaner, with the result that the number of dry-cleaning outlets fell from 5300 in 2000 to about 4500 in 2005.[11] Changing needs present potential market opportunities, which drive the company. Market-driven companies seek to adapt their product and service offerings to the demands of current and latent markets. This orientation is shown in Figure 1.3. Because marketing-orientated companies get close to their customers, they understand their needs and problems. When personal contact is insufficient or not feasible, formal marketing research is commissioned to enable the companies to understand customer motivations and behaviour. Part of the success of German machine tool manufacturers can be attributed to their willingness to develop new products with lead customers—those companies that, themselves, were innovative.[12] This contrasts sharply with the attitude of UK machine tool manufacturers, who saw marketing research only as a tactic to delay new product proposals and who feared that involving customers in new product design would have adverse effects on sales of their current products.

In short, the differences between market-orientated businesses and internally orientated businesses are summarized in Table 1.1. Market-driven businesses

Table 1.1 Marketing-orientated businesses

Market-orientated businesses	Internally orientated businesses
Customer concern throughout business	Convenience comes first
Know customer choice criteria and match with marketing mix	Assume price and product performance key to most sales
Segment by customer differences	Segment by product
Invest in market research (MR) and track market changes	Rely on anecdotes and received wisdom
Welcome change	Cherish status quo
Try to understand competition	Ignore competition
Marketing spend regarded as an investment	Marketing spend regarded as a luxury
Innovation rewarded	Innovation punished
Search for latent markets	Stick with the same
Be fast	Why rush?
Strive for competitive advantage	Happy to be me-too

display customer concern throughout the business; they understand the criteria customers use to choose between competing suppliers; they invest in market research, and track market changes; they regard marketing spend as an investment, and are fast and flexible in terms of their pursuit of new opportunities.

Creating and delivering customer value

Those companies that are marketing orientated aim to create customer value in order to attract and retain customers. No company is immune from this challenge. Even De Beers, the world's biggest diamond company, has found that its product has been challenged, as customers choose designer products instead. The intention of market-oriented companies is to deliver superior value to their target customers and, in doing so, they implement the marketing concept by meeting and exceeding customer needs better than the competition. One of the great benefits of having satisfied customers is that they tell others of their experiences, further enhancing sales. For example, recent research has shown that the experience of other customers with a product or service has a significant impact on purchase decision in sectors like automobiles and financial services.[13] Online businesses are significant users of word-of-mouth marketing. For example, TripAdvisor.com is a website where satisfied and dissatisfied customers post their reviews of hotels and destinations they have stayed at, and these kinds of reviews influence the purchase decisions of other customers.

No matter how famous your brand is, failure to implement the marketing concept can have severe consequences for the business. For example, Guinness, one of the leading drinks brands in Ireland and the UK, has been suffering from falling sales since 2001, as consumers' tastes and preferences change. In contrast, Ritz Carlton has developed an enviable reputation in the luxury hotel market. One of the company's mottos is that staff 'only have permission to say yes'.[14] This is a clear signal to everyone in the company that no effort should be spared in responding to the needs of its discerning customers. Customer value is dependent on how the customer perceives the benefits of an offering and the sacrifice that is associated with its purchase. Therefore:

$$\text{customer value} = \text{perceived benefits} - \text{perceived sacrifice}$$

Perceived benefits can be derived from the product (for example, the hotel room and restaurant), the associated service (for example, how responsive the hotel is to the specific needs of customers) and the image of the company (for example, is the image of the company/product favourable?) (see Exhibit 1.2). Conveying benefits is a critical marketing task and is central to positioning and branding, as we shall see in Chapters 5 and 6. *Perceived sacrifice* is the total cost associated with buying the product. This consists not just of monetary costs, but also the time and energy involved in the purchase. For example, with hotels, good location can reduce the time and energy required to find a suitable place to stay. But marketers need to be aware of another critical sacrifice in some buying situations; this is the potential psychological cost of not making the right decision. Uncertainty means that people perceive risk when purchasing. Therefore, hotels like the Marriott or restaurants like McDonald's aim for consistency so that customers can be confident of what they will receive when they visit these service providers.

The key to marketing success is to exceed the value offered by competitors. Consumers decide on purchases on the basis of judgements about the value offered by suppliers. Once a product has been purchased, customer satisfaction depends on its perceived performance compared to the buyer's expectations. Customer satisfaction occurs when perceived performance matches or exceeds expectations. Expectations are formed through pre-buying experiences, discussions with other people and suppliers' marketing activities. Companies need to avoid the mistake of setting customer expectations too high through exaggerated promotional claims, since this can lead to dissatisfaction if performance falls short of expectations.

In the current competitive climate, it is usually not enough simply to match performance and expectations. Expectations need to be exceeded for commercial success so that customers are delighted with the outcome. In order to understand the concept of customer satisfaction, the Kano model (see Figure 1.4) helps to separate characteristics that cause dissatisfaction, satisfaction and delight. Three characteristics underlie the model: 'must be', 'more is better' and 'delighters'.

Those characteristics recognized as 'must bes' are expected and thus taken for granted. For example, in a hotel, customers expect service at reception and a clean room. Lack of these characteristics causes annoyance but their presence only brings dissatisfaction up

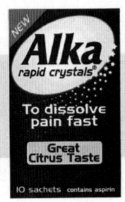

Exhibit 1.2 This advert for Alka Crystals demonstrates product benefits in a clever way by showing how it can be taken without water

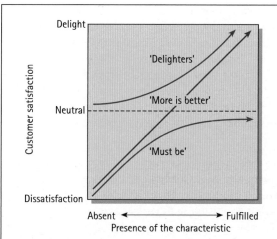

Figure 1.4 Creating customer satisfaction
Source: Joiner, B.L. (1994) *Fourth Generation Management*, New York: McGraw-Hill

response may cause positive satisfaction or even delight. The usability of search results is an example of 'more is better' and has become a key differentiating factor in the search engine industry, which has allowed Google to become the dominant player. 'Delighters' are the unexpected characteristics that surprise the customer. Their absence does not cause dissatisfaction, but their presence delights the customer. For example, a UK hotel chain provides free measures of brandy in the rooms of their adult guests. This delights many of its customers, who were not expecting this treat.

Over time, however, such 'delighters' become expected, and this is a problem that marketers must tackle. For example, some car manufacturers provided small, unexpected delighters such as pen holders and delay mechanisms on interior lights so that there is time to find the ignition socket at night. These are standard on most cars now and have become 'must be' characteristics because customers have come to expect them. This means that marketers must constantly strive to find new ways of delighting; innovative thinking and listening to

to a neutral level. 'More is better' characteristics can take satisfaction past neutral and into the positive satisfaction range. For example, no response to a telephone call can cause dissatisfaction, but a fast

customers are key ingredients in this (see Marketing in Action 1.1).

The effects of these kinds of changes can be seen in the case of Dell, one of the world's largest computer companies. Founded by Michael Dell, while he was still a student at the University of Texas in Austin, it rapidly became the biggest computer maker in the world, offering customized, low-cost computers that were sold direct to consumers. In terms of the market, it was delivering 'more is better'. But its enormous successes in the 1990s prompted a response from the competition. IBM sold its personal computer division to Lenovo, which has been matching Dell's low-price PCs. And companies like HP and Apple have come to the market with

Marketing in Action 1.1: Finding the music you want to hear

> **Study guide:** Below is a review of some new innovations in radio. Read and consider the differences in value offered by these new 'stations' versus traditional radio stations.

Businesses need to combine innovation and marketing to meet the evolving needs of the consumer. Nowhere is this more evident than in commercial radio. Radio is a huge business. For example, Communicorp, a radio group with businesses in Ireland, Bulgaria, Estonia, the Czech Republic, Hungary and Ukraine, generated revenues of over €47 million in 2006. The standard business model for radio has been a combined focus on particular segments of the market and on advertisers. So stations have targeted mature audiences, young audiences or ethnic audiences, or have been based on particular music genres such as rock, country or classical, as they sought to attract and hold listeners. Advertisers can then target these niche audiences by sponsoring shows or paying to have their ads carried on the station. And listeners get to enjoy particular presenters and the kinds of music they play.

But some new internet-based radio stations are threatening to offer significantly more value to listeners than traditional stations. One of the leading such stations is Last.fm, founded in London in 2002. Its core service is a customized internet radio station that streams music tailored to each individual's taste. The company's software then monitors a user's preferences and cross-matches them with those of like-minded users. Last.fm has grown rapidly to have users in 244 countries and in the region of 15 million unique users per month. Pandora.com, based in San Francisco, acts as a music discovery service. Recommendations are automated using a technology called the Music Genome Project, which weighs more than 400 different musical attributes and genres when selecting songs to add to a playlist. Users can respond immediately, indicating whether they like a selection or not, and can create a variety of personalized stations suited to their particular diverse tastes.

Internet radio offers greater value to listeners by allowing them to listen only to the music they want to hear, and to discover new music that they might also like. Consumers no longer rely on the 'hit and miss' service provided by radio programme producers. They can also create their own profile pages with the music that they like, and chat and listen to other listeners' music—in effect, becoming a partial social networking site. Users can search for a musical 'neighbour' who shares their taste, view that person's music journals, and send them a message or add them as a 'friend'. Many other online businesses, such as iLike and Finetune, offer a similar combination of social radio and music discovery, suggesting that this is a field of business that is likely to grow rapidly, presenting challenges to existing radio and interesting new opportunities for advertisers. Internet-based audio services have doubled their share of internet users from 7 per cent in 2002 to 14 per cent in 2006, but one of the major challenges facing the sector is the potential introduction of licence fees, which would significantly increase its costs of doing business.

Based on: Garrity (2007);[15] Guha (2007)[16]

innovative, low-price products. Dell is no longer leading the market, and problems with its customer service levels mean that it is also struggling to deliver on the 'must bes' in the computer business. In 2006 and 2007, it failed to meet analysts' profit targets and its share price slipped. Evidence of how serious the problems are can be seen in the return of Michael Dell as chief executive in 2007.

Delivering customer value

As well as being a philosophy that puts the customer at the centre of the business, marketing is also a business function that encompasses the variety of activities that must be conducted in order to deliver customer value. These include conducting marketing research to understand customer needs and their behaviour, segmenting markets into submarkets to be targeted by the company, developing products and brands, and positioning these in the marketplace, making pricing decisions, deciding on a **promotional mix**, selling and distributing products, and marketing planning and management. These are the kinds of issues that will be introduced briefly in the next section on the marketing mix and will be the focus of later chapters in this book. Markets and marketing are constantly changing, and new methods of delivering value—such as **customer relationship management** (CRM)—are being developed. These new techniques, along with issues of importance to the marketing profession such as marketing ethics, will also be discussed throughout this book.

Marketing, therefore, is an exciting and multifaceted profession. Marketing managers are responsible for ensuring that the organization delivers value to customers; but in doing so they may avail themselves of the services of researchers, salespeople, communication specialists, advertising agencies and retail specialists. The wide range of careers that fall within the realm of marketing is outlined in Appendix 1.1 at the end of this chapter.

The marketing mix

A key marketing activity is the management of the company's **marketing mix**. The marketing mix consists primarily of four major elements: **product**, **price**, promotion and **place**, though in different kinds of businesses, marketers have different areas of responsibility. These '4-Ps' are four key decision areas and form a major aspect of marketing concept implementation. Later, we will look at each of the 4-Ps in considerable detail. At this point, however, it will be useful to examine each element briefly so that we can understand the essence of marketing mix decision-making.

Product

The choice of what products/services and benefits should be offered to a group of customers is known as the 'product decision'. An important element is new product/service development. As technology and tastes change, products become out of date and inferior to those of the competition, so companies must replace them with features that customers value. For example, when Microsoft launched Windows XP in 2001, it offered home users new features such as Windows Movie Maker for editing and organizing home movies, and a Network Set-up Wizard so that all the computers in a home can share printers, files and an internet connection. Product decisions also involve choices regarding brand names, guarantees, packaging and the services that should accompany the product offering. Guarantees can be an important component of the product offering. For example, the operators of the AVE, Spain's high-speed train, capable of travelling at 300 kmph, are so confident of its performance that they guarantee to give customers a full refund of their fare if they are more than five minutes late.

Price

Because price represents, on a unit basis, what the company receives for the product or service that is being marketed, it is a key element of the marketing mix. All the other elements represent costs—for example, expenditure on product design (product), advertising and salespeople (promotion), and transportation and distribution (place). Marketers, therefore, need to be very clear about pricing objectives, methods and the factors that influence price setting; they must also take into account the necessity for discounting and offering allowances in some transactions.

Promotion

Decisions have to be taken with due attention to the promotional mix: advertising, personal selling, sales promotions, public relations, direct marketing and internet marketing. By these means, the target audience is made aware of the existence of a product or service, and the benefits (both economic and psychological) it confers to customers (see Exhibit 1.3). Each element of the promotional mix has its own set of strengths and weaknesses, and these will be explored later. A growing form of promotion is the use of the internet as a promotional tool. A key advantage of this medium is that small local

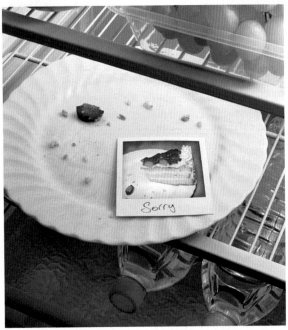

THE NEW POLAROID ONE
instant originals

Exhibit 1.3 Clever advertising like this for Polaroid has failed to prevent the company going into decline; its products have been replaced by superior technologies like digital photography, demonstrating that all elements of the marketing mix play a crucial role in organizational success

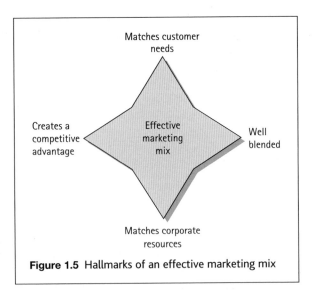

Figure 1.5 Hallmarks of an effective marketing mix

companies can expand the scope of their market at a relatively low cost.

Place

The aspect of place is to do with those decisions concerning the distribution channels that are to be used and their management, the location of outlets, methods of transportation, and the inventory levels to be held. The objective is to ensure that products and services are available in the proper quantities, at the right time and in the right place. Distribution channels consist of organizations such as retailers or wholesalers through which goods pass on their way to customers. Producers need to manage their relationships with these organizations well because they may provide the only cost-effective access to the marketplace.

An effective marketing mix (see Figure 1.5) is composed of four main features. Initially, the mix must be designed to match the needs of a target customer group. Second, it must contribute to the creation of a **competitive advantage**, which is a clear performance differential over the competition on factors

that are important to customers. Third, the marketing mix must match the resources that are available to the firm. Certain media—for example, television advertising—require a minimum threshold investment before they are regarded as feasible. In the UK a rule of thumb is that at least £5 million (€7 million) per year is required to achieve impact in a national advertising campaign. Clearly, those brands that cannot afford such a promotional budget must use other less expensive media (for example, posters or sales promotion) to attract and hold customers. Finally, an effective marketing mix should be well blended to form a consistent theme. For example, the use of exclusive outlets for upmarket fashion and cosmetic brands—Armani, Christian Dior and Calvin Klein, for example—is consistent with their strategic positioning (see Marketing in Action 1.2).

Thinking of the marketing mix simply in terms of the 4-Ps has been the subject of some criticism in recent years. For example, in service businesses like hair salons, the hairdresser is a key part of the service itself, while the décor of a restaurant or café is an important aspect of the enjoyment of that experience. Consequently, service marketers have argued for a '7-Ps' approach to incorporate (in addition to the original 4-Ps) the *people*, *process* and *physical evidence* aspects of services.[17] Even some of the earliest marketing writings identified up to 12 areas of responsibility for the marketer, including activities like fact-finding and servicing customers.[18] Whatever framework is used, the important issue is not to neglect decision-making areas that are critical to effective marketing. The strength of the 4-Ps approach is that it represents a memorable and practical framework for marketing decision-making, and has proved useful in the classroom and in practice for many years.

Marketing in Action 1.2: Marketing water

Study guide: Below is a description of the marketing mix used by one brand. Read it and consider how well it meets the hallmarks of an effective marketing mix.

An example of an effective marketing mix is that used by the Icelandic mineral water company, Glacial. The Icelandic countryside is pure and unspoiled, and several companies have tried to market Icelandic mineral water abroad without a great deal of success. So when Icelandic Water Holdings launched its new brand in 2004, it carefully developed an appropriate marketing mix. The name Glacial was chosen because it drew on Iceland's unspoiled and wild image. Square rather than round bottles were used to package the product, and the design on the label resembled an ice formation that differed on each face of the bottle to resemble the ever changing nature of a glacier. On the shelf, the different photographs on the bottle create a kind of landscape, which helps to capture the consumer's attention.

In terms of promotion, the company sought to generate maximum publicity and buzz around the brand. It launched the product at major events such as the Cannes Film Festival and the launch of the Microsoft Xbox 360 in Los Angeles. By targeting such high-profile events, it created an awareness for the brand among opinion leaders. Distribution has been secured by signing deals with large global companies like Anheuser-Busch, which distributes Budweiser and other leading global brands. And by pricing the product at the upper end of the range of mineral waters, Icelandic Glacial is positioned as a premium water.

Its superior position in the market is also supported by the assertion that its production and distribution is carbon neutral. Mineral waters come in for criticism, in that their transportation around the globe leaves a significant carbon footprint. For example, the US bottled water market alone is estimated to be worth US$11 billion. But Icelandic Water Holdings argues that it pumps and bottles its water using non-polluting geo-thermal power, which is a natural energy source derived from Iceland's volcanic countryside.

Based on: Anonymous (2007);[19] Birchall (2007)[20]

Marketing and business performance

Does marketing work? Surprisingly this is a controversial question, with many people arguing that, yes, of course it does, while others are less sure. The difficulty surrounds the intangibility of marketing. It is very difficult to predict in advance whether a marketing or promotional campaign is going to work. Sometimes campaigns like those for Levi's 501 jeans are stunningly successful. On the back of the famous ad featuring Nick Kamen in a launderette, sales of Levi's 501s rose 800 per cent. Not only that but sales of all jeans (even those of competitors) went up (see Exhibit 1.4).

Similarly, recent developments in retail banking in the UK demonstrate the importance and power of effective marketing. Loyalty to particular providers

Exhibit 1.4 The success of Levi's demonstrates the power of an effective marketing campaign

has been decreasing and in the five-year period 2000–04, the number of people switching current accounts doubled from 500,000 to 1 million. In response, HBOS began adopting marketing practices more usually associated with the retail trade than with banks, such as offering value-for-money products and introducing comparative advertising showing the different rates of interest charged by the big banks. The strategy worked. The bank attracted 1 million new bank account customers and 1.2 million new credit card customers in 2004, and profits rose by 22 per cent.[21]

In other companies, marketing is seen as the central engine of business growth. For example, Nestlé is a huge global company with 8000 products (a figure that grows to 20,000 when local variations are included) and an annual marketing budget of US$2.5 billion. The company's chief executive has a marketing background and the head of marketing is responsible for each of the company's seven strategic business units. This structure is designed to ensure that marketing thinking is central to the company's strategic decisions.[22] Another consumer products firm, Reckitt Benckiser, which markets leading brands like Harpic and Dettol, invests 12 per cent of sales annually in marketing, which is well above average.[23]

But, for some, the issue is not whether marketing works but rather that it works too well. In recent years, marketing has been the subject of a great deal of criticism.[24] It has been equated with trickery and deception, and with persuading people (often those on low incomes) to buy products they do not really need. Some of the main controversies surrounding marketing are summarized in Ethical Debate 1.1.

In short, marketing works. Succeeding in making it work in any particular situation is the challenge. In that regard some issues relating to the nature and impact of marketing need to be borne in mind.

Efficiency versus effectiveness

We can gain another perspective on customer orientation if we understand the distinction between **efficiency** and **effectiveness**. *Efficiency* is concerned with inputs and outputs. An efficient firm produces goods economically—it does things right. The benefit is that cost per unit of output is low and, therefore, the potential for offering low prices to gain market share, or charging medium to high prices and achieving high profit margins, is present. However, to be successful, a company needs to be more than just efficient, it needs to be effective as well. *Effectiveness* means doing the right things. This implies operating in attractive markets and making products that

	Ineffective	Effective
Inefficient	Goes out of business quickly	Survives
Efficient	Dies slowly	Does well Thrives

Figure 1.6 Efficiency and effectiveness

consumers want to buy. Conversely, companies that operate in unattractive markets or are not producing what consumers want to buy will go out of business—the only question is one of timing. The link between performance and combinations of efficiency and effectiveness is illustrated in Figure 1.6.

A company that is both inefficient and ineffective will go out of business quickly because it is a high-cost producer of products that consumers do not want to buy. This was the case with many web-based businesses that were formed during the dotcom boom of the late 1990s. A company that is efficient and ineffective may last a little longer because its low cost base may generate more profits from the dwindling sales volume it is achieving. Firms that are effective but inefficient are likely to survive because they are operating in attractive markets and are marketing products that people want to buy. The problem is that their inefficiency is preventing them from reaping the maximum profits from their endeavours. It is the combination of both efficiency and effectiveness that leads to optimum business success. Such firms do well and thrive because they are operating in attractive markets, are supplying products that consumers want to buy and are benefiting from a low cost base.

The global automotive industry is a classic study of the dynamics of efficiency and effectiveness. For many years now, the big three US auto manufacturers—Ford, General Motors and Chrysler—have been in trouble. In 2006, Ford and GM laid off some 55,000 workers between them in the USA, with Chrysler's German operations laying off a further 8500. This was on top of previous rounds of heavy job losses in 1980, 1991 and 2001. Several rounds of efficiency drives would appear to have had only the effect of lengthening the time period of the decline of these once leading firms. They would appear to be dying slowly, having not addressed the problem of effectiveness. In contrast, Toyota has risen to become the leading global car company through a combination of highly reliable, competitively priced vehicles (effectiveness) that are very efficiently produced using innovative and industry-leading production practices (efficiency).

Ethical Debate 1.1: Marketing—good or evil?

It is possible to look at marketing from different standpoints. A positive view holds that marketing provides significant benefits to society. For example, the innovative efforts of companies provide us, as consumers, with a world of choice and diversity. A search on Google allows us to find information on anything that we want; with Skype, we can make free phone calls to our friends and relatives on the other side of the world, and websites like Amazon and eBay allow us to shop from the comfort of our desks. The innovations of tomorrow will bring us new and appealing products, services and solutions. Second, as the practice of marketing improves, our particular needs are increasingly being met. If we eat only gluten-free products, love sky-diving and have a passion for Japanese origami, there are organizations that will fulfil these needs. As firms collect more information about their customers, they will tailor solutions to meet specific user requirements. Finally, the competition between firms continually forces them to improve their services and products, and deliver extra value to customers. For example, low-fares airlines have revolutionized air travel and enable people who traditionally flew infrequently to travel to new destinations much more often.

At the same time, marketing is also the subject of some trenchant criticism. For example, it is seen as not only fulfilling needs but creating unnecessary wants. Critics argue that companies use sophisticated marketing techniques to create aspirations and to get consumers to buy products that they don't really need, with the result that many consumers find themselves building up significant debts. Consumer credit levels are at an all-time high in developed economies like the US and the UK. Related to this is the rise of materialism in society. Proponents of this view suggest that the modern consumer has become obsessed with consumption, as illustrated, for example, by the growth in Sunday shopping, which has to a large extent displaced religious participation and different forms of leisure and community activities on Sundays. Psychologists argue that this rise in consumption has done little to make people feel happier and better about themselves. And, at the same time as materialism is rising, there are growing concerns that the world's resources are being rapidly depleted and that current levels of consumption are not sustainable into the future. Third, there are concerns with the way that marketers target vulnerable groups like children, where the skills of child psychologists are used to find more and novel ways to instil brand preferences in the very young. Critics also point to the way that, for example, young girls are portrayed as sexual objects in the marketing and advertising of toys like Bratz dolls. Finally, there are concerns with the ways that marketing activity appears to have invaded all aspects of society. Public leisure events such as sports, shows and concerts now usually have a corporate partner, with the result that events aimed at teenagers may be sponsored by an alcoholic drinks organization, for example. Pressures on the public funding of schools, hospitals, and so on, also creates opportunities for corporations to tie in with these entities, which is often ethically questionable.

Resolving such a debate is very difficult, but the core of the issue lies in the key components of the definition of marketing—namely value and profit. When organizations provide genuine value to customers, marketing is doing what it should, and both firms and society benefit. When firms create an illusion of value or seek to exploit customers for profit, then consumers and society do not benefit. Like all professions, marketing has its unscrupulous practitioners and there will always be individuals and organizations who will seek to exploit vulnerable customers. But, in an information-rich world, such practitioners can and should be named and shamed.

Suggested reading: James (2007);[25] Klein (2000);[26] Linn (2004)[27]

Marketing and performance

The adoption of the marketing concept will improve business performance—that is the basic premise (see Marketing in Action 1.3). Marketing is not an abstract concept, its acid test is the effect that its use has on key corporate indices such as profitability and market share. In recent years, studies in both Europe and North America have sought to examine the relationship between marketing and performance. The results suggest that the relationship is positive.

Narver and Slater, for instance, looked closely at the relationship between business performance and marketing orientation.[28] They collected data from 113 strategic business units (SBUs) of a major US corporation. In the main, their study found that the relationship between market orientation and profitability was strongly linear, with the businesses displaying the highest level of market orientation achieving the highest levels of profitability, and those with the lowest scores on market orientation having the lowest profitability figures. As the authors state: 'The findings give marketing scholars and practitioners a basis beyond mere intuition for recommending the superiority of a market orientation.'

A study by the consultants Bain & Company in the USA looked at the performance of 500 consumer brands in 100 categories between the years 1997 and 2001. It found that brands that belonged to companies that innovated and advertised were likely to see higher revenues. Companies that drew at least 10 per cent of their 2001 sales from new products introduced during the period were 60 per cent more likely to post higher sales growth. Also, those companies reporting double-digit revenue increases were 60 per cent more likely to out-spend other brands in their category on advertising. An example is Old Spice, a brand that is over 50 years old. It introduced sub-brands such as High Endurance deodorant in 1994 and Red Zone in 1999. Both products accounted for more that 75 per cent of Old Spice sales in 2001 and helped the brand to grow by 13 per cent that year, in a category that grew at an average of 1 per cent.[29]

A study published in the UK by Hooley, Lynch and Shepherd[30] sought to develop a typology of approaches to marketing, and to relate those approaches to business performance. They identified four groups of companies, namely 'marketing philosophers', 'sales supporters', 'departmental marketers' and 'unsures'. The marketing philosophers saw marketing as a function with prime responsibility for identifying and meeting customers' needs and as a guiding philosophy for the whole organization; they did not see marketing as confined to the marketing department, nor did they regard it merely as sales support. The sales supporters saw marketing's primary functions as being sales and promotion support. Marketing was confined to what the marketing department did, and had little to do with identifying and meeting customer needs. The departmental marketers not only shared the view of the marketing philosophers that marketing was about identifying and meeting customer needs, but also believed that marketing was restricted to what the marketing department did. The final group of companies—the unsures—tended to be indecisive regarding their marketing approach.

The attitudes, organization and practices of the four groups were compared, with the marketing philosophers exhibiting many distinct characteristics, as summarized below.

1. Marketing philosophers adopted a more proactive, aggressive approach towards the future.
2. They had a more proactive approach to new product development.
3. They placed a higher importance on marketing training.
4. They adopted longer time horizons for marketing planning.
5. Marketing had a higher status within the company.
6. Marketing had a higher chance of being represented at board level.
7. Marketing had more chance of working closely with other functional areas.
8. Marketing made a greater input into strategic plans.

Significantly, the marketing philosophers achieve a significantly higher ROI (return on investment) than the remainder of the sample. The departmental marketers performed at the sample average, while the unsures and sales supporters performed significantly worse. Hooley *et al.*'s conclusion was that marketing should be viewed not just as a departmental function but as a guiding philosophy for the whole organization.

It is surprising, then, that marketing has not had the influence in corporate boardrooms its importance would seem to justify. A recent study in the UK found that only 21 per cent of CEOs in the FTSE 100 had worked in marketing before going into general management, and only five of the FTSE 100 companies had dedicated marketing directors on their boards.[31] Research in the USA shows that the majority of chief executives in recent decades have had a finance background.[32] Doyle argues that the reason for marketing's relatively low status is that

Marketing in Action 1.3: The success of Walkers Sensations

Study guide: Below is a review of the successful launch of a new snack product. Read it and consider the extent to which effective marketing was central to its success.

Adult luxury snacking is a growing sector of the snack market. Valued at £237 million in 2002, this sector has undergone substantial growth of over 26 per cent since 1988. Walkers' foray into the evening snack market followed research that identified lunchtime and dinner as the most popular snacking times. Qualitative research found that price and indulgence were key attributes that consumers used when choosing between potato crisp brands. Everyday crisps fall into the low-price, low-indulgence category, while speciality crisps were seen as high-price, high-indulgence. Herein lay an opportunity to develop a reasonably priced, high-indulgence brand for the evening snack market. Walkers grasped this opening in the market and began developing the mainstream premium brand, Walkers Sensations.

Walkers decided to target this new luxury brand at an adult audience, principally 25–45-year-old parents of young children. In terms of usage occasion, it envisaged the brand to be consumed as part of evening relaxation. Extensive research further refined its positioning strategy, product and price. It was decided to offer the crisps in an array of flavours, from the familiar to the exotic. Packaging was key to creating an augmented product that would appeal to target customers. Photographs were used to convey the premium nature, and a reduced-in-size Walkers banner also succeeded in differentiating the product from the Walkers master brand. It was priced in line with its premium positioning, at 20 per cent above a large packet of Walkers crisps.

The launch of Walkers Sensations was also critical to reinforcing its distinctive brand values. TV and print advertising initially used celebrity endorsers such as Gary Lineker and Victoria Beckham. Later, 'It girl' Tara Palmer-Tomkinson replaced Victoria Beckham as one of the brand's celebrity faces. The ads have given the brand a sense of fun while effectively communicating the indulgent nature of the product. Walkers succeeded in achieving complete saturation of the market through intensive distribution. First appearing in stores in 2002, this new brand achieved phenomenal sales of £78 million in its first year.

Based on: Goldstone (2002);[33] Murphy and Goldstone (2003)[34]

the links between marketing investments and the long-term profitability of the organization have not been made clear.[35] Too often, marketers justify their investments in terms of increasing customer awareness, sales volume or market share. Doyle proposes the concept of **value-based marketing**, where the objective of marketing is seen as contributing to the maximization of **shareholder value**, which has become the overarching goal of chief executives in more and more companies. This approach helps clarify the importance of investment in marketing assets such as brands and marketing knowledge, and helps to dissuade management from making arbitrary cuts in marketing expenditure, such as advertising, in times of economic difficulty. The title CMO, or Chief Marketing Officer, has begun to emerge in some companies to reflect the importance of marketing to the overall performance of the organization. CMOs usually have a seat in the corporate boardroom.

The scope of marketing

Up to now our focus has been on the application of marketing in commercial contexts—that is, its use by companies with products or services to sell. But it is clear from simple observation that the marketing concept, and marketing tools and techniques, are in evidence in many other contexts too. For example, political parties are often criticized for their over-use of marketing. They are heavy users of marketing research to find out what the views of the voting public are; the candidates they put forward for election are often carefully selected and 'packaged' to appeal to voters. They are also extensive users of advertising and public relations to get their message across (see Exhibit 1.5).

Evidence of the application of marketing can be found in many other contexts. Educational institutions

Exhibit 1.5 Billboards like this one are a particularly popular advertising medium for political parties

have become more market-led as demographic changes have given rise to greater competition for students, whose choices are increasingly being influenced by the publication of performance-based league tables. Universities are responding by developing new logos and rebranding themselves, conducting promotional campaigns, and targeting new markets such as mature students and those from other countries around the world. The average marketing budget of private schools in the UK has risen from £33,966 in 2001 to £59,300 in 2006, and this investment has enabled private schools to grow their enrolments in spite of a national decline in the number of school-age children. They are also using the kinds of segmentation techniques employed by companies to identify potential 'customers', as well as customer service training to convert enquiries into 'sales'.[36] The use of marketing takes many forms in the arts and media. It has been argued that many media vehicles, such as newspapers and television channels, are being 'dumbed down' in order to appeal to certain market segments and to maximize revenues, in the same way many artistic organizations would be criticized for putting revenues ahead of quality and originality by producing art that appeals to a mass audience. The use of marketing can be found in almost all walks of life, such as when a city markets itself, as shown in Marketing in Action 1.4.

Marketing in Action 1.4: Marketing London

Study guide: Below is an illustration of marketing in a non-traditional context. Read it and consider any other examples of marketing in a novel context that you can think of.

Not only products and services but also places market themselves. This is often referred to as destination marketing. Tourism generates an estimated £15 billion a year for London's economy. However, the 11 September 2001 attacks in New York, the Iraq War and the London underground bombings of 2005 have created significant challenges for London in its efforts to attract visitors. The marketing body charged with this responsibility is VisitLondon and in 2002 it appointed Tamara Ingram, chief executive of Grey advertising agency, as its chairman to spearhead its marketing efforts.

Ingram has overseen an integrated marketing effort to rebrand London and increase its appeal to visitors. Traditionally, the London Tourist Board had sought primarily to bring tourists to the city, while VisitLondon aims to make London appealing to residents, people in the UK and people from overseas, whether they are business people or tourists. One of the first initiatives was the 'Totally London' campaign, which used London street signs, transport and typography in an integrated way to boost interest in the city's museums, retail outlets, parks and other attractions. Since then it has focused on particular segments of the market, such as, for example, the gay and lesbian communities, as well as producing study guides for international students. Events such as the Chinese New Year are used as a focal point for the Chinese market and a 'China in London' season, including films and cultural events, was promoted on the London Underground, in the print media and on a microsite on the VisitLondon web page. These kinds of initiatives help to strengthen economic links between London and China.

VisitLondon has used some novel marketing techniques to promote the city in international markets. For example, in Japan, it commissioned Japanese pop star Kyoko to record a single called 'Wonder London—Future Calling'. In the USA, six London taxi drivers toured twelve US cities in their iconic black cabs, offering free rides to commuters. These are examples of **buzz marketing**—that is, marketing initiatives designed to get consumers talking about a particular brand.

While visitor numbers have recovered from the London bombings, the city still faces challenges, particularly in the domestic market where low-cost airlines make travel to other European cities particularly attractive. But its marketing efforts appear to be working. In 2007, the city attracted 11 million domestic visitors, the only city in the UK to reverse falling domestic numbers. And with the profile being given to the city by the impending Olympic Games in 2012, it is likely that the appeal of London will continue to grow.

Based on: Garrahan (2006)[39]

The range of potential applications for marketing has given rise to much debate among marketing scholars regarding the scope of marketing.[37] In particular, the challenge has been to find a core concept that effectively integrates both business and non-business or social marketing. For example, initially the idea of a transaction was put forward, but not all marketing requires a transaction or sale. Kotler then put forward the notion of exchange, implying that any exchange between two parties can be considered marketing.[38] However, this is also clearly problematic as many exchanges, such as favours given by family members, are not marketing activities. For our purposes, the core of marketing is the notion of a customer and the need to understand and respond to the customer's needs.

Planning marketing activity

Finally, in many organizations, marketing can be a haphazard activity often done in response to particular opportunities or in times of difficulty or crisis. But attention to marketing must be consistent as markets change and nothing lasts for ever. For example, who would have thought it would be necessary to market gold? It is. Demand for gold has been falling as consumers switch their spending to luxury brands like Cartier and Louis Vuitton, and its image has been tarnished by its use on everything from biscuits to credit cards. In response the World Gold Council has developed an advertising campaign for gold jewellery.[40]

For marketing efforts to be effective, it is essential that a planned approach is taken. Planning is about deciding where we want to go and how we are going to get there. The process of **marketing planning** involves analysing the environment and the organization's capabilities, and deciding on courses of action and ways to implement those decisions. Having a plan gives managers a focal point for decisions and actions. It also stimulates achievement by giving the organization clear targets to aim at, which can be helpful in generating change in an organization.

The marketing planning process is shown in Figure 1.7 and we will revisit the issue of marketing planning in more detail in Chapter 12.

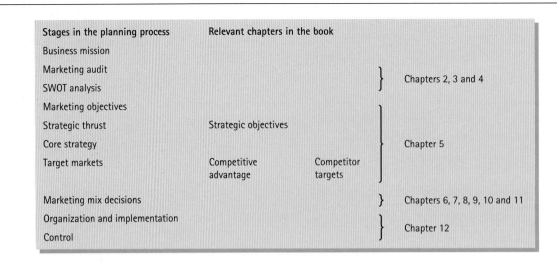

Stages in the planning process	Relevant chapters in the book		
Business mission			
Marketing audit			
SWOT analysis			Chapters 2, 3 and 4
Marketing objectives			
Strategic thrust	Strategic objectives		
Core strategy			Chapter 5
Target markets	Competitive advantage	Competitor targets	
Marketing mix decisions			Chapters 6, 7, 8, 9, 10 and 11
Organization and implementation			Chapter 12
Control			

Figure 1.7 The marketing planning process

Summary

This chapter has introduced the concept of marketing and discussed how and why organizations become market-oriented. In particular, the following issues were addressed.

1. What is meant by the marketing concept and a market orientation. The key idea here is that it is a business philosophy that puts the customer at the centre of things. Implementing the marketing concept requires a focus on customer satisfaction, an integrated effort throughout the company and a belief that corporate goals can be achieved through customer satisfaction.

2. The idea of customer value, which is the difference between the perceived benefits from consuming a product or service and the perceived sacrifice involved in doing so. Value can be derived by customers from the features of a product, the services supplied with it or indeed the image associated with it.

3. That customer value is delivered through the basic marketing mix of product, price, promotion and place. These 4-Ps and others are key decision points for marketers on an ongoing basis.

4. That marketing works and there is a strong relationship between a marketing philosophy and business performance. Academic research in the field of market orientation and ample evidence from practice attest to the power of marketing in assisting organizations to achieve their goals.

5. That the scope of marketing is broad, involving non-business as well as business contexts. Political parties, educational institutions, sporting organizations, religious organizations and others are regular users of marketing.

6. That marketing planning is an important activity to ensure marketing effectiveness. Organizations should avoid a haphazard approach to marketing and seek to conduct it in a carefully planned and structured manner.

Key terms

buzz marketing marketing initiatives designed to get consumers talking about a product or service

competitive advantage a clear performance differential over the competition on factors that are important to target customers

customer relationship management (CRM) the methodologies, technologies and e-commerce capabilities used by firms to manage customer relationships

customer satisfaction the fulfilment of customers' requirements or needs

customer value perceived benefits minus perceived sacrifice

effectiveness doing the right thing, making the correct strategic choice

efficiency a way of managing business processes to a high standard, usually concerned with cost reduction; also called 'doing things right'

marketing concept the achievement of corporate goals through meeting and exceeding customer needs better than the competition

marketing mix a framework for the tactical management of the customer relationship, including product, place, price, promotion (the 4-Ps); in the case of services, three other elements to be taken into account are process, people and physical evidence

marketing orientation companies with a marketing orientation focus on customer needs as the primary drivers of organizational performance

marketing planning the process by which businesses analyse the environment and their capabilities, decide upon courses of marketing action and implement those decisions

place the distribution channels to be used, outlet locations, methods of transportation

price (1) the amount of money paid for a product; (2) the agreed value placed on the exchange by a buyer and seller

product a good or service offered or performed by an organization or individual, which is capable of satisfying customer needs

production orientation a business approach that is inwardly focused either on costs or on a definition of a company in terms of its production facilities

promotional mix advertising, personal selling, sales promotion, public relations and direct marketing

shareholder value the returns to a company's shareholders, which grow when the company increases its dividends or its share price rises

value-based marketing a perspective on marketing that emphasizes how a marketing philosophy and marketing activities contribute to the maximization of shareholder value

Study questions

1. Discuss the differences between marketing as a philosophy and marketing as a set of business activities. How are the two ideas related?
2. Identify two examples of organizations that you consider provide customer satisfaction, and describe how they do it.
3. Marketing is sometimes considered to be an expensive luxury. Respond to this claim by demonstrating how a marketing orientation can have a positive impact on business performance.
4. Marketing is everywhere. Discuss.
5. Rather than assisting in the creation of value, marketing is responsible for many of society's ills. Discuss.
6. Visit www.marketingpower.com and www.cim.co.uk and discuss the different definitions of marketing presented by two of the world's leading marketing organizations.

Suggested reading

Brown, S. (2001) Torment Your Customers (They'll Love It), *Harvard Business Review*, October, 83–8.

Court, D. (2007) The Evolving Role of the CMO, *McKinsey Quarterly*, 3, 28–39.

Levitt, T. (1960) Marketing Myopia, *Harvard Business Review*, **38**, 45–56.

McGovern, G., D. Court, J.A. Quelch and **B. Crawford** (2004) Bringing Customers into the Boardroom, *Harvard Business Review*, **82** (11), 70–81.

Vandermerwe, S. (2003) Achieving Deep Customer Focus, *Sloan Management Review*, 45 (3), 26–35.

References

1. **Anonymous** (2003) Beyond the Model T: How Henry Ford's Legacy Has Shaped Modern Life, *Financial Times*, 16 June, 19; **Bulik, B.S.** (2004) The iPod Economy, *Advertising Age*, 18 October, 1; **Schlender, B.** (2005) How Big Can Apple Get?, *Fortune*, 28 February, 38–45.

2. **Drucker, P.F.** (1999) *The Practice of Management*, London: Heinemann.

3. **Rosenberg, L.J.** and **J.A. Czepeil** (1983) A Marketing Approach to Customer Retention, *Journal of Consumer Marketing*, **2**, 45–51.

4. **Grönroos, C.** (1989) Defining Marketing: A Market-oriented Approach, *European Journal of Marketing*, **23** (1), 52–60.

5. **Terazono, E.** (2007) Sales Blow for Men's Magazine Market, *Financial Times*, 16 February, 2.

6. **Fullerton, R.** (1988) How Modern is Modern Marketing? Marketing's Evolution and the Myth of the 'Production Era', *Journal of Marketing*, **52**, 108–25.

7. **Jones, D.** and **D. Monieson** (1990) Early Development of the Philosophy of Marketing Thought, *Journal of Marketing*, **54**, 102–13.

8. **Benton, R.** (1987) The Practical Domain of Marketing, *American Journal of Economics and Sociology*, **46** (4), 415–30.

9. **Done, K.** (2006) Boeing Lambasts Airbus's Product Strategy, *Financial Times*, July 13, 26.

10. **Davis, P.** (2005) Attack on 'Outdated' Marketing, *Financial Times*, Fund Management Supplement, 30 May, 1.

11. **Moules, J.** (2005) Spotless Service Undermined by Shrinking Revenues, *Financial Times*, 5 July, 5.

12. **Brown, R.J.** (1987) Marketing: A Function and a Philosophy, *Quarterly Review of Marketing*, **12** (3), 25–30.

13. **Satterthwaite, C.** (2004) Trust Me, and Martin and Sophie and the Boys, *Financial Times*, Creative Business, 16 November, 10.

14. **Freemantle, D.** (1998) *What Customers Like About You*, London: Nicholas Brealey Publishing.

15. **Garrity, B.** (2007) Hot Commodities, *Billboard*, **119** (12), 29–31.

16. **Guha, M.** (2007) Sole Listener is Target for Online Radio, *Financial Times*, 16 January, 12.

17. **Booms, B.H.** and **M.J. Bitner** (1981) Marketing Strategies and Organisation Structures for Service Firms, in **Donnelly, J.H.** and **W.R. George** (eds) *Marketing of Services*, Chicago: American Marketing Association, 47–52.

18. **Borden, N.** (1964) The Concept of the Marketing Mix, *Journal of Advertising Research*, June, 2–7.

19. **Anonymous** (2007) How 'Green' is that Water, Businessweek.com, 13 August.

20. **Birchall, J.** (2007) The Thirst to Build a Strong Brand, *Financial Times*, 28 November, 16.

21. **Croft, J.** (2005) Banks Shop Around to Set Out their Stalls, *Financial Times*, 5 April, 23.

22. **Benady, A.** (2005) Nestlé's New Flavour of Strategy, *Financial Times*, 22 February, 13.

23. **Anonymous** (2008) Cleaning Up, *The Economist*, 16 February, 67.

24. **Klein, N.** (2000) *No Logo*, London: Flamingo Press.

25. **James, O.** (2007) *Affluenza*, London: Vermilion.

26. **Klein, N.** (2000) op. cit.

27. **Linn, S.** (2004) *Consuming Kids: The Hostile Takeover of Childhood*, New York: The New Press.

28. **Narver, J.C.** and **S.F. Slater** (1990) The Effect of a Market Orientation on Business Profitability, *Journal of Marketing*, **54** (October), 20–35.

29. **Terazono, E.** (2003) Spending Money to Make Money, *Financial Times*, Creative Business, 17 June, 4–5.

30. **Hooley, G., J. Lynch** and **J. Shepherd** (1990) The Marketing Concept: Putting the Theory into Practice, *European Journal of Marketing*, **24** (9), 7–23.

31. **Terazono, E.** (2003) Always on the Outside Looking In, *Financial Times*, Creative Business, 5 August, 4–5.

32. **Fligstein, N.** (1987) Intraorganisational Power Struggles: The Rise of Finance Personnel to Top Leadership in Large Corporations, 1919–1979, *American Sociology Review*, **52**, 44–58.

33. **Goldstone, J.** (2002) Posh Nosh, *Brand Strategy*, May, 34.

34. **Murphy, C.** and **J. Goldstone** (2003) And for My Next Trick . . . , *Marketing*, 30 October, 22–3.

35. **Doyle, P.** (2000) *Value-based Marketing*, Chichester: John Wiley & Sons Ltd.

36. **Boone, J.** (2007) Private School's Marketing Pays Off, *Financial Times*, 4 May, 3.

37. See, for example, **Foxall, G.** (1984) Marketing's Domain, *European Journal of Marketing*, **18** (1), 25–40; **Kotler, P.** and **S. Levy** (1969) Broadening the Concept of Marketing, *Journal of Marketing*, **33**, 10–15.

38. **Kotler, P.** (1972) A Generic Concept of Marketing, *Journal of Marketing*, **36**, 46–54.

39. **Garrahan, M.** (2006) London Lures Back the Crowds, *Financial Times*, 7 March, 10.

40. **Morrison, K.** (2005) Into a New Golden Age, *Financial Times*, 6 January, 10.

Online **Learning**Centre

When you have read this chapter, log on to the Online Learning Centre for *Foundations of Marketing* at **www.mcgraw-hill.co.uk/textbooks/jobber**, where you'll find multiple-choice test questions, links and extra online study tools for marketing.

Appendix 1.1

Careers in marketing

Choosing a career in marketing can offer a wide range of opportunities. Table A1.1 outlines some of the potential positions available in marketing.

Table A1.1 Careers in marketing

Marketing positions	
Marketing executive/co-ordinator	Management of all marketing-related activities for an organization.
Brand/product manager	A product manager is responsible for the management of a single product or a family of products. In this capacity, he or she may participate in product design and development according to the results of research into the evolving needs of their customer base. In addition, marketing managers develop business plans and marketing strategies for their product line, manage product distribution, disseminate information about the product, and co-ordinate customer service and sales.
Brand/marketing assistant	At the entry level of brand assistant, responsibilities consist of market analysis, competitive tracking, sales and market share analysis, monitoring of promotion programmes, etc.
Marketing researcher/analyst	Market researchers collect and analyse information to assist in marketing, and determine whether a demand exists for a particular product or service. Some of the tasks involved include designing questionnaires, collecting all available and pertinent information, arranging and analysing collected information, presenting research results to clients, making recommendations.
Marketing communications manager	Manages the marketing communications activity of an organization manager such as advertising, public relations, sponsorships and direct marketing.
Customer service manager/executive	Manages the service delivery and any interactions a customer may have with an organization. Role can be quite varied, depending on industry.

Sales positions	
Sales executive/business development	Aims to develop successful business relationships with existing and potential customers. Manages the company's sales prospects.
Sales manager	Plans and co-ordinates the activities of a sales team, controls product distribution, monitors budget achievement, trains and motivates personnel, prepares forecasts.
Key account executive	Manages the selling and marketing function to key customers (accounts). Conducts negotiations on products, quantities, prices, promotions, special offers etc. Networks with other key account personnel influential in the buying decision process. Liaises internally with all departments and colleagues in supplying and servicing the key account. Monitors performance of the key account.
Sales support manager	Provides sales support by fielding enquiries, taking orders and providing phone advice to customers. Also assists with exhibitions, prepares documentation for brochures and sales kits, and commissions market research suppliers for primary data.
Merchandiser	Aims to maximize the display of a company's point-of-sale displays, and ensures that they are stocked and maintained correctly.
Sales promotion executive	Aims to communicate product features and benefits directly to customers at customer locations through sampling, demonstrations and the management of any sales promotion activities.
Telesales representative	Takes in-bound or makes out-bound calls, which are sales related.
Advertising sales executive	Sells a media organization's airplay, TV spot or space to companies for the purpose of advertising.

Table A1.1 continued

Retailing positions	
Retail management	Plans and co-ordinates the operations of retail outlets. Supervises the recruitment, training, conduct and work of staff. Maintains high levels of customer service. Manages stock levels.
Retail buyer	Purchases goods to be sold in retail stores. Manages and analyses stock levels. Obtains information about the range of products available. Manages vendor relations.
Advertising positions	
Account executive	Helps devise and co-ordinate advertising campaigns. Liaises with clients, obtaining relevant information from them such as product and company details, budget and marketing goals, and marketing research information. Briefs other specialists in the agency (such as creative team, media planners and researchers) on client requirements, to develop the details of a campaign. May present draft campaign suggestions to clients along with a summary of the expenditure involved, and negotiate and arrange for modifications if required. May supervise and co-ordinate the work of the relevant production departments so that the campaign is developed as planned to meet deadlines and budget requirements.
Media planner/buyer	Organizes and purchases advertising space on television, radio, in magazines, newspapers or on outdoor advertising. Liaises between clients and sellers of advertising space to ensure that the advertising campaign reaches the target market.
Public relations positions	
Public relations executive	Helps to develop and maintain a hospitable, friendly public environment for the organization. This involves liaising with clients, co-ordination of special events, lobbying, crisis management, media relations, writing and editing of printed material.
Press relations/ corporate affairs	Develops and maintains a good working relationship with the media. Creates press releases or responds to media queries.

Case 1 YouTube

YouTube has become an internet phenomenon

In its short existence, YouTube has become a classic example of a modern internet phenomenon. It is a video-sharing website that is used on a daily basis by people all over the world. It has been used to embarrass celebrities, to cause political storms, for entertainment, for self-promotion and for thousands of other reasons. The company was only 16 months old when Google was willing to pay US$1.65 billion to acquire it. What have been the reasons for its amazingly rapid growth and what are the future challenges it faces?

Background

Like some famous computer companies before it, YouTube was founded in a garage, by Chad Hurley, Steve Chen and Karid Jarem, in February 2005, and was officially launched to the world in December of that year from offices in San Francisco. YouTube is an online portal through which users can watch and share video content. Video had been available on the internet for some time, but Hurley and Chen wanted to make it easier to pass on the videos that they thought others would want to see. So instead of users having to download special software to view videos, they created a way in which video could be viewed directly on the web. Another important feature of the technology was that it put all its videos into a format that could be played by the Flash player that was found on virtually all PCs. Multiple formats had been a particular problem for video websites prior to this.

The initial vision for YouTube was that it would be a vehicle whereby young people in particular would have the facility to show off their talents as home movie makers, building on the increasing popularity of 'reality television' at the time. Consequently, some of the most popular early videos were parodies of social networks like MySpace.com or spoofs of leading movies like *Brokeback Mountain*. But as the site began to get popular, trailers of much-anticipated new movies began to appear on it. Advertisers were quick to recognize its potential, and viral advertisers like Carlsberg and Nike began putting ads on the site.

A key to YouTube's early success was that viewers had the facility to send a link via email to their friends, which enabled the creation of a community of users. YouTube's technology also made it easier for bloggers and others to 'grab' a video segment from YouTube and place it on their own web pages, extending the reach of its content to a much bigger audience. And it also let its users decide which videos were worth watching by providing the facility to rate and recommend videos in the same way as Amazon had been doing with books and CDs.

YouTube then benefited from the network effects that allow many companies to grow rapidly on the internet. In other words, the bigger a site's audience gets, the more success will feed off itself. The people who are attracted to putting a home video on YouTube because of the size of its audience, often produce content that attracts new viewers and on it goes in a virtuous cycle. Consequently, the volume of content appearing on the site and its level of usage grew exponentially. Fans upload 65,000 videos and over 100 million clips are viewed each day. By June 2007, Nielsen's NetRatings were showing that it had logged 55 million unique users each month, a rise of 300 per cent from June 2006. Part of the reason for YouTube's phenomenal popularity is that is both easy to use and edgy at the same time. Users can watch videos without even registering, so, as with shopping, all you have to do is 'walk in the door'. But also almost anything imaginable, from the funny to the weird to the sad, is available on the site. Because the site does not pre-screen uploads, which is efficient because it saves on the cost of hiring a team of editors, the site becomes host to all sorts of weird and wonderful material, from obscure bands to tearful video diaries, and so on. This endless supply of material allows users to be entertained for hours on the site.

Revenue streams

Having spent the early part of its life building up a global profile and user base, one of the key challenges facing YouTube is how to generate revenue from all these users. This represents a difficult challenge for the company as it will want to do so without alienating its existing client base. Part of the site's appeal at present is that it is seen as not overtly commercial, and it is viewed by many as a user-driven, grassroots entity. Several potential revenue streams have been initiated by the company, such as those listed below.

- *Sponsored brand channels:* sponsored channels are specially designed YouTube pages that allow users to view branded content. One of the earliest customers was Warner Brothers Records, which set up a page to promote a new album by Paris Hilton.
- *Display advertising:* there are a variety of display ad formats throughout the site, which can be segmented by age, gender, geography and time of day. One format is an in-video overlay that lasts for about 15 seconds and viewers have the choice of closing it, waiting for it to expire automatically or clicking on it to watch the full advert.
- *Contests:* companies can run competitions on the site, where viewers rate videos.
- *YouTube video ads:* companies can advertise their products on the site.
- *YouTube in-video ads:* ads that are placed in YouTube partners' video content.

YouTube controls the 'Featured Videos' that appear on its homepage, which can dramatically increase the popularity of a video.

The takeover by Google

As the site grew, speculation about whether it would be acquired by a bigger player like Google was widespread. For some time this did not look likely as Hurley and Chen had indicated that they wanted to remain independent and had been critical of Google's video-sharing site, Google Video. They were also concerned that Google had already dabbled in too many products beyond web search and was risking confusing its customers. But eventually the sale became an easy choice for YouTube. It was losing money incurring the costs of storing and delivering millions of videos, and it also risked further costs because of potential copyright lawsuits. Google offered it immense storage capacity, the largest online network of potential advertisers as well as teams of lawyers to help deal with any legal issues that may arise. For Google, it also represented a strategic change towards buying a large competitor rather than looking to build up Google Video.

The copyright dilemma

The issue of copyrighted material appearing on YouTube quickly became a controversial one for the company. For example, Viacom distributes the kind of short content that is so popular on YouTube and after months of negotiations regarding a revenue share failed, it ordered YouTube to remove over 100,000 video clips from its site. Even its sale to Google was nearly jeopardized by the problem because at the same time as it was negotiating with the search engine giant, Universal Music was preparing a lawsuit against the company alleging massive copyright infringement. But its case was helped when another music company, Warner Music, did a deal with YouTube to distribute its music videos in exchange for a licensing fee and a share of advertising.

The problem for many companies is that while the uploading of videos onto YouTube may be violating copyright, it is also turning out to be a useful way to generate some publicity about an upcoming movie or TV show. In response, YouTube is working on technology that would identify copyrighted video content and implement 'audio-fingerprinting' to ensure music companies are paid for use of their songs in YouTube clips. But some of the content providers argue that YouTube has been too slow in deploying this technology. At the same time, it has struck numerous partnership deals with content providers such as CBS, the BBC, Universal Music Group, Sony Music Group, Warner Music Group, NBA and the Sundance Channel.

The future

YouTube has been a stunning success story, which has given it a strong lead in the video distribution business. In early 2008, it became the most popular social media website in the UK, ahead of Wikipedia, Facebook and others, with 10.4 million unique visits in January of that year. However, competition is likely to come from a variety of sources. First, there are the many other video-sharing websites that have launched following the success of YouTube. Large organizations like News Corporation, which owns MySpace.com, Yahoo!Video, MSN Video and AOL, have developed online video offerings. Some of the big content creators like Disney, which owns the ABC television network, have streamed their most popular videos on their own websites, which are free to watch.

Other companies, such as Metacafe, are trying to pursue a different content model. There are millions of videos on YouTube, but critics argue that many are of dubious quality and barely watchable. Metacafe, makes an effort to be selective and promote only 'good' videos on its homepage. First, it rejects duplicates, which make up about half its submissions. Then it uses 100,000 volunteers as film critics in the same way that Wikipedia uses volunteers to write and vet articles. Third, it analyses clips using its VideoRank algorithm, which examines metrics like whether the video was watched all the way to the end, to determine its quality. Metacafe claims that it attracts 25 million unique users each month. Also, there are sites like Eefoof.com, Panjea.com, Revver and Blip.TV, which share up to 50 per cent of ad page revenue with the creators of videos. Eefoof uses the tagline 'Make it. Post it. Profit'. In response, YouTube has also begun offering a share of advertising revenues to video uploaders.

So, despite its phenomenal early success, the future is uncertain for YouTube. The most gloomy scenario is that it becomes the next Napster—the company that pioneered the digital downloading of music only to eventually be shut down by legal action undertaken by the major music labels. In the same way, YouTube has built the business of online video distribution but faces similar major legal issues over copyright and a wave of aggressive new rivals. Its early success will be no guarantee that it can rest on its laurels.

Questions

1. What kind of customer value does YouTube provide in the marketplace?
2. How do businesses like YouTube alter the ways that organizations and customers interact?
3. What are the challenges facing YouTube in the future?

This case was prepared from various published sources by Professor John Fahy, University of Limerick, as a basis for class discussion rather than to illustrate either effective or ineffective management.

Chapter 2
The Global Marketing Environment

Chapter Outline

The macroenvironment

Economic forces

Social forces

Political and legal forces

Physical forces

Technological forces

The microenvironment

Environmental scanning

Learning Outcomes

By the end of this chapter you will understand:

1   what is meant by the term 'marketing environment'
2   the distinction between the microenvironment and the macroenvironment
3   the impact of economic, social, political and legal, physical, and technological forces on marketing decisions
4   the growing importance of social responsibility and ethical marketing practices
5   how companies respond to environmental change.

Marketing Spotlight

Counterfeiting: a booming global business

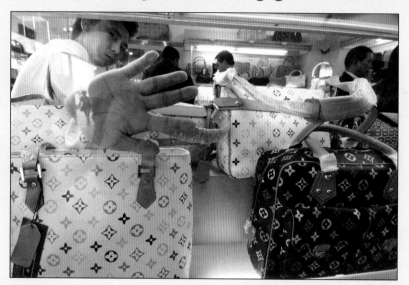

goods, and its value in 2005 was estimated to be US$350 billion.

The intensity of competition, particularly among clothing retailers, has also given rise to a trademark infringement problem. For example, in December 2006, Marks & Spencer was forced to destroy thousands of handbags when designer brand Jimmy Choo threatened it with legal action for allegedly copying its Cosmo silk bag. UK company Mosaic Fashions successfully sued the Irish chain Dunnes Stores for copying a Karen Millen sweater design. In the past it would have taken six months for designer items to find their way to the high street. But now, through the use of information technology and low-cost production, it can now be done in a matter of hours.

M odern business has become truly global. Products that you purchase in your favourite shops may well have been made on the other side of the world. Shoes may come from South East Asia, fruit from Chile and water from New Zealand. Designs of products that appear on television worn by celebrities can quickly be found in high-street stores. Modern media, like the internet and television, have become vehicles through which the aspirations of society are shaped. In this global and fast-moving environment, it is relatively easy to bend the rules, and the rapid growth of counterfeiting is just one illustration of this.

Many product categories suffer from extensive levels of counterfeiting. For example, effective brand building by a variety of companies over the years has created a league of premium brands like Burberry, Gucci, Yves St Laurent, Hugo Boss and many others. When sold in outlets like department stores and speciality shops, they typically command high prices. Their promotion creates the promise of an aspirational lifestyle characterized by wealth and luxury. But, in many instances, these products can be produced relatively cheaply in low-cost production locations around the world. Therefore they are ripe for counterfeiting. Replica versions of the top brands are produced in vast quantities and sold through unauthorized channels like discount stores, markets and online. The International Chamber of Commerce estimates that 7 per cent of world trade is in counterfeit

One of the fastest-growing sectors for counterfeiting is in the pharmaceutical drugs business. Because drugs are high-value items and are small and cheap to transport, they are very attractive to counterfeiters. As many of the consumers who need drugs cannot afford them they look to buy them online or from other unauthorized channels. It is estimated that about 10 per cent of the drugs sold in the developing world are fake. Lifestyle drugs like Viagra and Prozac have also proved to be very popular. Consumer health is being put at risk because the fakes may contain no active ingredients or harmful ingredients and many are making it into official distribution channels. Telling a real drug from a fake version is practically impossible.

Counterfeiting illustrates the global nature of business, the power of the internet as a distribution channel and the need for businesses to operate within a strict legal framework. For example, Christian Dior has filed a lawsuit against eBay alleging that 90 per cent of 'Christian Dior' products sold on the site between 2001 and 2005 were fakes. However, research has also shown that the majority of consumers are happy to purchase counterfeit products, particularly clothing and footwear. The desire to satisfy needs and wants suggests that counterfeiting is likely to be a global problem for some time.[1]

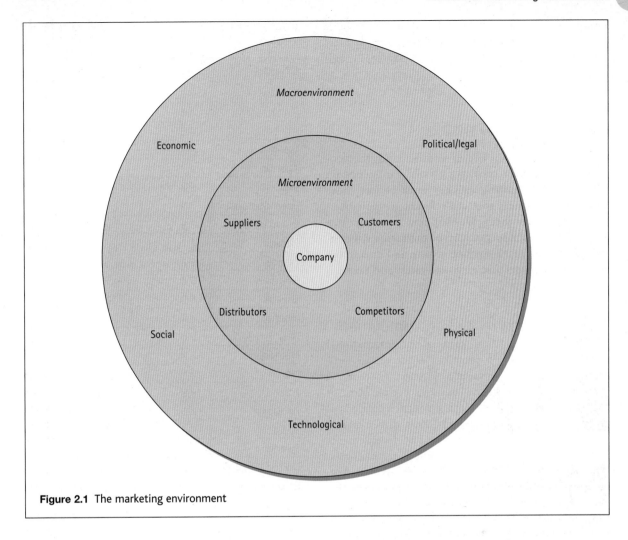

Figure 2.1 The marketing environment

A market-orientated firm needs to look outward to the environment in which it operates, adapting to take advantage of emerging opportunities and to minimize potential threats. In this chapter we will examine the **marketing environment** and how to monitor it. In particular, we will look at some of the major forces acting on companies, such as the economic, social, legal, physical and technological issues that affect corporate activities.

The marketing environment is composed of the forces and actors that affect a company's ability to operate effectively in providing products and services to its customers. It is useful to classify these forces into the **microenvironment** and the **macroenvironment** (see Figure 2.1). The microenvironment consists of the actors in the firm's immediate environment or business system that affect its capabilities to operate effectively in its chosen markets. The key actors are suppliers, distributors, customers and competitors. The macroenvironment consists of a number of broader forces that affect not only the

company, but also the other actors in the microenvironment. These can be grouped into economic, social, political/legal, physical and technological forces. These shape the character of the opportunities and threats facing a company, and yet are largely uncontrollable.

The macroenvironment

This chapter will focus on the major macroenvironmental forces that affect marketing decisions. Four forces—namely economic, social, political/legal and technological—have been the focus of most attention, with the result that the acronyms PEST or STEP are often used to describe macroenvironmental analysis. The growing importance of the impact of marketing activity on the physical environment means that this issue, too, will be a focus of attention. Later in the chapter we will introduce the four dimensions of the microenvironment, which will then be dealt with in greater detail throughout the book. The changing nature of the supply chain and customer behaviour will be dealt with in detail in the next chapter. Distribution will be examined in Chapter 11 and competitive forces in Chapter 12.

Economic forces

Through its effect on supply and demand, the economic environment can have a crucial influence on the success of companies. They must choose those economic influences that are relevant to their business and monitor them. We shall now examine three major economic influences on the marketing environment of companies: economic growth and unemployment; interest rates and exchange rates; and taxation and inflation.

Economic growth and unemployment

The general state of both national and international economies can have a profound effect on an individual company's prosperity. Economies tend to fluctuate according to the 'business cycle'. Most of the world's economies went through a period of significant growth from the mid-1990s, driven mainly by productivity gains brought about by developments in computing and telecommunications technologies. The fortunes of many sectors, such as retailing, services and consumer durables, closely mirror this economic pattern. In Ireland, which had very strong growth during the late 1990s, new car sales rose from a level of about 70,000 per year in the early part of the decade to over 200,000 in 2000. Similarly, the current buoyant growth of the Chinese and Indian economies is resulting in a boom in demand for cars, housing and consumer durables, as well as for commodities like oil and copper. A major marketing problem is predicting the next boom or slump. Investments made during periods of high growth can become massive cash drains if customer spending falls suddenly. The problems faced by many residential and commercial property developers and the banks that lent money to them in 2008 were partly caused by this trap.

Low growth rates are reflected in high unemployment levels, which in turn affect consumer spending power. Unemployment levels throughout some of the world's major economies are shown in Table 2.1. In times of economic recession, consumers tend to postpone spending and/or become more cost conscious, shifting more of their spending to discount stores. This is also the time when companies tend to cut back on advertising budgets, which has particular implications for marketing.

Table 2.1 Unemployment rates (per cent) in selected countries

Country	2006	2007
Canada	6.3	6.0
United States	4.6	4.6
Australia	4.8	4.4
Japan	4.1	3.9
Austria	4.7	4.4
Belgium	8.3	7.5
Czech Republic	7.1	5.3
Denmark	3.9	3.8
Finland	7.7	6.9
France	9.2	8.3
Germany	9.8	8.4
Greece	8.9	8.3
Ireland	4.4	4.5
Italy	6.8	6.1
Netherlands	3.9	3.2
Norway	3.5	2.6
Poland	13.8	9.6
Portugal	7.6	8.0
Spain	8.5	8.3
Sweden	7.0	6.1
United Kingdom	5.3	5.3
Euro Area	8.2	7.4

Source: OECD

Interest and exchange rates

One of the levers that the government uses to manage the economy is interest rates; the interest rate is the rate at which money is borrowed by businesses and individuals (see Exhibit 2.1). Throughout the world, interest rates are at historically low levels. One of the results of this has been a boom in consumer borrowing. House prices have been growing at double-digit rates in many countries, which has meant significant sales and profit rises for construction companies and global furniture retailers like IKEA. There has even been a surge in the number of television programmes dealing with property acquisition, purchasing holiday homes abroad and home improvement. While taking on debt to buy homes and cars has traditionally been considered acceptable, what is worrying policy-makers now is the high levels of consumer debt arising particularly from the over-use of credit cards. Total household borrowing as a percentage of gross domestic product (GDP) has risen considerably over the past two decades, but the rate of growth has been variable. Debt levels are below 40 per cent of GDP in Italy but over 100 per cent in the UK, the Netherlands and

Table 2.2 Interest rates (per cent) in selected countries

Country	2008
United States	2.08
Australia	7.91
Japan	0.75
Euro Area	4.74
China	4.50
India	6.92
UK	5.89
Denmark	5.25
Norway	6.26
Russia	10.25
Singapore	1.28
Brazil	11.18

Source: The Economist

Exhibit 2.1 Northern Rock used aggressive savings and lending rates in order to build its share of the market in the UK before suffering during the credit crunch of 2008

Denmark. Levels of credit card debt are at an all-time high in countries like Ireland, Australia and the USA. All loans eventually have to be paid back and, should interest rates rise, repayment costs will rise too. At the extreme this leads to situations where people may lose their homes, as has happened in the USA, and companies suffer from bad debts as people default on loans. In the UK in 2007, the leading banks saw a significant rise in bad debts, and consumers who had over-borrowed were unable to repay. Overall, changes in interest rates are usually followed quickly by changes in consumer behaviour. Table 2.2 shows the variation in the level of interest rates in some of the major economies around the world.

Exchange rates are the rates at which one currency buys another. With the formation of the European Union, exchange rates between most European countries are now fixed. However, the rates at which major currencies like the US dollar, the euro, sterling and the yen are traded are still variable. These floating rates can have a significant impact on the profitability of a company's international operations. For example, the declining US economy and falling interest rates there in 2007 and 2008 have led to a significant weakening of the US dollar against currencies like the euro and the Japanese yen. This in turn has meant that both European and Japanese goods became more expensive in the United States, causing problems for many European companies that are dependent on the US market. For example, the Irish luxury goods group, Waterford-Wedgwood has over 70 per cent of its sales in the USA, and has suffered significant

losses and share price falls in recent years. However, from the point of view of some US businesses, the falling dollar has brought very positive results, with, for example, tourism to the country increasing due to relatively lower prices for food and accommodation. Dramatic currency falls have also taken place in New Zealand in 2006 and Iceland in 2008.

Taxation and inflation

There are two types of taxes: direct and indirect. Direct taxes are taxes on income and wealth, such as income tax, capital gains tax, inheritance tax, and so on. Income tax is important for marketers because it determines the levels of disposable income that consumers have. When taxes fall, consumers keep a greater portion of their earnings and have more money to spend. It also increases the levels of discretionary income that they have—that is, the amount of money available after essentials such as food and rent have been paid for. At this point consumers move from needs to wants, and a great deal of marketing activity is aimed at trying to convince us where we should spend our discretionary income.

Indirect taxes include value-added tax (VAT), excise duties and tariffs, and are taxes that are included in the prices of goods and services that we buy. They have major implications for marketing mix variables such as price. Changes in VAT rates need to be passed on to customers and this can cause problems for firms trying to compete on the basis of low price, for example. Differences in indirect tax levels across national boundaries give rise to the problem of *parallel importing*, whereby goods are bought in a low-cost country for importation back into a high-cost country. This presents a problem for distributors in the high-cost country, who are not permitted to get access to this source of supply. Variations in tax levels impact on consumer demand. For example, lower tax levels on wine have resulted in consumers switching from beer. As a result, some interesting disputes have arisen with regard to how products should be classified. For example, Marks & Spencer had consistently argued that its teacakes should be classified as cakes (which carry a zero VAT rating) as opposed to chocolate biscuits, which carry a VAT rate of 20 per cent. The long-running legal battle between the company and the UK Treasury was finally ended in the European Court in 2008 when the court ruled in

M&S's favour, resulting in a £3.5 million rebate to the company for VAT paid on the product.

Finally, inflation is a measure of the cost of living in an economy. The inflation rate is calculated by monitoring price changes on a basket of products such as rent/mortgage repayments, oil, clothing, food items and consumer durables. The rising price of commodities like oil and wheat feed through to consumers in the form of higher fuel bills and higher bread and pasta prices. Rapid rises in inflation also reduce the future value of savings, investments and pensions. Governments are acutely sensitive to inflation figures and take action to keep inflation under control.

Overall economic movements feed through to marketing in the form of influencing demand for products and services, and the level of profitability that accrues to the firm from the sales of goods. Economic movements can sometimes be sudden and severe in their level of impact, as shown in Marketing in Action 2.1.

Marketing in Action 2.1: The credit crisis and the demise of Northern Rock

Study guide: Below is a review of the near collapse of the UK bank, Northern Rock. Read it and describe how it illustrates the importance of understanding changes in the economic environment.

For much of the global economy, the early part of this decade was boom time. Economic growth was good, inflation was low, employment levels were high and consumer demand was strong. Significantly, too, interest rates were low, which encouraged people to borrow money to invest in assets such as property and equities. But, in a break with tradition, consumers also borrowed to fund current expenditure on products like cars and holidays, and the level of income being diverted to savings decreased. In the deregulated financial services environment, banks and building societies competed aggressively for this business by offering attractively priced loans and mortgage products.

But to be able to lend out money, banks had to have money coming in and, with savings falling, they faced a problem. One of the solutions to this problem was the emergence of a form of financing known as asset-backed securities, which worked as follows. Banks in the USA offered loans to house purchasers with poor credit histories. Normally banks are reluctant to do this in case the borrower defaults on the loan, but in this instance, they got over this problem by selling on these loans or parts of them to other banks in the form of investment securities. These were then sold on again to other banks and investors. But because the original lending bank no longer carried the investment risk, the monitoring of the mortgages was poor and the criteria by which loans were issued were lax. With a downturn in the US economy, the inevitable happened. Large numbers of these 'subprime' mortgages began to default, making the resulting securities worthless. But because these loans had been sliced and repackaged several times, the location of the losses became unclear. Gradually some banks, like Citigroup in the USA and UBS in Europe, began to acknowledge that they had lost billions. But paralysis gripped the money markets and banks stopped lending to each other, or lent only at high rates, because they were uncertain that they would be repaid. The flows of funds to business and consumers dried up and the major central banks around the world had to intervene on several occasions in 2007 and 2008.

The highest-profile casualty of the so-called credit crunch was the UK bank, Northern Rock. In comparison to its peers, Northern Rock obtained a relatively high proportion of its finance in the 'wholesale' market, relying heavily on products like asset-backed securities rather than on private savings. When the world's banks stopped lending to each other, Northern Rock struggled to source finance to meet the day-to-day demands of its consumers. The Bank of England provided it with emergency finance in September 2007 and this news caused customers to panic. Long queues began to form outside Northern Rock branches and online as consumers sought to withdraw their money. It was the first 'run' on a British bank in 140 years and was averted only when the Bank of England underwrote its assets to the tune of £30 billion. Its share price fell from over £10 in June 2007 to less than 90 pence by early 2008. After attempts to sell the bank at this knockdown price failed, it was ultimately nationalized by the UK Government in February 2008.

The fall of Northern Rock was dramatic and unprecedented—and a sharp reminder of how uncontrollable external forces can impact on a business. In January 2007, the bank had announced pre-tax profits of £627 million for 2006. This marked 10 years of growth since its conversion in 1997 from a building society to become Britain's fifth biggest mortgage lender. But its business model, which provided it with cheaper finance than its competitors, became its undoing when the environment changed. Its failure to appreciate the risks it faced ultimately led to its demise.

Social forces

There are four social forces, in particular, that have had implications for marketing. These are: changes in the demographic profile of the population; cultural differences within and between nations; **social responsibility** and marketing ethics; and the influence of the **consumer movement**. We will now examine each of these in turn.

Demographic forces

The term demographics refers to changes in population. Three major forces are world population growth, changing age distribution and changes in household composition. Most of the forecast world population growth is expected to occur in Africa, Asia and Latin America. Many marketers tend to ignore African countries because they are home to the majority of the estimated four billion people worldwide that live in poverty (that is, survive on less than US$1500 a year). However, companies such as Hewlett-Packard, Unilever and Vodafone are increasingly focusing their attention on these so-called 'premarkets' (i.e. not yet sufficiently developed to be considered consumer markets) and are recognizing that they can return a profit while having a positive effect on the livelihoods of people. For example, Unilever is trying to sell more soap in African countries, which improves hygiene and cuts down on diseases, while mobile phone companies like Vodafone in Africa and Digicell in the Caribbean have generated significant profits from providing telephony in these regions.

Globalization has given rise to two other interesting demographic effects, namely population migration between countries and the rise of middle and wealthy classes in countries with a low average GDP per capita. Ireland is an interesting case in point where population falls in the 1980s have been replaced by a dramatic rise in inward migration by people attracted to its rapidly growing economy. The continued integration of Europe has resulted in significant movements of labour from the poorer areas of Central and Eastern Europe to the wealthier Western European countries. These patterns are being played out around the world, and the UN estimates that, in 2007, 200 million people settled outside the country in which they were born. These population movements bring with them increased demand for niche products and services. Global economic prosperity has also given rise to significant segments of wealthy consumers in countries with low average wages, such as Russia and China. For example, advertising expenditure in Nigeria has grown six-fold since 2000 as global companies seek to reach its growing middle class.[2]

A major demographic change that will continue to affect demand for products and services is the rising proportion of people over the age of 60 and the

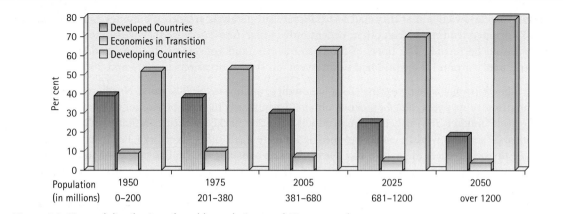

Figure 2.2 Size and distribution of world population aged 60 years and over
Source: UN, World Economic & Social Survey 2007

decline in the younger age group. Figure 2.2 shows projections for the growth of this segment up to 2050. The rise in the over-45-year-old group creates substantial marketing opportunities because of the high level of per capita income enjoyed by this group in developed countries. They have much lower commitments in terms of mortgage repayments than younger people, tend to benefit from inheritance wealth and are healthier than ever before. Pharmaceuticals, health and beauty, technology, travel, financial services, luxury cars, lavish food and entertainment are key growth sectors for this market segment. The overall implication of these trends is that many consumer companies may need to reposition their product and service offerings to take account of the rise in so-called 'grey' purchasing power.

Finally, one of the emerging demographic trends is the growth in the number of household units and falling household sizes. People are choosing to get married later or stay single, divorce rates are rising and family sizes are smaller than they traditionally have been. Combined with high incomes and busy lives, these trends have led to a boom in connoisseur convenience foods and convenience shopping. Companies like Northern Foods and Marks & Spencer, in particular, have catered for this market very successfully. Demand for childcare and homecare facilities has also risen.

Cultural forces

Culture is the combination of values, beliefs and attitudes that is possessed by a national group or subgroup. Cultural differences have implications for the way in which business is conducted. For example, because of the growth of markets like China, India and Singapore, more and more westerners are doing business in these countries and are finding significant differences in the ways things are done. Westerners tend to view contracts as set in stone, while those from the East take a more flexible view. In the East, a penchant for harmony means that decision-making tends primarily to be a rubber-stamping of a consensus already hammered out by senior management. The Western obsession with using logic to unravel complex situations is likely to be viewed as naive by those in the East. These kinds of differences are deeply culturally bound in the complex social networks of the East versus the greater levels of independence experienced by those living in the West.[3]

International marketers need to pay particular attention to the possible impact of culture. For example, MTV—which was the traditional, all-American music channel—now has 141 channels broadcasting in 32 languages to 160 countries. While these could be vehicles for the export of American culture to new countries, the company is careful to reflect local cultures; for example, 45 per cent of what is shown on MTV Arabia in the Middle East is locally produced and the remainder is translated.[4]

Even within particular countries, however, it is important to bear in mind that many subcultures also exist. The rapid movement of global populations, described above, has meant that ethnically based subcultures have sprung up in most developed countries, creating potentially lucrative niche markets for products and services. For example, recent US census data estimates that there are 35.3 million Hispanics in America with a buying power of US$452.4 billion.[5] In addition, social trends and fashions give rise to their own particular subcultures, whose members dress and behave in certain ways—hip hop fans, football hooligans, and so on. For example, when the Burberry brand was adopted by football hooligans

Marketing in Action 2.2: Burberry's 'problem' customers

> **Study guide:** Below is a review of recent problems encountered by the Burberry brand in the UK. Read it and think of other brands that are connected to particular subcultures.

Burberry, the iconic English brand, was founded by Thomas Burberry back in 1856. By 1924 its distinctive check pattern appeared in the lining of its now famous trench coat. This trademark-registered design, which was to become the company's signature look, was later extended to umbrellas, scarves and luggage. A period of international expansion began in the 1980s for the, by then, fashionable clothing brand, marked by the opening of its first flagship store in New York. Burberry was renowned for its luxury status, embraced by the affluent and refined in society.

Unfortunately, unintended and much less desirable markets have also begun to adopt the brand. In the UK, Burberry's distinctive check has become the uniform of the 'chav', a term used in the media to deride a certain type of youth. Chavs are predominantly white, lower-class adolescents who like to sport numerous brands, often counterfeit, as a badge of aspirational cool.

The brand has also become particularly associated with football hooligans, who are often seen at matches sporting Burberry shirts and baseball caps. In 2004, two British pubs banned the wearing of Burberry on their premises, putting forward the argument that the brand had become a uniform for football hooligans and yobs. The story received huge media attention and this association with lower-class vulgarity and anarchy is in stark contrast to Burberry's adverts, which contain images of young, beautiful, well-heeled people who also tend to be mainly white.

The adoption of luxury brands by unintended markets can cause quite a headache for brand owners, who must decide how best to react. Burberry's response was to pursue an aggressive strategy of taking the brand upmarket again. It hired supermodel Kate Moss to front its advertising, and expanded its range of retail stores. It also targeted key international markets like the USA, where the brand's image is much stronger. This approach appears to be working, with the company reporting an annual increase in profits of 25 per cent in 2008. Luxury brands must carefully manage their brand image and hope the fickleness of fashion will see their new 'problem' customers move on to their next unsuspecting victim.

Based on: Braddock (2003);[6] Killgren (2008);[7] O'Brien (2003);[8] Tomkins (2005)[9]

and 'chavs' as one of its signature brands, this became a significant problem for the company and caused a sharp slowdown in sales in the UK (see Marketing in Action 2.2).

Corporate social responsibility and marketing ethics

Companies have a responsibility to society that goes beyond their legal responsibilities, and they need to recognize this. Corporate social responsibility (CSR) refers to the ethical principle that a person or an organization should be accountable for how its acts might affect the physical environment and the general public. Concerns about the environment and public welfare are represented by pressure groups such as Greenpeace and ASH (Action on Smoking and Health).

Marketing managers need to be aware that organizations are part of a larger society and are accountable to that society for their actions. Such concerns led Perrier to recall 160 million bottles of its mineral water in 120 countries after traces of a toxic chemical were found in 13 bottles. The recall cost the company a total of £50 million, even though there was no evidence that the level of the chemical found in the water was harmful to humans. Perrier acted because it believed the least doubt in the consumers' minds should be removed in order to maintain its brand's image of quality and purity. In contrast, Coca-Cola took a week to accept responsibility for a wave of sickness caused by the contamination of its products in Belgium, and faces continued criticism over anti-union violence, worsening water shortages and childhood obesity. Companies are increasingly conscious of the need to communicate their socially responsible

Live an ethical lifestyle
And look fabulous
while doing it.

Shop online at adili.com

ADiLi.com
the best of ethical fashion

Exhibit 2.2 Adili is one of a number of fashion companies that have sprung up in response to concerns about the level of ethics in the production of clothing and fashion products

activities. The term 'Green marketing' is used to describe marketing efforts to produce, promote and reclaim environmentally sensitive products (see Marketing in Action 2.4).[10]

The societal marketing concept is a label often used to describe how the activities of companies should not only consider the needs of customers but also society at large (see Exhibit 2.2). This notion has given rise to movements like the Fairtrade Foundation and also to the formation of companies like Edun, the Dublin-based fashion company. Founded by U2's Bono and his wife Ali Hewson, the company manufactures a line of organic cotton shirts, jeans and hemp blazers. Its fashion line is made from non-subsidized cotton sourced in Peru and manufactured in Africa, while its second brand, Edun Live comprises mass-market clothes made from Tanzanian cotton and manufactured in Lesotho. The company's ethical goal is to support manufacturers in Africa and world farmers by championing organic, environmentally sustainable cotton products.[11]

Corporate social responsibility is no longer an optional extra but a key part of business strategy that comes under close scrutiny from pressure groups,

private shareholders and institutional investors, some of whom manage ethical investment funds. Businesses are increasingly expected to adapt to climate change, biodiversity, social equity and human rights in a world characterized by greater transparency and more explicit values.[12] Two outcomes of these developments have been the growth in social reporting and **cause-related marketing**. Some of the corporate social responsibility (CSR) and cause-related marketing activities of leading companies operating in Ireland are shown in Table 2.3.

Social reporting is where firms conduct independent audits of their social performance. These audits usually involve surveys of key stakeholders such as customers and employees. Social audits normally take the form of printed reports, but these are increasingly being replaced by the internet as the main communication medium. The advantages of the internet are that it is easy to update, the distribution of information is cost effective, it is searchable, can be produced swiftly and is environmentally friendly. However, it is also the medium most favoured by those who wish to criticize big businesses. For example, www.ryan-be-fair.org features comments from people claiming to be Ryanair staff who are critical of the company and its practices, while the Professional Pilots Rumour Network (www.pprune.org) is a popular site on which pilots share information and gossip. Most comments on the site are negative towards Ryanair except one staunch defender who goes by the pseudonym of Leo Hairy Camel. His identity is a matter of speculation but Leo Hairy Camel is an anagram of Michael O'Leary, the name of the company's outspoken chief executive.[13]

Cause-related marketing is a commercial activity by which businesses and charities or causes form a partnership with each other in order to market an image, product or service for mutual benefit. Cause-related marketing works well when the business and charity have a similar target audience. For example, American Express is a founding partner in Product Red, a corporate alliance that gives a share of profits from branded products to the Global Fund to fight AIDS, tuberculosis and malaria. One of the strongest commitments to cause-related marketing has been given by Canadian company MAC cosmetics, which is now part of the Estée Lauder group. It gives away all of the sales revenues for its Viva Glam lipstick range to the MAC AIDS Fund, which in turn distributes it to HIV groups. To date, it has given away over US$100 million.[14]

A related issue is that of marketing ethics. **Ethics** are the moral principles and values that govern the

Table 2.3 Corporate social responsibility activities of selected companies in Ireland

Company	CSR activities
Allied Irish Banks	The AIB Better Ireland programme focuses on helping disadvantaged children. AIB has donated over €10 million to 700 projects
Bank of Ireland	A member of the FTSE4Good Index; introduced an ethical business statement and environmental management system
Diageo	Developed Choice Zone to support education programmes to promote sensible drinking; contributed more than €3.5 million towards the Diageo Liberties Learning Initiative
IBM Ireland	A community volunteer programme registered over 12,000 volunteer hours in two years
Johnson & Johnson	Foundation of the Special Achievers Club in Janssen, Cork; mentoring programme in partnership with Tallaght Community School; CSR committee set up in 2004
KPMG	Training sessions for the ReadyforWork programme for the homeless; partner with Westland Row School in the Schools' Business Partnership
Marks & Spencer	Marks & Start is a community programme aiming to enable 2500 people each year to prepare for the world of work
O_2	Sponsored the O_2 Ability Awards; raising awareness of dyslexia with all employees
Tesco Ireland	Raised more than €2.6 million for national charities through a 'charity of the year' programme

Source: Responsible Business: Driving Innovation & Competitiveness, *Irish Times*, 27 May 2005, 12

actions and decisions of an individual or group.[15] They involve values about right and wrong conduct. There can be a distinction between the legality and ethicality of marketing decisions. Ethics concern personal moral principles and values, while laws reflect society's principles, and standards that are enforceable in the courts.

Not all unethical practices are illegal. For example, it is not illegal to include genetically modified (GM) ingredients in products sold in supermarkets; however, some organizations (such as Greenpeace) believe it is unethical to sell GM products when their effect on health has not been scientifically proven. Such concerns have led to supermarket chains, such as Iceland and Sainsbury's in the UK, removing GM foods from their own-label products. Similarly, mobile phone companies need to be responsive to the potential long-term risks posed by the use of these devices as some scientific studies have shown a link between mobile phone use and the development of brain tumours. Manufacturers are ensuring that handsets conform to international guidelines on the Specific Absorption Rate of radiation emissions and the industry has contributed millions of dollars to research on the issue.[16]

Many ethical dilemmas derive from a conflict between profits and business actions. For example, by using child labour the cost of producing items is kept low and profit margins are raised. In 2006, secret footage aired on a news bulletin on the UK's Channel 4 showed clearly underage workers making Tesco own-label clothing in a factory in Bangladesh. Tesco, it emerged, was unaware that the factory produced clothes for it—it is a member of the Ethical Trading Initiative, which is a UK-based group that requires independent monitoring of the global supply chain. Because of the importance of marketing ethics, each of the chapters in this book includes a key ethical debate discussing the positions taken by supporters and critics of marketing on a variety of core themes. The debate on corporate social responsibility (CSR) is summarized in Ethical Debate 2.1.

The consumer movement

The 'consumer movement' is the name given to the set of individuals, groups and organizations whose aim is to safeguard consumer rights. For example, the Consumers' Association in the UK campaigns on behalf of consumers and provides information about products, often on a comparative basis, allowing consumers to make more informed choices between products and services. This information is published in the organization's magazine *Which?* (www.which.org).

As well as offering details of unbiased product testing and campaigning against unfair business practices, the consumer movement has been active in areas such as product quality and safety, and information accuracy. Notable successes have been the Campaign for Real Ale (CamRA), improvements in car safety, the stipulation that advertisements for credit facilities

Ethical Debate 2.1: CSR or PR?

For many years now, debate has raged regarding how socially responsible companies should be. Businesses do not operate in isolation, but are intrinsically linked to the economic, social, physical and political environments in which they operate. To many, their record in being sensitive to the needs of these environments is not one to be proud of. The abuse of human resources in the form of poorly paid workers, working in dangerous conditions and child labour has been highlighted. Environmental damage through pollution, deforestation and the illegal dumping of waste has rightly been criticized. There is also the exploitation of consumers through the maintenance of artificially high prices and the corruption of the political process throughout the world. The list goes on. Riots between protesters and police at major government and economic conferences highlight the extent of the divide between business and some sections of society.

As a result of societal pressure for change, corporate social responsibility (CSR) has become part of the language of the corporate boardroom. All major corporations have CSR initiatives and publicize these in their annual reports and on their websites. For example, in 1953, Shell Oil Company set up the Shell Oil Foundation, which, since its formation, has contributed in the region of US$500 million to the development of the communities where Shell employees live and work. Marks & Spencer has its 'Plan A', a list of 100 worthy targets over five years. These include helping 15,000 children in Uganda get a better education, saving 55,000 tonnes of CO_2, recycling 48 million clothes hangers, converting over 20 million garments to Fairtrade cotton, and so on. Triple bottom-line accounting has grown, whereby firms demonstrate not only their economic performance but also their social and environmental performances.

At the same time, however, there are commentators who trenchantly argue that these kinds of investments are completely wrong. This position has been most famously argued by the US economist Milton Friedman. In his view, the mission of a business is to maximize the return to its owners and shareholders; he advocated that anything that detracts from that mission should be avoided, and that society's concerns are the responsibility of government. Similarly, Robert Reich, who served as US Labor Secretary under Bill Clinton, has argued that companies cannot be socially responsible and that activists are neglecting the important task of getting governments to solve problems. Added to this is the growing line of research which shows that CSR does not work—in other words, that CSR has a negative effect on corporate performance.

So it remains very much a matter of debate as to whether the current trend in CSR activity reflects a greater concern from businesses about their impact on the environment or whether this is simply a rather large public relations exercise. Many critics would suggest the latter as companies respond to increasing scrutiny from non-governmental organizations and the public at large. A CSR initiative may create a feel-good factor within a business and may satisfy commentators and shareholders, but the ultimate test is whether businesses will consistently put principle before profit. Ironically the two are not mutually exclusive as the experience of companies like the Body Shop, Ben & Jerry's, innocent Ltd and others has shown. Enlightened long-term self-interest would appear to be the best approach for corporations to take.

Suggested reading: Allen (2007);[17] Bakan (2004);[18] *The Economist* (2008);[19] James (2007)[20]

must display the true interest charges (annual percentage rates), and the inclusion of health warnings on cigarette packets and advertisements.

Such consumer organizations can have a significant influence on production processes. For example, pressure from environmental movements in Finland and Germany on UPMKymmene, Finland's largest company and Europe's biggest papermaking firm, ensured that the number of new trees planted matched the number of trees felled. German customers (which constitute the firm's biggest market), such as the publisher Springer, now have clauses on forest sustainability and biodiversity written into their

Table 2.4 Most ethically perceived brands in selected countries

Ranking	UK	France	Germany
1	Co-op	Danone	Adidas
2	Body Shop	Adidas	Nike
3	Marks & Spencer	Nike	Puma
4	Traidcraft	Nestlé	BMW
5	Cafedirect	Renault	Demeter
6	Ecover	Peugeot	gepa
7	Green & Black's	Philips	Volkswagen
8	Tesco	Carrefour	Sony
9	Oxfam	Coca-Cola	Trigema

Source: GfK NOP

contracts with paper companies.[21] In the UK, the Office of Fair Trading is seeking to enable consumers to more easily take legal action against companies that have harmed them through anti-competitive practices.

A 2007 study of 5000 consumers in Europe found that ethical consumerism was on the rise, and that respondents felt that business ethics had worsened (see Table 2.4).[22] The consumer movement should not be considered a threat to business, but marketers should view its concerns as offering an opportunity to create new products and services to satisfy the needs of these emerging market segments. For example, growing concern over rising obesity levels in the developed world has led McDonald's to make significant changes to its menu items and marketing approach. It introduced a number of healthy options to its menus, including salads and fruit bags, which helped the company to return to profitability after some years of poor performance.

Political and legal forces

Marketing decisions can also be influenced by political and legal forces, which determine the rules by which business is conducted. Political forces describe the close connections that politicians and senior business people often have. These relationships with politicians are often cultivated by organizations, both to monitor the political mood and also to influence it. Companies sometimes make sizeable contributions to the funds of political parties in an attempt to maintain favourable relationships. The alcohol industry, for example, has a vested interest in maintaining close ties with government whereby it hopes to counter proposals from pressure groups demanding curbs on the marketing of alcoholic drinks. The extent to

which businesses try to influence the political process is illustrated by the level of lobbying that takes place. It is estimated that there are 15,000 lobbyists in Brussels trying to influence EU policy-making by its 732 MEPs.[23] Some of the proposals that businesses have lobbied against include restrictions on online and mobile phone advertising to reduce spam, tougher packaging rules to reduce waste, and stricter testing and labelling for chemicals.

Political decisions can have major consequences for businesses. This is sharply illustrated by the US decision to invade Iraq, which resulted in some leading American companies becoming the targets for attack and some American products being boycotted. Usually, political forces have a more gradual and subtle effect, as illustrated by European politicians' pursuit of a common European union.

The European Union

In the past, the basic economic unit has been the country, which was largely autonomous with regard to the decisions it made about its economy and levels of supply and demand. But, for the past three decades, all this has been changing rapidly, driven mainly by the globalization of business. The world's largest companies, like Microsoft, General Electric, Wal-Mart and others, are now larger than most countries in economic terms. At the same time, countries have been merging together into economic areas to more effectively manage their affairs. Most European countries are now part of the European Union (EU), the North American countries have grouped together into an economic area known as NAFTA, and the Pacific Rim countries are part of a group known as the ASEAN.

The advent in 1986 of the Single European Act was the launch pad for a free-flowing internal market in the EU. The intention was to create a massive deregulated market of 320 million consumers by abolishing barriers to the free flow of products, services, capital and people among the then 12 member states. More recently, the Maastricht Treaty (1992), the Nice Treaty (2000) and the introduction of the euro (2002) have all been further steps towards the development of full economic union. Another significant milestone for the EU was the admission of a further 10 new countries in May 2004, bringing the total to 25. The current EU members are Austria, Belgium, Britain, the Czech Republic, Cyprus, Denmark, Estonia, Finland, France, Germany, Greece, Hungary, Ireland, Italy, Latvia, Lithuania, Luxembourg, Malta, the Netherlands, Poland, Portugal, Slovakia, Slovenia, Spain and Sweden. The common currency, the euro, is in use in 13 countries, making travel, price comparisons and cross-border trade easier. The development of the EU has had a number of business implications.

There has been a great deal of discussion about just how much the single European market will advance the level of pan-European marketing. On the one hand, the increasing mobility of European consumers, the accelerating flow of information across borders and the publicity surrounding the introduction of the euro has promoted a pan-European marketing approach; on the other hand, the persistence of local tastes and preferences means that the elimination of formal trade barriers may not bring about standardization of marketing strategies between countries. Standardization appears to depend on product type. In the case of many industrial goods, consumer durables (such as cameras, toasters, watches, radios) and clothing (Gucci shoes, Benetton sweaters, Levi's jeans) standardization is well advanced. However, for many fast-moving consumer goods (fmcg), standardization of products is more difficult to achieve because of local tastes. Even a pan-European brand like Garnier, owned by the French cosmetics group L'Oréal, has adapted its promotional campaign for its hair-colouring product Garnier Nutrisse. Because it felt that trust was an important element in selling hair-colouring products it sought to identify suitable celebrities in each market. In the UK, *Big Brother* host Davina McCall was chosen, while similarly appropriate local television presenters and actresses were chosen in France, Italy, Germany and Spain.[24] Each element of the marketing mix may be affected by the ongoing development of the single European market.

Pro-competitive legislation

Political action may also translate directly into legislation and less formal directives, which can have a profound influence on business conduct. One of the key areas in which regulators act is to ensure that competition is fair and legal, and operates in a way that ensures that consumers and society benefit. Formerly, the control of monopolies in Europe was enacted via Article 86 of the Treaty of Rome, which aimed to prevent the 'abuse' of a dominant market position. However, control was increased in 1990 when the EU introduced its first direct mechanism for dealing with mergers and takeovers: the Merger Regulation. This gave the Competition Directorate of the European Commission jurisdiction over 'concentrations with a European dimension'. Over the years, the Commission has challenged the activities of major global companies, most notably Microsoft. After a legal battle lasting nine years, Microsoft finally admitted defeat in 2007 after the European Commission charged that it had abused its dominance in the software market. It had to pay fines totalling €777 million and was forced to provide information to other companies in order that their software would 'interoperate' with Microsoft's. Competition bodies also operate at a national level, such as the Office of Fair Trading in the UK and the Competition Authority in Ireland, where they monitor local-level competition issues.

Consumer legislation

Regulators also enact legislation designed to protect consumers. Many countries throughout Europe have some form of Consumer Protection Act that is designed to regulate how businesses interact with consumers and how they advertise their products. These acts typically outlaw practices that are deemed to be unfair, misleading or aggressive. For example, promotions and product information must be clear and claims—such as that a product is friendly to the environment—must be backed up with evidence. This legislation is then enforced through a body such as the National Consumer Agency in Ireland. The need for this kind of consumer protection is illustrated by the marketing of products like breakfast cereals and soft drinks, as shown in Marketing in Action 2.3.

In short, political and legal decisions can very quickly change the rules of the business game. For example, in 2008, the French Government sought to abolish advertising on public television, a move that had significant implications for advertisers, who were spending in the region of €850 million on these channels. Similarly, the European Court's ruling in 2007 that the Baileys Minis series could remain on sale represented an important victory for Diageo, which had invested heavily in the development of the brand

Marketing in Action 2.3: What is a healthy breakfast?

Study guide: Below is a review of some research that is critical of marketing to children. Read it and consider how consumers, regulators and companies should respond to the issues raised.

The breakfast cereal market is a huge one, estimated to be worth £1.23 billion in the UK, and is critical for companies like Kellogg's. The major target for most breakfast cereal marketing is children, and cartoon characters such as Shrek, Tony the Tiger and the Simpsons regularly appear in advertising and on packaging. But what is in breakfast cereals and are they as healthy as they often claim to be? A study by the Consumer Association of Ireland found that none of the 36 children's cereals that it studied scored a healthy rating, meaning that it was high in fibre and low in sugar, salt and saturated fat. Two-thirds of the cereals contained at least 30 per cent sugar, with some own-label brands reaching 38 per cent sugar content. Kellogg's rejected the findings of the study, claiming that it did not take account of the vitamins and minerals included in its products.

Controversies like these are important because of the growing problem of obesity in society and particularly among children. It is estimated that one in five UK children is clinically obese, and this figure is forecast to rise to one in four by 2010. As a result there are increasing calls for a ban on the advertising of certain kinds of foods to children. Ofcom, the UK communications regulator, proposed a series of restrictions, including no advertising or sponsorship by food and drinks firms in programmes aimed at pre-school children, that celebrities and licensed characters not be used in food and drink adverts, and that promotional offers not be targeted at children aged under 10. These types of promotional offer have a powerful effect on children and research has even found that obese children double their intake of food after watching food advertisements on television.

The European Food Safety Authority has become concerned about research that shows a link between food colourings typically used in sweets and confectionery products and hyperactivity in children. Reports on children's toys have found that girls are being sexualized at an increasingly young age, and in 2006 Tesco was condemned for selling a Peekaboo pole-dancing kit on the toys and games section of its website. These developments illustrate the need for the regulation of businesses. Companies need to be careful about who their advertising is targeted at and what claims its makes. Where this does not happen, critics and consumer organizations are likely to highlight the problem and call for stricter regulation of corporate activities.

Based on: Cullen (2007);[25] Terazono (2006);[26] Wiggins (2007)[27]

---

extension. In many instances, firms and industries create voluntary codes of practice in order to stave off possible political and legal action.

Codes of practice

On top of the various laws that are in place, certain industries have drawn up codes of practice—sometimes as a result of political pressure—to protect consumer interests. The UK advertising industry, for example, has drawn up a self-regulatory Code of Advertising Standards and Practice designed to keep advertising 'legal, decent, honest and truthful' (see Exhibit 2.3). Similarly, the marketing research industry has drawn up a code of practice to protect people

from unethical activities such as using marketing research as a pretext for selling. However, many commentators are critical of the potential effectiveness of voluntary codes of conduct in industries like oil exploration and clothing manufacture.[28] Firms like Coca-Cola and PepsiCo in the USA have begun to restrict sales of soft drinks in schools, in an effort to appease critics and stave off regulation such as that imposed in France, which banned school-based vending machines.

Marketing management must be aware of the constraints on its activities brought about by the political and legal environment. It must assess the extent to

Exhibit 2.3 Advertising such as this for Hunky Dory crisps in Ireland was the subject of many complaints to the Advertising Standards Authority of Ireland and had to be withdrawn

which there is a need to influence political decisions that may affect operations, and the degree to which industry practice needs to be self-regulated in order to maintain high standards of customer satisfaction and service.

Physical forces

As we have seen, the consumer movement aims to protect the rights of consumers; environmentalists, in turn, aim to protect the physical environment from the costs associated with producing and marketing products and services. They are concerned with the *social* costs of consumption, not just the *personal* costs to the consumer. Six environmental issues are of particular concern. These are climate change, pollution, scare resource conservation, recycling and non-wasteful packaging, environmentally friendly ingredients, and animal testing Marketers need to be aware of the threats and opportunities associated with each of these issues.

Climate change

Climate change has been one of the most hotly debated topics in recent years. Most commentators argue that human activity is hastening the depletion of the ozone layer, resulting in a gradual rise in world temperatures, which is melting the polar ice caps and causing more unpredictable weather extremes like droughts and hurricanes. Movies like Al Gore's *An Inconvenient Truth* have helped to bring the debate into the mainstream. Contrarian views suggest that global warming is largely the result of a natural cycle. To date, the Kyoto Protocol, a global agreement on climate change, has been ratified by 175 countries and seeks agreed reductions in greenhouse gas emissions from all parties signed up to the agreement. In effect, for businesses, this means seeking ways to reduce CO_2 emissions and a ban on the use of chlorofluorocarbons (CFCs). For example, Land Rover, whose sport utility vehicles (SUVs) are a prime target for green-minded law-makers, aims to cut its fleet's average carbon dioxide emissions by 20 per cent before 2012. Such initiatives will be necessary as higher taxes on SUVs have caused their sales levels in Western Europe to fall quickly. Opportunities are also being created by the use of route-planning software by transport companies to reduce emissions, and internet matching systems to fill empty vehicles.

Climate change has the potential to have a major impact on business and society. For example, air travel is very much taken for granted and has boomed in recent years due to economic prosperity and the marketing activities of low-cost airlines. But aeroplanes are significant users of limited fossil fuels like oil, and CO_2 emissions from international aviation have doubled since 1990. Ultimately, this may mean consumers choosing to fly less or even being encouraged to fly less, which will have significant implications for the aviation industry. These kinds of changes have already happened in the business of patio heaters, which grew in popularity due to smoking bans and a preference by consumers for eating and drinking outdoors. But the gas-powered heaters can emit as much CO_2 per year as one and half cars, and companies like B&Q have decided to stop selling them.

Pollution

The quality of the physical environment can be harmed by the manufacture, use and disposal of products. The production of chemicals that pollute the atmosphere, the use of nitrates in fertilizer that pollutes rivers, and the disposal of by-products into the sea have caused considerable public concern. Rapidly growing economies like China and India have particular problems in this regard, with China having overtaken the USA as the world's biggest emitter of CO_2. Coal provides 80 per cent of China's energy and it is anticipated that it will continue to do so for the next half-century. Factory and car emissions have meant that air pollution has become a major problem in Beijing. Water pollution has also reached serious levels, with an estimated 90 per cent of the water running through cities polluted.[29]

Pressure from regulators and consumer groups helps to reduce pollution. Denmark has introduced a series of anti-pollution measures including a charge on pesticides and a CFC tax. In the Netherlands, higher taxes on pesticides, fertilizers and carbon monoxide emissions are proposed. Not all of the activity is simply cost raising, however. In Germany, one of the marketing benefits of its involvement in green technology has been a thriving export business in pollution-control equipment.

Consumer groups can exert enormous pressure on companies by influencing public opinion. For example, environmentalist protests convinced Shell to abandon its plans to dump its obsolete North Sea oil installation, *Brent Spar*, at sea. Environmentalists are a key component of the wider movement that monitors business practices and generates pressure for change.

Conservation of scarce resources

Recognition of the finite nature of the world's resources has stimulated a drive towards conservation. This is reflected in the demand for energy-efficient housing and fuel-efficient motor cars, for example. In Europe, Sweden has taken the lead in developing an energy policy based on domestic and renewable resources. The tax system penalizes the use of polluting energy sources like coal and oil, while less polluting and domestic sources such as peat and woodchip receive favourable tax treatment. In addition, nuclear power is to be phased out by 2010. More efficient use of energy and the development of energy-efficient products (backed by an energy technology fund) will compensate for the shortfall in nuclear energy capacity. Toyota's development of its Prius model—a hybrid petrol-electric car—has been an unprecedented success; so much so, that the company has struggled to meet demand for it (see Exhibit 2.4).

There is increasing recognition that water may become the next scarce resource that needs to be conserved due to rising global temperatures. This has

Exhibit 2.4 This Toyota advertisement demonstrates the company's environmental credentials

major implications for the lucrative global bottled water industry. A US study has found that global consumption of bottled water had grown by over 57 per cent in the five-year period to 2006 and the amount being spent on it was seven times the sum invested in providing safe drinking water in developing countries.[30] Furthermore, millions of barrels of crude oil are used in the making of plastic bottles for water, 90 per cent of which are disposed of after one use and take 1000 years to biodegrade. Water scarcity also has implications for soft drinks manufacturers like PepsiCo and Coca-Cola, which are accused of causing water shortages near production plants in developing countries.

Organizational responses to the issue of scarce resources can have interesting effects. For example, because of the finite supply of fossil fuels like oil, there has been a significant growth in bio-fuels, which are manufactured from grain. This has resulted in less grain available to make products like bread, which has driven up food prices around the world.

Recyclable and non-wasteful packaging

The past 20 years or so have seen significant growth in recycling throughout Europe. Cutting out waste in packaging is not only environmentally friendly but also makes commercial sense. Thus companies have introduced concentrated detergents and refill packs, and removed the cardboard packaging around some brands of toothpaste, for example. The savings can be substantial: in Germany, Lever GmbH saved 30 per cent by introducing concentrated detergents, 20 per cent by using lightweight plastic bottles, and the introduction of refills for concentrated liquids reduced the weight of packaging materials by a half. Many governments have introduced bans on the ubiquitous plastic bags available at supermarkets and convenience stores as they give rise to pollution and are slow to biodegrade, which has major implications for packaging manufacturers.

The growth in the use of the personal computer has raised major recycling issues as PCs contain many harmful substances and pollutants. EU legislation is forcing manufacturers to face up to the issue of how these products are recycled, with some of the costs being absorbed by the companies and the rest by the consumer. Hewlett-Packard has set up a team to re-examine how PCs are made and to design them with their disposal in mind. The team has conducted projects such as using corn starch instead of plastic in its printers, redesigning packaging and cutting down on emissions from factories.[31] The Waste Electrical and Electronic Equipment (WEEE) Directive became European law in 2003 and imposed the responsibility for the disposal of electrical products on manufacturers. Consumers are entitled to return old electrical goods to sellers, which are charged with recycling them, though the cost of this activity has largely been passed on to consumers through an additional recycling levy. One of the consequences of the Directive has been an increased focus by manufacturers on the ease of recycling of their products.

Use of environmentally friendly ingredients

The use of biodegradable and natural ingredients when practicable is favoured by environmentalists. The toy industry is one that has come in for criticism for its extensive use of plastics and other environmentally unfriendly products. Consequently, start-up companies like Green Toys and Anamalz have used a different approach. The former makes toys from recycled plastic milk containers, which are sold in recycled cardboard, while Anamalz uses wood instead of plastic. The humble light bulb is a classic example of a product made from environmentally unfriendly ingredients. It wastes huge amounts of electricity, radiating 95 per cent of the energy it consumes as heat rather than light, and its life span is relatively short. This is because existing light bulbs use electrodes to connect with the power supply and also include dangerous materials like mercury. Researchers at a company called Ceravision in the UK have developed an alternative that does not require electrodes or mercury, uses very little energy and should never need changing. These types of innovations illustrate the business opportunities that are created through the monitoring of the marketing environment.

Animal testing of new products

To reduce the risk of them being harmful to humans, potential new products such as shampoos and cosmetics are tested on animals before launch. This has aroused much opposition. One of the major concepts underlining the initial success of UK retailer the Body Shop was that its products were not subject to animal testing. This is an example of the Body Shop's ethical approach to business, which also extends to its suppliers. Other larger stores, responding to Body Shop's success, have introduced their own range of animal-friendly products.

In summary, while care for the physical environment represents a major challenge for commercial enterprises, it also represents a huge opportunity. New

Marketing in Action 2.4: Eco-marketing

Study guide: Below are some examples of companies that are capitalizing on the opportunities created by concern for the environment. Read the text and identify some other examples that you can think of.

Eco-marketing, or green marketing, is likely to be a booming business for the foreseeable future. Because of increased consumer concern for the environment, corporations will be keen to emphasize their green credentials. For example, in 2006, Ford Motor Co. announced that it was spending £1 billion on research and development projects to improve the fuel efficiency of its cars. But as we saw earlier in our discussion of CSR, consumers will also need to be wary of the green claims that are being made by some corporations. For example, a study in Ireland found that about 50 per cent of the products studied were making claims to be environmentally friendly that were potentially misleading. It found paint products that were claiming to be lead-free and even one standard unrecycled paper product that carried the slogan 'Kinder to Nature'.

But many organizations are finding that developing solutions to challenges posed by the physical environment can be very lucrative. A case in point is the Irish company Airtricity. It was founded in 1997 and has become one of the world's leading renewable energy companies, owning and operating wind farms throughout Europe. It is both a generator and a supplier of electricity and has built up a customer base of 38,000 commercial customers in Ireland. Voted Ireland's company of the year in 2007, it was sold to Scottish and Southern Energy plc in 2008 for €2.5 billion. The use of wind to generate electricity cuts down on the burning of fossil fuels like coal and oil, and in some countries this business is well developed (e.g. in Denmark, where 20 per cent of its total electricity demands are met by wind).

Even the business of investing in companies that are investing in the environment has become big business. Green investment products are one of the fastest-growing sectors of the fund management business. In most instances, these products allow investors to take a stake in a pool of companies engaged in environmental activities such as energy conservation, waste management, recycling or the development of environmentally friendly products. In other instances, investors provide seed capital for start-up businesses. To date, the performance of these funds has tended to compare very favourably to that of their peers.

Based on: Carswell (2008);[32] Reid (2007)[33]

products or solutions that are environmentally friendly are likely to be received positively in the marketplace (see Marketing in Action 2.4).

Technological forces

People's lives and companies' fortunes can both be affected significantly by technology. Technological advances have given us body scanners, robotics, camcorders, computers and many other products that have contributed to our quality of life. Many technological breakthroughs have changed the rules of the competitive game. For example, the launch of the computer has decimated the market for typewriters and has made calculators virtually obsolete. Companies, like Skype, that have pioneered telephone calls over the internet threaten to revolutionize the telecoms business and reduce revenues for international calling to virtually zero. Monitoring the technological environment may result in the spotting of opportunities and major investments in new technological areas. For example, ICI invested heavily in the biotechnology sector, and leads the market for equipment used in genetic fingerprinting. Japanese companies are investing heavily in areas such as microelectronics, biotechnology, new materials and telecommunications.

New potential applications for technology are emerging all the time. For example, the Piggy Wiggy supermarket chain in South Carolina has become the first US retailer to roll out a biometric payment system in its 120 stores. To pay, the customer places an index finger on a small screen, types in a number on an adjacent pad, selects an account from an electronic wallet and walks away. Cash, cheque books and credit cards are unnecessary.[34] The key to successful technological investment is, however, market potential, not technological sophistication for its own sake. The classic example of a high-tech initiative driven by technologists rather than pulled by the market is Concorde. Although technologically sophisticated, management knew before its launch that it never had any chance of being commercially viable. Large numbers of internet businesses have failed for the same reason.

One particular major technological change that is affecting marketing is the development of information technology. Information technology, or IT, describes the broad range of innovations within the fields of computing and telecommunications. Almost no aspect of marketing remains unaffected by developments in these areas, and at appropriate junctures throughout the book we have included a 'Technology Focus' section to highlight the impact of technology on some aspects of marketing. For example, many market research studies are being conducted via email; the efficiency of salesforces is being improved through salesforce automation; and the ease with which international marketing can be conducted has been enhanced by technologies such as videoconferencing and mobile telephony (see Exhibit 2.5). In Chapter 10 we will see that a whole new industry, called customer relationship management (CRM), has grown up in recent years; this uses database technologies to enable companies to improve their relationships with customers. The internet is also having a profound effect on how business is conducted, as we shall see in Chapter 10 and throughout the book.

The microenvironment

In addition to the broad macroeconomic forces discussed above, a number of microeconomic variables also impact on the opportunities and threats facing the organization. We shall introduce each of these in turn, and deal with them in greater detail throughout the book.

Exhibit 2.5 This advertisement for the Nokia E61 aims to highlight the value of the product as a tool for conducting business

Customers

As we saw in Chapter 1, customers are at the centre of the marketing effort and we shall examine customer behaviour in great detail in the next chapter. Ultimately customers determine the success or failure of the business. The challenge for the company is to identify unserved market needs and to get and retain a customer base. This requires a sensitivity to changing needs in the marketplace and also having the adaptability to take advantage of the opportunities that present themselves.

Distributors

Some companies, such as mail-order houses, online music companies and service providers, distribute directly to their customers. Most others use the services of independent wholesalers and retailers. As we shall see in Chapter 11, these middlemen provide many valuable services, such as making products available to customers where and when they want them, breaking bulk and providing specialist services such as merchandising and installation. Developments in distribution can have a significant impact on the performance of manufacturers. For example, the growing power of grocery retailers such as Wal-Mart and Tesco has affected the profitability of consumer foods manufacturers.

Suppliers

Not only are the fortunes of companies influenced by their distributors, they can also be influenced by their suppliers. Supply chains can be very simple or very complex. For example, the average car contains about 15,000 components. As a result the car industry is served by three tiers of suppliers. Tier-one companies make complete systems such as electrical systems or braking systems. They are served by tier-two suppliers, who might produce cables, for example, and are in turn supplied by tier-three suppliers who produce basic commodities such as plastic shields or metals. Just like distributors, powerful suppliers can extract profitability from an industry by restricting the supply of essential components and forcing the price up.

Competitors

Levels of competition vary from industry to industry. In some instances, there may be just one or two major players as is often the case in formerly state-run industries like energy or telecommunications. In others, where entry is easy or high profit potential exists, competition can be intense. For example, when Perrier launched its mineral water in response to a growing concern with healthy living, it spawned a rash of competitors in a rapidly growing industry. To be successful in the marketplace, companies must not only be able to meet customer needs but must also be able to gain a differential advantage over competitors. We will examine the issue of competition in greater detail in Chapter 12.

Environmental scanning

The practice of monitoring and analysing a company's marketing environment is known as **environmental scanning**. Two key decisions that management need to make are what to scan and how to organize the activity. Clearly, in theory, every event in the world has the potential to affect a company's operations, but a scanning system that could cover every conceivable force would be unmanageable. The first task, then, is to define a feasible range of forces that require monitoring. These are the 'potentially relevant environmental forces' that have the most likelihood of affecting future business prospects— such as, for example, changes in the value of the yen

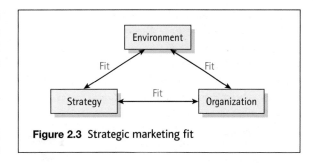

Figure 2.3 Strategic marketing fit

for companies doing business in Japan. The second prerequisite for an effective scanning system is to design a system that provides a fast response to events that are only partially predictable, emerge as surprises and grow very rapidly. This has become essential due to the increasing turbulence of the marketing environment.

In general, environmental scanning is conducted by members of the senior management team, though some large corporations will have a separate unit dedicated to the task. The most appropriate organizational arrangement for scanning will depend on the unique circumstances facing a firm. A judgement needs to be made regarding the costs and benefits of each alternative. The size and profitability of the company and the perceived degree of environmental turbulence will be factors that impinge on this decision. Environmental scanning provides the essential informational input to create strategic fit between strategy, organization and the environment (see Figure 2.3). Marketing strategy should reflect the environment even if this requires a fundamental reorganization of operations.

Companies respond in various ways to environmental change (see Figure 2.4).

Ignorance

If environmental scanning is poor, companies may not realize that salient forces are affecting their future prospects. They therefore continue as normal, ignorant of the environmental issues that are threatening their existence, or the opportunities that could be seized. No change is made.

Delay

The next response, once the force is understood, is to delay action. This can be the result of bureaucratic decision processes that stifle swift action. The slow response by Swiss watch manufacturers to the introduction of digital watches, for example, was thought, in part, to be caused by the bureaucratic nature of their decision-making. 'Marketing myopia' can slow

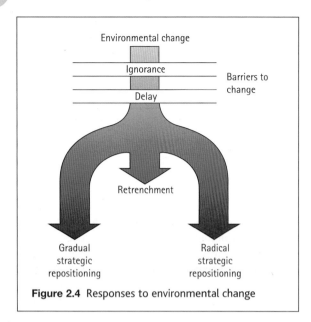

Figure 2.4 Responses to environmental change

delay is 'psychological recoil' by managers who see change as a threat and thus defend the status quo. These are four powerful contributors to inertia.

Retrenchment

This sort of response deals with efficiency problems but disregards effectiveness issues. As sales and profits decline, the management cuts costs; this leads to a period of higher profits but does nothing to stem declining sales. Costs (and capacity) are reduced once more, but the fundamental strategic problems remain. Retrenchment policies only delay the inevitable.

Gradual strategic repositioning

This approach involves a gradual, planned and continuous adaptation to the changing marketing environment.

Radical strategic repositioning

If its procrastination results in a crisis, a company could have to consider a radical shift in its strategic positioning—the direction of the entire business is fundamentally changed. For example, the UK clothing retailer Hepworths was radically repositioned as Next, a more upmarket outlet for women's wear targeted at 25–35-year-old working women. Radical strategic repositioning is much riskier than gradual repositioning because, if unsuccessful, the company is likely to fold.

response through management being product-focused rather than customer-focused. Management may believe that there will always be a need for made-to-measure suits, for example, and therefore delay responding to the growing popularity of casual wear. A third source of delay is 'technological myopia'; this occurs where a company fails to respond to technological change. The example of Pollitt and Wigsell—a steam engine manufacturer that was slow to respond to the emergence of electrical power—illustrates technological myopia. The fourth reason for

Summary

This chapter has introduced the concept of the marketing environment. In particular, the following issues were addressed.

1. That the marketing environment comprises a microenvironment and a macroenvironment. What happens in these environments is largely uncontrollable by firms but can have a significant impact on organizational performance.

2. There are five key components of the macroenvironment: economic forces, social forces, legal/political forces, technological forces and physical forces. Changes on each of these dimensions can present either opportunities or threats to the firm.

3. Economic forces comprise economic growth and unemployment, interest rates and exchange rates, as well as taxation and inflation. They largely impact upon how well-off consumers feel, and their resulting propensity to buy goods and services.

4. Social forces comprise demographic forces, cultural forces, corporate social responsibility and marketing ethics, as well as the consumer movement. The latter two forces have become particularly important as the impact of business on society receives greater attention.

5. 'Political and legal forces' describes the regulatory environment in which organizations operate. Regulation may be enacted at a national or European level, and is mainly designed to protect the interests of consumers and to ensure a fair competitive playing field for organizations.

6. Changes in the physical environment have been the focus of a great deal of attention in recent years. This encompasses concerns regarding climate change, pollution, scarce resource conservation, recycling and non-wasteful packaging, environmentally friendly ingredients and animal testing.

7. The term technology is used widely to describe information technology but also developments in nanotechnology, automation and so on. Technology is the engine as well as one of the outputs of modern business and needs to be carefully monitored as changes in this area can make businesses obsolete very quickly.

8. There are four key components of the microenvironment: suppliers, distributors, customers and competitors. These will be discussed in detail throughout the book.

9. That environmental scanning is the process of examining the company's marketing environment. Firms exhibit a number of different responses to environmental change, including no change through ignorance, delay and retrenchment, through to gradual or radical repositioning.

Key terms

cause-related marketing the commercial activity by which businesses and charities or causes form a partnership with each other to market an image, product or service for mutual benefit

consumer movement an organized collection of groups and organizations whose objective it is to protect the rights of consumers

environmental scanning the process of monitoring and analysing the marketing environment of a company

ethics the moral principles and values that govern the actions and decisions of an individual or group

macroenvironment a number of broader forces that affect not only the company but the other actors in the environment, e.g. social, political, technological and economic

marketing environment the actors and forces that affect a company's capability to operate effectively in providing products and services to its customers

microenvironment the actors in the firm's immediate environment that affect its capability to operate effectively in its chosen markets—namely, suppliers, distributors, customers and competitors

social responsibility the ethical principle that a person or an organization should be accountable for how its actions might affect the physical environment and the general public

Study questions

1. Visit the Warner Music Group website (www.wmg.com) and familiarize yourself with its business. Identify and discuss the major forces in the environment that are likely to impact on the company's prospects for the next five years.

2. Corporate social responsibility (CSR) activities are largely an exercise in public relations by major corporations. Discuss.

3. Discuss the alternative ways in which companies might respond to changes in the macroenvironment.

4. Discuss five business opportunities arising from the growth in concern for the physical environment.

5. After almost two decades of growth, many of the world's leading economies may be moving into a period of recession. Discuss four implications of this potential development for businesses.

6. Visit the following websites: www.barclays.com, www.hbosplc.com and www.hsbc.com. Compare and contrast the CSR initiatives being pursued by these major UK financial institutions.

Suggested reading

Bakan, J. (2004) *The Corporation*, London: Constable & Robinson.

Brownlie, D. (1999) Environmental Analysis, in M.J. Baker (ed.) *The Marketing Book*, Oxford: Butterworth-Heinemann.

The Economist (2008) Just Good Business: A Special Report on Corporate Social Responsibility, 19 January, 1–22.

Enkvist, P., T. Naucler and J. Oppenheim (2008) Business Strategies for Climate Change, *McKinsey Quarterly*, **2**, 24–33.

James, O. (2007) *Affluenza*, London: Vermilion.

Klein, N. (2000) *No Logo*, London: HarperCollins.

Schlosser, E. (2001) *Fast Food Nation*, London: Penguin.

References

1. Jack, A. (2007) Bitter Pills: The Fast-Growing, Deadly Industry in Fake Drugs, *Financial Times*, 14 May, 13; Lambkin, M. and Y. Tyndall (2007) Stealing Beauty, *Marketing Age*, Summer, 71–5; Rigby, E. (2005) Fashionistas May Soon Find Being up to Date Too Costly, *Financial Times*, 18 August, 22.

2. Green, M. (2008) Nigerians Heed the Call of Marketing, *Financial Times*, 8 April, 10.

3. Matthews, R. (2005) Where East can Never Meet West, *Financial Times*, 21 October, 13.

4. Edgecliffe-Johnson, A. (2007) MTV Tunes into a Local Audience, *Financial Times*, 16 October, 16.

5. Authers, J. (2003) US Grapples with 'Language of Love', *Financial Times*, 13 January, 9.

6. Braddock, K. (2003) When a Brand Becomes Guilty by Association, *Financial Times*, 17 July, 11.

7. Killgren, L. (2008) Enthusiastic US lifts Burberry, *Financial Times*, 29 May, 23.

8. O'Brien, D. (2003) Burberry Square, brand-channel.com, 16 June.

9. Tomkins, R. (2005) The Damage that the Wrong Kind of Customer can do, *Financial Times*, 18 January, 11.

10. For a discussion of some green marketing issues, see Pujari, D. and G. Wright (1999) Integrating Environmental Issues into Product Development: Understanding the Dimensions of Perceived Driving Forces and Stakeholders, *Journal of Euromarketing*, 7 (4), 43–63; Peattie, K. and A. Ringter (1994) Management and the Environment in the UK and Germany: A Comparison, *European Management Journal*, **12** (2), 216–25.

11. Carter, M. (2005) Ethical Business Practices Come into Fashion, *Financial Times*, 19 April, 14.

12. Elkington, J. (2001) *The Chrysalis Economy*, Capstone.

13. Hegarty, S. (2005) So Who is Leo Hairy Camel?, *Irish Times*, Weekend Review, 2 April, 3.

14. Jack, A. (2008) An Unusual Model for Good Causes, *Financial Times*, 5 June, 16.

15. Berkowitz, E.N., R.A. Kerin, S.W. Hartley and W. Rudelius (2000) *Marketing*, Boston, MA: McGraw-Hill.

16. Hunt, B. (2005) Companies With Their Reputations on the Line, *Financial Times*, 24 January, 10.

17. Allen, K. (2007) *The Corporate Takeover of Ireland*, Dublin: Irish Academic Press.

18. Bakan, J. (2004) *The Corporation*, London: Constable.

19. *The Economist* (2008) Just Good Business: A Special Report on Corporate Social Responsibility, 19 January.

20. James, O. (2007) *Affluenza*, London: Vermilion.

21. Business Portrait (1997) Early Riser Reaches the Top, *European*, 17–23 April, 32.

22. Grande, C. (2007) Businesses Behaving Badly, Say Consumers, *Financial Times*, 20 February, 15.

23. Minder, R. (2006) The Lobbyists Have Taken Brussels By Storm, *Financial Times*, 19 January, 11.

24. Terzano, E. (2004) A Campaign that Shows its Roots, *Financial Times*, Creative Business, 14 December, 12.

25. Cullen, P. (2007) Survey Finds 36 Children's Cereals Cannot be Rated Healthy, *Irish Times*, 4 June, 3.

26. Terazono, E. (2006) Ban on Junk Food Adverts 'Should be Bolder', *Financial Times*, 29 March, 5.

27. Wiggins, J. (2007) Fat Children Double Eating After Adverts, *Financial Times*, 25 April, 5.

28. Klein, N. (2000) *No Logo*, London: HarperCollins.

29. Coonan, C. (2008) Great Pall of China, *Innovation*, January, 36–7.

30. Ward, A. (2006) Global Thirst for Bottle Water Attacked, *Financial Times*, 13 February, 9.

31. Harvey, F. (2004) PC Makers Set to Face Costs of Recycling, *Financial Times*, 4 February, 13.

32. Carswell, S. (2008) Fishing for New Assets, *Innovation*, January, 26–7.

33. Reid, L. (2007) Products Not as Friendly to Environment as they Claim, *Irish Times*, 12 June, 1.

34. Birchall, J. (2005) US Supermarket Encourages Shoppers to Keep in Touch, *Financial Times*, 13 July, 22.

Case 2 innocent Ltd: being good is good for business

In a world of big commercial brands that promise to make you feel younger, look better or live longer, occasionally there are those that come along that try to be more grounded, more real and more authentic. A classic case in point was the Body Shop chain of cosmetic shops, which did not promise to reverse ageing or get rid of wrinkles but instead offered natural, authentic products and showed concern for the environment at the same time. innocent Ltd is a company in that mould. It has built a very successful business in the smoothie market by offering quality, fresh products and by behaving in an openly ethical manner. Its success has spawned a host of competitors and it now faces several challenges to its dominance of the sector.

Company background

innocent was founded in 1998 by three college friends—Richard Reed, Adam Balon and Jon Wright. In the summer of that year, the trio set up a stall at a small music festival in London. They started with £500 of fresh fruit and set up two bins, one with a 'yes' sign and the other with a 'no' sign. They also had another sign that asked customers 'Should we give up our jobs to make these drinks?' By the end of the festival, the 'yes' bin was overflowing and innocent Ltd was born. The vision of its founders, in the words of Richard Reed, was to be 'Europe's favourite little juice company', and innocent set about making products that contained 100 per cent pure, fresh ingredients with no additives. The unconventional approach that has characterized its development was illustrated through the use of both a lower-case 'i' rather than a capital letter 'I' in its name and its claim on its packaging that its smoothies contained no preservatives, no concentrates, no sweeteners, no additives and no funny business. Based on its initial success, its vision was subsequently broadened to be the Earth's favourite little food company by 2030.

Capitalizing on the growing trend towards healthy eating and living, innocent quickly became a marketing phenomenon. Its products were ideal for cash-rich, time-poor, health-conscious consumers, who do not eat enough fruit or have the time to prepare healthy meals. It achieved year-on-year sales growth levels of 100 per cent and reached an annual turnover in excess of £100 million in 2007. Its primary markets were the UK and Ireland, where estimates put its market share at 64 per cent, but the product was also sold in a variety of other countries throughout Europe, including the Netherlands, France, Germany and Scandinavia.

Company values and branding

One of the distinctive features of the company was the extent to which the beliefs and values of its founders were reflected in what it did and in the way that it did it. From the start, innocent aimed to be an authentic company that was honest with its business partners and its customers. Its ethos was to involve its customers in its strategic decisions, and to keep its products natural, simple and innovative. The company's core values were to be responsible, entrepreneurial, generous, commercial and natural.

The choice of the innocent name, which was a very unusual name for a brand of soft drinks, deliberately reflects this ethos. It represents the naturalness of the products and also that the company wants to do the right things in its key business decisions. When they couldn't afford a design company to develop the company's logo, the founders hired one of their friends, Dan Germain, to develop the now distinctive symbol of the apple with a halo, which again was illustrative of the company's core values.

These values were also reflected in how the company communicated with its customers, which was in a very relaxed and non-corporate style. This was most vividly illustrated in the packaging of its products. They were bright and colourful and contained text that was designed to bring a smile to your face. It included statements like 'shake before opening, not after' and invited customers to 'enjoy by' rather than 'use by'. Another label read 'My mum's started buying our smoothies (and that's after a year, the skinflint). They are as fat free as an apple or banana and that's because they are just fruit. Is that good enough for you mum? Right I'm off to smash some windows and have a fag.' This kind of statement effectively got the message across that the product was made from real fruit, but it did so in a humorous, non-preachy, non-corporate way. Yet another label read, 'Thou shall not commit adultery . . . that's one guideline we follow religiously; our smoothies are 100 per cent pure fruit. We call them innocent because we refuse to adulterate them in any way.'

Dan Germain, who subsequently became Head of Creative at innocent, has been quoted as saying 'lots of businesses spend a lot of money on creating an image and then telling people about it. What we do is tell people about our reality. Being innocent informs everything we are trying to do . . . paper from sustainable resources, a fresh tone on our labels, vans painted like cows, staff games in the park, going into the country to help pick elderberries for our juice. If we call the company innocent, we have a responsibility to be innocent.' He highlighted that innocent's major focus was on getting its products right and when that occurred it made branding easier.

Marketing activities

innocent's main business was smoothies. Having started off with three recipes, it has come up with almost 30 others over the years. Some of its most popular varieties have included strawberry and banana, mango and passion fruit, and pineapple, banana and coconut. It also introduced a range of kids' smoothies, which came in kid-friendly flavours complete with straws, and thickies, which were made with yoghurt and were thicker than regular smoothies. These products came in three different-sized packages, including 250 ml bottles, which were suitable for individuals who may want to consume the product while on the move, small cartons for its kids' range and large cartons for family consumption.

Because the product was a 100 per cent pure fruit smoothie, innocent was able to command a premium price for its range in the marketplace. List prices ranged from 99p for small bottles to £3.49 for its large cartons, prices that were generally higher than those of competitors such as own-label brands offered by supermarkets like Tesco. It cleverly deflected potential criticism of its prices by saying things like 'we would make them cheaper but they wouldn't be as tasty or as healthy because we'd have to use concentrates and other nasty stuff'. It was also innovative in how it has used sales promotions to encourage consumers to buy its product. An example of this is its 'Buy-one-get-one-tree' promotion, where a tree was planted by the company for every carton of smoothie purchased during the promotional period. Over 165,000 trees were planted in Africa and India.

Smoothies were widely distributed in supermarkets, convenience stores, cafés and delicatessens. Wholesale intermediaries were primarily used to distribute products to these retailers and the company also had a distinctive fleet of vehicles that reflected its laid-back image. Some were painted in the colours of different breeds of cows (and grew from really good grass man!!) and it also had its dancing grass vans (DGVs), which were vans that were covered in grass, making them distinctive and easy to spot. For example, one

DGV toured the UK and Scotland in 2002 providing samples of smoothies to over 1.3 million people.

Brightly coloured packaging and company vehicles are a key part of how the brand has built its presence in the marketplace. It did some advertising that was produced in-house to keep costs low but tended to focus mainly on gaining publicity through events and charity work. For example, it initially held a music festival called 'Fruitstock', which had the dual objective of thanking customers for their support as well as creating awareness of the brand. This was replaced by the 'innocent village fete', which has also been highly effective in enabling the company to reach its primary target markets. In 2007, a village fete was held in Regent's Park, London, and attracted over 60,000 people as well as raising over £150,000 for three chosen charities: the Samaritans, Friends of the Earth and Well Child.

A further distinctive feature of innocent's marketing was the extent to which it aimed to interact with and build relationships with its customers. A great deal of this was achieved by the fact that it tried to get out and interact with customers at village fetes or through its distinctive company vehicles. But, in addition, all its communications, such as that on its packaging and on its website, was designed to be two-way. Consumers were invited to contact the company on the 'banana' phone number, which was a hotline that anyone at head office would answer, or to visit the company anytime at its headquarters in London – Fruit Towers, a parody on the classic TV comedy series, *Fawlty Towers*. Consumers were encouraged to submit smoothie recipes as well as content and slogans for product packaging and advertising, and any 'sorry smoothie' stories, if they'd had a bad innocent experience. Its website, www.innocentdrinks.co.uk, provided entertainment through images and videos from various village fetes, and it also had pages on YouTube and Facebook. Visitors to its site were invited to joint the innocent family to receive emails of news, chances to win free drinks, as well as invitations to village fetes. In return, they were a source of market information in that they were occasionally asked questions like 'What you reckon we should do next, as we sometimes get confused?'

Sustainability

In keeping with its core values, innocent aimed to be an ethical company that 'wanted to leave things a little better than we find them'. Each year, it gave 10 per cent of its profits to charity, most of which goes to the innocent Foundation set up in 2004, with the aim of building sustainable futures for the world's poorest people. The foundation has worked with 18 partner organizations around the world such as Womankind Worldwide and the Microloan Foundation. Its partnership with Womankind supported Irula tribal women living in the Nadu coastal region of India, which was devastated by the 2004 tsunami and subsequent flooding. It helped to support over 430 families in setting up a brick production unit, which provided the income and bricks needed to rebuild homes. The Microloan Foundation provided small loans, basic business training and continuing guidance to vulnerable groups of women in sub-Saharan Africa.

Over the years, the Foundation has also been involved in several other projects, including, for example, the Big Knit. This involved older people from Age Concern around the UK, innocent customers and Sainsbury's staff knitting little woolly hats to place on the top of innocent smoothie bottles. The bottles were then sold in Sainsbury's and for every one sold, 50p went to Age Concern to help keep older people warm in winter. The project generated significant press coverage and innocent's sales increased by over 40 per cent during the period. It also won the Business in the Community National Example of Excellence for Cause Related Marketing at the 2007 BitC Awards.

Ethical behaviour has also permeated the company's key strategic decisions. All its bananas are bought from plantations that have been accredited by the Rainforest Alliance, an independent ethical auditing body that looked at farm workers' rights and well-being, as well as protecting ecosystems on the farms

innocent Drinks award winning promotion with Age Concern was intended to be both eye-catching and fun

and encouraging biodiversity. One hundred per cent recycled materials are used in packaging and labelling. Bottles are made from recycled plastic, while bottle caps are made from polyethylene, which is completely recyclable. Labels are made from 25 per cent recycled paper and 75 per cent paper from forests that have been certified by the Forest Stewardship Council. In 2007, innocent started measuring its carbon footprint from farm to fridge to recycling bin and, by the end of the year, had reduced it by 15 per cent. It has also encouraged its suppliers to go green and in the space of eight months, one of its carton co-packers had reduced its footprint by 60 per cent.

New challenges

In a short space of time, innocent Ltd has had a remarkable rise to fame. But having built a reputation as an ethical and 'innocent' company, it has faced many challenges in sustaining that reputation. For example, in May 2007, it was accused by one of its customers of having sold its soul to Satan when it announced its decision to trial its kids' smoothies in McDonald's. It has also been in trouble with the Advertising Standards Authority (ASA) for its campaigns for the 'Superfoods smoothie', where it claimed that the product was a 'natural detox'. It said the drink contained even more antioxidants than the average five a day, referring to the government's recommendation to eat at least five portions of fruit and vegetables per day. The ASA criticized the advertisement, claiming that 'neutralizing' free radicals did not amount to removing toxins and that innocent could not provide scientific evidence to support its detox claim. The brand's rise has been meteoric; continuing to grow so strongly may prove to be an even greater challenge.

Questions

1. What environmental trends created the opportunity for innocent to build its dominant position in the smoothie market?
2. Evaluate innocent's marketing mix. What are its strengths and weaknesses?
3. Analyse innocent's relationships with its customers. How have these relationships assisted with the development of the brand?
4. Critique the claim that innocent is an ethical company.

This case was prepared by Professor John Fahy, University of Limerick, from various published sources as a basis for class discussion rather than to illustrate either effective or ineffective management.

Chapter 3
Understanding Customer Behaviour

Learning Outcomes

By the end of this chapter you will understand:

1 the dimensions of customer behaviour, who buys, how they buy and the choice criteria used
2 the differences between consumer and organizational buyer behaviour
3 the main influences on consumer behaviour—the buying situation, personal and external influences
4 the main influences on organizational buying behaviour—the buy class, product type and purchase importance
5 the marketing implications of the various dimensions of consumer behaviour.

Neuro-marketing

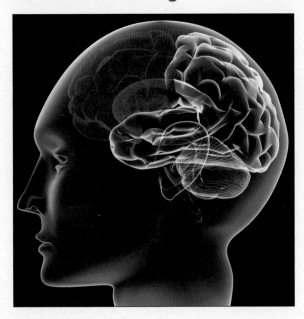

Our lives are full of choices. We choose which college we would like to attend, what courses we would like to study, what careers we would like to pursue. On a daily basis we make choices about the food we eat, the clothes we buy, the music we listen to, and so on. The processes by which we make all these choices are of great interest to marketers. Companies with products or services to sell want to know us, what we like and dislike, and how we go about making these consumption decisions. In essence, they would like to get inside our heads, and developments in the field of neuro-marketing mean that, increasingly, they are doing exactly that.

Neuro-marketing is an application of the techniques of neuroscience to the field of marketing. Neuroscience is the study of the brain and the nervous system; it draws on a variety of subject areas, such as genetics, physiology and evolutionary history. By studying the human brain, marketers can get a better understanding of how consumers respond to marketing stimuli like advertising and brands, and how we go about making our buying decisions. To get answers to these kinds of questions in the past, researchers tended to rely on the techniques of psychology, whereby consumers were asked to talk about and explain their consumption patterns. Neuroscience, however, allows us to examine precisely which part of the brain responds to stimuli, and from this we can infer how the consumer is likely to react. Different parts of the brain are associated with different emotions, such as empathy or reward, and brain scans can reveal whether these are activated when exposed to marketing stimuli.

A typical neuro-marketing study is an experiment that was carried out on the impact of Pepsi and Coke advertising on preferences towards these brands. Subjects were asked to take sips of Pepsi and Coke from unmarked cups and were also shown images of the Pepsi and Coke brands. The respondents expressed a significant preference for Coke over Pepsi but it was clear from the brain scans conducted that this was due to the advertising imagery for Coke rather than its taste. The appeal of neuro-marketing is that it can get beyond the expressed behaviour of consumers to reveal their true emotions. For example, market researchers are acutely aware that many consumers, when participating in studies, give the kinds of answers they think the researchers are looking for. For example, they might express a liking for a new product idea even though they would never intend to buy it. In a study in the US on advertisements during the Super Bowl, brain research revealed a Disney World ad to have the most positive brain signals while the audience favourite in other polls was a Bud Light advert.

Brain research can be used in a variety of areas. For example, a company called NeuroFocus tracks brain responses to television advertisements to determine whether consumers are paying attention, their level of emotional engagement with the advert and their memory retention. This promises to provide a much more accurate analysis of the extent to which consumers watch TV adverts than that provided by current technologies such as people meters. In the future, it would appear that marketers will be peering in ever greater detail inside our heads—something that also raises important ethical issues regarding how these technologies are used and whether they will be employed to exploit consumers. It would appear that we are moving to a new chapter in the study of consumer behaviour.[1]

In Chapter 1 we saw that an in-depth knowledge of customers is a prerequisite of successful marketing; indeed, understanding customers is the cornerstone upon which the marketing concept is built. How customers behave can never be taken for granted and new trends emerge all the time, such as the emergence of tattoos as fashion items. There are a variety of influences on the purchasing habits of customers and these are constantly changing and evolving. As a result, products that may only recently have been seen as 'must haves' quickly go out of fashion to be replaced by something else. Successful marketing requires a great sensitivity to these subtle drivers of behaviour and an ability to anticipate how they influence demand. In this chapter we will explore the nature of customer behaviour; we will examine the frameworks and concepts used to understand customers; and we will review the dimensions we need to consider in order to grasp the nuances of customer behaviour and the influences upon it.

The dimensions of customer behaviour

At the outset, a distinction needs to be drawn between the purchases of private consumers and those of organizations. Most consumer purchasing is individual, such as the decision to purchase a chocolate bar on seeing an array of confectionery at a newsagent's counter, though it may also be by a group such as a household. In contrast, in organizational or business-to-business (B2B) purchasing there are three major types of buyer. First, the industrial market concerns those companies that buy products and services to help them produce other goods and services such as the purchase of memory chips for MP3 players. These industrial goods can range from raw materials to components to capital goods such as machinery. Second, the reseller market comprises organizations that buy products and services to resell. Mail-order companies, retailers and supermarkets are examples of resellers (see the Oasis case at the end of this chapter). Third, the government market consists of government agencies that buy products and services to help them carry out their activities. Purchases for local authorities and defence are examples of this.

Understanding the behaviour of this array of customers requires answers to the following core questions (see Figure 3.1).

- *Who* is important in the buying decision?
- *How* do they buy?
- *What* are their choice criteria?

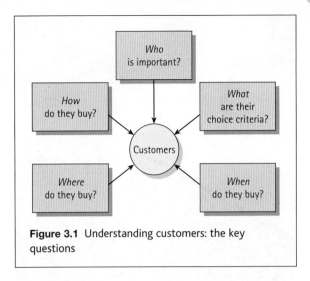

Figure 3.1 Understanding customers: the key questions

- *Where* do they buy?
- *When* do they buy?

The answers to these questions can be derived from personal contact with customers and, increasingly, by employing marketing research, which we will examine in Chapter 4. In this chapter we examine consumer and organizational buyer behaviour. The structure of this analysis will be based on the first three questions: who, how and what. These are often the most intractable aspects of customer behaviour; it is usually much more straightforward to answer the last two questions, about where and when customers buy.

Who buys?

Blackwell, Miniard and Engel[2] describe five roles in the buying decision-making process.

1. *Initiator:* the person who begins the process of considering a purchase. Information may be gathered by this person to help the decision.
2. *Influencer:* the person who attempts to persuade others in the group concerning the outcome of the decision. Influencers typically gather information and attempt to impose their choice criteria on the decision.
3. *Decider:* the individual with the power and/or financial authority to make the ultimate choice regarding which product to buy.
4. *Buyer:* the person who conducts the transaction. The buyer calls the supplier, visits the store, makes the payment and effects delivery.
5. *User:* the actual consumer/user of the product.

Multiple roles in the buying group may, however, be assumed by one person (see Exhibit 3.1). In a toy

**Simplicity is knowing they're getting all
the goodness they need.**
The Philips Juicer. With an extra large feeding tube it's never been
simpler to add essential vitamins and minerals to your family's daily diet.

Want to know more about your health & wellbeing? Visit www.philips.com/simplicity

PHILIPS
sense and simplicity

Exhibit 3.1 This advertisement for the Philips Juicer is
clearly targeted at parents of young children, who are
concerned about their nutrition and health

purchase, for example, a girl may be the initiator
and attempt to influence her parents, who are the
deciders. The girl may be influenced by her sister to
buy a different brand. The buyer may be one of the
parents, who visits the store to purchase the toy
and brings it back to the home. Finally, both children
may be users of the toy. Although the purchase was
for one person, in this example marketers have four
opportunities—two children and two parents—to
affect the outcome of the purchase decision. For
example, Samsung has sponsored the European
Computer Gaming Championships in a bid to build
its brand image among young people, who are known
to have a significant influence on the purchasing
behaviour of adults when it comes to buying technology. While it does not have a very favourable image
among over-40s, the company's research has found
that positive attitudes towards the Samsung brand
have increased by 25 per cent in the 18–29 age group
since it changed its marketing focus.[3]

The role of children in influencing household purchasing is very significant. The expression 'pester
power' is often used to by advertisers to describe the
process by which children subtly influence or more
overtly nag their parents into buying a product.

Young children are very brand aware. Studies show
that over 80 per cent of children aged between three
and six recognize the Coca-Cola logo.[4] Tweens—that
is, children in the 8–12 age group—are estimated to
account for some 60 per cent of all household expenditure.[5] For example, as over two-thirds of households buying a new car are influenced in the decision
by their children, Toyota in Australia has very successfully included chickens, puppies and kittens in its
advertising.[6]

The roles played by the different household members
vary with the type of product under consideration
and the stage of the buying process. For example,
men now do a very significant portion of household
grocery shopping, while women are increasing visitors
to DIY and hardware shops. Men were faster to
adopt the internet as a shopping medium, but have
recently been surpassed by women. Other interesting
differences have also been observed. Women, who
tend to take their time and browse in a retail environment, are more time conscious and goal-directed
online, while males tend to surf and browse many
websites when shopping on the internet. The impact
of these kinds of gender differences on marketing
practice are explored in Marketing in Action 3.1.
Also, the respective roles may change as the purchasing process progresses. In general, one or other
partner will tend to dominate the early stages, then
joint decision-making tends to occur as the process
moves towards final purchase. Joint decision-making
is more common when the household consists of two
income-earners.

Most organizational buying tends to involve more
than one individual and is often in the hands of a
decision-making unit (DMU), or **buying centre**, as
it is sometimes called. This is not necessarily a fixed
entity and may change as the **decision-making
process** continues. Thus a managing director may be
involved in the decision that new equipment should
be purchased, but not in the decision as to which
manufacturer to buy it from. The marketing task is
to identify and reach the key members in order to
convince them of the product's worth. But this is a
difficult task as the size of the decision-making groups
in organizations is on the increase. It can also be
difficult as the 'gatekeeper' is an additional role in
organizational buying. Gatekeepers are people like
secretaries who may allow or prevent access to a key
DMU member. The salesperson's task is to identify a
person from within the decision-making unit who is
a positive advocate and champion of the supplier's
product. This person (or 'coach') should be given all
the information needed to win the arguments that
may take place within the decision-making unit.

Marketing in Action 3.1: Sex and shopping

Study guide: Below are some examples of how marketers respond to consumer behaviour differences based on gender. Read the text and think of your own examples of gender-based consumer behaviour differences.

The different shopping behaviour of men and women has been the focus of a great deal of study over the years, and the stereotypes of the reluctant male shopper and the avid female shopper are the stuff of everything from sitcom to serious study. Increasingly researchers are going back in time to try to understand why these patterns appear to exist. Evolutionary psychologists argue that they are rooted in the hunter-gatherer dichotomy of early man, where hunting was the responsibility of males and gathering that of females. A recent study in the USA tested the proposition that women were more effective than men at remembering food locations. A total of 41 women and 45 men were recruited and taken to a farmer's market containing 90 food stalls. After visiting just six of the stalls and having something to eat, they were taken to the centre of the market and asked to point to the stalls using an arrow on a dial. On average, the women were more accurate than the men, which the researchers concluded showed that they are better at locating the sources of food.

Whatever the origins of such behaviour, there is no doubt that important differences exist that marketers have to take account of. For example, two-thirds of all customers at department stores are female, and while they like to walk around and explore the various floors, men like everything they are interested in to be in the same place. As a result, Bijenkorf in Amsterdam has experimented with having all male clothing, accessories, skincare and gadgets in one place. Selfridges has taken a similar approach, opening a new men's area in its London store, while Magasin du Nord in Copenhagen has introduced a personal shopping service for men, which includes clothing selections and grooming. Making shopping easy and quick still appears to be the priority for most males, thus perpetuating the stereotype.

In spite of their apparent aversion to shopping, male consumers can also represent an important market segment. For example, Fopp record and DVD shops, now part of the HMV chain, is distinctive in its focus on male shoppers. In concentrating on what it terms 'Fifty Quid Bloke', Fopp has targeted high-income males between 25 and 45, who have discerning tastes in books, music and film, to create a distinctive proposition in a very competitive marketplace. Following on from the rapid growth of male grooming products (the fastest-growing segment of the cosmetics business) is the growth in spas targeted at males. The number of spas in the USA has grown by 115 per cent since 2000, but two-thirds of their guests to date are women. When marketing to women, spa treatments focus on beauty and spirituality, whereas for men the appeal is more towards improved golf or ski performance as well as stress reduction. Once introduced to spas, most men agree that they are great, though few will admit it. Male consumers continue to be both important and challenging in equal measure.

Based on: Anonymous (2007);[7] Brooke (2007);[8] Kean (2007);[9] Yee (2005)[10]

The marketing implications of understanding who buys lie within the areas of marketing communications and segmentation. An identification of the roles played within the buying centre is a prerequisite for targeting persuasive communications. As we saw earlier, the person who actually uses or consumes the product may not be the most influential member of the buying centre, nor the decision-maker. Even when they do play the predominant role, communication to other members of the buying centre can make sense when their knowledge and opinions act as persuasive forces during the decision-making process.

How they buy

The decision-making process for consumers and organizations is shown in Figure 3.2. This diagram

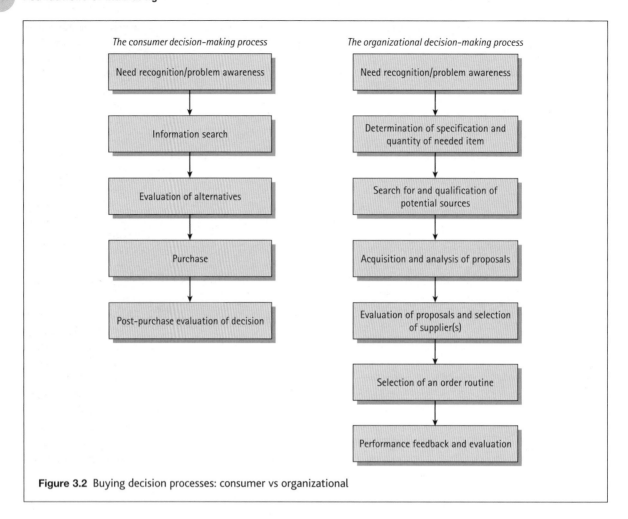

The consumer decision-making process

Need recognition/problem awareness

↓

Information search

↓

Evaluation of alternatives

↓

Purchase

↓

Post-purchase evaluation of decision

The organizational decision-making process

Need recognition/problem awareness

↓

Determination of specification and quantity of needed item

↓

Search for and qualification of potential sources

↓

Acquisition and analysis of proposals

↓

Evaluation of proposals and selection of supplier(s)

↓

Selection of an order routine

↓

Performance feedback and evaluation

Figure 3.2 Buying decision processes: consumer vs organizational

shows that buyers typically move through a series of stages, from a recognition that a problem exists to an examination of potential alternatives to a purchase and the subsequent evaluation of the purchase. Organizational buying is typically more complex and may involve more stages. However, the exact nature of the process will depend on the buying situation. In certain situations some stages will be omitted; for example, in a routine rebuy situation such as re-ordering photocopying paper, the purchasing officer is unlikely to pass through the third, fourth and fifth stages of organizational decision-making (search for suppliers and analysis, and evaluation of their proposals). These stages will be bypassed as the buyer, recognizing a need, routinely re-orders from an existing supplier. In general, the more complex the decision and the more expensive the item, the more likely it is that each stage will be passed through and that the process will take more time.

Need recognition/problem awareness

Need recognition may be functional and occur as a result of routine depletion (e.g. petrol, food) or

unpredictably (e.g. the breakdown of a car or washing machine). In other situations, consumer purchasing may be initiated by more emotional or psychological needs. For example, the purchase of Chanel perfume is likely to be motivated by status needs rather than by any marginal functional superiority over other perfumes.

Two issues govern the degree to which the buyer intends to resolve the problem: the magnitude of the discrepancy between the desired and present situation, and the relative importance of the problem.[11] A problem may be perceived but if the difference between the current and desired situation is small then the consumer may not be sufficiently motivated to move to the next step in the decision-making process. For example, a person may be considering upgrading their mobile phone from their existing model to a 3G phone. The 3G model may be viewed as desirable, but if the individual considers the difference in benefits to be small then no further purchase activity may take place. Conversely, a large discrepancy may be perceived but the person may not proceed to **information search** because the relative importance of the problem is small. A person may feel that a 3G model has significant advantages over an existing model, but that the relative importance of these advantages compared with other purchase needs (for example, a personal computer or a holiday) are small. The existence of a need, therefore, may not activate the decision-making process in all cases, due to the existence of 'need inhibitors'.[12] The marketing of mobile phones, with its emphasis on both the design features of new phones and their increased 'cool' factor is geared towards overcoming need inhibitors.

The need recognition stage has a number of implications for marketing. First, marketing managers must be aware of the needs of consumers and the problems they face. Sometimes this awareness may be due to the intuition of the marketer who, for example, spots a new trend (such as the early marketing pioneers who spotted the trend towards fast food, which has underpinned the global success of companies like McDonald's and Kentucky Fried Chicken). Alternatively, marketing research could be used to assess customer problems or needs (see Chapter 4). Second, marketers should be aware of need inhibitors. For example, in the personal computer industry, fears of not being able to use a computer might suggest developing an easy-to-use computer. Apple Computers provided such opportunities through its 'Test drive a Mac' dealer promotion when it launched the Macintosh. Third, marketing managers should be aware that needs may arise because of stimulation. Their activities, such as developing advertising campaigns and training salespeople to sell product benefits, may act as cues to need arousal.

Not all consumer needs are immediately obvious. Consumers often engage in exploratory consumer behaviour such as being early adopters of new products and retail outlets, taking risks in making product choices, recreational shopping and seeking variety in purchasing products. Such activities can satisfy the need for novel purchase experiences, offer a change of pace and relief from boredom, and satisfy a thirst for knowledge and consumers' curiosity.[13]

Information search

The second stage in the buyer decision-making process will begin when problem recognition is sufficiently strong. In the case of an organizational buying decision, the DMU will draw up a description of what is required and then begin a search for potential alternatives. When marketers can influence the specification that is drawn up, it may give their company an advantage at later stages in the buying process.

In a consumer situation, the search may be internal or external. Internal search involves a review of relevant information from memory. This review would include potential solutions, methods of comparing solutions, reference to personal experiences and marketing communications. If a satisfactory solution is not found then an external search begins. This involves personal sources such as friends, family, work colleagues and neighbours, and commercial sources such as advertisements and salespeople. Third-party reports such as *Which?* reports, and product testing reports in print and online media may provide unbiased information, and personal experiences may be sought such as asking for demonstrations, and viewing, touching or tasting the product. A great deal of information searching now takes place on the internet and one of the significant growth businesses has been intelligent agents—that is, websites such as buy.com and mysimon.com, which allow buyers to find out information about a wide range of products and compare online vendors. Many of these sites also provide product reviews and price comparisons free of charge (see Marketing in Action 3.2). In addition, sites like Amazon.com provide ongoing product and service recommendations for their customers. The objective of information search is to build up the **awareness set**—that is, the array of brands that may provide a solution to the problem.

Evaluation of alternatives and the purchase

Reducing the awareness set to a smaller group of options for serious consideration is the first step in evaluation. The awareness set passes through a screening filter to produce an **evoked set**: those products or services that the buyer seriously considers before making a purchase. In a sense, the evoked set is a shortlist of options for careful evaluation. The screening process may use different choice criteria from those used when making the final choice, and the number of choice criteria used is often fewer.[14] In an organizational buying situation, each DMU member may use different choice criteria. One choice criterion used for screening may be price. For example, transportation companies whose services are below a certain price level may form the evoked set. Final choice may then depend on criteria such as reliability, reputation and flexibility. The range of choice criteria used by customers will be examined in more detail later in this chapter.

Consumers' level of involvement is a key determinant of the extent to which they evaluate a brand. Involvement is the degree of perceived relevance and personal importance accompanying the brand choice.[15]

Marketing in Action 3.2: Online information search

> **Study guide:** Below is a review of the ways in which the internet assists with the information search phase of the buying decision process. Read it and consider examples of how you have used the internet in this way.

The internet is an information medium and, from its inception, has promised to revolutionize consumer shopping behaviour. To date, this revolution has not happened, though important changes are steadily taking place. Its impact on the information search stage of the buying process can be seen at three levels, namely host websites, comparison websites and peer websites.

Host websites are those of product vendors. Any buying decision can now be preceded by a visit to a company website to examine the product and read detailed information about it. For service companies, this can be an important way of bringing the experience to life for customers. For example, many hotels now offer surfers an opportunity to take a video tour of their facilities so that prospective customers can have an idea of what to expect before booking.

Comparison websites have been one of the biggest growth areas in online marketing. Typically these are sites that use intelligent agents to speedily search online stores and aggregate results in a form of one-stop shopping. Searches generate product and price information as well as reviews of products and online stores. Some of the global leaders include shopping.yahoo.com, mysimon.com and shopping.com, but there are many others. So far, they have been successful in generating a great deal of traffic but are not very profitable. For example, shopping.com has 6.2 million unique visitors and was bought by eBay for US$620 million in 2005, but it is estimated that it now has lower revenues than when that deal was done. Specialist comparison websites have also been developed, such as those for the financial services industry (e.g. moneysupermarket.com, nextag.com and confused.com). These sites compare the cost of loans, mortgages, insurance and the like, and facilitate online purchasing.

Finally, the growth of peer-to-peer websites is likely to be very important. For example, a site like TripAdvisor.com has had a significant impact on the travel industry. It contains reviews of destinations, airlines, hotels and restaurants written by other consumers, which can be checked in advance of a travel decision. However, like the reviews that are posted on sites like Amazon and elsewhere, it is important to remember that such sites are open to manipulation, such as consumers being paid to write favourable reviews. Social networks like Facebook and MySpace can also be a source of information on consumption decisions. In short, the biggest challenge facing the modern shopper is sifting through all the product information that is available in advance.

Based on: Fenton (2008)[16]

When a purchase is highly involving, the consumer is more likely to carry out extensive evaluation. High-involvement purchases are likely to include those incurring high expenditure or personal risk, such as car or home buying. In contrast, low-involvement situations are characterized by simple evaluations about purchases. Consumers use simple choice tactics to reduce time and effort rather than maximize the consequences of the purchase.[17] For example, when purchasing baked beans or breakfast cereals, consumers are likely to make quick choices rather than agonize over the decision. Research by Laurent

and Kapferer has identified four factors that affect involvement.[18]

1   *Self-image*: involvement is likely to be high when the decision potentially affects one's self-image. Thus purchase of jewellery, clothing and cosmetic surgery invokes more involvement than choosing a brand of soap or margarine.

2   *Perceived risk*: involvement is likely to be high when the perceived risk of making a mistake is high. The risk of buying the wrong house is much higher than that of buying the wrong chewing

gum, because the potential negative consequences of the wrong decision are higher. Risk usually increases with the price of the purchase.

3   *Social factors*: when social acceptance is dependent upon making a correct choice, involvement is likely to be high. Executives may be concerned about how their choice of car affects their standing among their peers in the same way that peer pressure is a significant influence on the clothing and music tastes of teenagers.

4   *Hedonistic influences*: when the purchase is capable of providing a high degree of pleasure, involvement is usually high. The choice of restaurant when on holiday can be highly involving since the difference between making the right or wrong choice can severely affect the amount of pleasure associated with the experience.

The distinction between high-involvement and low-involvement situations is important because the variations in how consumers evaluate products and brands lead to contrasting marketing implications. The complex evaluation in the high-involvement situation suggests that marketing managers need to provide a good deal of information about the positive consequences of buying. Print media may be appropriate in the high-involvement case since they allow detailed and repeated scrutiny of information. Car advertisements often provide information about the comfort, reliability and performance of the model. The salesforce also has an important role to play in the high-involvement situation by ensuring that the customer is aware of the important attributes of the product and correctly evaluates their consequences.

For low-involvement situations, the evaluation of alternatives is much more rudimentary and many purchases are made simply on impulse. In this case, attempting to gain 'top-of-mind awareness' and providing positive reinforcement through advertising, as well as seeking to gain trial (e.g. through sales promotion) may be more important than providing masses of information about the consequences of buying the brand. Furthermore, as this is of little interest, the consumer is not actively seeking information but is a passive receiver. Consequently, advertising messages should be short with a small number of key points, but with high repetition to enhance learning.[19] Television or radio may be the best media in this instance, since they facilitate the passive reception of messages. Also, they are ideal media for the transmission of short, highly repetitive messages. Advertising of many consumer products such as soap powder, toothpaste, tissue paper and the like follow this format.

Post-purchase evaluation of the decision

The creation of customer satisfaction is the real art of effective marketing. Marketing managers want to create positive experiences from the purchase of their products or services. Nevertheless, it is common for customers to experience some post-purchase concerns; this is known as **cognitive dissonance**. Such concerns arise because of an uncertainty surrounding the making of the right decision. This is because the choice of one product often means the rejection of the attractive features of the alternatives.

There are four ways in which dissonance is likely to be increased: due to the expense of the purchase; when the decision is difficult (e.g. there are many alternatives, many choice criteria, and each alternative offers benefits not available with the others); when the decision is irrevocable; and when the purchaser is inclined to experience anxiety.[20] Thus it is often associated with high-involvement purchases. Shortly after purchase, car buyers may attempt to reduce dissonance by looking at advertisements and brochures for their model, and seeking reassurance from owners of the same model. Rover buyers, say, are more likely to look at Rover advertisements and avoid Renault or Ford ads. Clearly, advertisements can act as positive reinforcers in such situations, and follow-up sales efforts can act similarly. Car dealers can reduce this 'buyer remorse' by contacting recent purchasers by letter to reinforce the wisdom of their decision and to confirm the quality of their after-sales service.

Many leading retailers in the USA are aiming to reduce dissonance by posting customer reviews of products and services online. Companies like Sears, Target, Home Depot and Macy's have all launched online product reviews. The risks of a negative review are outweighed by the value of obtaining customer feedback and also by providing future customers with a better idea of what to expect (see also Marketing in Action 3.2).[21] Managing expectations is a key part of reducing dissonance.

What are the choice criteria?

The various attributes (and benefits) a customer uses when evaluating products and services are known as choice criteria. They provide the grounds for deciding to purchase one brand or another. Different members of the buying centre may use different choice criteria. For example, purchasing managers who are judged by the extent to which they reduce purchase expenditure are likely to be more cost

Table 3.1 Choice criteria used when evaluating alternatives

Type of criteria	Examples
Technical	Reliability Durability Performance Style/looks Comfort Delivery Convenience Taste
Economic	Price Value for money Running costs Residual value Life cycle costs
Social	Status Social belonging Convention Fashion
Personal	Self-image Risk reduction Morals Emotions

conscious than production engineers who are evaluated in terms of the technical efficiency of the production process they design. Four types of choice criteria are listed in Table 3.1, which also gives examples of each.

Technical criteria are related to the performance of the product or service, and include reliability, durability, comfort and convenience. Reliability is particularly important in industrial purchasing. Many buying organizations are unwilling to trade quality for price. For example, Jaguar cars under Sir John Egan moved from a price-orientated purchasing system to one where quality was central, and purchasing managers were instructed to pay more provided the price could be justified in terms of improved quality of components.

Economic criteria concern the cost aspects of purchase and include price, running costs and residual values (e.g. the trade-in value of a car). However, it should not be forgotten that price is only one component of cost for many buying organizations. Increasingly, buyers take into account life cycle costs—which may include productivity savings, maintenance costs and residual values as well as initial purchase price—when evaluating products. Marketers can use life cycle cost analysis to

break into an account. By calculating life cycle costs with a buyer, new perceptions of value may be achieved.

Social criteria concern the impact that the purchase makes on the person's perceived relationships with other people, and the influence of social norms on the person. For example, in the early days the manufacturers of personal computers and mobile phones, such as Apple, IBM and Motorola, sought to sell them on the basis of their technical and economic criteria. But as the technology underpinning these products becomes similar for all vendors, new forms of differentiation, such as colour, shape, materials and appearance have become important. Technology products are increasingly being sold as fashion items, and fashions in turn are an expression of consumer identities. Nowadays phones, MP3 players and PCs are sold very much as fashion items. For example, Korea's LG Electronics scored a big hit when it teamed up with Prada to launch a line of Prada phones.

Personal criteria concern how the product or service relates to the individual psychologically. Emotions are an important element of customer decision-making (see Exhibit 3.2).

Exhibit 3.2 This advertisement for Bang & Olufsen highlights both the rational and emotional factors likely to influence purchase

The rejection of new-formula Coca-Cola in 1985, despite product tests that showed it to be preferred on taste criteria to traditional Coca-Cola, has been explained in part by emotional reactions to the withdrawal of an old and well-loved brand.[22] Saab ran a two-page advertising campaign that combined technical and economic appeals with an emotional one. The first page was headlined '21 Logical Reasons to Buy a SAAB'. The second page ran the headline 'One Emotional Reason'. The first page supported the headline with detailed body copy explaining the technical and economic rationale for purchase. The second page showed a Saab powering along a rain-drenched road. Personal criteria are also important in organizational purchasing. Risk reduction can affect choice decisions since some people are risk averse and prefer to choose 'safe' brands. The IBM advertising campaign that used the slogan 'No one ever got the sack for buying IBM' reflected its importance. Suppliers may be favoured on the basis that certain salespeople are liked or disliked, or due to office politics where certain factions within the company favour one supplier over another.

Marketing managers need to understand the choice criteria being used by customers to evaluate their products and services. Such knowledge has implications for priorities in product design, and the appeals to use in advertising and personal selling.

Influences on consumer behaviour

As noted above (in the discussion of the evaluation of alternatives), not all decisions follow the same decision-making process; nor do all decisions involve the same buying centre or use identical choice criteria. The following is a discussion of the major influences on the process, buying centre and choice criteria in consumer behaviour. They are classified into three groups: the buying situation, personal influences and social influences (see Figure 3.3). Later, we will look at the major influences on organizational buyer behaviour.

The buying situation

There are three kinds of buying situation: extended problem solving, limited problem solving and habitual problem solving.

The first of these, extended problem solving, involves a high degree of information search, as well as close examination of the alternative solutions using many choice criteria.[23] It is commonly seen in the purchase

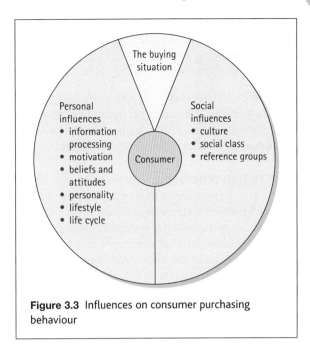

Figure 3.3 Influences on consumer purchasing behaviour

of cars, video and audio equipment, houses and expensive clothing, where it is important to make the right choice. Information search and evaluation may focus not only on which brand/model to buy, but also on where to make the purchase. The potential for cognitive dissonance is greatest in this buying situation. Extended problem solving is usually associated with three conditions: the alternatives are differentiated and numerous; there is an adequate amount of time available for deliberation; and the purchase has a high degree of involvement.[24] As we noted earlier, marketers can help in this buying situation by providing information-rich communications via advertising and the salesforce.

A great deal of consumer purchases come under the mantle of limited problem solving. The consumer has some experience with the product in question so that information search may be mainly internal through memory. However, a certain amount of external search and evaluation may take place (e.g. checking prices) before the purchase is made. This situation provides marketers with some opportunity to affect the purchase by stimulating the need to conduct a search (e.g. advertising) and reducing the risk of brand switching (e.g. warranties).

Habitual problem solving is what happens when a consumer repeat-buys a product while carrying out little or no evaluation of the alternatives, such as groceries purchased on a weekly shopping trip. He or she may recall the satisfaction gained by purchasing a brand, and automatically buy it again. Advertising may be effective in keeping the brand name in the consumer's mind and reinforcing already favourable attitudes towards it.

Personal influences

The six personal influences on consumer behaviour are: information processing, motivation, **beliefs** and **attitudes**, personality, lifestyle and life cycle.

Information processing

The term 'information processing' refers to the process by which a stimulus is received, interpreted, stored in memory and later retrieved.[25] It is therefore the link between external influences including marketing activities and the consumer's decision-making process. Two key aspects of information processing are perception and learning.

Perception is the complicated means by which we select, organize and interpret sensory stimulation into a meaningful picture of the world.[26] Three processes may be used to sort, into a manageable amount, the masses of stimuli that could be perceived. These are **selective attention**, **selective distortion** and **selective retention**. Selective attention is the process by which we screen out those stimuli that are neither meaningful to us nor consistent with our experiences and beliefs. It has obvious implications for advertising as studies have shown that consumers consciously attend to only between 5 and 25 per cent of the advertisements to which they are exposed.[27] A number of factors influence attention. We pay more attention to stimuli that contrast with their background than to stimuli that blend in with it. The name Apple is regarded as an attention-grabbing brand name because it contrasts with the technologically orientated names usually associated with computers. The size, colour and movement of a stimulus also affect attention. Position is also critical; objects placed near the centre of the visual range are more likely to be noticed than those on the periphery. This is why there is intense competition to obtain eye-level positions on supermarket shelves. We are also more likely to notice those messages that relate to our needs (benefits sought)[28] and those that provide surprises (for example, substantial price reductions).

When consumers distort the information they receive according to their existing beliefs and attitudes this is known as selective distortion. We may distort information that is not in accord with our existing views. Methods of doing this include thinking that we misheard the message, and discounting the message source. Consequently it is very important to present messages clearly without the possibility of ambiguity

Exhibit 3.3 This is a still from the award-winning BRAVIA Campaign 'Colour like-no-other' of Sony Europe; it demonstrates the visual power of colour and is also a highly appropriate way of conveying the key value proposition of a brand of LCD television

and to use a highly credible source. **Information framing** can affect interpretation. 'Framing' refers to ways in which information is presented to people. Levin and Gaeth[29] asked people to taste minced beef after telling half the sample that it was 70 per cent lean and the other half that it was 30 per cent fat. Despite the fact that the two statements are equivalent, the sample that had the information framed positively (70 per cent lean) recorded higher levels of taste satisfaction. Information framing has obvious implications for advertising and sales messages. The weight of evidence suggests that messages should be positively framed. Colour is another important influence on interpretation (see Exhibit 3.3). Blue and green are viewed as cool, and evoke feelings of security. Red and yellow are regarded as warm and cheerful. Black is seen as an indication of strength. By using the appropriate colour in pack design it is possible to affect the consumer's feelings about a product. However, it is important to remember that colour is also subject to different interpretations across different cultures.

Selective retention refers to the fact that only a selection of messages may be retained in memory. We tend to remember messages that are in line with existing beliefs and attitudes. Selective retention has a role to play in reducing cognitive dissonance: when reading reviews of a recently purchased car, positive messages are more likely to be remembered than negative ones.

Learning is the result of **information processing**; the term refers to any change in the content or organization of long-term memory.[30] There are numerous ways in which learning can take place. These include conditioning and cognitive learning. **Classical conditioning** is the process of using an established relationship between a stimulus and a response to cause the learning. Thus, in advertising, humour that is known to elicit a pleasant response may be used in the belief that these favourable feelings will be a condition of the product. The energy drink Red Bull uses humour in its advertising to appeal to its target market of young adults.

Operant conditioning differs from classical conditioning in terms of the role and timing of the reinforcement. In this case, reinforcement results from rewards: the more rewarding the response, the stronger the likelihood of the purchase being repeated. Operant conditioning occurs as a result of product trial. The use of free samples is based on the principles of operant conditioning. For example, free samples of a new shampoo are distributed to a large number of households. Because the use of the shampoo is costless it is used (desired response), and because it has desirable properties it is liked (reinforcement) and the likelihood of its being bought is increased. Thus the sequence of events is different for classical and operant conditioning. In the former, by association, liking precedes trial; in the latter, trial precedes liking. A series of rewards (reinforcements) may be used over time to encourage the repeat buying of the product.

The learning of knowledge, and the development of beliefs and attitudes without direct reinforcement is referred to as **cognitive learning**. The learning of two or more concepts without conditioning is known as **rote learning**. Having seen the headline 'Lemsip is for flu attacks', the consumer may remember that Lemsip is a remedy for flu attacks without the kinds of conditioning and reinforcement previously discussed. **Vicarious learning** involves learning from others without direct experience or reward. It is the promise of the reward that motivates. Thus we may learn the type of clothes that attract potential admirers by observing other people. In advertising, the 'admiring glance' can be used to signal approval of the type of clothing being worn or the alcoholic beverage

being consumed. We imagine that the same may happen to us if we dress in a similar manner or drink a similar drink. **Reasoning** is a more complex form of cognitive learning and is usually associated with high-involvement situations. For example, some advertising messages rely on the recipient to draw their own conclusions through reasoning, having been presented with some facts or assertions.

Whatever the type of learning that has taken place, the creation of product positioning is the result of the learning process. The market objective is to create a clear and favourable position in the mind of the consumer.[31] As we saw at the start of the chapter, some marketing companies are beginning to experiment with neuroscience, where brain activity is monitored while consumers are shown pictures of products, people and activities in order to try to better understand information processing and preference formation.

Motivation

To understand **motivation** we must look at the relationship between needs, drives and goals.[32] The basic process involves needs (deprivations) that set drives in motion (deprivations with direction) to accomplish goals (anything that alleviates a need and reduces a drive). Motives can be grouped into five categories, as proposed by Maslow.[33]

1   *Physiological*: the fundamentals of survival, e.g. hunger or thirst.
2   *Safety*: protection from the unpredictable happening in life, e.g. accidents, ill-health.
3   *Belongingness and love*: striving to be accepted by those to whom we feel close and to be an important person to them.
4   *Esteem and status*: striving to achieve a high standing relative to other people; a desire for prestige and a good reputation.
5   *Self-actualization*: the desire for self-fulfilment in achieving what one is capable of for one's own sake, i.e. actualized in what one potentially is.

It is important to understand the motives that drive consumers because it is these that determine **choice criteria**. In Western markets, the first four stages of Maslow's hierarchy have largely been satisfied. Consequently, many brands now emphasize the need for self-actualization in their advertising.

Beliefs and attitudes

A thought that a person holds about something is known as a 'belief'. In a marketing context, it is a thought about a product or service on one or more choice criteria. Marketing people are very interested in consumer beliefs because these are related to attitudes. In particular, misconceptions about products can be harmful to brand sales. Duracell batteries were believed by consumers to last three times as long as Ever Ready batteries, but in continuous use they lasted over six times as long. This prompted Duracell to launch an advertising campaign to correct this misconception.

An 'attitude' is an overall favourable or unfavourable evaluation of a product or service. The consequence of a set of beliefs may be a positive or negative attitude towards the product or service. Changing attitudes is an important step in convincing consumers to try a brand. For example, the marketers of Skoda cars first had to overcome significantly negative attitudes towards the brand before they succeeded in growing its sales levels in the UK market.

Understanding beliefs and attitudes is an important task for marketers. For example, the attitudes of the 'grey market', those over the age of 50 years, are not well understood. Some companies, such as Gap, have explicitly targeted this segment, but Gap was forced to close its Forth & Towne outlets after heavy losses. At the same time, 25 per cent of Apple's recently launched iPhones have been bought by people over 50.[34] This large and relatively well-off group is likely to be the subject of significant marketing effort in the years to come.

Personality

Just from our everyday dealings with people we can tell that they differ enormously in their personalities. **Personality** is the sum of the inner psychological characteristics of individuals, which lead to consistent responses to their environment.[35] A person may tend to be warm/cold, dominant/subservient, introvert/extrovert, sociable/a loner, adaptable/inflexible, competitive/co-operative, and so on. For example, luxury goods manufacturers are faced with the challenge of understanding and marketing to today's highly successful young businessmen, sometimes labelled 'alpha males'. While they too like to buy traditional luxury goods such as shoes, suits and gadgets, an increasing proportion of their spending is on the adrenalin buzz of experiences such as racing fast cars, private aircraft and gambling.[36] If we find from marketing research that our product is being purchased by people with certain personality profiles, then our advertising could show people of the same type using the product.

This concept—personality—is also relevant to brands. 'Brand personality' is the characterization of brands as perceived by consumers. Brands may be characterized as 'for young people' (Tommy

Hilfiger), 'for winners' (Nike), or 'self-important' (L'Oréal). This is a dimension over and above the physical (e.g. colour) or functional (e.g. taste) attributes of a brand. By creating a brand personality a marketer may generate appeal to people who value that characterization. For example, one of the longest-running fictional brands is James Bond; a variety of car makers and technology companies have attempted to bring his cool, suave and sexy personality into their brands by placing them in Bond movies.

Lifestyle

Lifestyle patterns have been the subject of much interest as far as marketing research practitioners are concerned (see Exhibit 3.4). The term 'lifestyle' refers to the pattern of living as expressed in a person's activities, interests and opinions. Lifestyle analysis (psychographics) groups consumers according to their beliefs, activities, values and demographic characteristics (such as education and income). For example, the advertising agency Young & Rubicam, identified seven major lifestyle groups that can be found throughout Europe and the USA.

1 *The mainstreamers*: the largest group. Attitudes include conventional, trusting, cautious and family centred. Leisure activities include spectator sports and gardening; purchase behaviour is habitual, brand loyal and in approved stores.
2 *The aspirers*: members of this group are unhappy, suspicious and ambitious. Leisure activities include trendy sports and fashion magazines; they buy fads, are impulse shoppers and engage in conspicuous consumption.
3 *The succeeders*: those that belong to this group are happy, confident, industrious and leaders. Leisure activities include travel, sports, sailing and dining out. Purchase decisions are based on criteria like quality, status and luxury.
4 *The transitionals*: members of this group are liberal, rebellious, self-expressive and intuitive. They have unconventional tastes in music, travel and movies; and enjoy cooking and arts and crafts. Shopping behaviour tends to be impulsive and to involve unique products.
5 *The reformers*: those that belong to this group are self-confident and involved, have broad interests and are issues orientated. They like reading, cultural events, intelligent games and educational TV. They have eclectic tastes, enjoy natural foods, and are concerned about authenticity and ecology.
6 *The struggling poor*: members of this group are unhappy, suspicious and feel left out. Their

A MORTGAGE & A LIFE!

Just because it's your first home doesn't mean you can't have a life anymore! We will find you the best mortgage to suit your particular lifestyle and we'll make sure you can still live your life, your way!

Lifestyle Mortgages, your lifestyle, your choice!

Independent Mortgage Brokers

Lo Call 1890 441 441

Lifestyle Mortgages, Level One, Liosbaun Retail Park, Tuam Road, Galway
Email info@lifestylemortgages.ie **Web** www.lifestylemortgages.ie

Lifestyle Mortgages is regulated by the Financial Regulator. Warning: If you do not keep up repayments on your mortgage or any loan secured on it. Terms and conditions apply.

Exhibit 3.4 This advertisement attempts to reassure consumers that moving to a new stage of life (i.e. home ownership) does not mean that existing lifestyles have to be sacrificed

interests are in sports, music and television; their purchase behaviour tends to be price based, but they are also looking for instant gratification

7 *The resigned poor*: those in this group are unhappy, isolated and insecure. Television is their main leisure activity and shopping behaviour is price based, although they also look for the reassurance of branded goods.

Lifestyle analysis has implications for marketing since lifestyles have been found to correlate with purchasing behaviour.[37] A company may choose to target a particular lifestyle group (e.g. the mainstreamers) with a product offering, and use advertising that is in line with the values and beliefs of this group. For example, United Biscuits has brought out the McV a:m range, which is a range of cereal bars, muesli fingers and marmalade muffins designed for people who do not have time to eat a proper breakfast.[38] As information on the readership/viewership habits of lifestyle groups becomes more widely known so media selection may be influenced by lifestyle research.

Increasingly, even very niche lifestyles are the focus of marketing attention. For example, flash mobbing was a recent fad where groups of people in their 20s and 30s, mobilized by email and text messages would gather in public places to engage in unconventional activities such as waving bananas in the air or speaking without the use of the letter 'O'. Record companies have adopted the approach in organizing concerts for some of their artists. Details of the location of the concert are kept secret until the last minute and revealed only to those who register at the Flash Fusion Concerts website.[39]

Life cycle

In addition to the factors we have already examined, consumer behaviour may depend on the 'life stage' people have reached. A person's life cycle stage is of particular relevance since disposable income and purchase requirements may vary according to life cycle stage. For example, young couples with no children may have high disposable income if both work, and may be heavy purchasers of home furnishings and appliances since they may be setting up home. When they have children, their disposable income may fall, particularly if they become a single-income family and the purchase of baby and child-related products increases. At the empty-nester stage, disposable income may rise due to the absence of dependent children, low mortgage repayments and high personal income. Research has shown that when children leave a home, a mother is likely to change 80 per cent of the branded goods she buys regularly and that they are more likely than any other group to decide which brands they want to buy once in a store than beforehand.[40] Both these issues have important marketing implications.

Social influences

The three social influences on consumer behaviour are: culture, social class and reference groups.

Culture

As we noted in Chapter 2, **culture** refers to the traditions, taboos, values and basic attitudes of the whole society within which an individual lives. It provides the framework within which individuals and their lifestyles develop, and consequently affects consumption. For example, in Japan it is generally women that control the family finances and make all the major household spending decisions. As a result, many financial services firms are developing investment products targeted specifically at Japanese women.

The most notable trend in the past three decades has been the increased internationalization of cultures.

Products and services that, previously, may only have been available in certain countries are now commonplace. For example, speciality cuisines like Japanese sushi, Korean barbeque and Cajun food can now be found in major cities throughout the world. Allied to this, though, is the growing domination of some cultures. For example, the successes of American fast-food chains and movie production companies represent a major challenge to smaller, local enterprises in many parts of the world.

Social class

Long regarded as an important determinant of consumer behaviour, in the UK the idea of social class is based largely on occupation (often that of the chief income earner). This is one way in which respondents in marketing research surveys are categorized, and it is usual for advertising media (e.g. newspapers) to give readership figures broken down by social class groupings. However, the use of traditional social class frameworks to explain differences in consumer behaviour has been criticized because certain social class categories may not relate to differences in disposable income (for example, many self-employed manual workers can have very high incomes). The National Statistics Socio-economic Classification system (NS-SEC) in the UK aims to take account of this situation by identifying eight categories of occupation, as shown in Table 3.2. Consumption patterns are likely to vary significantly across these categories. For example, research on the social class of British grocery shoppers has found that the highest proportion of AB (managerial/professional) shoppers

frequent Sainsbury's; Asda attracts a significantly higher share of people in lower supervisory and technical occupations; while Tesco's profile mirrored that of society in general.[41] However, some recent consumer trends would suggest that differences across the groups might be blurring, as illustrated in Marketing in Action 3.3.

Reference groups

A group of people that influences an individual's attitude or behaviour is called a **reference group**. Where a product is conspicuous (for example, clothing or cars) the brand or model chosen may have been strongly influenced by what buyers perceive as acceptable to their reference group; this may consist of the family, a group of friends or work colleagues. Some reference groups may be formal (e.g. members of a club or society), while others may be informal (friends with similar interests). Reference groups influence their members by the roles and norms expected of them. An opinion leader is someone in a reference group from whom other members seek guidance on a particular topic. This means that opinion leaders can exert enormous power over purchase decisions. For example, pop stars such as Jennifer Lopez, Britney Spears and Celine Dion have developed wide ranges of products, ranging from music to clothes to perfumes, which are essentially aspirational brands selling the qualities of their celebrity and lifestyle.

A related issue is the 'herd mentality' of consumption behaviour. People are social animals and tend to

Table 3.2 Social class categories

Analytic class	Operational categories	Occupations
1	Higher managerial and professional occupations	Employers in large organizations; higher managerial and professional
2	Lower managerial and professional occupations	Lower managerial occupations; higher technical and supervisory occupations
3	Intermediate occupations	Intermediate clerical/administrative, sales/service, technical/auxiliary and engineering occupations
4	Small employers and own-account workers	Employers in small, non-professional and agricultural organizations, and own-account workers
5	Lower supervisory and technical occupations	Lower supervisory and lower technical craft and process operative occupations
6	Semi-routine occupations	Semi-routine sales, service, technical, operative, agricultural, clerical and childcare occupations
7	Routine occupations	Routine sales/service, production, technical, operative and agricultural occupations
8	Never worked and long-term unemployed	Never worked, long-term unemployed and students

Marketing in Action 3.3: The 'unpredictable' consumer

Study guide: The paragraphs below show that consumers do not necessarily behave in the way that marketers might like them to. Read the text and consider the extent to which you create your own identity through consumption.

The largest population groups in the UK by disposable income are groups 2 and 3 in Table 3.2. Traditionally, this group, sometimes known as 'middle England', has been seen as quite homogeneous and easy to reach through a classic marketing mix of good product, competitive price and widespread distribution.

But recent research suggests that many consumers in this group no longer behave in such a predictable manner. Many middle-market consumers are engaged by upmarket brands but are also just as willing to buy cheaper low-brow brands if they feel that the latter meet their needs. As a result, they regularly mix a variety of expensive and cheap brands in an effort to demonstrate their individualism and self-expression. An example would be a consumer who flies on a budget airline but then stays at a five-star hotel.

The motivation to behave in this way seems to be driven by a desire for a greater sense of individualism. Consumers are reacting to the ubiquity of brands; they argue that by buying certain clothing brands, for example, they know that they will see others wearing the same clothes as well. So, whether it is the purchase of fashion, food or interiors, the attitude of these consumers appears to be that they are willing to combine expensive and cheap brands in order to create a look that is both 'individual and makes you feel smart'.

What these developments demonstrate is that the marketing practices of today and yesterday may not be suitable tomorrow as how consumers react to and engage with brands is continually evolving. This is captured by the difficulty in distinguishing between 'mass market' and 'premium brands'. Tesco may be a mass-market brand but it has a premium dimension through its 'Finest' range. Newcastle Brown ale is a quintessentially north-of-England, working-class drink but it is the number one performing alcohol brand in the USA, where it has been adopted by wealthy career women in chic San Diego bars. The noodle chain Wagamama started life as a healthy option for students, but is now frequented by all levels in society. At the same time, so-called luxury brands, like Ralph Lauren, Burberry, Chanel and BMW, are seen by ordinary customers as being increasingly attainable.

Based on: Carter (2003);[42] Rigby (2005);[43] Shaughnessy (2007)[44]

follow the crowd, therefore companies are looking at ways of exploiting this to increase sales. For example, researchers in the USA created an artificial music market in which people downloaded previously unknown songs. What they found was that when consumers could see how many times the tracks had been downloaded, they tended to select the most popular tracks. Similarly, 'smart cart' technology is being pioneered in supermarkets to exploit this herd instinct. Each cart has a scanner that reads products that have been chosen and relays it to a central computer. When a shopper walks past a shelf of goods, a screen on the shelf can tell her/him how many people in the shop have already selected that particular product. Studies have shown that if the number is high, s/he is more likely to choose it, so this method can be used to increase sales without offering discounts, for example.[45]

In summary, the behaviour of consumers is affected by a variety of factors. The buying situation, a range of personal influences and some social influences all combine to make up the nature of the relationships that individuals have with products and services. We will now turn to the factors that influence the buying behaviour of organizations.

Influences on organizational buying behaviour

Organizational buying is characterized by a number of unique features. Typically, the number of customers is small and order sizes large. For example, Tesco, Asda, Sainsbury's and Morrisons account for over 70 per cent of supermarket sales in the UK, so getting or losing an account with these resellers can be crucial. Organizational purchases are often complex and risky, with several parties having input into the purchasing decision as would be the case with a major IT investment. The demand for many organizational goods is derived from the demand for consumer goods, which means that small changes in consumer demand can have an important impact on the demand for industrial goods (see Marketing in Action 3.4). For example, the decline in the sale of VCRs has had a knock-on effect on the demand for VCR component parts. When large organizational customers struggle, this impacts on their suppliers. Most major car manufacturers such as Ford, General Motors, Daimler-Chrysler and Volkswagen have all demanded significant price cuts from their suppliers in recent years. However, at the same time suppliers have faced rising steel and raw material costs, which has affected profitability and forced some out of business.[46] Organizational buying is also characterized by the prevalence of negotiations between buyers and sellers; and in some cases reciprocal buying may take place where, for example, in negotiating to buy computers a company like Volvo might persuade a supplier to buy a fleet of company cars.

Marketing in Action 3.4: Riding the Wii!

> **Study guide:** Below are some examples of the nature of derived demand in organizational purchasing. Read the text and think of examples of where a fall in consumer demand has had a knock-on effect on component suppliers.

In recent years there have been some stunning technological successes, such as the iPod, the PlayStation and the plasma television. What is important to remember, however, is that the success of these products in the consumer marketplace also means a big boom for the makers of the components that go to make up these innovations.

A typical case in point is the Nintendo Wii. This product took the games market by storm when it was launched in 2004 and it sold over 30 million units in 2007. But the makers of its components have been significant beneficiaries as well. Mitsumi Electric, a Japanese electronics company, provides the Wii's wireless LAN and parts for its controllers, as well as helping to assemble the machine. It saw its operating profit surge by 500 per cent between 2006 and 2007, and roughly 40 per cent of this gain is directly linked to Nintendo. Tabuchi Electric, which makes the AC adaptor for the Wii, increased its operating profit by almost 500 per cent for the first quarter of 2007, while Hosiden, a small parts maker in Osaka, has also experienced a big rise in sales and profits. Indeed, one of the biggest challenges facing the suppliers of a runaway success like the Wii is to be able to expand production to meet the sudden surge in demand. For this reason, some companies like Nintendo maintain a policy of having two suppliers for each core component.

A core task for component makers is to be able anticipate new directions in technology. For example, Intel has become famous for supplying the microprocessors used in personal computers, something that has been captured in its famous advertising slogan: 'Intel Inside'. But as personal computers become ever smaller and many of their functions become available through next-generation mobile phones, the company will need to continue to innovate to meet the needs of new customers as well as face the challenges presented by new competitors. Similarly, as it anticipates a significant growth in the developing world for low-cost cars, the German components supplier Bosch is aiming to be one of the world's market leaders in supplying parts to low-cost manufacturers such as Tata in India. This represents a new departure for a company usually associated with premium European brands such as Mercedes.

Based on: Milne (2006);[47] Sanchanta (2007)[48]

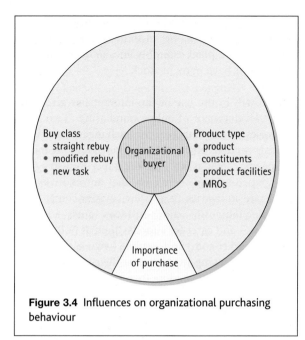

Figure 3.4 Influences on organizational purchasing behaviour

Figure 3.4 shows the three factors that influence organizational buying behaviour and the choice criteria that are used: the buy class, the product type and the importance of purchase.[49]

The buy class

Organizational purchases may be distinguished as either a **new task**, a **straight rebuy** or a **modified rebuy**.[50] A new task occurs when the need for the product has not arisen previously so that there is little or no relevant experience in the company, and a great deal of information is required. A straight rebuy occurs where an organization buys previously purchased items from suppliers already judged acceptable. Routine purchasing procedures are set up to facilitate straight rebuys. The modified rebuy lies between the two extremes. A regular requirement for the type of product exists, and the buying alternatives are known, but sufficient change (e.g. a delivery problem) has occurred to require some alteration to the normal supply procedure.

The buy classes affect organizational buying in the following ways. First, the membership of the DMU changes. For a straight rebuy possibly only the purchasing officer is involved, whereas for a new buy senior management, engineers, production managers and purchasing officers may be involved. Modified rebuys often involve engineers, production managers and purchasing officers, but not senior management, except when the purchase is critical to the company. Second, the decision-making process may be much longer as the buy class changes from a straight rebuy to a modified rebuy and to a new task. Third, in terms of influencing DMU members, they are likely to be much more receptive to new task and modified rebuy situations than straight rebuys. In the latter case, the purchasing manager has already solved the purchasing problem and has other problems to deal with. So why make it a problem again?

The first implication of this buy class analysis is that there are big gains to be made if a company can enter the new task at the start of the decision-making process. By providing information and helping with any technical problems that can arise, the company may be able to create goodwill and 'creeping commitment', which secures the order when the final decision is made. The second implication is that since the decision process is likely to be long, and many people are involved in the new task, supplier companies need to invest heavily in sales personnel for a considerable period of time. Some firms employ 'missionary' sales teams, comprising their best salespeople, to help secure big new task orders.

The product type

Products can be classified according to four types: materials, components, plant and equipment, and maintenance repair and operation (MRO):

1. materials—to be used in the production process, e.g. aluminium
2. components—to be incorporated in the finished product, e.g. headlights
3. plant and equipment—for example, bulldozers
4. products and services for MRO—for example, spanners, welding equipment and lubricants.

This classification is based on a customer perspective—how the product is used—and may be employed to identify differences in organizational buyer behaviour. First, the people who take part in the decision-making process tend to change according to product type. For example, senior management tend to get involved in the purchase of plant and equipment or, occasionally, when new materials are purchased if the change is of fundamental importance to company operations, e.g. if a move from aluminium to plastic is being considered. Rarely do they involve themselves in component or MRO supply. Similarly, design engineers tend to be involved in buying components and materials, but not normally MRO and plant equipment. Second, the decision-making process tends to be slower and more complex as product type moves along the following continuum:

$$MRO \rightarrow components \rightarrow materials \rightarrow plant\ and\ equipment$$

The importance of purchase

A purchase is likely to be perceived as being important to the buying organization when it involves large sums of money, when the cost of making the wrong decision, e.g. in terms of production downtime, is high and when there is considerable uncertainty about the outcome of alternative offerings. In such situations, many people at different organizational levels are likely to be involved in the decision and the process will be long, with extensive search for and analysis of information. Thus extensive marketing effort is likely to be required, but great opportunities present themselves to sales teams who work with buying organizations to convince them that their offering has the best pay-off; this may involve acceptance trials (e.g. private diesel manufacturers supply railway companies with prototypes for testing), engineering support and testimonials from other users. Additionally, guarantees of delivery dates and after-sales service may be necessary when buyer uncertainty regarding these factors is pronounced.

Features of organizational purchasing practice

A number of trends have occurred within the purchasing function that have marketing implications for supplier firms. The relentless drive for efficiency by businesses has been one of the key factors behind the growth of just-in-time purchasing, online purchasing and centralized purchasing At the same time, these developments have often strengthened relationships between buyers and their suppliers, and we have seen a significant growth in relationship marketing and reverse marketing.

The **just-in-time (JIT)** concept aims to minimize stocks by organizing a supply system that provides materials and components as they are required.[51] The total effects of JIT can be enormous. Purchasing inventory and inspection costs can be reduced, product design can be improved, delivery streamlined, production downtime reduced, and the quality of the finished item enhanced. Very close co-operation is required between a manufacturer and its suppliers. An example of a company that employs a JIT system is the Nissan car assembly plant in Sunderland in the UK. Nissan adopts what it terms 'synchronous supply': parts are delivered only minutes before they are needed. For example, carpets are delivered by Sommer Allibert, a French supplier, from its facility close to the Nissan assembly line in sequence for fitting to the correct model. Only 42 minutes elapse between the carpet being ordered and its being fitted

to the car. This system also carries risks, however. For example, the Kobe earthquake in Japan shut down those car plant assembly lines in nearby regions that did not have parts in stock.

The growth in the use of the internet has given rise to the development of online purchasing. Two main categories of marketplaces, or exchanges, have been created: **vertical electronic marketplaces** are industry specific, such as sites for the paper industry (e.g. www.paperexchange.com) or the automotive and healthcare industries (e.g. www.covisint.com); **horizontal electronic marketplaces** cross industry boundaries and cater for supplies such as MROs (e.g. www.dgmarket.com) and services (www.elance.com). Companies seeking supplies post their offers on these websites. Potential vendors then bid for the contracts electronically. Some companies report significant improvements in efficiency from managing their purchasing this way, through reducing the amount of procurement staff involved in processing orders and increasing the potential global spread of vendors. This heightened competition presents challenges for suppliers.

Where several operating units within a company have common requirements and where there is an opportunity to strengthen a negotiating position by bulk buying, centralized purchasing is an attractive option. Centralization encourages purchasing specialists to concentrate their energies on a small group of products, thus enabling them to develop an extensive knowledge of cost factors and the operation of suppliers.[52] For example, increasing concerns over the costs of healthcare has meant that many hospitals have centralized purchasing in procurement departments rather than devolving the activity to doctors and nurses as had been the case in the past. As a result, many contracts are put out to tender, often on a pan-European basis, with vendors selected on the basis of quality, cost and ability to deliver over a number of years. The net effect of this is that orders are much more difficult to secure but, once secured, are likely be more long lasting. At the same time, organizational buying has become increasingly characterized by very close relationships between buyers and sellers (see Exhibit 3.5). **Relationship marketing** is the process of creating, developing and enhancing relationships with customers and other stakeholders. For example, Marks & Spencer has trading relationships with suppliers that stretch back almost a century. Such long-term relationships can have significant advantages for both buyer and seller. Risk is reduced for buyers as they get to know people in the supplier organization and know who to contact when problems arise. Communication is thus improved,

**YOU WANT A
PARTNER TO HELP
YOU FEEL GOOD
ABOUT DOING WELL.**
HELLO NEIGHBOUR.

WELCOME

ABN AMRO is a local bank that works to the highest ethical principles
We focus on initiatives that protect the environment, promote social
well-being and stimulate economic growth. We even won a gold medal
for our approach to sustainable development*. So no matter where you
are, we'll protect your interests and your surroundings.

www.abnamro.com

Making more possible ABN·AMRO

Exhibit 3.5 This advertisement for ABN-Amro demonstrates the
importance of relationships in business-to-business marketing

The traditional view of marketing is that supplier firms will actively seek out the requirements of customers and attempt to meet those needs better than the competition. However, purchasing is now taking on a more proactive, aggressive stance in acquiring the products and services needed to compete. This process, whereby the buyer attempts to persuade the supplier to provide exactly what the organization wants, is called **reverse marketing**.[54] Syngenta, an international supplier of chemicals, uses reverse marketing very effectively to target suppliers with a customized list of requirements concerning delivery times, delivery success rates and how often sales visits should occur. The growth of reverse marketing presents two key benefits to suppliers who are willing to listen to the buyer's proposition and carefully consider its merits: first, it provides the opportunity to develop a stronger and longer-lasting relationship with the customer; second, it could be a source of new product opportunities that may be developed to a broader customer base later on.

Finally in B2B contexts, a firm may not actually make a purchase but rather it simply leases a product. A lease is a contract by which the owner of an asset (e.g. a car) grants the right to use the asset for a period of time to another party in exchange for the payment of rent.[55] The benefits to the customer are that a leasing arrangement avoids the need to pay the cash purchase price of the product or service, is a hedge against fast product obsolescence, may have tax advantages, avoids the problem of equipment disposal and, with certain types of leasing contract, avoids some maintenance costs. These benefits need to be weighed against the costs of leasing, which may be higher than outright buying.

and joint problem solving and design management can take place with suppliers becoming, in effect, strategic partners. Sellers gain through closer knowledge of buyer requirements, and many companies have reorganized their salesforces to reflect the importance of managing customer relationships effectively—a process known as key account management. New product development can benefit from such close relationships. The development of machine-washable lambs' wool fabrics and easy-to-iron cotton shirts came about because of Marks & Spencer's close relationship with UK manufacturers.[53] The issue of relationship marketing will be dealt with in more detail in Chapter 7.

Summary

This chapter has examined the nature of customer behaviour and the key influences on customer behaviour. The following key issues were addressed.

1. The differences between consumer and organizational buying behaviour. In the latter, the buying decision process involves more stages, the input of more parties and greater levels of negotiation. Technical and economic choice criteria tend to play a greater role in organizational buying.

2. Who buys—the five roles in the buying decision-making process: initiator, influencer, decider, buyer and user. Different people may play different roles, particularly in a family purchase and, for marketers, identifying the decider is critical.

3. The buying decision process, involving the stages of need recognition, search for alternatives, evaluation of alternatives, purchase and post-purchase evaluation. In the case of high-involvement purchases, consumers will typically go through all these stages, whereas in a low-involvement situation, they may move directly from need recognition to purchase.

4. The main choice criteria used in making purchase decisions—namely technical, economic, social and personal criteria. In consumer buyer behaviour, social and personal criteria are very important as consumers build their identities through product and service selection.

5. The main influences on consumer buying behaviour: the buying situation, personal influences and social influences. At any given time, there are myriad factors that may influence a consumer's purchase decision. For example, personality, stage of life cycle, reference groups and vicarious learning—to mention a few—may combine to drive a purchase decision in a certain direction.

6. The main influences on organizational buying behaviour: the buy class, the product type and the importance of purchase. For example, a major investment in plant and equipment that is critical to the organization and is a new task purchase will necessitate the involvement of many parties in the organization and will take time before a decision is made.

7. The key features of organizational purchasing practice: just-in-time purchasing, online purchasing, centralized purchasing, relationship marketing, reverse marketing and leasing. Organizational purchasing at one level presents opportunities for reverse marketing and relationship building with suppliers, but at a different level is driven by efficiency concerns that are managed through centralized and online purchasing.

Key terms

attitude the degree to which a customer or prospect likes or dislikes a brand

awareness set the set of brands that the consumer is aware may provide a solution to a problem

beliefs descriptive thoughts that a person holds about something

buying centre a group that is involved in the buying decision; also known as a decision-making unit (DMU) in industrial buying situations

choice criteria the various attributes (and benefits) people use when evaluating products and services

classical conditioning the process of using an established relationship between a stimulus and a response to cause the learning of the same response to a different stimulus

cognitive dissonance post-purchase concerns of a consumer arising from uncertainty as to whether a decision to purchase was the correct one

cognitive learning the learning of knowledge, and development of beliefs and attitudes without direct reinforcement

culture the traditions, taboos, values and basic attitudes of the whole society in which an individual lives

decision-making process the stages that organizations and people pass through when purchasing a physical product or service

evoked set the set of brands that the consumer seriously evaluates before making a purchase

horizontal electronic marketplaces online procurement sites that cross several industries and are typically used to source low-cost supplies such as MRO items

information framing the way in which information is presented to people

information processing the process by which a stimulus is received, interpreted, stored in memory and later retrieved

information search the identification of alternative ways of problem solving

just-in-time (JIT) the JIT concept aims to minimize stocks by organizing a supply system that provides materials and components as they are required

lifestyle the pattern of living as expressed in a person's activities, interests and opinions

modified rebuy where a regular requirement for the type of product exists and the buying alternatives are known but sufficient (e.g. a delivery problem has occurred) to require some alteration to the normal supply procedure

motivation the process involving needs that set drives in motion to accomplish goals

new task refers to the first-time purchase of a product or input by an organization

operant conditioning the use of rewards to generate reinforcement of response

perception the process by which people select, organize and interpret sensory stimulation into a meaningful picture of the world

personality the inner psychological characteristics of individuals that lead to consistent responses to their environment

reasoning a more complex form of cognitive learning where conclusions are reached by connected thought

reference group a group of people that influences an individual's attitude or behaviour

relationship marketing the process of creating, maintaining and enhancing strong relationships with customers and other stakeholders

reverse marketing the process whereby the buyer attempts to persuade the supplier to provide exactly what the organization wants

rote learning the learning of two or more concepts without conditioning

selective attention the process by which people screen out those stimuli that are neither meaningful to them nor consistent with their experiences and beliefs

selective distortion the distortion of information received by people according to their existing beliefs and attitudes

selective retention the process by which people retain only a selection of messages in memory

straight rebuy refers to a purchase by an organization from a previously approved supplier of a previously purchased item

vertical electronic marketplaces online procurement sites that are dedicated to sourcing supplies for producers in one particular industry

vicarious learning learning from others without direct experience or reward

Study questions

1. What are the differences between organizational buying behaviour and consumer buying behaviour?
2. Choose a recent purchase that included not only yourself but also other people in making the decision. What role(s) did you play in the buying centre? What roles did these other people play and how did they influence your choice?
3. Review your decision to choose the educational establishment you are attending in terms of need recognition, information search, evaluation of alternatives and post-selection evaluation.
4. Review the choice criteria influencing some recent purchases such as a hairstyle, a meal, etc.
5. Describe the recent trends in just-in-time purchasing, online purchasing and centralized purchasing. Discuss the implications of these trends for marketers in vendor firms.
6. Look at the following advertisements for Lynx deodorant and Red Bull: http://www.youtube.com/watch?v=_ni8fYRcXuI; http://www.youtube.com/watch?v=PM8y78z_C-o. Using the information processing theory discussed in this chapter, explain how these adverts impact upon the viewer.

Suggested reading

Anderson, J.C., J.A. Narus and **W. van Rossum** (2006) Customer Value Propositions in Business Markets, *Harvard Business Review*, **84** (3), 90–9.

Ford, D. (1997) *Understanding Business Markets*, London: Academic Press.

Silverstein, M.J. and **N. Fiske** (2003) Luxury for the Masses, *Harvard Business Review*, **81** (4), 48–58.

Thompson, E.S. and **A.W. Laing** (2003) 'The Net Generation': Children and Young People, the Internet and Online Shopping, *Journal of Marketing Management*, **19** (3/4), 491–513.

Underhill, P. (2000) *Why we Buy: The Science of Shopping*, London: Texere.

References

1. **McClure, S., Li, J., Tomlin, D., Cypert, K., Montague, L. and Montague, R.** (2004) Neural Correlates of Behavioural Preference in Culturally Familiar Drinks, *Neuron*, **44**, 379–87; **Vence, D.** (2006) Pick Someone's Brain: Neurological Research Seeks Brand Effects, *Marketing News*, 1 May, 11–14.

2. **Blackwell R.D., P.W. Miniard** and **J.F. Engel** (2000) *Consumer Behavior*, Orlando, FL: Dryden, 174.

3. **Pesola, M.** (2005) Samsung Plays to the Young Generation, *Financial Times*, 29 March, 11.

4. **Jones, H.** (2002) What are they Playing At?, *Financial Times*, Creative Business, 17 December, 6.

5. **Shrimsley, R.** (2004) Children's Power is Out of Control: Blame the Parents, *Financial Times*, 26 November, 14.

6. **Lindstrom, M.** (2003) The Real Decision Makers, *Brandchannel.com*, 11 August.

7. **Anonymous** (2007) Sex, Shopping and Thinking Pink, *Economist*, 25 August, 78.

8. **Brooke, S.** (2007) It's Different for Guys, *Financial Times: Life & Arts*, 28 April, 7.

9. **Kean, D.** (2007) Deep Inside the Mind of the Bloke, *Financial Times*, 15 May, 16.

10. **Yee, A.** (2005) Spas Woo Men by Scrubbing Up Macho Side, *Financial Times*, 17 September, 16.

11. **Hawkins, D.I., R.J. Best** and **K.A. Coney** (1989) *Consumer Behaviour: Implications for Marketing Strategy*, Boston, MA: Irwin, 536.

12. **O'Shaughnessey, J.** (1987) *Why People Buy*, New York: Oxford University Press, 161.

13. **Baumgartner, H.** and **J.-Bem Steenkamp** (1996) Exploratory Consumer Buying Behaviour: Conceptualisation and Measurement, *International Journal of Research in Marketing*, **13**, 121–37.

14. **Kuusela, H., M.T. Spence** and **A.J. Kanto** (1998) Expertise Effects on Prechoice Decision Processes and Final Outcomes: A Protocol Analysis, *European Journal of Marketing*, **32** (5/6), 559–76.

15. **Blackwell R.D., P.W. Miniard** and **J.F. Engel** (2000) *Consumer Behavior*, Orlando, FL: Dryden, 34.

16. **Fenton, B.** (2008) Counting the Cost of the Online Land Grab, *Financial Times*, 19 February, 21.

17. **Elliott, R.** and **E. Hamilton** (1991) Consumer Choice Tactics and Leisure Activities, *International Journal of Advertising*, **10**, 325–32.

18. **Laurent, G.** and **J.N. Kapferer** (1985) Measuring Consumer Involvement Profiles, *Journal of Marketing Research*, **12** (February), 41–53.

19. **Rothschild, M.L.** (1978) *Advertising Strategies for High and Low Involvement Situations*, Chicago: American Marketing Association Educator's Proceedings, 150–62.

20. **Hawkins, D.I., R.J. Best** and **K.A. Coney** (1989) *Consumer Behaviour: Implications for Marketing Strategy*, Boston, MA: Irwin.

21. **Birchall, J.** (2006) Retailers Give Customers the Final Word, *Financial Times*, 6 October, 13.

22. **Mowen, J.C.** (1988) Beyond Consumer Decision-making, *Journal of Consumer Research*, **5** (1), 15–25.

23. **Hawkins, D.I., R.J. Best** and **K.A. Coney** (1989) *Consumer Behaviour: Implications for Marketing Strategy*, Boston, MA: Irwin, 30.

24. **Engel, J.F., Blackwell, R.D.** and **P.W. Miniard** (1990) *Consumer Behaviour*, Orlando, FL: Dryden, 29.

25. **Engel, J.F., Blackwell, R.D.** and **P.W. Miniard** (1990) *Consumer Behaviour*, Orlando, FL: Dryden, 363.

26. **Williams, K.C.** (1981) *Behavioural Aspects of Marketing*, London: Heinemann.

27. **Hawkins, D.I., R.J. Best** and **K.A. Coney** (1989) *Consumer Behaviour: Implications for Marketing Strategy*, Boston, MA: Irwin, 275.

28. **Ratneshwar, S., L. Warlop, D.G. Mick** and **G. Seegar** (1997) Benefit Salience and Consumers' Selective Attention to Product Features, *International Journal of Research in Marketing*, **14**, 245–9.

29. **Levin, L.P.** and **G.J. Gaeth** (1988) Framing of Attribute Information Before and After Consuming the Product, *Journal of Consumer Research*, **15** (December), 374–8.

30. **Hawkins, D.I., R.J. Best** and **K.A. Coney** (1989) *Consumer Behaviour: Implications for Marketing Strategy*, Boston, MA: Irwin, 317.

31. **Ries, A.** and **J. Trout** (1982) *Positioning: The Battle for your Mind*, New York: Warner.

32. **Luthans, F.** (1981) *Organisational Behaviour*, San Francisco: McGraw-Hill.

33. **Maslow, A.H.** (1954) *Motivation and Personality*, New York: Harper & Row, 80–106.

34. **Guerrera, F.** and **J. Birchall** (2007) Boom Time, *Financial Times*, 6 December, 13.

35. **Kassarjan, H.H.** (1971) Personality and Consumer Behaviour: A Review, *Journal of Marketing Research*, November, 409–18.

36. **Silverman, G.** (2005) The Challenge is to Feed the Alpha Male's Insatiable Appetites, *Financial Times*, 5 July, 12.

37. **O'Brien, S.** and **R. Ford** (1988) Can We At Last Say Goodbye to Social Class?, *Journal of the Market Research Society*, **30** (3), 289–332.

38. **Urry, M.** (2003) United Biscuits' Biggest Breakfast Plan, *Financial Times*, 22 August, 21.

39. **Tomkins, R.** (2005) Flash Mobbing Gives Up its Wild Past and Goes Into Marketing, *Financial Times*, 26 July, 13.

40. **Carter, M.** (2005) A Brand New Opportunity in the Empty Nest, *Financial Times*, 5 December, 14.

41. **Anonymous** (2005) This Sceptred Aisle, *Economist*, 6 August, 29.

42. **Carter, M.** (2003) The Low-down on the Low-brow Consumer, *Financial Times*, 27 November, 13.

43. **Rigby, E.** (2005) Canny Consumers Dictate the In-store Trend, *Financial Times*, 12 July, 24.

44. **Shaughnessy, H.** (2007) Blurring the Lines of Branding, *Innovation*, July, 43–4.

45. **Anonymous** (2006) Swarming the Shelves, *Economist*, 11 November, 90.

46. **Simon, B.** (2005) Car Parts Groups Face a Depressed Future, *Financial Times*, 18 May, 31.

47. **Milne, R.** (2006) Bosch Targets Growth in Low-Cost Cars, *Financial Times*, 3 March, 28.

48. **Sanchanta** (2007) Nintendo Wii Success Helps Component Makers Score, *Financial Times*, 17 September, 25.

49. **Cardozo, R.N.** (1980) Situational Segmentation of Industrial Markets, *European Journal of Marketing*, **14** (5/6), 264–76.

50. **Robinson, P.J., C.W. Faris** and **Y. Wind** (1967) *Industrial Buying and Creative Marketing*, Boston, MA: Allyn & Bacon.

51. **Hutt, M.D.** and **T.W. Speh** (1997) *Business Marketing Management*, 3rd edn, New York: Dryden Press, 40.

52. **Briefly, E.G., R.W. Eccles** and **R.R. Reeder** (1998) *Business Marketing*, Englewood Cliffs, NJ: Prentice-Hall, 105.

53. **Thornhill, J.** and **A. Rawsthorn** (1992) Why Sparks are Flying, *Financial Times*, 8 January, 12.

54. **Blenkhorn, D.L.** and **P.M. Banting** (1991) How Reverse Marketing Changes Buyer–Seller Roles, *Industrial Marketing Management*, **20**, 185–91.

55. **Anderson, F.** and **W. Lazer** (1978) Industrial Lease Marketing, *Journal of Marketing*, **42** (January), 71–9.

Online **LearningCentre**

When you have read this chapter, log on to the Online Learning Centre for *Foundations of Marketing* at **www.mcgraw-hill.co.uk/textbooks/jobber**, where you'll find multiple-choice test questions, links and extra online study tools for marketing.

Case 3 Oasis

An example of clothing lines from Oasis for 2009

The fashion business is one that has been changing radically in recent years. The success of 'fast fashion' retailers like Zara and H&M has meant that styles and designs come and go more quickly than ever, while advances in information technology and highly efficient planning mean that new products can be developed more quickly and brought from low-cost manufacturing sites in Asia and Eastern Europe to Western markets in a very short space of time. All of this means that the buying function for fashion retailers has become even more critical. Buyers must be able to anticipate what styles and designs are likely to appeal to customers for the coming season. These decisions have far-reaching consequences. Get them wrong and retailers and their suppliers suffer losses caused by unsold stock or the need to discount them heavily.

Company background

Oasis is a UK-based own-label women's fashion retailer aimed at 18–30-year-olds. It was launched in 1991 and is now part of the Mosaic Fashions group,

which has been owned by acquisitive Icelandic company, Baugur, since 2003. Oasis has over 300 UK outlets, run as stand-alone stores or concessions in department stores, and operates franchises in 19 countries in Europe, the Middle East and the Far East. After opening an Oasis outlet in Beijing, the retailer plans to launch 100 concessions in China. Annual turnover for Oasis averages £200 million and its headquarters are based in Shoreditch, London, in the same premises as some of its sister companies. In addition to Oasis, Mosaic Fashions comprises retailers Karen Millen, Coast, Principles, Warehouse, Odille, Anoushka G and Shoe Studio. In addition, parent company Baugur has invested in various UK retail chains, including House of Fraser, Jane Norman and All Saints, designer labels Matthew Williamson and PPQ, food retailer Iceland, and toy store Hamleys.

Oasis sells own-label products, which are exclusive to its stores, designed and developed centrally at head office by buying, merchandising and design teams, supported by services including marketing, learning

Table C3.1 Oasis sub-brands

Sub-brand	Product types
Future Organic	Denim and T-shirt range made from environmentally friendly organic cotton fabrics
Premium Denim	Branded range available only in Oasis outlets, featuring fabric tags and customized packaging
New Vintage	Designs inspired by clothing from vintage markets and updated by the Oasis design team
Odille	The Odille lingerie range was launched as a sub-brand of Oasis in 2004, and now includes swimwear and nightwear; Odille has since become a brand in its own right, being sold in several UK department stores and distributed in the USA via outlets of lingerie retailer Victoria's Secret
Escape	Lifestyle and travel products including accessories and homeware

and development, finance, human resources and information technology. The design team develops products by researching trends, sourcing suitable fabrics and trims, and sketching ideas. The buying team collaborates with the in-house designers to select and develop those products they believe will appeal most to potential customers. They view the Oasis core target customer as being in her late 20s, while recognizing that its ranges also attract a substantial number of customers under 25 and over 30. The company describes its collections as being 'wearable' and able to 'transcend seasons while still having a fashionable edge'. Oasis caters for fashion followers by offering styles that combine fashionability and practicality, often remaining wearable in terms of style and quality for more than one season (see Table C3.1). Oasis launched a transactional website in 2006, selling a selected range of the company's products; it contains an interactive fitting room, blog and career information.

Product development processes

Buying and merchandising are the key decision-making units within Oasis. When the buyers have selected the designs they consider to be the most appropriate for the typical customer, they then decide which suppliers would be suitable to manufacture them. Fashion retailers rarely own factories, so the buyers deal with suppliers in various countries, who will organize the manufacture of the products on their behalf. Oasis sources products globally, choosing manufacturers that have the most suitable skills and sufficient production capacity to make the products. In common with most UK fashion retailers, Oasis imports a large proportion of its garments from the Far East, due to competitive prices and good standards of manufacture, with a limited amount of specialist products such as knitwear being made in the UK. This reflects the fact that over 95 per cent of clothing and footwear sold in the UK is imported.

Within Oasis, the buying director is in charge of three buying managers, each of whom is responsible for a team of buyers, assistant buyers and buying clerks. Buyers work closely with merchandisers, designers and quality assurers (QAs) in order to successfully develop the product range. Buyers also liaise with the in-house marketing department, providing garments for promotional photo shoots. At Oasis, the buyer's job involves negotiating prices for products with suppliers, buying products in the right colours and quantities within the right timescale, and ensuring that the garments fit correctly.

Buying a range at Oasis starts with the design team presenting initial concepts of product styles and colours for the season, based on various sources of inspiration, including shopping trips to Paris, Milan and New York. (In the fashion business, a 'season' is approximately six months: either spring and summer or autumn and winter.) The designers group clothes according to their end use, such as casual wear or work wear. A department planning meeting is held for buyers, designers and merchandisers to review design sketches and decide which styles should be made into prototype samples by suppliers. The buying team then specifies appropriate selling prices and the samples are reviewed and reformulated if required at a team meeting, which is referred to as 'vision day'. Buyers in Oasis review the proposed range of products regularly and, at a 'pre-selection' meeting, the whole team analyses samples of all of the products that will be sold in-store in a specific month.

After these preparatory meetings, the buyers are ready to present the finalized range of samples to the buying and design directors and merchandise controller at a 'range review' meeting, around seven weeks before it is delivered to the stores. This enables the team to analyse the whole range and make any final adjustments by amending or replacing garments. A small proportion of the budget is retained to introduce any high-fashion items at this point, before each item in the range goes into production with the specified supplier. The merchandise team is responsible for calculating the figures for the range, such as order quantities, and liaising with suppliers to ensure that the products arrive in-store at the correct time. Buyers and QAs liaise with suppliers to ensure that the fit and quality of the garments, and the fabric from which they are made, meet the standards specified by Oasis. The company has an overseas sourcing office in Hong Kong, staffed with employees to liaise with Chinese suppliers on behalf of Oasis.

Oasis requires its suppliers to conform to an ethical code of practice that covers relevant social and environmental issues. Oasis states on its website that it 'is committed to operating ethically with its suppliers and their employees', and its suppliers must ensure that:

- employees' rights, working hours, wages, work environment, disciplining procedure and residential facilities (if appropriate) must meet Oasis's standards
- they do not use child labour
- they do not use enforced labour in any part of the supply chain
- Health & Safety standards are met.

The Oasis design, buying, merchandising and QA teams often work on different stages of three seasons simultaneously. Forward planning is essential in the fashion business, to allow time for product development, manufacturing and transport, so initial preparation for a season's range may start more than a year in advance of products going into stores. Delivery of products is organized so that Oasis stores receive new styles every week. When each season has finished, the performance of the range is judged on the amount of items reduced in the sale, the profit margin and how it has performed compared to the original plan. The buyers review their ranges' strengths and weaknesses to help them devise an action plan for the next season.

Oasis buying manager Beth Jelly considers the most difficult aspect of her job to be 'judging what the customer will want to buy, well ahead of the selling season' and estimating each product's life cycle. Buyers receive feedback from customers in various forms to enable them to meet customers' needs more effectively. Staff from Oasis stores give weekly feedback to head office, including a SWOT (strengths, weaknesses, opportunities and threats) analysis of the current range. The buyers occasionally work anonymously in the changing rooms of Oasis stores to gain direct feedback from customers on their opinions of their products, and to discuss the ranges with retail staff.

References

Baugur website (2008) www.baugurgroup.com.

Goworek, H. (2007) *Fashion Buying*, Blackwell Publishing.

Hawkes, S. (2008) Baugur Raises £100m with Booker Stake Sale, *The Times*, 25 June 2008.

Key Note (2006) *Clothing and Footwear Industry*, www.keynote.co.uk.

Mosaic website (2008) www.mosaic-fashions.co.uk.

Oasis website (2008) www.oasis-stores.com.

Retail Intelligence (2007) *Clothing Retailing: UK 2007*, Mintel.

Questions

1. Describe the buying decision process for fashion retailers. What are the key stages of the buying process?
2. Are there any ways in which the buying process can be improved?
3. Describe the key factors that influence the behaviour of the buyers for the Oasis chain?
4. How does the behaviour of consumer fashion buyers influence that of the buyers in fashion outlets?

This case was prepared by Helen Goworek, Senior Lecturer in Marketing, Nottingham Trent University, as a basis for class discussion rather than to illustrate either effective or ineffective management.

Chapter 4
Marketing Research and Information Systems

Learning Outcomes

By the end of this chapter you will understand:

1. the importance of marketing research
2. the different types of marketing research available
3. the approaches to conducting research
4. the stages in the marketing research process
5. the nature and purpose of marketing information systems.

Searching for 'cool'

Trend spotting is one of the biggest marketing research challenges facing companies marketing to the 16–34 age group. It is sometimes described as the search for 'cool', which is an invisible, intangible but very valuable commodity. Marketers know that if 'cool' people start talking or eating or dressing or shopping in a certain way, then 'non-cool' people will follow them. Understand what cool people are doing today and you can see what everyone else will be doing a year from now.

But cool is an elusive quality. And it will not be discovered through conventional market research techniques such as surveys or focus group interviews. Many leading companies employ professional trend spotters ('cool hunters') to seek it out. In what might sound like the ideal job, trend spotters, who are usually in their 20s, spend their time going to parties, making new friends online, travelling to far-flung destinations and hanging out in 'cool' places like New York's Soho district. They are then responsible for providing regular reports on the latest happenings in music, fashion, lifestyle and technology. Perhaps the biggest challenge for both the trend spotter and their employer is to sift through the mass of

information that is available to truly identify the drivers of youth behaviour. Separating fads from real trends is not easy, as the obsession with everything online demonstrated in the late 1990s. In addition, there are now a variety of boutique research firms providing trend-spotting services—including, for example, the Zandl Group and www.trendwatching.com.

One company that uses trend spotters to maintain its cool positioning in the marketplace is the urbanwear brand, Diesel. The Diesel brand started out in Italy in 1975 and has since grown to annual global sales levels in the region of US$680 million. The company employs 50 25-year-old trend spotters from around the world who travel wherever they want to research and seek out new trends and ideas. Maintaining its cool image is extremely important to a brand that is now so large that it has become mainstream. Therefore it must constantly seek to be innovative in its product design— for example, producing a new line like 55 DSL, which targets skateboarders and snowboarders, as well as being creative in its advertising and online marketing (www.diesel.com).[1]

The importance of marketing research

Marketing research is enormously important. Truly market-led companies recognize that they need to always be in touch with what is happening in the marketplace. Customer needs are continually changing, often in ways that are very subtle. For some companies, no major strategic decisions are made without first researching the market. But this activity goes far beyond commercial organizations. For example, organizations ranging from political parties to record companies are heavy users of marketing research and often stand accused of over-dependence on it to shape everything from manifestos to new albums. Marketing research can play a role in many different activities. Research can be useful to help understand what customers want, to decide whether to launch a new product or not, to get feedback from customers about ongoing levels of service, to measure the effectiveness of a sponsorship campaign, and so on.

The marketing research industry is massive, estimated to be worth over US$24 billion globally in 2006 and US$10,597 million in Europe, or nearly half the total global spend. Table 4.1 provides details of levels of marketing research expenditure throughout the world. Market research also tends to follow market development. For example, some of the highest growth rates for market research have been in countries like Latvia and Bulgaria, whose growing economies have attracted the interest of marketers.[2] Defining the boundaries of marketing research is not easy. Casual discussions with customers at exhibitions or through sales calls can provide valuable informal information about their requirements, competitor activities and future happenings in the industry. More formal approaches include the conduct of marketing research studies or the development of marketing information systems. This chapter focuses on these formal methods of information provision. First, we will describe the different types of marketing research and the approaches used to conduct research studies. Then we will look at the process of marketing research and its uses in more detail. Finally, we examine the development of marketing information systems and the ethics of market research.

Types of marketing research

In the first instance we need to distinguish between ad hoc and continuous research.

Table 4.1 Global marketing research expenditure 2006 (selected countries)

Country	Turnover in US$ million	Spend per capita in US$
UK	2369	39.19
Sweden	335	36.92
France	2214	35.33
USA	8232	27.49
Norway	126	27.10
Germany	2206	26.73
Australia	532	25.76
Denmark	131	24.11
Finland	125	23.96
Switzerland	166	22.76
Netherlands	346	21.17
New Zealand	86	20.76
Canada	652	20.04
Ireland	84	19.97
Belgium	167	16.06
Luxembourg	6	13.09
Singapore	55	12.23
Italy	706	12.16
Japan	1380	10.79
China	583	0.44

Source: Esomar Global Market Research, 2007

Ad hoc research

Ad hoc research focuses on a specific marketing problem, collecting data at one point in time from one sample of respondents. Examples of ad hoc studies are usage and attitude surveys, product and concept tests, advertising development and evaluation studies, corporate image surveys and customer satisfaction surveys. Ad hoc surveys are either custom-designed or omnibus studies, and these account for over 60 per cent of market research expenditure globally.

Custom-designed studies

This type of study is based on the specific needs of the client. The research design is based on the research brief given to the marketing research agency or internal marketing researcher. Because they are tailor-made, such surveys can be expensive.

Omnibus surveys

An alternative to the custom-designed study is the **omnibus survey** in which space is bought on

Exhibit 4.1 Face-to-face interviews and telephone surveys are two of the most popular ways to conduct ad hoc research

questionnaires for face-to-face or telephone interviews (see Exhibit 4.1). An interview may cover many topics, as questionnaire space is bought by a number of clients, who benefit from cost sharing. Usually the type of information sought is relatively simple (e.g. awareness levels and ownership data). Often the survey will be based on demographically balanced samples of 1000–2000 adults. However, more specialist surveys covering the markets for children, young adults, mothers and babies, the 'grey' market and motorists exist.

Continuous research

Continuous research involves the interviewing of the same sample of people repeatedly. The main types of continuous research are consumer panels, retail audits and television viewership panels.

Consumer panels

When large numbers of households are recruited to provide information on their purchases over time, together they make up a **consumer panel**. For example, a grocery panel would record the brands, pack sizes, prices and stores used for a wide range of supermarket brands. By using the same households over a period of time, measures of brand loyalty and switching can be achieved, together with a demographic profile of the type of person who buys particular brands. Recent years have seen a significant growth in the use of technology in consumer panel research, with studies being conducted online or over the telephone as well as face to face. Once participants are familiar with the researchers and have indicated a willingness to participate then these more remote research approaches can work very effectively.

The rapid growth of online blogs and discussion forums has given rise to a variant on the traditional customer panel. These types of discussion boards are everywhere on the internet, discussing anything from the fat content of potato crisps to the merits of new electronic gadgets. In most instances, they have not been formally created by corporations but the frank nature of the debate that often takes place on them makes them appealing to managers. Some companies track these discussion groups to see what is being said about their brands and what trends are emerging. It is also a very cost-effective form of research as much of the monitoring can be done electronically. However, because this monitoring is generally covert, it may be disturbing for participants to learn that what they have to say is being studied by companies.

Retail audits

Another type of continuous research is the **retail audit**. By gaining the co-operation of retail outlets (e.g. supermarkets), sales of brands can be measured by means of laser scans of barcodes on packaging, which are read at the checkout. Although brand loyalty and switching cannot be measured, retail audits can provide an accurate assessment of sales achieved by store. A major provider of retail audit data is ACNielsen. For example, its BookScan service provides weekly sales data on over 300,000 titles collected from point-of-sale information from a variety of retailers.

Television viewership panels

A television viewership panel measures audience size on a minute-by-minute basis. Commercial breaks can be allocated ratings points (the proportion of the target audience watching)—the currency by which television advertising is bought and judged. In the UK, the system is controlled by the Broadcasters' Audience Research Board (BARB) (www.barb.co.uk), and run by AGB and RSMB. AGB handles the measurement process and uses 'people meters' to record whether a set is on/off, which channel is being watched and, by means of a hand console, who is watching. Because of concerns about the extent to which viewers actually watch advertising, audience measurement companies are now providing measures of the viewership of advertising breaks as well as programmes. Technological developments continue to revolutionize TV audience measurement. Personal video recorders (PVRs), build up a profile of viewers' likes and dislikes, and record their favourite programmes automatically, but the box also relays every button press on its remote control back to the manufacturer, providing exact details of what programmes people watch on what channels.

Exhibit 4.2 Loyalty card schemes are used extensively by organizations to build up databases of customers

Marketing databases

Companies collect data on customers on an ongoing basis. The data are stored on marketing databases, containing each customer's name, address, telephone number, past transactions and, sometimes, demographic and lifestyle data. Information on the types of purchase, frequency of purchase, purchase value and responsiveness to promotional offers may be held (see Chapter 10). For example, retailers are encouraging the collection of such data through introducing loyalty card schemes, which are popular with supermarkets, department stores and petrol retailers (see Exhibit 4.2). Customers collect points that can be redeemed for cashback or gifts while at the same time the retailer collects valuable information about the customer each time the card is used.

Banks have become heavy users of this type of information as they seek to manage more carefully consumers that have taken on debts such as mortgages and credit cards. Banks get information from a number of sources, including their own records, their links to other payment organizations, such as Visa and Mastercard, and specialist credit checking agencies. Through the examination of this information, they can develop relatively accurate predictions of which customers are likely to default on a loan, or they can intervene earlier before debts become significant. For example, if consumers have switched more of their regular shopping, such as groceries, from cash to credit cards, this may indicate a cash shortage and the increased risk of a missed payment on a loan.

Customer relationship management (CRM) systems

A potential problem with the growth of marketing databases is that separate ones are created in different departments of the company. For example, the sales department may have an account management database containing information on customers, while call centre staff may use a different database created at a different time also containing information on customers. This fragmented approach can lead to problems, when, for example, a customer transaction is recorded on one but not the other database. Issues like this have led to the development of customer relationship management (CRM) systems where a single database is created from customer information to inform all staff who deal with customers. CRM is a term for the methodologies, technologies and e-commerce capabilities used by companies to manage customer relationships[3] (see Chapter 10). Companies such as Tesco make some of their CRM data available to suppliers in order that they can respond better to the needs of their ultimate customer: the grocery shopper.

Website analysis

Continuous data can also be provided by analysing consumers' use of websites. Measurements of the areas of the site most frequently visited, which products are purchased and the payment method used can be made. Indeed one of the challenges of website analysis is coping with the vast volumes of data that can be produced. Whatever the challenges of measuring the size of the audience from an advertising point of view, there are several aspects of how consumers behave while visiting a website that owners should record and monitor. First, where did they come from —for example, did they come via a search engine or from a link on another site? Second, where do they go once they are on the site? What options are selected, what visuals are viewed, and so on. Did they respond to particular offers, promotions or site design changes? And, if the company is an online retailer, what percentage of consumers proceeded to the checkout and, for those that didn't, at what stage in the process did they drop out? Some of the challenges of measuring website audiences are discussed in Marketing in Action 4.1.

Approaches to conducting marketing research

There are two main ways for a company to carry out marketing research, depending on the situation facing it. It might either carry out the work itself or employ the services of a market research agency. The advantage of using an agency is that it will have the specialist skills and experience of conducting studies; these advantages may be offset, however, by the prohibitively high cost of using the agency's services. Where the study is small in scale, such as gathering information from libraries or interviewing a select number of industrial customers, companies may choose to conduct the work themselves. This is

Marketing in Action 4.1: Website audience measurement

> **Study guide:** Below is a review of some of the key metrics used to measure website audiences. Read it and consider the advantages and disadvantages of each measure.

Internet advertising is the fastest-growing sector of the advertising industry, but before you decide where to advertise you need to be able to estimate how many people are likely to see your advert. Fortunately websites are rich in the data they provide but, unfortunately, they produce so much that it makes the selection decision very difficult. Should you go by hits, unique users, time spent on a site, or indeed by click-through, impressions, sessions, queries or engagement? The internet advertising planner is faced with some very difficult decisions.

In the early days of e-commerce, many internet companies proudly trumpeted the number of hits their websites received. A hit is recorded when a web user clicks on any one element (such as an image, text, etc.) of one web page. However, this was an easy figure to manipulate—simply increasing the number of graphics on a page increased the number of hits. Page views (the number of pages a visitor looks at) became the next currency by which websites were measured, but this is equally suspect. Many modern websites use a technology that allows pages to update parts of themselves, such as a share-price ticker, without having to reload and redraw the rest of the page. But the problem is that a user spending the entire day on Yahoo!Finance, for example, counts as only one page view. Unique users (when a person visits a website) is another popular metric. But it, too, is problematic because 2 million unique users could mean anything from 2 million people visiting the site once, to one person visiting it 2 million times. It is impossible to know for sure. As websites like MySpace and YouTube have become more interactive, advertisers have become more interested in other measures. 'Duration' and 'time spent' suggest how long one or more people are interacting with a page, which in turn gives an indication of how 'engaged' they are.

Basic customer behaviour patterns on a website are tracked through technologies such as logfiles, which are a record of all activity on a site, and cookies, which are files located on the visitor's hard drive. For example, click-through or click-stream analysis looks at logfiles to see where users go when they visit a site. Web analytics combines these basic metrics with demographic and subscription information to provide a more detailed analysis of visitor behaviour. Website owners can know a lot about what visitors to their site do but getting this information requires careful planning.

Based on: Anonymous (2007);[4] Guenther (2003);[5] Phippen, Sheppard and Furnell (2004)[6]

---

particularly feasible if a company has a marketing department and/or a marketing research executive on its staff. Other companies prefer to design the research themselves and then employ the services of a fieldwork agency to collect the data. Alternatively, where resources permit and the scale of the study is larger, companies may employ the services of a market research agency to conduct the research. The company will brief the agency about its market research requirements and the agency will do the rest. The typical stages involved in completing a market research study are described next; full-service agencies generally conduct all the activities described below.

The leading marketing research firms in the world are shown in Table 4.2.

Stages in the marketing research process

Figure 4.1 provides a description of a typical marketing research process. Each of the stages illustrated will now be discussed. Some leading companies' different approaches to research problems are discussed in Marketing in Action 4.2.

Initial contact

The process usually starts with the realization that a marketing problem (e.g. a new product development or advertising decision) requires information to aid its solution. Marketing management may contact internal marketing research staff or an outside agency. Let

Table 4.2 World's leading marketing research firms, 2006

Name	Country	Employees	Turnover (US$m)
The Nielsen Company	USA	39,517	3,696.0
IMS Health, Inc.	USA	7,400	1,958.6
Taylor Nelson Sofres plc	UK	14,570	1,851.1
The Kantar Group	UK	6,900	1,401.4
GfK AG	Germany	7,900	1,397.3
Ipsos Group SA	France	6,503	1,077.0
Synovate	UK	5,726	739.6
IRI	USA	3,600	665.0
Westat, Inc.	USA	1,906	425.8
Arbitron, Inc.	USA	1,045	329.3

Source: Esomar, Global Market Research, 2007

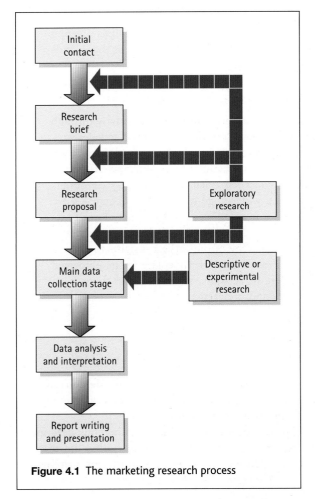

Figure 4.1 The marketing research process

us assume that the research requires the assistance of a marketing research agency. A meeting will be arranged to discuss the nature of the problem and the client's research needs. If the client and its markets are new to the agency, some rudimentary exploratory research (e.g. a quick online search for information about the client and its markets) may be conducted prior to the meeting.

Research brief

At a meeting to decide what form the research will need to take, the client explains the marketing problem and outlines the company's research objectives. The marketing problem might be the need to attract new customers to a product group, and the research objectives to identify groups of customers (market segments) who might have a use for the product and the characteristics of the product that appeal to them most.

Other information that should be provided for the research agency includes the following.[7]

1   *Background information*: the product's history and the competitive situation.
2   *Sources of information*: the client may have a list of industries that might be potential users of the product. This helps the researchers to define the scope of the research.
3   *The scale of the project*: is the client looking for a 'cheap and cheerful' job or a major study? This has implications for the research design and survey costs.
4   *The timetable*: when is the information required?

The client should produce a specific written **research brief**. This may be given to the research agency prior to the meeting and perhaps modified as a result of it but, without fail, should be in the hands of the agency before it produces its **research proposal**. The research brief should state the client's requirements and should be in written form so that misunderstandings are minimized. In the event of a

Marketing in Action 4.2: Getting to know customers

Study guide: Below are some examples of how firms use market research to solve business problems. Read them and think of other examples of ways in which companies can get close to their customers.

When it comes to trying to understand customers, organizations can take a variety of different approaches. For example, one of the world's largest retailer's, Wal-Mart, has had a tradition of doing very little consumer research. It preferred to test-market items from suppliers in its stores and then simply ordered those that sold well. But in recent years, as its sales growth has slowed and it has faced intense competition from other retailers like Target, it has begun to invest more heavily in market research. In early 2004, it carried out a study of 6000 existing customers and found that a significant number wanted more in terms of fashion items and contemporary styles from the organization. In response, it created the Metro 7 sub-brand, which is targeted at fashion-conscious female customers with an urban lifestyle. Metro 7 is located in about 500, mostly urban, Wal-Mart stores as well as on the company's website. In keeping with the fast-fashion trends in this sector, its range is refreshed monthly to reflect evolving styles. As well as meeting the needs of its customers, more fashionable clothing is also attractive to Wal-Mart as these kinds of products are more profitable than many of its grocery and household lines. It is also increasing its investment in market research and consumer insights to identify further growth opportunities and to try to move away from its heavy reliance on an 'every day low prices' approach.

Retailers generally are in a very good position to know a lot about customers, particularly through the analysis of shopping patterns and also by monitoring how consumers respond to sales promotions. This in turn has put pressure back on manufacturers to ensure that they also try to get to know their customers better. Companies like confectionery manufacturer Mars have begun to take novel approaches to this problem. For example, Mars has opened seven café-style outlets in Chicago, which include 'chocolate lounges' where a wide range of premium chocolates are available for purchase. Essentially, Mars has ventured into retailing in order to get closer to its customers. It has also conducted focus-group interviews with potential customers to get a better understanding of what they would like to see in the cafés. One of the earliest insights to emerge from this research is that consumers expressed a preference for dark chocolate for its perceived health benefits. Whether on the part of manufacturers or retailers, it is clear that there is an increasing emphasis on trying to understand our tastes and preferences.

Based on: Birchall (2005);[8] Grant (2005)[9]

dispute later in the process, the research brief (and proposal) form the benchmarks against which it can be settled. It is typical to brief two or three agencies as the extra time involved is usually rewarded by the benefits of more than one viewpoint on the research problem . . . and a keener quote!

Research proposal

A research proposal lays out what a marketing research agency promises to do for its client, and how much this will cost. Like the research brief, the proposal should be written in a way that avoids misunderstandings. A client should expect the following to be included.

1 *A statement of objectives*: to demonstrate an understanding of the client's marketing and research problems.

2 *What will be done*: an unambiguous description of the research design—including the research method, the type of sample, the sample size (if applicable) and how the fieldwork will be controlled.

3 *Timetable*: if and when a report will be produced.

4 *Costs*: how much the research will cost and what, specifically, is/is not included in those costs.

When assessing a proposal, a client needs to ensure that it is precise, jargon-free and that it addresses all the issues the client expects.

Exploratory research

Prior to the main data collection stage, **exploratory research** is employed to carry out the preliminary exploration of a research area. This usually occurs between acceptance of the research proposal and the main data collection stage, but can also take place prior to the client/agency briefing meeting and before submission of the research proposal, as an aid to its construction. Exploratory research techniques allow the researcher to understand the people who are to be interviewed in the main data collection stage, and the market that is being researched. The main survey stage can thus be designed with this knowledge in mind rather than being based on the researcher's ill-informed prejudices and guesswork.

A project may involve all or some of the following exploratory research activities:

- secondary research
- qualitative research (group discussions and depth interviews)
- observation.

Secondary research

Because the data come to the researcher 'second-hand' (i.e. other people have compiled it), this type of study is known as **secondary research**. (When the researcher actively collects new data—for example, by interviewing respondents—this is called primary research.) Secondary research should be carried out before primary research. Without the former, an expensive primary research survey might be commissioned to provide information that is already available from secondary sources. Increasingly a significant amount of market information is available for purchase through companies like Mintel, Euromonitor and others.

Secondary data can be found via examination of internal records and reports of research previously carried out for a company. External sources include government and European Commission statistics, publishers of reports and directories on markets, countries and industries, trade associations, banks, newspapers, magazines and journals. Given the amount of potential sources of information that are available globally, for many the first port of call is an internet search engine. The search engine business has grown dramatically in recent years and has led to expressions such as 'to google', after the popular search engine Google, entering the general lexicon. The range of sources of information available to researchers in the European Union is included in Appendix 4.1 (at the end of this chapter), which lists some of the major sources classified by research question.

Qualitative research

Group discussions and depth interviews are the main types of **qualitative research**. This kind of research aims to establish customers' attitudes, values, behaviour and beliefs.

Group discussions, sometimes referred to as **focus groups**, involve unstructured or semi-structured discussions between a moderator or group leader, who is often a psychologist, and a group of consumers (see Exhibit 4.3). The moderator has a list of areas to cover within the topic, but allows the group considerable freedom to discuss the issues that are important to them. By arranging groups of six to twelve people to discuss their attitudes and behaviour, a good deal of knowledge may be gained about the consumer. This can be helpful when constructing questionnaires, which can be designed to focus on what is important to the respondent (as opposed to the researcher) and worded in language the respondent uses and understands. Sometimes focus groups are used to try to generate new product ideas, through the careful selection of participants who have a flair for innovation or a liking for all things new.

The traditional focus group takes place face to face, but the rise of the internet has led to the creation of online focus groups. The internet offers 'communities of interests', which can take the form of chatrooms or websites dedicated to specific interests or issues. These are useful forums for conducting focus groups or at least for identifying suitable participants. Questions can be posed to participants who are not under time pressure to respond. This can lead to

Exhibit 4.3 Focus group interviews such as this one are a very popular form of market research

richer insights since respondents can think deeply about the questions put to them online. Another advantage is that they can comprise people located all over the world at minimal cost. Furthermore, technological developments mean it is possible for clients to communicate secretly online with the moderator while the focus group is in session. The client can ask the moderator certain questions as a result of hearing earlier responses. Clearly, a disadvantage of online focus groups compared with the traditional form is that the body language and interaction between focus group members is missing.[10]

Depth interviews involve the interviewing of individual consumers about a single topic for perhaps one or two hours. The aims are broadly similar to those of the group discussion, but depth interviews are used when the presence of other people could inhibit the expression of honest answers and viewpoints, when the topic requires individual treatment (as when discussing an individual's decision-making process) and where the individual is an expert on a particular topic. For example, depth interviews have been used to conduct research on wealthy Americans to try to understand their attitudes and opinions on money and how they spend it. This was deemed to be a method that was superior to focus groups or surveys, where it was felt that respondents would be reluctant to talk about these issues. A technique called 'snowballing' was also used, where interviewees would recommend others that they thought would be willing to participate in the research.[11]

Care has to be taken when interpreting the results of qualitative research because the findings are usually based on small sample sizes, and the more interesting or surprising viewpoints may be disproportionately reported. This is particularly significant when qualitative research is not followed by a quantitative study.

Qualitative research accounts for 14 per cent of all expenditure on marketing research, of which 70 per cent is spent on group discussions, 15 per cent on in-depth interviews and 15 per cent on other qualitative techniques. Because of its ability to provide in-depth understanding, it is of growing importance within the field of consumer research.[12]

Observation

Observation can also help in exploratory research when the product field is unfamiliar, and may be either informal (where marketers take note of shopping patterns, etc.) or formal (where an observation study is designed and conducted). Observation studies can have a number of advantages. First, they do not rely on the respondent's willingness to provide information; second, the potential for the interviewer to bias the study is reduced; and, third, some types of information can be collected only by observation (for example, a traffic count). Observation studies can be conducted either by human or mechanical means, such as video recording, and may be conducted with or without the customer's knowledge. Camera phones are the latest technology to be used for observation studies, with problems arising when they are used covertly. Samsung, the world's leading manufacturer of camera phones, has even banned their use in its factories, fearing industrial espionage.[13] Observation studies are particularly popular in the retail trade where a great deal can be learned by simply watching the behaviour of shoppers in a supermarket or clothing shop. The growth of observation as a research technique has given rise to the development of the field of **marketing ethnography** (see Marketing in Action 4.3).

The objective of exploratory research, then, is not to collect quantitative data and form conclusions but to become better acquainted with the market and its customers. This allows the researcher to base the quantitative survey on informed assumptions rather than guesswork.

The main data collection stage

The design of the main data collection procedures will be done following careful exploratory research. The most usual approach is to undertake survey research to describe customers' beliefs, attitudes, preferences, behaviour, and so on. In general, the research design will be based on the following framework.

- Who and how many people to interview: the sampling process.
- How to interview them: the survey method.
- What questions to ask: questionnaire design.

The sampling process

Figure 4.2 offers an outline of the **sampling process**. This starts with the definition of the population—that is, the group that forms the subject of study in a particular survey. The survey objective will be to provide results that are representative of this group. Sampling planners, for example, must ask questions like 'Do we interview purchasing managers in all software development firms or only those that employ more than 50 people?'

Once the population has been defined, the next step is to search for a sampling frame—that is, a list or other record of the chosen population from which a sample can be selected. Examples include the

Marketing in Action 4.3: Marketing ethnography

Study guide: Below is a review of the use of ethnographic techniques in researching markets. Read it and then conduct your own small-scale ethnographic study to see what insights you can generate.

One of the criticisms of research techniques like focus-group interviews is that they are somewhat contrived. Groups of people, who may or may not know each other, are brought together in boardroom-type settings and expected to provide insights into their thoughts, feelings and opinions. In such settings consumers may find it difficult or be unwilling to fully engage. As a result, many research companies are borrowing from the kinds of techniques that are employed by anthropologists and biologists, which place an emphasis on the observation of species in their natural settings. This emerging field is known as marketing ethnography.

In ethnographic studies, researchers decide what human behaviours they want to observe. They then go out into the field and record what consumers do, how they live their lives, how they shop, and so on. Having recorded these activities, consumers are interviewed to try to gain insights into the motivations and attitudes that underpin their actions. When all these data have been collected, they are analysed using qualitative software packages that search for common patterns of behaviour and generate clusters of consumers. Finally, the presentation of research findings via video can be very powerful. This allows marketing executives to know consumers in a more intimate way than other forms of research, such as the focus group. More importantly, it provides a mechanism for senior executives to get close to consumer groups they may never come into contact with in their own daily lives because of physical distance and/or social class disparities.

Several leading companies are extensive users of ethnographic research. For example, Procter & Gamble has used it to understand party planning in American homes. Researchers observed both adults planning a dinner party and teenagers planning a gathering, and generated over 100 general insights that enabled the company to plan products and services. Specific themes that emerged from the research included: making parties fun for the host, overcoming unpleasant surprises and ensuring that the party met preconceived expectations. Technology companies like Xerox and Intel use the technique to try to understand the different ways in which technology is used around the world. For example, Xerox researchers examining mobile phone use found that one Malaysian man used the GPS function on his phone every day to find Mecca; this is typical of the kind of unexpected findings that ethnography can uncover. Intel's research in China revealed that parents saw PC use as a distraction for young children, which resulted in its development of a computer aimed at the home educational market. Employed in a business setting, ethnography has some key strengths. It provides an unbiased record of key variables such as what is happening, where is it happening, the order in which it happens, as well as who is doing what and what is being communicated verbally and non-verbally.

Based on: Berner (2006);[14] Durante and Feehan (2006);[15] Thomas (2005)[16]

electoral register and the *Kompass* directory of companies. Researchers then choose between three major sampling methods: simple random sampling (where the sample is drawn at random and each individual has a known and equal chance of being selected); stratified random sampling (where the population is broken into groups and a random sample is drawn from each group); and quota sampling (where interviewers are instructed to ensure that the sample comprises a required number of individuals meeting pre-set conditions, such as a set percentage of small, medium-sized and large companies).

Finally, the researcher must select an appropriate sample size. The larger the sample size the more likely it is that the sample will represent the population. Statistical theory allows the calculation of sampling error (i.e. the error caused by not interviewing

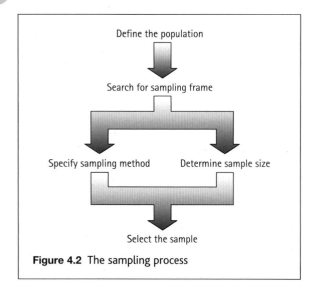

Figure 4.2 The sampling process

everyone in the population) for various sample sizes. In practice, the number of people interviewed is based on a balance between sampling error and cost considerations. Fortunately, sample sizes of around 1000 (or fewer) can provide measurements that have tolerable error levels when representing populations counted in their millions.

The survey method

Four options are available to those choosing a survey method: face-to-face interviews, telephone interviews, mail surveys or internet surveys. Each method has its own strengths and limitations; Table 4.3 gives an overview of these.

A major advantage of face-to-face interviews is that response rates are generally higher than for telephone interviews or mail surveys.[17] It seems that the

personal element in the contact makes refusal less likely. Face-to-face interviews are more versatile than telephone and mail surveys. The use of many open-ended questions on a mail survey would lower response rates,[18] and time restrictions for telephone interviews limit their use. Probing for more detail is easier with face-to-face interviews. A certain degree of probing can be achieved with a telephone interview, but time pressure and the less personalized situation will inevitably limit its use.

Face-to-face interviews do, however, have their drawbacks. They are more expensive than telephone and mail questionnaires. Telephone and mail surveys are cheaper because the cost of contacting respondents is much less expensive, unless the population is very concentrated. The presence of an interviewer can cause bias (e.g. socially desirable answers) and lead to the misreporting of sensitive information. For example, O'Dell[19] found that only 17 per cent of respondents admitted borrowing money from a bank in a face-to-face interview compared to 42 per cent in a comparable mail survey.

In some ways, telephone interviews are a halfway house between face-to-face and mail surveys. They generally have a higher response rate than mail questionnaires but a lower rate than face-to-face interviews; their cost is usually three-quarters of that for face-to-face but higher than for mail surveys; and they allow a degree of flexibility when interviewing. However, the use of visual aids is not possible and there are limits to the number of questions that can be asked before respondents either terminate the interview or give quick (invalid) answers in order to speed up the process. The use of computer-aided telephone interviewing (CATI) is growing. Centrally

Table 4.3 A comparison of survey methods

	Face to face	Telephone	Mail	Internet
Questionnaire				
Use of open-ended questions	High	Medium	Low	Low
Ability to probe	High	Medium	Low	Low
Use of visual aids	High	Poor	High	High
Sensitive questions	Medium	Low	High	Low
Resources				
Cost	High	Medium	Low	Low
Sampling				
Widely dispersed populations	Low	Medium	High	High
Response rates	High	Medium	Low	Low
Experimental control	High	Medium	Low	Low
Interviewing				
Control of who completes questionnaire	High	High	Low	Low/high
Interviewer bias	Possible	Possible	Low	Low

Table 4.4 Relative levels of expenditure on survey methods, 2006 (selected European countries)

Country	Face-to-face	Telephone	Mail	Internet	Other	Total*
Denmark	9	27	15	14	0	65
Finland	7	22	10	10	45	94
France	19	16	2	10	38	85
Ireland	50	12	0	3	0	65
Italy	39	35	1	3	2	80
Netherlands	13	19	8	22	14	76
Spain	31	26	2	10	13	82
Sweden	6	34	10	22	16	88
Switzerland	20	55	4	6	1	86
UK	26	18	6	13	17	80

*Total is the total for quantitative market research expenditure; the remainder is accounted for by qualitative techniques such as focus-group interviews
Source: Esomar, Global Market Research, 2007

located interviewers read questions from a computer monitor and input answers via the keyboard. Routing through the questionnaire is computer-controlled, thus assisting the process of interviewing.

Given a reasonable response rate, mail survey research is normally a very economical method of conducting research. However, the major problem is the potential for low response rates and the accompanying danger of an unrepresentative sample. Nevertheless, using a systematic approach to the design of a mail survey, such as the Tailored Design Method (TDM),[20] has been found to have a very positive effect on response rates. The TDM recommends, as ways of improving response rates, both the careful design of questionnaires to make them easy to complete, as well as accompanying them with a personalized covering letter emphasizing the importance of the research. Studies using the TDM on commercial populations have generated high response rates.[21]

The internet has become a very popular medium for conducting survey research. Online research expenditures exceeded US$3 billion in 2006, a rise of over 14 per cent on the previous year, with the largest growth being recorded in the UK, which rose by over 90 per cent on the previous year.[22] The internet questionnaire is usually administered by email or signals its presence on a website by registering key words or using banner advertising on search engines to drive people to the questionnaire. The major advantage of the internet as a marketing research vehicle is its low cost, since printing and postal costs are eliminated, making it even cheaper than mail surveys. In other ways, its characteristics are similar to mail

surveys: the use of open-ended questions is limited; control over who completes the questionnaire is low; interviewer bias is low; and response rates are likely to be lower than for face-to-face and telephone interviews.

When response is by email, the identity of the respondent will automatically be sent to the survey company. This lack of anonymity may restrict the respondent's willingness to answer sensitive questions honestly. A strength of the internet survey is its ability to cover global populations at low cost, although sampling problems can arise because of the skewed nature of internet users. These tend to be from the younger and more affluent groups in society. For surveys requiring a cross-sectional sample this can be severely restricting.

The relative levels of expenditure on the different research methods are shown in Table 4.4.

Questionnaire design

To obtain a true response to a question, three conditions are necessary. First, respondents must understand the question; second, they must be able to provide the information; and, third, they must be willing to provide it. Figure 4.3 shows the three stages in the development of the questionnaire: planning, design and pilot.

The planning stage involves the types of decision discussed so far in this chapter. It provides a firm foundation for designing a questionnaire, which provides relevant information for the marketing problem that is being addressed.

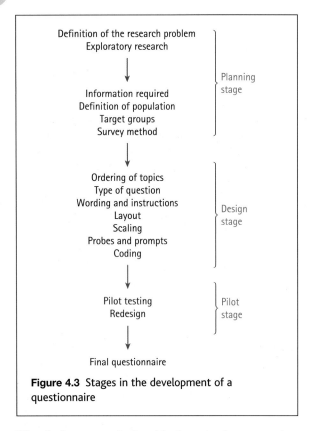

Definition of the research problem
Exploratory research

Planning stage

Information required
Definition of population
Target groups
Survey method

Ordering of topics
Type of question
Wording and instructions
Layout
Scaling
Probes and prompts
Coding

Design stage

Pilot testing
Redesign

Pilot stage

Final questionnaire

Figure 4.3 Stages in the development of a questionnaire

questions, in order to relax the respondent, and leave sensitive questions until last. Effective questionnaires are well structured and have a logical flow. Second, the type of question needs to be decided. Generally, three types are used: dichotomous questions (allow two possible answers, such as 'Yes'/'No'), multiple-choice questions, which allow more than two answers, and open questions, where the respondents answer by expressing their opinions.

Great care needs to be taken with both the wording and instructions used in the questionnaire and its layout. Questionnaire designers need to guard against asking ambiguous or leading questions, and using unfamiliar words (see Table 4.4). In terms of layout, the questionnaire should not appear cluttered and, where possible, answers and codes should each form a column so that they are easy to identify.

The use of 'scales' is very common in questionnaire design. For example, respondents are given lists of statements (e.g. 'My company's marketing information system allows me to make better decisions') followed by a choice of five positions on a scale ranging from 'strongly agree' to 'strongly disagree'. 'Probes' are used to explore or clarify what a respondent has said. Following a question about awareness of brand names, the exploratory probe 'Any others?' would seek to identify further names. Sometimes respondents use vague words or phrases like 'I like going on

The design stage deals with the actual construction of the survey instrument and involves a number of important decisions. The first relates to the ordering of topics. It is sensible to start with easy-to-answer

Exhibit 4.4 The Whiskas brand used a play on market research with its famous slogan '8 out of 10 cats prefer Whiskas' and has continued this theme

Table 4.5 Poorly worded questions

Question	Problem and solution
What type of wine do you prefer?	'Type' is ambiguous: respondents could say 'French', 'red' or 'claret', say, depending on their interpretation. Showing the respondent a list and asking 'from this list . . .' would avoid the problem
Do you think that prices are cheaper at Asda than at Aldi?	Leading question favouring Asda; a better question would be 'Do you think that prices at Asda are higher, lower or about the same as at Aldi?' Names should be reversed for half the sample
Which is more powerful and kind to your hands: Ariel or Bold?	Two questions in one: Ariel may be more powerful but Bold may be kinder to the hands. Ask the two questions separately
Do you find it paradoxical that X lasts longer and yet is cheaper than Y?	Unfamiliar word: a study has shown that less than a quarter of the population understand such words as paradoxical, chronological or facility. Test understanding before use

holiday because it is nice'. A clarifying probe such as, 'In what way is it nice?' would seek a more meaningful response. 'Prompts', on the other hand, aid responses to a question. For example, in an aided recall question, a list of brand names would be provided for the respondent. Coding involves the assignment of numbers to specific responses in order to facilitate analysis of the questionnaire later on.

Once the preliminary questionnaire has been designed it should be piloted with a representative subsample, to test for faults; this is known as the 'pilot stage'. Piloting tests the questionnaire design and helps to estimate costs. Face-to-face piloting, where respondents are asked to answer questions and comment on any problems concerning a questionnaire read out by an interviewer, is preferable to impersonal piloting where the questionnaire is given to respondents for self-completion and they are asked to write down any problems found.[23] Once the pilot work proves satisfactory, the final questionnaire can be administered to the chosen sample.

Data analysis and interpretation

Computers are invariably used to carry out the quantitative analysis of questionnaire data. Basic marketing analyses can be carried out using such software analysis packages as Microsoft Excel on a personal computer. More sophisticated analyses can be conducted using packages such as SPSS-PC and NUD.IST.

Basic analysis of questionnaire data may be at the descriptive level (e.g. means, frequency tables and standard deviations) or on a comparative basis (e.g. t-tests and cross-tabulations). More sophisticated analysis may search for relationships (e.g. regression analysis), group respondents (e.g. cluster analysis), or

establish cause and effect (e.g. analysis of variance techniques used on experimental data).

When interpreting marketing research results, great care must be taken. One common failing is to infer cause and effect when only association has been established. For example, establishing a relationship that sales rise when advertising levels increase does not necessarily mean that raising advertising expenditure will lead to an increase in sales. Other marketing variables (e.g. salesforce effect) may have increased at the same time as the increase in advertising. A second cautionary note concerns the interpretation of means and percentages. Given that a sample has been taken, any mean or percentage is an estimate subject to 'sampling error'—that is, an error in an estimate due to taking a sample rather than interviewing the entire population. A market research survey which estimates that 50 per cent of males but only 45 per cent of females smoke, does not necessarily suggest that smoking is more prevalent among males. Given the sampling error associated with each estimate, the true conclusion might be that there is no difference between males and females.

Report writing and presentation

Crouch suggests that the key elements in a research report are as follows:[24]

1 title page
2 list of contents
3 preface—outline of agreed brief, statement of objectives, scope and methods of research
4 summary of conclusions and recommendations
5 previous related research—how previous research has had a bearing on this research
6 research method
7 research findings

8   conclusions
9   appendices.

Sections 1–4 provide a concise description of the nature and outcomes of the research for busy managers. Sections 5–9 provide the level of detail necessary if any particular issue (e.g. the basis of a finding, or the analytical technique used) needs checking. The report should be written in language the reader will understand; jargon should be avoided.

Marketing information systems

By carefully following each of the stages described above, researchers can improve the quality of the market information they collect. However, the variety of information that is currently available to companies means that it is sensible to set up a **marketing information system**. A marketing information system has been defined as:

> . . . a system in which marketing information is formally gathered, stored, analysed and distributed to managers in accord with their informational needs on a regular planned basis.[25]

The system is built on an understanding of the information needs of marketing management, and supplies that information when, where and in the form that the manager requires it. Marketing information system (MkIS) design is important since the quality of a marketing information system has been shown to influence the effectiveness of decision-making.[26] The MkIS comprises four elements: internal continuous data, internal ad hoc data, environmental scanning, and marketing research (see Figure 4.4).

Companies possess an enormous amount of marketing and financial data (internal continuous data) that may never be used for marketing decision-making unless organized by means of an MkIS. This includes, for example, information that is available from the company's salesforce, such as number of accounts opened, customer attitudes, etc., as well as financial data such as that regarding sales and profitability.

Company data can also be used for a specific (ad hoc) purpose (this is known as internal ad hoc data). For example, management may look at how sales have reacted to a price increase or a change in advertising copy. Although this could be part of a continuous monitoring programme, specific one-off analyses are inevitably required from time to time. Capturing the

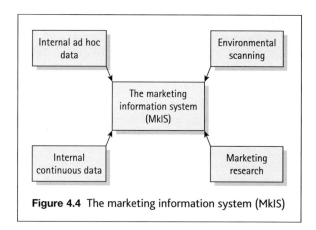

Figure 4.4 The marketing information system (MkIS)

data on the MkIS allows specific analyses to be conducted when needed.

The environmental scanning procedures discussed in Chapter 2 also form part of the MkIS. Although often amorphous in nature, environmental analysis—whereby the economic, social, legal, technological and physical forces are monitored—should be considered part of the MkIS. These are the forces that shape the context within which suppliers, the company, distributors and the competition do business. As such, environmental scanning provides an early warning system for the forces that may affect a company's products and markets in the future. In this way, scanning enables an organization to act upon, rather than react to, opportunities and threats.

As discussed in this chapter, marketing research is primarily concerned with the provision of information about markets and measuring the reactions of consumers to various marketing actions.[27] As such it is a key part of the MkIS because it makes a major contribution to marketing mix planning.

The use of marketing information systems and marketing research

It is important to understand the factors that affect the use of marketing information systems and marketing research. Systems and marketing research reports that remain unused have no value in decision-making.

Marketing information systems should be designed to provide information on a selective basis (for example, by means of a direct, interactive capability).[28] Senior management should conspicuously support use of the system. These recommendations are in line with Ackoff's view[29] that a prime task of an information system is to eliminate irrelevant information by tailoring information flows to the individual manager's needs. It also supports the prescription of Piercy and

Evans that the system should be seen to have top management support,[30] and is consistent with Kohli and Jaworski's view that a market orientation is essentially the organization-wide generation and dissemination of, and responsiveness to, market intelligence.[31]

One of the biggest challenges facing the modern marketing company is the sheer volume of customer information available to it. For example, when continuous data like internal sales records, loyalty card data and website analysis data are combined, the amount of information held about customers can grow very quickly. For example, a US study found that France Telecom's databases held 29.2 terabytes of data, which was equivalent to the printed collec-

tion of the Library of Congress six times over.[32] Converting this data into usable and timely information for managers is a critical management challenge.

Marketing research is more likely to be used if researchers appreciate not only the technical aspects of research, but also the need for clarity in report presentation and the political dimension of information provision. It is unlikely that marketing research reports will be used in decision-making if the results threaten the status quo or are likely to have adverse political repercussions. Therefore, perfectly valid and useful information may sometimes be ignored in decision-making for reasons other than difficulties with the way the research was conducted.

Ethical Debate 4.1: Market research—fact or fiction?

Market research is one of the most visible faces of marketing. At some stage or other, nearly everyone participates in a survey, whether it is in a retail environment, a university or at home via telephone, post or, increasingly, by pressing the red button on their television remote controls. Consumers are also invited to participate in focus groups, depth interviews and ethnographic research. While all this research provides answers, it also seems to be raising some very fundamental questions.

The first concerns the widespread usage to which research is being put. It is virtually impossible now to pick up a newspaper or watch the television without seeing the results of some survey or other being presented. It may be about the most mundane of matters, such as how much time is spent cleaning the kitchen floor or who people think is the most eligible film star. The more outrageous the survey or its findings, the more likely it is to be picked up by news bulletins or discussed on talk radio shows. In other words, surveys have become the news and for 24-hour news channels they represent a relatively cheap and useful time filler. For example, many people missed the irony of Sky News charging viewers to vote by text on whether they thought they were paying too much for their mobile phone bills.

The sheer prevalence of surveys and their findings raises two other fundamental questions: who sponsored the study and how was it conducted? The former is crucial because it demonstrates that many of the surveys in the media are, in truth, public relations pieces being put out by particular companies or brands. For example, our floor cleaning survey is likely to have originated from a cleaning products company; that the majority of workers favour emailing colleagues over face-to-face meetings is likely to come from a business communications company, and so on. Sometimes, this can be relatively harmless fun but in other instances it can be very serious if the subject matter relates to food, family health and the like. The surfeit of visual, audio and print media means that there is always an outlet for these kinds of PR exercises. The consumer should take care to know who sponsored any study that receives media coverage.

After reading this chapter, you should also be critical of how studies are being conducted. What was the sampling frame and the sample size? What questions were asked, and were they unbiased or leading questions? For all the survey findings that are presented regularly, this type of background detail rarely is. In its absence, it is impossible to conclude that the research was conducted scientifically. Unfortunately, time-pressed consumers rarely seek out this information and tend to take survey results at face value.

Market research suffers from other problems, too. In some instances it is used to gather competitor intelligence. Questionable practices include using student projects to gather information without the student revealing the identity of the sponsor of the research, pretending to be a potential supplier who is conducting a telephone survey to understand the market, posing as a potential customer at an exhibition, bribing a competitor's employee to pass on proprietary information, and covert surveillance such as through the use of hidden cameras. The practice of selling in the guise of marketing research, commonly known as 'sugging', also occurs from time to time. Despite the fact that it is not usually practised by bona fide marketing research agencies but, rather, unscrupulous selling companies who use marketing research as a means of gaining compliance to their requests, it is the marketing research industry that suffers from its aftermath.

Market research is an important vehicle by which organizations can learn more about their customers, and develop products and services that meet their needs. Properly conducted, it can yield invaluable insights, and can be the difference between success and failure in business. But its reputation is being sullied by the prevalence of 'bogus' surveys and other questionable practices. This raises the issue of whether research deals with the facts or is an exercise in fiction.

Summary

This chapter has examined the nature and role of marketing research and marketing information systems. The following key issues were addressed.

1. The importance of marketing research: marketing research is key if an organization is to be truly market-led. It can provide answers to all sorts of marketing questions that the organization may face.

2. The types of marketing research: marketing research can be either ad hoc (to solve specific problems at a point in time) or continuous (to gather information on an ongoing basis). Ad hoc research is more popular, but a range of continuous research techniques, such as online consumer panels, loyalty cards and website analysis, provides firms with a steady stream of consumer information.

3. The approaches to conducting research: marketing research can be conducted either by the organization itself or by employing the services of a professional marketing research firm. Large-scale, complex research work is best conducted by a professional firm.

4. The stages in the market research process: these include initial contact, the research brief, the research proposal, exploratory research, the main data collection phase, data analysis and report writing/presentation.

5. Qualitative research techniques: these comprise focus groups, depth interviews and observation. The latter, combined with the use of ethnographic techniques, is an increasingly popular way of collecting customer information.

6. The four main survey methods, namely face-to-face, telephone, mail and internet: each has its unique advantages and disadvantages, and the decision as to which to use should be guided by the nature of the study, the respondents and the cost.

7. The nature of marketing information systems: these are systems in which marketing information is formally gathered, stored and distributed on a regular, planned basis.

Key terms

ad hoc research a research project that focuses on a specific problem, collecting data at one point in time with one sample of respondents

consumer panel household consumers who provide information on their purchases over time

continuous research repeated interviewing of the same sample of people

depth interviews the interviewing of consumers individually for perhaps one or two hours with the aim of understanding their attitudes, values, behaviour and/or beliefs

exploratory research the preliminary exploration of a research area prior to the main data collection stage

focus group a group, normally of six to eight consumers, brought together for a discussion focusing on an aspect of a company's marketing

marketing ethnography the study of consumer behaviour in its naturally occurring context, through observation and/or discussion

marketing information system a system in which marketing information is formally gathered, stored, analysed and distributed to managers in accordance with their informational needs on a regular, planned basis

marketing research the gathering of data and information on the market

omnibus survey a regular survey, usually operated by a market research specialist company, which asks questions of respondents

qualitative research exploratory research that aims to understand consumers' attitudes, values, behaviour and beliefs

research brief written document stating the client's requirements

research proposal a document defining what the marketing research agency promises to do for its client and how much it will cost

retail audit a type of continuous research tracking the sales of products through retail outlets

sampling process a term used in research to denote the selection of a subset of the total population in order to interview them

secondary research data that has already been collected by another researcher for another purpose

Study questions

1. What are the differences between secondary and primary data? Explain the roles played by each.
2. Outline the main stages in the marketing research process, identifying particularly the kinds of difficulties that might be faced at each stage.
3. Market research is being trivialized by the number of surveys that are being reported in the media. Discuss
4. Discuss recent developments in the measurement of website audiences.
5. What is meant by a marketing information system? Discuss, using examples, the main components of such a system.
6. Visit www.surveymonkey.com and learn about how to create and administer a survey.

Suggested reading

Carson, D., A. Gilmore and **K. Gronhaug** (2001) *Qualitative Marketing Research*, London: Sage Publications.

Cooke, M. and **N. Buckley** (2008) Web 2.0, Social Networks and the Future of Market Research, *International Journal of Market Research*, **50** (2), 267–92.

Fahy, J. (1998) Improving Response Rates in Cross-Cultural Mail Surveys, *Industrial Marketing Management*, **27**, 459–67.

Grossnickle, J. and **O. Raskin** (2001) *The Handbook of Online Marketing Research: Knowing Your Customers Using the Net*, New York: McGraw-Hill.

Lorange, P. (2004) Memo to Marketing, *Sloan Management Review*, **46** (2), 16–20.

Ulwick, A. and **L. Bettencourt** (2008) Giving Customers a Fair Hearing, *Sloan Management Review*, **49** (3), 62–68.

References

1. **Grossman, L.** (2003) The Quest for Cool, *Time Canada*, **162** (10), 44; **Langer, J.** (2001) Forecasting Traps can Trip up Trend Spotters, *Advertising Age*, **72** (14), 18; **Terazono, E.** (2003) Squaring the Mainstream Circle, *Financial Times: Creative Business*, 24 June, 2–3; **Wood, D.** (2004) Up on What's Going Down, *Financial Times*, Creative Business, 4 May, 6.

2. **Fielding, M.** (2007) Explore New Territory, *Marketing News*, 1 March, 25–8.

3. **Foss, B.** and **M. Stone** (2001) *Successful Customer Relationship Marketing*, London: Kogan Page.

4. **Anonymous** (2007) Many Ways to Skin a Cat, *Economist*, 1 December, 72–3.

5. **Guenther, K.** (2003) Nothing Measured, Nothing Gained, *Online*, **27** (6), 53–5.

6. **Phippen, A., L. Sheppard** and **S. Furnell** (2004) A Practical Evaluation of Web Analytics, *Internet Research*, **14** (4), 284–93.

7. **Crouch, S.** and **M. Housden** (1999) *Marketing Research for Managers*, Oxford: Butterworth Heinemann, 253.

8. **Birchall, J.** (2005) What Wal-Mart Women Really Really Want, *Financial Times*, 10 October, 11.

9. **Grant, J.** (2005) The Search for Dark Secrets, *Financial Times*, 29 November, 14.

10. **Gray, R.** (1999) Tracking the Online Audience, *Marketing*, 18 February, 41–3.

11. **Birchall, J.** (2005) Rich, But Not Fortune's Fools, *Financial Times*, 13 December, 13.

12. **Goulding, C.** (1999) Consumer Research: Interpretive Paradigms and Methodological Ambiguities, *European Journal of Marketing*, **33** (9/10), 859–73.

13. **Harper, J.** (2003) Camera Phones Cross Moral, Legal Lines, *Washington Times*, Business, 15 July, 6.

14. **Berner, R.** (2006) The Ethnography of Marketing, *Businessweek.com*, 12 June.

15. **Durante, R.** and **M. Feehan** (2006) Watch and Learn, *Marketing News*, 1 February, 59–61.

16. **Thomas, K.** (2005) Anthropologists Get to the Bottom of Customers' Needs, *Financial Times*, 24 August, 9.

17. **Yu, J.** and **H. Cooper** (1983) A Quantitative Review of Research Design Effects on Response Rates to Questionnaires, *Journal of Marketing Research*, 20 February, 156–64.

18. **Falthzik, A.** and **S. Carroll** (1971) Rate of Return for Close v Open-ended Questions in a Mail Survey of Industrial Organisations, *Psychological Reports*, **29**, 1121–2.

19. **O'Dell, W.F.** (1962) Personal Interviews or Mail Panels?, *Journal of Marketing*, **26**, 34–9.

20. **Dillman, D.** (1978) *Mail and Telephone Surveys: The Total Design Method*, New York: John Wiley & Sons.

21. See **Fahy, J.** (1998) Improving Response Rates in Cross-cultural Mail Surveys, *Industrial Marketing Management*, 27 (November), 459–67; **Walker, B., W. Kirchmann** and **J. Conant** (1987) A Method to Improve Response Rates in Industrial Mail Surveys, *Industrial Marketing Management*, **16** (November), 305–14.

22. **Esomar** (2007) *Global Market Research, 2007*, www.esomar.org.

23. **Reynolds, N.** and **A. Diamantopoulos** (1998) The Effect of Pretest Method on Error Detection Rates: Experimental Evidence, *European Journal of Marketing*, **32** (5/6), 480–98.

24. **Crouch, S.** (1992) *Marketing Research for Managers*, Oxford: Butterworth Heinemann, 253.

25. **Jobber, D.** and **C. Rainbow** (1977) A Study of the Development and Implementation of Marketing Information Systems in British Industry, *Journal of the Marketing Research Society*, **19** (3), 104–11.

26. **Van Bruggen, A., A. Smidts** and **B. Wierenga** (1996) The Impact of the Quality of a Marketing Decision Support System: An Experimental Study, *International Journal of Research in Marketing*, **13**, 331–43.

27. **Moutinho, L.** and **M. Evans** (1992) *Applied Marketing Research*, Colorado Springs, CO and Wokingham: Addison-Wesley, 5.

28. **Jobber, D.** and **M. Watts** (1986) Behavioural Aspects of Marketing Information Systems, *Omega*, **14** (1), 69–79; **Wierenga, B.** and **P.A.M. Oude Ophis** (1997) Marketing Decision Support Systems: Adoption, Use and Satisfaction, *International Journal of Research in Marketing*, **14**, 275–90.

29. **Ackoff, R.L.** (1967) Management Misinformation Systems, *Management Science*, **14** (4), 147–56.

30. **Piercy, N.** and **M. Evans** (1983) *Managing Marketing Information*, Beckenham: Croom Helm.

31. **Kohli, A.** and **B. Jaworski** (1990) Market Orientation: The Construct, Research Propositions and Marketing Implications, *Journal of Marketing*, **54**, 1–18.

32. **London, S.** (2004) Choked by a Data Surfeit, *Financial Times*, 29 January, 17.

Online **LearningCentre**

Appendix 4.1

Sources of European marketing information

Is there a survey of the industry?

Euromonitor GMID Database has in-depth analysis and current market information in the key areas of country data, consumer lifestyles, market sizes, forecasts, brand and country information, business information sources and marketing profiles.

Reuters Business Insight Reports are full-text reports available online in the sectors of healthcare, financial services, consumer goods, energy, e-commerce and technology.

KeyNote Reports cover size of market, economic trends, prospects and company performance.

Mintel Premier Reports cover market trends, prospects and company performance.

Snapshots on CD-Rom The 'Snapshots' CD series is a complete library of market research reports, providing coverage of consumer, business-to-business and industrial markets. Containing 2000 market research reports, this series provides incisive data and analysis on over 8000 market segments for the UK, Europe and the United States.

British Library Market Research is a guide to British Library Holdings. It lists titles of reports arranged by industry. Some items are available on inter-library loan; others may be seen at the British Library in London.

International Directory of Published Market Research, published by Marketsearch.

How large is the market?

European Marketing Data and Statistics Now available on the Euromonitor GMID database.
International Marketing Data and Statistics Now available on the Euromonitor GMID database.
CEO Bulletin
A–Z of UK Marketing Data
European Marketing Pocket Book
The Asia Pacific Marketing Pocket Book
The Americas Marketing Pocket Book

Where is the market?

Regional Marketing Pocket Book
Regional Trends gives the main economic and social statistics for UK regions.
Geodemographic Pocket Book

Who are the competitors?

British companies can be identified using any of the following.
Kompass (most European countries have their own edition)
Key British Enterprises
Quarterly Review—KPMG
Sell's Products and Services Directory (Gen Ref E 380.02542 SEL)

For more detailed company information consult the following.
Companies Annual Report Collection Carol: Company Annual Reports online at www.carol.co.uk
Fame DVD (CD-Rom service)
Business Ratio Reports
Retail Rankings

Overseas companies sources include:
Asia's 7,500 Largest Companies
D&B Europa
Dun's Asia Pacific Key Business Enterprises
Europe's 15,000 Largest Companies
Major Companies of the Arab World
Million Dollar Directory (US)
Principal International Businesses

What are the trends?

Possible sources to consider include the following.
The Book of European Forecasts Now available on the Euromonitor GMID database.
Marketing in Europe
European Trends
Consumer Europe Now available on the Euromonitor GMID database.
Consumer Goods Europe
Family Expenditure Survey
Social Trends
Lifestyle Pocket Book
Drink Trends
Media Pocket Book
Retail Business

Mintel Market Intelligence
OECD (Organisation for Economic Co-operation and Development)

EU statistical and information sources
'Eurostat' is a series of publications that provide a detailed picture of the EU; they can be obtained by visiting European Documentation Centres (often in university libraries) in all EU countries; themes include general statistics, economy and finance, and population/social conditions
Eurostat Yearbook
European Access is a bulletin on issues, policies, activities and events concerning EU member states.
Marketing and Research Today is a journal that examines social, political, economic and business issues relating to Western, Central and Eastern Europe.
European Report is a twice-weekly news publication from Brussels on industrial, economic and political issues.

Abstracts and indexes

Business Periodicals Index
ANBAR Marketing and Distribution Abstracts
ABI Inform
Research Index
Times Index
Elsevier Science Direct
Emerald
Wiley Interscience and Boldideas

Guides to sources

A great variety of published information sources exists; the following source guides may help you in your search.
Marketing Information
Guide to European Marketing Information
Compendium of Marketing Information Sources
Croner's A–Z of Business Information Sources
McCarthy Cards: a card service on which are reproduced extracts from the press covering companies and industries; it also produces a useful guide to its sources: *UK and Europe Market Information: Basic Sources*

Statistics

Guide to Official Statistics
Sources of the Unofficial UK Statistics

Sources: the authors thank the University of Bradford School of Management Library for help in compiling this list

Case 4 Inchydoney Island Lodge and Spa

Exponential growth in spas has occurred in Ireland over the last five years, with much of this growth being represented in the hotel or resort spa sector. The growth is not only in response to changing consumer expectations but is also playing a key role in educating consumers with regard to spa experiences. Within a short period of time, the health and wellness industry has grown from offering a few select, dedicated health farms and spas to offering a significant choice to the consumer, including:

- destination spa or purpose-built facility, whose sole purpose is to offer a comprehensive, full-service wellness spa experience for overnight or day guests
- dedicated full-service spa in a hotel or resort, which offers a dedicated and comprehensive full-service wellness spa experience separate to the hotel business
- other hotel spas with small but well-appointed spas offering spa services and pampering packages
- specialized retreats and health farms, which differ from a spa and offer specialized services including holistic treatments and experiences.

Trends in the market

People visit spas for a variety of reasons, including pampering, relaxation, fitness, health and spirituality. What appears to unite all customer groups is the desire to feel better, but it is how they seek to feel better that varies. Some of the motivations of those who visit spas include the following.

- A desire to feel better via pampering and indulgence: outer beauty is a key draw for the majority of spa-goers, who assume that cosmetic treatments (e.g. facials, manicures) will be available at all spa facilities.
- A means of escape: consumers generally feel better when removed from the normal day-to-day environment and circumstances. Many people visit spa facilities to relieve or reduce stress, or simply to indulge their senses.
- A desire to gain a holistic approach to well-being: for those who are looking for serenity, understanding and self-acceptance.
- A desire for improved wellness, to feel better by changing one's spirit or body: for those who want to discover how lifestyle choices can lead to optimal health.
- Rehabilitation: for those who need to recover after an illness.

- Expert advice: on skincare and diet, products and techniques to use at home to recreate the spa experience.
- A way to achieve fitness: for people who want to get in shape by attending fitness classes, or adopting a healthier lifestyle.

Over the past few years, an upmarket spa has become a prerequisite for many Irish hotels as they attempt to attract customers in an increasingly competitive market. One hotel that has excelled in the area of providing a top-quality spa experience is Inchydoney Island Lodge and Spa.

The Inchydoney Island Lodge and Spa

The Inchydoney Island Lodge and Spa is an award-winning hotel located near Clonakilty in County Cork. In a setting overlooking two beaches, it has become renowned as Ireland's most exclusive and tranquil retreat. The Lodge and Spa combines its great location, luxurious accommodation, unique seawater therapies and top-class dining to create an attractive offering to customers. It was voted Best Four Star Hotel at the Hotel and Catering Review Gold Medal Awards 2006, and was voted Ireland's Leading Spa Resort at the World Travel Awards in 2004 and 2007.

Spa retreat

The spa at the Inchydoney Island Lodge and Spa hotel specializes in thalassotherapy. Thalassotherapy comes from the Greek word for 'sea', and refers to a variety of treatments that use seawater and seaweed, each designed to tone, moisturize and revitalize the body and skin, and in many cases improve circulation. Other marine and ocean derivatives feature in thalassotherapy too, including algae, mud and sand. All are cleaned and purified before use. Different forms of thalassotherapy have different effects, helping users to:

- relax
- tone muscles
- cleanse skin
- reduce the appearance of cellulite
- boost the immune system
- improve sleep quality.

Thalassotherapy is also thought to help people with circulatory problems (such as hypertension and arteriosclerosis), respiratory conditions (such as asthma and bronchitis), post-traumatic disorders (such as muscle atrophy) and chronic inflammations (such as rheumatic arthritis). Interestingly, there is no scientific evidence for the efficacy of thalassotherapy, although many people give anecdotal evidence about how it has helped them.

The Inchydoney Island Lodge and Spa has a fully equipped thalasso pool that is split into two parts—one for swimming and the other for water massage. It offers a wide array of thalassotherapy treatments, such as mud baths, underwater showers, hydro-massage, aromatherapy, and seaweed, mud and algae wraps, as well as massage and beauty therapies. Guests at the hotel can enjoy unlimited use of the heated seawater therapy pool, with its bubble seats, micro jets and massage jets, as well as the sauna, steam room, gym and relaxation room. In the competitive spa market, one of Inchydoney's key competitive advantages is that it is home to Ireland's only accredited thalassotherapy spa. There are a number of thalassotherapy spas in Britain and many more across luxurious hotels in European countries, such as the Mare Nostrum in Greece, the Trianon Palace and Spa, Westin Hotel in France, and the Sheraton Fuerteventura Beach, Golf and Spa Resort in Spain.

Despite this advantage, competition is intense. Spa treatments in Ireland are now more varied than ever. Some take inspiration from their beautiful natural surroundings using home-grown products including seaweed, peat, seawater and local plant extracts. Others have imported spa services from around the world. It is not unusual to find Ayurveda, reiki, lomi lomi massage and balneotheraphy all at one spa. Some of Inchydoney's most significant competitors in Ireland include the following.

- The Aghadoe Heights Hotel and Spa: a luxurious five-star hotel located overlooking the Lakes of Killarney. This spa applies customized treatments using particular specialist brands, such as Aveda, Biodraga, Neom and Futuresse.
- ESPA at the Ritz-Carlton, Powerscourt, County Wicklow: the luxurious treatments here are inspired by Eastern philosophies and use the award-winning ESPA product range. ESPA has also created a selection of signature experiences unique to the Ritz-Carlton, Powerscourt, including the 'Garden of Inspiration Body Ritual' and the 'Garden of Inspiration Botanical Facial Ritual'. It is the first ESPA-branded spa to launch at a Ritz-Carlton in Europe.
- Sheraton Fota Island Golf Resort and Spa, located on Fota Island in County Cork: the spa

offers an extensive range of signature treatments, hydrotherapy, thermal suites, as well as holistic relaxation and pampering.
- Park Hotel Kenmare, County Kerry: here the Sámas Experience comprises three elements— thermal suite, holistic treatment of your choice and 'Pure Relaxation'.
- Molton Brown Spa Killarney Plaza: located in the heart of Killarney Town at the gateway to the Ring of Kerry. The treatments offered here reflect the impulse of the seasons—whether one is in need of renewal (spring), radiance (summer), replenishment (autumn) or regeneration (winter).
- Muckross Park Hotel and Cloisters Spa: situated in Killarney's National Park with 25,000 acres of forest, mountains and lakes. Cloisters Spa offers itself as a sanctuary for mind and body, with 12 treatment rooms, a vitality pool and thermal suite including a herbal sauna.

In light of these changes in the spa market, two issues emerge as critical to the future development of marketing strategies for Inchydoney.

1. How important is thalassotherapy to Irish consumers when choosing a destination spa?
2. What differentiates Inchydoney from other leading thalassotherapy spas across Europe?

Inchydoney Island Lodge and Spa recognizes that marketing research needs to be conducted to generate the answers to the above questions. It is envisaged that the information gathered will enable the marketing team to develop marketing strategies that will be effective in attracting and meeting consumers' needs, both nationally and internationally.

Questions

1. Develop specific research objectives for Inchydoney Island Lodge and Spa.
2. Identify potential sources of secondary data that could be used to research the Irish and international markets.
3. Develop a research plan to meet the research objectives that you have set. In particular, provide details of and justify the data collection methods you would use and any sampling procedures that you would employ.

This case was prepared by Rose Leahy and Nollaig O'Sullivan, Cork Institute of Technology, from published sources as a basis for class discussion rather than to illustrate either effective or ineffective management.

Chapter 5
Market Segmentation, Targeting and Positioning

Chapter Outline

Segmenting consumer markets

Consumer segmentation criteria

Segmenting organizational markets

Criteria for successful segmentation

Target marketing

Positioning

Repositioning

Learning Outcomes

By the end of this chapter you will understand:

1   the process of market segmentation and why it is important
2   the methods used to segment both consumer and organizational markets
3   the criteria for effective segmentation
4   the process of market targeting and the four target market strategies—undifferentiated, differentiated, focused and customized marketing
5   the concept of positioning and the keys to successful positioning
6   the concept of repositioning and the repositioning options available to the firm.

Segmentation, targeting and positioning by Boffi

Home furnishings is one of the most diverse businesses on the planet. In different countries throughout Europe different styles and designs are commonplace, which is the result of a combination of physical, cultural, social and architectural influences. Climate conditions influence the nature and style of home furnishings but so, too, do local tastes and preferences. While there are some major pan-European brands, like Sweden's IKEA, that operate in this arena, it remains one where there is ample opportunity for market segmentation because of the diversity evident in the marketplace. One company that is exploiting this diversity to build a niche position for itself is the Italian manufacturer, Boffi.

Boffi was founded in 1934 just north of Milan in Italy, where it manufactured kitchens. In the early 1980s it expanded into bathrooms and both product ranges remain the mainstay of its business today. Like many of its contemporaries in the Milan region, Boffi relies on the traditional Italian strengths of design, superior craftsmanship and small-scale production. But as global companies like IKEA began developing standardized, low-price furniture, the marketplace became much more challenging for these kinds of operators. However, by focusing on the high end of the market and selling its products for high prices, Boffi has been able to withstand this competition successfully.

There are three main elements to the Boffi strategy. The first is its focus on the high-end segment of the market, which is a growing sector as income levels rise in Europe and also in emerging economies like Russia, India and China. It sees itself as operating in the luxury goods business, which includes products like top-of-the-range watches and helicopters. A fitted kitchen using Boffi cabinets and appliances can cost a customer up to €200,000. Some of its bathroom products include a Japanese-designed bathtub complete with water feature that sells for €9000 and a stone bath retailing for €22,000. Second, it gives added prestige to its products by linking with famous designers. It has built up a panel of over 30 designers around the world, which gives its products uniqueness and appeal. And, third, it has bucked the trend to concentrate production in low-cost countries, instead keeping it in Italy where it feels it can generate some advantages through innovation and craftsmanship rather than low price. It has a small manufacturing workforce of about 100 staff, who focus on final assembly, and the company generated sales of €62 million in 2006.

As befits such a high-end product range, it is sold only in exclusive stores in most of the major cities around the world, such as London, Paris, Los Angeles and Madrid. Boffi either owns these shops or has a share in them. This enables it to control the merchandising and retail image of the product to ensure its exclusiveness. A significant portion of its sales also goes to the commercial sector, such as exclusive hotels and office buildings.

Boffi has been successful because it has clearly used its strengths to focus on a particular segment of the market and to concentrate on serving that particular segment well. Though large parts of the market are excluded from its products due to their high price levels, the company is still profitable in a highly competitive business. This is the essence of market segmentation, targeting and positioning.[1]

In our review of customer behaviour in Chapter 3, we saw that there are a variety of influences on the purchase decisions of customers. Their needs and wants vary and no matter how good a company's product or service is, not all customers will want it or will be willing to pay the same price for it. For example, airlines such as British Airways and SAS recognize that business and pleasure travellers are different in terms of their price sensitivity and the level of service required. As we saw above, in the home furnishings market, the type of person who buys luxury leather suites is very different from the type of person who buys conventional sofas; their reasons for purchase are different (style and prestige versus economy) and the type of furniture they want is different in terms of appearance and materials. Therefore, to implement the marketing concept and satisfy customer needs successfully, different product and service offerings must be made to the diverse customer groups that typically comprise a market.

The technique used by marketers to get to grips with the diverse nature of markets is called **market segmentation**. Market segmentation is defined as 'the identification of individuals or organizations with similar characteristics that have significant implications for the determination of marketing strategy'.

Thus, market segmentation involves the division of a diverse market into a number of smaller submarkets that have common features. The objective is to identify groups of customers with similar requirements so that they can be served effectively, while being of a sufficient size for the product or service to be supplied efficiently (see Exhibit 5.1). Usually, particularly in consumer markets, it is not possible to create a marketing mix that satisfies every individual's particular requirements exactly. Market segmentation, by grouping together customers with similar needs, provides a commercially viable method of serving these customers. It is therefore at the heart of strategic marketing, since it forms the basis by which marketers understand their markets and develop strategies for serving their chosen customers better than the competition.

There are a number of reasons why it is sensible for companies to segment their markets (see Figure 5.1). Most notably, it allows companies the opportunity to enhance their

Yaris Colour Collection

Admit it. Your car is a giant handbag. A fast and powerful one, but a handbag all the same. So shouldn't your biggest accessory ooze style? Why not pop into a Toyota showroom and try on Crystal Silver. If it's not quite right, then there's four other gorgeous colours to um and ah over. And just like the best handbags, it has a stylishly designed interior that's crammed full of extras you wouldn't be without, all from £7995. Visit toyota.co.uk or call 0845 275 5555 before your best friend does.

TODAY TOMORROW TOYOTA

Exhibit 5.1 This advertisement for the Toyota Yaris unashamedly targets female buyers

Better matching of customer needs
Enhanced profitability
Enhanced opportunities for growth
Improved customer retention
More effective targeting of communications
Opportunities for segment dominance

Figure 5.1 The benefits of market segmentation

profits. Many customers are willing to pay a premium for products or services that match their needs. For example, first-class air travellers regularly pay thousands of pounds for long-haul flights, though the additional costs of catering for these customers is only marginally higher than that of catering for economy-class customers. Similarly, the premium-priced segment of the car market is one of the fastest-growing segments, having risen by 82 per cent in the 10 years to 2004, and is expected to continue to grow. At the same time, profit margins in this segment are three times that of the mainstream segment, meaning that brands like Lexus, BMW and Mercedes will compete aggressively to exploit this opportunity.[2]

Second, through segmenting markets, companies can examine growth opportunities and expand their product lines. For example, in marketing its over-the-counter cough medicines, the Pfizer corporation offers different products for different types of cough under the Benylin brand. In its children's medicines range, it offers separate products for chesty coughs, dry coughs and night coughs, while there are five different cough brands in its adult range. Finally, in many competitive markets, companies are not able to compete across all segments effectively; by segmenting markets,

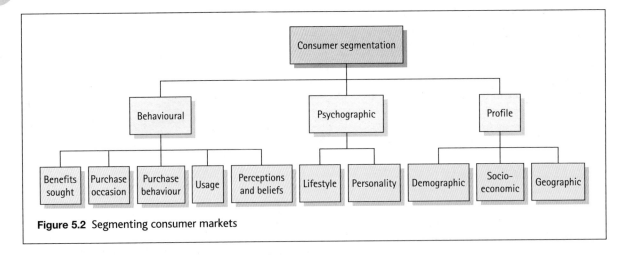

Figure 5.2 Segmenting consumer markets

companies can identify which segments they might most effectively compete in and develop strategies suited for that segment. For example, in the audio equipment business, one of the leading brands is Bose, which has built a global reputation as a manufacturer of high-quality sound systems that are only available through select stores and at premium prices. By pursuing this strategy, Bose has successfully differentiated itself from competitors like Sony, Samsung and Pioneer and, despite its premium prices, still has sales revenues of over US$1 billion per annum.

Segmenting consumer markets

Consumer segmentation criteria may be divided into three main groups: behavioural, psychographic and profile variables. Since the purpose of segmentation is to identify differences in behaviour that have implications for marketing decisions, behavioural variables, such as benefits sought from the product and buying patterns, may be considered the ultimate bases for segmentation. **Psychographic segmentation** is used when researchers believe that purchasing behaviour is correlated with the personality or lifestyle of consumers. Having found these differences, the marketer needs to describe the people who exhibit them and this is where **profile segmentation** such as socio-economic group or geographic location is valuable.[3] For example, a marketer may see whether there are groups of people who value low calories in soft drinks and then attempt to profile them in terms of their age, socio-economic groupings, etc. Figure 5.2 shows the major segmentation variables used in consumer markets and Table 5.1 describes each of these variables in greater detail.

Consumer segmentation criteria

Table 5.1 shows the variety of criteria that might be considered when segmenting a consumer market. In practice there is no prescribed way of segmenting a market, and different criteria and combinations of criteria may be used. In the following paragraphs we will examine some of the more popular bases for segmentation.

Benefits sought

Benefit segmentation provides an understanding of why people buy in a market, and can aid the identification of opportunities. It is a fundamental method of segmentation because the objective of marketing is to provide customers with benefits that they value. For example, a basic product like toothpaste can confer a variety of benefits, ranging from decay prevention to fresh breath, and great taste to white teeth. Companies like Colgate have developed sub-brands that provide each of these benefits, such as Colgate Cavity Protection (decay prevention), Colgate Total Advanced Fresh Gel (fresh breath), Colgate Max Fresh Cool Mint (taste) and Colgate Simply White and Ultra-brite Advanced Whitening (white teeth). Similarly, in the clothing market, one of the most rapidly growing segments is the plussize market—that is, women's size 14 and up. In the USA, this market is estimated to be worth US$17.2 billion. The challenge for manufacturers is to produce clothing for this market that fits well and is still fashionable.[4] Focusing on benefits helps companies to spot business development opportunities, as demonstrated in Marketing in Action 5.1.

Purchase behaviour

The degree of brand loyalty in a market is a useful basis for segmenting customers. Solus buyers are totally

Table 5.1 Consumer segmentation methods

Variable	Examples
Behavioural	
Benefits sought	Convenience, status, performance
Purchase occasion	Self-buy, gift
Purchase behaviour	Solus buying, brand switching, innovators
Usage	Heavy, light
Perceptions and beliefs	Favourable, unfavourable
Psychographic	
Lifestyle	Trendsetters, conservatives, sophisticates
Personality	Extroverts, introverts, aggressive, submissive
Profile	
Age	Under 12, 12–18, 19–25, 26–35, 36–49, 50–64, 65
Gender	Female, male
Life cycle	Young single, young couples, young parents, middle-aged empty-nesters, retired
Social class	Upper middle, middle, skilled working, unwaged
Terminal education age	16, 18, 21 years
Income	Income breakdown according to study objectives and income levels per country
Geographic	North vs south, urban vs rural, country
Geodemographic	Upwardly mobile young families living in larger owner-occupied houses, older people living in small houses, European regions based on language, income, age profile and location

brand loyal, buying only one brand in the product group. For example, a person might invariably buy Ariel Automatic washing powder. Most customers, however, practise brand-switching behaviour. Some may have a tendency to buy Ariel Automatic but also buy two or three other brands; others might show no loyalty to any individual brand but switch brands on the basis of special offers (e.g. money off) or because they are variety seekers who look to buy a different brand each time. A recent trend in retailing is 'biographics'. This is the linking of actual purchase behaviour to individuals. The growth in loyalty schemes in supermarkets, such as the Tesco Clubcard scheme, has provided the mechanism for gathering this information. Customers are given cards that are swiped through an electronic machine at the checkout so that points can be accumulated towards discounts and vouchers. The more loyal the shopper, the higher the number of points gained. The supermarket also benefits by knowing what a named individual purchases and where. Such biographic data can be used to segment and target customers very precisely. For example, it would be easy to identify a group of customers who were ground coffee purchasers and target them through direct mail. Analysis of the data allows the supermarkets to stock products in each of their stores that are more relevant to their customers' age, lifestyle and expenditure. Japanese convenience stores are extensive users of this kind of customer informa-

tion and, because of space restrictions there, shelves are restocked up to three times per day.[5]

Usage

Another way of segmenting customers is on the basis of whether they are heavy users, light users or non-users of a selected product category. The profiling of heavy users allows this group to receive the most marketing attention (particularly promotion efforts) on the assumption that creating brand loyalty among these people will pay great dividends. Sometimes the 80:20 rule applies, where about 80 per cent of a product's sales come from 20 per cent of its customers. Skype is an example of a telecommunications company that has focused very effectively on the opportunities created by the growing need for telephone contact among people living in different parts of the world. By offering free calls over the internet, Skype quickly built a customer base of 246 million registered users worldwide.[6] However, attacking the heavy-user segment can have drawbacks if all of the competition are also following this strategy. Analysing the light and non-user categories may provide insights that permit the development of appeals that are not being mimicked by the competition. The identity of heavy, light and non-user categories, and their accompanying profiles for many consumer goods, can be accomplished by using survey information such as that provided by the Target Group Index

Marketing in Action 5.1: Grey Goose takes flight

Study guide: Below is a review of the successful launch of Grey Goose Vodka. Read it and try to think of examples of other market segments that are currently unserved.

Segmentation strategies often have the effect of identifying the presence of segments where none appeared to exist before. A classic case in point is that of the super-premium vodka segment identified by Sidney Frank, the founder of Grey Goose Vodka. Frank had noticed that in spirit categories like brandy and whisky, there were many prestigious upmarket brands like vintage malt whiskies but that this was not the case with vodka, which had been dominated by mainstream brands like Smirnoff and Absolut. In his view, there was a market for a super-premium vodka at a super-premium price, and he set about creating one.

To command such a segment of the market, Frank felt that the brand had to tell a good story. So he made the decision to manufacture it in France, which does not have a vodka tradition but is the country where many of the world's best luxury brands come from. The company was founded in 1997 and the brand was initially targeted at the US market. Its value proposition was that it was carefully crafted by French vodka artisans, using water from pristine French springs and filtered through Champagne limestone in the Cognac region of France. It was packaged in a carefully designed bottle with smoked glass and a silhouette of flying geese, and was launched at twice the price of Absolut, then the premium-brand leader. It was instantly successful and by the time the brand was sold to the Bacardi group in 2002 for US$2 billion, it had racked up sales of over 1.5 billion cases per annum in the USA.

The success of Grey Goose spawned a whole new category in vodka. Existing and new competitors rushed to bring out their own brands of super-premium vodka. Absolut launched the Level brand in 2004 as a direct competitor to Grey Goose. Diageo launched Ciroc vodka in 2003, which is made in France from grapes as opposed to corn, wheat and potatoes. Different raw materials, different methods of manufacture and the inclusion of flavourings such as mint, coconut, coffee and vanilla have all combined to make the super-premium vodka category one of the most innovative and competitive in the drinks industry. It has also prevented the sector from suffering the downturn that has been experienced by other spirits brands.

Based on: Breen (2005)[7]

(TGI) (www.tgisurveys.com). This is a large-scale annual survey of buying and media habits in the UK.

Lifestyle

Lifestyle segmentation aims to categorize people in terms of their way of life, as reflected in their activities, interests and opinions (see Exhibit 3.2). As we saw in Chapter 3, lifestyle is an important personal factor driving consumer behaviour, and advertisers have identified several different lifestyle groupings. Lifestyle is also a powerful method of segmentation as particular lifestyle groups have fairly predictable media habits. For example, people who enjoy outdoor activities such as hiking and watersports will be likely to read magazines, watch television programmes and visit websites dealing with these topics.

Marketers can then use these media to reach their chosen segments.

Lifestyle segmentation describes the way in which many advertising agencies attempt to relate brands (e.g. Martini) to a particular lifestyle (e.g. aspirational). A good example of this is recent efforts by Emap to segment the market for music by fan behaviour. Emap is a media company that owns three UK music magazine titles, 27 radio stations, 7 digital music television channels and 17 music websites. In 2003, it surveyed 2200 15–39-year-olds, who completed a detailed questionnaire about their music listening and purchasing habits, as well as other lifestyle and attitude traits. This was supplemented by 30 in-depth focus groups on the subject of fans' relationship with music and, in late 2005, the study

Love Life

Love LoSalt

LoSalt is the great tasting way to a healthier lifestyle, containing only one-third the sodium of regular table, sea and rock salts.
LoSalt is low in sodium salt and high in natural potassium

BALANCED FOR LIFE
BALANCED FOR FLAVOUR

www.losalt.com

Exhibit 5.2 Healthy living is a growing market; brands like Lo Salt aim to capitalize on the trends towards healthier lifestyles

was repeated. It identified four major segments. 'Savants' are passionate about music and represent about 9 per cent of the age group studied. They are mainly male and include sub-segments such as 'insiders'—in bands themselves, 'curators'—mainly early to mid-30s, who are aficionados of good music, and 'hoodies'—mainly teenage schoolboys. 'Enthusiasts' represent 16 per cent of the group and include 'miss dynamites'—knowledgeable and worldly-wise mid- to late-teen girls; 'iPod tourists', mostly males in their mid-20s with a passion for niche music; and 'party grandees' males in their late 20s and 30s, who still have an active social life. The two remaining segments, 'Casuals' and 'Indifferents', were less interested in music.[8] This type of segmentation and the labels used to describe the different segments are very popular in advertising circles as they enable mental images of certain groups to be formed, as well as providing a description of the lifestyles of these segments.

Age

Age is a factor that has been used in the segmentation of a host of consumer markets.[9] As we saw in Chapter 3, children have become a very important market and now have their own television programmes, cereals, computer games and confectionery. One of the biggest children's marketers, Disney, has brought out a new web-based video game called *Virtual Magic Kingdom*, in an effort to stay relevant to its market, who are spending an increasing amount of time on the internet. While playing the game, children can collect 'game points' that can be used at the real theme parks in Orlando, Paris, and so on.[10] Similarly, a KPMG study found that only one-fifth of fund management firms were targeting 'Generation Y' customers—that is, those born in the 1980s—even though this group will have to be more financially adept than their parents due to changes in pension regimes.[11] In contrast, leading UK newspapers such as *The Times* and the *Guardian* have started including free entertainment listings with the papers as a way of attracting younger customers and boosting sales.[12]

As we saw in Chapter 2, age distribution changes within the European Union are having a profound effect on the attractiveness of various age segments to marketers, with people over 50 years of age likely to become increasingly important in the future. Sometimes labelled the 'grey market', people are now living longer, with life expectancies rising into the 80s in developed countries around the world. Many 'grey consumers' are healthy, active, well educated, financially independent and have a lot of leisure time, making them a very attractive market. For example, research by Marks & Spencer found that women over 55 spend 20 per cent more on clothing that their 35-year-old counterparts and this is reflected in the company's use of over-50s celebrities like Twiggy in its advertising.[13]

Social class

Social class is another important segmentation variable. As we saw in Chapter 3, social class groupings are based primarily on occupation. However, people who hold similar occupations may have very dissimilar lifestyles, values and purchasing patterns. Nevertheless, research has found that social class has proved to be useful in discriminating between owning a dishwasher, having central heating and privatization share ownership, for example, and therefore should not be discounted as a segmentation variable.[14] In addition, social classes tend to vary in their media consumption, meaning that these groups can be targeted effectively by advertisers. For example, tabloid newspapers tend to target working-class people, whereas traditional broadsheets see the middle and upper classes as their primary audience. It is important to monitor how consumer behaviour changes within the social classes. For example, sales of ultra-luxury car brands such as Rolls-Royce and Maybach are struggling as the super-rich shun conspicuous consumption. However, the more discreet sales of mega yachts are growing at a rate of 30% annually.[15]

Geography

At a very basic level, markets can be segmented on the basis of country, regions within a country or on the basis of city size. More popular in recent years has been the combination of geographic and demographic variables into what are called **geodemographics**. In countries that produce population census data, the potential exists for classifying consumers on the combined basis of location and certain demographic (and socio-economic) information. Households are classified into groups according to a wide range of factors, depending on what is asked on census returns. In the UK, variables such as household size, online behaviour, occupation, family size and ethnic background are used to group small geographic areas (known as enumeration districts) into segments that share similar characteristics. Several companies produce analyses of this information—for example, Experian—but the best known is that produced by CACI Market Analysis (www.caci.co.uk) entitled ACORN (from its full title—A Classification

Of Residential Neighbourhoods). The main ACORN groupings and their characteristics are shown in Table 5.2. CACI uses 125 demographic statistics and 287 lifestyle variables to produce a detailed consumer picture; all 1.9 million postcodes in the UK are classified in this way, enabling some very precise targeting of the market.

Geodemographic information, like that in the ACORN groupings, has been used to select recipients of direct mail campaigns, to identify the best locations for stores and to find the best poster sites. This is possible because consumers in each group can be identified by means of their postcodes. Another area where census data are employed is in buying advertising spots on television. Agencies depend on information from viewership panels, which record their viewing habits so that advertisers can get an insight into who watches what. In the UK, census analyses are combined with viewership data via the postcodes of panellists.[16] This means that advertisers who wish to reach a particular geodemographic group can discover the type of programme they prefer to watch and buy television spots accordingly.

A major strength of geodemographics is that it can link buyer behaviour to customer groups. Buying habits can be determined by means of large-scale syndicated surveys—for example, the TGI and MORI Financial Services—or from panel data (for example,

Table 5.2 The ACORN targeting classification

Categories	% in UK population	Groups	% in UK population
A: Wealthy Achievers	25.4	1 Wealthy Executives 2 Affluent Greys 3 Flourishing Families	8.6 7.9 9.0
B: Urban Prosperity	11.5	4 Prosperous Professionals 5 Educated Urbanites 6 Aspiring Singles	2.1 5.5 3.8
C: Comfortably Off	27.4	7 Starting Out 8 Secure Families 9 Settled Suburbia 10 Prudent Pensioners	3.1 15.5 6.1 2.7
D: Moderate Means	13.8	11 Asian Communities 12 Post-Industrial Families 13 Blue Collar Roots	1.5 4.7 7.5
E: Hard Pressed	21.2	14 Struggling Families 15 Burdened Singles 16 High Rise Hardship 17 Inner City Adversity	13.3 4.2 1.6 2.1

Source: © CACI Limited (data source BMRB and OPCS/GRO(S)); © Crown Copyright; all rights reserved; ACORN is a registered trademark of CACI Limited; reproduced with permission
Note: Due to rounding, the percentages total 99.2

the grocery and toiletries markets are covered by AGB's Superpanel). By 'geocoding' respondents, those ACORN groups most likely to purchase a product or brand can be determined. This can be useful for branch location since many service providers use a country-wide branch network and need to match the market segments to which they most appeal to the type of customer in their catchment area. The merchandise mix decisions of retailers can also be affected by customer profile data. Media selections can be made more precise by linking buying habits to geodemographic data.[17]

In short, a wide range of variables can be used to segment consumer markets. Flexibility and creativity are the hallmarks of effective segmentation analysis. Often, a combination of variables will be used to identify groups of consumers that respond in the same way to marketing mix strategies.

Segmenting organizational markets

As we noted in Chapter 3, organizational markets, in contrast to consumer markets, tend to be characterized by relatively small numbers of buyers. Nevertheless, there are also many cases where it will be appropriate to segment organizational markets.

Organizational segmentation criteria

Some of the most useful bases for segmenting organizational markets are described below.

Organizational size

Market segmentation in this case may be by size of buying organization. Large organizations differ from medium-sized and small organizations in having greater order potential, more formalized buying and management processes, increased specialization of function, and special needs (e.g. quantity discounts). The result is that they may form important target market segments and require tailored marketing mix strategies. For example, the salesforce may need to be organized on a key account basis where a dedicated sales team is used to service important industrial accounts. List pricing of products and services may need to take into account the inevitable demand for volume discounts from large purchasers, and the salesforce will need to be well versed in the art of negotiation (see Marketing in Action 5.2).

Industry

Industry sector—sometimes identified by the Standard Industrial Classification (SIC) codes—is another com-

mon segmentation variable. Different industries may have unique requirements from products. For example, software applications suppliers like Oracle and SAP can market their products to various sectors, such as banking, manufacturing, healthcare and education, each of which has unique needs in terms of software programs, servicing, price and purchasing practice. By understanding each industry's needs in depth, a more effective marketing mix can be designed. In some instances, further segmentation may be required. For example, the education sector may be further divided into primary, secondary and further education, as the product and service requirements of these sub-sectors may differ.

Geographic location

The use of geographic location as a basis for differentiating marketing strategies may be suggested by regional variations in purchasing practice and needs (see Exhibit 5.3). The purchasing practices and expectations of companies in Central and Eastern Europe are likely to differ markedly from those in Western Europe. Their more bureaucratic structures may imply a fundamentally different approach to doing business that needs to be recognized by companies attempting to enter these emerging industrial markets. These differences, in effect, suggest the need

Exhibit 5.3 This advertisement for HSBC Global Banking and Markets shows that it operates on a global scale and can meet the banking needs of companies doing business in different parts of the world

Marketing in Action 5.2: New market segments for Lenovo

> **Study guide:** Below is a review of how Lenovo segments the market for personal computers. Read it and summarize the different marketing strategies that it uses for each segment.

Lenovo is a Chinese computer company that made waves in 2005 when it purchased IBM's famous but ailing personal computer division. It was an acquisition that moved Lenovo from the eighth largest to the third largest PC manufacturer in the world, and marked the emergence of Chinese companies as major global players. IBM traditionally had been a leader in the PC business and had built up a particular reputation for serving the needs of large enterprises. But as Lenovo took over the loss-making division, it recognized that it needed to expand the business into new segments.

Since the acquisition, Lenovo has concentrated on expanding IBM's product range into the small to medium-sized business (SMB) sector, a sector in which it had built a strong level of expertise in China. The two market segments have very different patterns of buyer behaviour. Most sales to the SMB sector tend to be transactional, while making sales to the corporate market requires building relationships with large multinational organizations. Lenovo was able to exploit its powerful reseller network of over 10,000 retailers and businesses in the SMB sector in China and at the same time piggyback on IBM's strong relationships and reputation in the corporate sector globally. Different branding strategies were used for both segments. Though Lenovo acquired the rights to use IBM's famous 'Think' brand on all its products for five years, it has chosen to target this range at the corporate sector because of its premium image in the market. And, in February 2006, it launched its Lenovo 3000 range of desktops and laptops globally with a focus on the SMB sector.

In 2008, Lenovo moved aggressively into the consumer market, which is currently dominated by companies like Dell and HP. Previously, it had been strong in this segment only in China, where it had targeted the rapidly growing consumer segment in over 600 cites. But by launching a range of six products, three desktops and three laptops, Lenovo wants to build a global reputation for high-quality, innovatively designed consumer machines. For example, the IdeaPad U110 is a laptop with a bright-red top and 11-inch screen, while the Y710 has a keyboard with special controls for video gamers. In terms of distribution, Lenovo is aiming to primarily sell these products online, like Dell. Its profile in the consumer market has been enhanced through its sponsorship of the 2006 Turin Winter Olympics, the 2008 Beijing Olympic Games as well as a deal with Barcelona soccer star Ronaldinho, which sees him become worldwide ambassador for the brand.

Based on: Collins (2006);[18] Dickie (2005);[19] Hamm (2008)[20]

for regional segments since marketing needs to reflect these variations.

Choice criteria

The factor of choice criteria segments the organizational market on the basis of the key criteria used by buyers when they are evaluating supplier offerings. One group of customers may rate price as the key choice criterion, another segment may favour productivity, while a third may be service orientated. These varying preferences mean that marketing and sales strategies need to be adapted to cater for each segment's needs. Three different marketing mixes would be needed to cover the three segments, and salespeople would have to emphasize different

benefits when talking to customers in each segment. Variations in key choice criteria can be powerful predictors of buyer behaviour.

Purchasing organization

Another segmentation variable is that of decentralized versus centralized purchasing, because of its influence on the purchase decision.[21] Centralized purchasing is associated with purchasing specialists who become experts in buying a range of products and are particularly popular in sectors like grocery retailing. Specialization means that they become more familiar with cost factors, and the strengths and weaknesses of suppliers than do decentralized generalists. Furthermore, the opportunity for volume buying means that their power to demand price concessions from suppliers is enhanced. They have also been found to have greater power within the decision-making unit (DMU—see Chapter 3) vis-à-vis technical people like engineers, than decentralized buyers who often lack the specialist expertise and status to challenge the technicians' preferences. For these reasons, purchasing organization provides a good base for distinguishing between buyer behaviour, and can have implications for marketing activities. For example, the centralized purchasing segment could be served by a national account salesforce, whereas the decentralized purchasing segment might be covered by territory representatives.

Interesting opportunities often appear at the intersection of consumer and industrial markets. For example, a small German technology company called Wagner has become the biggest supplier of spray guns for painting in the USA, with an 85 per cent market share. It used its expertise, built up through working with professional painters, to make products that also appeal to DIY painters. Its vast range of 3000 products enables it to span both consumer and industrial markets, with prices ranging from US$50 up to US$2 million for large industrial systems. Though most manufacturers concentrate on industrial segments, two-thirds of Wagner's sales in the USA now come from consumer spray guns.

Criteria for successful segmentation

To determine whether a company has properly segmented its market, five criteria are usually considered.

1   *Effective*: the segments identified should consist of customers whose needs are relatively homogenous within a segment, but significantly different from those in other segments. If buyer needs in different segments are similar, then the segmentation strategy should be revised.
2   *Measurable*: it must be possible to identify customers in the proposed segment, and to understand their characteristics and behaviour patterns. For example, some personality traits, like 'outgoing' or 'conservative', might be difficult to pin down, whereas variables like age or occupation would be more clear-cut.
3   *Accessible*: The company must be able to formulate effective marketing programmes for the segments that it identifies. In other words, it must be clear what kinds of promotional campaign might work best for the segment, how the prod-

ucts might best be distributed to reach the segment, and so on.
4   *Actionable*: The company must have the resources to exploit the opportunities identified through the segmentation scheme. Certain segments—for example, in international markets—might be identified as being very attractive but the company may not have the resources or knowledge necessary to serve them.
5   *Profitable*: Most importantly, segments must be large enough to be profitable to serve. This is what is meant by the clichéd expression 'Is there a market in the gap?' Very small segments may be unprofitable to serve, though advances in production and distribution technologies mean that, increasingly, micro-segments can be profitable (see the section on customized marketing, below). Sometimes large segments may remain untapped. For example, Britain's Asian population has a combined spending power of £14 billion and has been largely ignored by anything other than niche brands. This prompted mobile phone company O_2 to sponsor the UK's six largest *mela*—the summer festivals run each year by Asian communities across the UK—in an effort to build its brand within this lucrative market.[22]

Target marketing

Once the market segments have been identified, the next important activity is the selection of target markets. **Target marketing** refers to the choice of specific segments to serve, and is a key element in marketing strategy. An organization needs to evaluate the segments and to decide which ones to serve using the five criteria outlined above. For example, CNN targets its news programmes to what are known as 'influentials'. This is why, globally, CNN has focused so much of its distribution effort into gaining access to hotel rooms. Business people know that, wherever they are in the world, they can see international news on CNN in their hotel. Its sports programming is also targeted, with plenty of coverage of upmarket sports such as golf and tennis.

The aim of evaluating market segments is for a company to arrive at a choice of one or more segments to concentrate on. Target market selection is the choice of what and how many market segments in which to compete. There are four generic target marketing strategies from which to choose: undifferentiated marketing, differentiated marketing, focused marketing and customized marketing (see Figure 5.3). Each option will now be examined.

Figure 5.3 Target marketing strategies

Undifferentiated marketing

Market analysis will occasionally reveal no pronounced differences in customer characteristics that have implications for a marketing strategy. Alternatively, the cost of developing a separate market mix for different segments may outweigh the potential gains of meeting customer needs more exactly. Under these circumstances a company may decide to develop a single marketing mix for the whole market. This absence of segmentation is called **undifferentiated marketing**. Unfortunately this strategy can occur by default. For example, companies that lack a marketing orientation may practise undifferentiated marketing through lack of customer knowledge. Furthermore, undifferentiated marketing is more convenient for managers since they have to develop only a single product. Finding out that customers have diverse needs, which can be met only by products with different characteristics, means that managers have to go to the trouble and expense of developing new products, designing new promotional campaigns, training the salesforce to sell the new products, and developing new distribution channels. Moving into new segments also means that salespeople have to start prospecting for new customers. This is not such a pleasant activity as calling on existing customers who are well known and liked.

Differentiated marketing

Specific marketing mixes can be developed to appeal to all or some of the segments when market segmentation reveals several potential targets. This is called **differentiated marketing**; it is a very popular market targeting strategy that can be found in sectors as diverse as cars, hotels and fashion retailing (see Exhibit 5.4). For example, Arcadia's segmentation of the fashion market revealed distinct customer groups for which specific marketing mixes could be employed. In response the group has a portfolio of shops that are distinctive in terms of shop name, style of clothing, décor and ambience. In all, the company has eight separate brands including, for example, Miss Selfridges (aimed at the 18–24 age group), Dorothy Perkins (aimed at women in their 20s and 30s) and Evans (which stocks women's clothes that

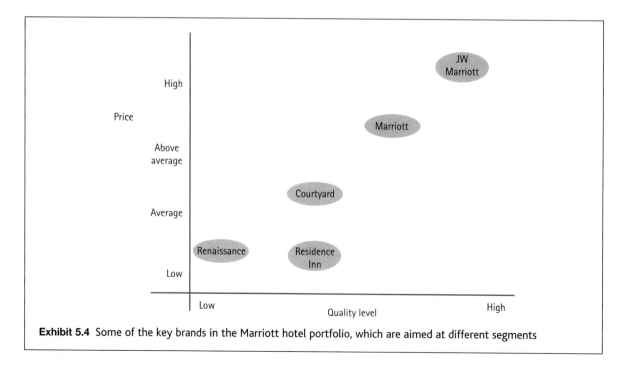

Exhibit 5.4 Some of the key brands in the Marriott hotel portfolio, which are aimed at different segments

Marketing in Action 5.3: Differentiating Gap Inc.'s brands

Study guide: Below is a review of Gap Inc.'s portfolio of brands. Read it and consider both the advantages and disadvantages of a differentiated marketing strategy.

Gap Inc. began life as a retailer of Levi's jeans in San Francisco in 1969 and then extended its range, selling basics likes khakis, chinos, jeans and T-shirts. Gap Inc. presented itself as a premium brand in the smart-casual business and quickly established a strong foothold in the market. Responding to competition in the market, Gap acquired Banana Republic in 1983. Banana Republic was a lifestyle brand targeting customers with a taste for travelling, and its stores had an exotic, safari-style theme. By the early 1990s, overall sales in the Gap corporation were slowing and its brands were under pressure from some new, fashionable competitors like Abercrombie & Fitch. Its response was to bring out a new line of discount clothing aimed at value-conscious family shoppers. Old Navy was launched in 1994, positioned as 'big, loud, fun and cheap'. Over 280 Old Navy stores were opened in the following three years, making a significant contribution to Gap Inc. revenues.

But the positions occupied by each of the brands in the marketplace began to become less clear. The similarities between Gap and Old Navy were starting to become visible, with both stores retailing basics like khakis and jeans at different price points and both using the same style of advertising, featuring celebrities like MTV hosts. When customers saw little difference between the two brands they started opting for the cheaper alternative. To counter this, Gap relaunched its brand, going back to basics and focusing on its core exclusivity. In doing so, it brought the brand closer to Banana Republic in the modern fashion casuals segment. All this confusion in the marketplace was having a significant impact on the bottom line.

In response, Gap's strategy was to go back to its classic image of basics; Old Navy was to stay aimed at the value-conscious segment of the market and Banana Republic was repositioned for the 25–35 age group offering sophisticated casual wear and business casual wear, and given a designer feel. However, many commentators were sceptical that the differentiated strategy was working, citing the decision to use Madonna to front a Gap advertising campaign as a further example of the confusion. And, increasingly, Gap was losing sales to focused marketers like American Eagle and Abercrombie & Fitch, who have been eating into its market share. It would appear that a clear strategy for its three major brands is becoming more important than ever.

Based on: Anonymous (2003);[23] Birchall (2007);[24] Collard (2004);[25] Gayatri and Madhav (2004);[26] Manning-Schaffel (2002)[27]

---

are size 16+). Similarly, as part of its turnaround strategy, Marks & Spencer sought to move away from one brand (St Michael) with wide market appeal to a range of sub-brands such as Autograph (an upmarket brand) and Per Una, which is aimed at fashion-conscious women up to the age of 35. A differentiated target marketing strategy exploits the differences between marketing segments by designing a specific marketing mix for each segment. One potential disadvantage of a differentiated compared to an undifferentiated marketing strategy is the loss of cost economies. However, the use of flexible manufacturing systems can minimize such problems. The challenges of pursuing a differentiated marketing strategy are outlined in Marketing in Action 5.3.

Focused marketing

Just because a company has identified several segments in a market does not mean that it should serve them all. Some may be unattractive or out of step with its business strengths. Perhaps the most sensible route would be to serve just one of the market segments. When a company develops a single marketing mix aimed at one target (niche) market it is practising **focused marketing**. This strategy is particularly appropriate for companies with limited resources. Small companies may stretch their resources too far by competing in more than one segment. Focused marketing allows research and development expenditure to be concentrated on meeting the needs of one set of customers, and managerial activities can thus be devoted to understanding and catering for those needs. Large organizations may not be interested in serving the needs of this one segment, or their energies may be so dissipated across the whole market that they pay insufficient attention to their requirements.

An example of a firm pursuing a focused marketing approach is Bang & Olufsen, the Danish audio electronics firm; it targets its stylish music systems at upmarket consumers who value self-development, pleasure and open-mindedness. Anders Kwitsen, the company's chief executive, describes its positioning as 'high quality, but we are not Rolls-Royce—more BMW'. Focused targeting and cost control mean that B&O defies the conventional wisdom that a small manufacturer could not make a profit by marketing consumer electronics in Denmark.[28] In the USA, 60 per cent of Bang & Olufsen revenues come from home theatre systems that can cost up to US$250,000.[29] It is not uncommon for focused marketers to switch their attention from one segment to another as trends in the market change. For example, Connect Support Services is a London-based computer support company that began life serving the needs of a small number of large corporate clients. But as the negotiation of big contracts became increasingly time-consuming and costly, the company switched its focus to smaller firms with between 5 and 500 PCs, significantly growing its overall number of customers and its turnover.[30] By focusing on innovation, product quality and focused marketing captured by the 'Vorsprung durch Technik' slogan, Audi has transformed itself from a mass-market brand of car to a luxury brand.

Some successful focused marketers frequently move on to become differentiated marketers. For example, low-cost airlines like Ryanair and easyJet have successfully targeted the business traveller while continuing to be popular with holiday travellers.

Customized marketing

The requirements of individual customers in some markets are unique, and their purchasing power sufficient to make viable the design of a discrete marketing mix for each customer. Segmentation at this disaggregated level leads to the use of **customized marketing**. Many service providers, such as advertising and marketing research agencies, architects and solicitors, vary their offerings on a customer-by-customer basis. They will discuss face to face with each customer their requirements, and tailor their services accordingly. Customized marketing is also found within organizational markets because of the high value of orders and the special needs of customers. Locomotive manufacturers will design and build prod-

ucts according to specifications given to them by individual rail transport providers. Similarly, in the machine tools industry, the German company Emag is a global leader in making 'multitasking' machines that cut metals used in industries like aerospace and vehicles. It practises customized marketing by manufacturing basic products at a cost-effective production site in eastern Germany but then finishing off or customizing these products in factories around the world that are located close to the customer.[31] Customized marketing is often associated with close relationships between suppliers and customers in these circumstances because the value of the order justifies a large marketing and sales effort being focused on each buyer.

One of the most fascinating developments in marketing in recent years has been the introduction of **mass customization** in consumer markets. This practice was initially pioneered by Japanese companies, who exploited their strengths in production systems and logistics to deliver customized products such as men's suits, bicycles and golf clubs to private consumers.[32] So when a Japanese man went to buy a suit he wasn't faced with a rack of ready-made suits, but rather a range of materials and colours from which he could choose. His measurements were then taken and a tailor-made suit was available for him within a week, but at a price that compared favourably with that of mass-produced garments. More and more products are now being customized to the needs of particular individuals. For example, at the Mercedes Sindelfingen plant near Stuttgart, every model passing through the plant has a pre-assigned customer, many of whom configure their cars via the internet. Furthermore, many customers take delivery of their cars at the plant rather than from a dealer as has traditionally been the case. The role of technology is assisting the process of customized marketing, as discussed in Technology Focus 5.1.

Positioning

So far, we have examined two key aspects of the marketing management process, namely market segmentation (where we look at the different needs and preferences that may exist in a market) and market targeting (where we decide which segment or segments of the market we are going to serve). We now arrive at one of the most important and challenging aspects of marketing: **positioning**. Positioning can be defined as:

'. . . the act of designing the company's offering so that it occupies a meaningful and distinct position in the target customer's mind.'

Technology Focus 5.1: Markets of one

How far have we progressed towards the 'promised land' of one-to-one marketing? Well, it would appear that there has been a great deal of progress. For example, all of Amazon's estimated 50 million US customers, and millions more around the world, could claim to have a customized relationship with the company given the personal recommendations on products and services that they periodically receive. Similarly, most leading websites have a facility for creating a personal interface. Google customers can create a personalized iGoogle page that contains all key information sources, favourite websites and 'gmail' messages. But, increasingly, this is happening not just with technology companies but all leading brands. For example, NikeiD allows customers to design their own personal versions of Nike shoes and apparel. Initially only available online, Nike has followed up the success of this service by opening NikeiD studios in Nike Town stores around the world. Consumers create designs in the studio which can then be delivered either via the Nike Town stores or direct to their homes.

Many other product categories are getting in on the act. German consumers can make their own cereal from 75 organic ingredients at www.mymuesli.com. M&M's can be customized at www.mymms.com. Perhaps most ambitious is www.mydnafragrance.com, which offers to create a customized perfume. Consumers use a DNA home collection kit to provide the company with a DNA sample that is then used to create a personalized fragrance. Theranostics is a growth area in medicine where patients are first examined to see if they will benefit from a particular treatment. For example, Dako, a Danish diagnostics company, has developed a test for the protein Her-2, which shows whether women with breast cancer will respond to Genetech's Herceptin treatment.

Customization is one of the real strengths of the internet. At a site like www.pandora.com, consumers can build a personal portfolio of radio stations. Sites like www.youtube.com and www.myspace.com allow them to build their personal brands. Most websites allow for the creation of detailed personal histories of sites visited and products viewed. Offline, products like digital video recorders (DVRs) allow us to customize our TV viewing. But the interactivity of these devices provides manufacturers with a detailed picture of our viewing habits. So we are moving to a world where not only are our products customized, but also our advertising and even the price at which we buy products can be customized. It is a slow and gradual process, but there is ever greater evidence of 'segments of one' in consumer markets.

Suggested reading: Godin (1999);[33] Peppers and Rodgers (1996)[34]

This is the challenge that faces all organizations. All firms make products or provide services but, as we saw in Chapter 1, consumers buy benefits. Positioning is essentially that act of linking your product or service to the solutions that consumers seek and ensuring that, when they think about those needs, your brand is one of the first that comes to mind. For example, there is a segment of the car-buying market that values safety as one of its key purchasing criteria. Over the years, Swedish car manufacturer Volvo successfully positioned itself as one of the safest cars in the market through a combination of its design and its advertising messages. When asked which car they thought was the safest, Volvo was consistently mentioned by customers though technical tests showed that it was not significantly safer than other brands in the market. This is the power of effective positioning: ensuring that your brand occupies a meaningful and distinct place in the target customer's mind.

Effective positioning created an interesting problem for Coca-Cola (see Exhibit 5.5). Though not exclusively marketed towards females, 80 per cent of Diet Coke sales are to women. Research by the company showed that men were also interested in a low-calorie drink but were reluctant to drink Diet Coke. So Coca-Cola Zero, which has been dubbed 'bloke Coke' was targeted at the male market using very male-orientated advertising. Though its ingredients are virtually indistinguishable from those of Diet Coke, its market appeal is very different.[35]

Exhibit 5.5 Diet Coke and Coke Zero: virtually identical drinks that are positioned very differently

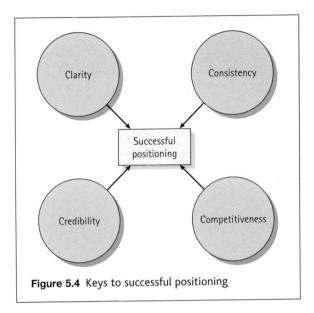

Figure 5.4 Keys to successful positioning

Positioning is both important and difficult. It is important because, today, we live in an over-communicated society.[36] Consumers are constantly exposed to advertising messages, some estimates put the number as high as 1000 messages per day. Add to this the volumes of information available through the print and broadcast media and the internet, and it is easy to see why consumers could suffer from information overload. To cut through this clutter, a company needs messages that are simple, direct and that resonate with the customer's needs. Failure to gain a position in the customer's mind significantly increases the likelihood of failure in the marketplace.

Developing a positioning strategy

Deciding what position to try to occupy in the market requires consideration of three variables, namely the customers, the competitors and the company itself. In terms of customers we must examine what attributes matter to them—there is little point in seeking a position that is unimportant from the customer's point of view. In many markets, competitors are already well entrenched, so the next challenge is to find some differential advantage that ideally cannot easily be matched. Third, as implied by the resource-based view of the firm, the company should look at building a position based on its unique attributes as this increases the likelihood that advantage can be sustained.[37]

Once the overall positioning strategy is agreed, the next step is to develop a positioning statement. A positioning statement is a memorable, image-enhancing, written summation of the product's desired stature. The statement can be evaluated using the criteria shown in Figure 5.4. Coca-Cola has become the world's most valuable brand through its effective exploitation of catchy positioning slogans like 'Things go better with Coke' in the 1960s and 'It's the real thing' in its 1970s advertising.

Figure 5.5 Some classic advertising slogans
Source: www.adslogans.co.uk

1   *Clarity*: the idea must be perfectly clear, both in terms of target market and differential advantage. Complicated positioning statements are unlikely to be remembered. Simple messages such as

'BMW—The Ultimate Driving Machine', 'Carlsberg—Probably the Best Lager in the World' and 'L'Oréal—Because I'm Worth it' are clear and memorable (see Figure 5.5).

2 *Consistency*: because people are bombarded with messages daily, a consistent message is required to break through this noise. Confusion will arise if, this year, we position on 'quality of service' and next year change this to 'superior product performance'. Some companies, like BMW, have used the same positioning—in BMW's case, 'The Ultimate Driving Machine'—for decades.

3 *Credibility*: the selected differential advantage must be credible in the minds of target customers. An attempt to position roll-your-own cigarette tobacco as an upmarket exclusive product failed due to lack of credibility. Similarly, Toyota's lack of credibility as an upmarket brand caused it to use 'Lexus' as the brand name for its top of the range cars.

4 *Competitiveness*: the chosen differential advantage must possess a competitive edge. It should offer something of value to the customer that the competition is failing to supply. For example, the success of the iPod was based on the differential advantage of seamless downloading of music from iTunes, Apple's dedicated music store, to a mobile player producing high quality sound.

The perceptual map is a useful tool for determining the position of a brand in the marketplace. It is a visual representation of consumer perceptions of a brand and its competitors, using attributes (dimensions) that are important to consumers. The key steps in producing a perceptual map are as follows.

1 Identify a set of competing brands.
2 Identify—using qualitative research (e.g. group discussions)—the important attributes consumers use when choosing between brands.
3 Conduct quantitative marketing research where consumers score each brand on all key attributes.
4 Plot brands on a two-dimensional map (or maps).

Figure 5.6 shows a perceptual map for seven supermarket chains. The results show that the supermarkets are grouped into two clusters: the high-price, wide product range group; and the low-price, narrow product range group. These are indicative of two market segments and show that supermarkets C and D are close rivals, as measured by consumers' perceptions, and have very distinct perceptual positions in the marketplace compared with E, F and G. Perceptual maps are useful in considering strategic moves. For example, an opportunity may exist to create a differential advantage based on a combina-

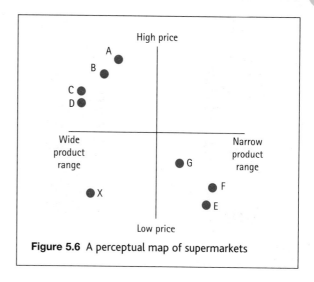

Figure 5.6 A perceptual map of supermarkets

tion of wide product range and low prices (as shown by the theoretical position at X).

Repositioning

Occasionally, perhaps because of changing customer tastes or poor sales performance, a product or service will need to be repositioned. **Repositioning** involves changing the target markets, the differential advantage or both (see Figure 5.7). The first option is to keep product and target market the same but to change the image of the product. For example, many companies marketing products to older customers are realizing that they need to be very careful in not portraying this group as kindly, slightly doddery souls when many remain reasonably healthy and active into old age. Therefore, the Complan brand of powdered energy drinks has changed its image from one of a caring, sickbed 'meal replacement' drink to a pro-active brand with a sense of humour, by using tongue-in-cheek cartoon characters on its packaging and in its advertising, engaged in lively activities like skateboarding and crowd surfing.[38] Similarly, Levi's is attempting to change the image of its famous 501 jeans from the 1950s retro-American made famous by the Nick Kamen launderette advertisement to something that is more relevant to today's youth culture, by employing ads shot in contemporary Los Angeles.[39] An alternative approach is to keep the same target market but to modify the product. For example, in the intensely competitive mass car market, Ford brands like the Mondeo have had a reputation for being dull, so Ford is investing heavily in trying to make its car designs more appealing to the consumer. A new design team was assembled and at the 2005 Frankfurt Motor Show, the new Ford Iosis was unveiled with a radical new design featuring

Product

	Same	Different
Same	Image repositioning	Product repositioning
Different	Intangible repositioning	Tangible repositioning

Target market

Figure 5.7 Alternative repositioning strategies

doors that opened upwards, a sharply sloping windscreen and large wheels.

Some repositioning strategies involve retaining the product but changing the market segment it is aimed at. Lucozade, a carbonated drink, is a famous example of this kind of so-called 'intangible repositioning'. Manufactured by Beecham's Foods, it was initially targeted at sick children. Marketing research found that mothers were drinking it as a midday pick-me-up and the brand was consequently repositioned to

aim at this new segment. Subsequently the energy-giving attributes of Lucozade have been used to appeal to a wider target market —young adults—by means of advertisements featuring leading athletes and soccer players. The history of Lucozade shows how a combination of repositioning strategies over time has been necessary for successful brand building. Several other brands have sought to repeat what Lucozade has done. For example, Rubex, the vitamin C drink, has transformed its positioning from a cold and flu drink to one that assists young people in overcoming the effects of a hard night's clubbing, while Red Bull has moved from a drink associated with clubbing to a more mainstream energy drink. Cadbury's has sought to reposition Roses and Flake into the rapidly growing premium chocolate segment, while Jose Cuervo spent US$65 million on a promotional campaign entitled 'Vive Cuervo' (Live Cuervo) to broaden the appeal of tequila, which has traditionally been associated with student parties.[40]

For a further example of intangible repositioning see Marketing in Action 5.4.

Marketing in Action 5.4: Repositioning cider

Study guide: Below is a review of the successful repositioning of Bulmers cider. Read it and think of other examples of brands that have been successfully or unsuccessfully repositioned.

One of the best examples of effective repositioning has been that achieved by the Irish cider brand Bulmers. Originally manufactured by Showerings and now owned by the C&C group, Bulmers has been the leading cider brand in Ireland. But, for many years, cider had an unenviable reputation. It was largely seen as the drink of young males, and was often consumed outdoors in public parks and urban areas. Irrespective of what drink was being drunk, 'cider parties' became the generic term to describe gatherings of young adults in public places, often engaged in anti-social behaviour, which gave the product very negative associations. At the same time, cider was a niche category of the beer market characterized by falling sales, low prices and low profitability.

While it might have been tempting to view the business as being in terminal decline and to exit it, Bulmers instead chose to try to reposition the brand and to increase its appeal to new market segments. Its repositioning objectives were to challenge existing perceptions of cider and to communicate Bulmers' values and benefits. Television was chosen as the primary medium to use to try to change attitudes. The main message that was being communicated was the tradition of cider making and a love of and respect for nature, which was encapsulated in the tag-lines 'nothing added but time' and 'time dedicated to you'. Sports programming was also heavily targeted, with a particular emphasis on sports like golf and rugby, where again there would not have been a tradition of cider advertising, which distinguished Bulmers from its competitors. The TV campaign was supported by press, radio, outdoor and sponsorship activity.

Changes in other elements of the marketing mix were also critical to the repositioning of cider. The two-litre plastic bottle or flagon, which was most associated with the negative image of cider, was discontinued and cans were introduced instead. And the company was also quick to seize on the innovation of the long-necked bottle, as used by Budweiser. In terms of pricing, cider was traditionally marketed at price points below stout, ale and lager. C&C has gradually raised the price of cider, first to the level of stout and then up to and just higher than that of lager, which has helped to give it a premium image.

The repositioning effort has been hugely successful. Bulmers' share of the beer and cider market in Ireland has grown from 2.8 per cent in the early 1990s to over 10 per cent today. In addition, the brand was successfully introduced into the UK in 2004, under the Magners label. Here, too, the image of cider had been negative, with the product seen as a cheap intoxicant sold primarily in shops and off-licences. But with strong visual advertising showing the product being made 'from apple orchard to glass', and sold primarily through pubs as a refreshing summer drink, its sales have grown dramatically. By 2006, it had claimed 16 per cent of the UK cider market.

Based on: Murray Brown (2005);[41] Shoesmith (2007)[42]

When both product and target market are changed, a company is said to be practising 'tangible repositioning'. For example, a company may decide to move up- or downmarket by introducing a new range of products to meet the needs of its new target customers. British Midland found it necessary to use both target and product repositioning in the face of growing competition in the airline business. The company was worried about its local British image and set about transforming itself into a global airline. It joined the Star alliance led by Lufthansa and United Airlines, and commenced a long-haul service to the USA. It also spent £15 million on a corporate rebranding initiative to change its name from British Midland to bmi to create a more international appeal.

The decision to reposition a brand should not be taken lightly as there are risks attached to this strategy. For example, in an effort to counteract stagnant sales in the mature men's magazine segment, titles such as *Esquire* and *Arena* repositioned themselves as 'lads' mags' (a market that had been growing rapidly), interspersing scantily clad models and drinking yarns with profiles of politicians. However, the strategy failed badly with lots of readers departing the magazines and not returning when the titles moved back to their original positioning. Sales of *Esquire* in 2003 were 30,000 units down from its peak of 100,000.[43]

Summary

This chapter has examined the key activities of market segmentation, market targeting and positioning. The following issues were addressed.

1. The process of market segmentation: not all consumers in the market have the same needs and we can serve them better by segmenting the market into groups with homogeneous needs.

2. The variety of bases available for segmenting both consumer and industrial markets, and often a combination of bases, are used to effectively segment markets. In consumer markets, behavioural variables such as benefits sought and purchase behaviour are particularly powerful bases for segmentation. Choice criteria is a key factor in segmenting organizational markets.

3. The five criteria for successful segmentation: effective, measurable, accessible, actionable and profitable.

4. The four generic target marketing strategies: undifferentiated marketing, differentiated marketing, focused marketing and customized marketing. Differentiated and focused marketing have their unique strengths and weaknesses, while customized marketing continues to grow in popularity.

5. What is meant by the concept of positioning, why it is important, and the need for clarity, consistency, credibility and competitiveness in a positioning statement. Consumers buy benefits, not products or services, and positioning is the key to conveying these benefits.

6. The concept of repositioning and the four repositioning strategies: image repositioning, product repositioning, intangible repositioning and tangible repositioning. Repositioning is challenging and should be undertaken with great care.

Key terms

benefit segmentation the grouping of people based on the different benefits they seek from a product

customized marketing a market coverage strategy where a company decides to target individual customers and to develop separate marketing mixes for each

differentiated marketing a market coverage strategy where a company decides to target several market segments and to develop separate marketing mixes for each

focused marketing a market coverage strategy where a company decides to target one market segment with a single marketing mix

geodemographics the process of grouping households into geographic clusters based on such information as type of accommodation, occupation, number and age of children, and ethnic background

lifestyle segmentation the grouping of people according to their pattern of living as expressed in their activities, interests and opinions

market segmentation the process of identifying individuals or organizations with similar characteristics that have significant implications for the determination of marketing strategy

mass customization the opposite to mass production, which means that all products produced are customized to the predetermined needs of a specific customer

positioning the choice of target market (*where* the company wishes to compete) and differential advantage (*how* the company wishes to compete)

profile segmentation the grouping of people in terms of profile variables such as age and socio-economic group so that marketers can communicate to them

psychographic segmentation the grouping of people according to their lifestyle and personality characteristics

repositioning changing the target market or differential advantage, or both

target marketing selecting a segment as the focus for a company's offering or communications

undifferentiated marketing a market coverage strategy where a company decides to ignore market segment differences and to develop a single marketing mix for the whole market

Study questions

1. Discuss the advantages of market segmentation.
2. You have been asked by a client company to segment the ice cream market. Use at least three different bases for segmentation and describe the segments that emerge.
3. Many consumer goods companies have recently been experimenting with the possibilities of a customized target marketing strategy. What are the advantages and limitations of such a strategy?
4. A friend of yours wants to launch a new breakfast cereal on the market but is unsure how to position the product. Develop a perceptual map of the breakfast cereal market identifying brands that compete in the same space and also if there are gaps where there are currently no major brands.
5. What is the difference between positioning and repositioning? Choose a brand that has been repositioned in the marketplace and describe both its old positioning and its new positioning. Is its repositioning strategy best described as image, product, intangible or tangible repositioning?

6. Visit www.adverteyes.biz/. Review some of the past positioning statements for your favourite brands. What are your views on the frequency with which some brands change their positioning statements?

Suggested reading

Pine, J.B. and **J.H. Gilmore** (2000) *Markets of One —Creating Customer-unique Value through Mass Customization*, Boston, MA: Harvard Business School Press.

Ries, A. and **J. Trout** (2001) *Positioning: The Battle for Your Mind*, New York: Warner.

Weinstein, A. (2006) A Strategic Framework for Defining and Segmenting Markets, *Journal of Strategic Marketing*, **14** (2), 115–27.

Yankelovich, D. and **D. Meer** (2006) Rediscovering Market Segmentation, *Harvard Business Review*, **84** (2), 122–31.

Zeithaml, V., **R. Rust** and **K. Lemon** (2001) The Customer Pyramid: Creating and Serving Profitable Customers, *California Management Review*, **43** (4), 118–42.

References

1. **Marsh, P.** (2007) A Recipe to Beat Low-Cost Rivals, *Financial Times*, February 12, 12.
2. **Mackintosh, J.** (2004) A Global Drive for the Affluent: Carmakers Seek New Markets for Their Luxury Brands, *Financial Times*, 3 December, 21.
3. **Van Raaij, W.F.** and **T.M.M. Verhallen** (1994) Domain-specific Market segmentation, *European Journal of Marketing*, **28** (10), 49–66.
4. **Foster, L.** (2004) The Plus-size Market Shapes Up, *Financial Times*, 10 December, 13.
5. **Fahy, J.** and **F. Taguchi** (1995) Reassessing the Japanese Distribution System, *Sloan Management Review*, **36** (2), 49–61.
6. **Lillington, K.** (2007) Skype's the Limit, *Irish Times Business*, 2 November, 7.
7. **Breen, J.** (2005) Hot Shots, *Irish Times Magazine*, 6 August, 28–9.
8. **Jennings, D.** (2007) *Net, Blogs and Rock'n'Roll*, London: Nicholas Brealey Publishing.
9. **Tynan, A.C.** and **J. Drayton** (1987) Market Segmentation, *Journal of Marketing Management*, **2** (3), 301–35.
10. **Yee, A.** (2005) Disney Woos Visitors Via the Web, *Financial Times*, 27 January, 30.
11. **Anonymous** (2007) The Boomers' Babies, *Economist*, 11 August, 60.
12. **Grimshaw, C.** (2003) The Entertainment Bandwagon, *Financial Times*, Creative Business, 22 July, 14.
13. **O'Dea, A.** (2007) Coming of Age, *Marketing Age*, Winter, 20–6.
14. **O'Brien, S.** and **R. Ford** (1988) Can We at Last Say Goodbye to Social Class?, *Journal of the Market Research Society*, **30** (3), 289–332.
15. **Anonymous** (2005) Conspicuous Non-consumption, *The Economist*, 8 January, 55–6.
16. **Garrett, A.** (1992) Stats, Lies and Stereotypes, *Observer*, 13 December, 26.
17. **Mitchell, V.W.** and **P.J. McGoldrick** (1994) The Role of Geodemographics in Segmenting and Targeting Consumer Markets: A Delphi Study, *European Journal of Marketing*, **28** (5), 54–72.
18. **Collins, J.** (2006) Lenovo Faces up to Rivals' Challenge, *Irish Times Business*, 5 May, 6.
19. **Dickie, M.** (2005) Lenovo Targets Small Business, *Financial Times*, 30 September, 33.
20. **Hamm, S.** (2008) Lenovo Thinks Beyond the ThinkPad, *Businessweek.com*, January 3.
21. **Corey, R.** (1978) *The Organisational Context of Industrial Buying Behaviour*, Cambridge, MA: Marketing Science Institute, 6–12.
22. **Carter, M.** (2003) O_2's Cultural Pitch for the Ethnic Pound, *Financial Times*, 3 July, 13.
23. **Anonymous** (2003) Outsider Who Plugged the Gap, *The Business*, 24 August, 13.
24. **Birchall, J.** (2007) Founder's Son Dons the Mantle at Gap After Chief's Departure, *Financial Times*, 24 January, 24.
25. **Collard, J.** (2004) How Gap Bounced Back, *Financial Times*, 21 February, 48.
26. **Gayatri, D.** and **T. Phani Madhav** (2004) Gap and Banana Republic: Changing Brand Strategies with Fashion, Case 504-087-1, *European Case Clearing House*.
27. **Manning-Schaffel, V.** (2002) Can Gap Mend its Brand?, *Brandchannel.com*, 1 April.
28. **Richards, H.** (1996) Discord Amid the High Notes, *The European*, 16–22 May, 23.
29. **Gapper, J.** (2005) When High Fidelity Becomes High Fashion, *Financial Times*, 20 December, 11.
30. **Bird, J.** (2003) A Switch to Safety in Numbers, *Financial Times*, 30 January, 11.
31. **Marsh, P.** (2004) Mass-produced for Individual Tastes, *Financial Times*, 22 April, 12.
32. **Westbrook R.** and **P. Williamson** (1993) Mass Customisation: Japan's New Frontier, *European Management Journal*, **11** (1), 38–45.
33. **Godin, S.** (1999) *Permission Marketing: Turn Strangers into Friends and Friends into Customers*, New York: Simon & Schuster.
34. **Peppers, D.** and **M. Rodgers** (1996) *The One to One Future*, New York: Doubleday.
35. **Madden, C.** (2007) Coca-Cola Zero: The Real Thing or the Same Thing?, *Irish Times*, 16 March, 12.
36. **Ries, A.** and **J. Trout** (2001) *Positioning: The Battle For Your Mind*, New York: Warner.

37. **Fahy, J.** (2001) *The Role of Resources in Global Competition*, London: Routledge.

38. **Dowdy, C.** (2005) Advertisers Smoke Out Images of Pipes and Slippers, *Financial Times*, 7 November, 30.

39. **Benady, A.** (2005) Levi's Looks to the Bottom Line, *Financial Times*, 15 February, 14.

40. **Silver, S.** (2003) Tequila Tries to Get Out of the Slammer, *Financial Times*, 22 May, 15.

41. **Murray Brown, J.** (2005) An Irish Cider Kicks its Image up the Field, *Financial Times*, 4 October, 14.

42. **Shoesmith, C.** (2007) Rival Cider Delivers New Blow to C&C, *Irish Times*, 25 August, 17.

43. **Grimshaw, C.** (2003) Let's Get Serious, *Financial Times*, Creative Business, 28 January, 12.

When you have read this chapter, log on to the Online Learning Centre for *Foundations of Marketing* at **www.mcgraw-hill.co.uk/textbooks/jobber**, where you'll find multiple-choice test questions, links and extra online study tools for marketing.

Case 5 The changing face of luxury fashion: Burberry, Beckham and Big Brother

Paradise for anybody wanting to stay *en vogue* is the Choice store at the Bluewater shopping centre in Kent, England. Emporio Armani, Vivienne Westwood, Prada, Paul Smith and Gucci are just a few of the many designer labels that are tempting shoppers to splash out on a new wardrobe. Being at the cutting edge of fashion comes at a price, but it seems that the advertising slogan 'Because I'm worth it' is not just appropriate for the cosmetics brand L'Oréal but for contemporary consumption culture in general. According to Ledbury Research, the global luxury goods market was worth £75 billion in 2006 and is booming, with annual sales growth in double figures. Strong demand in large emerging markets, including China, India and Russia, has become an important source of this growth. In the UK, the luxury goods market accounts for approximately 5 per cent of the world total. The changing face of luxury consumption in the UK is, however, representing a new generation of luxury consumers. Shoppers at the Bluewater Choice store resemble less the rich and famous but more the latte drinkers in a nearby Starbucks. The consumption of luxury today gives the impression of no longer being 'exclusive' but 'inclusive'. Today's luxury shopper could be a teacher, a banker or a plumber.

This movement towards luxury mass consumption has been referred to as the democratization of luxury. The changing economic and social fabric of British society in the last decade or so has helped to transform consumer attitudes and behaviour. First, increasing disposable incomes have given consumers the financial means to purchase luxury items. A larger number of consumers than ever before are able to afford luxury goods. The emergence of the affluent masses has evolved as a defining feature of contemporary luxury consumption. This phenomenon is also demonstrated by the increasing independence and spending power of professional women, which has helped revive the luxury fashion industry. A second factor can be referred to as the 'Beckham syndrome'. Celebrities such as David Beckham, a footballer with pop star status, have become important fashion and lifestyle icons, especially for younger people. Aspirational role models from the worlds of sport, music, fashion and entertainment are bringing luxury brands from the glossy pages of fashion magazines to the front pages of the popular press. The popular hip hop music scene has also helped to glorify designer brands. The rapper 50 Cent includes numerous references to

Gucci, Fendi, Prada, Moschino, Christian Dior and Chanel in the song 'I know what you like'. Finally, it has never been easier for consumers to access luxury fashion. Designer labels are no longer restricted to boutiques in exclusive settings but available in the high street, whether in Croydon, Hull or Plymouth. The internet has also lowered the barriers to entry for fashion designers to reach out to a broader audience. Customers can click to purchase luxury fashion brands at online designer boutiques (e.g. jimmychoo. com), department stores (e.g. harrods.com) or virtual fashion malls (e.g. designermall.co.uk).

Market segments

The luxury fashion market has traditionally been segmented according to two very separate and distinct customer groups—namely the 'affluents' and the 'non-affluents'. Those who could afford luxury fashion brands were targeted by slick advertising campaigns in quality newspapers or fashion magazines. Social grades, determined by the occupation of the chief income earner, were often used to identify these customers. The reality today is, however, that the luxury landscape has evolved and luxury consumption is no longer determined by the size of one's wallet or purse. Luxury consumers are members of a 'big tent' coalition encompassing all ages, income brackets, occupations and socio-economic standings. This means that marketers need to identify and understand the luxury consumer not based solely on demographics—luxury can mean different things to different people.

One alternative is therefore to segment the luxury fashion market based on consumer attitudes and potential buying habits. The following three sub-segments, or 'mindsets', were identified as being the most prominent in terms of high-yield returns within the luxury fashion industry. First, Fashion Traditionalists represent the conservative luxury consumer who values high levels of quality and service. Authenticity plays an important role in the decision-making process. Tradition luxury fashion brands with a strong heritage, such as Burberry, Jaeger and Austin, are preferred choices. Second, Fashion Leaders are trendsetters for whom image matters. Individualistic in nature, luxury brands reflect who they are and what image they wish to reflect to the outside world. They want to stay one step ahead of their peers and are more likely to buy brands that are based on style.

The third sub-segment is Fashion Followers, made up of self-stylists who are happy to mix and match clothes bought at high-street retailers such as Topshop, Mango or Zara with upmarket designer brands. They are also more likely to 'trade up'—that is, to spend more on selected items to meet their aspirational needs. Quality is not so important—it is more about appearance and fitting in with the latest trends.

The increasing mainstream or mass appeal of luxury fashion has important implications for the industry. A positive knock-on effect is the opportunity for luxury brands to attract a broader customer base and thereby increase sales. Fashion Teens, for example, is a high-growth segment with significant market potential. According to the market research firm NPD Group (www.npdgroup.com), designer labels account for approximately 15 per cent of purchases by 13–17-year-olds in the USA. Teens have become increasingly independent and confident as they start to experiment with luxury fashion. They adore shopping and worship brands. An important source of inspiration and information is fashion and lifestyle blogs and websites. Fashion Teens are luxury customers in their own right, and either have their own financial resources or the ability to influence their parents or guardians to subsidize the occasional extravagance.

Challenges for luxury fashion brands

However, the ubiquitous nature of luxury fashion can prove to be costly in the longer term. Despite anti-counterfeit legislation on a national and European level, the counterfeit industry continues to grow. Fake designs are costing the fashion industry tens of millions of pounds in lost sales, and risk diluting brand value. Consumers can pick up a fake Louis Vuitton bag at numerous street markets across the country or online at a bargain price. High-street retailers have also been targeted for copying designs. The designer Jimmy Choo forced the high-street chains New Look, Oasis and Marks & Spencer to withdraw products for alleged design infringements. Street credibility is paramount for Fashion Fakers. It doesn't matter if the designer brands are genuine or fake—it's the image that matters. It is sometimes difficult even to distinguish what is a fake and what is genuine. The development of so-called 'Big Brother' technology such as radio-frequency identification (RFID) tags could be one way to confirm product identification and thereby combat counterfeiting. However, changes in attitude have meant that counterfeit ownership has become increasingly socially acceptable. Britney Spears was even reported to be carrying a replica Chanel purse. According to the law firm Davenport Lyons (www.davenportlyons.com), almost two-thirds of UK consumers are proud to tell their family and friends that they have bought a fake luxury item.

The consumption of luxury today is prevalent and complex. There appears to be something for everyone. The dilemma for many luxury fashion brands is to be exclusive and authentic while appealing to a growing mainstream market. This is not an easy task given the increasingly competitive environment within the fashion sector. Mass retailers such as Zara and Topshop, and even the supermarket chain Tesco, are redefining how luxury fashion is presented— offering similar designs but at a significantly lower price. A growing number of internationally renowned designers are also collaborating with mass retailers. Karl Lagerfeld and Stella McCartney have designed collections for high-street chain H&M. Designs were sold out within hours as shoppers scrambled to get their hands on a bargain. However, the trend towards luxury fashion for the masses has resulted in greater fragmentation. The luxury market is no longer highly polarized between two extremes, namely prestige and mass marketing. The establishment of different levels of luxury, ranging from ultra luxury to affordable luxury, is a reflection of luxury's mass appeal. This may come as a relief to the *Luxe Ultras*—the epitome of luxury. Money is no obstacle and they acquire the most exclusive luxury fashion brands on offer. They search for brands that reflect their ultra-luxury status—willing to pay £10,000 for a HENK case. This gives luxury a truly new meaning. And, yet, internet auction sites have offers for similar designs at the fraction of the original price. Will luxury ever be the same?

Questions

1. Identify and describe the key market segments in the luxury fashion business.
2. To what extent does the teen segment represent a viable segment of the market?
3. What type of market targeting strategy has been pursued to date by luxury fashion brands? Does this strategy need to change?

This case was prepared by Glyn Atwal, ESC Rennes School of Business, France, from various published sources as a basis for classroom discussion rather than to show effective or ineffective management. The author would like to thank Ledbury Research for insights into the luxury industry.

Chapter 6
Brand and Product Management

Learning Outcomes

By the end of this chapter you will understand:

1 the differences between products and brands
2 the key aspects of building and managing a
  successful brand
3 how to manage a diverse product or brand portfolio
4 how product performance evolves over time
5 the importance of innovation and the new product
  development process
6 some of the ethical issues related to branding and
  product management.

Experiential marketing

Most brands operate in markets that can be described as mature. Growth rates in these markets are relatively modest, and competition is well established and intense. Therefore brands must work harder and harder to find ways to differentiate themselves and appeal to consumers that have limitations both in time and disposable income. Where traditionally many brands would have tried to connect with customers through major advertising campaigns, many are now complementing these with activities where the brand engages directly and in a real way with customers. This is what is known as 'experiential marketing'.

For example, one of the most popular forms of experiential marketing has been the increased association of brands with events like rock concerts and music festivals. This allows marketers to use relevant ways of communicating with audiences for such events, such as through online media and buzz marketing. In the early part of this decade, the Guinness brand was associated with the Witnness music festival in Ireland, where even the altered spelling of the word 'witness' highlighted the Guinness association. Pre-publicity for the event also featured a play on the idea of a witness. Consumers and the media joined in a search for clues and were invited to participate in the discovery of Witnness. This generated huge publicity about the event and the various acts that would be performing there. Because the target audience was considered to be marketing literate and cynical with regard to corporate marketing efforts, this approach was more subtle and gave consumers a feeling of ownership and involvement with the event.

Experiential marketing has also become very popular within the retail trade as stores and locations seek to find new ways of appealing to potential customers. The focus has moved from being a venue where products are sold to one where consumers can have a shopping experience or where they can shop as part of other activities. Many major shopping malls now have cinemas attached, others have leisure facilities such as gymnasiums and swimming pools, and some have theatres and galleries. Luxury store Prada, New York, has a cultural performance space, Louis Vuitton's Paris flagship store has an art gallery and a bookstore, while Gucci's Ginza store in Tokyo also has an art gallery as well as an event space. Nespresso has opened a number of Nespresso Boutiques to create the 'ultimate coffee experience'.

The ideal **experiential marketing** effort is an ownable, sensory brand experience that makes customers feel like the product or service is theirs. These motivated customers then become product advocates, who influence family, friends and co-workers to try the product. For example, Delta Airlines has developed its SKY360 lounge in New York to create a customer experience. Visitors to the lounge are met by actual flight attendants and ticket agents. They sample food items available on Delta and are asked to try new entertainment systems that are built into the backs of seats. The lounge has WiFi connections and computer terminals for anyone who wants to book a flight with Delta. Creating an experience around a brand is likely to be one of the key ways in which companies will seek to differentiate themselves in the future.[1]

As we saw in Chapter 1, the essence of marketing is the delivery of value to some customer group. Products and brands are often the embodiment of that value proposition. For example, Kodak may well manufacture film but it understands that its business is allowing its customers to collect and retain memories. That's just as well because film technology is rapidly being replaced by digital technology and by consumers collecting and sharing memories via mobile phones, CDs or online. Old 'technologies' like 35 mm film and paper printing are quickly becoming outdated, with up to 30 per cent of digital camera owners never printing their pictures. Kodak has responded by phasing out its declining film-based business, involving 26,000 job cuts, and shifting its focus to digital photography and online file sharing through Kodak Easyshare Gallery.[2] But, with the pace of consumer and technological change being even faster than Kodak anticipated, its share price has been hit and the value of the Kodak brand, once one of the highest in the world, fell to number 82 in the top 100 in 2007.

This chapter will deal with all these issues. First, we will examine the difference between a product and a brand, which is one of the most important distinctions that students of marketing must grasp. Then we will take a comprehensive look at the different aspects of managing modern brands. Many firms, such as global corporations like Diageo or Colgate, can have an extensive range of brands, so we will also examine how to manage these portfolios of brands or products. As the Kodak example shows, the demand for products can change very rapidly, so we will look, too, at how to manage products and brands effectively over time. An important element of this is innovation and ensuring a steady supply of new products, which is also discussed. Finally, the chapter closes with an introduction to some additional issues involved in managing products.

Products vs brands

A product can be anything that has the capacity to satisfy customer needs. In everyday speech we often distinguish between products and services, with products being tangible (e.g. a car) and services mainly intangible (e.g. a medical examination). When we look at what the customer is buying, it is essentially a benefit, whether the means are tangible or intangible. For example, a car provides the benefit of transportation; the medical examination provides the benefit of a health check. Consequently, it is logical to include services within the definition of the product. Hence, there are physical products such as a watch, car or gas turbine, and service products such as medical services, insurance or banking. All of these provide benefits to customers—for example, a gas turbine provides power, and insurance reduces financial risk. The principles discussed in this chapter apply equally to physical and service products. However, because there are special considerations associated with service products (e.g. intangibility) and as service industries (e.g. tourism, consulting) form an important and growing sector, the next chapter is dedicated to services marketing in detail.

Branding is the process by which companies distinguish their product offerings from the competition (see Exhibit 6.1). The word 'brand' is derived from the old Norse word 'brandr', which means 'to burn'

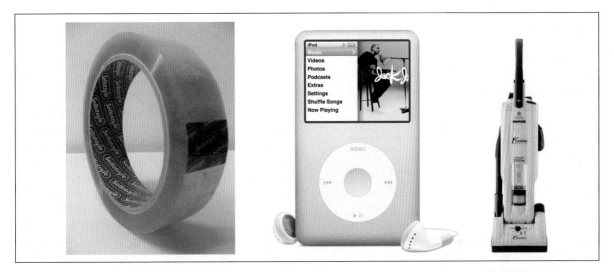

Exhibit 6.1 There are many different brands of adhesives, MP3 players and vacuum cleaners, but Sellotape, iPod and Hoover have been so successful that they have come to be associated with these product categories—they are what are known as **generic brands**

as brands were and still are the means by which livestock owners mark their animals to identify ownership.[3] Building and maintaining a brand is one of the critical tasks of the marketing manager. We now live in a world where the technical differences between products are becoming fewer and fewer. For example, Volkswagen cars share a similar platform with Skoda, Seat and Audi. In most cases, consumers will not know (and often will not care) where the products are made. What will determine which company's product is purchased will be how consumers feel about the **brand**. Branding permits customers to develop associations (e.g. prestige, status, economy) and eases the purchase decision.[4] The power of brands to affect perceptions is particularly noticeable in blind product testing, where customers often fail to distinguish between competing offerings even though they may have a high level of loyalty to one brand.

For some time now it has been conventional for marketers to think in terms of different levels of product (see Figure 6.1). At the most basic level, there is the core benefit provided by the product, such as cars that provide transportation or telephones that provide a means of communication. Understanding the core benefits provided by products is important in terms of identifying potential sources of competition. For example, sales of paper diaries manufactured by

companies like Filofax have fallen because the same benefit is delivered, arguably more effectively, through handheld devices like BlackBerrys and the diaries available on personal computers. Similarly, the popularity of MP3 players is having a significant effect on the demand for music CDs. Around the basic benefit is the 'actual product' the consumer purchases, which comprises certain features, styling, and so on, which go to make up the brand. For example, a Nokia mobile phone is an actual product, which is a blend of design, style, features and packaging assembled to meet the needs of the market. There is also a third level of product, namely the 'augmented product'. This is the additional bundle of benefits that are added to a product, and typically include elements like guarantees, additional services, additional **brand values** and the types of product-related experience discussed at the start of this chapter. For example, the new Lexus GS includes extras like a keyless entry system, air-conditioned front seats, Bluetooth connectivity for mobile phones, parking-assist sensors and a rear electric sunshade.

Viewing a product in terms of these three levels is very important in helping to make product management decisions. In order to differentiate their brands in a crowded and competitive marketplace, companies are always looking for new ways to augment their

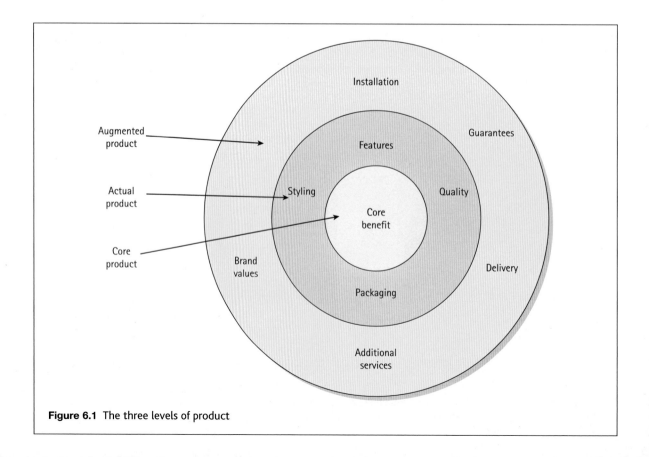

Figure 6.1 The three levels of product

product and add additional values to it. On the other hand, it is quite interesting that, for example, the low-fares airlines like Ryanair and easyJet have gone in the opposite direction. Instead of looking at ways to augment their product, these companies have stripped away aspects of the actual and augmented product and focused heavily on the core benefit: transportation at a low price. In their view, aspects of the actual and augmented product did not deliver valuable benefits to consumers and there was merit in going back to the core benefit of moving people from A to B. This shift in strategic thinking has revolutionized air travel and low-fares airlines are now growing faster and are significantly more profitable than traditional airlines.

Branding

Developing a brand is difficult, expensive and takes time. We have seen that brands enable companies to differentiate their products from competitive offerings, but we must look at the benefits of brands in more detail.

The benefits of brands

Strong brands deliver the following benefits to companies.

Company value

The financial value of companies can be greatly enhanced by the possession of strong brands. For example, Nestlé paid £2.5 billion (€3.6 billion) for Rowntree, a UK confectionery manufacturer—a sum six times its balance sheet value. However, the acquisition gave Nestlé access to Rowntree's stable of brands, including KitKat, Quality Street, After Eight and Polo.

Consumer preference and loyalty

Strong brand names can have positive effects on consumer perceptions and preferences. This in turn leads to brand loyalty where satisfied customers continue to purchase a favoured brand. Over time some brands, such as Apple, Harley-Davidson and Virgin, become cult brands: consumers become passionate about the brand and levels of loyalty go beyond reason[5] (see Marketing in Action 6.1). The strength of brand loyalty can be seen when companies try to change brands, such as Coca-Cola's proposed introduction of New Coke, or when the brand is threatened with extinction such as Bewley's Cafés in Dublin.[6]

Barrier to competition

The impact of the strong, positive perceptions held by consumers about top brands means it is difficult

Marketing in Action 6.1: Brand communities

Study guide: Below is a review of the development of brand communities. Read it and consider whether you are a member of any brand community.

The relationship between consumers and brands is a complex one, but what is increasingly becoming evident is the emergence of brand communities: groups of people tied together by their admiration for certain brands. A brand community has been formally defined as a 'specialized, non-geographically bound community based on a structured set of relationships among admirers of a brand'. Others take a broader view and also include motivated employees, strategic partners and investors who are committed to a brand.

What is interesting is that brand communities take on all the major trappings of social communities. First, there is a shared consciousness, which is the intrinsic connection that members feel to one another, and their collective sense of difference from others not in the community. Second, there are the shared rituals and traditions that perpetuate the community's values. The third indicator of community is a sense of moral responsibility or obligation to the community as a whole and to its individual members.

These traits can be found in the behaviour of people, including customers, of cult or iconic brands such as Harley-Davidson. Harley is a 106-year-old brand that still ranks in the global top 50 brands in terms of value. The Harley Owners Group—initially set up to counter the damage to the company's image caused by an association with Hell's Angels—consists of 866,000 members who organize bike rides, training courses, social events and charity fundraisers. They pore over motorcycle magazines and wear Harley-branded gear to feel like rugged individualists. Over 250,000 attended the brand's centenary, held in Milwaukee in 2003.

Many other brands are rapidly reaching similar iconic status—for example, Absolut, Amazon, Apple, Ben & Jerry's, IKEA, Lexus, Singapore Airlines, Tiffany's, and so on. Brand communities are likely to form around any brand, but are most likely where brands have a strong image, a rich and lengthy history, threatening competition and are publicly consumed. The growth of the internet has helped to foster brand communities by providing a medium where information about the brand can be gathered and where exchanges between community members on a global basis are facilitated. Many leading brands, such as CNN and Disney, host online communities through bulletin boards, forums and chatrooms. Heineken allows individuals to establish their own virtual bars where, as bartender, they can chat to other visitors and meet their friends.

Based on: McWilliam (2000);[7] Muniz and O'Guinn (2001);[8] Upshaw and Taylor (2001)[9]

for new brands to compete. Even if the new brand performs well on blind taste tests, this may be insufficient to knock the market leader off the top spot. This may be one of the reasons that Virgin Coke failed to dent Coca-Cola's domination of the cola market.

High profits

Strong, market-leading brands are rarely the cheapest. Brands such as, Kellogg's, Coca-Cola, Mercedes, Nokia and Microsoft are all associated with premium prices. This is because their superior brand equity means that consumers receive added value over their less powerful rivals. Strong brands also achieve distribution more readily and are in a better position to resist retailer demands for price discounts. Research into return on investment for US food brands supports the view that strong brands are more profitable. The number one brand's average return was 18 per cent, number two achieved 6 per cent, number three returned 1 per cent, while the number four position was associated with a minus 6 per cent average return on investment.[10]

Base for brand extensions

A strong brand provides a foundation for leveraging positive perceptions and goodwill from the core brand to brand extensions. Examples include Pepsi Max, Lucozade Sport, Smirnoff Ice and Microsoft Internet Explorer. The new brand benefits from the added value that the brand equity of the core brand bestows on the extension.

Consumers as well as companies benefit from brands. The buying decision is simplified because consumers can select brands that they are familiar with or have a preference for. Much of the time, this comes down to the extent to which the consumer trusts the brand.

Some of the most trusted brands in Europe include Nokia, Visa, Nivea and Sony.

Brands are now everywhere. Supermarket shelves carry thousands of them, distributors are no longer resellers of other people's brands, but have become brands in their own right, and celebrities have become very tuned in to the importance of creating a brand. Ethical Debate 6.1 examines the implications of these developments.

Building brands

Building brands involves making decisions about the brand name and how the brand is developed and positioned in the marketplace.

Naming brands

Three brand name strategies can be identified: family, individual and combination.

A **family brand name** is used for all products—for example, Philips, Heinz and Google. The goodwill attached to the family brand name benefits all brands, and the use of the name in advertising helps the promotion of all of the brands carrying the family name. The risk is that if one of the brands receives unfavourable publicity or is unsuccessful the reputation of the whole range of brands can be tarnished. This is also known as 'umbrella branding'. Some companies create umbrella brands for part of their brand portfolios to give coherence to their range of products. For example, Sony has created PlayStation for its range of video game consoles.

The **individual brand name** does not identify a brand with a particular company—for example,

Ethical Debate 6.1: Brand values and the value of a brand

Brands are at the heart of what marketing is about. Whether it is a piece of technology, a sports star or a soft drink, they all can benefit from adopting the principles of branding. In a competitive marketplace, brands differentiate one offering from another and assist consumers with making decisions.

But inherent in the notion of a brand is the concept of value. When a consumer chooses a certain brand, they are doing so on the basis that a given brand delivers a certain level of value. But how accurate is this perception? For example, when a consumer buys a leading brand of running shoe, is she buying a higher level of value than if she bought a lesser-known brand or a cheaper running shoe? Consumers who are brand loyal would typically argue that a leading brand equates with better quality, but the research evidence does not always support this position. For example, a study published in the *British Journal of Sports Medicine* in 2007 showed that low- to medium-cost running shoes in each of three brands provided the same (if not better) cushioning of in-shoe pressure than high-cost running shoes.[11] A high-price brand, in this case, does not equate to greater levels of value as measured by product quality.

Critics of branding argue that brands do not provide value but rather an illusion of value. Vast sums are spent creating brands that are essentially not really all that different. Consumers pay more for leading brands in the belief that these are superior to other brands in terms of quality and specifications, when often this is not the case. A way out of this dilemma is to fully understand what we mean by consumer value. As shown in Chapter 3, consumers choose products for rational as well as emotional reasons. Brands are selected not only for their technical attributes but also for personal and social reasons. Should a consumer not have the option to select a brand if that brand, for example, makes them feel good about themselves or gives them the feeling that they are impressing their peers? Consumer societies are about choice and, increasingly, consumers have the information that they need to make informed choices. But, despite this, the debate concerning the real value of brands is likely to continue to rage into the future.

Suggested reading: Adamson (2006);[12] Klein (2000)[13]

Procter & Gamble does not use its company name on its brands—Duracell, Head & Shoulders, Pampers, Pringles, and so on (we will look at this later, in Table 6.5). This may be necessary when it is believed that each brand requires a separate, unrelated identity. In some instances, the use of a family brand name when moving into a new market segment may harm the image of the new **product line**. One famous example is the decision to use the Levi's family brand name on a new product line—Levi's Tailored Classics—despite marketing research information which showed that target customers associated the name Levi's with casual clothes, thus making it incompatible with the smart suits the company was launching. This mistake was not repeated by Toyota, which abandoned its family brand name when it launched its upmarket executive car, simply called the Lexus.

In the case of combination brand names, family and individual brand names are combined, this capitalizes on the reputation of the company while allowing the individual brands to be distinguished and identified (e.g. Kellogg's All Bran, Nokia N70, Microsoft Windows XP).

Much careful thought should be given to the choice of brand name since names convey images. For example, Renault chose the brand name Safrane for one of its executive saloons because research showed that this brand name conveyed an image of luxury, exotica, high technology and style. The brand name Pepsi Max was chosen for the diet cola from Pepsi targeted at men as it conveyed a masculine image in a product category that was associated with women. So one criterion for deciding on a good brand name is that it evokes positive associations.

Brand names are equally important in the context of industrial and technological products. Good brands give industrial manufacturers the opportunity to compete on bases other than price, which is becoming increasingly important due to low-cost competition from countries like China. One recent study found that the most valuable industrial brands in the world were 3M (industrial products), Tyco (industrial products), Honeywell (industrial products), Caterpillar (construction machines), United Technologies (lifts, air conditioners), Emerson (motors, control systems) and Ingersoll-Rand (industrial products).[14] The value of a good brand name can be seen in the prices paid for some of the top domain names in the world, such as diamond.com (US$7.5 million), vodka.com (US$3 million) and cameras.com (US$1.5 million).[15]

Another important criterion is that the brand name should be memorable and easy to pronounce. Short names such as Esso, Shell, Daz, Ariel, Novon and Mini fall into this category. For example UBS, Europe's third largest bank, has dropped its family names UBS Warburg and UBS PaineWebber in favour of the simple UBS name. There are exceptions to this general rule, as in the case of Häagen-Dazs, which was designed to sound European in the USA where it was first launched. A brand name may suggest product benefits—as in the case of Right Guard (deodorant), Alpine Glade (air and fabric freshener), Head & Shoulders (anti-dandruff shampoo), Compaq (portable computer)—or express what the brand is offering in a distinctive way, such as Toys 'R' Us. Technological products may benefit from numerical brand naming (e.g. Audi A4, Airbus A380, Yamaha YZF R125). This also overcomes the need to change brand names when marketing in different countries.

Some specialist companies have been established to act as brand name consultants. Market research is used to test associations, memorability, pronunciation and preferences. It is important to seek legal advice to ensure that a brand name does not infringe an existing brand name. Interesting controversies can arise relating to brand names and trademarks such as Victoria Beckham's efforts to stop Peterborough United Football Club trademarking their decades-old nickname 'Posh'. More controversially, some companies are also trying to obtain the legal rights to slogans—such as Nestlé for the KitKat slogan 'Have a Break'. Table 6.1 summarizes those issues that are important when choosing a brand name, while Table 6.2 shows how brand names can be categorized.

Developing brands

A brand is created by means of the augmentation of a core product to add brand values. The core product offers core benefits (see Figure 6.1). Crisps are a satisfying snack, but all crisps can achieve that benefit.

Table 6.1 Brand name considerations

A good brand name should:
1 evoke positive associations
2 be easy to pronounce and remember
3 suggest product benefits
4 be distinctive
5 use numerals when emphasizing technology
6 not infringe an existing registered brand name

Table 6.2 Brand name categories

People:	Cadbury, Mars, Heinz
Places:	Singapore Airlines, Deutsche Bank
Descriptive:	I Can't Believe It's Not Butter, the Body Shop, T-mobile
Abstract:	KitKat, Kodak, Prozac
Evocative:	Egg, Orange
Brand extensions:	Dove Deodorant, Virgin Direct, Playtex Affinity
Foreign meanings:	LEGO (from 'play well' in Danish), Thermos (meaning 'heat' in Greek)

Source: adapted from Miller, R. (1999) Science Joins Art in Brand Naming, *Marketing*, 27 May, 31–2.

Branding allows marketers to create added values that distinguish one brand from another. This is sharply illustrated by the contrasting fortunes of Golden Wonder and Walkers. Golden Wonder was founded in 1947 and invented flavoured crisps in 1962. But despite its popularity with generations of Britons, years of falling sales saw the company placed in administration in 2006.[16] In contrast, Walkers has created a sense of fun around its products, as well as emphasizing product quality through the use of celebrity endorsers like Gary Lineker in its advertising (see Marketing in Action 1.3) and has gone on to dominate the crisps business in the UK. Successful brands are those that create a set of brand values that are superior to those of other, rival, brands. So brand building involves a deep understanding of both the functional (e.g. ease of use) and emotional (e.g. confidence) values that customers use when choosing between brands, and the ability to combine them in a unique way to create an augmented product that customers will prefer.

Building successful brands is an extremely challenging marketing task. In fact, of Britain's top 50 brands, only 18 per cent have been developed since 1975.[17] This also implies that when a brand becomes established, it tends to endure for a very long time.

Table 6.3 The top 20 most valuable brands worldwide

	Company	2008 brand value (US$ billions)	Country of origin	% change from 2007
1	Google	86.06	USA	30
2	General Electric	71.38	USA	15
3	Microsoft	70.89	USA	29
4	Coca-Cola	58.21	USA	17
5	China Mobile	57.23	China	39
6	IBM	55.34	USA	65
7	Apple	55.21	USA	123
8	McDonald's	49.50	USA	49
9	Nokia	43.96	Finland	39
10	Marlboro	37.32	USA	−5
11	Vodafone	36.96	UK	75
12	Toyota	35.13	Japan	5
13	Wal-Mart	34.55	USA	−6
14	Bank of America	33.09	USA	15
15	Citigroup	30.32	USA	−10
16	Hewlett-Packard	29.29	USA	17
17	BMW	28.01	Germany	9
18	ICBC	28.00	Canada	70
19	Louis Vuitton	25.74	France	14
20	American Express	24.82	USA	7

Source: Brandz Top 100

Table 6.3 lists the world's leading brands, some of which are over 100 years old, so we can see that brand building is a long-term activity. There are many demands on people's attention; generating awareness, communicating brand values and building customer loyalty usually takes many years, which is why the rapid rise to prominence of brands like Amazon and Google is so admirable. Similarly, the Korean company Samsung has moved from being seen as a company that produced cheap television and microwave ovens to a leading global, premium brand in sectors like mobile phones, memory chips and flat panels. This was achieved through doubling its marketing spend to US$3 billion, advertising that showed the company's prowess in technology, product placement in futuristic films like *Matrix Reloaded* and sponsorship of the Athens Olympics, which increased general awareness of the brand.[18] The value of the Samsung brand is now greater than that of the once dominant Sony. League tables like those presented in Table 6.3 are also illustrative in charting the demise of once venerable brands like Ford, Gap, Kodak, Pizza Hut and Motorola, all of whose value fell by between 10 and 20 per cent between 2006 and 2007.

Management must be prepared to provide a consistently high level of brand investment to establish and maintain the position of a brand in the marketplace. Unfortunately, it can be tempting to cut back on expenditure in the short term, particularly when there is a downturn in the economy. Such cutbacks need to be resisted in order for the brand to be supported, as it is one of the key drivers of shareholder value.[19]

Figure 6.2 is an analytical framework that can be used to dissect the current position of a brand in the marketplace, and to form the basis of a new brand positioning strategy. The strength of a brand's position in the marketplace is built on six elements: brand domain, brand heritage, brand values, brand assets, brand personality and brand reflection. The first of these, brand domain, corresponds to the choice of target market (where the brand competes); the other five elements provide avenues for creating a clear differential advantage with these target consumers. These elements are expanded on briefly below.

1   *Brand domain*: the brand's target market, i.e. where it competes in the marketplace.

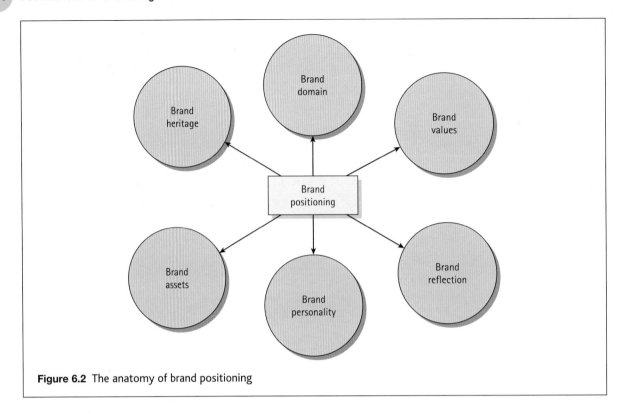

Figure 6.2 The anatomy of brand positioning

2 *Brand heritage*: the background to the brand and its culture. How it has achieved success (and failure) over its life. For example, English wines like Chapel Down have been successful despite the country's lack of a wine heritage.

3 *Brand value*: the core values and characteristics of the brand.

4 *Brand assets*: what makes the brand distinctive from other competing brands (symbols, features, images and relationships, etc.).

5 *Brand personality*: the character of the brand described in terms of other entities, such as people, animals or objects. Celebrity endorsement of brands gives them personality. Sales of Kia Kaha, a small New Zealand-based company, were significantly boosted when Michael Campbell won the US Open golf tournament wearing its clothing.[20]

6 *Brand reflection*: how the brand relates to self-identity; how the customer perceives him/herself as a result of buying/using the brand.

Brand managers can form an accurate portrait of how brands are positioned in the marketplace by analysing each of the elements listed above. Brand building is expensive and great care needs to be taken with brand investment decisions. For example, Unilever spent over £7 million on just redesigning its logo to make it more 'open and friendly'. The new logo combines the sun ('the ultimate symbol of vitality'), a bird ('a symbol of freedom') and a shirt ('representing fresh laundry and looking good').[21]

Brand management issues

Finally, firms may face a number of issues with respect to the management of brands. We will turn to these now.

Manufacturer brands versus own-label brands

Manufacturer brands are created by producers and bear their own chosen brand names. The responsibility for marketing the brand lies in the hands of the producer. Examples include Kellogg's Cornflakes, Gillette Sensor razors and Ariel washing powder. The value of the brand lies with the producer and, by building major brands, producers can gain distribution and customer loyalty.

Own-label brands (sometimes called distributor brands) are created and owned by distributors. Sometimes the entire **product mix** of a distributor may be own-label, as was the case for some time with

Table 6.4 The growing share of own-label globally

Product area	Own-label share (%)	Own-label growth (%)	Price differential vs manufacturer's brand (%)
Refrigerated food	32	9	−16
Paper, plastic and wraps	31	2	−24
Frozen food	25	3	−20
Pet food	21	11	−42
Shelf stable food	19	5	−27
Nappies and feminine hygiene	14	−1	−34
Healthcare	14	3	−37
Non-alcoholic beverages	12	3	−32
Home care	10	2	−36

Source: ACNielsen (2005) 'The Power of Private Label 2005' report

Marks & Spencer's St Michael brand, or only part of the mix may be own-label, as is the case with many supermarket chains. In many developed economies, sales of own-label products are growing at a faster rate than manufacturer brands (see Table 6.4). Own-label branding, if associated with the tight quality control of suppliers, can provide consistent high value for customers, and be a source of retail power as own-label brands compete effectively with **manufacturer brands**. Hard discounters such as Aldi and Lidl, which sell primarily own-label brands, control 15 per cent of the European retailing market. The power of low-price supermarket **own-label brands** has focused many producers of manufacturer brands on introducing so-called fighter brands (i.e. their own low-price alternatives). For example, in 2006, Unilever expanded its range of value brands to include ice cream and bouillon, and sold its frozen foods division (a sector where own-label brands are very strong).[22]

A major decision that producers have to face is whether to agree to supply own-label products for distributors The danger is that should customers find out about this, they may believe that there is no difference between the manufacturer brand and its cheaper own-label equivalent. For other producers, supplying own-label goods may be a means of filling excess capacity and generating extra income from the high sales volumes contracted with distributors.

Brand extension and stretching

Tangible value is added to a company by the goodwill associated with a respected brand name, and through the higher sales and profits that result. This higher financial value is called brand equity. Brand names with high **brand equity** are candidates to be used on other new brands since their presence has the potential to enhance their attractiveness. A **brand extension** is the use of an established brand name on a new brand within the same broad market. For example, the Anadin brand name has been extended to related brands: Anadin Extra, Ultra, Soluble, Paracetamol and Ibuprofen (see Exhibit 6.2). Unilever has successfully expanded its Dove soap brand into deodorants, shower gel, liquid soap and bodywash.[23] **Brand stretching** is when an established brand name is used for brands in unrelated markets. A popular trend at present is where celebrities extend their brand into a variety of product categories, such as Jennifer Lopez who markets jlo clothes, sunglasses, swimwear, fragrances, accessories and lingerie.

Some companies have been very successful in their employment of brand extensions and stretching; Richard Branson's Virgin company is a classic example. Beginning in 1970 as Virgin Records the company grew through Virgin Music (music publishing), Megastores (music retailing), Radio, Vodka, Cola, Atlantic Airways (long-haul routes), Express (short-haul routes), Rail, Direct (direct marketing of financial services) and One (one-stop banking) to now encompass over 200 businesses. Most recently, Virgin has expanded into healthcare through the opening of its chain of Virgin Active healthcare centres. Other famous companies have been less successful. For example, the McCafe has been a successful extension of the McDonald's brand in

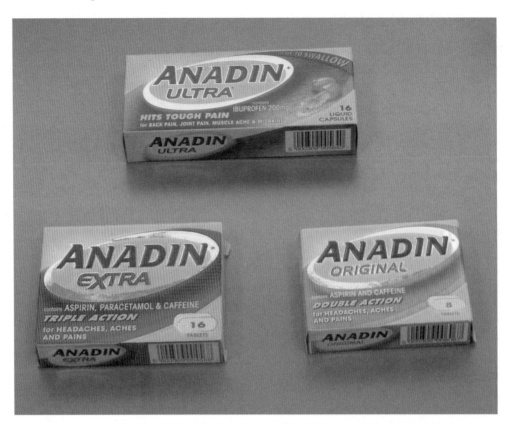

Exhibit 6.2 Anadin has successfully extended its core brand to appeal to different market segments

the USA, but McDonald's Switzerland created the McDonald's train and McDonald's airplane for family holidays, as well as the McDonald's business-class hotel, the Golden Arch. However, these proved to be unprofitable.[24]

The use of the brand extension is an important marketing tool. A study by ACNielsen showed that brand extensions account for approximately 40 per cent of new grocery launches.[25] Two key advantages of brand extension in releasing new products are that it reduces risk and is less costly than alternative launch strategies.[26] Both distributors and consumers may perceive less risk if the new brand comes with an established brand name. Distributors may be reassured about the saleability of the new brand and therefore be more willing to stock it. Consumers appear to attribute the quality associations they have of the original brand to the new one.[27] Launch costs can also be reduced by using brand extension. Since the established brand name is already well known, the task of building awareness of the new brand is eased. Consequently, advertising, selling and promotional costs are reduced. Furthermore, there is the likelihood of achieving advertising economies of scale since advertisements for the original brand and its extensions reinforce each other.[28]

These arguments can, however, be pushed too far. Brand extensions that offer no functional, psychological or price advantage over rival brands often fail.[29] There is also a danger that marketing management will underfund the launch, believing that the spin-off effects of the original brand name will compensate. This can lead to low awareness and trial. 'Cannibalization', which refers to a situation where the new brand gains sales at the expense of the established brand, can also occur. Anadin Extra, for example, could cannibalize the sales of the original Anadin brand. There is also the danger that bad publicity for one brand can affect the reputation of other brands under the same name. The Virgin brand name was in danger of being tarnished at one time because of poor punctuality of its trains. Massive investment in new rolling stock and locomotives has cured the problem.[30]

If a brand name is extended too far there can be a loss of credibility, and this is something that management needs to guard against. This is particularly relevant when using brand stretching. Virgin's extension into rail services has been unsuccessful, while the use of the Pierre Cardin name for such disparate products as clothing, toiletries and cosmetics, for example, diluted the brand name's credibility.[31] Brand extensions are likely to be successful if they make sense to the consumer. If the values and aspirations of the new target segment(s) match those of the original segment, and the qualities of the brand name are likewise highly prized then success is likely.

Pan-European and global branding

The expanding economic union in Europe and the growing globalization of business has created an interest in the prospects for pan-European and **global branding** respectively. A pan-European brand is one that has successfully penetrated the European market, while a global brand is one that has achieved global penetration levels. In Europe, the promise of pan-European branding has caused leading manufacturers to seek to extend their market coverage and to build their portfolio of brands. Nestlé has widened its brand portfolio by the acquisition of such companies as Rowntree (confectionery) and Buitoni-Perugina (pasta and chocolate). Mars has replaced its Treets and Bonitos brands with M&M's, and changed the name of its third-largest UK brand, Marathon, to Snickers, the name that is used in the rest of Europe. Many other brands, such as Toyota, Amazon, Coca-Cola, BMW and Nokia, are global successes.

Pan-European and global brands have a number of advantages. The most important of these is that they can attain tremendous economies of scale. Gillette's global success with its Sensor razor was based on a highly standardized approach: the product, brand name, the message ('The Best a Man Can Get'), advertising visuals and packaging were all standardized; only the voiceovers in the advertisements were changed to cater for 26 languages across Europe, the USA and Japan. Using the same advertising approach throughout the world saved the company approximately US$20 million.[32] The uniform image of many global brands is reassuring to consumers. For example, McDonald's customers know what to expect irrespective of where in the world they visit a McDonald's. Being globally scaled also means that many companies become the preferred provider. For example, consulting companies like Pricewaterhouse-Coopers may be attractive to potential clients because of their ability to offer a worldwide service.

However, while many brands seek pan-European or global status, national differences make it difficult to implement a standardized branding strategy across countries. For example, the fact that the French eat four times more yoghurt than the British, and the British buy eight times more chocolate than the

Italians reflects the kinds of national differences that will affect the marketing strategies of manufacturers.[33] The question is not whether brands can be built on a global scale (clearly they can), but which parts of the brand can be standardized and which must be varied across countries. For example, Unilever found that for detergent products, brand image and packaging could be standardized but the brand name, communications execution and brand formulation needed to vary across countries.[34] For its fabric conditioner it used the image of a cuddly teddy bear across countries, but the product was named differently in Germany (Kuschelweich), France (Cajoline), Italy (Coccolini), Spain (Mimosin), the USA (Snuggle) and Japan (Fa-Fa). Brand image and packaging were the same but the name and formulation (fragrance, phosphate levels and additives) differed between countries. The global/local dilemma is one that is regularly faced by many of the world's largest multinationals, as shown in Marketing in Action 6.2.

Co-branding

A popular strategy for some companies today is co-branding where two brands are combined. This may take the form of **product-based co-branding** or **communications-based co-branding**. Product-based co-branding involves the linking of two or more existing brands from different companies to form a product in which both brand names are visible to the consumer. There are two variants of this approach. **Parallel co-branding** occurs when two independent brands join forces to form a combined brand such as HP and Apple iPod to form the HP iPod. **Ingredient co-branding** is where one supplier explicitly chooses to position its brand as an ingredient of a product, such as when U2 launched the album *How to Dismantle an Atomic Bomb* pre-installed on an Apple iPod. Intel is one of the best-known ingredient brands through its popular slogan 'Intel inside', seen on PCs worldwide.

There are a number of advantages to product-based co-branding. First, the co-branding alliance can capture multiple sources of brand equity and therefore add value and provide a point of differentiation. Combining Häagen-Dazs ice cream and Bailey's liqueur creates a brand that adds value through distinctive flavouring that is different from competitive offerings. Second, a co-brand can position a product for a particular target market. For example, Volkswagen teamed up with Trek mountain bikes to develop the Jetta Trek, a special edition of the Volkswagen Jetta. The car was equipped with a bike

Marketing in Action 6.2: The global/local dilemma

> **Study guide:** Below is a review of the long-running arguments for and against a global marketing strategy. Read it and decide where you stand on this debate.

Major multinational corporations adopt different approaches to the global/local choice. Unilever and Nestlé have become huge organizations through the acquisition of local brands over time. But they are now discovering that many of these brands contribute very little to the bottom line. For example, by 1999, Unilever found that 75 per cent of its brands contributed less than 10 per cent of the company's sales. In 2004, it announced that it was trimming its brand portfolio from 1600 to 400 over five years. The luxury goods group, LVMH, cut its range from 73 in 2000 to 58 in 2006, and P&G, Heinz and Sara Lee have all taken similar approaches. Other companies have spent heavily on renaming local brands such as Mars' decision to rename Marathon as Snickers, and P&G's decision to rename its popular Fairy laundry detergent as Dawn, with the aim of giving these brands global consistency.

In contrast, the German consumer group Henkel is going in the opposite direction. Like Unilever, Henkel has grown through the acquisition of local companies, but rather than focusing on global leaders it maintains a portfolio of national and international brands. Persil, its premium brand in the laundry detergent business, is not suitable for the US market where washing machines on average use more water at lower temperatures than Europe, so for this reason it paid US$2.9 billion for the Dial group in 2003 to acquire the US washing powder Purex. After the failure of Fa, its range of personal care products, in the USA, it acquired the deodorants Right Guard, Soft & Dri and Dry Idea from P&G for US$275 million. In the company's view, Americans tend to prefer to suppress sweating, while continental Europeans want to conceal any odour without blocking perspiration.

Which approach is best remains unclear. P&G's decision to market the Dawn brand in Europe saw its share in Germany fall from 11.9 per cent in mid-2000 to 4.7 per cent in late 2001. Clearly, German consumers trusted the Fairy brand, whereas the Dawn brand meant little to them. It appears that multinationals need to strike a balance between those brands that have global appeal and those that have strong local connections. In addition, some aspects of the marketing mix, like product formulation, are easier to standardize, while others, such as packaging, pricing and distribution, are often best localized. So in the laundry detergent business, Henkel sells Losk in Russia, Neo-Mat in Greece and Tursil in Turkey, though all powders are similar in formulation.

Based on: **Anonymous (2005);**[35] **Frost (2005);**[36] **Grant (2005);**[37] **Wiesmann (2006)**[38]

---

rack and a Trek mounted on top, and appealed to some 15 million mountain bikers. Finally, co-branding can reduce the cost of product introduction since two well-known brands are combined, accelerating awareness, acceptance and adoption.[39]

Communications-based co-branding involves the linking of two or more existing brands from different companies or business units for the purposes of joint communications. For example, one brand can recommend another, such as Whirlpool's endorsement of Ariel washing powder.[40] Also the alliance can be used to stimulate interest or provide promotional opportunities, such as the deal between McDonald's and Disney, which gives the former exclusive global rights to display and promote material relating to new Disney movies in its outlets. In the USA, the breakfast cereal Cheerios carries an on-pack coupon offering a saving of US$1.50 on a box of Pampers disposable nappies, and the box of Pampers carries a similar coupon for Cheerios. Communications alliances are very popular in sponsorship deals, such as Shell's brand name appearing on Ferrari cars. Table 6.5 lists some examples of co-branding.

Table 6.5 Co-branding: some examples

Parallel co-brands

Häagen-Dazs and Baileys Cream Liqueur form Häagen-Dazs with Baileys flavour ice cream

Ford Focus and *Elle* women's magazine form Ford Focus Elle car

John Deere and St Lawrence Homes form the John Deere Signature Community in North Carolina

Ingredient co-brands

Intel as a component in Hewlett-Packard computers

Nutrasweet as an ingredient in Diet Coke

Scotchgard as stain protector in fabrics

Communications-based co-brands

Ariel and Whirlpool: joint advertising campaign

McDonald's and Disney: joint store promotions

Shell and Ferrari: sponsorship

Managing brand and product portfolios

Some companies have a large portfolio of brands (see Table 6.6 and Exhibit 6.3). They normally fall within a company's product line and mix. A product line is a group of brands that are closely related in terms of their functions and the benefits they provide (e.g. Dell's range of personal computers or Samsung's line of television sets). The *depth* of the product line refers to the number of variants offered within the product line. A 'product mix' is the total set of brands or products marketed in a company. It is the sum of the product lines offered. Thus, the *width* of the product mix can be gauged by the number of product lines an organization offers. Philips, for example, offers a wide product mix comprising the brands found within its product lines of television, audio equipment, video recorders, camcorders, and so on. Coca-Cola, for

Table 6.6 Sample brand portfolios of leading companies

Johnson & Johnson	Procter & Gamble	Nestlé	Unilever	L'Oréal	Diageo
Band-Aid	Always	Nescafé	Omo	Vichy	Guinness
Neutrogena	Bounce	Perrier	Surf Comfort Domestos	Garnier	Baileys
RoC	Duracell Pantene Pampers	Vittel KitKat Quality Street	Cif	La Roche-Posay Maybelline	Smirnoff J&B Bundaberg
Johnson's	Tampax	Purina	Dove	Lancôme	Captain Morgan
bebe	Crest	Rolo	Timotei	Ralph Lauren perfumes	Moët & Chandon
Clean & Clear	Vicks	Nespresso	Organics	Helena Rubinstein	Jose Cuervo
Aveeno	Head & Shoulders	Carnation	Knorr	Giorgio Armani perfumes	Tanqueray
Acuvue	Gillette Fusion	Lean Cuisine	Ben & Jerry's	Cacharel	Malibu
Pepcid	Camay	Buitoni	Lipton	Biotherm	
Tylenol	Hugo	Nesquik	Ragu		Archers
Imodium	Cover Girl	Libby's	Pot Noodle	Body Shop	Bells
Stayfree Piz Buin	Old Spice Pringles Oral B	Chef Purina Friskies	Hellmann's		Piat d'Or
Benecol	Naomi Campbell	Dreyer's	SlimFast Lux Impulse	Diesel	Bertrams VO
Reach toothbrushes	Lacoste	Poland Spring	Bertolli	Redken	Hennessey

Exhibit 6.3 Unilever is home to some of Europe's best-known brands such as Knorr

the competing needs of products so as to achieve the best performance for the company as a whole. Specifically, management needs to decide which brands to invest in, hold or withdraw support from.

The Boston Consulting Group's (BCG's) growth-share matrix is a technique borrowed from strategic management that has proved useful in helping companies to make product mix and/or product line decisions (see Figure 6.3). The matrix allows portfolios of products to be depicted in a 2 × 2 box, the axes of which are based on market growth rate and relative market share. The size of the circles reflects the proportion of revenue generated by each product line. Market growth rate forms the vertical axis and indicates the annual growth rate of the market in which each product line operates; in Figure 6.3 this is shown as 0–15 per cent although a different range could be used depending on economic conditions. Market growth rate is used as a proxy for market attractiveness.

Relative market share refers to the market share of each product relative to its largest competitor, and is shown on the horizontal axis. This acts as a proxy for competitive strength. The division between high and low market share is 1. Above this figure a product line has a market share greater than its main competitor. For example, if our product had a market share of 40 per cent and our main competitor's share was 30 per cent this would be indicated as 1.33 on the horizontal axis. Having plotted the position of each product on the matrix, a company can begin to think about setting the appropriate strategic objective for each line.

example, is deemed to be more vulnerable to market trends than its rival Pepsi because of its greater dependence on sales of sugary drinks, whereas Pepsi has a broader portfolio of drinks and food.

The process of managing groups of brands and product lines is called **portfolio planning**. This can be a very complex and important task. Some product lines will be strong, others weak. Some will require investment to finance their growth, others will generate more cash than they need. Somehow companies must decide how to distribute their limited resources among

The market leaders in high-growth markets are known as *stars*. They are already successful and the prospects for further growth are good. Resources

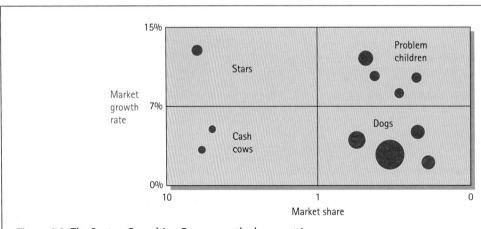

Figure 6.3 The Boston Consulting Group growth-share matrix

should be invested to maintain/increase the leadership position. Competitive challenges should be repelled. These are the cash cows of the future (see below) and need to be protected.

Problem children (also known as *question marks*) are cash drains because they have low profitability and require investment to enable them to keep up with market growth. They are so called because management has to consider whether it is sensible to continue the required investment. The company faces a fundamental choice: to increase investment (build) to attempt to turn the problem child into a star, or to withdraw support, either by harvesting (raising the price while lowering marketing expenditure) or divesting (dropping or selling it). In a few cases a third option may be viable: to find a small market segment (niche) where dominance can be achieved.

The high profitability and low investment associated with high market share in low-growth markets mean that *cash cows* should be defended. Consequently, the appropriate strategic objective is to hold sales and market share. The excess cash that is generated should be used to fund stars, problem children that are being built, and research and development for new products. For example, the C&C group sold its soft drinks business (a cash cow) to Britvic for €249 million, a deal aimed to fund its star division: cider.[41]

Dogs are weak products that compete in low-growth markets. They are the also-rans that have failed to achieve market dominance during the growth phase and are floundering in maturity. For those products that achieve second or third position in the marketplace (*cash dogs*) a small positive cash flow may result and, for a few others, it may be possible to reposition the product into a defendable niche. For the bulk of dogs, however, the appropriate strategic objective is to *harvest*—that is, to generate a positive cash flow for a time—or to *divest*, which allows resources and managerial time to be focused elsewhere.

The strength of the BCG's growth-share matrix is its simplicity. Once all of the company's products have been plotted it is easy to see how many stars, problem children, cash cows and dogs there are in the portfolio. Cash can be allocated as necessary to the different product lines to ensure that a balanced portfolio is maintained. However, the tool has also attracted a litany of criticism.[42] Some of the key problems with using the technique are as follows.

1   The matrix was based on cash flow but perhaps profitability (e.g. return on investment) is a better criterion for allocating resources.

2   Since the position of a product on the matrix depends on market share, this can lead to an unhealthy preoccupation with market share gain. In addition, market definition (which determines market share) can be very difficult.

3   The matrix ignores interdependences between products. For example, a dog may need to be marketed because it complements a star or a cash cow (it may be a spare part or an accessory, for example). Alternatively, customers and distributors may value dealing with a company that supplies a full product line. For these reasons dropping products because they fall into a particular box may be naive.

4   Treating market growth rate as a proxy for market attractiveness, and market share as an indicator of competitive strength is to oversimplify matters.

There are many other factors that have to be taken into account when measuring market attractiveness (e.g. market size, the strengths and weaknesses of competitors) and competitive strengths (e.g. exploitable marketing assets, potential cost advantages) besides market growth rates and market share. This led to the introduction of more complex portfolio matrices such as the McKinsey/GE market attractiveness–competitive position matrix, which used a variety of measures of market attractiveness and competitive strength.

The main contribution of the portfolio matrices generally has been to demonstrate that *different products should have different roles* in the product portfolio. For example, to ask for a 20 per cent return on investment (ROI) for a star may result in under-investment in an attempt to meet the profit requirement. On the other hand, 20 per cent ROI for a cash cow or a harvested product may be too low. However, the models should be used only as an aid to managerial judgement, and other factors that are not adequately covered by the models should be considered when making product mix decisions (see Marketing in Action 6.3).

Managing brands and product lines over time: the product life cycle

Both individual brands and product lines need to be managed over time. A useful tool for conceptualizing the changes that may take place during the time that a product is on the market is called the **product life cycle**. The classic product life cycle (PLC) has four

Marketing in Action 6.3: Sony's portfolio decisions

> **Study guide:** Below is a review of some of the leading product lines in Sony's portfolio. Read it, plot along the lines mentioned on a BCG matrix and advise Sony on what it should do.

Sony is one of Japan's most famous companies; its unique ability to produce top-quality miniature consumer electronics gave the world products like the Walkman personal stereo and the camcorder. However, for the past few years the company has been struggling to maintain its once dominant position. The reason for this is that too many of Sony's products are in unprofitable and declining businesses—in other words, it has too many 'dogs' in its portfolio.

For example, Sony is one of the top manufacturers of cathode-ray TVs. It sold over 7 million of these sets in 2005 and this product range was one of its biggest cash generators. But this business has collapsed in the developed world in recent years as consumers have switched to flat-panel TVs, and Sony has ceded market leadership to brands like Samsung and Panasonic. It has now entered the rapidly growing home theatre system and flat-screen TV business, but does not have market leadership in this sector (a problem child division). It also has a presence in the personal computer (PC) business, through its Vaio brand, but here again it is faced with some tough choices. PCs are an intensely price-competitive, low-margin and low-growth business, where Sony faces entrenched competitors like Dell, HP and Lenovo. Given its inability to differentiate the Vaio from the other brands in the marketplace it is questionable whether Sony should persist in this business. Other 'dog' businesses in which it is operating include its compact disc and minidisc product ranges, its car audio equipment and Sony Chemical—all low-growth or declining sectors.

The company has other divisions in its portfolio that appear to offer greater prospects. For example, its main 'cash cow' business is its camcorders. Though the business is no longer rapidly growing, Sony is the unquestioned market leader, and because it makes most of the product's components in-house, camcorders still deliver double-digit margins. Its 'star' division in recent years has been its video games business. The PlayStation brand is one of the best known in the industry and contributed two-thirds of Sony's operating profit in 2005. As this business matures, Sony needs to maintain a dominant position against rivals like the Xbox and Nintendo Wii, which it is trying to do with its PlayStation 3, in order to make this division a future cash cow. Sony has plenty of 'problem children' too, like its Walkman MP3 range, which trails well behind the dominant Apple iPod, though this is a growing business. But it is its investment in the Blu-ray disc, the next generation of DVD technology, that is likely to be its new 'star'. Having succeeded in convincing most of the big Hollywood studios to adopt its technology instead of the HD-DVD technology being promoted by Toshiba and Microsoft, Sony has won an intensely fought format war, which should drive sales of its high-definition DVD players and discs into the future.

Sony demonstrates the dynamic nature of company portfolios. Brands and divisions that were the stars or cash cows of the past may need to be divested in order to concentrate resources on delivering new stars for the future as consumer tastes and technologies change rapidly.

Based on: Anonymous (2008);[43] Gapper (2006);[44] Nakamoto (2005)[45]

---

stages (see Figure 6.4): introduction, growth, maturity and decline.

The PLC emphasizes the fact that nothing lasts for ever. For example, the drop in demand for elaborate tea services has seen dramatic declines at the makers of porcelain and fine bone china products, like Royal Worcester and Royal Doulton. There is a danger that management may fall in love with certain products, as in the case of a company that was founded on the success of a particular product. The PLC underlines the fact that companies have to accept that products need to be terminated and new products developed to replace them. Without this sequence a company may find itself with a group of products all in the decline stage of their PLC. A nicely balanced product array

Table 6.7 Marketing objectives and strategies over the product life cycle

	Introduction	**Growth**	**Maturity**	**Decline**
Strategic marketing objective	Build	Build	Hold	Harvest/manage for cash
Strategic focus	Expand market	Penetration	Protect share	Productivity
Brand objective	Product awareness/trial	Brand preference	Brand loyalty	Brand exploitation
Products	Basic	Differentiated	Differentiated	Rationalized
Promotion	Creating awareness/trial	Creating awareness/trial repeat purchase	Maintaining awareness/repeat purchase	Cut/eliminated
Price	High	Lower	Lowest	Rising
Distribution	Patchy	Wider	Intensive	Selective

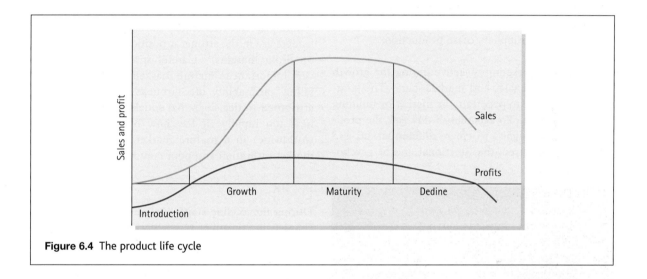

Figure 6.4 The product life cycle

would see the company marketing some products in the mature stage of the PLC, a number at the growth stage and the prospect of new product introductions in the near future.

The PLC emphasizes the need to review marketing objectives and strategies as products pass through the various stages. Changes in market and competitive conditions between the PLC stages suggest that marketing strategies should be adapted to meet them. Table 6.7 shows a set of stylized marketing responses to each stage. Note that these are broad generalizations rather than exact prescriptions, but they do serve to emphasize the· need to review marketing objectives and strategies in the light of environmental change.

Introduction

When a product is first introduced on to the market its sales growth is typically low and losses are incurred as a result of heavy development and initial promo-

tional costs. Companies will be monitoring the speed of product adoption and, if it is disappointing, may terminate the product at this stage.

The strategic marketing objective is to build sales by expanding the market for the product. The brand objective will be to create product (as well as brand) awareness so that customers will become familiar with generic product benefits. The product is likely to be fairly basic, with an emphasis on reliability and functionality rather than special features to appeal to different customer groups. Promotion will support the brand objectives by gaining awareness for the brand and product type, and stimulating trial. Advertising has been found to be more effective at the start of the life of a product than in later stages.[46] Typically, price will be high because of the heavy development costs and the low level of competition. Distribution will be patchy as some dealers will be wary of stocking the new product until it has proved successful in the marketplace.

Growth

This second stage is marked by a period of faster sales and profit growth. Sales growth is fuelled by rapid market acceptance and, for many products, repeat purchasing. Profits may begin to decline towards the latter stages of growth as new rivals enter the market attracted by the twin magnets of fast sales growth and high profit potential. For example, the internet search engine business has been growing rapidly and delivering very high profits for some incumbent firms like Google. But the profitability of this sector has attracted a range of new entrants, such as Jeteye.com, Blinkx.com and Icerocket.com, all of which are providing new and innovative search solutions. Similarly, in developed countries, the growth in pet ownership has given rise to a rapidly growing pet products and pet services sector. The end of the growth period is often associated with 'competitive shake-out', whereby weaker suppliers cease production.

The strategic marketing objective during the growth phase is to build sales and market share. The strategic focus will be to penetrate the market by building brand preference. To accomplish this task the product will be redesigned to create differentiation, and promotion will stress the functional and/or psycho-logical benefits that accrue from the differentiation. Awareness and trial are still important, but promotion will begin to focus on repeat purchasers. As development costs are defrayed and competition increases, prices will fall. Rising consumer demand and increased salesforce effort will widen distribution.

Maturity

Sales will eventually peak and stabilize as saturation occurs, hastening competitive shake-out. Mobile phone adoption rates, for example, have surpassed 100 per cent in some Western European countries. The survivors now battle for market share by introducing product improvements, using advertising and sales promotional offers, dealer discounting and price cutting; the result is strain on profit margins, particularly for follower brands. The need for effective brand building is felt most acutely during maturity as brand leaders are in the strongest position to resist pressure on profit margins.[47] Careful strategic decisions are very important in mature markets. For example, the falling profitability of Starbucks in 2007 has been attributed to decisions that sought to grow the business too rapidly (it has now over 30,000 outlets worldwide) in a mature market, which has led to market saturation and poor control over cafés.[48]

Decline

During the decline stages—when new technology or changes in consumer tastes work to reduce demand for the product—sales and profits fall. Suppliers may decide to cease production completely or reduce product depth. Promotional and product development budgets may be slashed, and marginal distributors dropped as suppliers seek to maintain (or increase) profit margins. Products like cathode ray tube (CRT) televisions have fallen out of favour as consumers have switched to flat-panel screens. For example, Dixons dropped the price of a CRT TV from £1300 in 2004 to £300 in 2005, and the range still failed to sell.[49] The effect of these changes on TV manufacturers have been dramatic. The French TV company, Thomson, lost €159 million in 2006 and announced that most of its manufacturing and distribution operations in Europe would close.[50] The increase in consumers making their travel arrangements online has led to a significant fall in the number of travel agents operating in the UK. In 2000, there were 1820 registered members of the Association of British Travel Agents (ABTA) but by 2005 this had fallen to 1397.[51]

Like the BCG's growth-share matrix, the PLC theory has been the subject of a significant amount of criticism. First, not all products follow the classic S-shaped curve. The sales of some products 'rise like

Exhibit 6.4 Companies like Green & Black's are prospering in a market where sales of dark chocolate are rising much faster than those of milk chocolate

a rocket then fall like the stick'. This is normal for fad products such as Rubik's cubes, which in the 1980s saw phenomenal sales growth followed by a rapid sales collapse as the youth market moved on to another craze. Blockbuster movies have a similarly short life cycle. For example, *X-Men, The Last Stand* grossed US$123 million in its first four days in cinemas, which was more than it earned for the remaining four months of its run.[52] Second, the duration of the PLC stages is unpredictable. The PLC outlines the four stages a product passes through without defining their duration. For example, e-books have languished in the introduction stage of the product life cycle for longer than anticipated. Clearly this limits its use as a forecasting tool since it is not possible to predict when maturity or decline will begin. Finally, and perhaps most worryingly, it has been argued that the PLC is the *result* of marketing activities, not the cause. Clearly, sales of a product may flatten out or fall simply because it has not received enough marketing attention, or because there has been insufficient product redesign or promotional support. Using the PLC, argue its critics, may lead to inappropriate action (e.g. harvesting or dropping the product) when the correct response should be increased marketing support (e.g. product replacement, positioning reinforcement or repositioning). Like many marketing tools, the PLC should not be viewed as a panacea to marketing thinking and decision-making, but as an aid to managerial judgement.

Nevertheless, the dynamic nature of brands and product lines focuses attention on the key marketing challenge of developing new products and services. It is to this issue that we turn next.

New product development

The introduction of new products to the marketplace is the life blood of corporate success. Changing customer tastes, technological advances and competitive pressures mean that companies cannot afford to rely on past product successes.

Instead they have to work on new product development programmes and nurture an innovative climate in order to lay the foundations for new product success. A case in point is Motorola. Struggling behind the market leader, Nokia, Motorola achieved enormous success with its sleek, brightly coloured Razr V3 mobile phone. But follow-up efforts have been less successful. The Razr2 and the Moto Q have not met with the same positive customer reaction. Its share of the global mobile phone market has fallen to

around 12 per cent and it has lost second place to Korea's Samsung.[53] The reality of new product development is that it is a risky activity and most new products fail. However, failure has to be tolerated; it is endemic in the whole process of developing new products.

Some new products reshape markets and competition by virtue of the fact that they are so fundamentally different from products that already exist. However, a shampoo that is different from existing products only by means of its brand name, fragrance, packaging and colour is also a new product. In fact four broad categories of new product exist.[54]

1. *Product replacements*: these account for about 45 per cent of all new product launches, and include revisions and improvements to existing products (e.g. the Ford Mondeo replacing the Sierra), repositioning (existing products such as Lucozade being targeted at new market segments) and cost reductions (existing products being reformulated or redesigned so that they cost less to produce).

2. *Additions to existing lines*: these account for about 25 per cent of new product launches and take the form of new products that add to a company's existing product lines. This produces greater product depth. An example is the launch by Weetabix of a brand extension, Oatabix, to compete with other oat-based cereals.

3. *New product lines*: these total around 20 per cent of new product launches and represent a move into a new market. For example, in Europe, Mars has launched a number of ice cream brands, which make up a new product line for this company. This strategy widens a company's product mix.

4. *New-to-the-world products*: these total around 10 per cent of new product launches, and create entirely new markets. For example, the video games console, the MP3 player and the camcorder have created new markets because of the highly valued customer benefits they provide.

Of course, the degree of risk and reward involved will vary according to the new product category. New-to-the-world products normally carry the highest risk since it is often difficult to predict consumer reaction Often, market research will be unreliable in predicting demand as people do not really understand the full benefits of the product until it is on the market and they get the chance to experience them. Furthermore, it may take time for products to be accepted. For example, the Sony Walkman was initially rejected by marketing research since the concept of being seen in a public place wearing head-phones was alien to most people. After launch, how-ever, this behaviour was accepted by younger age groups. At the other extreme, adding a brand varia-tion to an existing product line lacks significant risk but is also unlikely to proffer significant returns.

Managing the new product development process

New product development is expensive, risky and time consuming—these are three inescapable facts. Gillette, for example, spent in excess of £100 million over more than 10 years developing its Sensor razor brand. The new product concept was to develop a non-disposable shaver that would use new technology to produce a razor that would follow the contours of a man's face, giving an excellent shave (due to two spring-mounted platinum-hardened chromium blades) with fewer cuts. This made commercial sense given that shaving systems are more profitable than dis-posable razors and allow more opportunity for creat-ing a differential advantage. Had the brand failed, Gillette's position in the shaving market could have been irreparably damaged.

A seven-step new product development process is shown in Figure 6.5; this consists of idea generation,

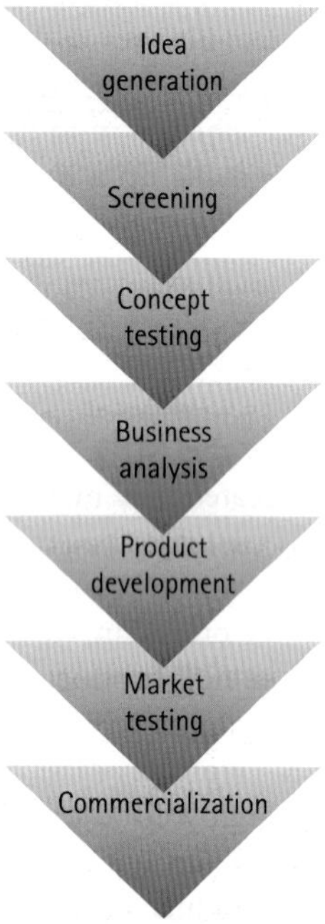

Figure 6.5 The seven-stage new product development process

screening, concept testing, business analysis, product development, market testing and commercialization. Although the reality of new product development may resemble organizational chaos, the discipline imposed by the activities carried out at each stage leads to a greater likelihood of developing a product that not only works, but also confers customer benefits. We should note, however, that new prod-ucts pass through each stage at varying speeds: some may dwell at a stage for a long period while others may pass through very quickly.[55]

Idea generation

The sources of new product ideas can be internal to the company: scientists, engineers, marketers, sales-people and designers, for example. Some companies use the **brainstorming** technique to stimulate the creation of ideas, and use financial incentives to per-suade people to put forward ideas they have had. 3M's Post-it adhesive-backed notepaper was a suc-cessful product that was thought of by an employee who initially saw the product as a means of prevent-ing paper falling from his hymn book as he marked the hymns that were being sung. Because of the innovative culture within 3M, he bothered to think of commercial applications and acted as a product champion within the company to see the project through to commercialization and global success.

Sources of new product ideas can also be external to the company. Examining competitors' products may provide clues to product improvements. Distributors can also be a source of new product ideas directly, since they deal with customers and have an interest in selling improved products. A major source of good ideas is the customers themselves. Their needs may not be satisfied with existing products and they may be genuinely interested in providing ideas that lead to product improvement. For example, the Dutch elec-tronics group, Philips employs anthropologists and cognitive psychologists to gather insights into the desires and needs of people around the world to enable it to compete more effectively with Asian rivals such as Sony who are more renowned for their design capabilities.[56] Internet-based social communities are a powerful source of innovation, with like-minded indi-viduals willing to share ideas and innovations for the common good. The open source software movement is one of the most powerful examples of consumer-led innovation.

In organizational markets, keeping in close contact with customers who are innovators and market leaders in their own marketplaces is likely to be a fruitful source of new product ideas.[57] These 'lead customers' are likely to recognize required improvements ahead of other customers as they have advanced needs and are likely to face problems before other product users. Some recent innovations such as GE's Light Speed VCT, which provides a three-dimensional image of a beating heart, and Staples' Wordlock, a padlock that uses words instead of numbers, have been developed in co-operation with lead customers.

A 2006 study by IBM of global chief executives found that, overall, employees were the most significant source of innovative ideas, followed by business partners, customers and consultants—in that order.[58]

Screening

Once new product ideas have been developed they need to be screened in order to evaluate their commercial value. Some companies use formal checklists to help them judge whether the product idea should be rejected or accepted for further evaluation. This ensures that no important criterion is overlooked. Criteria may be used that measure the attractiveness of the market for the proposed product, the fit between the product and company objectives, and the capability of the company to produce and market the product. Other companies may use a less systematic approach, preferring more flexible open discussion among members of the new product development committee to gauge likely success.

Concept testing

Once a product idea has been deemed worthy of further investigation, it can be framed into a specific concept for testing with potential customers. The concept may be described verbally or pictorially so that the major features are understood. In many instances the basic product idea will be expanded into several product concepts, each of which can be compared by testing with target customers. **Concept testing** thus allows the views of customers to enter the new product development process at an early stage. The buying intentions of potential customers are a key factor in judging whether any of the concepts are worth pursuing further.

Business analysis

Estimates of sales, costs and profits will be made, based on the results of the concept test, as well as on considerable managerial judgement. This is known as the **business analysis** stage. In order to produce sensible figures a marketing analysis will need to be undertaken. This will identify the target market, its size and projected product acceptance over a number of years. Consideration will be given to various prices and the implications for sales revenue (and profits)

discussed. By setting a tentative price this analysis will provide sales revenue estimates. Costs will also need to be estimated. If the new product is similar to existing products (e.g. a brand extension) it should be fairly easy to produce accurate cost estimates. For radical product concepts, costings may be nothing more than informal guesstimates.

When the quantity needed to be sold to cover costs is calculated, *break-even analysis* may be used to establish whether the project is financially feasible. *Sensitivity analysis*, in which variations from given assumptions about price, cost and customer acceptance, for example, are checked to see how they impact on sales revenue and profits, can also prove useful at this stage. 'Optimistic', 'most likely' and 'pessimistic' scenarios can be drawn up to estimate the degree of risk attached to a project. If the product concept appears commercially feasible this process will result in marketing and product development budgets being established based on what appears to be necessary to gain customer awareness and trial, and the work required to turn the concept into a marketable product.

Product development

This stage involves the development of the actual product. It is usually necessary to integrate the skills of designers, engineers, production, finance and marketing specialists so that product development is quicker, less costly and results in a high-quality product that delights customers. For example, the practice of 'simultaneous engineering' means that designers and production engineers work together rather than passing the project from one department to another once the first department's work is finished. Costs are controlled by a method called target costing. Target costs are worked out on the basis of target prices in the marketplace, and given as engineering/design and production targets.

A key marketing factor in many industries is the ability to cut time to market by reducing the length of the product development stage. There are two reasons why product development is being accelerated. First, markets such as those for personal computers, consumer electronics and cars change so fast that to be slow means running the risk of being out of date before the product is launched. Second, cutting time to market can lead to competitive advantage. This may be short-lived but is still valuable while it lasts. For example, Zara's ability to reduce time to market for new styles gave it a competitive advantage in the fashion industry. Marketing has an important role to play in the product development stage. R&D and engineering may focus on the functional aspects of the product, whereas seemingly trivial factors may have an important bearing on customer choice.

Product testing concentrates on the functional aspects of a product, as well as on consumer acceptance. Functional tests are carried out in the laboratory and in the field to check such aspects as safety, performance and shelf-life. Products also need to be tested with consumers to check their acceptability in use. Care at this stage can avoid expensive product recalls later, such as that faced by Mitsubishi Motors, which had to recall more than 80,000 vehicles because of faulty wheels. For consumer goods this often takes the form of in-house product placement. 'Paired companion tests' are used when the new product is used alongside a rival so that respondents have a benchmark against which to judge the new offerings. Alternatively, two (or more) new product variants may be tested alongside one another. A questionnaire is administered at the end of the test, which gathers overall preference information as well as comparisons on specific attributes. For example, two soups might be compared on taste, colour, smell and richness.

Market testing

Up to this point in the development process, although potential customers have been asked if they intend to buy the product, they have not been placed in the position of having to pay for it. **Market testing** takes measurement of customer acceptance one crucial step further than product testing, by forcing consumers to put their money where their mouth is, so to speak. The basic idea is to launch the new product in a limited way so that consumer response in the marketplace can be assessed. There are two major methods: the simulated market test and **test marketing**.

Simulated market tests take a number of forms, but the main idea behind them is to set up a realistic market situation in which a sample of consumers choose to buy goods from a range provided by the organizing company (usually a market research organization). For example, a sample of consumers may be recruited to buy their groceries from a mobile supermarket that visits them once a week. They are provided with a magazine in which advertisements and sales promotions for the new product can appear. This method allows the measurement of key success indicators such as penetration (the proportion of consumers who buy the new product at least once) and repeat purchase (the rate at which purchasers buy again) to be made. If penetration is high but repeat purchase low, buyers can be asked why they rejected the product after trial. Simulated market tests are therefore useful as a preliminary to test marketing by

spotting problems, such as in packaging and product formulation, that can be rectified before test market launch. They can also be useful in eliminating new products that perform so badly compared to the competition in the marketplace that test marketing is not justified.

When the new product is launched in one, or a few, geographical areas chosen to be representative of its intended market, this is known as test marketing. Towns or television areas are chosen in which the new product is sold into distribution outlets so that performance can be gauged face to face with rival products. Test marketing is the acid test of new product development since the product is being promoted as it would be in a national launch, and consumers are being asked to choose it against competitor products as they would if the new product went national. It is a more realistic test than the simulated market test and therefore gives more accurate sales penetration and repeat purchasing estimates. By projecting test marketing results to the full market an assessment of the new product's likely success can be gauged. However, test marketing does have a number of potential problems. Test towns and areas may not be representative of the national market, and thus sales projections may be inaccurate. For this reason, when Guinness was test-marketing its brand extension Guinness Mid-Strength, a low-alcohol version of Guinness, it chose Limerick as the most nationally representative location in the Irish market. Competitors may invalidate the test market by giving distributors incentives to stock their product, thereby denying the new product shelf space. Also, test markets need to run for long enough to enable the measurement of repeat purchase rates for a product since this is a crucial indicator of success for many products (e.g. groceries and toiletries). One of the main advantages of test marketing is that the information it provides facilitates the 'go/no go' national launch decision.

Commercialization

An effective commercialization strategy relies on marketing management making clear choices regarding the target market (*where* it wishes to compete), and the development of a marketing strategy that provides a differential advantage (*how* it wishes to compete). These two factors define the new product positioning strategy, as discussed in Chapter 5.

An understanding of the **diffusion of innovation process** is a useful starting point for choosing a target market.[59] This explains how a new product spreads throughout a market over time. Particularly important is the notion that not all people or organizations who comprise a market will be in the same

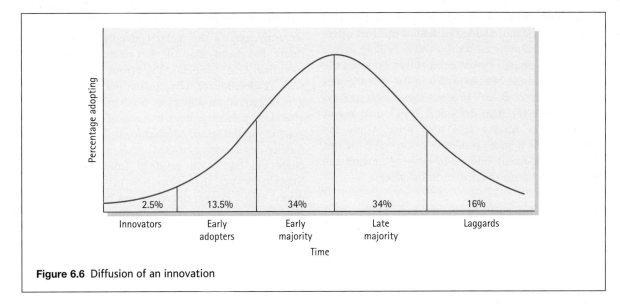

Figure 6.6 Diffusion of an innovation

state of readiness to buy a new product when it is launched. In other words, different actors in the market will have varying degrees of 'innovativeness'— that is, their willingness to try something new. For example, some consumers will be much quicker to adopt a new technology like the Blackberry wireless handheld device than others. Figure 6.6 shows the diffusion of innovation curve that categorizes people or organizations according to how soon they are willing to adopt an innovation.

The curve in Figure 6.6 shows that those actors (innovators and early adopters) who are willing to buy a new product soon after launch are likely to form a minor part of the total number of actors who will eventually be willing to buy it (see Exhibit 6.5). As the new product is accepted and approved by these customers, and the decision to buy the new product therefore becomes less risky, so the bulk of the market comprising the early and late majority begin to try the product themselves. Finally, after the product has gained full market acceptance, a group suitably described as the laggards adopts the product. By the time laggards have begun buying the product, innovators and early adopters have probably moved on to something new. For example in Europe, only innovators and early adopters have personal video recorders (PVRs) and video on demand (VoD). The early majority have broadband and 3G mobile phones. The late majority have digital television, while some laggards are now acquiring their first mobile phone.

These diffusion of innovation categories play a crucial role in the choice of target market. The key is to understand the characteristics of the innovator and early adopter categories, and to target them at launch.

Exhibit 6.5 The diffusion of e-books has, to date, been very slow; what is uncertain is how long it will take before improvements in technology make the e-book a real competitor against the print version you are now reading

For example, innovators are often adventurous and like to be different; they are willing to take a chance with an untried product.[60] In consumer markets they tend to be younger, better educated, more confident and more financially affluent, and consequently can afford to take a chance on buying something new. In organizational markets, they tend to be larger and more profitable companies if the innovation is costly, and have more progressive, better-educated management. They may themselves have a good track record in bringing out new products, and may have been the first to adopt innovations in the past. As such they may be easy to identify.

As far as the commercialization strategy goes, the second key decision is with regard to the choice of a marketing strategy that will establish a differential advantage. The more added benefits a product offers a customer, the more customers will be willing to buy it. This is illustrated by the competition between the Sony PS3 and the Nintendo Wii in the video games console business. Sony's product focuses on quality, with its Blue-ray high-definition DVD disc player giving real-life images at a high price, while the Nintendo Wii is more modestly priced and focuses on the fun element offered by players moving the controller to mimic the action on the screen.

In summary, bringing out new products and services is the key to long-term corporate success. It is a risky activity, but a systematic approach is likely to improve the chances of success.

Product management issues

There are three major product management issues that also have important ethical implications: product safety, planned obsolescence and deceptive packaging. We will now look at each of these in turn.

Product safety

Recently, one of the major concerns about product safety has been that of the safety of genetically modified (GM) products. Vociferous pressure groups such as Greenpeace have spoken out about the dangers of genetic modification. Such concerns, and the attendant publicity, have led one of the pioneers of genetic modification, Monsanto, to back away from further development of GM foods, and supermarket chains to ban such produce from their shelves. Supporters state that many new products are introduced with a certain degree of risk being acceptable. For example, a new pharmaceutical product may harm a tiny percentage of users but the utilitarianist principle of 'the greatest good for the greatest number' would support its launch. It is the reality of modern-day business that new products such as cars, pharmaceuticals and foods undergo extensive safety testing before launch. Anything less would violate the consumer's 'right to safety'. Product safety in Europe is enshrined in the General Product Safety Regulations Directive, which officially took effect in the EU in 2005. Organizational concerns with the attendant negative publicity caused by defective products means that expensive product recalls are now commonplace, as discussed in Marketing in Action 6.4.

Marketing in Action 6.4: Oops, sorry!

> **Study guide:** Below is a review of several recent product recalls. Read it and think of other examples of product recalls. How well have they been handled by the companies concerned?

What do Sony, Mattel, Cadbury Schweppes, Toyota, Guidant and H&M have in common? They are just some of the many companies that have been forced into expensive product recalls in the past few years. Companies spend vast sums building brands and adding layers of emotional value, but these recalls demonstrate that product quality cannot be ignored and that technical defects can prove to be very expensive. In the UK in 2006, there was a total of 179 product recalls, up by one-fifth on the previous year.

A case in point is Sony, a company that has long been associated with product quality and innovation. But, in 2006, it was forced into an expensive recall of its lithium ion batteries. Portable PCs account for about 50 per cent of sales of these products and Sony is the second largest manufacturer, with a global market share of around 25 per cent. But the chemistry of lithium ion packs is inherently unstable, and they are difficult and dangerous to manufacture. When some Sony batteries in Dell laptops began to explode, the company was forced into recalling 7 million batteries with significant knock-on effects on its profitability and share price. Another one of Japan's best-known companies, Toyota, has suffered similar damage to its brand's reputation for quality through numerous product recalls. In the USA and Japan, its two most important markets, it recalled over 6 million vehicles in between 2005 and 2007 for a variety of quality problems.

In certain industries, like food, product recalls are a very frequent occurrence because of the attendant health risks, particularly for children. For example, Nestlé recalled baby milk in Europe in late 2005 after products were found to be contaminated by a chemical used in the packaging. Heinz recalled eight baby food varieties in 2003 that were incorrectly labelled as milk-free. But Cadbury Schweppes was criticized in 2006 for being very slow in recalling some of its chocolate brands, which had been contaminated with salmonella. Six months after the problem had been discovered, some of the brands were still on the shelves.

Product recalls are expensive and can also do lasting damage to a brand. As product problems are almost impossible to totally eliminate what is important is how companies deal with the problems when they arise. The approach taken by the toy maker Mattel contrasts with that of Cadbury. It had to recall 21 million toys made in China after it was discovered that popular brands like 'Sarge' cars contained dangerous leaded paints, while potentially lethal magnets were used in its Barbie and Batman toy lines. The company's CEO stepped in immediately and acknowledged the problem, and it aggressively got the word out about the recall, though Mattel was criticized for not initially informing the US Consumer Product Safety Commission that there could be a problem.

Based on: Nakamoto and Nuttall (2006);[61] Silverstein (2007);[62] Tait (2007);[63] Wiggins (2006)[64]

Planned obsolescence

Many of the products on the market have not been designed to last for a long time. From the producers' point of view this is sensible as it creates a repeat-purchase situation. Hence, cars rust, computer software is quickly outdated and fashion items are replaced by the latest styles. Consumers accept that nothing lasts for ever, but the main thrust of this issue concerns what is an acceptable length of time before replacement is necessary. One driving force is competition. To quell the Japanese invasion, car manufacturers such as Ford and Volkswagen have made the body shells of their cars much more rust-resistant than they were before. Furthermore, it has to be recognized that many consumers welcome the chance to buy new clothes, new appliances with the latest features, and the latest model of car. Critics argue that planned obsolescence reduces consumers' 'right to choose' since some consumers may be quite content to drive an old car so long as its body shell is free from rust and the car functions well. As we have noted, the forces of competition may act to deter the excesses of planned obsolescence.

Deceptive packaging

This is something that can happen when, say, a product is presented in an oversized package, giving the impression that the consumer is getting more than is actually the case. This is known as 'slack' packaging[65] and has the potential to deceive when the packaging is opaque. Products such as soap powders and breakfast cereals have the potential to suffer from 'slack' packaging. A second area where packaging may be deceptive is through misleading labelling. This may take the form of the 'sin of omission'—for example, the failure of a package to state that a product contains GM soya. This relates to the consumer's 'right to be informed', and can include the stating of ingredients (including flavouring and colourants), nutritional contents and country of origin on labels. Nevertheless, labelling can still be misleading. For example, in the UK, the 'country of origin' is only the last country where the product was 'significantly changed'. So oil pressed from Greek olives in France can be labelled 'French' and foreign imports that are packed in the UK can be labelled 'produce of the UK'. Consumers should be wary of loose terminology. For example, Bachelors Sugar Free Baked Beans actually contain 1.7 g of sugar per 100 g, Kerry's Low Low Spread, which is marketed as low in fat, contains 38 g of fat per 100 g, and Walkers Lite crisps are a hefty 22 per cent fat. Consequently, the British Food Standards Agency (FSA) is promoting a 'traffic light' labelling system whereby foods high in calories, salt, sugar and fat will be clearly stamped with a red light, while more wholesome options are green-lighted, This is being opposed by many leading manufacturers and retailers, who favour a system whereby levels of sugar, fats and salt are given as a percentage of an adult's 'guideline daily amount'.[66] Similarly EU legislation aims to outlaw vague claims such as 'vitalize your body and mind' (Red Bull) or 'cleanse and refresh your body and soul' (Kombucha).[67]

The need for more stringent regulation of product labelling and advertising was starkly illustrated by the controversy surrounding ready-to-drink Ribena in New Zealand in 2007. As part of an experiment, two 14-year-old schoolgirls tested the product and found that it contained almost no vitamin C, despite the claims of its manufacturer, GlaxoSmithKline, that it had four times the vitamin C of oranges. Similarly, in the USA, Kraft Foods was sued by a consumer for selling tubs of guacamole that contained less than 2 per cent avocado.

Summary

In this chapter we have explored a number of issues involved in the marketing of products and brands. The following key issues were addressed.

1. The important distinction between products and brands. A product is anything that is capable of satisfying customer needs. Brands are the means by which companies differentiate their offerings from those of their competitors.

2. The key aspects involved in building brands, including decisions regarding the brand name, and developing and positioning brands. Firms can choose from family, individual and combination brand names, and developing the brand requires key decisions regarding its customer value proposition.

3. The key issues involved in brand management, including the challenges presented by the growth of own-label brands, brand extension decisions, pan-European and global branding decisions and co-branding decisions.

4. The challenge of managing a diverse group of products and brands, and the role of portfolio planning in assisting with this process. Many firms own significant portfolios of products and ongoing decisions need to be made regarding which ones should be invested in and which should be wound down.

5. The challenge of managing products and brands over time and the role of the product life cycle concept in assisting with this process. Products at different stages of growth require different marketing strategies and, despite its weaknesses, the product life cycle offers a helpful way of thinking about these decisions.

6. The importance of new product development and the process by which products are taken from the idea stage through to commercialization. Careful management is required during all the main stages, including idea generation, screening, concept testing, business analysis, product development, market testing and commercialization.

7. Product safety is a key challenge, as demonstrated by the rise in the number of product recalls globally. Packaging and labelling are also critical decisions, with much greater scrutiny taking place regarding the actual content of products.

Key terms

brainstorming the technique whereby a group of people generate ideas without initial evaluation; only when the list of ideas is complete is each one then evaluated

brand a distinctive product offering created by the use of a name, symbol, design, packaging, or some combination of these, intended to differentiate it from its competitors

brand equity the goodwill associated with a brand name, which adds tangible value to a company through the resulting higher sales and profits

brand extension the use of an established brand name on a new brand within the same broad market

brand stretching the use of an established brand name for brands in unrelated markets

brand values the core values and characteristics of a brand

business analysis a review of the projected sales, costs and profits for a new product to establish whether these factors satisfy company objectives

communications-based co-branding the linking of two or more existing brands from different companies or business units for the purposes of joint communication

concept testing testing new product ideas with potential customers

diffusion of innovation process the process by which a new product spreads throughout a market over time

experiential marketing the term used to describe marketing activities that involve the creation of experiences for consumers

family brand name a brand name used for all products in a range

generic brands brand names that have become so popular that product categories actually become known by the brand name

global branding achievement of brand penetration worldwide

individual brand name a brand name that does not identify a brand with a particular company

ingredient co-branding the explicit positioning of a supplier's brand as an ingredient of a product

manufacturer brands brands that are created by producers and bear their chosen brand name

market testing the limited launch of a new product to test sales potential

own-label brands brands created and owned by distributors or retailers

parallel co-branding the joining of two or more independent brands to produce a combined brand

portfolio planning managing groups of brands and product lines

product life cycle a four-stage cycle in the life of a product, illustrated as a curve representing the demand; the four stages being introduction, growth, maturity and decline

product line a group of brands that are closely related in terms of the functions and benefits they provide

product mix the total set of products marketed by a company

product-based co-branding the linking of two or more existing brands from different companies or business units to form a product in which the brand names are visible to the consumer

test marketing the launch of a new product in one or a few geographic areas chosen to be representative of the intended market

Study questions

1. Explain the difference between a product and a brand.
2. Think of five brand names. To what extent do they meet the criteria of good brand naming as laid out in Table 6.1? Do any of the names legitimately break these guidelines?
3. What are the advantages and disadvantages of co-branding? Suggest two co-branding alliances that you think might be successful, explaining why.
4. The product life cycle is more likely to mislead marketing management than provide useful insights. Discuss.
5. Many companies comprise a complex group of business units, which in turn often have wide product lines. Discuss the techniques available to the marketer for managing this complexity.
6. Outline the main stages in the new product development process, identifying the potential sources of failure at each stage.
7. Visit www.rdtrustedbrands.com. Review the most trusted brands in different categories in your area. How do these brands go about building this trust?

Suggested reading

Berthon, P., M. Holbrook and **J.M. Hulbert** (2003) Understanding and Managing the Brand Space, *Sloan Management Review*, **44** (2), 49–54

Gladwell, M. (2000) *The Tipping Point: How Little Things Can Make a Big Difference*, London: Abacus.

Hill, S., R. Ettenson and **D. Tyson** (2005) Achieving the Ideal Brand Portfolio, *Sloan Management Review*, **46** (2), 85–91.

Holman, R., H. Kaas and **D. Keeling** (2003) The Future of Product Development, *McKinsey Quarterly*, **3**, 28–40.

Joachimsthaler, E. and **D.A. Aaker** (1997) Building Brands Without Mass Media, *Harvard Business Review*, January/February, 38–51.

Kumar, N. and **J.B. Steenkamp** (2007) *Private Label Strategy: How to Meet the Store Brand Challenge*, Harvard Business School Press.

Moon, Y. (2005) Break Free From the Product Life Cycle, *Harvard Business Review*, **83** (5), 86–95.

Roberts, K. (2004) *The Future Beyond Brands: Lovemarks*, New York: Powerhouse Books.

References

1. **Borden, J.** (2008) Experiential Marketing Takes the Industry by Storm in 2008, *Marketing Week*, 15 January, 23–6; **Friedman, V.** (2006) Gucci's Temple to the 'Selling Ceremony', *Financial Times*, 3 November, 12.

2. **Yee, A.** (2005) Great Pictures, but Where are the Profits?, *Financial Times*, 1 September 23; **Yee, A.** (2006) Banishing the Negative: How Kodak is Developing its Blueprint for a Digital Transformation, *Financial Times*, 26 January, 15.

3. **Keller, K.** (2003) *Strategic Brand Management*, New Jersey: Pearson.

4. **Chernatony, L. de** (1991) Formulating Brand Strategy, *European Management Journal*, **9** (2), 194–200.

5. **Roberts, K.** (2004) *The Future Beyond Brands: Lovemarks*, New York: Powerhouse Books.

6. **Healy, A.** (2004) Campaigners Appeal for Cafes to be Rescued, *Irish Times*, 25 November, 6.

7. **McWilliam, G.** (2000) Building Stronger Brands Through Online Communities, *Sloan Management Review*, Spring, 43–54.

8. **Muniz, A.** and **T. O'Guinn** (2001) Brand Community, *Journal of Consumer Research*, **27** (4), 412–33.

9. **Upshaw, L.** and **E. Taylor** (2001) Building Business by Building a Masterbrand, *Brand Management*, **8** (6), 417–26.

10. **Reyner, M.** (1996) Is Advertising the Answer?, *Admap*, September, 23–6.

11. **Clingham, R., G.P. Arnold, T.S. Drew, L.A. Cochrane** and **R.J. Abboud** (2007) Do you Get Value for Money When you Buy an Expensive Pair of Running Shoes? *British Journal of Sports Medicine*, October, 1–5.

12. **Adamson, A.** (2006) *Brand Simple: How the Best Brands Keep it Simple and Succeed*, New York: Palgrave Macmillan.

13. **Klein, N.** (2000) *No Logo*, London: HarperCollins.

14. **Marsh, P.** (2005) Industry Plays the Name Game, *Financial Times*, 8 February, 12.

15. **Palmer, M.** (2007) What's in a Name? A Lot if it's Your Domain, *Financial Times*, 14 March, 24.

16. **Davoudi, S.** (2006) When that Well-known Flavour Fell from Favour, *Financial Times*, 10 January, 22.

17. **Brady, J.** and **I. Davis** (1993) Marketing's Mid-life Crisis, *McKinsey Quarterly*, **2**, 17–28.

18. **Anonymous** (2005) As Good As It Gets, *Economist*, 15 January, 60–2.

19. **Doyle, P.** (2000) *Value-based Marketing*, Chichester: John Wiley & Sons.

20. **Richards, H.** (2005) A Clothing Hit—on the Back of a Golfing Hero, *Financial Times*, 13 July, 16.

21. **Jones, A.** (2004) Unilever's Friendly Facelift Costs £7m, *Financial Times*, 13 May, 1.

22. **Wiggins, J.** (2006) Unilever Set to Take on Own-Brand Competition, *Financial Times*, 10 February, 20.

23. **Pandya, N.** (1999) Soft Selling Soap Brings Hard Profit, *Guardian*, 2 October, 28.

24. **de Mesa, A.** (2004) How Far can a Brand Stretch?, *Brandchannel.com*, 23 February.

25. **Sullivan, M.W.** (1990) Measuring Image Spillovers in Umbrella-branded Products, *Journal of Business*, July, 309–29.

26. **Sharp, B.M.** (1990) The Marketing Value of Brand Extension, *Marketing Intelligence and Planning*, **9** (7), 9–13.

27. **Aaker, D.A.** and **K.L. Keller** (1990) Consumer Evaluation of Brand Extensions, *Journal of Marketing*, **54** (January), 27–41.

28. **Roberts, C.J.** and **G.M. McDonald** (1989) Alternative Naming Strategies: Family versus Individual Brand Names, *Management Decision*, **27**, (6), 31–7.

29. **Saunders, J.** (1990) Brands and Valuations, *International Journal of Advertising*, **9**, 95–110.

30. **Sharp, B.M.** (1990) The Marketing Value of Brand Extension, *Marketing Intelligence and Planning*, **9** (7), 9–13.

31. **Aaker, D.A.** (1990) Brand Extensions: The Good, the Bad and the Ugly, *Sloan Management Review*, Summer, 47–56.

32. **Reisenbeck, H.** and **A. Freeling** (1991) How Global are Global Brands?, *McKinsey Quarterly*, **4**, 3–18.

33. **Barwise, P.** and **T. Robertson** (1992) Brand Portfolios, *European Management Journal*, **10** (3), 277–85.

34. **Halliburton, C.** and **R. Hünerberg** (1993) Pan-European Marketing—Myth or Reality, Proceedings of the European Marketing Academy Conference, Barcelona, May, 490–518.

35. **Anonymous** (2005) Local Tastes, *Economist*, 12 November, 80–1.

36. **Grant, J.** (2005) Procter Doctor: How Lafley's Prescription is Revitalizing a Tired Consumer Titan, *Financial Times*, 22 December, 17.

37. **Frost, R.** (2005) Should Global Brands Thrash Local Favorites?, *Brandchannel.com*, 7 March.

38. **Wiesmann, G.** (2006) Brands that Stop at the Border, *Financial Times*, 6 October, 13.

39. **Brech, P.** (2002) Ford Focus Targets Women with *Elle* Tie, *Marketing*, 8 August, 7.

40. **Keller, K.** (2003) *Strategic Brand Management*, New Jersey: Pearson.

41. **Brown, J.M.** (2007) Soft Drinks Sale to Britvic Enables C&C to Concentrate on High Margin Alcohol, *Financial Times*, 15 May, 22.

42. See, e.g., **Day, G.S.** and **R. Wensley** (1983) Marketing Theory with a Strategic Orientation, *Journal of Marketing*, Fall, 79–89; **Hasplagh, P.** (1982) Portfolio Planning: Uses and Limits, *Harvard Business Review*, January/February, 58–73; **Wensley, R.** (1981) Strategic Marketing: Betas, Boxes and Basics, *Journal of Marketing*, Summer, 173–83.

43. **Anonymous** (2008) Everything's Gone Blu, *Economist*, 12 January, 53.

44. **Gapper, J.** (2006) Sony is Scoring Low at its Own Game, *Financial Times*, 6 November, 17.

45. **Nakamoto, M.** (2005) Screen Test: Stringer's Strategy Will Signal to What Extent Sony Can Stay in the Game, *Financial Times*, 21 September, 17.

46. **Vakratsas, D.** and **T. Ambler** (1999) How Advertising Works: What Do We Really Know?, *Journal of Marketing*, **63**, January, 26–43.

47. **Doyle, P.** (1989) Building Successful Brands: The Strategic Options, *Journal of Marketing Management*, **5** (1), 77–95.

48. **Anonymous** (2008) Starbucks v McDonald's: Coffee Wars, *Economist*, 12 January, 54–5.

49. **Rigby, E.** and **A. Edgecliffe-Johnson** (2006) Dixons to Pull the Plug on Old Fashioned TV Sets, *Financial Times*, 19 January, 4.

50. **Anonymous** (2006) A Grim Picture, *Economist*, 4 November, 74.

51. **Garrahan, M.** (2005) Is this Journey's End for the Travel Agent?, *Financial Times: Global Traveller*, 14 November, 2.

52. **Anonymous** (2007) Endless Summer, *Economist*, 28 April, 69–70.

53. **Anonymous** (2005) Pretty in Pink, *Economist*, 5 November, 68; **Pimlott, D.** and **P. Taylor** (2008) Motorola Shares Fall 20% on Profit Warning, *Financial Times*, 24 January, 24; **Taylor, P.** (2007) Motorola Puts Faith in Function, Not Form, *Financial Times*, 17 May, 24.

54. **Booz, Allen** and **Hamilton** (1982) *New Product Management for the 1980s*, New York: Booz, Allen & Hamilton, Inc.

55. **Cooper, R.G.** and **E.J. Kleinschmidt** (1986) An Investigation into the New Product Process: Steps, Deficiencies and Impact, *Journal of Product Innovation Management*, June, 71–85.

56. **Tomkins, R.** (2005) Products That Aim Straight For Your Heart, *Financial Times*, 29 April, 13.

57. **Parkinson, S.T.** (1982) The Role of the User in Successful New Product Development, *R&D Management*, **12**, 123–31.

58. **Anonymous** (2007) The Love-In, *Economist Special Report on Innovation*, 13 October, 18.

59. **Rogers, E.M.** (1983) *Diffusion of Innovations*, New York: Free Press.

60. **Rogers, E.M.** (1983) *Diffusion of Innovations*, New York: Free Press.

61. **Nakamoto, M.** and **C. Nuttal** (2006) Sony Battles to Restore Credibility After Recall Warning, *Financial Times*, 4 October, 26.

62. **Silverstein, B.** (2007) A Brand's Worst Nightmare, *Brandchannel.com*, 10 September.

63. **Tait, N.** (2007) Recall of Goods Increases by a Fifth, *Financial Times*, 19 February, 4.

64. **Wiggins, J.** (2006) Recalls, Recriminations and Reputations, *Financial Times*, 3 August, 17.

65. **Smith, N.C.** (1995) Marketing Strategies for the Ethics Era, *Sloan Management Review*, Summer, 85–97. See also **T.W. Dunfee, N.C. Smith** and **W.T. Ross Jr** (1999) Social Contracts and Marketing Ethics, *Journal of Marketing*, **63** (July), 14–32.

66. **Pope, C.** (2007) New Labels Hit a Red Light, *Irish Times*, 15 January, 13.

67. **Hegarty, S.** (2003) You Are What You Think You Eat, *Irish Times*, Weekend Review, 19 July, 1.

Online **LearningCentre**

When you have read this chapter, log on to the Online Learning Centre for *Foundations of Marketing* at **www.mcgraw-hill.co.uk/textbooks/jobber**, where you'll find multiple-choice test questions, links and extra online study tools for marketing.

Case 6 Gorenje Group: the curious case of the £10,000 fridge and building a new European brand

Aleksander Uranc, marketing director of Gorenje Group, was delighted to see months of planning come to fruition. Tomorrow, he would unveil the world's most expensive refrigerator to the waiting media at the world's most famous department store, Harrods of London. Most fridges retail at £250–£650 (€300–€800), with premium fridges fetching close on £1500 (€,000). But a refrigerator costing £10,000 (€14,605) is a world first. The Gorenje 'Eyecatcher' fridge, which will go on display, is designed by famous Ferrari designer Pininfarina, and encrusted with over 7000 Swarovski crystals for discerning fashion- and design-conscious customers. The fridge has a touch-screen user interface, with temperature controls, alongside a built-in radio, recipe book and voice memo recorder/player capabilities.

The 'Eyecatcher' fridge from Gorenje

In the extremely competitive world of home appliances, which is dominated by several large corporate multinationals, Gorenje has tried to develop its brand and compete on an international scale. Gorenje is a Slovenian appliance manufacturer, which has emerged as one of the great success stories of Eastern European industry, surviving and thriving in the post Cold-War era. The company is the pride of Slovenia, a small country that was formerly part of Yugoslavia. From a relatively small domestic market, it has taken Europe by storm. It has withstood testing challenges such as competing against low-cost rivals from Asia and competitors with huge marketing budgets, as well as established retail distribution networks. Through collaboration with a range of well-known international designers/collaborators, such as Pininfarina, Ora Ïto and Swarovski, the company has helped to gradually reposition and define itself as an innovation-led brand.

But Gorenje needs to continue to build its brand internationally. Working with a prestigious retail partner like Harrods bodes well for the product launch. Only five of these limited edition 'Eyecatcher' premium fridges have been produced, and all five have been handcrafted, raising money for charity. It is hoped that this innovative campaign will lead to positive brand associations, raising Gorenje's profile in the UK and internationally. As Aleksander looks at the display in the cathedral of consumption that is Harrods, he hopes that the launch will garner excellent media coverage, and will re-energize Gorenje as a premium home brand for the future.

Background to Gorenje

The company's name comes from a tiny village in the former Yugoslavia. Gorenje grew to become a colossus of Yugoslavian industry, diversifying into ceramics, furniture, medical equipment and television sets. At its zenith, the company had over 20,000 employees and its slogan was 'everything for the home'. It benefited from a closed economy where it could reap huge dividends through state subsidies and focus on exporting, which accounted for 30 per cent of its business in the 1970s. It tried to build a reputation for solid, reliable products, and successfully built up relationships with several large key retailers.

During the 1980s, Yugoslavia faced financial austerity, with mounting IMF debts and inflation. The growing economic crises lead to a deterioration of relations among the several Yugoslav republics, which saw a renaissance of nationalism within these countries and a vicious downward spiral leading to bloody conflict. The collapse of Yugoslavia had the potential to destroy the company. Its profitable Yugoslav markets accounted for 40 per cent of its revenues and the Slovenian market on its own would not sustain the company's long-term viability. Slovenia itself was relatively untouched by the war that occurred in Croatia, Bosnia, Serbia and other former Yugoslav states. Not only were Gorenje's key markets cut off, so too were key suppliers, leading to enormous manufacturing and logistical pressures.

In the late 1990s, Gorenje entered a period of stability, due to a successful privatization and further penetration into export markets. The company began setting up distribution networks and subsidiaries throughout the growing Eastern European markets. The importance of design was added to its focus on cost efficiency, leading to the development of appliances for the mid-/upper price segment of the market. In the wake of very strong low-cost competition from Asia, this strategy helped the company survive, while others have had to outsource to countries such as China. Through its alliances with external award-winning designers, the brand has been enhanced. It now manufactures over 3.5 million large household appliances annually in its production plants in Slovenia, the Czech Republic and Serbia.

Product and brand strategy

Originally the company focused on 'everything for the home', but now Gorenje is focusing primarily on large domestic appliances such as fridges, cookers, laundry and integrated kitchens (see Table C6.1). The company's product line has continually evolved,

and has moved away from manufacturing basic home appliances to becoming more design led, contemporary and technologically sophisticated. Most of Gorenje's products are covered by a five-year parts and labour guarantee, which highlights the firm's focus on building high-quality, reliable products.

The marketplace is continually changing. Some of the main consumer trends include: energy consumption, new technological features, single-person households, ageing populations and rising global disposable income. Governments are now launching policy initiatives promoting environmentally friendly products. Within the home appliance sector, there is a big drive towards promoting eco-friendly products that comply with 'green' regulations. This has provided Gorenje with an opportunity to sell higher-spec appliances at higher price points. Also appliances have moved away from being seen as simply 'white goods'. Now they have to be reliable, have numerous technological functions, but also be aesthetically appealing, and

Table C6.1 Gorenje at a glance

Background

- Core business is the production and sale of large household appliances
- Slovenia's largest exporter
- Exports over 90% of its products
- Sales of €1.1 billion; net profit €22 million
- Has 4% of the European home appliance market
- Employs 10,816 people
- Company's mission is to create innovative, technically accomplished, superbly designed, user- and environment-friendly appliances for the home.
- Winner of the Red Dot Design Award 2005 and the Designer Manufacturer's Award 2006

Location of the Gorenje Group

Headquarters based in Velenje, Slovenia. Slovenia is small country based in Eastern Europe, bordering Italy, Austria, Hungary and Croatia, with a population of 2 million

Principal brands

- Gorenje
- Sidex
- Körting
- Mora

75% of sales are derived from the Gorenje brand. Mora was originally a Czech brand, the Körting brand is from West Germany. Mora, Sidex and Körting are lower-priced brands, while Gorenje occupies the mid-tier price bracket

Types of product sold	Markets
- Refrigerators - Cookers - Dishwashers - Microwave ovens - Tumble dryers - Wine coolers - Integrated kitchens	Sells to over 70 countries worldwide, including the UK, Spain, Sweden, Turkey, Germany, France and Eastern Europe Sales to EU: 57% Sales to Eastern Europe: 37% Sales to other countries: 6%

typically incorporate aluminium finishes. The ever increasing technological features for a simple fridge have changed to include, for example, features such AA+ energy rating, ice cube makers, water dispensers, anti-bacterial coating, intelligent temperature controls and dynamic visual display controls. These features require constant refinement and input from research and development, so as to stay competitive.

Gorenje is the company's main brand. But it also has several other brands in its portfolio. The co-branded Gorenje–Pininfarina, and Gorenje–Ora-Ïto brands (discussed below) are premium prestige brands. The Sidex brand is marketed at a lower price point compared to the Gorenje brand, in markets like France. The Körting brand is tremendously successful in countries such as Italy and Greece. In the United States it sells primarily to own-label retailers, which resell the product under their own brand names. Germany is by far Gorenje's biggest market for its units, with a 50:50 spread between the Gorenje brand and sales to own-label resellers. Therefore, Gorenje has utilized a strong own-brand strategy, yet it makes sure that own-label sales do not account for more than 30 per cent of its overall revenue, to ensure a continued focus on its core brand.

Strategic partnerships— innovative design

In order to boost the brand image of Gorenje and enhance its brand allure, the company has joined forces with several different design partners. This partnership strategy has yielded countless design awards and dramatic success in the market. Three of the most successful Gorenje partnerships have included those with Pininfarina, Ora-Ïto and Swarovski. These partnerships have paved the way for the brand to be seen as cutting edge, innovative and design focused. This strategy was essential if the company wanted to achieve higher price points and to withstand low-price competition from the Far East in the sector.

Pininfarina

Gorenje and Pininfarina formed this unlikely partnership way back in 1990. The Italian company was initially famous for producing car designs for Fiat, Alfa Romeo, Peugeot and Ferrari. In the early 1990s, it diversified into the design of non-automotive products such as furniture, interior design, fashion and technology products. Together, they have launched a co-branded product line that has helped reposition the Gorenje brand as modern, technologically sophisticated, with a trendy designer cachet. The partner-

ship has produced several different product lines, with co-branded refrigerators, hobs and ovens. Furthermore, the partnership has continually evolved with new design iterations, and all are priced at the ultra-premium end of the market, with a strong emphasis on design and technological innovation.

Swarovski

Turning fridges into jewellery pieces and high-concept art is a luxury branding exercise. This Austrian company is internationally renowned as a supplier of crystals to the fashion and jewellery industry. Together, the companies have developed the world's most expensive fridge, encrusted with 7000 glittering Swarovski crystals. These limited edition one-off pieces are used to showcase Gorenje's technical sophistication and innovative design. These fridges provide the necessary 'bling' to attract media and customer attention.

Ora-Ïto

The young French designer has worked with some of the world's most illustrious brands, such as Louis Vuitton, Heineken, Swatch, Gucci, Apple, and many more. Using this designer's flair for futuristic and provocative designs, Gorenje has produced integrated kitchens of the future. These high-quality and distinctive pieces, engineered by Gorenje, incorporate the latest advanced technology. They are stylish, innovative and inspired by a unique design—a combination that has positioned Gorenje as a very contemporary brand, with a design-led focus.

The competitive landscape

In Europe alone there are estimated to be over 250 home appliance brands. Now the industry is facing huge consolidation, with companies such as Bosch-Siemens Hausgeräte, Indesit, Electrolux and Haier dominating market share (see Table C6.2). Coupled with this, distribution channels are also consolidating. The company faces huge challenges from large competitors in a mature market, and new incumbent threats from Asia.

The next step

By 2010 Gorenje hopes to sell 4.3 million units annually. It is focused on becoming the most original, design-orientated trendsetter of home appliances in the world. It has set an ambitious target of achieving 5 per cent annual growth, which is to be achieved through increasing the added value of its products, more effective marketing strategies, more innovation, enhancing the sales network and improving cost efficiencies within the group's manufacturing operations. Aleksander is going to be very busy in achiev-

Table C6.2 Gorenje Group's main competitors

Electrolux	Indesit	Bosch-Siemens Hausgeräte (BSH)
Sells more than 40 million units every year under several different brands, including Tricity Bendix, AEG-Electrolux, Frigidaire and Zanussi.	The Italian company produces 15 million appliances a year, using Ariston, Cannon, Creda, Hotpoint, Indesit and Scholtes brands. Sales of €3.2 billion.	Produces two main home appliance brands under the separate Bosch and Siemens brands. It owns premium brand, Neff, and regional brands, Ufesa and Thermador. Sales of €8.3 billion on 40 million units.
Miele	**Haier**	**FagorBrandt**
German manufacturer, prides itself on high quality and the longevity of its products. Uses the slogan 'Forever better'. Produces 5 million units a year, with sales in excess of €2.54 billion.	The world's fourth largest white goods manufacturer, and a rising star from China. Its access to low-cost manufacturing sites, and focus on innovation, enables it to be a strong future competitor.	FagorBrandt owns the premium high-end Brandt, De Dietrich and Ocean brands, and five other regional brands. De Dietrich is the group's key brand for the future.
LG	**Fisher & Paykel**	**Whirlpool**
This South Korean industrial *chaebol* produces a wide array of appliance products, from fridges to vacuum cleaners.	This New Zealand-based home appliance maker has entered the European market with a portfolio of innovative design-led appliances.	This company sells Whirlpool, Maytag, KitchenAid, Jenn-Air, Amana, Brastemp and Bauknecht. With annual sales of €18 billion and a presence in 170 countries, it is the industry leader.

ing this target, and the Harrods launch is just one of the necessary branding initiatives. Trying to woo the hearts, minds and wallets of European customers, trying to build brand recognition and a positive brand image in the midst of strong large competitors, with well-established brand names, and even larger marketing budgets, is always going to be difficult. The company has to successfully differentiate its product portfolio among the myriad strong competition. It must strive to create a premium brand image as well as considering its other sub-brands, the supply of own-label products and its co-branding initiatives. Furthermore, the company needs to achieve the necessary volume sales to reap economies of scale.

Questions

1. Discuss how Gorenje has gone about building a European home appliance brand. What are the strengths and weaknesses of its approach?
2. What are Gorenje's brand values?
3. What are the key brand management issues facing the company as it grows the size and international scope of its business?
4. Evaluate the width and depth of Gorenje's product portfolio. What changes would you make?

This case was written by Niko Slavnic, IEDC, Slovenia, and Conor Carroll, University of Limerick. Copyright © Conor Carroll & Niko Slavnic (2008). The material in the case has been drawn from a variety of published sources, interviews, archival records and research reports.

Chapter 7
Services Marketing Management

Learning Outcomes

By the end of this chapter you will understand:

1. the nature and special characteristics of services
2. the differences between products and services
3. the composition of the services marketing mix
4. the key issues in managing services enterprises
5. the special importance of relationship marketing in services businesses
6. the nature and characteristics of not-for-profit marketing.

Vapiano: a new food concept

Eating is one of the most pleasurable activities we can engage in, and food is one of the biggest service industries in the world. Restaurants range from the ubiquitous fast-food outlets like McDonald's and Burger King to the top-of-the-market venues of famous celebrity chefs. It is also a business with a very high failure rate. Many amateur chefs try their hand at setting up a restaurant or catering business, and many quickly realize that it is not as easy as it might at first have appeared. Understanding the needs of a local market, getting the service concept right and then delivering it consistently are difficult challenges.

One innovative food service company that is growing rapidly is the German chain Vapiano. It derives its name from the Italian slang for relaxing, or 'taking life easy and living long and well'. In a unique approach, it tries to combine the principles of standardization used by global corporations like McDonald's with the delivery of high-quality, customized food. The initial concept for the restaurant was to be similar to the experience of cooking with friends, where you met with and could speak to the chef. But when Kent Hahne, now the company CEO, became an investor in the project he brought with him the work practices he was accustomed to as a McDonald's franchisee. The combination gave rise to an innovative new kind of restaurant that has proved very popular to date.

Customers at Vapiano are presented with a menu and a chip card, which keeps an electronic record of what they order from the different food and drink stations. Food is available from three stations—salads, pizza and pasta; each station can have up to four lines, depending on popularity, with each line corresponding to the chef who will cook the food. The chip cards are read by computer at each station. While this ordering process has a distinctly fast-food feel to it, the options available to the customer are more akin to what can be found in an upmarket restaurant. For example, nine different pasta shapes can be combined with 20 sauces and a variety of extras. Meals are cooked from scratch using fresh ingredients in front of the customer, which adds to the experiential element of the concept. The average bill size in the USA is US$18, which breaks down as US$9–US$10 for lunch and US$22–US$25 for dinner. The standardized processes and use of technology help to keep staff costs low, improving profit margins.

Vapiano International currently owns or has franchised 31 outlets in nine countries, and 2007 saw its first openings in the USA, Budapest and Istanbul. It plans to open 80 additional restaurants in the next four to eight years, expanding its presence in the USA, Eastern Europe and the Middle East. Potential franchisees receive all the customary support, such as site selection, operations services and management training. Similar to McDonald's, the company has now developed what it calls the 'Vapiano Bible', which is a 350-page training manual for restaurant managers.

Vapiano has shown that there are always new opportunities in mature service businesses like restaurants. As consumers become increasingly time poor, casual dining is on the increase. So, too, is the desire to eat healthily, and being able to see food cooked from scratch using fresh ingredients is also likely to appeal to many consumers. Vapiano claims that it is the 'future of fresh casual dining' and time will tell whether it is correct.[1]

For a number of decades now, it has been recognized that the marketing of **service** enterprises presents some additional challenges for the marketing manager. In the main, these challenges stem from the unique characteristics of services. For example, in many instances, services are produced and consumed at the same time, unlike traditional goods businesses where products are made in a factory, stored and then delivered, sometimes through a long distribution channel, to the market. This means that running a services business creates some unique issues. It does not to imply, however, that the principles of marketing covered in earlier chapters of this book do not apply to services, they do, but some additional considerations need to be borne in mind as well.

The services sector continues to become increasingly important. Throughout much of the developed world, its growth has been very rapid and accounts for up to 60 to 70 per cent of the gross national product of some countries, thus far outweighing that of manufacturing and agriculture.

The unique characteristics of services

There are four key distinguishing characteristics of services, namely intangibility, inseparability, variability and perishability (see Figure 7.1).

Intangibility

Pure services cannot be seen, tasted, touched or smelled before they are bought—that is, they are intangible. Rather a service is a deed, performance or effort, not an object, device or thing.[2] **Intangibility** may mean that a customer may find difficulty in evaluating a service before purchase. For example, it is virtually impossible to judge how enjoyable a holiday will be before taking it because the holiday cannot be shown to a customer before consumption, unlike a physical product like a mobile phone.

For some services, their intangible nature leads to difficulty in evaluation even after consumption. For example, it is not easy to judge how thorough a car service has been immediately afterwards—there is no way of telling if everything that should have been checked has been checked.

The challenge for the service provider is to use tangible cues to service quality. For example, a holiday firm may show pictures of the holiday destination, display testimonials from satisfied holidaymakers and provide details in a brochure of the kind of entertainment available. The staff of US-based computer services company the Geek Squad are clearly distinguishable through their short-sleeved white shirts, black ties and badges, and their colourful 'Geek Mobiles' in which they drive to house calls.[3] Service companies, like hotels, invest heavily in tangibles

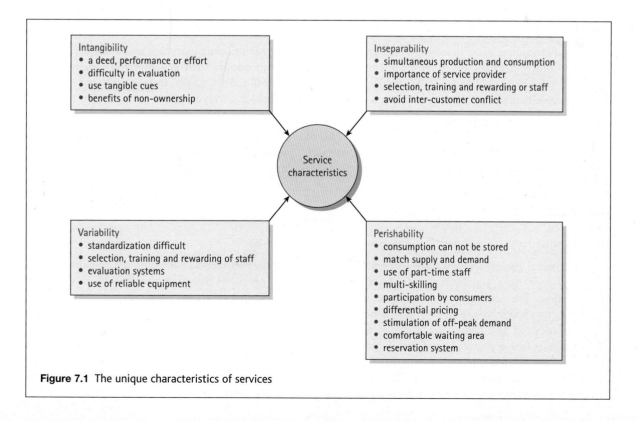

Figure 7.1 The unique characteristics of services

such as the décor of rooms and staff uniforms (see Marketing in Action 7.1).

The task is to provide an indication of likely service quality. McDonald's does this by controlling the physical settings of its restaurants and by using the golden arches as a branding cue. By having a consistent offering, the company has effectively dealt with the difficulties that consumers have in evaluating the quality of a service. Standard menus and ordering procedures have also ensured uniform and easy access for customers, while allowing quality control.[4]

Intangibility also means that the customer cannot own a service. Payment is for use or performance. For example, a car may be hired or a medical operation performed. Service organizations sometimes stress the benefits of non-ownership such as lower capital costs and the spreading of payment charges.

Marketing in Action 7.1: Rebranding Holiday Inn

> **Study guide:** Below is a review of the rebranding of the Holiday Inn hotel chain, with a focus on the changes being made to hotel tangibles. Read it and think of an example of another service business. Identify the tangibles in this business and how they might be updated.

Holiday Inn is part of the Intercontinental Hotel Group (IHG), which is one of the world's largest hotel groups, with almost 4000 outlets in over 100 countries. The original Holiday Inn chain was founded in the USA in 1952 and quickly grew its reputation as a middle-market family hotel. As well as continuing to serve this segment, it also targets business travellers and competes in a crowded sector against a variety of other well-known brands, such as Ramada Inn, Best Western and Quality Inn. It sister brand, Holiday Inn Express, targets more budget-conscious travellers.

In 2007, IHG decided to rebrand Holiday Inn to take advantage of what it determined to be a gap in the market between it and more upmarket brands such as Marriott and Hilton. The overall cost of the initiative was estimated to be US$1 billion, with a minimum investment of US$200,000 from each hotel owner. The rebranding was expected to move at a rate of 150 hotels per month and finish by 2010. A particular focus of the effort was on tangibles such as the hotel signage and upgrading of lobbies, which influence the important first impressions that customers get. For example, the group spent two years developing perfumes and a music list to complement its image. Holiday Inns will smell of fresh odours such as lemongrass, paired with the music of bands like U2, while the Express chain will have a musky, woody scent and be complemented by the soft pop sounds of Jack Johnson and John Mayer.

The decision to rebrand Holiday Inn was taken after research on 18,000 customers, which took two years and cost £20 million. The overall level of investment in the tangible aspects of the hotel experience demonstrates how important they are perceived to be when delivering services. Holiday Inn expects that the investment will deliver a memorable customer experience as well as increased room revenue.

Based on: Blitz (2007);[5] Ranson (2007);[6] Sibun (2007)[7]

Inseparability

Unlike physical goods, services have **inseparability** —that is, they have simultaneous production and consumption. For example, a haircut, a medical operation, psychoanalysis, a holiday and a pop concert are produced and consumed at the same time. This contrasts with a physical good that is produced, stored and distributed through intermediaries before being bought and consumed. This illustrates the importance of the service provider, who is an integral part of the satisfaction gained by the consumer. How service providers conduct themselves may have a crucial bearing on repeat business over and above the technical efficiency of the service task. For example, how courteous and friendly the service provider is may play a large part in the customer's perception of the service experience. The service must be provided not only at the right time and in the right place but also in the right way.[8]

Often, in the customer's eyes, the photocopier service engineer or the insurance representative *is* the company. Consequently, the selection, training and rewarding of staff who are the frontline service people is of fundamental importance in the achievement of high standards of service quality. This notion of the inseparability of production and consumption gave rise to the idea of relationship marketing in services, as we shall see later. In such circumstances, managing buyer–seller interaction is central to effective marketing and can be fulfilled only in a relationship with the customer.[9]

Furthermore, the consumption of the service may take place in the presence of other consumers. This is apparent with restaurant meals, air, rail or coach travel, and many forms of entertainment, for example. Consequently, enjoyment of the service is dependent not only on the service provided, but also on other consumers. Therefore service providers need to identify possible sources of nuisance (e.g. noise, smoke, queue jumping) and make adequate provision to avoid inter-customer conflict. For example, a restaurant layout should provide reasonable space between tables and non-smoking areas so that the potential for conflict is minimized.

Marketing managers should not underestimate the role played by customers in aiding other customers in their decision-making. A study into service interactions in IKEA stores found that almost all customer–employee exchanges related to customer concerns about 'place' (e.g. 'Can you direct me to the pick-up point?') and 'function' (e.g. 'How does this chair work?'). However, interactions between customers took the form of opinions on the quality of materials used in products, advice on bed sizes and how to move around the in-store restaurant. Many customers appeared to display a degree of product knowledge or expertise bordering on that of contact personnel.[10]

Variability

Service quality may be subject to considerable **variability**, which makes standardization difficult (see Exhibit 7.1). Two restaurants within the same chain may have variable service owing to the capabilities of their respective managers and staff. Two marketing courses at the same university may vary considerably in terms of quality, depending on the lecturer. Quality variations among physical products may be subject to tighter controls through centralized production, automation and quality checking before dispatch. Services, however, are often conducted at multiple locations, by people who may vary in their attitudes (and tiredness), and are subject to simultan-

Simply come back tomorrow. ANNUAL TICKET

Exhibit 7.1 This clever advertisement for Berlin Zoo focuses on the problem of variability in services – if you missed the animals because they were hiding, you can always come back again!

eous production and consumption. The last characteristic means that a service fault (e.g. rudeness) cannot be quality checked and corrected between production and consumption, unlike a physical product such as misaligned car windscreen wipers.

The potential for variability in service quality emphasizes the need for rigorous selection, training and rewarding of staff in service organizations. Training should emphasize the standards expected of personnel when dealing with customers. *Evaluation systems* should be developed that allow customers to report on their experiences with staff. Some service organizations, notably the British Airports Authority, tie reward systems to customer satisfaction surveys, which are based, in part, on the service quality provided by their staff.

Service standardization is a related method of tackling the variability problem. For example, a university department could agree to use the same software platform when developing course delivery. The use of reliable equipment rather than people can also help in standardization—for example, the supply of drinks via vending machines or cash through bank machines.

Exhibit 7.2 The various DisneyWorld theme parks are renowned for their queuing systems, which is how they deal with the problem of excessive demand for their most popular activities

However, great care needs to be taken regarding equipment reliability and efficiency. For example, the security of internet banking facilities impacts upon consumers' willingness to use this medium for financial transactions.

Perishability

The fourth characteristic of services is their **perishability** in the sense that consumption cannot be stored for the future. A hotel room or an airline seat that is not occupied today represents lost income that cannot be gained tomorrow. If a physical good is not sold, it can be stored for sale later. Therefore it is important to match supply and demand for services. For example, if a hotel has high weekday occupancy but is virtually empty at weekends, a key marketing task is to provide incentives for weekend use. This might involve offering weekend discounts, or linking hotel use with leisure activities such as golf, fishing or hiking.

Service providers also have the problem of catering for peak demand when supply may be insufficient. A physical goods provider may build up inventory in slack periods for sale during peak demand. Service providers do not have this option. Consequently alternative methods need to be considered. For example, supply flexibility can be varied through the use of part-time staff doing peak periods. Multi-skilling means that employees may be trained in many tasks. Supermarket staff can be trained to fill shelves, and work at the checkout at peak periods. Participation by consumers may be encouraged in production

(e.g. self-service breakfasts in hotels). Demand may be smoothed through differential pricing to encourage customers to visit during off-peak periods (for example, lower-priced cinema and theatre seats for afternoon performances). If delay is unavoidable then another option is to make it more acceptable, for example, by providing effective queuing systems, a comfortable waiting area with seating and free refreshments (see Exhibit 7.2). Finally, a reservation system as commonly used in restaurants, hair salons, and theatres can be used to control peak demand and assist time substitution.

In summary, intangibility, inseparability, variability and perishability combine to distinguish services from products. But it is important to remember that they are not completely distinct and in most instances it is a matter of degree. For example, a marketing research study would provide a report (physical good) that represents the outcome of a number of service activities (discussions with client, designing the research strategy, interviewing respondents and analysing the results). Figure 7.2 shows a physical goods–service continuum with the position of each offering dependent upon its ratio of the tangible/intangible elements. At the pure goods end of the scale is clothing, as the purchase of a skirt or socks is not normally accompanied by a service. Machinery purchase may involve more service elements in the form of installation and maintenance. Software design is positioned on the service side of the continuum since the value of the product is dependent on design expertise rather than the cost of the

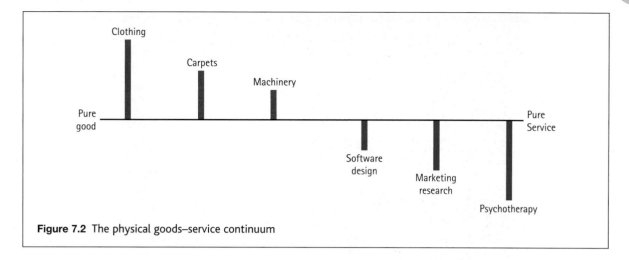

Figure 7.2 The physical goods–service continuum

physical product (disk). Finally, psychotherapy may be regarded as a pure service since the client receives nothing tangible from the transaction. Opportunities for competitive advantage often lie in the service components. For example, cinemas are once again suffering falling audiences as films are quickly released on DVD and watched at home by viewers.[11] Improving the service component represents one of the few avenues for cinemas to wrest back patrons.

The services marketing mix

The **services marketing mix** is an extension of the 4-Ps framework introduced in Chapter 1. The essential elements of product, promotion, price and place remain but three additional variables—people, physical evidence and process—are included to produce a 7-Ps mix.[12] The need for the extension is due to the high degree of direct contact between the firm and the customer, the highly visible nature of the service assembly process, and the simultaneity of production and consumption. While it is possible to discuss people, physical evidence and process within the original 4-Ps framework (for example, people could be considered part of the product offering) the extension allows a more thorough analysis of the marketing ingredients necessary for successful services marketing. As we shall see, the management of each element of the marketing mix is influenced by the unique characteristics of services discussed above.

Product

As we saw above, services are intangible. This means that service customers suffer higher perceived risk in their decision-making and that the three elements of the extended marketing mix—people, physical evidence and process—are crucial in influencing the

customer's perception of service quality. These will be discussed later.

In the previous chapter we noted that branding decisions are crucial for effective marketing. The brand name of a service influences the perception of that service. Research on service organizations has identified four characteristics of successful brand names, as follows.[13]

1   *Distinctiveness*: it immediately identifies the services provider and differentiates it from the competition.
2   *Relevance*: it communicates the nature of the service and the service benefit.
3   *Memorability*: it is easily understood and remembered.
4   *Flexibility*: it not only expresses the service organization's current business but also is broad enough to cover foreseeable new ventures.

Wagamama, the successful Japanese noodle chain, literally translates as 'wilful naughty child', but the distinctiveness of its name and service has proven to be attractive in foreign markets. Credit cards provide examples of effective brand names: Visa suggests internationality and MasterCard emphasizes top quality. Obviously the success of the brand name is heavily dependent on the service organization's ability to deliver on the promise it implies. Sometimes service brand names are changed, such as the decisions by Aviva, the UK's biggest insurer group, to drop its Norwich Union brand, which had existed for over 200 years, and by Eagle Star to change its name to that of its parent, Zurich.

Promotion

The intangible element of a service may be difficult to communicate. For example, it may be difficult to represent courtesy, hard work and customer care in

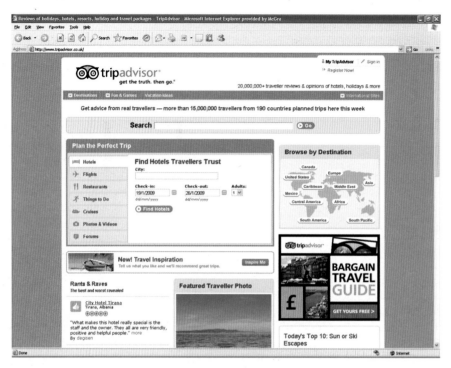

Exhibit 7.3 The website TripAdvisor.com has become one of the most popular sites for consumers to talk about both their positive and negative experiences with travel destinations, hotels and airlines

an advertisement. Once again the answer is to use tangible cues that will help customers understand and judge the service. A hotel, for example, can show the buildings, swimming pool, friendly staff and happy customers; an investment company can provide tangible evidence of past performance; testimonials from satisfied customers can also be used to communicate services benefits. Netto, the Danish-based supermarket chain, used testimonials from six customers in its UK advertising to explain the advantages of shopping there.

Advertising can be used to communicate and reinforce the image of a service. For example, store image can enhance customer satisfaction and build store loyalty.[14] The new media can also be used to promote services. For example, some online retailers use targeted emails to encourage customers to visit their sites. The travel and leisure retailer Lastminute.com sends more than two million emails to customers every week with the content tailored to fit the recipient's age and lifestyle.[15]

Word of mouth is critical to success for services because of their experiential nature (see Exhibit 7.3). For example, talking to people who have visited a resort or hotel is more convincing than reading holiday brochures. Promotion, therefore, must acknowledge the dominant role of personal influence in the choice process and stimulate word-of-mouth communication. Cowell suggests four approaches:[16]

1 persuading satisfied customers to inform others of their satisfaction (e.g. American Express rewards customers who introduce others to its service)
2 developing materials that customers can pass on to others
3 targeting opinion leaders in advertising campaigns
4 encouraging potential customers to talk to current customers (e.g. open days at universities).

Communication should also be targeted at employees because of their importance in creating and maintaining service quality. Internal communications can define management expectations of staff, reinforce the need to delight the customer and explain the rewards that follow from giving excellent service. External communications that depict service quality can also influence internal staff if they include employees and show how they take exceptional care of their customers.

Care should be taken not to exaggerate promises in promotional material since this may build up unachievable expectations. For example, Delta Airlines used the advertising slogan 'Delta is ready when you are'. This caused problems because it built up customers' expectations that the airline would always be ready—an impossible task. This led Delta to change its slogan to the more realistic 'We love to fly and it shows'.[17]

Price

Price is a key marketing tool for three reasons. First, as it is often difficult to evaluate a service before purchase, price may act as an indicator of perceived quality. For example, in a travel brochure the price charged by hotels may be used to indicate their quality. Some companies expect a management consultant to charge high fees, otherwise they cannot be particularly good. Second, price is an important tool in controlling demand: matching demand and supply is critical in services because they cannot be stored. Creative use of pricing can help to smooth demand. Third, a key segmentation variable with services is price sensitivity. Some customers may be willing to pay a much higher price than others. Time is often used to segment price-sensitive and price-insensitive customers. For example, Royal Bank of Scotland generates about one-third of its income for its corporate lending and capital markets division where it has a reputation for the keenness of its prices—in other words, the level of interest that it charges its customers for their borrowings.[18]

Place

Distribution channels for services are usually more direct than for many physical goods. Because services are intangible, the services marketer is less concerned with storage, the production and consumption is often simultaneous, and the personal nature of services means that direct contact with the service provider (or at best its agent) is desirable. Agents are used when the individual service provider cannot provide a sufficiently wide selection for customers. Consequently agents are often used for the marketing of travel, insurance and entertainment. However, increased use of the internet means that direct dealings with the service provider are becoming more frequent.

Growth for many service companies means opening new facilities in new locations. Whereas producers of physical goods can expand production at one site to serve the needs of a geographically spread market, the simultaneous production and consumption of hotel, banking, catering, retailing and accounting services, for example, means that expansion often means following a multi-site strategy. The evaluation of store locations is therefore a critical skill for services marketers. Much of the success of top European supermarket chains has resulted from their ability to choose profitable new sites for their retailing operations and Tesco's dominance of the UK market has been attributed to its pre-emption of many of the best store locations around the country.

People

Because of the simultaneity of production and consumption in services, the firm's personnel occupy a key position in influencing customer perceptions of product quality.[19] In fact, service quality is inseparable from the quality of the service provider. John Carlzon, head of the airline SAS, called this interaction 'moments of truth'. He explained that SAS faced 65,000 moments of truth per day and that the outcomes determined the success of the company. Research on customer loyalty in the service industry has shown that only 14 per cent of customers who stopped patronizing service businesses did so because they were dissatisfied with the quality of what they had bought. More than two-thirds stopped buying because they found service staff indifferent or unhelpful.[20]

In order for service employees to be in the frame of mind to treat customers well, they need to feel that their company is treating them well. An important marketing task, then, is to set standards to improve the quality of service provided by employees and monitor their performance. Without training and control, employees tend to be variable in their performance, leading to variable service quality. The relationship between staff satisfaction and customer satisfaction is a complex one, as shown in Marketing in Action 7.2.

The selection of suitable people is the starting point of the process as the nature of the job requires appropriate personality characteristics. Once selected, training is required to familiarize recruits to the job requirements and the culture of the organization. Socialization then allows recruits to experience the culture and tasks of the organization. Service quality may also be affected by the degree to which staff are empowered or given the authority to satisfy customers and deal with their problems. For example, each member of staff of Marriott Hotels is allowed to spend up to £1000 on their own initiative to solve customer problems.[21] Maintaining a motivated workforce in the face of irate customers, faulty support systems and the boredom that accompanies some service jobs is a demanding task. Some service companies give employee-of-the-month awards in recognition of outstanding service. Reward and remuneration is also important. For example, the US retailer Costco competes against Wal-Mart in the discount warehouse sector. But its pay and conditions are far superior to its main rival and it has a staff turnover rate of 17 per cent annually compared with 70 per cent for the sector.[22]

Marketing in Action 7.2: The happy staff–happy customers link

> **Study guide:** Below are some perspectives on the happy staff–happy customers debate. Read the text and think of examples of service organizations that you have visited that have both apparently happy and unhappy staff. What are the implications of each for your experience of the service?

There is a long-held belief in services marketing that a well-motivated, happy workforce increases the chances that customers will be pleased with their service experience. Some companies, like Virgin Group, go even further, arguing that a virtuous cycle of happy staff leading to happy customers leading to happy shareholders exists. Because satisfied customers are likely to spend more, this gives rise to higher profits and, ultimately, better returns to the company's owners.

Another popular recent trend has been the emergence of the 'best companies to work for' rankings, which rate organizations in terms of how happy their employees are with their working conditions and remuneration. And there is now a Great Places to Work Institute dedicated to understanding what makes workplaces great. Companies with a reputation for the quality of their working conditions include SAS, which operates in the competitive computer software industry. Its campus in North Carolina has extensive sports facilities, childcare and early schooling, and its own primary healthcare centre, which are all free to staff. It also has a long-term 'wellness' programme and a lifestyle education scheme, with the result that the average SAS worker is off sick for only 2.5 days per year. The company's staff turnover rate is around 4 per cent, which is much lower than the 20 per cent average for the software industry, which has the direct monetary benefit of saving about US$85 million a year in recruitment and training costs. Its annual revenues are now about US$2 billion and it has always been profitable.

But the links between this kind of investment in happy staff and happy customers is not as clear as it would intuitively appear to be. For example, research in the UK at 13 retail organizations in financial services, food retailing, telecommunications and insurance revealed a very mixed picture. In some instances there was a correlation between happy staff and happy customers but in others the staff were happy and the customers unhappy, and even vice versa. A further interesting finding was that, where employees are more satisfied than customers, company profits tend to rise, and vice versa. A significant problem for service companies is that, despite all the people-orientated initiatives that have been tried in recent times such as team-building exercises and culture change programmes, there has been no discernible increase in employee engagement with their companies. A Gallup study of 450 companies in 124 countries has consistently shown over the past seven years that no more than 30 per cent of employees are actively engaged in their jobs.

The implications of these findings are very important and demonstrate that the relationship between happy staff and happy customers is a complex one. Initiatives aimed at staff satisfaction should in the first instance be judged by their impact on customer satisfaction.

Based on: Anonymous (2007);[23] Mitchell (2007)[24]

Physical evidence

As we saw above, customers look for clues to the likely quality of a service by inspecting the tangible evidence. For example, prospective customers may gaze through a restaurant window to check the appearance of the waiters, the décor and furnishings. The ambience of a retail store is highly dependent on décor, and colour can play an important role in establishing mood because colour has meaning. For example, the reception area of the Petshotel chain in the USA is typically furnished with floral soft furnishings, armchairs, a wide-screen television and stainless steel bowls filled with doggie biscuits. This and its slogan, 'All the comforts of home', is designed to put pet owners at ease that their dogs will be well looked after while they are away.[25]

The layout of a service operation can be a compromise between the operation's need for efficiency, and marketing's desire for effectively serving the customer. For example, the temptation to squeeze in an extra table in a restaurant or seating in an aircraft may be at the expense of customer comfort. Changes in the physical evidence are often part of a marketer's effort to reposition a brand. For example, the desire by McDonald's to improve the image of its brand has seen it invest in lime-green 'egg' chairs in many of its European restaurants, as well as putting in iPods so that customers can sit and listen to music. This moves the brand much closer to a company like Starbucks rather than its traditional competitors such as Burger King.

Process

This is the procedures, mechanisms and flow of activities by which a service is acquired. Process decisions radically affect how a service is delivered to customers. For example, a self-service cafeteria is very different from a restaurant. Marketing managers need to know if self-service is acceptable (or indeed desirable). Queuing may provide an opportunity to create a **differential advantage** by reduction/elimination, or making the time spent waiting more enjoyable. Certainly waiting for service is a common experience for customers and is a strong determinant of overall satisfaction with the service and customer loyalty. Research has shown that an attractive waiting environment can prevent customers becoming irritated or bored very quickly, even though they may have to wait a long time. Both appraisal of the wait and satisfaction with the service improved when the attractiveness of the waiting environment (measured by atmosphere, cleanliness, spaciousness and climate) was rated higher.[26] Providing a more effective service (shorter queues) may be at odds with operations as the remedy may be to employ more staff.

Reducing delivery time—for example, the time between ordering a meal and receiving it—can also improve service quality. This need not necessarily cost more if customers can be persuaded to become involved in the production process, as reflected in the successful growth of self-service breakfast bars in hotels. The drive for efficiencies also means that service companies outsource parts of the service process, which has significant risks for service performance and reputation. For example, British Airways' decision to sell its catering business and outsource its meals to Gate Gourmet was problematic when its new supplier's industrial relations problems disrupted its supply of meals. Process problems were also at the root of much of the disruption experienced during the opening of Terminal 5 at Heathrow in London.

Managing services enterprises

Successfully implementing the services marketing mix and coping with the unique challenges of services enterprises places a number of demands on managers. First, the variability and inseparability of services presents some unique challenges in managing service productivity. Second, all the company's activities must be geared towards delivering a given level of service quality, which can be key in differentiating the offerings of one provider from those of another. Finally, a focus on quality and service excellence creates the opportunity for building long-term relationships with clients that can be very beneficial to the company.

Managing service productivity

Productivity is a measure of the relationship between an input and an output. For example, if more people can be served (output) using the same number of staff (input), productivity per employee has risen. Clearly there can be conflict between improving service productivity (efficiency) and raising service quality (effectiveness). For example, a doctor who reduces consultation time per patient, or a university that increases tutorial group size, raise productivity at the risk of lowering service quality.

Clearly, a balance must be struck between productivity and service quality. There are ways of improving productivity without compromising quality. As we saw earlier, customers can be involved in the service delivery process, such as in self-service restaurants and petrol stations, and supply and demand for services can be balanced through either capacity expansion or demand management techniques. Advances in technology also greatly assist in improving service productivity, as shown in Technology Focus 7.1.

Managing service quality

Intuitively, it makes sense to suggest that improving service quality will increase customer satisfaction, leading to higher sales and profits (see Marketing in Action 7.3). The increased use of customer satisfaction studies in industries like telecommunications means that poor ratings can have a significant impact on customer retention and revenues. Companies with a reputation for poor service or for not handling customer complaints effectively often see their market performance suffer.

Technology Focus 7.1: Automatic service!

Technology can be used to improve service productivity and also service quality. For example, airport X-ray surveillance equipment raises the throughput of passengers (productivity) and speeds the process of checking in (service quality). Automatic cash dispensers in banks increase the number of transactions per period (productivity) while reducing customer waiting time (service quality). Automatic vending machines increase the number of drinks sold per establishment (productivity) while improving accessibility for customers (service quality).

Technology has also become an increasingly important component of service delivery. For example, in 2007, companies spent US$280 billion on outsourced call centres, many of which are customer service centres. As consumers become increasingly frustrated by the service provided by many call centres, further investments in software are necessary to improve service. For example, 'demographic mapping' software provides information on the products callers are more likely to buy based upon their location, the time of day of the call, and whether they are calling from a mobile or land line. This enables calls to be more efficiently routed.

The internet has had a dramatic effect on some service businesses. For example, the travel industry has undergone dramatic change. The role of the travel agent has changed as consumers book travel and holidays online. This change in consumer behaviour towards the self-organization of travel plans has brought with it new opportunities. Tour operators used to offer packages including transfers from airports to hotels, but this is not available for independent travellers. This created an opportunity for the UK company, Holidaytaxis.com, which is an advance online booking system for airport transfers. It also offers a shuttle bus service, Shuttletransfers.com, for groups, as well as Businesstaxis.com, which has seen it move into the lucrative corporate market.

In summary, technology has played, and will continue to play, a crucial role in how service organizations interact with customers. The real challenge for organizations is finding the correct balance between the efficiencies generated through the use of technology and the quality and flexibility of service that can be provided by people. Innovative solutions are being pioneered by software companies like Liveperson.com, which provides a facility whereby a pop-up window appears if a consumer quits an application inviting the user to either phone or text a real customer service person for assistance.

Indeed, it has been shown that companies that are rated higher on service quality perform better in terms of market share growth and profitability.[27] Yet for many companies high standards of service quality remain elusive. There are four causes of poor perceived quality (see Figure 7.3). These are the barriers that separate the perception of service quality from what customers expect.[28]

Barriers to the matching of expected and perceived service levels

Misconceptions barrier: this arises from management's misunderstanding of what the customer expects. Lack of marketing research may lead managers to misconceive the important service attributes that customers use when evaluating a service, and the way in which customers use attributes in evaluation.

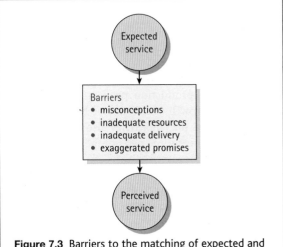

Figure 7.3 Barriers to the matching of expected and perceived service levels

Marketing in Action 7.3: Customer service excellence at Singapore Airlines

> **Study guide:** Below is a review of Singapore Airlines' customer service strategy. Read it and think of other examples of businesses that offer great service.

Singapore Airlines (SIA) has an outstanding reputation for the quality of its customer service and is a frequent winner of awards in this area. For example, in 2003 it was awarded 'Airline of the Year' and 'Best Trans-Pacific Airline' by OAG in the UK, and received the 'World's Best Service Award' from US magazine *Travel & Leisure*. In previous years it has won awards in categories such as 'Best Long-Haul Airline', 'Best First Class', 'Best Economy Class', 'Best Foreign Airline' and 'Best Crisis Management'.

So what makes this company so good? In short, it has had a focus on delighting its customers since its formation and, over the years, has built up a reputation for consistently good service. In terms of in-flight service, SIA emphasizes the quality of its food (designed by an international culinary panel of chefs), seats are designed to be comfortable, the in-flight entertainment system (Krisworld) provides individual video screens for each passenger, and so on. But what separates SIA from other airlines that offer similar tangibles is the empathy and responsiveness shown by cabin crew in responding to the needs of particular customers. This quality service is captured by the 'Singapore girl', which is the iconic image standing for Asian charm and hospitality that appears in all the company's marketing.

Like all service leaders, there is a commitment to customer service that runs all the way down from senior management and throughout the organization. For example, as a former CEO of SIA commented, 'our passengers are our raison d'être. If SIA is successful, it is because we have never allowed ourselves to forget that important fact.' Systems have been put in place that allow quality of service to flourish. For example, SIA has a service development department that hones and tests any change before it is introduced. It also employs an innovation approach it calls 40-30-30, where it focuses 40 per cent of resources on training, 30 per cent on review of process and procedures, and 30 per cent on creating new products and services. Training is key and new stewardesses undergo training for four months, longer than any other airline. It also has one attendant for every 22 seats, which is a higher ratio than all of its competitors.

The results of this strategy speak for themselves. Even though SIA fares are often more expensive than those of other airlines, the company has been consistently profitable since the beginning in an industry renowned for its cyclicality and difficult years.

Based on: Heracleous, Wirtz and Johnston (2004);[29] Kingi (2003)[30]

Inadequate resources barrier: managers may understand customer expectations but be unwilling to provide the resources necessary to meet them. This may arise because of a cost reduction or productivity focus, or simply because of the inconvenience it may cause.

Inadequate delivery barrier: managers may understand customer expectations and supply adequate resources but fail to select, train and reward staff adequately, resulting in poor or inconsistent service. This may manifest itself in poor communication

skills, inappropriate dress, and unwillingness to solve customer problems.

Exaggerated promises barrier: even when customer understanding, resources, and staff management are in place, a gap between customer expectations and perceptions can still arise through exaggerated promises. Advertising and selling messages that build expectations to a pitch that cannot be fulfilled may leave customers disappointed even when receiving a good service.

Meeting customer expectations

A key to providing service quality is the understanding and meeting of customer expectations. To do so requires a clear picture of the criteria used to form these expectations, recognizing that consumers of services value not only the outcome of the service encounter but also the experience of taking part in it. For example, an evaluation of a haircut depends not only on the quality of the cut but also the experience of having a haircut. Clearly, a hairdresser needs not only technical skills but also the ability to communicate in an interesting and polite manner. The following 10 criteria may be used when evaluating the outcome and experience of a service encounter.[31]

1 *Access*: is the service provided at convenient locations and times with little waiting?
2 *Reliability*: is the service consistent and dependable?
3 *Credibility*: can customers trust the service company and its staff?
4 *Security*: can the service be used without risk?
5 *Understanding the customer*: does it appear that the service provider understands customer expectations?
6 *Responsiveness*: how quickly do service staff respond to customer problems, requests and questions?
7 *Courtesy*: do service staff act in a friendly and polite manner?
8 *Competence*: do service staff have the required skills and knowledge?
9 *Communication*: is the service described clearly and accurately?
10 *Tangibles*: how well managed is the tangible evidence of the service (e.g. staff appearance, décor, layout)?

These criteria form a useful checklist for service providers wishing to understand how their customers judge them. A self-analysis may show areas that need improvement but the most reliable approach is to check that customers use these criteria and conduct marketing research to compare performance against competition. Where service quality is dependent on a succession of service encounters (for example, a hotel stay may encompass check-in, the room itself, the restaurant, breakfast and check-out) each should be measured in terms of their impact on total satisfaction so that corrective action can be taken if necessary.[32]

Developing and managing customer relationships

Delivering excellent service quality creates the opportunity to build an ongoing relationship with customers (see Exhibit 7.4). The idea of **relationship marketing** can be applied to many industries. It is particularly important in services since there is often direct contact between service provider and consumer —for example, doctor and patient, hotel staff and guests. The quality of the relationship that develops will often determine its length. Not all service encounters have the potential for a long-term relationship, however. For example, a passenger at an international airport who needs road transportation will probably never meet the taxi driver again, and the choice of taxi supplier will be dependent on the passenger's position in the queue rather than free choice. In this case the exchange—cash for journey—is a pure transaction: the driver knows that it is unlikely that there will ever be a repeat purchase.[33] Organizations, therefore, need to decide when the practice of relationship marketing is most applicable. The following conditions suggest the use of relationship marketing activities.[34]

- There is an ongoing or periodic desire for the service by the customer, e.g. insurance or theatre service versus funeral service.
- The customer controls the selection of a service provider, e.g. selecting a hotel versus entering the first taxi in an airport waiting line.
- The customer has alternatives from which to choose, e.g. selecting a restaurant versus buying water from the only utility company service in a community.

Exhibit 7.4 Scandinavian Airlines has developed a reputation for the quality of service it offers to its business-class customers

The existence of strong customer relationships brings benefits both for organizations and customers. There are six benefits to service organizations in developing and maintaining strong customer relationships.[35] The first is *increased purchases*. Customers tend to spend more because, as the relationship develops, trust grows between the partners. Second is *lower costs*. The start-up costs associated with attracting new customers are likely to be far higher than the cost of retaining existing customers. Third, loyal customers generate a significant *lifetime value*. If a customer spends £80 in a supermarket per week, resulting in £8 profit, and uses the supermarket 45 times a year over 30 years, the lifetime value of that customer is almost £11,000. Fourth, the intangible aspects of a relationship are not easily copied by the competition, generating a *sustainable competitive advantage* (again, see Marketing in Action 7.3). Fifth, satisfied customers generate additional business due to the importance of *word-of-mouth* promotion in services industries. Finally, satisfied, loyal customers raise *employees' job satisfaction* and decrease staff turnover.

The net result of these six benefits of developing customer relationships is high profits. A study has shown across a variety of service industries that profits climb steeply when a firm lowers its customer defection rate.[36] Firms could improve profits from 25 to 85 per cent (depending on industry) by reducing customer defections by just 5 per cent. The reasons are that loyal customers generate more revenue for more years and the costs of maintaining existing customers are lower than the costs of acquiring new ones.

Entering into a long-term relationship can also reap benefits for the customer. First, since the intangible nature of services makes them difficult to evaluate beforehand, purchase relationships can help to reduce the risk and stress involved in making choices. Second, strong relationships allow the service provider to deliver a higher-quality service, which can be customized to particular needs. Maintaining a relationship reduces the customer's switching costs and, finally, customers can reap social and status benefits from the relationship, such as when restaurant managers get to know them personally.

Two key aspects of building relationships are bonding and service recovery. We will turn to these next.

Bonding

Retention strategies vary in the degree to which they bond the parties together. One framework that illustrates this idea distinguishes between three levels of retention strategy based on the types of bond used to cement the relationship.[37]

1 *Level 1*: at this level the bond is primarily through financial incentives—for example, higher discounts on prices for larger-volume purchases, or frequent flyer or loyalty points resulting in lower future prices. The problem is that the potential for a sustainable competitive advantage is low because price incentives are easy for competitors to copy even if they take the guise of frequent flyer or loyalty points.

2 *Level 2*: this higher level of bonding relies on more than just price incentives and consequently raises the potential for a sustainable competitive advantage. Level 2 retention strategies build long-term relationships through social as well as financial bonds, capitalizing on the fact that many service encounters are also social encounters. Customers become clients, the relationship becomes personalized and the service customized. Characteristics of this type of relationship include frequent communication with customers, providing personal treatment like sending cards, and enhancing the core service with educational or entertainment activities such as seminars or visits to sporting events. Some hotels keep records of their guests' personal preferences such as their favourite newspaper and alcoholic drink.

3 *Level 3*: this top level of bonding is formed by financial, social and structural bonds. Structural bonds tie service providers to their customers through providing solutions to customers' problems that are designed into the service delivery system. For example, logistics companies often supply their clients with equipment that ties them into their systems.

Service recovery

Service recovery strategies should be designed to solve the problem and restore the customer's trust in the firm, as well improve the service system so that the problem does not recur in the future.[38] They are crucial because an inability to recover service failures and mistakes lose customers directly as well as through their tendency to tell other actual and potential customers about their negative experiences. This is particularly the case where consumers have paid a great deal for a service, such as first-class air passengers.

The first ingredient in a service recovery strategy is to set up a tracking system to identify system failures. Customers should be encouraged to report service problems since it is those customers that do not complain that are least likely to purchase again. Second, staff should be trained and empowered to respond to service complaints. This is important because research has shown that the successful resolution of a complaint can cause customers to feel more positive about the firm than before the service failure. For example, when P&O had to cancel a round-the-world cruise because of problems with its ship, the *Aurora*, it reportedly offered passengers their money back plus a discount on their next booking. Many passengers said they planned to travel on a P&O cruise in the future.[39]

Finally, a service recovery strategy should encourage learning so that service recovery problems are identified and corrected. Service staff should be motivated to report problems and solutions so that recurrent failures are identified and fixed. In this way, an effective service recovery system can lead to improved customer service, satisfaction and higher customer retention levels.

Marketing in non-profit organizations

Non-profit organizations attempt to achieve some other objective than profit. This does not mean that they are uninterested in income as they have to generate cash to survive. However, their primary goal is non-economic—for example, to provide cultural enrichment (an orchestra), to protect birds and animals (Royal Society for the Protection of Birds, Royal Society for the Prevention of Cruelty to Animals), to alleviate hunger (Oxfam), to provide education (schools and universities), to foster community activities (community associations), and to supply healthcare (hospitals) and public services (local authorities). Their worth and standing is not dependent on the profits they generate. They are discussed in this chapter as most non-profit organizations operate in the services sector. Indeed, non-profit organizations account for over half of all service provision in most European countries.

Marketing is of growing importance to many non-profit organizations because they need to generate funds in an increasingly competitive arena (see Exhibit 7.5). Even organizations that rely on government-sponsored grants need to show how their work is of benefit to society; they must meet the needs of their customers. Many non-profit organizations rely on membership fees and donations, which means that communication to individuals and organizations is required, and they must be persuaded to join or make a donation. This requires marketing skills, which are increasingly being applied. As we saw in Chapter 1, political parties, universities, hospitals and aid agencies are now frequent users of marketing.

Exhibit 7.5 This advertisement for Macmillan Cancer Support aims to generate awareness of this important organization

Characteristics of non-profit marketing

There are a number of characteristics of non-profit marketing that distinguish it from that conducted in profit-orientated organizations.[40]

Education vs meeting current needs
Some non-profit organizations see their role not only as meeting the current needs of their customers but also educating them in terms of new ideas and issues, cultural developments and social awareness. These goals may be in conflict with maximizing revenue or audience figures. For example, a public broadcasting organization like the BBC may trade off audience size for some of its objectives, or an orchestra may decide that more esoteric pieces of classical music should be played rather than more popular pieces.

Multiple publics
Most non-profit organizations serve several groups, or publics. The two broad groups are *donors*, who may be individuals, trusts, companies or government bodies, and *clients*, who include audiences, patients and beneficiaries.[41] The need to satisfy both donors and clients is a complicated marketing task. For example, a community association may be partly funded by the local authority and partly by the users (clients) of the association's buildings and facilities. To succeed, both groups have to be satisfied.

The BBC has to satisfy not only its viewers and listeners, but also the government, which decides the size of the licence fee that funds its activities. Non-profit organizations need to adopt marketing as a coherent philosophy for managing multiple public relationships.[42]

Measurement of success and conflicting objectives

For profit-orientated organizations success is ultimately measured in terms of profitability. For non-profit organizations, measuring success is not so easy. In universities, for example, is success measured in terms of research output, number of students taught, the range of qualifications or the quality of teaching? The answer is that it is a combination of these factors, which can lead to conflict—more students and a larger range of courses may reduce the time available for research. Decision-making is therefore complex in non-profit-orientated organizations.

Public scrutiny

While all organizations are subject to public scrutiny, public-sector non-profit organizations are never far from the public's attention. The reason is that they are publicly funded from taxes. This gives them extra newsworthiness and they have to be particularly careful not to become involved in controversy.

Marketing procedures for non-profit organizations

Despite these differences, the marketing procedures relevant to profit-orientated organizations can also be applied to non-profit organizations. Target marketing, differentiation and marketing-mix decisions need to be made. We will now discuss these issues with reference to the special characteristics of non-profit organizations.

Target marketing and differentiation

As we have already discussed, non-profit organizations can usefully segment their target publics into donors and clients (customers). Within each group, sub-segments of individuals and organizations need to be identified. These will be the targets for persuasive communications and the development of services. The needs of each group must be understood (see Marketing in Action 7.4). For example, donors may judge which charity to give to on the basis of awareness and reputation, the confidence that funds will not be wasted on excessive administration, and the perceived worthiness of the cause. The charity needs, therefore, not only to promote itself but also to gain publicity for its cause. Its level of donor funding will depend upon both these factors. The brand name

of the charity is also important. 'Oxfam' suggests the type of work the organization is mainly concerned with—relief of famine—and so is instantly recognizable. 'Action in Distress' is also suggestive of its type of work.

Market segmentation and targeting are key ingredients in the marketing of political parties. Potential voters are segmented according to their propensity to vote (obtainable from electoral registers) and their likelihood of voting for a particular party (obtainable from door-to-door canvassing returns). Resources can then be channelled to the segments most likely to switch votes in the forthcoming election, via direct mail and doorstep visits. Focus groups provide a feedback mechanism for testing the attractiveness of alternative policy options and gauging voters' opinions on key policy areas such as health, education and taxation. By keeping in touch with public opinion, political parties have the information to differentiate themselves from their competitors on issues that are important to voters. While such marketing research is unlikely to affect the underlying beliefs and principles upon which a political party is based, it is a necessary basis for the policy adaptations required to keep in touch with a changing electorate. [43]

Developing a marketing mix

Many non-profit organizations are skilled at *event marketing*. Events are organized to raise funds, including dinners, dances, coffee mornings, book sales, sponsored walks and theatrical shows. Not all events are designed to raise funds for the sponsoring organization. For example, the BBC has organized the Comic Relief and Children in Need telethons to raise money for worthy causes.

The pricing of services provided by non-profit organizations may not follow the guidelines applicable to profit-orientated pricing. For example, the price of a nursery school place organized by a community association may be held low to encourage poor families to take advantage of the opportunity. Some non-profit organizations exist to provide free access to services—for example, the National Health Service in the UK. In other situations, the price of a service provided by a non-profit organization may come from a membership or licence fee. For example, the Royal Society for the Protection of Birds (RSPB) charges an annual membership fee; in return members receive a quarterly magazine and free entry to RSPB bird watching sites. The BBC receives income from a licence fee, which all televisions owners have to pay. The level of this fee is set by government, making relations with political figures an important marketing consideration.

Marketing in Action 7.4: ActionAid targets the youth market

Study guide: Below is a review of the techniques used by ActionAid to promote itself. Read it and think of other examples of promotional techniques being used by not-for-profit organizations.

ActionAid was founded in 1972; its vision is a world without poverty, where every person can exercise their right to a life of dignity. The organization works with poor and marginalized communities in Africa, Asia and Latin America to help overcome the causes of poverty. It has five priority areas, namely education, HIV and AIDS, food, emergencies, and women and girls. As well as seeking to effect change in these areas it also lobbies governments and organizations such as the World Bank, the World Trade Organization, the International Monetary Fund and the EU to change policies that exacerbate poverty.

Young people are an important source of support for its activities and in trying to reach this group it has adopted some novel approaches. For example, at music festivals it set up a tent that offered karaoke during the day and club music at night. As well as dancing and relaxation, festival-goers were offered the chance to find out about trade issues and sign petitions. It also produced a strong slogan, 'Bollocks to Poverty', which it was felt was hard-hitting, direct and likely to appeal to this audience. The strategy appears to have worked. ActionAid reported that the campaign resulted in a four-fold increase in traffic to its website and more than 100,000 people signed a petition at one of its summer festivals.

Young people are a key market segment for aid agencies. They are likely to hold strong views about such issues and to be willing to back up those views with action, whether in the form of donations or volunteer work. Using music festivals to reach them is a clever approach as many of the artists playing at such festivals are likely to endorse the efforts of aid agencies. For example, Chris Martin, lead singer of the popular band Coldplay, had taken to having the slogan, 'Make Trade Fair' written on his hands. With their idols supporting the cause, young people were more likely to both hear and act on the message.

Based on: Chakrabortty (2005)[44]

Like most services, distribution systems for many non-profit organizations are short, with production and consumption simultaneous. This is the case for hospital operations, consultations with medical practitioners, education, nursery provision, cultural entertainment and many more services provided by non-profit organizations. Such organizations have to think carefully about how to deliver their services with the convenience that customers require. For example, Oxfam has 750 shops around the UK that sell second-hand clothing, books, music and household items that have been donated to it. It has also formed alliances with online retailers such as abebooks.co.uk to list and sell second-hand books, from which Oxfam receives a commission.

Many non-profit organizations are adept at using promotion to further their needs. The print media are popular with organizations seeking donations for worthy causes such as famine in Africa. Direct mail is also used to raise funds. Mailing lists of past donors

are useful here, and some organizations use lifestyle geodemographic analyses to identify the type of person who is more likely to respond to a direct mailing. Non-profit organizations also need to be aware of publicity opportunities that may arise because of their activities. Many editors are sympathetic to such publicity attempts because of their general interest to the public. Sponsorship is also a vital income source for many non-profit organizations.

Public relations has an important role to play in generating positive word-of-mouth communications and establishing the identity of the non-profit organization (e.g. a charity). Attractive fundraising settings (e.g. sponsored lunches) can be organized to ensure that the exchange proves to be satisfactory to donors. A key objective of communications efforts should be to produce a positive assessment of the fundraising transaction and to reduce the perceived risk of the donation so that donors develop trust and confidence in the organization and become committed to the cause.[45]

Summary

In this chapter, we examined the particular issues that arise when marketing services businesses. The following key issues were addressed.

1. There are four unique characteristics of services, namely intangibility, inseparability, variability and perishability. As a result marketers must find ways to 'tangibilize' services, must pay attention to service quality, must find ways to ensure service consistency, and must find ways to balance supply and demand for services.

2. The services marketing mix is broader than the marketing mix that is used for products in that attention needs to be paid to the issues of people, physical evidence and process.

3. Frontline employees are critical to the success of a service organization and great attention needs to be paid to their selection, training and motivation. Employee empowerment is a key element of service quality and service recovery.

4. Because of service variability and inseparability, good productivity can be difficult to achieve. Advances in technology have had a significant impact on both service productivity and service quality.

5. Service quality is a crucial element of services marketing. Essentially, it involves measuring how service perceptions match up against the expectations that customers have of the service provider.

6. Service businesses have the opportunity to build strong relationships with customers. Two key aspects of relationship building are bonding and service recovery.

7. Non-profit organizations attempt to achieve some objectives other than profit. Their two key publics are donors and clients; the needs of these two groups often conflict. In managing this complexity, non-profit organizations use conventional services marketing techniques.

Key terms

differential advantage a clear performance differential over competition on factors that are important to target customers

exaggerated promises barrier a barrier to the matching of expected and perceived service levels caused by the unwarranted building up of expectations by exaggerated promises

inadequate delivery barrier a barrier to the matching of expected and perceived service levels caused by the failure of the service provider to select, train and reward staff adequately, resulting in poor or inconsistent delivery of service

inadequate resources barrier a barrier to the matching of expected and perceived service levels caused by the unwillingness of service providers to provide the necessary resources

inseparability a characteristic of services, namely that their production cannot be separated from their consumption

intangibility a characteristic of services, namely that they cannot be touched, seen, tasted or smelled

misconceptions barrier a failure by marketers to understand what customers really value about their service

perishability a characteristic of services, namely that the capacity of a service business, such as a hotel room, cannot be stored—if it is not occupied, there is lost income that cannot be recovered

relationship marketing the process of creating, maintaining and enhancing strong relationships with customers and other stakeholders

service any deed, performance or effort carried out for the customer

services marketing mix product, place, price, promotion, people, process and physical evidence

variability a characteristic of services, namely that being delivered by people the standard of their performance is open to variation

Study questions

1. The marketing of services is no different to the marketing of physical goods. Discuss.

2. What are the barriers that can separate expected from perceived service? What must service providers do to eliminate these barriers?

3. Discuss the role of service staff in the creation of a quality service. Can you give examples from your own experiences of good and bad service encounters?

4. Discuss the benefits to organizations and customers of developing and maintaining strong customer relationships.

5. One of the biggest difficulties with services is that they cannot be stored. Discuss the strategies open to marketers to balance supply and demand for services.

6. How does marketing in non-profit organizations differ from that in profit-orientated companies. Choose a non-profit organization and discuss the extent to which marketing principles can be applied.

7. Visit www.epinions.com and www.tripadvisor.com. Discuss the impact of the existence of these websites on organizations that provide good and poor levels of service.

Suggested reading

Ahmed, P.K. and **R. Mohammed** (2003) Internal Marketing: Issues and Challenges, *European Journal of Marketing*, **37** (9), 1177–87.

Berry, L.L., V. Shankar, J. Turner Parish, S. Cadwallader and **T. Dotzel** (2006) Creating New Markets Through Service Innovation, *Sloan Management Review*, **47** (2), 56–63.

Kumar, V., J.A. Petersen and **R.P. Leone** (2007) How Valuable is Word of Mouth? *Harvard Business Review*, **85** (10), 139–56.

McDermott, L., M. Steed and **G. Hastings** (2005) What is and What is Not Social Marketing: The Challenge of Reviewing the Evidence, *Journal of Marketing Management*, **21** (5/6), 545–53.

Shugan, S.M. and **X. Jinhong** (2004) Advance Selling for Services, *California Management Review*, **46** (3), 37–55.

Urban, G. (2004) The Emerging Era of Customer Advocacy, *Sloan Management Review*, **45** (2), 77–82.

References

1. **Wiesmann, G.** (2008) Fusion of Fast Food and Elegance, *Financial Times*, 2 April, 14; **Zibart, E.** (2007) Vapiano, A Fine European Import, *Washington Post*, 8 June, WE16.

2. **Berry, L.L.** (1980) Services Marketing is Different, *Business Horizons*, May–June, 24–9.

3. **Foster, L.** (2004) The March of the Geek Squad, *Financial Times*, 24 November, 13.

4. **Edgett, S.** and **S. Parkinson** (1993) Marketing for Services Industries: A Review, *Service Industries Journal*, **13** (3), 19–39.

5. **Blitz, R.** (2007) Holiday Inn in $1bn Makeover, *Financial Times*, 25 October, 21.

6. **Ranson, K.** (2007) Holiday Inn Gets a $1bn Rebrand, *Travelweekly.co.uk*, 24 October.

7. **Sibun, J.** (2007) £1bn Rebrand for Holiday Inn Chain, *Telegraph.co.uk*, 25 October.

8. **Berry, L.L.** (1980) Services Marketing is Different, *Business Horizons*, May–June, 24–9.

9. **Aijo, T.S.** (1996) The Theoretical and Philosophical Underpinnings of Relationship Marketing, *European Journal of Marketing*, **30** (2), 8–18; **Grönoos, C.** (1990) *Services Management and Marketing: Managing the Moments of Truth in Service Competition*, Lexington, MA: Lexington Books.

10. **Baron, S., K. Harris** and **B.J. Davies** (1996) Oral Participation in Retail Service Delivery: A Comparison of the Roles of Contact Personnel and Customers, *European Journal of Marketing*, **30** (9), 75–90.

11. **Parkes, C.** (2005) Cinemas Feel the Pinch as Viewers Stay on the Sofa, *Financial Times*, 26 June, 25.

12. **Booms, B.H.** and **M.J. Bitner** (1981) Marketing Strategies and Organisation Structures For Service Firms, in **Donnelly J.H.** and **W.R. George** (eds) *Marketing of Services*, Chicago: American Marketing Association, 47–51.

13. **Berry, L.L., E.E. Lefkowith** and **T. Clark** (1980) In Services: What's in a Name?, *Harvard Business Review*, Sept–Oct, 28–30.

14. **Bloemer, J.** and **K. de Ruyter** (1998) On the Relationship Between Store Image, Store Satisfaction and Store Loyalty, *European Journal of Marketing*, **32** (5/6), 499–513.

15. **Cole, G.** (2003) Window Shopping, *Financial Times*, IT Review, 5 February, 4.

16. **Cowell, D.** (1995) *The Marketing of Services*, London: Heinemann, 35.

17. **Sellers, P.** (1988) How to Handle Customer Gripes, *Fortune*, 118 (October), 100.

18. **Thal Larsen, P.** (2006) Good Performer in Corporate Lending and Capital Markets, *Financial Times*, 1 March, 21.

19. **Rafiq, M.** and **P.K. Ahmed** (1992) The Marketing Mix Reconsidered, *Proceedings of the Annual Conference of the Marketing Education Group*, Salford, 439–51.

20. **Schlesinger, L.A.** and **J.L. Heskett** (1991) The Service-driven Service Company, *Harvard Business Review*, Sept–Oct, 71–81.

21. **Bowen, D.E.** and **L.L. Lawler** (1992) Empowerment: Why, What, How and When, *Sloan Management Review*, Spring, 31–9.

22. **Birchall, J.** (2005) Pile High, Sell Cheap and Pay Well, *Financial Times*, 11 July, 12.

23. **Anonymous** (2007) Doing Well By Being Rather Nice, *Economist*, 1 December, 74.

24. **Mitchell, A.** (2007) In the Pursuit of Happiness, *Financial Times*, 14 June, 14.

25. **Birchall, J.** (2005) Top Dogs Lead the Way as Pet Market Bears its Teeth, *Financial Times*, 3 August, 28.

26. **Pruyn, A.** and **A. Smidts** (1998) Effects of Waiting on the Satisfaction With the Service: Beyond Objective Time Measures, *International Journal of Research in Marketing*, 15, 321–34.

27. **Buzzell, R.D.** and **B.T. Gale** (1987) *The PIMS Principles: Linking Strategy to Performance*, New York: Free Press, 103–34.

28. **Parasuraman, A., V.A. Zeithaml** and **L.L. Berry** (1985) A Conceptual Model of Service Quality and its Implications for Future Research, *Journal of Marketing*, Fall, 41–50.

29. **Heracleous, L., J. Wirtz** and **R. Johnston** (2004) Cost-effective Service Lessons from Singapore Airlines, *Business Strategy Review*, 15 (1), 33–8.

30. **Kingi, S.** (2003) Customer Service at Singapore Airlines, *European Case Clearing House*, 503-114-1.

31. **Parasuraman, A., V.A. Zeithaml** and **L.L. Berry** (1985) A Conceptual Model of Service Quality and its Implications for Future Research, *Journal of Marketing*, Fall, 41–50.

32. **Danaher, P.J.** and **J. Mattsson** (1994) Customer Satisfaction During the Service Delivery Process, *European Journal of Marketing*, 28 (5), 5–16.

33. **Egan, C.** (1997) Relationship Management, in Jobber, D. (ed.) *The CIM Handbook of Selling and Sales Strategy*, Oxford: Butterworth-Heinemann, 55–88.

34. **Berry, L.L.** (1995) Relationship Marketing, in Payne, A., M. Christopher, M. Clark and H. Peck (eds) *Relationship Marketing for Competitive Advantage*, Oxford: Butterworth-Heinemann, 65–74.

35. **Zeithaml, V.A.** and **M.J. Bitner** (2002) *Services Marketing*, New York: McGraw-Hill, 174–8.

36. **Reichheld, F.F.** and **W.E. Sasser Jr** (1990) Zero Defections: Quality Comes To Services, *Harvard Business Review*, Sept–Oct, 105–11.

37. **Berry, L.L.** and **A. Parasuraman** (1991) *Managing Services*, New York: Free Press, 136–42.

38. **Kasper, H., P. van Helsdingen** and **W. de Vries Jr** (1999) *Services Marketing Management*, Chichester: Wiley, 528.

39. **Witzel, M.** (2005) Keep your Relationship With Clients Afloat, *Financial Times*, 31 January, 13.

40. **Bennett, P.D.** (1988) *Marketing*, New York: McGraw-Hill, 690–2.

41. **Shapiro, B.** (1992) Marketing for Non-Profit Organisations, *Harvard Business Review*, September–October, 123–32.

42. **Balabanis, G., R.E. Stables** and **H.C. Philips** (1997) Market Orientation in the Top 200 British Charity Organisations and its Impact on their Performance, *European Journal of Marketing*, 31 (8), 583–603.

43. **Butler, P.** and **N. Collins** (1994) Political Marketing: Structure and Process, *European Journal of Marketing*, 28 (1), 19–34.

44. **Chakrabortty, A.** (2005) Charities Tune into Youth, *Financial Times*, 25 October, 13.

45. **Hibbert, S.** (1995) The Market Positioning of British Medical Charities, *European Journal of Marketing*, 29 (10), 6–26.

Case 7 Paddy Power: from gambling to entertainment

Once associated primarily with smoky, dimly lit outlets and middle-aged males, the betting industry has undergone some radical changes. The retail face of the business has become dominated by a number of chains consisting of bigger, brighter and better-designed outlets. And the industry has been revolutionized by the internet. Online betting has grown rapidly and has attracted consumers who would have felt uncomfortable going into traditional betting shops, such as younger people and females. To increase their appeal to these new segments, betting companies have offered odds, not just on horse races, but on all other sports and indeed on almost anything, such as who will be the winner of a reality TV show and will the next celebrity baby be a boy or a girl. Using this approach, gambling has been marketed as simply a bit of fun, with the result that it has become much more mainstream and the business has boomed. Like any growing business is has attracted its fair share of new entrants and competition has become intense.

Company background

Paddy Power was founded in 1988 through the merger of three existing Irish high-street bookmakers, giving it an initial chain of 38 outlets. From this base, it grew rapidly and in the short space of 10 years this number had increased to 100. By 2008, it had become the largest bookmaker in Ireland, with 183 outlets, and was growing quickly in the UK through its 58 shops in the London area. A further eight outlets were acquired in May 2008, when it expanded into Northern Ireland for the first time through the acquisition of McGranaghan Racing in Belfast. The company was also very open to examining new ways of reaching its customers. For example, in 1996 it launched a telephone betting service, Dial-a-Bet, and in 2000, its website, www.paddypower.com, was launched.

The company went public in 2001, floating on both the Dublin and London stock exchanges. At this time it redefined its mission to become a broader-based, entertainment company that made betting more accessible and fun. To this end it increased its range of services. Paddypowercasino.com was launched in 2004, which was essentially an online casino, where players could play virtual poker, blackjack, roulette and a variety of other games. February 2005 saw the launch of paddypowerpoker.com to capitalize on the growing global popularity of online poker, where players pitted their skills against other real players from around the world. Indeed many individuals had given up their day jobs to become full-time, online poker players. A range of games, such as Texas Hold'em, and five- and seven-card stud were played and paddypowerpoker.com provided varying ranges of buy-in to suit different income and skill levels. Other services launched included paddy-powerbingo.com, aimed at the female market, and paddypowertrader.com, a spread betting website that enabled consumers to bet on the performance of a variety of financial products such as shares, indices, currencies and commodities. The vast majority of Paddy Power's services were aimed at the personal consumer, but it also provided some business services such as conditional rebates. For example, assume a car dealer ran a promotion such as 'Buy a BMW and if England win the World Cup we will give you your money back'. The dealer could then hedge this offer with Paddy Power. If England won, Paddy Power paid the dealer, who in turn returned the price of the car to the buyer.

Key financial information for the company is shown in Table C7.1. It demonstrates the growing profitability of the company and the increased role played by its online businesses in contributing to group turnover and profitability.

Marketing activities

Since its flotation on the stock market in 2001 the company's marketing strategy has been to:

- create awareness for the brand in new and existing markets
- raise the profile of its betting services
- recruit active and loyal users to its services.

Key to the successful achievement of these objectives was the positioning of the firm as 'fun, fair and friendly', in an effort to distinguish itself from its competitors. In terms of fun, it offered all sorts of novelty bets, such as who will be the next President of the USA; it has sponsored events like the world's first *Father Ted* festival and it even set up a stand at the Vatican taking bets on the election of the new pope— a stunt that got coverage from hundreds of major international media corporations, such as NBC and CNN.

Table C7.1 Key financial information (€ millions)

	2007	2006	2005	2004	2003
Non-retail betting	926	832	577	471	363
Retail betting	1102	963	794	689	551
Total turnover	2028	1795	1372	1160	914
Non-retail operating profit	38.4	29.4	20.7	13.4	2.2
Retail operating profit	33.7	16.0	9.4	17.7	17.4
Group operating profit	72.1	45.5	30.1	31.1	19.6
Pre-tax profits	75.8	49.7	31.3	27.5	17.6
Cash balances	87.9	87.1	52.3	47.2	39.2

Source: Paddy Power Annual Reports

It also carefully cultivated the image of being fair, or of being the punter's (gambler's) friend, through its 'money-back specials'. For example, in 2006, it refunded bets on the Pakistan cricket team when it was deemed to have forfeited the fourth test against England following a ball tampering incident. In a press release, a Paddy Power spokesperson said, 'in these circumstances, we don't look at our rules but we ask ourselves what we would consider to be a fair result if we were the punter'. In a similar approach it offered to refund money to customers if their team was knocked out through a penalty shoot-out in the 2006 soccer World Cup. By doing so, Paddy Power bailed out the unfortunate backers of England, Argentina, France and Switzerland.

This fun, friendly image was also reflected in the firm's retail outlets and in its communications with its customers. For example, its shops were designed to be modern, attractive and air-conditioned. The customer experience was enhanced through top-quality audio and video equipment and other innovative facilities such as interactive information terminals. It increased its call capacity at its Dial-a-Bet call centre to 360 lines, and invested in the training and development of its staff to provide an efficient and friendly service. It designed its website to be fun and interactive through the inclusion of novelties such as the Wedding Speech Sweepstakes Kit, which enabled users to organize a sweepstake based on the length of the speeches at a wedding. Spanish- and German-language versions of its website were launched in 2006.

Publicity and promotion

Through its redefinition as an entertainment company, Paddy Power sought to bring fun and irreverence into everything that it did. This became very manifest in its ability to spot and exploit publicity opportunities and also in its controversial advertising.

Paddy Power has consistently been in trouble with consumers and regulators due to the nature and content of its advertising. Because of restrictions on advertising gambling on radio and television, it focused primarily on outdoor media. In 2001, it ran a campaign showing elderly people walking across a road being approached by an oncoming pick-up truck. Each person had odds on their heads and the tagline read 'let's make things more interesting'. The advert was the most complained about that year in the UK and Ireland, with most critics claiming that it was demeaning to old people. Paddy Power argued that the odds referred to which person would cross the road first, not who would be knocked down, but the advert was banned. It managed to recover the situation by issuing an apology to pensioners, and journalists were persuaded to allow supporters and critics of the campaign to air their views. Significant publicity was received, with the result that traffic to its UK and Irish websites more than trebled during this period.

In 2005, the company was in trouble again when it ran an outdoor campaign version of Leonardo Da Vinci's image of the *Last Supper*, which suggested that Jesus spent time gambling with his apostles. Jesus had a stack of poker chips in front of him, while some of the other apostles played roulette; the tag-line read, 'There's a place for fun and games.' When the Advertising Standards Authority asked the company to remove the offending posters, it didn't but instead covered them with a sticker that read 'There's a place for fun and games. Apparently this isn't it.' The campaign had cost Paddy Power €200,000 but the controversy generated such publicity that its costs were effectively recouped. Other controversial campaigns included 'Where have all the women gone?' for paddypowerbingo.com (see Chapter 9) and an advert for paddypowertrading.com, which was accused of implying that online gambling increased sexual prowess.

But by living up to its ethos of having fun, Paddy Power has been masterful in spotting and exploiting publicity opportunities. For example, because of restrictions on its sponsorship of sports it has had to be creative in terms of highlighting its association with teams and events. During the 2007 Rugby World Cup, it got the Tongan player Epi Taione to change his name to Paddy Power by deed poll to highlight the firm's sponsorship of the Tongan team. The International Rugby Board vetoed the stunt but not before it received massive international media coverage. It has also got around such restrictions by sponsoring well-known fans of leading teams or by having its name on the equipment used by players.

Another example of its ability to run with a publicity-generating activity is the paddypower.com World Strip Poker Championship. This initially began as an April Fool's joke but public interest in the idea meant that it was staged for real. The eight-hour event involving 200 men and women from 12 countries was won by John Young, a freelance writer from London. The competition raised €10,000 for Cancer Research and it even got into the *Guinness Book of Records*.

Paddy Power has also organized or sponsored several other events. These have included one of the world's long-running 'No Limit Texas Hold'em' tournaments —the Irish Poker Open—which attracted 708 players in 2007. Its five-a-side soccer tournament in London attracted over 400 teams, while the Irish Karaoke Championships attracted an entry from 88 pubs. It also sponsored the successful television series *Big Brother* in 2001, receiving significant television and press coverage during the eight-week event, estimated to be worth an equivalent of £1.5 million in advertising spend.

Building relationships with its customers was also a key part of its marketing activity. For example, innovations like Bet & Watch allowed customers to use the facility to view every horse race in Ireland and the UK live online. At paddypowercasino.com, the Players Club Loyalty programme was formed to reward players for consistent game play, while at paddypowerpoker.com, players were given bonus 'Paddy points' that could be redeemed against entry to tournaments, to purchase gifts from its loyalty store or to move up the ranks of its VIP programme. In order to create an online poker playing community, the site allowed users to chat and interact as they played, and interactive promotions were regularly released to entertain players between and outside of games. The site also sought to educate players about the game by providing poker tutorials, educational articles, poker software tools, news and other exciting content. Similar value-added content was provided at paddypowertrader.com.

A successful entertainment company

Paddy Power became a successful entertainment company by broadening the appeal of betting. Instead of focusing on high-value customers (the high rollers of the gambling world) it sought to democratize betting by making it something that was fun and accessible to everyone. Through adopting this approach it became the largest betting firm in Ireland and, through a primarily online presence, the fifth biggest operator in the UK. Its online business represented 45 per cent of group turnover compared with 12 per cent and 17 per cent for major competitors such as William Hill and Ladbrokes respectively. Its high media profile, often achieved controversially, would also appear to have benefited it to a great extent. Its brand recognition in Ireland consistently reached 90 per cent, while it was 60 per cent in the UK, behind much more established brands such as Ladbrokes, William Hill and Coral Bookmakers.

Questions

1. Analyse the ways in which advances in technology have changed the betting business. What are the implications for betting firms?
2. How did Paddy Power go about building its service brand? What are the unique attributes of the brand?
3. Evaluate the services marketing mix used by Paddy Power. What are its strengths and weaknesses?
4. Analyse Paddy Power's customer relationship development initiatives. How successful have they been?
5. Due to concerns from some quarters about the social impact of gambling, advertising is strictly controlled in the UK and Ireland. Paddy Power has circumvented this with some irreverent advertising campaigns and activities that subsequently caused offence to some groups and fell foul of the Advertising Standards Authority. What is your view of the tactics used by Paddy Power? Are there ethical issues to be considered?'

This case was prepared by Professor John Fahy, University of Limerick, from various published sources as a basis for class discussion rather than to illustrate either effective or ineffective management.

Chapter 8
Pricing Strategy

Learning Outcomes

By the end of this chapter you will understand:

1   the three basic approaches to setting prices
2   the importance of adopting an integrated approach
     to price setting
3   the key factors that influence price-setting decisions
4   the major issues involved in managing pricing decisions
     over time.

Name your price!

Until recently, it was always companies that decided the price to charge for their products. As we shall see in this chapter they consider a variety of factors such as the costs of production, competitor prices, positioning strategy, and so on, when arriving at these decisions. But, in a novel approach, some organizations are now allowing their customers to set their own prices. Consumers pay whatever they feel the product or service is worth.

The most celebrated example of this in recent years occurred in the rapidly changing music industry. Music is a sector that has been transformed by the internet. The digital downloading and sharing of music, first illegally and then legally, has changed the way that music is packaged and distributed, with knock-on consequences for the major record labels. Sales of CDs, once the staple source of income for record companies, have collapsed, to be replaced by digital downloads and live shows. But the cost of making digital downloads available is much lower than that of CDs and this has encouraged artists to experiment with different pricing formulas. When one of the world's top bands, Radiohead, offered consumers the option to pay what they liked for their new album, a watershed had clearly been reached.

Radiohead brought out the new album, *In Rainbows*, in October 2007. But it was released as a digital download only from the band's website, Radiohead.com. Fans who visited the site to download the album were then invited to pay whatever they liked. In taking this approach, the band was cutting out the record company, distributors and retailers, all of whom would eat into the margins made from sales of the album. So, even if fans offered to pay, for example, just £5 for the album instead of the usual £15 for a new release, Radiohead may still do better, as a result of their reduced costs of production and distribution. Typically bands get 12 per cent of the average album price, so, as long as consumers offer to pay at least about one-tenth of what they would normally pay for an album, the artist is not losing out.

Opinions on whether the experiment was successful or not are divided. By November of that year, just 38 per cent of the people downloading the album had paid any more than the required 45p handling charge. Of those paying something, the average amount was estimated at US$6 (£2.88), substantially less than the regular CD price. But it can also be argued that US$6 is far better than nothing, which is what bands receive for illegal downloads. Combined with the publicity received and the promotion given to the band's accompanying £40 box set, the experiment could have been considered to have worked.

This example shows how dynamic marketing can be. In the face of rapid changes, organizations can come up with novel approaches that have huge ramifications for an industry. Radiohead were well established and free from contract restrictions so they could take this novel approach. But companies like Priceline.com allow consumers to name their price for a whole host of products and services, like air travel and car hire. There are no guarantees that existing models, whereby organizations set prices and consumers have to accept them, will last for ever.[1]

Because price is the revenue earner, it is the 'odd one out' of the marketing mix. The price of a product is what the company gets back in return for all the effort that is put in to manufacturing and marketing the product. The other elements of the marketing mix —product, promotion, place, physical evidence, and so on—are costs. Therefore, no matter how good the product, how creative the promotion or how efficient the distribution, unless price covers costs, the company will make a loss. It is therefore essential that managers understand how to set prices, because both undercharging (lost margins) and overcharging (lost sales) can have a dramatic effect on profitability (see Marketing in Action 8.1).

The importance of price is illustrated by the launch of the Mercedes A Class model in Germany. Initially, the company had chosen a price tag of DM29,500, based on the belief that the DM30,000 mark was psychologically important. However, after further market research that examined the value offered to customers in comparison to competitor brands such as the BMW 3 series and the VW Golf, the price was set at DM31,000. Mercedes still hit its sales target of 200,000, but the higher price increased its income by DM300 million a year.[2]

One of the key factors that marketing managers need to remember is that price is just one element of the marketing mix: it should not be set in isolation, but should be blended with product, promotion and place to form a coherent mix that provides superior customer value. The sales of many products, particularly those that are a form of self-expression, such as

Marketing in Action 8.1: The *Harry Potter* series: high sales, low profits

Study guide: Below is a review of pricing for the immensely successful *Harry Potter* series of books. Read it and consider the relationship between prices and profits.

J.K. Rowling's *Harry Potter* series is one of the best known and most successful book series of all time. The seven-book series consists of: *Harry Potter and the Philosopher's Stone, Harry Potter and the Chamber of Secrets, Harry Potter and the Prisoner of Azkaban, Harry Potter and the Goblet of Fire, Harry Potter and the Order of the Phoenix, Harry Potter and the Half-blood Prince* and *Harry Potter and the Deathly Hallows*; each was more successful than its predecessor. *Order of the Phoenix* broke many records when it was published. Amazon.com, in what it described as the largest event in 'e-commerce history' received 1.3 million pre-orders worldwide.

But while sales levels reached dizzy heights, profitability levels for retailers were eroded by intense price competition. For example, in the case of *Order of the Phoenix*, the recommended retail price was £16.99. However, Tesco, given its immense size, was able to order 750,000 copies and offer them at £9.97. Customers voted with their wallets and Tesco sold 317,400 editions of the book in the first 24 hours of sale.

The pattern was repeated for *Harry Potter and the Half-blood Prince* in 2005. With a recommended retail price again of £16.99, the average price was £9.40. KwikSave grabbed most attention by offering a limited number of volumes at £4.99, well below cost price. The book sold over 3 million copies in seven days but specialist book retailers like Ottakars sold just 65,000 copies in the first day, giving it a market share of 3.5 per cent as against its usual launch share of 8 per cent. The final book in the series, *Harry Potter and the Deathly Hallows*, became a best-seller six months before it was launched, as again it could be pre-ordered at a discounted price at Amazon.com, Wal-Mart and elsewhere.

This level of price competition meant that there was very little margin available to the retailer. Discounters like the supermarkets and online shops used the book to drive traffic to their stores/sites in the hope that other products would be sold as well. Paradoxically, some reported that the retail price being charged for *Order of the Phoenix* in the supermarkets was less than the wholesale price they had paid, implying that it would have been better for them to order the book from Tesco or Asda than the publishers.

Based on: Graff and McLaren (2003);[3] Voyle (2003);[4] Wilson and Woodhouse (2005)[5]

drinks, cars, perfume and clothing, could suffer from prices that are too low. As we shall see, price is an important part of positioning strategy since it often sends quality cues to customers.

Understanding how to set prices is an important aspect of marketing decision-making, not least because of changes in the competitive arena. Greater price competition is becoming a fact of life, with the use of technology helping to drive down costs, greater levels of globalization and retail competition helping to depress price levels, and developments like the internet and the introduction of the euro giving rise to greater levels of price transparency. Price setting and price management are therefore key activities that influence the profitability of the firm.

Basic methods of setting prices

Shapiro and Jackson[6] identified three methods used by managers to set prices (see Figure 8.1). The first of these—cost-based pricing—reflects a strong internal orientation and, as its name suggests, is based on costs (see Marketing in Action 8.2). The second is competitor-orientated pricing, where the major emphasis is on the price levels set by competitors and how our prices compare with those. The final approach is market-led pricing, so called because it

focuses on the value that customers place on a product in the marketplace and the nature of the marketing strategy used to support the product. In this section we will examine each of these approaches, and draw out their strengths and limitations.

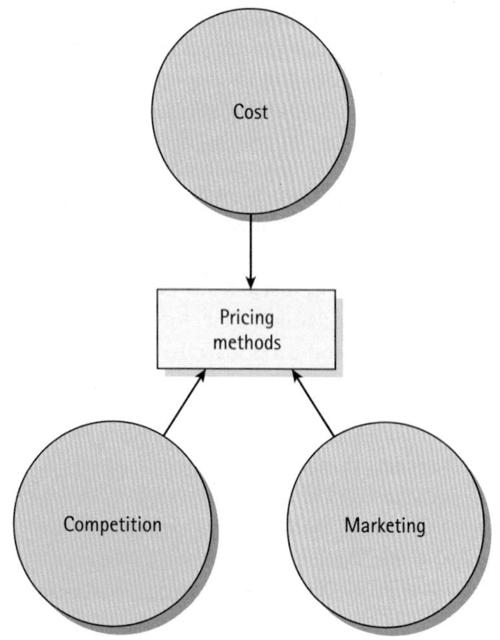

Cost-based pricing

Cost-based pricing is a useful approach to price setting in that it can give an indication of the minimum price that needs to be charged in order to break even. Cost-based pricing can best be explained by using a simple example (see Table 8.1). Imagine that you are given the task of pricing a new product and the cost figures given in Table 8.1 apply. Direct costs such as labour and materials work out at £2 per unit. As output increases, more people and materials will be needed and so total costs increase. Fixed costs (or overheads) per year are calculated at £200,000. These costs (such as office and manufacturing facilities) do not change as output increases. They have to be paid whether 1 or 200,000 units are produced.

Once we have calculated the relevant costs, it is necessary to estimate how many units we are likely to sell. We believe that we produce a good-quality product and therefore sales should be 100,000 in the first year. Therefore total (full) cost per unit is £4 and using the company's traditional 10 per cent mark-up a price of £4.40 is set.

So that we may understand the problems associated with using **full cost pricing**, we should assume

Figure 8.1 Pricing methods

Table 8.1 Cost-based pricing

Year 1	
Direct costs (per unit)	= £2
Fixed costs	= £200,000
Expected sales	= 100,000
Cost per unit	
Direct costs	= £2
Fixed costs (200,000 ÷ 100,000)	= £2
Full costs	= £4
Mark-up (10 per cent)	= £0.40
Price (cost plus mark-up)	= £4.40
Year 2	
Expected sales	= 50,000
Cost per unit	
Direct costs	= £2
Fixed costs (200,000 ÷ 50,000)	= £4
Full costs	= £6
Mark-up (10 per cent)	= £0.60
Price (cost plus mark-up)	= £6.60

that the sales estimate of 100,000 is not reached by the end of the year. Because of poor economic conditions or as a result of setting the price too high, only 50,000 units are sold. The company believes that this level of sales is likely to be achieved next year. What happens to price? Table 8.1 gives the answer: it is raised because cost per unit goes up. This is because fixed costs (£200,000) are divided by a smaller expected sales volume (50,000). The result is a price rise in response to poor sales figures. This is clearly non-sense and yet can happen if full cost pricing is followed blindly. A major UK engineering company priced one of its main product lines in this way and suffered a downward spiral of sales as prices were raised each year, with disastrous consequences.

So, the first problem with cost-based pricing is that it leads to an increase in the price as sales fall. Second, the procedure is illogical because a sales estimate is made *before* a price is set. Third, it focuses on internal costs rather than customers' willingness to pay.

Finally, there may be a technical problem in allocating overheads in multi-product firms.[7]

The real value of this approach is that it gives an indication of the minimum price necessary to make a profit. Once direct and fixed costs have been measured, 'break-even analysis' can be used to estimate the sales volume needed to balance revenue and costs at different price levels. Therefore, the procedure of calculating full costs is useful when other pricing methods are used since full costs may act as a constraint. If they cannot be covered then it may not be worthwhile launching the product. In practice, some companies will set prices below full costs (known as direct cost pricing or **marginal cost pricing**). As we saw in the previous chapter this is a popular strategy for services companies. For example, where seats on an aircraft or rooms in hotels are unused at any time, that revenue is lost. In such situations, pricing to cover direct costs plus a contribution to overheads is sensible to reduce the impact of excess capacity, though this approach is not sustainable in the long term.

Marketing in Action 8.2: The success of Renault's Logan

Study guide: Below is review of the pricing strategy used for the launch of the Renault Logan. Read it and consider the advantages and disadvantages of cost-based pricing.

To take advantage of the growing prosperity of Central and Eastern Europe, the French motor company Renault bought the ageing Romanian manufacturer Dacia in 1999. Its strategy was to produce a car that was modern, reliable and affordable for sale in developing markets in Europe, Asia and Latin America. Driving efficiencies were a key part of this strategy and every effort was made to keep costs to a minimum. Expensive curves and creases in the car design were eliminated, and components from other vehicles were even reused. The result was a cheap-looking saloon car. The model was priced inexpensively and was only expected to cover its investment costs and make a modest contribution to profits.

But the car has turned out to be a runaway success. Priced at €7500 in France, it sold 9000 units in three months after going on sale there in June 2005, despite receiving no advertising support. Global sales in 2005 were expected to hit 160,000 units, well ahead of the planned level of 100,000 units. By the end of 2006, over 450,000 vehicles had been sold, which was substantially ahead of targeted sales levels. The brand has also been a hit in Romania to such an extent that the company has raised its prices there and did not even bother to launch the planned cheapest version at €5000. Profits are far ahead of expectations and the success of the car has left its Romanian factory struggling to keep up with demand. In 2006, an estate version of the car was launched, in 2007 the Logan van was launched and a pick-up version was planned for 2008.

This example illustrates the risks of cost-based pricing. Fortunately for the company, sales exceeded expectations but the opportunity to reap larger profits had been missed. It demonstrates the need to understand the potential level of value that consumers can attribute to a new innovation.

Based on: English (2004);[8] Mackintosh (2005)[9]

Exhibit 8.1 Advertisements such as this one from Ryanair frequently land the company in court for false, misleading or offensive messages; its advertising also regularly targets its major competitors

Competitor-orientated pricing

Competitor-orientated pricing may take any one of three forms:

1 where firms follow the prices charged by leading competitors
2 where producers take the going-rate price
3 where contracts are awarded through a **competitive bidding** process.

Some firms are happy simply to benchmark themselves against their major competitors, setting their prices at levels either above, the same as or below them (see Exhibit 8.1). This is very popular in the financial services area where, for example, the price of a loan (that is, the interest rate) is often very similar across a wide range of competitors. It can be a risky approach to take, particularly if the firm's cost position is not as good as that of its competitors (see 'Cost-based pricing', above, and Marketing in Action 8.3).

In other circumstances, all competitors receive the same price because it is the going rate for the product. **Going-rate prices** are most typically found in the case of undifferentiated commodities such as coffee beans or cattle meat. The challenge for the marketer in this situation is to find some creative ways of differentiating the product in order to charge a different price.

In addition, many contracts are won or lost on the basis of competitive bidding. The most usual process is the drawing up of detailed specifications for a product and putting the contract out to tender. Potential suppliers quote a price, which is known only to themselves and the buyer (known as a 'sealed bid'), or the bidding may take place in a public auction where all competitors see what prices are being bid. All other things being equal, the buyer will select the supplier that quotes the lowest price. A major focus for suppliers, therefore, is the likely bid price of competitors. Increasing price pressures, European competition legislation and the growing use of technology has resulted in more and more supply contracts being subject to competitive bidding. For example, traditionally, many hospital supply companies sold directly to doctors and nurses in hospitals, which meant that suppliers invested in developing selling skills and building relationships with these customers. Now, the norm is that supply contracts are put out to tender, with the winning bidder often securing the contract for a period of three to five years. Thus supply firms have had to develop skills in different areas such as tender preparation and pricing. Online auctions present suppliers with a whole new set of demands (see Chapter 3).

The main advantage of the competitor-orientated pricing approach is that it is simple and easy to use, except in the case of competitive bidding, where it may be difficult to guess what prices competitive bids will come in at. Increased price transparency in Europe, brought about by the introduction of the euro and the growing use of the internet as a tool for comparing prices, will perhaps increase the level of attention being given to competitor-orientated pricing. It also suffers, however, from two significant flaws. First, it does not take account of any differential advantages the firm may have, which may justify its charging a higher price than the competition. As we have seen, the creation of a differential advantage is a fundamental marketing activity, and firms should seek to reap the rewards of this investment. This reaffirms the importance of blending pricing with the other elements of the marketing mix rather than viewing it as an isolated decision. Second, as noted above, competitor-orientated pricing is risky where a firm's cost position is weaker than that of its competitors.

Market-led pricing

A key marketing consideration when setting prices is estimating a product's value to the customer. In brief, the more value a product gives compared to the competition, the higher the price that can be charged. Simply because one product costs less to make than another does not imply that its price should be less. The logic of this position is borne out by Glaxo's approach when it launched Zantac, an ulcer treatment drug. It set the price for the drug at 50 per cent more than that of SmithKline Beecham's Tagamet, which was then the world's best-selling drug. Thanks to its fewer side-effects, Zantac overtook Tagamet and the resulting superior revenues transformed Glaxo from a mid-sized UK company to a global powerhouse.[10]

In this section we shall explore a number of ways of estimating value to the customer. Marketers have at their disposal, three useful techniques for uncovering customers' value perceptions: trade-off analysis, experimentation and **economic value to the customer (EVC)** analysis.

Trade-off analysis

Measurement of the trade-off between price and other product features—known as trade-off analysis or conjoint analysis—enables their effects on product preference to be established.[11] Respondents are not asked direct questions about price, instead product profiles consisting of product features and price are described, and respondents are asked to name their preferred profile. From their answers the effect of price and other product features can be measured using a computer model. For example, respondents are shown different combinations of features such as speed, petrol consumption, brand and price in the case of a car and asked which combinations they prefer. This exercise enables one to measure the impact on preferences of increasing or reducing the price. Companies like 3M, who are renowned for their product innovation, use trade-off analysis at the test marketing stage for new products. Different combinations of variables such as the brand, packaging, product features and price are tested to establish the price level customers are prepared to pay.[12]

Experimentation

A limitation of trade-off analysis is that respondents are not asked to back up their preferences with cash expenditure. Consequently there can be some doubt whether what they say they prefer would be reflected in an actual purchase when they are asked to part with money. 'Experimental pricing research' attempts to overcome this drawback by placing a product on sale at different locations with varying prices. Test marketing (see Chapter 6) is often used to compare the effectiveness of varying prices. For example, the same product could be sold in two areas using an identical promotional campaign, but with different prices between areas. Obviously, the areas would need to be matched (or differences allowed for) in

terms of target customer profile so that the result would be comparable. The test needs to be long enough so that trial and repeat purchase at each price can be measured. This is likely to be between 6 and 12 months for products whose purchase cycle lasts more than a few weeks.

EVC analysis

Experimentation is more usual when pricing consumer products. However, industrial markets have a powerful tool at their disposal when setting the price of their products: economic value to the customer (EVC) analysis. Many organizational purchases are motivated by economic value considerations since reducing costs and increasing revenue are prime objectives for many companies. If a company can produce an offering that has a high EVC, it can set a high price and yet still offer superior value compared to the competition. A high EVC may be because the product generates more revenue for the buyer than competition or because its operating costs (such as maintenance, operation or start-up costs) are lower over its lifetime. EVC analysis is usually particularly revealing when applied to products whose purchase price represents a small proportion of the lifetime costs to the customer.[13]

For example, assume a manufacturer is buying a robot to use on its production line. The robot costs €100,000 but this represents only one-third of the customer's total life cycle costs. An additional €50,000 is required for start-up costs such as installation and operator training, while a further €150,000 needs to be budgeted for in post-purchase costs such as maintenance, power, etc. Assume also that a new product comes on the market that due to technological advances reduces start-up costs by €20,000 and post-purchase costs by €50,000. Total costs then have been reduced by €70,000 and the EVC that the new product offers is €170,000 (€300,000–€130,000). Thus the EVC figure is the total amount that the customer would have to pay to make the total life cycle costs of the new and existing robot the same. If the new robot was priced at €170,000 this would be the case—any price below that level would create an economic incentive for the buyer to purchase the new robot.

The main advantage of market-led pricing is that it keeps customer perceptions and needs at the forefront of the pricing decision. However, in practice it is sensible for a company to adopt an integrated approach to pricing, paying attention not only to customer needs but also to cost levels (cost-based pricing) and competitor prices (competitor-orientated pricing).

Marketing in Action 8.3: The price of money

> **Study guide:** Below is a review of how banks arrive at the price of the loans that they give us. Read it and examine the price of any 'debt' that you have. Is it the most competitive price in the market?

While money is the medium through which trade is conducted, it is also one of the world's most tradable commodities. We don't always have it when we want it, therefore we purchase using our credit cards, we take out personal loans and, if we need to purchase 'big ticket' items like housing, we take out mortgages. But how do the suppliers of these products, namely retail banks, arrive at the price that they charge us? Evidently it would appear that they employ a combination of cost-based, competitor-orientated and market-led pricing.

A study by the European Commission in 2006 found marked variations throughout Europe in the cost of financial products. The most expensive mortgages were to be found in Germany, Spain and Portugal, while Denmark and Poland's were among the cheapest. Personal loans were most expensive in Denmark, the Netherlands and Ireland, and cheapest in Hungary and Poland. The UK and Greece were most expensive for credit cards, and Belgium was cheapest. Given that banks are essentially in the business of taking in money in retail deposits and lending it to consumers who need it, what explains the major price variations? What the market is willing to accept is clearly an important factor. Many consumers tend not to look very closely at the cost of money, or are confused by the different prices quoted, such as the annual percentage rate (APR) or cost/thousand. For example, the rates charged on credit cards are normally significantly higher than those on personal loans, yet consumers continue to build up large levels of credit card debt.

Intensity of competition is also a key factor. When it comes to financial products there tends to be a high level of consumer inertia. Consumers tend to be slow to switch mortgages even though doing so could result in savings of thousands of euros over the life of the loan. In the absence of competition, prices remain high until profits become very attractive to potential new entrants. For example, Halifax entered the Irish mortgage market, attracted by the potential high profits there. It priced its loans below those of existing competitors and offered consumers over €1000 to switch to its loans. Even with these incentives, the company estimated that it could still make good returns.

But while banks are frequently criticized for excessive profiteering, recent experiences show how important it is for them to cover their costs. This was starkly illustrated by the collapse of Northern Rock during the credit crisis of 2007 and 2008. Unlike many of its peers, which rely on deposits as their primary source of money to lend, Northern Rock had borrowed heavily on the inter-bank market to lend to its consumers. But when the price of these borrowings suddenly rose, the margins on its lending were reduced and its profits fell dramatically. Unable to cover its costs, the bank had to be rescued by the Bank of England. Financial products generally carry small margins making price-setting critical. Increased price transparency and cross-border competition further reduce the margin for error.

Based on: McCaffrey (2006);[14] Slattery (2006)[15]

Key factors influencing price-setting decisions

Aside from the basic dimensions of cost, competitive prices and customer value, various aspects of the firm's marketing strategy will also affect price-setting decisions. In particular, marketing decisions such as positioning strategies, new product launch strategies,

product-line strategies, competitive marketing strategies, distribution channel strategies and international marketing strategies will have an impact on price levels.

Positioning strategy

As we saw in Chapter 5, a key decision that marketing managers face is positioning strategy, which involves the choice of target market and the creation

Exhibit 8.2 For TKMaxx, advertising like this is a key component of its positioning strategy

of a differential advantage. Each of these factors can have an enormous impact on price. Price can be used to convey a differential advantage and to appeal to a certain market segment (see Exhibit 8.2). Leading European retail chains such as Aldi and Lidl target cost-conscious grocery shoppers through a policy of lowest prices on a range of frequently purchased household goods. At the other end of the spectrum, many firms will charge very high prices in order to appeal to individuals with a high net worth. Products such as yachts, luxury cars, golf club memberships, luxury holidays, and so on, are sold in this way. Price is a powerful positioning tool because, for many people, it is an indicator of quality. This is particularly the case for products where objective measurement of quality is not possible, such as drinks and perfume, and for services where quality cannot be assessed before consumption.

Because price perceptions are so important to customers, many companies engage in what is called **psychological pricing**—that is, the careful manipulation of the reference prices that consumers carry in their heads. Consequently, the price of most grocery products end in '.99' because the psychological difference between £2.99 and £3.00 is much greater than the actual difference.

New product launch strategy

When launching new products, price should be carefully aligned with promotional strategy. Figure 8.2 shows four marketing strategies based on combinations of price and promotion. Similar matrices could also be developed for product and distribution, but for illustrative purposes promotion will be used here. A combination of high price and high promotion expenditure is called a 'rapid skimming strategy'. The high price provides high-margin returns on investment and the heavy promotion creates high levels of product awareness and knowledge. The launches of

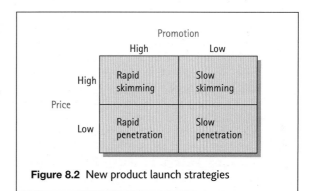

Figure 8.2 New product launch strategies

Microsoft's Xbox and Apple's iPod are examples of a rapid skimming strategy (see also Marketing in Action 8.4). A 'slow skimming strategy' combines high price with low levels of promotional expenditure. High prices mean big profit margins, but high levels of promotion are believed to be unnecessary, perhaps because word of mouth is more important and the product is already well known (Rolls-Royce, say) or because heavy promotion is thought to be incompatible with product image, as with cult products. One company that uses a skimming pricing policy effectively is German car components supplier Bosch. It has applied an extremely profitable skimming strategy, supported by patents, to its launch of fuel injection and anti-lock brake systems.[16] Companies that combine low prices with heavy promotional expenditure are practising a 'rapid penetration strategy'. The aim is to gain market share rapidly, perhaps at the expense of a rapid skimmer. For example, low-fares airlines like easyJet and Ryanair have successfully attacked incumbents like British Airways and Lufthansa using this strategy, as has Direct Line in the sale of general insurance products. Finally, a 'slow penetration strategy' combines low price with low promotional expenditure. Own-label brands use this strategy: promotion is not necessary to gain distribution and low promotional expenditure helps to maintain

Marketing in Action 8.4: Skimming the market

> **Study guide:** Below is a review of price skimming strategies in some popular product categories. Read it and consider whether price skimming is ethical or not.

In a number of product markets, like phones, MP3 players and games consoles, rapid skimming strategies are becoming ever more prevalent. A particular case in point is the Apple iPhone. An 8-gigabyte version of the phone was launched in July 2007 with a price tag of US$599. But, by just September of that year, its price had fallen by US$200 and a new 16-gigabyte model was launched on the market at a price of US$499. Innovators and early adopters who had purchased the phone at the full initial price were outraged and were ultimately offered a US$100 gift voucher by Apple.

The iPhone is an example of a classic rapid skimming strategy. Buzz marketing was used intensively to generate demand for the product, with a promise that it would do for mobile phones what the iPod had done for MP3 players. Its ease of use, combined with its functionality and its Apple 'cool', were extolled in blogs, reviews and commentaries. This low-cost form of promotion, combined with a high initial price, meant high profits for Apple. By January 2008, 4 million handsets had been sold and price reductions assisted it in its goal to sell 10 million devices by the end of that year.

There are several explanations for the rise in the use of rapid skimming strategies. The first is the cost of production. Products like the iPhone represent the convergence of several technologies, such as music players, computers and telecommunications. Packing all this functionality into one product is expensive. Second is the speed of imitation by competitors. Innovative new designs are now very quickly reverse-engineered and replicated, with new low-cost versions quickly reaching the shop floor. A rapid skimming strategy is the best way to recoup the high costs of research and development before competitors erode margins. Finally, consumer behaviour also plays an important role. The desire to be the first person with a new product is a strong feature of today's consumers, as demonstrated by the queues that frequently form for new phones, games consoles and fashion items. Price does not seem to be a major factor for these early adopters, and technology companies are exploiting this.

However, managing a skimming strategy is easier said than done. Drop the price too quickly and you risk the wrath of customers, as Apple has done. Drop the price too slowly, as Sony did with its PlayStation 3, and you risk losing out on sales and market penetration. On the back of the global success of its PlayStation 2, Sony launched the PlayStation 3 at a price of US$600 in 2006, compared with US$399 for the Microsoft Xbox and US$249 for the Nintendo Wii. By the time the PlayStation 3 brand was eventually retailing at US$399 one year later, Sony had seen its dominant position in the global games console market eroded and it had fallen to number three behind Microsoft and Nintendo. The timing of pricing decisions is critical for the success of new products.

Based on: Sanchanta (2007);[17] Stern (2008)[18]

high profit margins for these brands. This price/promotion framework is useful when thinking about marketing strategies at launch.

The importance of picking the right strategy is illustrated by the failure of TiVo in the UK. TiVo make personal video recorders (PVRs), which are high-technology recorders capable of storing up to 40 hours of television and with features such as the facility to rewind live television programmes and memorize selections so that favourite programmes are automatically recorded. But the product has failed to take off and TiVo has withdrawn from the UK market. Part of the reason for the failure is that consumers did not seem to fully understand what PVRs can do and therefore couldn't justify spending in the region of £300 plus a monthly subscription fee for a recorder. Some analysts estimate that the product should be priced in the region of £100 for it to take off, suggesting that a penetration rather than a skimming strategy would have been more appropriate.[19]

High price (skimming) strategies and low price (penetration) strategies may be appropriate in different situations. A skimming strategy is most suitable in situations where customers are less price sensitive, such as where the product provides high value, where customers have a high ability to pay and where there are under high pressure to buy. However, setting the price too high can lead to problems generating sales. For example, when Nissan launched its 350Z sports car, it was priced at levels similar to top sports cars like the Porsche Boxster and BMW Z4. However, poor sales levels forced it to cut its retail price by €10,000, a move that brought it closer to the next level of sports cars like the Mazda RX-8. Penetration pricing strategies are more likely to be driven by company circumstances where the company is seeking to dominate the market, where it is comfortable to establish a position in the market initially and make money later, and/or where it seeks to create a barrier to entry for competitors.

Product-line strategy

Marketing-orientated companies also need to take account of where the price of a new product fits into its existing product line. Where multiple segments appear attractive, modified versions of the product should be designed, and priced differently, not according to differences in costs, but in line with the respective values that each target market places on a product. All the major car manufacturing companies have products priced at levels that are attractive to different market segments, namely economy cars, family saloons, executive cars, and so on.

Some companies prefer to extend their product lines rather than reduce the price of existing brands in the face of price competition. They launch cut-price 'fighter brands' (see Chapter 6) to compete with the low-price rivals. This has the advantage of maintaining the image and profit margins of existing brands. For example, Apple introduced the iPod Shuffle, retailing at US$99, to compete with low-price MP3 players, and also introduced the Mac Mini computer to compete against cheaper PCs coming on to the market from companies like Lenovo. By producing a range of brands at different price points, companies can cover the varying price sensitivities of customers and encourage them to trade up to the more expensive, higher-margin brands.

Competitive marketing strategy

The pricing of products should also be set within the context of the firm's competitive strategy. Four strategic objectives are relevant to pricing: build, hold, harvest and reposition.

Build objective

For price-sensitive markets, a build objective for a product implies a price lower than that of the competition. If the competition raise their prices we would be slow to match them. For price-insensitive markets, the best pricing strategy becomes less clear-cut. Price in these circumstances will be dependent on the overall positioning strategy thought appropriate for the product.

Hold objective

Where the strategic objective is to hold sales and/or market share, the appropriate pricing strategy is to maintain or match the price relative to the competition. This has implications for price changes: if the competition reduces prices then our prices would match this price fall.

Harvest objective

A harvest objective implies the maintenance or raising of profit margins, even though sales and/or market share are falling. The implication for pricing strategy would be to set premium prices. For products that are being harvested, there would be much greater reluctance to match price cuts than for products that were being built or held. On the other hand, price increases would swiftly be matched.

Reposition objective

Changing market circumstances and product fortunes may necessitate the repositioning of an existing product. This may involve a price change, the direction and magnitude of which will be dependent on the new positioning strategy for the product.

The above examples show how developing clear strategic objectives helps the setting of price and clarifies the appropriate reaction to competitive price changes. Price setting, then, is much more sophisticated than simply asking 'How much can I get for this product?' The process starts by asking more fundamental questions like 'How is this product going to be positioned in the marketplace?' and 'What is the appropriate strategic objective for this product?' Answering these questions is an essential aspect of effective price management.

Channel management strategy

When products are sold through intermediaries such as distributors or retailers, the list price to the customer must reflect the margins required by them. Some products, such as cars, carry margins of typically less than 10 per cent, therefore car dealers must rely on sales of spare parts and future servicing of new cars to generate returns. Other products, such as jewellery, may carry a margin of several hundred per cent. When Müller yoghurt was first launched in the UK, a major factor in gaining distribution in a mature market was the fact that its high price allowed attractive profit margins for the supermarket chains. Conversely, the implementation of a penetration pricing strategy may be hampered if distributors refuse to stock a product because the profit per unit is less than that available on competitive products.

The implication is that pricing strategy is dependent on understanding not only the ultimate customer but also the needs of distributors and retailers who form the link between them and the manufacturer. If their needs cannot be accommodated, product launch may not be viable or a different distribution system (such as direct selling) might be required.

International marketing strategy

The firm's international marketing strategy will also have a significant impact on its pricing decisions. The first challenge that managers have to deal with is that of **price escalation**. This means that a number of factors can combine to put pressure on the firm to increase the prices it charges in other countries. These include the additional costs of shipping and transporting costs to a foreign market, margins paid to local distributors, customs duties or tariffs that may be charged on imported products, differing rates of sales taxes and changes to the price that may be

Exhibit 8.3 The online music retailer CD Wow has been accused of parallel importing

driven by exchange rates and differing inflation rates. All of these combine to mean that the price charged in a foreign market is often very different to that charged on the home market. Sometimes it is higher, but it can also be lower if circumstances dictate that low prices are necessary to gain sales, as would be the case in countries where levels of disposable income are low. In such instances it is important for firms to guard against **parallel importing**—this is when products destined for an international market are re-imported back into the home market and sold through unauthorized channels at levels lower than the company wishes to charge. For example, the online music company CD Wow was fined £41 million when it was charged with selling cut-price CDs in the UK that it had imported from Hong Kong (see Exhibit 8.3). But trading of products across borders within the European Union is legal, so companies like Chemilines have been able to build a successful business importing pharmaceuticals from EU accession

Table 8.2 EU car price comparison, 1 January 2008

Pre-tax prices: all prices in euros				
Country	**Audi A3**	**Mercedes E220**	**Toyota Avensis**	**VW Golf**
Germany	19,080	34,500	19,781	13,698
Spain	18,263	34,397	16,730	13,372
France	16,984	34,569	17,986	12,787
Ireland	17,777	34,500	18,751	13,707
UK	16,329	30,318	18,342	12,900
Greece	17,710	34,500	16,507	11,027
Denmark	16,061	34,476	15,833	10,986
Sweden	16,310	31,754	16,855	12,636

Source: European Commission

states for sale in the UK, where prices can be up to 30 per cent higher.[20]

While most firms seek to standardize as many elements of the marketing mix as possible when operating internationally, pricing is one of the most difficult to standardize for the reasons outlined above. Sometimes the price differences are driven by cost variations, but sometimes they are also due to the absence of competitors or different customer value perceptions, which can lead to accusations of ripping off customers. Now that international prices are much easier to compare through, for example, the introduction of the euro, price differences across markets have become much more controversial (see Table 8.2, where some big differences in the pre-tax prices of new cars can be observed throughout Europe, and also Ethical Debate 8.1).

Ethical Debate 8.1: What is a fair price?

Price is one of the most hotly debated aspects of marketing. News reports regularly present stories of price variations for products across Europe, leading to claims that some consumers are being unfairly ripped off by companies charging inflated prices. For example, one study found that consumers in Ireland pay €10.99 for four Gillette Mach-3 blades compared with just €6.84 in London, that they pay €9.39 for a packet of Pampers newborn nappies compared with only €4.79 in the Netherlands, and that they pay higher prices for several other well-known brands.[21] These variations are difficult to justify, given the nature of modern consumer markets. Global pharmaceutical companies have been accused of overcharging for critical medicines, particularly in the world's poorer countries where diseases like HIV and AIDS are rampant. Telecommunications companies charge significant premiums for calls made or texts sent while roaming in other countries. And international travellers have complained for years about being ripped off by taxi companies, car hire firms, hotels and other service outlets when they visit new countries.

There are several ways in which organizations can exploit consumers by overcharging for goods and services. One of the most common is price fixing, which is illegal and banned throughout Europe. Rather than compete on price, companies collude with each other to ensure that everyone charges the same or similar prices. For example, 23 individuals and companies in Ireland were charged with price fixing in the home heating oil business. The cartel met regularly to fix the price charged to consumers in response to changes in the overall oil price. Estimates put it that they may have increased the price by up to 10 per cent, or €4.4 million, per year, which shows the attraction of fixing prices to unscrupulous companies. It is the job of regulatory authorities like the Competition Authority of Ireland and the Office of Fair Trading (OFT) in the UK to identify and investigate possible price collusion. For example, in 2008, the OFT has been investigating possible collusion between British supermarkets and their suppliers. The 'big four' supermarkets—Tesco, Asda, Sainsbury's and Morrisons—along with suppliers like Britvic, Coca-Cola, Mars, Nestlé, Procter & Gamble, Reckitt Benckiser and Unilever, have been asked to hand over documents. Price fixing is most likely to be found in industries where brand differentiation is difficult, such as oil, paper, glass and chemicals.

Equally controversial is the practice of deceptive pricing—in other words, where prices are not the same as they may first appear. Low-cost airlines have been significant users of deceptive pricing. For example, quoted fares may be as low as 99 cents but when all additional items, such as taxes, baggage charges, fuel surcharges, seat charges and credit card charges, are added in, fares may end up being well in excess of €70. These companies are also users of opt-outs. That is, unless consumers specifically opt out of additional items like travel insurance they will be charged for these as well. Furthermore, many of the headline low-fares offers are very limited in their availability, often restricted to just a few seats. EU regulators have targeted the industry to clean up its act on pricing. Airlines must now give a clear indication of the total price and extra charges have to be indicated at the start rather than the end of the booking.

All this means that consumers need to be very careful when judging the price of a good or service. Ultimately this debate rests on the issue of price and value. Consumers can vote with their feet. If they feel that a price is excessive, in most cases they can switch to substitute products or to other vendors. Consumers need to inform themselves and companies need to take great care in setting price levels. As this chapter shows, pricing must be an integral part of a company's marketing strategy.

Managing price changes

So far, our discussion has concentrated on those factors that affect pricing strategy; but in a highly competitive world, pricing is dynamic—managers need to know when and how to raise or lower prices, and whether or not to react to competitors' price moves. Many large corporations, such as Wal-Mart, Carrefour and Dell, build their marketing strategies around price leadership. First, we will discuss initiating price changes before analysing how to react to competitors' price changes.

Three key issues associated with initiating price changes are: the circumstances that may lead a company to raise or lower prices, the tactics that can be used, and estimating competitor reaction. Table 8.3 illustrates the major points relevant to each of these considerations.

Circumstances

Marketing research (for example, **trade-off analysis** or experimentation) which reveals that customers place a higher value on the product than is reflected in its price could mean that a price increase is justified. Rising costs, and hence reduced profit margins, may also stimulate price rises. Another factor that leads to price increases is excess demand. This regularly happens, for example, in the residential property market where the demand for houses can often grow at a faster pace than houses can be built by construction companies, resulting in house price inflation. A company that cannot supply the demand created by its customers may choose to raise prices in an effort to balance demand and supply. This can be an attractive option as profit margins are automatically widened. The final circumstance when companies may decide to raise prices is when embarking on a harvest objective. Prices are raised to increase margins even though sales may fall.

In the same way, price cuts may be provoked by the discovery that a price is high compared to the value that customers place on a product, by falling costs and by excess supply leading to excess capacity. A further circumstance that may lead to price falls is the adoption of a build objective. When customers are thought to be price sensitive, price cutting may be used to build sales and market share, though doing so involves the risk of provoking a price war.

Tactics

There are many ways in which price increases and cuts may be implemented. The most direct is the 'price jump', or fall, which increases or decreases the

Table 8.3 Initiating price changes

	Increases	Cuts
Circumstances	Value greater than price Rising costs Excess demand Harvest objective	Value less than price Excess supply Build objective Price war unlikely Pre-empt competitive entry
Tactics	Price jump Staged price increases Escalator clauses Price unbundling Lower discounts	Price fall Staged price reductions Fighter brands Price bundling Higher discounts
Estimating competitor reaction	Strategic objectives Self-interest Competitive situation Past experience	

price by the full amount at one go. A price jump avoids prolonging the pain of a price increase over a long period, but may raise the visibility of the price increase to customers. This happened in India, where Hindustan Lever, the local subsidiary of Unilever, used its market power to raise the prices of its key brands at a time when raw materials were getting cheaper. As a result operating margins grew from 13 per cent in 1999 to 21 per cent in 2003. Subsequently, though, sales fell sharply due to competition from P&G and Nirma, a local brand, as well as consumer disaffection.[22] Using staged price increases might make the price rise more palatable but may elicit accusations of 'always raising your prices'. A one-stage price fall can have a high-impact, dramatic effect that can be heavily promoted but also has an immediate impact on profit margins. Staged price reductions have a less dramatic effect but may be used when a price cut is believed to be necessary although the amount necessary to stimulate sales is unclear. Small cuts may be initiated as a learning process that proceeds until the desired effect on sales is achieved.

'Escalator clauses' can also be used to raise prices. The contracts for some organizational purchases are drawn up before the product is made. Constructing the product—for example, a new defence system or motorway—may take a number of years. An escalator clause in the contract allows the supplier to stipulate price increases in line with a specified index (for example, increases in industry wage rates or the cost of living).

Another tactic that effectively raises prices is **price unbundling**. Many product offerings actually consist of a set of products to which an overall price is set (for example, computer hardware and software). Price unbundling allows each element in the offering to be priced separately in such a way that the total price is raised. A variant on this process is charging for services that were previously included in the product's price. For example, manufacturers of mainframe computers have the option of unbundling installation and training services, and charging for them separately.

Yet another approach is to maintain the list price but lower discounts to customers. In periods of heavy demand for new cars, dealers lower the cash discount given to customers, for example. Similarly if demand is slack, customers can be given greater discounts as an incentive to buy (see Exhibit 8.4). However, there are risks if this strategy is pursued for too long a period of time. For example, due to poor sales of its car models, GM pursued a four-year price discounting strategy in the US market, with disastrous effects.

Exhibit 8.4 This advertisement for Orange demonstrates the popular use of discounts by telephone companies as a vehicle for getting and keeping customers

One iteration of the scheme, which was known as 'Employee Discounts for Everyone', offered buyers a discount averaging US$400–US$500 off the price of a new car. This took the total in incentives available to the buyer to over US$7000, or over 20 per cent off the suggested retail price of the car.[23] The resulting price war with Ford and Chrysler, who followed with similar schemes, has hurt profits. But, more worryingly, the effect of the campaign seems to be that GM customers simply bring forward purchases that they were going to make anyway to avail themselves of the discounts, and customer attention has switched to price rather than the value offered by the product.[24]

Quantity discounts can also be manipulated to raise the transaction price to customers. The percentage discount per quantity can be lowered, or the quantity that qualifies for a particular percentage discount can be raised.

Those companies contemplating a price cut have three choices in addition to a direct price fall.

1   A company defending a premium-priced brand that is under attack from a cut-price competitor may choose to maintain its price while introducing

a fighter brand. The established brand keeps its premium-price position while the fighter brand competes with the rival for price-sensitive customers.

2 Where a number of products and services that tend to be bought together are priced separately, price bundling can be used to effectively lower price. For example, televisions can be offered with 'free three-year repair warranties' or cars offered with 'free service for two years'.

3 Finally, discount terms can be made more attractive by increasing the percentage or lowering the qualifying levels.

Estimating competitor reaction

The extent of competitor reaction is a key factor in the price change decision. A price rise that no competitor follows may turn customers away, while a price cut that is met by the competition may reduce industry profitability. Four factors affect the extent of competitor reaction: their strategic objectives, what is in their self-interest, the competitive situation at the time of the price change, and past experience.

Firms should attempt to gauge their competitors' strategic objectives for their products. By observing pricing and promotional behaviour, talking to distributors and even hiring their personnel, estimates of whether competitor products are being built, held or harvested can be made. This is crucial information—their response to our price increase or cut will depend upon it. They are more likely to follow our price increase if their strategic objective is to hold or harvest. If they are intent on building market share, they are more likely to resist following our price increase. Conversely, they are more likely to follow our price cuts if they are building or holding, and more likely to ignore our price cuts if they are harvesting.

When estimating competitor reactions, self-interest is also important. Managers initiating price changes should try to place themselves in the position of their competitors. What reaction is in their best interests? This may depend on the circumstances of the price change. For example, if price is raised in response to cost inflation, the competitor firms are more likely to follow than if price is raised because of the implementation of a harvest objective. Price may also depend on the competitive situation. For example, if competition has excess capacity a price cut is more likely to be matched than if this is not the case. Similarly, a price rise is more likely to be followed if competition is faced with excess demand.

Looking at their reactions to previous price changes can also help one to judge competitor reaction. While past experience is not always a reliable guide it may provide an insight into the way in which competitor firms view price changes and the likely actions they might take.

Reacting to competitors' price changes

Companies need to analyse their appropriate reactions when their competitors initiate price changes. Three issues are relevant here: when to follow, what to ignore and the tactics to use if the price change is to be followed. Table 8.4 summarizes the main considerations.

Table 8.4 Reacting to competitors' price changes

	Increases	Cuts
When to follow	Rising costs Excess demand Price-insensitive customers Price rise compatible with brand image Harvest or hold objective	Falling costs Excess supply Price-sensitive customers Price fall compatible with brand image Build or hold objective
When to ignore	Stable or falling costs Excess supply Price-sensitive customers Price rise incompatible with brand image Build objective	Rising costs Excess demand Price-insensitive customers Price fall incompatible with brand image Harvest objective

Tactics
  Quick response
  Slow response
	Margin improvement urgent
	Gains to be made by being customer's friend
		Offset competitive threat
		High customer loyalty

When to follow

When competitive price increases are due to general rising cost levels or industry-wide excess demand, they are more likely to be followed. In these circumstances the initial pressure to raise prices is the same on all parties. Following a price rise is also more likely when customers are relatively price insensitive, which means that the follower will not gain much advantage by resisting the price increase. Where brand image is consistent with high prices, a company is more likely to follow a competitor's price rise as to do so would be consistent with the brand's positioning strategy. Finally, a price rise is more likely to be followed when a company is pursuing a harvest or hold objective because, in both cases, the emphasis is more on profit margin than sales/market share gain.

When they are stimulated by general falling costs or excess supply, price cuts are likely to be followed. Falling costs allow all companies to cut prices while maintaining margins, and excess supply means that a company is unlikely to allow a rival to make sales gains at its expense. Price cuts will also be followed in price-sensitive markets since allowing one company to cut price without retaliation would mean large sales gains for the price cutter. This has happened in the UK toiletries market where Boots has failed to follow Tesco in aggressive price cutting on products like shampoo and skin cream. Boots' profits and share price have been falling while Tesco's continue to grow.[25] The image of the company can also affect reaction to price cuts. Some companies position themselves as low-price manufacturers or retail outlets. In such circumstances they would be less likely to allow a price reduction by a competitor to go unchallenged for to do so would be incompatible with their brand image. Finally, price cuts are likely to be followed when the company has a build or hold strategic objective. In such circumstances an aggressive price move by a competitor would be followed to prevent sales/market share loss (see Exhibit 8.5). In the case of a build objective, the response may be more dramatic, with a price fall exceeding the initial competitive move. For example, Vodafone halved the monthly tariff for wireless datacards from £30 to £15, which put it on a par with 3, the industry leader, in a bid to grow its share of the mobile data services market.

When to ignore

In most cases, the circumstances associated with companies not reacting to a competitive price move are simply the opposite of the above. Price increases are likely to be ignored when costs are stable or

Exhibit 8.5 This advert cleverly shows the competitive reaction of a ferry company as it attempts to capitalise on the convenience of travelling with a car which is unavailable to passengers who choose to fly

falling, which means that there are no cost pressures forcing a general price rise. In the situation of excess supply, companies may view a price rise as making the initiator less competitive and therefore allow the rise to take place unchallenged, particularly when customers are price sensitive. Companies occupying low-price positions may regard a price rise in response to a price increase from a rival to be incompatible with their brand image. Finally, companies pursuing a build objective may allow a competitor's price rise to go unmatched in order to gain sales and market share.

Price cuts are likely to be ignored in conditions of rising costs, excess demand and when servicing price-insensitive customers. Premium-price positioners may be reluctant to follow competitors' price cuts for to do so would be incompatible with their brand image. For example, some luxury brands, such as Lacoste, have suffered heavily because of pursuing a strategy of discounting when faced with excess capacity while competitors chose not to follow.[26] Lastly, price cuts may be resisted by companies using a harvest objective.

Tactics

If a company decides to follow a price change, it can do this quickly or slowly. A quick price reaction is likely when there is an urgent need to improve profit margins. Here, the competitor's price increase will be welcomed as an opportunity to achieve this objective.

In contrast, a slow reaction may be the best approach when a company is pursuing the image of customers' friend. The first company to announce a price increase is often seen as the high-price supplier. Some companies have mastered the art of playing low-cost supplier by never initiating price increases and following competitors' increases slowly.[27] The key to this tactic is timing the response: too quick and customers do not notice; too long and profit is foregone. The optimum period can be found only by experience but, during it, salespeople should be told to stress to customers that the company is doing everything it can to hold prices for as long as possible.

If a firm wishes to ward off a competitive threat, a quick response to a competitor's price fall is called for. In the face of undesirable sales/market share erosion, fast action is needed to nullify potential competitor gains. However, reaction will be slow when a company has a loyal customer base willing to accept higher prices for a period so long as they can rely on price parity over the longer term.

Summary

Price is a major element in developing an effective marketing strategy because it is the only component of the marketing mix that directly generates revenue—all the others are costs. In this chapter the following key issues were addressed.

1. There are three bases upon which prices are set, namely cost, competition and market value. We noted that all three should be taken into account when setting prices. Costs represent a floor above which prices must be set to build a viable business, while competition and customers will influence the overall height of prices.

2. That the pricing levels set may also be influenced by a number of other marketing strategy variables, namely, positioning strategy, new-product launch strategy, product-line strategy, competitive strategy, channel management strategy and international marketing strategy. The pricing decision must be integrated with all other elements of the marketing mix.

3. That prices are dynamic, therefore marketers are faced with decisions relating to initiating price changes or responding to the price changes made by competitors. Whether prices are rising or falling, various factors need to be taken into account and these are important decisions as they affect the overall profitability of the firm.

4. That there are key issues surrounding the ethics of price setting. Price fixing is illegal, and other unethical practices such as deceptive pricing and product dumping are frequently targeted by regulators. Greater levels of price transparency are assisting consumers to avoid being exploited by unscrupulous companies.

Key terms

competitive bidding drawing up detailed specifications for a product and putting the contract out to tender

economic value to the customer (EVC) the amount a customer would have to pay to make the total life cycle costs of a new and a reference product the same

full cost pricing pricing so as to include all costs, and based on certain sales volume assumptions

going-rate prices prices at the rate generally applicable in the market, focusing on competitors' offerings rather than on company costs

marginal cost pricing the calculation of only those costs that are likely to rise as output increases

parallel importing when importers buy products from distributors in one country and sell them in another to distributors who are not part of the manufacturer's normal distribution; caused by significant price differences for the same product between different countries

price escalation the additional costs incurred in taking products to an international market, including transportation costs, distribution

costs, taxes and tariffs, exchange rates and inflation rates

price unbundling pricing each element in the offering so that the price of the total product package is raised

psychological pricing taking into consideration the psychological impact of the price level that is being set

trade-off analysis a measure of the trade-off customers make between price and other product features, so that their effects on product preference can be established

Study questions

1. Accountants are always interested in profit margins; sales managers want low prices to help push sales; and marketing managers are interested in high prices to establish premium positions in the marketplace. To what extent do you agree with this statement in relation to the setting of prices?
2. Why is value to the customer a more logical approach to setting prices than cost of production? What role can costs play in the setting of prices?
3. How would you justify the price differences for a cup of coffee that you might encounter if you purchase it in a local coffee shop versus a top-class hotel?
4. Discuss how a company pursuing a build strategy is likely to react to both price rises and price cuts by competitors.
5. Discuss the specific issues that arise when pricing products for international markets.
6. Visit www.vodafone.co.uk, www.o2.co.uk, www.orange.co.uk and www.easymobile.co.uk, and compare the prices these companies charge for their products. How difficult is it to make an accurate comparison of the cost of a mobile phone package? Why do you think this is so?

Suggested reading

Anderson, E. and D. Simester (2003) Mind Your Pricing Cues, *Harvard Business Review*, **81** (9), 96–103.

Davis, G. and E. Brito (2004) Price and Quality Competition between Brands and Own Brands: A Value Systems Perspective, *European Journal of Marketing*, **38** (1/2), 30–56.

Florissen, A., B. Maurer, B. Schmidt and T. Vahlenkamp (2001) The Race to the Bottom, *McKinsey Quarterly*, **3**, 98–108.

Jobber, D. and D. Shipley (1998) Marketing-orientated Pricing Strategies, *Journal of General Management*, **23** (4), 19–34.

Marn, M., Roegner, E. and C. Zawada (2003) Pricing New Products, *McKinsey Quarterly*, **3**, 40–50.

Mohammed, R. (2005) *The Art of Pricing: How to Find the Hidden Profits to Grow Your Business*, London: Crown Business.

Sahay, A. (2007) How Dynamic Pricing Leads To Higher Profits, *Sloan Management Review*, **48** (4), 53–60.

References

1. **Carroll, J.** (2007) Fasten Your Seatbelts, This Will be Turbulent, *The Ticket*, 28 December, 2; **Edgecliffe-Johnson, A.** (2007) Little Gold at End of Band's Rainbow, *Financial Times*, 7 November, 4; **Naughton, J.** (2007) Radiohead Find There's Gold at the End of *In Rainbows*, *Observer*, 18 November (www.guardian.co.uk).
2. **Lester, T.** (2002) How To Ensure that the Price is Exactly Right, *Financial Times*, 30 January, 15.
3. **Graff, V.** and **G. McLaren** (2003) *Harry Potter* Price Cut Sparks War of Bookstores, *Independent*, 20 June, 5.
4. **Voyle, S.** (2003) Harry and a Fierce Scramble for the Elusive Potter Gold, *Financial Times*, 20 June, 22.
5. **Wilson, B.** and **C. Woodhouse** (2005) Potter Price War, *Evening Standard*, 1 April, 28.
6. **Shapiro, B.P.** and **B.B. Jackson** (1978) Industrial Pricing to Meet Customer Needs, *Harvard Business Review*, Nov/Dec, 119–27.
7. **Christopher, M.** (1982) Value-in-use Pricing, *European Journal of Marketing*, **16** (5), 35–46.
8. **English, A.** (2004) Renault to Sell £3200 Car in Romania, Telegraph.co.uk, 3 June.

9. **Mackintosh, J.** (2005) Renault's Surprise Romanian Success, *Financial Times*, 29 September, 30.

10. **London, S.** (2003) The Real Value in Setting the Right Price, *Financial Times*, 11 September, 15.

11. **Kucher, E.** and **H. Simon** (1987) Durchbruch bei der Preisentscheidung: Conjoint-Measurement, eine neue Technik zur Gewinnoptimierung, *Harvard Manager*, 3, 36–60.

12. **Lester, T.** (2002) How To Ensure That the Price is Exactly Right, *Financial Times*, 30 January, 15.

13. **Forbis, J.L.** and **N.T. Mehta** (1979) Economic Value to the Customer, *McKinsey Staff Paper*, Chicago: McKinsey and Co. Inc., February, 1–10.

14. **McCaffrey, U.** (2006) Republic's Lenders Still Banking on Mortgages, *Irish Times, Business This Week*, 21 July, 3.

15. **Slattery, L.** (2006) Moving Mortgage is Worth a Little Effort, *Irish Times, Business This Week*, 10 November, 9.

16. **Simon, H.** (1992) Pricing Opportunities—And How to Exploit Them, *Sloan Management Review*, Winter, 55–65.

17. **Sanchanta, M.** (2007) A Price Cut Too Late for PlayStation 3, *Financial Times*, 6 December, 25.

18. **Stern, S.** (2008) Keep the Focus on Value or You Will Pay the Price, *Financial Times*, 27 May, 12.

19. **Cane, A.** (2003) TiVo, Barely Used . . . , *Financial Times*, Creative Business, 25 February, 12.

20. **Jack, A.** (2005) Drugs Groups Seek Cure for Irritation of Parallel Trading, *Financial Times*, 10 August, 18.

21. **Cullen, P.** (2007) Cheated at the Checkout, *Irish Times, Weekend Review*, 28 July, 1.

22. **Anonymous** (2004) Slow Moving: Can Unilever's Indian Arm Recover From Some Self Inflicted Wounds, *Economist*, 6 November, 67–8.

23. **Simon, B.** (2005) GM's Price Cuts Drive Record Sales, *Financial Times*, 5 July, 28.

24. **Simon, B.** (2005) Detroit Giants Count Cost of Four-year Price War, *Financial Times*, 19 March, 29.

25. **Buckley, C.** (2005) Boots Bears Brunt of Slump, *Sunday Business Post*, Money & Markets, 3 April, 2.

26. **Dowdy, C.** (2003) Wealth, Taste and Cachet at Bargain Prices, *Financial Times*, 9 October, 17.

27. **Ross, E.B.** (1984) Making Money with Proactive Pricing, *Harvard Business Review*, Nov/Dec, 145–55.

When you have read this chapter, log on to the Online Learning Centre for *Foundations of Marketing* at **www.mcgraw-hill.co.uk/textbooks/jobber**, where you'll find multiple-choice test questions, links and extra online study tools for marketing.

Case 8 Sony's PlayStation 3: the fall of the king?

Three giants have been sharing the video games console market over the last seven years: Sony, Microsoft and Nintendo. The recent launch of their so-called 'next-gen' consoles has revived the war that they wage against each other, as they all aim to sell far more than a mere console, but rather the real entertainment centre of any house. Yet, in trying to reach this objective, they rely on different marketing and pricing strategies.

A new king is born . . . or is it?

On the eve of the launch of its PlayStation 3 (PS3), Sony was by far the leader in the console market, thanks to its best-selling PlayStation 2. From 2000 to 2006, this console sold about 100 million units all over the world. Sony considered that these figures would speak for themselves, and that the reputation of the company would considerably help the launch of the PS3 to be a success. Yet, things went very differently . . .

The PS3 was launched in November 2006 throughout Japan and the United States. Back then, two versions of the console were proposed, one with a 20 Gb hard-drive, and the second one, more expensive, with a 60 Gb hard-drive. Besides some other differences (see Appendix 1), both models were equipped with a high-definition Blu-ray DVD player and a powerful graphic chipset. The European launch in late March 2007 was slightly different, as only the 60 Gb model was made available, since Sony had decided that the 20 Gb would be launched in this market only if there was a demand for it. However, this never happened, and the 20 Gb model was even completely abandoned some months later due to its relatively low sales.

The PS3 was claimed to be the most powerful console on the market. Sony hoped it would set new norms not only in the video game industry but also in the multimedia entertainment industry at large. Indeed, Sony presented its huge calculation and graphic power on the one hand, and the Blu-ray player on the other, as the two key advantages over its two main competitors: Microsoft's Xbox 360 and Nintendo's Wii. In that sense, Sony did not consider the PS3 to be a mere console, but an actual home entertainment centre, as described on the PlayStation website:[1] 'PS3 delivers the next generation of interactive entertainment. Enjoy Blu-ray disc movies, cutting edge high definition games, easy music, video and photo storage, free access to PlayStation Network (PSN) and much more' . . . Definitely 'much more', as the console was bound to evolve over time. Phil Harrison, who was then President of Sony Computer Entertainment Worldwide Studios, declared in February 2007: 'The launch of a platform like PS3 is not a fixed specification the day you buy the console. The chipset stays the same but the software changes over time. We'll continue to refine it, not just for developer experience, but for consumers too.'

This consumer experience was enhanced by many online services, accessible through the PlayStation Network (PSN). It enabled web surfing, free online gaming (except for MMORPGs[2] such as *World of Warcraft*), voice and video chat, and instant messaging services. PSN also offered access to the PlayStation Store, an online shop where gamers could find both free and paid-for digital content: playable demos, games and movies trailers, and exclusive games (including games from previous versions of the PlayStation or older consoles such as the Sega Genesis). Sony announced that high-definition films and music would also be found in the future. What's more, the PSN should give access to PlayStation Home in a few months or so, which is a kind of 'Second Life-like' virtual world where players will be able to form communities, create their own avatar and have a hugely customizable virtual space at their disposal to fill with their own content (photographs, movies, items unlocked in games, etc.). Finally, the PlayStation Network also makes it possible to read the content of the PS3 hard drive on the PSP (PlayStation Portable), through a WiFi connection.

Furthermore, as previously mentioned, the PS3 had a Blu-ray player. Its integration into the PS3 aimed to push this technology so that it would become the future DVD standard.[3] This proved to be a very costly decision for Sony. Indeed, the production of the (very expensive) Blu-ray diodes encountered many problems that explained a large part of the delay of the PS3. Moreover, two studies published at the end of 2006 showed that very few PS3 consumers were interested in Blu-ray functionality.

This state-of-the-art equipment was costly. In the United States, for example, the launch price of the 20 GB version was US$499 and US$599 for the 60 Gb. Despite this high price, many people queued to get it on the very day of its release, even sometimes one week before the console hit the shelves. In fact, Sony had many production problems, and had already been obliged to delay the release of the console. This greatly increased fans' impatience. Moreover, these problems forced Sony to deliver limited quantities to the Japanese and American markets, something that the firm felt obliged to do. As a consequence, many people bought a PS3 only to make a profit by quickly reselling it on eBay for a far higher price (for instance, from 16 to 22 November 2006, 28,500 PS3s were sold at an average of US$1276).

The European launch did not encounter such problems since Sony had more time to prepare for it. Hence, on 23 March 2007, 1 million PS3s were available at a €599 retail price (a little bit more in the UK, as the £425 price was equivalent to €635). Once again, the price apparently did not hinder its commercial success. Online retailers were besieged; for example, six times more pre-orders for the PS3 than the Xbox 360 were taken by the online retailer www.play.com —and 15 times more than the Wii! In the UK, the PS3 became the fastest-selling home console, with 165,000 of the 200,000 consoles available for the British market sold within two days of the launch (vs 105,000 Wii and 70,000 Xbox 360 consoles during the same period of time after their market release).

These figures, however, contrasted with the low attendance at many of the special evening events Sony organized to celebrate the European launch. Be it in Paris or London, only a handful of people queued to get theirs on day one, which differed greatly from what had happened for the PS2 launch. According to some analysts, while shortages were announced before the launch of the PS2 and provoked massive queuing, the million PS3s available on 'D-day' made customers somehow reluctant to queue all day until midnight for a console they could peacefully buy some days later. Yet, Sony did take care of the ones who did. For instance, those who waited until midnight at the London Virgin Megastore to buy their PS3 also received a free 46-inch high-definition television and a taxi home! Nevertheless, the way sales evolved in the following weeks and months raised one crucial question: is the PS3 an idol with feet of clay?

Fierce competition

Indeed, sales were far lower than expected, as the PS3 suffered from the competition. First, the Xbox 360 (X360), by Microsoft, was nearly as powerful as Sony's console, even though one of the major differences between the two lay in the absence of a Blu-ray player. Moreover, Microsoft's console was released one year earlier (late November/early December 2005), and 5.3 million units had already been sold when the PS3 was launched. Like the PS3, the X360 came with many online free and non-free services, through Xbox Live. These services included: chat, instant messaging, exclusive games and video-on-demand (VoD) to counter Sony's Blu-ray technology. Nonetheless, the X360 suffered from many technical problems, too, which have been heavily relayed on video gaming websites, blogs and video sharing websites (such as YouTube). This poor image for the product obliged Microsoft to react quickly in the face of customer dissatisfaction.

The latest competitor on this market was the Wii, by Nintendo. Technically speaking, this console was far less powerful than the other two, but was differentiated by its revolutionary gameplay. Its primary controller, the Wiimote, had motion-sensing capabilities that allowed the user to interact with and manipulate items on screen by moving. Consequently, players became really active, and video games took on a previously unknown social dimension. This enabled the Wii to benefit from a large public relations campaign. Furthermore, the Wii was far less costly than the X360 or the PS3: in Europe, for example, it cost €249 (£179.99) with one Wiimote and the game *Wii Sports*. The Wii also allowed gamers to create their own personalized avatar (called 'Mii') usable in many games, and offered many web services (weather, news, a virtual shop that enabled the downloading of games from older consoles, and social networking services). This clever strategy, which targeted non-gamers as well as traditional gamers fond of Nintendo's products, proved a massive success: as of 16 July 2008, the Wii had sold 28.65 million units, while 19.60 million X360s and only 13.96 million PS3s have been sold.[4] Such a success even exceeded Nintendo's highest forecasts, and the company frequently suffered from many shortages. This success has also been amplified by many people who testified that they physically benefited from the activity associated with the use of their console. This has resulted in the release of the WiiBoard and the game *Wiifit*. With this, people could practise many sports (gym, fitness, ski simulation, etc.) or even yoga. However, in response, rumours emerged in the first months of 2008, that Microsoft would be developing an X360 controller with motion-sensing capabilities as well. This would enable Microsoft to target non-players, who would also benefit from its superior graphics.

The relatively low price of the Wii, compared to its competitors, helps to explain its great success. Microsoft and Sony have been obliged to reduce the price of their own consoles. Even before the Japanese launch, Sony had already announced a 20 per cent price cut, as its console appeared too expensive. And, in July 2007, Sony decreased the price of the PS3 in the United States by US$100 (followed by a €100 rebate in Europe some weeks later). Similarly, Microsoft offered a US$50 rebate in the United States and €50 in Europe some weeks later; a further discount was offered in mid-March 2008. Yet, a study published by iSuply showed that Sony was losing between US$240 and US$300 on each PS3 sold, whereas Microsoft was estimated to be losing US$120 per console. Instead revenues were being generated on the sale of games and licences.[5] At the same time, both companies increased the number of versions of their consoles, to get prices as low as possible, even though it meant a slight decrease in the quality of their product (see Appendix 1). In contrast, Nintendo was profitable from the very beginning due to the technical choices it made. In addition, the high level of demand for its products meant that it avoided the need for any price cuts, despite many rumours that emerged when its competitors changed their prices.

As well as competing on price, the three companies developed massive communication campaigns aiming directly at their customers: TV and radio commercials, internet ads and contests, PR campaigns, etc. As an example, the promotional budget for the launch of the Wii was more than US$200 million—the biggest communication campaign Nintendo had ever conducted.

References

1   http://uk.playstation.com/ps3/.
2   Massively Multiplayer Online Role-Playing Games.
3   At the moment the PS3 was launched, two standards were competing to become the future DVD standard: HD-DVD (mainly, Toshiba) and Blu-ray. Toshiba halted the production and sale of HD-DVD in February 2008, due to low sales and the decision of many motion pictures studios to stop supporting HD-DVD.
4   Source: http://www.vgchartz.com.
5   Any editor who wishes to develop and sell a game for a console has to pay the console manufacturer for a licence.

Questions

1. Did Nintendo, Sony and Microsoft rely on the same methods of setting the *initial* price of their consoles?
2. What are the key factors that influenced the three firms' price-setting decisions?
3. Analyse the price-changing strategies of Sony and Microsoft. What do you think of Nintendo's decision not to decrease the price of its Wii?

This case was prepared by Loïc Plé, IÉSEG School of Management, France, from various published sources as a basis for class discussion rather than to show effective or ineffective management.

Table C8.1 The multiple versions of the PS3

Feature	20 Gb (NSTC*)	40 Gb (PAL/NSTC*)	60 Gb (NSTC*)	60 Gb (PAL*)	80 Gb (NSTC*)
In production	No	Yes	No	No	Yes
Colours (glossy finish for all)	Piano Black	Piano Black Ceramic White (USA, Asia and Japan only) Satin Silver (Asia and Japan only)	Piano Black	Piano Black	Piano Black
USB 2.0 ports	4	2	4	4	4
802.11 b/g WiFi	No	Yes	Yes	Yes	Yes
Flashcard readers	No	No	Yes	Yes	Yes
Chrome trim	No	Yes	Yes	Yes	Yes
SACD support	Yes	No	Yes	Yes	Yes
PS2 retro compatibility	Yes (hardware)	No	Yes (hardware)	Yes (software emulation)	Yes (software emulation)
First available	November 2006	October 2007	November 2006	March 2007	August 2007

Plus all models include Blu-ray/DVD/CD drive, HDMI 1.3a, Bluetooth 2.0, Gigabit Ethernet
* NTSC and PAL are two analogue television systems
Source: adapted from http://en.wikipedia.org/w/index.php?title=PlayStation_3&oldid=205287355

Table C8.2 The multiple versions of the X360

Features	Elite	Premium	Arcade	Core
In production	Yes	Yes	Yes	No
Suggested retail price (as of 14 March 2008)	US$449.99 GB£259.99 €369.99	US$349.99 GB£199.99 €269.99	US$279.99 GB£159.99 €199.99	US$279.99 GB£199.99 (until discontinuation)
First available	November 2005	August 2007	October 2007 (replaces the Core)	November 2005
Appearance	Matte black, chrome disc drawer	Matte white, chrome disc drawer	Matte white	Matte white
Included storage	120 Gb HDD	20 Gb HDD	256 Mb mem. unit	No
Ethernet cable	Yes	Yes	No	No
Xbox 360 Headset	Yes	Yes	No	No
Included audio/video cables/adapters	HDMI 1.2 (HD) Hybrid component/ composite digital/analogue audio dongle	Hybrid component/ composite	Composite	Composite
HDMI port	Yes	Yes (From July 2007 onwards)	Yes	No
Bundled games	*Hexic HD*	*Hexic HD*	Xbox Live Arcade compilation disc	Region specific

Source: adapted from http://en.wikipedia.org/w/index.php?title=Xbox_360&oldid=205207401

Chapter 9
Integrated Marketing Communications 1: Mass Communications Techniques

Chapter Outline

Integrated marketing communications (IMC)

Stages in developing an integrated communications campaign

Advertising

Sales promotion

Public relations and publicity

Sponsorship

Other promotional tools

Learning Outcomes

By the end of this chapter you will understand:

1 the concept of integrated marketing communications
2 the key characteristics of the seven major promotional tools
3 how to develop an integrated communications campaign—target audience analysis, objective setting, budgeting, message and media decisions, and campaign evaluation
4 the nature and importance of advertising in the promotional mix
5 the roles of sales promotion, public relations/publicity and sponsorship in the promotional mix.

Advertising at Marks & Spencer

One of the most fascinating challenges in marketing is the creation of communications messages. Part art, part science, this activity can have a huge impact on the fortunes of organizations. Memorable TV, press or outdoor campaigns can transform companies and drive the sales of their products and services. Many other campaigns fail to make any impact in the marketplace. The difficulty in advance of running a campaign is that it is virtually impossible to know whether it will work or not. Great campaigns like the Levi's 501s campaign (which we looked at in Chapter 1) or the Adidas 'Impossible is Nothing' campaign, discussed in Case 9, have struck a chord with consumers in ways that could not have been predicted in advance. This is all part of the challenge of creating great marketing.

A case in point has been the contrasting fortunes of Marks & Spencer over the past few years. M&S is one of Britain's most venerable companies; it built its reputation on high-quality, affordable clothing and high-quality food products. By the late 1990s, it had come to dominate British retailing, but as ever nothing is certain in business. Competition from speciality retailers such as Next, Gap and Zara began to eat in to its clothing sales, while its offerings were criticized for being staid, boring and not in touch with the needs of the modern consumer. Several management reshuffles did little to stem its rapid decline.

By the turn of the century, M&S was losing market share across all divisions except food, and while significant cost-cutting was being carried out, it became imperative for the company to increase its sales, particularly in sectors like women's wear, where it had previously been dominant. The company's marketing people needed to create communications messages that would appeal to the modern woman. In its first attempt to do this, it tried a risky, and ultimately disastrous, strategy. As much of the advertising that is aimed at women is criticized for projecting images of impossibly skinny or beautiful people, M&S went in a more natural direction with its 'I'm normal' campaign. The accompanying TV visuals showed the size 16 British woman, Amy Davis, running naked up a hill. As a strategy to sell clothing, it didn't work and the brand's reputation hit rock bottom. In contrast, to Dove's later 'campaign for real beauty', this projection of reality rather than allure in advertising did not work.

The revival of M&S's fortunes came from the creation of the 'Your M&S' campaign, which was rooted in the fact that Marks & Spencer had become the subject of several takeover attempts as its fortunes flagged. The idea was to re-instil M&S's core historical values of quality, service and value, and to try to convey to the British consumer that this company 'belonged' to them. Well-known British celebrities such as Twiggy, Lizzie Jagger and Erin O'Connor were used to front the adverts, and a blouse worn by Twiggy in one ad sold more units in one week than any other product in the history of M&S. Campaigns for food used the tagline 'This is not just food, this is M&S food' and, when hot chocolate puddings appeared in one of its commercials, sales increased by 288 per cent. The overall result of the 'Your M&S' campaign was an estimated additional 18 million customer visits in its first year, as well as a sharp rise in sales and profits.

The ad campaign was named the most effective British advertising effort in 2006 by the Institute of Practitioners in Advertising. Although M&S is not completely out of its troubles, this example shows how effective advertising helps to turn around even the most difficult of situations. But it also demonstrates the very fine line between success and failure in advertising and promotion, which is what makes it such a challenging and exciting business.[1]

As the above example shows, promoting products and services is a key marketing activity but, unfortunately, some people think that promotion is all there is to marketing. Readers of this book will by now, however, recognize that there is much more to marketing than just promotion. Promotional activities can be broad—that is, aimed at the market as a whole. These are known as mass communication techniques and will be the focus of this chapter. However, recent years have seen a significant increase in promotion that is targeted at individuals. This is known as direct communication and we will examine these developments in the next chapter. The overall range of techniques available to the marketer is usually known as the 'promotional mix' and comprises seven main elements.

1 *Advertising*: any paid form of non-personal communication of ideas or products in the prime media (television, press, posters, cinema and radio).
2 *Sales promotion*: incentives to consumers or the trade that are designed to stimulate purchase.
3 *Publicity*: the communication of a product or business by placing information about it in the media without paying for the time or space directly.
4 *Sponsorship*: the association of the company or its products with an individual, event or organization.
5 *Direct marketing*: the distribution of products, information and promotional benefits to target consumers through interactive communication in a way that allows response to be measured.
6 *Internet marketing*: the distribution of products, information and promotional benefits to consumers and businesses through internet technologies.
7 *Personal selling*: oral communication with prospective purchasers with the intention of making a sale.

In addition to these key promotional tools, the marketer can also use other techniques, such as exhibitions and product placement in movies, songs or video games, which have been growing in popularity in recent years. Before proceeding any further, however, it is important to stress that promotional mix decisions should not be made in isolation. As we saw with pricing, all aspects of the marketing mix need to be blended together carefully. The promotional mix used must be aligned with the decisions made with regard to product, pricing and distribution, in order to communicate benefits to a target market.

Integrated marketing communications (IMC)

Given the variety of techniques available to marketers, a key marketing decision is the choice of the promotional blend needed to communicate to the **target audience**. Each of the seven major promotional tools has its own strengths and limitations; these are summarized in Table 9.1. Marketers will carefully weigh these factors against promotional objectives to decide the amount of resources they should channel into each tool. For example in 2002, the consumer foods giant Unilever, spent €7.3 billion on marketing, with just over half of this, €4 billion, being spent on advertising.[2]

Usually, the following five considerations will have a major impact on the choice of the promotional mix.

1 *Resource availability and the cost of promotional tools:* to conduct a national advertising campaign may require several million pounds. If resources are not available, cheaper tools such as direct marketing or publicity may have to be used.
2 *Market size and concentration:* if a market is small and concentrated then personal selling may be feasible, but for mass markets that are geographically dispersed, selling to the ultimate customer would not be cost-effective. In such circumstances advertising or direct marketing may be the correct choice.
3 *Customer information needs:* if a complex technical argument is required, personal selling may be preferred. If all that is required is the appropriate brand image, advertising may be more sensible.
4 *Product characteristics:* because of the above arguments, industrial goods companies tend to spend more on personal selling than advertising, whereas consumer goods companies tend to do the reverse.
5 *Push versus pull strategies:* a **distribution push** strategy involves an attempt to sell into channel intermediaries (e.g. retailers) and is dependent on personal selling and trade promotions. A **consumer pull** strategy bypasses intermediaries to communicate to consumers directly. The resultant consumer demand persuades intermediaries to stock the product. Advertising and consumer promotions are more likely to be used.

As the range of promotional techniques expands, there is an increasing need to co-ordinate the messages and their execution. This problem is often exacerbated by the fact that, for example, advertising

Table 9.1 Key characteristics of seven key promotional mix tools

Advertising
- Good for awareness building because it can reach a wide audience quickly
- Repetition means that a brand positioning concept can be effectively communicated; TV is particularly strong
- Can be used to aid the sales effort: legitimize a company and its products
- Impersonal: lacks flexibility and questions cannot be answered
- Limited capability to close the sale

Personal selling
- Interactive: questions can be answered and objectives overcome
- Adaptable: presentations can be changed depending on customer needs
- Complex arguments can be developed
- Relationships can be built because of its personal nature
- Provides the opportunity to close the sale
- Sales calls are costly

Direct marketing
- Individual targeting of consumers most likely to respond to an appeal
- Communication can be personalized
- Short-term effectiveness can easily be measured
- A continuous relationship through periodic contact can be built
- Activities are less visible to competitors
- Response rates are often low
- Poorly targeted direct marketing activities cause consumer annoyance

Internet promotion
- Global reach at relatively low cost
- The number of site visits can be measured
- A dialogue between companies, and their customers and suppliers can be established
- Catalogues and prices can be changed quickly and cheaply
- Convenient form of searching for and buying products
- Avoids the necessity of negotiating and arguing with salespeople

Sales promotion
- Incentives provide a quick boost to sales
- Effects may be only short term
- Excessive use of some incentives (e.g. money off) may worsen brand image

Publicity
- Highly credible as message comes from a third party
- Higher readership than advertisements in trade and technical publications
- Lose control: a press release may or may not be used and its content distorted

Sponsorship
- Very useful for brand building and generating publicity
- Provides an opportunity to entertain business partners
- Can be used to demonstrate the company's goodwill to its local community or society in general
- Becoming increasingly popular due to the fragmentation of traditional media

is controlled by the advertising department, whereas personal selling strategies are controlled by the sales department, leading to a lack of co-ordination. This has led to the adoption of **integrated marketing communications** by an increasing number of companies. Integrated marketing communications is the system by which companies co-ordinate their marketing communications tools to deliver a clear, consistent, credible and competitive message about the organization and its products. For example, it means that website visuals are consistent with the images portrayed in **advertising** and that the messages conveyed in a direct marketing campaign are in line with those developed by the public relations department.

The application of this concept of integrated marketing communications can lead to improved consistency and clearer positioning of companies and their brands in the minds of consumers.

A simple model of the communication process is shown in Figure 9.1. The source (or communicator)

encodes a message by translating the idea to be communicated into a symbol consisting of words or pictures, such as an advertisement. The message is transmitted through media, such as television or the internet, which are selected for their ability to reach the desired target audience in the desired way. 'Noise'—distractions and distortions during the communication process—may prevent transmission to some of the target audience. The vast amount of promotional messages a consumer receives daily makes it a challenge for marketers to cut through this noise. When a receiver sees or hears the message it is decoded. This is the process by which the receiver interprets the symbols transmitted by the source. Communicators need to understand their targets before encoding messages so that they are credible. Otherwise the response may be disbelief and rejection. In a **personal selling** situation, feedback from buyer to salesperson may be immediate as when objections are raised or a sale is concluded. For other types of promotion, such as advertising and sales promotion, feedback may rely on marketing research to

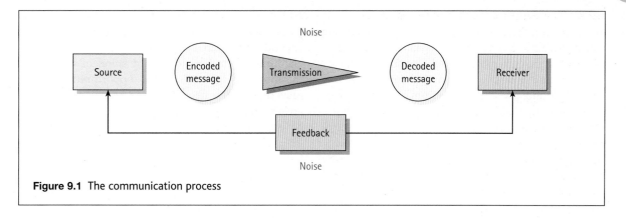

Figure 9.1 The communication process

estimate reactions to commercials, and increases in sales due to incentives.

Stages in developing an integrated communications campaign

For many small and medium-sized firms, marketing communications planning involves little more than assessing how much the firm can afford to spend, allocating it across some media and, in due course, looking at whether sales levels have increased or not. It is clear that to avoid wasting valuable organizational resources, marketing communications should be planned and evaluated carefully. The various stages involved in doing this are outlined in Figure 9.2.

The process begins by looking at the firm's overall marketing strategy, its positioning strategy and its intended target audience. What is the firm trying to achieve in the marketplace and what role can marketing communications play? If, for example, the firm is trying to reposition a brand or change consumer attitudes, then advertising is likely to play an important role in this, but it must be integrated with the other marketing mix elements. Objectives need to be set for the IMC campaign and they should be quantifiable. For example, the objective is to increase sales by a given amount or to increase awareness among the youth market by a given percentage. Only after these stages are complete should the company begin thinking about what it is going to say (the message decisions) and where and how it is going to say it (the promotional mix decisions). These are complex decisions, which are discussed in detail in this and the next chapter. A budget for the campaign needs to be agreed, usually at board level in the company. Then after the campaign has been run, it is imperative that it is fully evaluated to assess its effectiveness. We will

Figure 9.2 A framework for implementing integrated marketing conditions

now examine some of the key mass communications techniques in more detail.

Advertising

Advertising is very big business. In 2005, almost £19 billion was spent on advertising in the UK. There has long been considerable debate about how advertising works. The consensus is that there can be no single all-embracing theory that explains how all advertising works because it has varied tasks. For example, advertising that attempts to make an instant sale by incorporating a return coupon that can be used to order a product is very different from corporate image advertising that is designed to reinforce attitudes. One view of advertising sees it as being powerful enough to encourage consumers to buy by moving them through the stages of awareness, interest, desire and action (known by the acronym AIDA). An alternative approach—the awareness, trial, reinforcement (ATR) model—sees a key role of advertising as being to defend brands, by reinforcing beliefs so that existing customers may be retained. Advertising is likely to have different roles depending on the nature of the product and the degree of involvement of the customer (see Chapter 3).

Developing advertising strategy

Each of the steps identified in Figure 9.2 is appropriate irrespective of whether the firm is conducting an advertising campaign, a **direct marketing** or **sales promotion** campaign, all that changes is the detail involved. Here we examine some specific advertising issues.

Defining advertising objectives

Although, ultimately, advertising is a means of stimulating sales and increasing profits, a clear understanding of its communication objectives is of more operational value. Advertising can have a number of communications objectives. First, it can be used to create awareness of a brand or a solution to a company's problem. Awareness creation is critical when a new product is being launched or when the firm is entering a new market. Second, advertising can be used to stimulate trial, such as car advertising encouraging motorists to take a test drive. Third, and as we saw in Chapter 5, advertising is used to help position products in the minds of consumers, such as L'Oréal's repeated use of the slogan 'Because I'm worth it' or Ronseal's 'It does exactly what it says on the tin'. Other objectives of advertising include the correction of misconceptions about a product or service, reminding customers of sales or special offers, and providing support for the company's salesforce.

Setting the advertising budget

The amount that is spent on advertising governs the achievement of communication objectives. There are four methods of setting advertising budgets. A simple method is the 'percentage of sales' method, whereby the amount allocated to advertising is based on current or expected revenue. However, this method is weak because it encourages a decline in advertising expenditure when sales decline, a move that may encourage a further downward spiral of sales. Furthermore, it ignores market opportunities, which may suggest the need to spend more (not less) on advertising. For example, General Motors cut its advertising expenditure for the first half of 2007 by 27 per cent though sales of its models in the USA have been falling.

Alternatively, companies may set their advertising budgets based upon matching competitors' expenditures, or using a similar percentage of sales figure as their major competitor. Again this method is weak because it assumes that the competition has arrived at the optimum level of expenditure, and ignores market opportunities and communication objectives. Sometimes firms make a decision on the basis of what they think they can afford. While affordability needs to be taken into account when considering any corporate expenditure, its use as the sole criterion for budget setting neglects the communication objectives that are relevant for a company's products, and the market opportunities that may exist, to grow sales and profits.

The most effective method of setting advertising budgets is the 'objective and task' method. This has the virtue of being logical since the advertising budget depends upon communication objectives and the costs of the tasks required to achieve them. It forces management to think about objectives, media exposure levels and the resulting costs. In practice, the advertising budgeting decision is a highly political process.[3] Finance may argue for monetary caution, whereas marketing personnel, who view advertising as a method of long-term brand building, are more likely to support higher advertising spend. During times of economic slowdown, advertising budgets are among the first to be cut, though this can be the time when advertising expenditure is most effective.

Message decisions

An **advertising message** translates a company's basic selling proposition or **advertising platform** into words, symbols and illustrations that are attractive and meaningful to the target audience. In the 1980s, IBM realized that many customers bought its computers because of the reassurance they felt when dealing with a well-known supplier. The company used this knowledge to develop an advertising campaign based on the advertising platform of reassurance/low risk. This platform was translated into the advertising message 'No one ever got the sack for buying IBM'. As we shall see below, the choice of

Exhibit 9.1 In 2007, Cadbury's used the visual of a gorilla playing drums to promote its Dairy Milk brand. The risky strategy was rewarded with the advert becoming a huge television and viral marketing hit. How you interpret its message is up to you!

media available to the advertiser is vast, therefore one of the challenges of message formulation is to keep the message succinct and adaptable across various media. For example, a recent campaign for eBay just focused on the word 'It'. Imagery of the word 'It' appeared on posters, print and TV, and migrated online as a viral campaign. The 'It' was finally revealed as part of eBay's slogan, 'Whatever it is, you can get it on eBay'.[4]

Most of those who look at a press advertisement read the headline but not the body copy. Because of this, some advertisers suggest that the company or brand name should appear in the headline otherwise the reader may not know the source of the advertisement. For example, the headlines 'Good food costs less at Sainsbury's' and 'United Colors of Benetton' score highly because in one phrase or sentence they link a customer benefit or attribute with the name of the company. Even if no more copy is read, the advertiser has got one message across by means of a strong headline.

Messages broadcast via television also need to be built on a strong advertising platform (see Marketing in Action 9.1). Because TV commercials are usually of a duration of 30 seconds or less, most communicate only one major selling appeal—sometimes called the 'single-minded proposition'—which is the single most motivating and differentiating thing that can be said about the brand.[5] A variety of creative treatments can be used, from lifestyle, to humour, to shock advertising (see Exhibit 9.1). Cosmetic brands like Estée Lauder have traditionally favoured the lifestyle approach to advertising though many have now moved to using top models and celebrities in their advertising. Until recently sex was used very frequently as a shock or attention-getting tactic in advertising, though recent research suggests that its ability to gain attention is waning.[6] Comparative advertising is another popular approach frequently used by companies like low-cost airlines, supermarkets and banks to demonstrate relative price advantages. It can be a risky approach as it often leads to legal battles over claims made, such as the legal action between Asda and Tesco over the former's claim that it was 'officially' the lowest price supermarket.[7]

Television advertising is often used to build a brand personality. The brand personality is the message the advertisement seeks to convey. Lannon suggests that people use brand personalities in different ways,[8] such as acting as a form of self-expression, reassurance, a communicator of the brand's function and an indicator of trustworthiness. The value of the brand personality to consumers will differ by product category and this will depend on for what purpose they use brand imagery. In 'self-expressive' product categories, such as perfumes, cigarettes, alcoholic drinks and clothing, brands act as 'badges' for making public an aspect of personality ('I choose this brand [e.g. Tommy Hilfiger] to say this about myself').

Marketing in Action 9.1: Creating and sending messages

Study guide: Below is a review of the advertising messages being used by some of Europe's leading telecommunications companies. Read it and consider the advantages and disadvantages of the approaches being used.

Advertising is a highly creative process. Companies have messages that they want to communicate and they work with advertising agencies to find ways to get their message across. Often this can be quite challenging. Take a product like a mobile phone network. Technically, a phone network is a system of masts that communicate signals to each other. Consequently, it is probably not the most exciting technology in the world, but the various mobile phone operators need to be able to find ways of connecting with customers in order to develop their businesses.

Orange has been one of the great successes in mobile phone branding. When Orange was launched in 1994, the mobile phone market was a confusing place, with consumers having difficulty keeping pace with the technology and understanding the range of tariffs on offer. Orange's strategy ran counter to that of its competitors by focusing on its quirky name and colour, and not even mentioning mobile phones. This was captured in the slogan 'The future's bright, the future's Orange', which was reassuring for customers faced with these challenges. This emotional appeal worked and it doubled its subscriber base in 1995 and became the youngest UK company to enter the FTSE Index the following year. Now as part of French Telecom, it has successfully employed a similar strategy throughout Europe, making it one of the leading brands in markets like France, Israel and Switzerland.

Similarly, the world's largest mobile phone group, Vodafone, is currently focusing on an emotional appeal through the slogan 'Make the most of now.' This is captured by the iconic 'Mayfly' TV campaign, which extols the virtues of living life to the full. Mayflies have a life expectancy of one day and viewers are asked to imagine what life would be like if we embraced it in this way. Again mobile phones or networks do not feature anywhere in the advert but the implication of the campaign is that time is precious and that mobile phones help people to make the most of their time. The new generation of mobile phones that are complete with 3G services further enhances the time-saving value that consumers can get from their phones. Ironically, only time will tell whether this campaign will have the effect of increasing the adoption of 3G phones in general or increasing Vodafone's share of the market. But the kind of advertising adopted by some of the leading mobile phone operators shows the level of creativity that is employed to generate messages that appeal to consumers.

Based on: Cane (2005);[9] Carter (2005)[10]

Campaigns developed by some leading brands are examined in Marketing in Action 9.1.

As the challenge of holding the viewer's attention to advertising increases, organizations are coming up with increasingly novel creative treatments. For example, Honda and Channel 4 combined to produce the first live TV advertisement in 2008. A live sky-diving jump was broadcast in which 19 stuntmen spelt out the car maker's brand name in an advert that had the slogan 'Difficult is worth doing'. The pre- and post-publicity surrounding the initiative also benefited Honda.

Media decisions

Because of the proliferation of media now available to an advertiser, such as hundreds of TV channels or radio stations, the media selection decision has become a very important one. Some of the overall effects of the changes in technology on advertising are discussed in Technology Focus 9.1.

Choice of media class (for example, television versus press) and media vehicle (e.g. a particular newspaper or magazine) are two key decisions. Both of these will be examined next.

Technology Focus 9.1: New forms of television advertising

Developments in technology are changing the way that mass communications works on a variety of levels. First, there is the proliferation of media vehicles, which presents both challenges and opportunities. A small number of terrestrial TV or radio channels have been replaced by a very large number of digital channels. As audiences fragment, they become harder to reach, but also the opportunity for focusing on smaller segments increases. Second, television advertising, in particular, is interruptive. Technology like that provided by remote controls and personal video recorders (PVRs) enables viewers to avoid these interruptions. Again this presents a big challenge for advertisers, but also an opportunity for more precise targeting of adverts. PVRs memorize viewing patterns and when these are fed back to advertisers, specific adverts can be directed to specific consumers. Third, new technologies give rise to new innovations like branded TV channels and user-generated advertising.

With the growth of the internet, video-sharing websites like YouTube compete with television as a source of entertainment. As a result, car companies like BMW and Audi have pioneered online brand channels. The BMW film series, *The Hire*, was a series of short (eight-minute) films created for the internet in 2001. In keeping with BMW's reputation for quality, it was keen to ensure that the films were not seen as simply glorified advertisements. The British actor Clive Owen was the main star, and leading directors like John Frankenheimer, Guy Ritchie and Ang Lee were hired as well. The films proved to be immensely popular, with the result that the series was extended and ran until 2005. It is estimated that it was viewed 100 million times over four years and many of the films still appear on viral video websites. Millions of people also registered on the BMW website, giving the company a large database of BMW and potential BMW owners. The Audi TV channel was launched in the UK in 2005 and features information about Audi vehicles, but also entertainment featuring sport and cooking celebrities. But this does not mean that all branded programmes have migrated to the internet. For example, the series *Luxury Unveiled*, featuring one-hour documentaries on brands like Cartier and Chanel, was made for television with an eye on the emerging markets for luxury products like Russia and China.

The most unique feature of the internet in the past few years has been the growth in user-generated content, which underpins sites like MySpace, YouTube and Flickr. So it comes as no surprise that there has also been a growth in user-generated advertising. As much of what appears on video-sharing sites like YouTube is spoof advertising, some companies are seeking to harness this creativity in a positive way by inviting users to create adverts and submit them to corporate competitions. For example, Mastercard invites user-created adverts to be sent to its website, Priceless.com. Wal-Mart's School My Way initiative invites high-school students in the USA to create web pages and videos, and enter a competition with the winners to be shown in a cable television commercial.

Other brands that have encouraged users to develop adverts include Nike, Toyota and L'Oréal. User-generated content can be extremely risky, however. Some adverts may show the company in a very negative light, such as a General Motors competition that attracted claims that it was contributing to global warming, and many will remain online long after the company has decided to change the theme or focus of its advertising. But its real strength is that it encourages consumers to interact with the brand and also helps brand owners to understand how consumers feel about and relate to their brands. It also brings a diversity to the creative process that no one company or agency can provide.

Traditional television advertising is far from dead, but it is changing. Rather than being a producer-driven and interruptive force, it appears that it will increasingly become an interactive medium, driven as much by consumers who seek it out and contribute to its creation.

Table 9.2 Media class options

1 Television
2 Press
   National newspapers
   Regional newspapers
   Trade and technical
   Magazines
3 Posters
4 Cinema
5 Radio

Table 9.2 lists the major media class options (the media mix). The media planner faces the choice of using television, press, cinema, posters, radio or a combination of media classes. Creative factors have a major bearing on the choice of media class. For example, if the objective is to position the brand as having a high-status, aspirational personality, television would be better than posters. However, if the communication objective is to remind the target audience of a brand's existence, a poster campaign may suffice.

Each medium possesses its own set of creative qualities and limitations. Television can be used to demonstrate the product in action, or to use colour and sound to build an atmosphere around the product, thus enhancing its image. Although TV was traditionally one of the most powerful advertising

mediums, concerns about fragmentation of the TV audience have led many leading advertisers to move away from it. Furthermore, recent research has again questioned whether viewers actually watch ads when they are on, finding that consumers may spend as little as 23 per cent of the time the ads are on watching them, with the remainder spent talking, reading, surfing between channels or doing tasks such as cleaning, ironing or office work.[11] Unilever has responded by reducing the amount of advertising it places on television, switching instead to outdoor and internet advertising. Despite these developments, television is still the largest advertising medium (see Figure 9.3) and some research shows it plays a significant role in brand building.[12]

Press advertising is useful for providing factual information and offers an opportunity for consumers to re-examine the advertisement at a later stage. Advertisers are increasingly using colour print ads to ensure that their brands stand out. Leaders in this field include the likes of Orange and easyJet, as well as retail chains like Marks & Spencer. Colour advertising in newspapers has risen by 53 per cent as against an 8 per cent growth in mono advertising.[13] Magazines can be used to target particular markets and one growing sector is customer magazines, whereby leading brands such as BMW and Mercedes produce colour magazines of pictures and editorial about their products. Posters are a very good

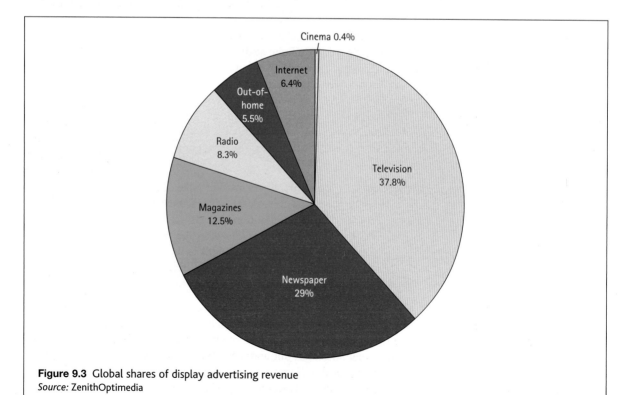

Figure 9.3 Global shares of display advertising revenue
Source: ZenithOptimedia

support medium, as their message has to be short and succinct because consumers such as motorists will normally only have time to glance at the content. Lavazza, the Italian coffee brand, is an extensive user of poster sites in airports and metropolitan areas where its glamorous, fashion magazine-style adverts are used to build awareness and image of the brand. Outdoor advertising continues to be favoured as the growth of cities, metros and long commuting times make the medium appealing, though it is increasingly subject to regulation. Radio is limited to the use of sound and is therefore more likely to be useful in communicating factual information rather than building image, while cinema benefits from colour, movement and sound, as well as the presence of a captive audience. Cinema is a particularly good medium for brands trying to reach young audiences.

A number of other factors also affect the **media class decision**. An important consideration is the size of the advertising budget. Some media are naturally more expensive than others. For example, £500,000 may be sufficient for a national poster campaign but woefully inadequate for television. The relative cost per opportunity to see (OTS) is also relevant. The target audience may be reached much more cheaply using one medium rather than another. However, the calculation of OTS differs according to media class, making comparisons difficult. For example, in the UK, an OTS for the press is defined as 'read or looked at any issue of the publication for at least two minutes', whereas for posters it is 'traffic past site'. A further consideration is competitive activity. A company may decide to compete in the same medium as a competitor or seek to dominate an alternative medium. For example, if a major competitor is using television, a firm may choose posters, where it could dominate, thus achieving a greater impact. Finally, for many consumer goods producers, the views of the retail trade (for example, supermarket buyers) may influence the choice of media class. Advertising expenditure is often used by salespeople to convince the retail trade to increase the shelf space allocated to existing brands, and to stock new brands. For example, if it is known that supermarkets favour television advertising in a certain product market, the selling impact on the trade of £3 million spent on television may be viewed as greater than the equivalent spend of 50:50 between television and the press.

The choice of a particular newspaper, magazine, television spot, poster site, etc., is called the **media vehicle decision**. Although creative considerations still play a part, cost per thousand calculations are the dominant influence. This requires readership and viewership figures. In the UK, readership figures are produced by the National Readership Survey, based on 36,000 interviews per year. Television viewership is measured by the Broadcasters' Audience Research Board (BARB), which produces weekly reports based on a panel of 5100 households equipped with metered television sets (people meters). Traffic past poster sites is measured by Outdoor Site Classification and Audience Research (OSCAR), which classifies 130,000 sites according to visibility, competition (one or more posters per site), angle of vision, height above ground, illumination and weekly traffic past site. Cinema audiences are monitored by Cinema and Video Industry Audience Research (CAVIAR) and radio audiences are measured by Radio Joint Audience Research (RAJAR).

Media buying is a specialist area and a great deal of money can be saved on rate card prices by powerful media buyers. Media buying is accomplished through one of three methods: full service agencies, media specialists and media buying clubs. Full service agencies, as the name suggests, provide a full range of advertising services for their clients including media buying. Independent media specialists grew in the early 1990s as clients favoured their focused expertise and negotiating muscle. Media buying clubs were formed by full service agencies joining forces to pool buying power. However, the current trend is back to full service agencies, but with one major difference: today the buying is done by separate profit-making subsidiaries. With very few exceptions, all the world's top media-buying operations are now owned by global advertising companies such as WPP and Publicis.

Executing the campaign

When an advertisement has been produced and the media selected, it is sent to the chosen media vehicle for publication or transmission. A key organizational issue is to ensure that the right advertisements reach the right media at the right time. Each media vehicle has its own deadlines after which publication or transmission may not be possible.

Evaluating advertising effectiveness

Measurement can take place before, during and after campaign execution. Pre-testing takes place before the campaign is run and is part of the creative process. In television advertising, rough advertisements are created and tested with target consumers. This is usually done with a focus group, which is shown perhaps three alternative commercials and the group members are asked to discuss their likes, dislikes and understanding of each one. Stills from the proposed commercial are shown on a television screen with a voiceover. This provides an inexpensive but realistic portrayal of what the commercial will be like if it is shot. The results provide important input from the target consumers themselves rather than relying solely on **advertising agency** views. Such research is not without its critics, however. They suggest that the impact of a commercial that is repeated many times cannot be captured in a two hour group discussion. They point to the highly successful Heineken campaign—'Refreshes the parts other beers cannot reach' —which was rejected by target consumers in the pre-test.[14] Despite this kind of criticism, advertising research is a booming business because of the uncertainty surrounding the effectiveness of traditional media like television, and the rise of new media such as the internet and mobile advertising.

Post-testing can be used to assess a campaign's effectiveness once it has run. Sometimes formal post-testing is ignored through laziness, fear or lack of funds. However, checking how well an advertising campaign has performed can provide the information necessary to plan future campaigns. The top three measures used in post-test television advertising research are image/attitude change, actual sales and usage, though other financial measures such as cash flow, shareholder value and return on investment are increasingly being used. Image/attitude change is believed to be a sensitive measure, which is a good predictor of behavioural change. Those favouring the actual sales measure argue that, despite difficulties in establishing cause and effect, sales change is the ultimate objective of advertising and therefore the only meaningful measure. Testing recall of adverts is also popular. Despite the evidence suggesting that recall may not be a valid measure of advertising effectiveness, those favouring recall believe that because the advertising is seen and remembered it is effective.

Organizing for campaign development

There are four options open to an advertiser when organizing for campaign development. First, small companies may develop the advertising in co-operation with people from the media. For example, advertising copy may be written by someone from the company, but the artwork and final layout of the advertisement may be done by the newspaper or magazine. Second, the advertising function may be conducted in-house by creating an advertising department staffed with copy-writers, media buyers and production personnel. This form of organization locates total control of the advertising function within the company, but since media buying is on behalf of only one company, buying power is low. Cost-conscious companies such as Ryanair do most of their advertising work in-house. Third, because of the

specialist skills that are required for developing an advertising campaign, many advertisers opt to work with an advertising agency. Larger agencies offer a full service, comprising creative work, media planning and buying, planning and strategy development, market research and production. Because agencies work for many clients, they have a wide range of experience and can provide an objective outsider's view of what is required and how problems can be solved. Four large global conglomerates—Omnicom, WPP Group, Interpublic and Publicis—with combined sales revenues of over US$34 billion in 2006, dominate the industry. These corporations have grown in response to major multinational companies like Samsung and Nestlé, who want their global advertising handled by one firm.[15] A fourth alternative is to use in-house staff (or their full service agency) for some advertising functions, but to use specialist agencies for others. The attraction of the specialist stems, in part, from the large volume of business that each controls. This means that they have enormous buying power when negotiating media prices. Alternatively, an advertiser could employ the services of a 'creative hot-shop' to supplement its own or its full service agency's skills. Saatchi & Saatchi began life as a creative hot-shop before developing into a full service agency.

The traditional system of agency payment was by commission from the media owners. This was because advertising agencies were originally set up on behalf of media owners who wished to provide advertising services to enhance the likelihood of selling advertising space. Hence, it was natural that payment should be from them. Under the commission system, media owners traditionally offered a 15 per cent discount on the rate card (list) price to agencies. For example, a £1 million television advertising campaign would result in a charge to the agency of £1 million minus 15 per cent (£850,000). The agency invoiced the client at the full rate card price (£1 million). The agency commission therefore totalled £150,000.

Large advertisers have the power to demand some of this 15 per cent in the form of a rebate. For example, companies like Unilever and P&G have reduced the amount of commission they allow their agencies. Given that P&G spent an estimated US$8.5 billion in 2006 it could probably demand very low commission levels, but these companies chose not to exercise all of their muscle as low commission rates ultimately may lead to poor-quality advertising. The second method of paying agencies is by fee. For smaller clients, commission alone may not be sufficient to cover agency costs. Also, some larger clients are advocating fees rather than commission, on the basis that this removes a possible source of agency bias towards media that pay commission rather than a medium like direct mail for which no commission is payable.

Payment by results is the third method of remuneration. This involves measuring the effectiveness of the advertising campaign using marketing research, and basing payment on how well communication objectives have been met. For example, payment might be based on how awareness levels have increased, brand image improved or intentions-to-buy risen. Another area where payment by results has been used is media buying. For example, if the normal cost per thousand to reach men in the age range 30–40 is £4.50, and the agency achieves a 10 per cent saving, this might be split 8 per cent to the client and 2 per cent to the agency.[16] Procter & Gamble uses the payment by results method to pay its advertising agencies, which include Saatchi & Saatchi, Leo Burnett, Grey and D'Arcy Masius Benton & Bowles. Remuneration is tied to global brand sales, so aligning their income more closely with the success (or otherwise) of their advertising.[17]

Ethical Debate 9.1: Informing or misleading?

Advertising is everywhere; it is the means by which organizations communicate with potential customers. But many opponents argue that advertising is at best wasteful and at worst downright misleading, offensive and dangerous. On the other hand, advocates argue that, in modern societies, consumers are savvy enough to be able to assess advertising for what it is.

Misleading advertising can take the form of exaggerated claims and concealed facts. For example, the low-cost airline Ryanair is frequently in trouble around Europe for its provocative advertising. A recent comparative campaign in the UK was headlined 'Robbed by Lastminute.com' and showed a burglar with 'online agent' written on its top. Lastminute.com complained that the ad was misleading and that the cartoon robber 'denigrated and discredited' its business, a claim that was upheld by the Advertising Standards Authority (ASA). Similarly, broadband operators have been criticized for advertising promised download speeds that, in reality, were not delivered.

Advertising can also deceive by omitting important facts from its message. Such concealed facts may give a misleading impression to the audience. The advertising of food products like breakfast cereals is particularly susceptible to misleading advertising, such as omitting details of sugar and salt levels, or making bogus scientific claims of health benefits. Some companies, like Kellogg's, use celebrity presenters of science programmes (e.g. Philippa Forrester, presenter of *Tomorrow's World*) to endorse their products, which can give the impression that claims are scientifically grounded. Many industrialized countries have their own codes of practice that protect the consumer from deceptive advertising. For example, in the UK the ASA (www.asa.org.uk) administers the British Code of Advertising Practice, which insists that advertising should be 'legal, decent, honest and truthful'. Shock advertising, such as that pursued in the past by companies like Paddy Power, Benetton and FCUK, is often the subject of many complaints to the ASA (see Exhibit 9.2).

Critics argue that advertising images have a profound effect on society. They claim that advertising promotes materialism and takes advantage of human frailties. Advertising is accused of stressing the importance of material possessions, such as the ownership of a car or the latest in consumer electronics. Critics argue that this promotes the wrong values in society. A related criticism is that advertising takes advantage of human frailties such as the need to belong or the desire for status. For example, a UK Government white paper has proposed a ban on junk food advertising at certain times, in the same way as cigarette and alcohol advertising is restricted. Supporters of advertising counter that these ads do not prey on human frailties but basic psychological characteristics that would be served even if advertising did not exist.

One particularly controversial area is that of advertising to children. Critics argue that children are especially susceptible to persuasion and that they therefore need special protection from advertising. For example, a UK study found that children increased their consumption of sweet and savoury foods by 134 per cent after watching fast-food, breakfast cereal and soft drinks

Exhibit 9.2 Advertising by the betting company Paddy Power regularly tests the boundaries of good taste; this advertisement for its online bingo site was part of a 'Where have all the women gone' series and was subjected to restrictions in both the UK and Ireland

advertisements on television, with obese children significantly more likely to up their consumption.[18] Others counter by claiming that the children of today are remarkably 'streetwise' and can look after themselves. They are also protected by parents who can, to some extent, counteract advertising influences. Many European countries have regulations that control advertising to children. For example, in Germany, the advertising of specific types of toy is banned, and in the UK alcohol advertising is controlled. The Broadcasting Commission of Ireland (BCI) has introduced a new code for children's advertising that bans 'Christmas-themed' advertising before 1 November each year, and also bans celebrities and sports stars from advertising food and soft drinks aimed at children. However, the difficulties involved in regulating advertising in this way are illustrated by the advertising industry's response to such restrictions, which was to suggest that companies would simply move this kind of advertising to non-Irish TV channels such as Sky, UTV and MTV, which also broadcast in Ireland.[19]

Advertising has always been controversial and it looks like it will continue to be so for some time to come.

Sales promotion

As we have already seen, sales promotions are incentives to consumers or the trade that are designed to stimulate purchase. Examples include money off and free gifts (consumer promotions), and discounts and salesforce competitions (trade promotions). A vast amount of money is spent on sales promotion and many companies are engaging in joint promotions. Some of the key reasons for the growth in sales promotion include the following.

- *Increased impulse purchasing*: the rise in impulse purchasing favours promotions that take place at the point of purchase.
- *The rising cost of advertising and advertising clutter*: these factors erode advertising's cost-effectiveness.

- *Shortening time horizons*: the attraction of the fast sales boost of a sales promotion is raised by greater rivalry and shortening product life cycles.
- *Competitor activities*: in some markets, sales promotions are used so often that all competitors are forced to follow suit.
- *Measurability*: measuring the sales impact of sales promotions is easier than for advertising since its effect is more direct and, usually, short term. The growing use of electronic point-of-sale (EPOS) scanner information makes measurement easier.

If sales require a 'short, sharp shock', sales promotion is often used to achieve this. In this sense it may be regarded as a short-term tactical device. The long-term sales effect of the promotion could be positive, neutral or negative. If the promotion has attracted new buyers who find that they like the brand, repeat purchases from them may give rise to a positive long-term effect.[20] Alternatively, if the promotion (e.g. money off) has devalued the brand in the eyes of consumers, the effect may be negative.[21] Where the promotion has caused consumers to buy the brand only because of its incentive value with no effect on underlying preferences, the long-term effect may be neutral.[22] An international study of leading grocery brands has shown that the most likely long-term effect of a price promotion for an existing brand is neutral. Such promotions tend to attract existing buyers of the brand during the promotional period rather than new buyers (see Marketing in Action 9.2).[23]

Sales promotion strategy

As with advertising, a systematic approach should be taken to the management of sales promotions involving the specification of objectives for the promotion,

decisions on which techniques are most suitable and an evaluation of the effectiveness of the promotion.

Sales promotions can have a number of objectives. The most usual goal is to boost sales over the short term. Short-term sales increases may be required for a number of reasons, including the need to reduce inventories or meet budgets prior to the end of the financial year, moving stocks of an old model prior to a replacement, and to increase stock-holding by consumers and distributors in advance of the launch of a competitor's product. A highly successful method of sales promotion involves encouraging trial. Home sampling and home couponing are particularly effective methods of inducing trial. Certain promotions, by their nature, encourage repeat purchasing of a brand over a period of time. Any promotion that requires the collection of packet tops or labels (e.g. free mail-ins and promotions such as bingo games) attempts to increase the frequency of repeat purchasing during the promotional period. Some promotions are

Marketing in Action 9.2: Newspapers and sales promotion

Study guide: Below is a review of the sales promotion strategies being pursued by newspaper owners. Read it and consider the advantages and disadvantages of the approaches being used.

As discussed earlier in the chapter, newspapers are an important advertising medium. But, in the information age, it is a sector that is facing many challenges. The ownership of newspaper titles is increasingly held by large media corporations such as News Corporation, Fairfax Media and Independent Newspapers, which may hold up to hundreds of titles in different countries around the world. As a result, competition between titles is intense. But, in addition, many consumers are switching to broadcast and digital media to obtain their news, and newspaper readership is relatively static or falling. For example, over the past decade, newspaper sales in Europe have been falling in most countries, with the exception of Ireland and Spain. Indeed, one of the leading French newspapers, *Le Monde*, saw its circulation fall by over 11 per cent between 2001 and 2006, in common with many other titles in France and the UK. The movement of advertising revenues, such as the very profitable classified advertising, to the internet has also had a significant impact on the cost position of newspapers.

Faced with these challenges, it is interesting that newspapers have turned to sales promotion to assist. Premiums have been the most popular form of promotion used, with free gifts like magazines, CDs and DVDs being given away, often with Sunday titles. Spanish newspapers are heavy users of these kinds of promotions, with everything from airline tickets to classic film collections to lotteries for cars and holidays being used to promote titles. Many of the promotions are self-liquidating, with increases in the cover price being used to recoup the cost of promotions.

In Spain, these promotions seem to have been effective in stemming falling sales, but it is very questionable whether this strategy is sustainable in the long term. Premiums are just as likely to encourage brand switching as they are to increase overall sales. And when over-used or employed for long periods, 'promotion fatigue' is likely to set in. While sales promotions may give the ailing newspaper sector a short-term boost, more integrated marketing strategies will be necessary to tackle the migration of readers and advertisers to digital media.

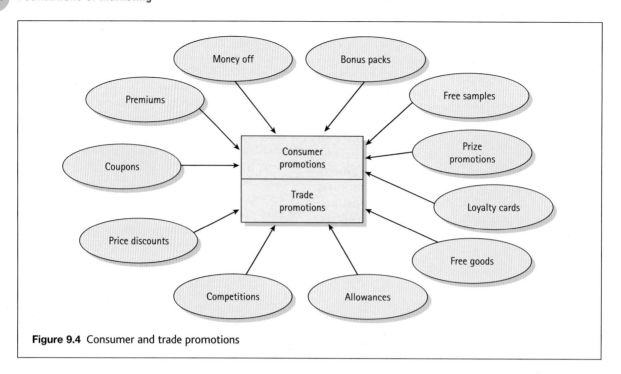

Figure 9.4 Consumer and trade promotions

designed to encourage customers to purchase larger pack sizes. Finally, trade promotions are usually designed to gain distribution and shelf space. Discounts, free gifts and joint promotions are methods used to encourage distributors to stock brands.

Selecting the type of sales promotion to use

There is a very wide variety of promotional techniques that a marketer can consider using (see Figure 9.4). Major consumer sales promotion types are money off, bonus packs, premiums, free samples, coupons, prize promotions and loyalty cards. A sizeable proportion of sales promotions are directed at the trade, including price discounts, free goods, competitions and allowances.

Consumer promotion techniques

Money-off promotions provide direct value to the customer and therefore an unambiguous incentive to purchase. They have a proven track record of stimulating short-term sales increases. However, price reductions can easily be matched by competitors and if used frequently can devalue brand image. **Bonus packs** give added value by giving consumers extra quantity at no additional cost and are often used in the drinks, confectionery and detergent markets. The promotion might be along the lines of 'Buy 10 and get 2 extra free' (see Exhibit 9.3). Because the price is not lowered, this form of promotion runs less risk of devaluing the brand image. When two or more items are banded together the promotion is called a

multibuy. These are frequently used to protect market share by encouraging consumers to stock up on a particular brand when two or more items of the same brand are banded together, such as a shampoo and conditioner. Multibuys can also generate range trial

Exhibit 9.3 This Boots promotion is an example of a bonus pack

when, for example, a jar of coffee is banded with samples of other coffee varieties such as lattes and mochas. **Premiums** are any merchandise offered free or at low cost as an incentive to purchase a brand; they can come in three forms: free in- or on-pack gifts, free in-the-mail offers and self-liquidating offers, where consumers are asked to pay a sum of money to cover the costs of the merchandise. The main role of premiums is in encouraging bulk purchasing and maintaining share. Breakfast cereal manufacturers have been extensive users of in-pack and self-liquidating premiums. For example, Kellogg's latest 'Big Breakfast' promotion for its mini portion packs and cereal bars includes gifts, a scratchcard competition, trade incentives and extensive point-of-purchase support.

Free samples of a brand may be delivered to the home or given out in a store and are used to encourage trial. For new brands or brand extensions this is an effective, if sometimes expensive, way of generating trial. Coupons can be delivered to the home, appear in magazines or newspapers, or appear on packs, and are used to encourage trial or repeat purchase. They are a popular form of sales promotion, although they are usually less effective in raising initial sales than money-off promotions because there is no immediate saving and the appeal is almost exclusively to existing consumers.[24] There are three main types of prize promotion: competitions, draws and games. These are often used to attract attention or stimulate interest in a brand. Competitions require participants to exercise a certain degree of skill and judgement and entry is usually dependent on purchase at least. For example, in an attempt to revitalize its ailing PG Tips tea brand, Unilever put 'mind game' puzzles on the backs of packs and directed entrants to a PG Tips website for solutions. Draws make no demand on skill and judgement, the result simply depends on chance.

Finally, a major development in retailing is the offering of loyalty cards to customers. Points are gained every time money is spent at an outlet, which can be used against purchases at the store in future. The intention is to attract customers back to the store but, as we shall see in the next chapter, loyalty cards are an excellent source of customer information, which can be used in direct marketing campaigns. Loyalty cards are very popular in the UK, with over 90 per cent of people holding at least one card and 78 per cent having two or more. Card schemes can be specific to one company such as the Tesco Clubcard, or a joint venture between several companies such as the Nectar card, which involves companies like Hertz, Sainsbury's, BP, Beefeater and Ford, and boasts over 11 million customers. Similarly, online retailers use schemes like MyPoints, which reward shoppers for reading emails, visiting sites, completing surveys and making purchases.

The role of loyalty cards in retaining customers has been the focus of much attention as it is known that keeping customers has a direct impact on profitability. A study conducted by PricewaterhouseCoopers showed that a 2 per cent increase in customer retention has the same profit impact as a 10 per cent reduction in overhead costs.[25] Customer retention programmes are aimed at maximizing a customer's lifetime value to the company. For example, airlines can identify their best customers (often business travellers) by analysis of their database and reward them for their loyalty. By collecting and analysing data the airlines identify and profile their frequent flyers, learn how best to develop a relationship with them, and attempt to acquire new customers with similar profiles.

Despite their growth, loyalty schemes have attracted their critics. Such schemes may simply raise the cost of doing business and, if competitors respond with me-too offerings, the final outcome may be no more than a minor tactical advantage.[26] Shell, for example, reportedly spent £20 million on hardware and software alone to launch its Smart Card, which allows drivers to collect points when purchasing petrol.[27] A second criticism is that the proliferation of loyalty schemes is teaching consumers promiscuity. Evidence from a MORI (www.mori.co.uk) poll found that 25 per cent of loyalty card holders are ready to switch to a rival scheme if it has better benefits.[28] Far from seeing a loyalty scheme as a reason to stay with a retailer, consumers may be using such schemes as criteria for switching.

Trade promotion techniques

The trade may be offered (or may demand) discounts in return for purchase, which may be part of a joint promotion whereby the retailer agrees to devote extra shelf space, buy larger quantities, engage in a joint competition and/or allow in-store demonstrations. An alternative to a price discount is to offer more merchandise at the same price (free goods); for example, the 'baker's dozen' technique involves offering 13 items (or cases) for the price of 12. Manufacturers may use competitions, such as providing prizes for a distributor's salesforce, in return for achieving sales targets for their products. Finally, a manufacturer may offer an allowance (a sum of money) in return for retailers providing promotional facilities in store (display allowance). For example, allowances would be needed to persuade a supermarket to display cards on its shelves indicating that a brand was being sold at a special low price.

The pharmaceutical industry is one of the biggest users of trade promotion. For example, in 2004, pharmaceutical companies in the USA spent US$14.7 billion on marketing to healthcare professionals as against US$3.6 billion on direct-to-consumer advertising activities. Trade promotions involve gifts, samples and industry-sponsored training courses. It is a highly competitive business with roughly 102,000 pharmaceutical 'detailers' or salespeople all trying to meet with the top prescribers among America's 870,000 physicians.[29]

The final stage in a sales promotion campaign involves testing the promotion. As with advertising, both pre-testing and post-testing approaches are available. The major pre-testing techniques include **group discussions** (testing ideas on groups of potential targets), **hall tests** (bringing a sample of customers to a room where alternative promotions are tested) and **experimentation** (where, for example, two groups of stores are selected and alternative promotions run in each). After the sales promotion has been implemented the effects must be monitored carefully. Care should be taken to check sales both during and after the promotion so that post-promotional sales dips can be taken into account (a lagged effect). In certain situations a sales fall can precede a promotion (a lead effect). If consumers believe a promotion to be imminent they may hold back purchases until it takes place. Alternatively, if a retail sales promotion of consumer durables (e.g. gas fires, refrigerators, televisions) is accompanied by higher commission rates for salespeople, they may delay sales until the promotional period.[30] If a lead effect is possible, sales prior to the promotion should also be monitored.

Public relations and publicity

If it wishes to succeed, a company must be dependent on many groups. The marketing concept focuses on customers and distributors, but the needs and interests of other groups (such as employees, shareholders, the local community, the media, government and pressure groups) are also important (see Figure 9.5). **Public relations** is concerned with all of these groups, and public relations activities include **publicity**, corporate advertising, seminars, publications, lobbying and charitable donations. PR can accomplish many objectives:[31] it can foster prestige and

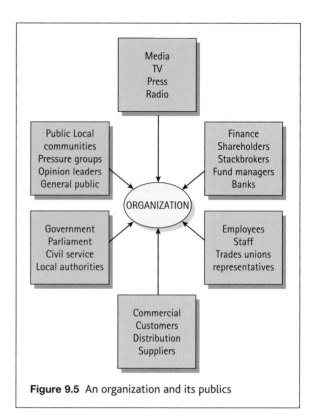

Figure 9.5 An organization and its publics

reputation, which can help companies to sell products, attract and keep good employees, and promote favourable community and government relations; it can promote products by creating the desire to buy a product through unobtrusive material that people read or see in the press, or on radio and television; awareness and interest in products and companies can be generated; it can be used to deal with issues or opportunities, or to overcome misconceptions about a company that may have been generated by bad publicity; and it can have a key role to play in fostering goodwill among customers, employees, suppliers, distributors and the government. For example, Vodafone used a carefully orchestrated public relations strategy in its legal battle with Eddie Jordan over the sponsorship of Jordan's Formula 1 team. Vodafone, which easily won the case, was concerned that it would be seen as a Goliath beating up Jordan's David. It hired a communications expert and at the end of each day of the trial, the media were given a summary of the trial plus a clear analysis of Vodafone's legal position.

Three major reasons for the growth in public relations are a recognition by marketing teams of the power and value of public relations, increased advertising costs leading to an exploration of more cost-effective communication routes, and improved understanding of the role of public relations (see Marketing in Action 9.3).

Marketing in Action 9.3: Dyson: good and bad publicity

> **Study guide:** Below is a review of some of the media coverage given to Dyson Appliances Ltd. Read and consider the advantages and disadvantages of using publicity as a promotional tool.

Dyson Appliances Ltd has had something of a rollercoaster ride in the British press. The company was founded by James Dyson in 1993 and at first it was revered as a template for British manufacturing. Dyson had revolutionized the vacuum cleaning business with his invention of the bagless cyclone vacuum cleaner—a 'high suction' machine that dispensed of the need for bags (see Exhibit 9.4). The success of the innovation catapulted Dyson to market share leadership in the £530 million industry, which is served by large multinational players like Electrolux. James Dyson's personal profile also soared. He was acclaimed as a living example of the great British inventor

Exhibit 9.4 The innovations of Dyson Appliances Ltd have received extensive coverage in the media

and he became one of a select group of business people picked by Tony Blair to be part of his innovation review group.

But, in 2002, Dyson announced that it was moving its production of vacuum cleaners from the small town of Malmesbury in Wiltshire to Malaysia with the loss of 800 jobs. While Dyson is far from alone in shifting manufacturing to lower-cost locations, what seemed to really cause problems was how the move was handled. Dyson justified the move as a way of keeping the company in good financial shape, but this sounded hollow to staff who knew they were working in a very profitable company. Others speculated that the reasons for the move related to specific local issues such as opposition to a planned expansion at the plant. So from being the great inventor, Dyson had, in the eyes of some, become the pursuer of cheap labour. This was exacerbated in 2003 when it was announced that all Dyson production in the UK, including that of its best-selling washing machines, was to move to Malaysia. Commenting on the move, a union official remarked that 'Dyson is no longer a UK product'.

This negative publicity was also damaging Dyson's position in the market. Its market share in vacuum cleaners in 2003 was 15 per cent in volume terms down from 20 per cent in 2002. Furthermore, low-cost rivals such as Samsung and LG from South Korea, who sell products at less than 50 per cent of the price of the Dyson brand, began to make inroads in the market. And perhaps of most concern to the company was the finding of some research, which indicated that only 35 per cent of owners of a Dyson vacuum cleaner would buy another.

Based on: Collins (2003);[32] Marsh (2003);[33] Moorish (2002)[34]

Table 9.3 Potentially newsworthy topics

Being or doing something first	Financial issues
Marketing issues	Financial statements
New products	Acquisitions
Research breakthroughs: future new products	Sales/profit achievements
Large orders/contracts	**Personal issues**
Sponsorships	Training awards
Price changes	Winners of company contests
Service changes	Promotions/new appointments
New logos	Success stories
Export success	Visits by famous people
Production issues	Reports of interviews
Productivity achievements	**General issues**
Employment changes	Conferences/seminars/exhibitions
Capital investments	Anniversaries of significant events

Publicity is a major element of public relations. It can be defined as the communication about a product or organization by the placing of news about it in the media without paying for the time or space directly. The three key tasks of a publicity department are responding to requests for information from the media, supplying the media with information on important events in the organization and stimulating the media to carry the information and viewpoint of the organization.[35] Information dissemination may be through news releases, news conferences, interviews, feature articles, photocalls and public speaking (at conferences and seminars, for example). No matter which of these means is used to carry the information, publicity has three important characteristics.

1   *The message has high credibility:* the message has greater credibility than advertising because it appears to the reader to have been written independently (by a media person) rather than by an advertiser. Because of this enhanced credibility it can be argued that it is more persuasive than a similar message used in an advertisement.

2   *No direct media costs:* since space or time in the media does not have to be bought there is no direct media cost. However, this is not to say that it is cost free. Someone has to write the news release, take part in the interview or organize the news conference. This may be organized internally by a press officer or publicity department, or externally by a public relations agency.

3   *No control over publication:* unlike advertising, there is no guarantee that the news item will be published. This decision is taken out of the control of the organization and into the hands of an editor. A key factor in this decision is whether the item is judged to be newsworthy. Newsworthy items include where a company does something first, such as a new product

or research breakthrough, new employees or company expansions, sponsorships, etc. A list of potentially newsworthy topics is provided in Table 9.3. Equally there is no guarantee that the content of the news release will be published in the way that the news supplier had intended or that the publicity will occur when the company wants it to.

Sponsorship

Sponsorship has been defined by Sleight as:[36]

'a business relationship between a provider of funds, resources or services and an individual, event or organisation which offers in return some rights and association that may be used for commercial advantage'.

Potential sponsors have a wide range of entities and activities from which to choose, including sports, arts, community activities, teams, tournaments, individual personalities or events, competitions, fairs and shows. Sport sponsorship is by far the most popular sponsorship medium as it offers high visibility through extensive television coverage, the ability to attract a broad cross-section of the community and to service specific niches, and the capacity to break down cultural barriers (see Exhibit 9.5). For example, the Olympics, the biggest global sporting event, attracted over US$1.4 billion in sponsorship for the 2004 Athens Games, which represented one-third of the revenue generated by the Games. Such is the scramble for sponsorship opportunities that even a soccer team's pre-season tour can be sponsored; this was the case with a tour of China by Spanish club Real Madrid, which was sponsored by local cigarette company Hong Ta Shan.

Exhibit 9.5 Sports sponsorship is still one of the most popular forms of sponsorship; brands achieve recognition and positive associations through their involvement with leading sports people and events

Vodafone is very active in sports sponsorship, with a portfolio that includes the England cricket team, the Australian rugby team, the McLaren Formula 1 team and the UEFA Champions League. These links help to build the image of Vodafone as being a global force.

Sponsorship can be very expensive. For example, each official sponsor of the 2006 World Cup soccer tournament in Germany paid up to £45 million each for the privilege. Therefore organizations need to have a carefully thought-out and well-planned sponsorship strategy. The five principal objectives of sponsorship are to gain publicity, create entertainment opportunities, foster favourable brand and company associations, improve community relations, and create promotional opportunities.

Gaining publicity

Sponsorship provides ample opportunity to create publicity in the news media. Worldwide events such as major golf, football and tennis tournaments supply the platform for global media coverage. Such **event sponsorship** can provide exposure to millions of people. For example, DHL, the German-owned package delivery company, signed a deal to sponsor major league baseball in the USA. This was part of a strategy by DHL to raise its awareness level in the US market where it has a small share and which is also home to its two major global rivals, UPS and FedEx.[37] Similarly, Red Bull's entry into Formula 1 motor racing through its sponsorship of the Jaguar team is seen as part of a strategy of broadening its market appeal. The publicity opportunities of sponsorship can provide major awareness shifts. For example, Canon's sponsorship of football in the UK raised awareness of the brand name from 40 per cent to 85 per cent among males. Similarly Texaco's prompted recall improved from 18 per cent to 60 per cent because of its motor racing sponsorship.[38]

Creating entertainment opportunities

A major objective of much sponsorship is to create entertainment opportunities for customers and the trade. Sponsorship of music, the arts and sports events can be particularly effective. For example, Barclays Capital sponsored a fashion show at London's Natural History Museum for 450 of its clients that were attending a global borrowers and investors forum. Often, key personalities are invited to join the sponsor's guests to add further attractiveness to the event. Similarly, sponsors of the Global Challenge yacht race, such as Norwich Union, BP and BT, used the event to entertain their best clients on board sponsored boats in desirable locations like Boston and Cape Town.[39]

Fostering favourable brand and company associations

A third objective of sponsorship is to create favourable associations for the brand and company. For example, sponsorship of athletics by SmithKline Beecham for its Lucozade Sport brand reinforces its market position and its energy associations. Similarly, Procter & Gamble spent the entire marketing budget for its shampoo Wash & Go, totalling €8.4 million, on sponsoring football's English Premier League. The intention was to position it as a sports brand with the tag-line 'A simply great supporter of football'.[40] Both the sponsor and the sponsored activity become involved in a relationship with a transfer of values from activity to sponsor. The audience, finding the sponsor's name, logo and other symbols threaded through the event, learns to associate sponsor and activity with one another. Figure 9.6 shows some broad values conferred on the sponsor from five sponsorship categories.

Improving community relations

Sponsorship of schools—for example, by providing low-cost personal computers as Tesco has done—and supporting community programmes can foster a socially responsible, caring reputation for a company. Many multinational companies get involved in community initiatives in local markets. For example, Nortel Networks, the Canadian telecommunications company, has had a very successful association with the Galway Arts Festival, one of the leading festivals in the Republic of Ireland. Similarly, UBS has sponsorships with the Tate art gallery, the London Symphony Orchestra and some inner-city schools like the Bridge Academy in London.

Creating promotional opportunities

Sponsorship events provide an ideal opportunity to promote company brands. Sweatshirts, bags, pens, and so on, carrying the company logo and name of the event can be sold to a captive audience. One of the attractions of O_2's sponsorship of the former Millennium Dome (now known as the O_2) was to showcase the latest in mobile phone technology and WiFi services as part of improving the overall visitor experience at the Dome.[41] For example, O_2 customers can avoid having to get a paper ticket and instead receive a barcode on their phones that allows them access to an event. By doing so, O_2 is hoping

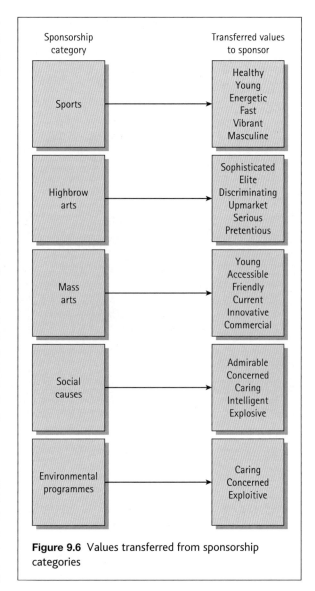

Figure 9.6 Values transferred from sponsorship categories

to both win new customers and persuade existing customers to buy new services.

New developments in sponsorship

Sponsorship has experienced a major growth in the past 15 years. Some of the factors driving the rise in sponsorship expenditure include, the escalating costs of media advertising, restrictive government policies on tobacco and alcohol advertising, the fragmentation of traditional mass media, the proven record of sponsorship and greater media coverage of sponsored events.[42] Accompanying the growth of event sponsorship has been the phenomenon of **ambush marketing**. Originally, the term referred to the activities of companies that tried to associate themselves with an event without paying any fee to the event owner. Nike has been a particularly successful ambush marketer at various Olympic Games and indeed emerged as the name Asian viewers most closely associated with the Athens Games even though it was not one of the event's official sponsors.[43] The activity is legal so long as no attempt is made to use an event symbol, logo or mascot. More recently, ambush marketing activities have become more subtle with, for example, companies sponsoring the television coverage of an event rather than the event itself. Regulations are catching up with the ambush marketers, such as provisions in the London Olympics Bill that would outlaw the words 'gold', 'summer' and '2012' in advertisements by non-sponsors of the 2012 Olympics.

The selection of an event or individual to sponsor requires that consideration is given to a number of key questions. These include the firm's communication objectives, its target market, the promotional opportunities presented, the costs involved and the risks associated with the sponsorship. The latter point is examined in Marketing in Action 9.4. As with all

Marketing in Action 9.4: The perils of sponsorship

> **Study guide:** Below is a review of some examples of where sponsorships have resulted in negative publicity for the companies involved. Read it and consider what advice you would give to a prospective sponsor.

Sponsorship is a powerful promotional tool but one that is also not without its risks. This is particularly true when the sponsorship is linked to a celebrity or sports star. One of the most celebrated examples in recent years is that of Kate Moss, one of Britain's top fashion models. She had successful endorsement arrangements with a variety of leading clothing and cosmetics brands but attracted huge negative publicity when video images emerged of her appearing to snort cocaine. She was quickly dropped by a number of brands including H&M, Chanel and Burberry, who feared that their images might be tarnished by association with her. Ironically, before her cocaine scandal, she was earning a reputed £4.5 million per year. But since the scandal, she has been signing a whole new set of endorsement contracts, ranging from one with Nikon cameras worth £1.5 million, to another with Calvin Klein worth £500,000, to others including Bulgari, Longchamp and Virgin Mobile. Overall, her earnings in 2006 were reputed to have soared to £11 million, suggesting that the controversy had done no damage to her brand reputation.

To avoid the risks attached to sponsoring individuals, many organizations choose instead to develop associations with teams or events. However, this can prove to be just as problematic, as demonstrated by the negative publicity generated by the Tour de France in recent years. The Tour de France is one of the world's most difficult and most famous professional cycling races, and an iconic sports event in its host country. But for some time now the event has been dogged by allegations of drug taking by cyclists and even orchestrated blood doping by whole teams. Each of the major teams in the event has a commercial sponsor. For example, Deutsche Telecom's sponsorship of Team Telekom and later Team T-mobile in the event sparked a cycling craze in Germany after Jan Ullrich, the team leader, rode to victory in 1997. But the relationship turned sour after former cyclists and team doctors confessed to using performance-enhancing drugs when Ullrich failed a drugs test in 2006.

Even sponsoring a TV programme has its risks. One of the most successful TV shows in recent years has been Channel 4's reality show, *Big Brother*. But it became mired in a racist controversy in 2007 during arguments between Shilpa Shetty, an Indian actress, and some of the other contestants, particularly Jade Goody. The media regulator Ofcom received a record 33,000 emails and telephone calls in protest over the alleged racist treatment of Shetty. The programme's sponsor, Carphone Warehouse, suspended its sponsorship of the show, which was worth £3 million, despite market research showing that most people did not blame the sponsor for the controversy. The irony for Carphone Warehouse is that controversies like this significantly increase the viewership of such programmes, though it was unwilling to risk damage to its brand.

Based on: Anonymous (2007);[45] Grande (2007);[46] Vernon (2006)[47]

communications initiatives, the sponsorship should be carefully evaluated against the initial objectives to assess whether it was successful or not. For example, Volvo's £2 million sponsorship of tennis resulted in 1.4 billion impressions (number of mentions or sightings, audience size), which it calculated was worth £12 million in media advertising.[44] Similarly, BT estimated that media coverage of its sponsorship of the Global Challenge yacht race covered costs by a multiple of three and the official website attracted more than 30 million hits per race.

Other promotional tools

Because of the fragmentation of traditional audiences such as press and television, a variety of other promotional techniques are becoming more commonplace. Two popular mass communications tools include exhibitions and product placement, which are examined below. In addition, other companies use their brands to create entertainment opportunities. For example, Guinness opened the Guinness Storehouse in Dublin in 2000. By 2002, it had seen its one millionth visitor and it has become the number one fee-paying tourist attraction in Ireland.[48]

Exhibitions

Exhibitions are unique in that, of all the promotional tools available, they are the only one that brings buyers, sellers and competitors together in a commercial setting. In Europe, the Cologne trade exhibitions bring together 28,000 exhibitors from 100 countries with 1.8 million buyers from 150 countries.[49] Exhibitions are a particularly important part of the industrial promotional mix and can be a key source of information on buyers' needs and preferences.

Exhibitions are growing in their number and variety. Aside from the major industry exhibitions such as motor shows and property shows, more specialized lifestyle exhibitions are emerging in niche markets. For example, the Cosmo show, featuring cosmetics and targeting young women, attracts over 55,000 visitors. The 1999 event was the launch pad for Olay Colour (formerly Oil of Ulay) to reveal its new identity and for the launch of Cussons' new moisturizer, Aqua Source.

Exhibitions can have a variety of objectives, including identifying prospects and determining their needs, building relationships, providing product demonstrations, making sales, gathering competitive intelli-

gence and fostering the image of the company. They require careful planning and management to ensure that they run smoothly. And a post-show evaluation needs to take place to determine its effectiveness. Fortunately, there are a variety of variables that can easily be quantified, which can be used to measure success. These include number of visitors to the stand, number of leads generated, number of orders received and their value, and so on. Following up the trade show through contact with prospects and customers is also important.

Product placement

Product placement is the deliberate placing of products and/or their logos in movies, television, songs and video games, usually in return for money (see Exhibit 9.6). While it has been big business in some countries, like the United States, for some time, restrictions preventing product placement have only recently been relaxed in Europe. For example, Steven Spielberg's sci-fi film *Minority Report* featured more than 15 major brands, including Gap, Nokia, Pepsi, Guinness, Lexus and Amex, with their logos appearing on video billboards throughout the film. These product placements earned Dreamworks and 20th Century Fox US$25 million, which went some way towards reducing the US$102 million production costs of the film.[50] Similarly, when the hip-hop artist Busta Rhymes had a smash hit with 'Pass the Courvoisier', US sales of the cognac rose by 14 per cent in volume and 11 per cent in value. Allied Domecq, the brand's owner, claims it did not pay for the plug, but McDonald's is more upfront, offering hip-hop artists US$5 each time they mention Big Mac in a song.[51] The value of product placement deals in the USA grew from £174 million in 1974 to £3.5 billion in 2004, and is forecast to grow to US$7 billion by 2009.[52]

Product placement has grown significantly in recent years for the following reasons: media fragmentation means it is increasingly hard to reach mass markets; the brand can benefit from the positive associations it gains from being in a film or TV show; many consumers do not realize that the brand has been product-placed; repetition of the movie or TV show means that the brand is seen again and again; careful choice of movie or TV show means that certain segments can be targeted; and promotional and merchandising opportunities can be generated on the shows' websites. For example, the clothes and accessories worn by actresses in popular TV shows like *Sex and the City* and *Desperate Housewives* have been in great demand from viewers and some have quickly

Exhibit 9.6 The 2008 James Bond film *Quantum of Solace* features product placements from Sony, Aston Martin, Smirnoff, Virgin Atlantic and other leading brands. In this image Daniel Craig is wearing a limited edition watch from OMEGA, the Seamaster Plant Ocean 600m which was created for the film. Copyright OMEGA 2008

sold out. Show producers are increasingly looking at the merchandising opportunities that their shows can present. Technological developments in the online gaming sector allow for different products to be placed in games at different times of the day or in different geographic locations, expanding the marketing possibilities available to companies (see Marketing in Action 9.5). Product placement is significantly more restricted in Europe than it is in the USA, though the Audiovisual Media Services Directive adopted by the EU in 2007 permits greater levels of placement on EU television programmes but not news, current affairs, sport and children's programming.

Though product placement is becoming very popular, it is important to remember that there are risks involved. If the movie or TV show fails to take off it can tarnish the image of the brand and reduce its potential exposure. Audiences can become annoyed by blatant product placement, also damaging the image, and brand owners may not have complete control over how their brand is portrayed. Also the popularity of product placement is fast giving rise to claims that it constitutes deceptive advertising.

Lobby groups in the USA claim that one of the difficulties with product placement is that it can't be controlled by the consumer in the way the traditional advertising breaks can through zapping, and want it restricted.

Product placement is subject to the same kinds of analysis as all the other promotional techniques described in this chapter. For example, in the James Bond movie *Die Another Day*, the Ford Motor Company had three of its car brands 'starring' in the film: an Aston Martin Vanquish, a Thunderbird and a Jaguar XKR. Movie-goers were interviewed both before and after seeing the film to see if their opinions of the brands had changed. In addition, the product placement was part of an integrated campaign including public relations and advertising, which ensured that even people who had not seen the film were aware of Ford's association with it. During the film's peak viewing periods in the USA and UK, Ford's research found that the number of times its name appeared in the media increased by 34 per cent and that Ford corporate messages appeared in 29 per cent of the Bond-related coverage.[53]

Marketing in Action 9.5: Product placement and gaming

> **Study guide:** Below is a review of product placement in video games. Read it and try to think of examples of products that you have seen 'placed' in movies, songs or video games.

Video gaming is a growing industry, with a particular appeal to young males, therefore it is an attractive forum for product placement by firms wanting to target that segment of the market. It is estimated that over 70 per cent of 18–34-year-old males are gamers and that they spend 30 billion 'eyeball hours' on this activity, but to date only 0.07 per cent of advertising spend is allocated to video games. There are several advantages in placing a product in a game as opposed to a TV show or movie. First, the product can be used as part of the game play, such as a car or a snowboard, making its inclusion more realistic. Second, placing an ad in a video game ensures a highly engaged audience as the player will be giving the game his full attention. A further appeal is that the placement is potentially viewed every time the game is played, as opposed to the once-off appearances of a product in many TV shows and movies.

Early versions of in-game placements tended to be static billboard-type adverts such as a hoarding around a sports field, or simple placements such as a visit to McDonald's in *The Sims*. The new generation of games allow for more dynamic placement and the use of multimedia formats such as music, animation and video. This is particularly true of games that are played online. For example, a character can pick up a can of Coke in a game that is played at 2 pm, but if the game is being played later in the day, the same character can be seen picking up a brand of beer. The real advantage of dynamic placement is that the ad can simply be moved from game to game depending on popularity. Placements can also be geographically customized to where gamers live, allowing for even greater levels of segmentation.

In-game expenditure is growing rapidly. In the USA, expenditure in 2006 was US$55 million, which is forecast to soar to US$805 million by 2012. The proportion being spent on static adverts is rapidly giving way to dynamic adverts, and advertisers pay according to how much the ad is seen—the standard 'cost per thousand' metric used by other media. Leading brands that have featured in video games include, McDonald's, Intel, Red Bull and Coca-Cola, and several automotive brands like Castrol, Bridgestone and Elf. Like many forms of promotion, the major challenge is in assessing its level of effectiveness. For example, if a product is placed in a game, to what extent can changes in sales or awareness of the product be attributed to this. However, recent research has shown that game placement can be very effective. A study conducted in the USA, using survey, panel and eye-tracking technology, found that a half-second exposure to a placement is sufficient for a player to notice it, and that 75 per cent of gamers engaged with at least one placement per minute.

Based on: Anonymous (2007);[54] Enright (2007);[55] Nuttall (2005);[56] Williams (2005)[57]

Summary

This chapter has provided an overview of the promotional mix and examined some important mass communications techniques. The following key issues were addressed.

1. The promotional mix is broad, comprising seven elements, namely advertising, sales promotion, publicity, sponsorship, direct marketing, internet and online marketing, and personal selling. Decisions regarding which combination to use will be driven by the nature of the product, resource availability, the nature of the market and the kind of strategies being pursued by the company.

2. Because of the breadth of promotional techniques available, it is important to adopt an integrated approach to marketing communications. This means that companies carefully blend the promotional mix elements to deliver a clear, consistent, credible and competitive message in the marketplace.

3. It is important to take a systematic approach to communications planning. The various steps involved include consideration of the company's marketing and positioning strategy, identifying the target audience, setting communications objectives, creating the message, selecting the promotional mix, setting the promotional budget, executing the strategy and evaluating the strategy.

4. Advertising is a highly visible component of marketing, but it is only one element of the promotional mix. Advertising strategy involves an analysis of the target audience, setting objectives, budgeting decisions, message and media decisions, and evaluating advertising effectiveness. Significant ethical issues surround the use of advertising, which is also undergoing many changes due to developments in technology.

5. Sales promotions are a powerful technique for giving a short-term boost to sales or for encouraging trial. Some of the most popular consumer promotion techniques include premiums, coupons, loyalty cards and money-offs, while discounts and allowances are popular trade promotion techniques.

6. Publicity plays a very important role in the promotional mix. It is the mechanism through which organizations communicate with their various publics. It has more credibility than advertising and incurs no direct media costs, but firms cannot control the content or timing of publication.

7. Sponsorship is a popular form of promotion. The most common types of sponsorship include sports, the arts, community activities and celebrities. Its principal objectives are to generate publicity for the sponsor, create entertainment opportunities and foster favourable brand and company associations.

8. Product placement is a rapidly growing form of promotion, which is also controversial because of its subtle nature. Product placement is the deliberate placing of products in movies, television programmes, songs and video games, often in exchange for money.

Key terms

advertising any paid form of non-personal communication of ideas or products in the prime media (i.e. television, the press, posters, cinema and radio, the internet and direct marketing)

advertising agency an organization that specializes in providing services such as media selection, creative work, production and campaign planning to clients

advertising message the use of words, symbols and illustrations to communicate to a target audience using prime media

advertising platform the aspect of the seller's product that is most persuasive and relevant to the target consumer

ambush marketing any activity where a company tries to associate itself or its products with an event without paying any fee to the event owner

bonus pack pack giving the customer extra quantity at no additional cost

consumer pull the targeting of consumers with communications (e.g. promotions) designed to create demand that will *pull* the product into the distribution chain

direct marketing (1) acquiring and retaining customers without the use of an intermediary; (2) the distribution of products, information and promotional benefits to target consumers through interactive communication in a way that allows response to be measured

distribution push the targeting of channel intermediaries with communications (e.g.

promotions) to *push* the product into the distribution chain

event sponsorship sponsorship of a sporting or other event

exhibition an event that brings buyers and sellers together in a commercial setting

experimentation the application of stimuli (e.g. two price levels) to different matched groups under controlled conditions for the purpose of measuring their effect on a variable (e.g. sales)

group discussion a group, usually of six to eight consumers, brought together for a discussion focusing on an aspect of a company's marketing strategy

hall tests bringing a sample of target consumers to a room that has been hired so that alternative marketing ideas (e.g. promotions) can be tested

integrated marketing communications the concept that companies co-ordinate their marketing communications tools to deliver a clear, consistent, credible and competitive message about the organization and its products

media class decision the choice of prime media (i.e. the press, cinema, television, posters, radio) or some combination of these

media vehicle decision the choice of the particular newspaper, magazine, television spot, poster site, etc.

money-off promotions sales promotions that discount the normal price

personal selling oral communication with prospective purchasers with the intention of making a sale

premiums any merchandise offered free or at low cost as an incentive to purchase

product placement the deliberate placing of products and/or their logos in movies and television programmes, usually in return for money

public relations the management of communications and relationships to establish goodwill and mutual understanding between an organization and its public

publicity the communication of a product or business by placing information about it in the media without paying for time or space directly

sales promotion incentives to customers or the trade that are designed to stimulate purchase

sponsorship a business relationship between a provider of funds, resources or services and an individual, event or organization that offers in return some rights and association that may be used for commercial advantage

target audience the group of people at which an advertisement or message is aimed

Study questions

1. What is meant by integrated marketing communications? Explain the advantages of taking an integrated approach to marketing communications.
2. Select three recent advertising campaigns with which you are familiar. Discuss the target audience, objectives and message executions adopted in each case.
3. It is frequently argued that much promotional expenditure is wasteful. Discuss the ways in which the effectiveness of the various promotional techniques described in this chapter can be measured.
4. Discuss the role of sponsorship in the promotional mix.
5. There is no such thing as bad publicity. Discuss.
6. Discuss the reasons why product placement has become such a popular promotional technique for some product categories. What are the ethical issues surrounding the growth of product placement?
7. Visit www.youtube.com. Examine some adverts for a brand or organization of your choice. Discuss the message that the adverts are attempting to convey, as well as the creative treatment used.

Suggested reading

Fahy, J., F. Farrelly and **P. Quester** (2004) Competitive Advantage Through Sponsorship: A Conceptual Model and Research Propositions, *European Journal of Marketing*, **38** (8), 1013–31.

Fitzgerald, M. and **D. Arnott** (2000) *Marketing Communications Classics*, London: International Thomson Publishing.

Kohli, C., L. Leuthesser and **R. Suri** (2007) Get Slogan? Guidelines for Creating Effective Slogans, *Business Horizons*, **50** (5), 415–22.

Nunes, P.F. and J. Merrihue (2007) The Continuing Power of Mass Advertising, *Sloan Management Review*, **48** (2), 63–9.

Raghubir, P., J. Inman and H. Grande (2004) The Three Faces of Consumer Promotions, *California Management Review*, **46** (4), 23–43.

Robinson, D. (2006) Public Relations comes of Age, *Business Horizons*, **49** (3), 247–56.

References

1. Pfanner, E. (2006) Fashioning a Makeover, *International Herald Tribune*, 12 November, www.iht.com; Rigby, E. (2005) Jazzy Lights and Music Fail to Hide M&S's Need to Increase Sales, *Financial Times*, 9 November, 23; Sweney, M. (2006) A Successful Ad Campaign has Revived the Fortunes of Marks & Spencer, *Guardian*, 6 November, www.guardian.co.uk.

2. Benady, A. (2003) Hundreds of Brands, Billions to Spend, *Financial Times*, Creative Business, 25 February, 2–3.

3. Piercy, N. (1987) The Marketing Budgeting Process: Marketing Management Implications, *Journal of Marketing*, **51** (4), 45–59.

4. Saatchi & Saatchi Compton (1985) *Preparing the Advertising Brief*, 9.

5. Silverman, G. (2006) Is 'it' the Future of Advertising?, *Financial Times*, 24 January, 11.

6. Anonymous (2004) Sex Doesn't Sell, *Economist*, 30 October, 46–7.

7. Rigby, E. (2005) Tesco's Victory Over Asda Advert Ends Year-Long Row, *Financial Times*, 18 August, 5.

8. Lannon, J. (1991) Developing Brand Strategies across Borders, *Marketing and Research Today*, August, 160–7.

9. Cane, A. (2005) Vodafone Rings the Changes, *Financial Times*, 11 October, 15.

10. Carter, M. (2005) Orange Rekindles Emotional Ties, *Financial Times*, 20 September, 13.

11. Ritson, M. (2003) It's the Ad Break . . . and the Viewers are Talking, Reading and Snogging, *Financial Times Creative Business*, 4 February, 8–9; Silverman, G. (2005) Advertisers are Starting to Find Television a Turn-off, *Financial Times*, 26 July, 20.

12. Terazono, E. (2005) TV Fights for its 30 Seconds of Fame, *Financial Times*, 20 September, 13.

13. Grimshaw, C. (2003) Standing Out in the Crowd, *Financial Times*, Creative Business, 6 May, 7.

14. Bell, E. (1992) Lies, Damned Lies and Research, *Observer*, 28 June, 46.

15. Anonymous (2005) Consumer Republic, *Economist*, 19 March, 63, 66.

16. Smith, P.R. (1993) *Marketing Communications: An Integrated Approach*, London: Kogan Page, 116.

17. See Tomkins, R. (1999) Getting a Bigger Bang for the Advertising Buck, *Financial Times*, 24 September, 17; and Waters, R. (1999) P&G Ties Advertising Agency Fees to Sales, *Marketing Week*, 16 September, 1.

18. Wiggins, J. (2007) Fat Children Double Eating After Adverts, *Financial Times*, 25 April, 5.

19. Oliver, E. (2004) Advertisers Uneasy Over Regulator Code for Children, *Irish Times*, 27 March, 16.

20. Rothschild, M.L. and W.C. Gaidis (1981) Behavioural Learning Theory: Its Relevance to Marketing and Promotions, *Journal of Marketing*, **45** (Spring), 70–8.

21. Tuck, R.T.J. and W.G.B. Harvey (1972) Do Promotions Undermine the Brand?, *Admap*, January, 30–3.

22. Brown, R.G. (1974) Sales Response to Promotions and Advertising, *Journal of Advertising Research*, **14** (4), 33–9.

23. Ehrenberg, A.S.C., K. Hammond and G.J. Goodhardt (1994) The After-effects of Price-related Consumer Promotions, *Journal of Advertising Research*, **34** (4), 1–10.

24. Davidson, J.H. (1998) *Offensive Marketing*, Harmondsworth: Penguin, 249–71.

25. Murphy, J. (1997) The Art of Satisfaction, *Financial Times*, 23 April, 14.

26. Dowling, G.R. and M. Uncles (1997) Do Loyalty Programs Really Work?, *Sloan Management Review*, **38** (4), 71–82.

27. Burnside, A. (1995) A Never Ending Search for the New, *Marketing*, 25 May, 31–5.

28. Murphy, C. (1999) Addressing the Data Issue, *Marketing*, 28 January, 31.

29. Anonymous (2005) An Overdose of Bad News, *Economist*, 19 March, 69–71.

30. Doyle, P. and J. Saunders (1985) The Lead Effect of Marketing Decisions, *Journal of Marketing Research*, **22** (1), 54–65.

31. Lesly, P. (1991) *The Handbook of Public Relations and Communications*, Maidenhead: McGraw-Hill, 13–19.

32. Collins, N. (2003) Dyson's Not Making Suckers of Anyone, *Daily Telegraph*, 25 August, 18.

33. Marsh, P. (2003) Dust is Settling on the Dyson Market Clean-up, *Financial Times*, 12 December, 12.

34. Moorish, J. (2002) In Malmesbury, There are Few Tears for Mr Dyson and his Miracle Cleaner, *Independent on Sunday*, 10 February, 14.

35. Lesly, P. (1991) *The Handbook of Public Relations and Communications*, Maidenhead: McGraw-Hill, 13–19.

36. Sleight, S. (1989) *Sponsorship: What it is and How to Use it*, Maidenhead, McGraw-Hill, 4.

37. **Ward, A.** (2005) DHL Goes For Home Run in Rival's Back Yard, *Financial Times*, 6 April, 31.

38. **Mintel** (1991) *Sponsorship: Special Report*, London: Mintel International Group Ltd.

39. **Friedman, V.** (2003) Banks Step on to the Catwalk, *Financial Times*, 3 July, 12.

40. **McKelvey, C.** (1999) Washout, *Marketing Week*, 2 December, 27–9.

41. **Carter, M.** (2007) Sponsorship Branding Takes on New Name, *Financial Times*, 13 March, 12.

42. **Miles, L.** (1995) Sporting Chancers, *Marketing Director International*, **6** (2), 50–2.

43. **Bowman, J.** (2004) Swoosh Rules Over Official Olympic Brands, *Media Asia*, 10 September, 22.

44. **Smith, P.R.** (1993) *Marketing Communications: An Integrated Approach*, London: Kogan Page, 116.

45. **Anonymous** (2007) The Cartel of Silence, *Economist*, 9 June, 71.

46. **Grande, C.** (2007) Big Brother Sponsor Injects New Reality, *Financial Times*, 19 January, 3.

47. **Vernon, P.** (2006) The Fall and Rise of Kate Moss, *Guardian.co.uk*, 14 May.

48. **Parmar, A.** (2003) Guinness Intoxicates, *MarketingNews*, 10 November, 4, 6.

49. **O'Hara, B., F. Palumbo** and **P. Herbig** (1993) Industrial Trade Shows Abroad, *Industrial Marketing Management*, **22**, 233–7.

50. **Anonymous** (2002) The Top Ten Product Placements in Features, *Campaign*, 17 December, 36.

51. **Tomkins, R.** (2003) The Hidden Message: Life's a Pitch, and Then You Die, *Financial Times*, 24 October, 14; **Armstrong, S.** (2005) How To Put Some Bling into Your Brand, *Irish Times, Weekend*, 30 July, 7.

52. **Silverman, G.** (2005) After the Break: The 'Wild West' Quest to Bring the Consumers to the Advertising, *Financial Times*, 18 May, 17.

53. **Dowdy, C.** (2003) Thunderbirds Are Go, *Financial Times*, Creative Business, 24 June, 10.

54. **Anonymous** (2007) Got Game, *Economist*, 9 June, 69–71.

55. **Enright, A.** (2007) Inside In-Game Advertising, *Marketing News*, 15 September, 26–30.

56. **Nuttall, C.** (2005) There's a New Game in Town for Television Advertisers, *Financial Times*, 17 May, 14.

57. **Williams, H.** (2005) Medium is New Home for Message, *Financial Times*, Creative Business, 6 September, 7.

Case 9 Adidas vs Nike: who will score next?

Adidas, a German brand, was created in 1949 by Adi Dassler. The company was originally built according to three principles, which still permeate the company:

1 creating the best sports shoe
2 protecting athletes from injuries, and
3 offering them a durable product.

The group defines itself as being customer focused, trying to constantly improve the quality, the look, the feel and image of its products. Unfortunately, at the end of the 1980s and the beginning of the 1990s, the world market leader in sports shoes experienced its first serious financial and commercial problems. Adidas was overtaken by a fierce competitor that emerged during the 1970s, namely Nike. To regain its place at the head of the industry, Adidas has, among other things, purchased Reebok in mid-2005.

The rise of the leader

In 1964 Phil Knight and Bill Bowerman started the Blue Ribbon Sports Company, because they considered that sports shoes available in the market did not fit their needs in terms of quality. The name changed to Nike (the Greek goddess of Victory) seven years later when the now world-renowned logo was created and adopted. It sounds difficult to believe, but the Nike logo (the 'Swoosh') was, in fact, designed by a college student for no more than . . . US$35!

In 1985, the Air Jordan shoe opened a brand new era in sports shoes marketing and soon became one of the world's most popular sports shoes ever. According to Yves Marchand, a former Nike Europe executive, 'Before that, a product was not linked to a person, but to a sport. The Air Jordan established a triangulation between a star, a product and a consumer.'

Then, in 1987, Nike developed an innovative and memorable ad campaign using the Beatles song 'Revolution'. The rest is history, and the brand reached its current status as world leader in the sports shoes industry (see Table C9.1).

The marketing world of football is at war

Even though Nike has been the leader in its long-running battle with Adidas, there is a sport where the German company has always had an advantage: football.

Phil Knight was not very enamoured with this sport, and always evaluated it from a certain distance. However, conscious that football could not be ignored, especially in Europe, he finally decided to aim for leadership in this segment as well. To achieve this objective, Nike used one of the tools that explained its success in other sports: promotion. From 1994, promotional expenditure increased dramatically. Back then, the market was dominated by Adidas (with a market share of 45 per cent) and Puma (at 12 per cent), while the rest was scattered between relatively small brands such as Umbro, Lotto and Kappa, that could not afford to invest huge amounts of cash. Nike attacked these brands first, because this was easier than directly confronting Adidas.

The best example of this strategy is what happened during the 1994 World Cup. The Brazilian football team was sponsored by Umbro. However, Nike convinced about 10 of the team's players to wear its shoes, for US$200,000 each. At this time, this was a very high level of expenditure, but it turned out to be a great investment as Brazil went on to win the tournament. Nike could capitalize on the image of the team through the players it had sponsored, without being the official team sponsor. Thus, the brand's absence of legitimacy in football became history and, two years later, Nike became Brazil's official sponsor, with a US$200 million contract for 10 years. And,

Table C9.1 Adidas and Nike: some key figures

Company	Total turnover of company (2006–07)	Total net profit (2006–07)	Market share (sports shoes only) (2004)
Adidas/Reebok	€10 billion	€500 million	34%
Nike	€12.8 billion	€1.1 billion	38%

Source: Les Echos, 12 February 2007, 11; BW Online, 'Adidas' World Cup Shutout', 3 April 2006

during the 2006 World Cup in Germany, Nike sponsored eight teams (Australia, Brazil, South Korea, United States, Croatia, Mexico, Netherlands and Portugal), while Adidas had only six (Germany, France,[1] Spain, Japan, Trinidad and Tobago, and Argentina).

At about the same time, Nike began a spectacular advertising campaign, with French football legend Eric Cantona leading other star players in a football version of 'good vs evil'. This was at odds with the rules of this sector and product category, since football shoe brands did not use a lot of marketing communication. Nike shattered all the norms, hiring renowned scriptwriters such as Terry Gilliam and John Woo, who developed real scenarios around star players that Nike was sponsoring. Many commercials followed this one—for example, the one showing Brazilian players in an airport (World Cup 1998), and another with Ronaldo, Figo and Henry playing in a cargo hold (World Cup 2002). Every time, the individual was at the heart of the commercial, reflecting what Nike defines as its mission: 'To bring inspiration and innovation to every athlete★ in the world' (★'If you have a body, you are an athlete').

The sorts of special effects used in these commercials are very expensive, and those developed for the 2002 World Cup and Euro 2004 are rumoured to have cost from €10 million to €15 million each. But all this expenditure has paid off: the increase in Nike's and Adidas's turnovers since 1994 can partially be explained by these huge advertising budgets and by advertising efficiency (see Figure C9.1).

Confronted with this challenge on its home turf, Adidas had to fight back and did so using a multipronged approach. First, research and development was conducted to stimulate innovation and create very advanced new products such as 'One', an 'intelligent' model launched at the end of 2004, which

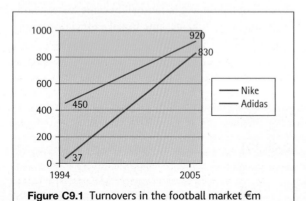

Figure C9.1 Turnovers in the football market €m

included a microchip and was priced at €250. Second, marketing expenditures were also increased dramatically. Adidas began to make commercials with some of its popular stars, such as that with Zidane, Beckham and Del Piero for Euro 2000. The company also became the one and only official equipment manufacturer (i.e. authorized by FIFA) for the 2006 World Cup.

'+10' vs 'Joga Bonito'

The 2006 German World Cup was the occasion for the two brands, Adidas and Nike, to launch new advertising campaigns. Among other promotional activities, Adidas pursued its 'Impossible is Nothing' campaign, which had begun two years earlier in athletics and was based on the history of the company. In these commercials, Adidas pitted some stars of yesteryear against their present-day counterparts. For example, old videos of footballers Beckenbauer or Platini were inserted into the commercials of the last '+10' campaign, which revolves around the idea that one player plus 10 others equals a team. This collective dimension is essential in Adidas's communication strategy, as are shared emotions, friendliness and simplicity, which Adidas considers as values that are naturally associated with football. Beyond the TV commercials (there were three of them), the '+10' campaign also relied on other forms of media. On the internet, the German brand organized a game, in partnership with Google Earth and, in France, Go Sport. The aim was for consumers to answer 10 questions about football and find stadiums all over the World using Google Earth. The winner received 11 tickets to attend World Cup matches with 10 friends.

As for Nike, the 2006 World Cup was the occasion to initiate in February 'Joga Bonito'—Portuguese for 'play beautifully'—a US$100 million multichannel campaign. It was based on TV ads, SMS, posters and magazines, and centred on a dedicated website (www.joga.com), a social networking site for soccer fans, launched in partnership with Google. Members from 140 countries could blog, create their own community around their favourite team or player, and download and upload videos, which could even be seen on an iPod or PSP, and so on. It also launched Joga TV, whose presenter was Eric Cantona. This website has represented a huge turnaround for Nike, since it is a completely different way to attract consumers compared with its traditional top-down mass-media messages. According to Trevor Edwards, Nike's vice-president for global brand management, 'Gone are the days of the one big ad, the one big shoe, and the hope that when we put it all together it makes a big impact.'

The results of this strategy are hard to measure, and even though Nike claims that its football equipment sales are booming, it also admits that the community has developed too recently for the actual market impact to be evaluated. At any rate, 'by enrolling consumers in shaping the marketing, Nike is figuring out what kind of micro-content audiences want and is nurturing deeper bonds of loyalty and advocacy,' says Pete Blackshaw, chief marketing officer at Nielsen Buzzmetrics. Furthermore, Nike has won the Golden Cyber Lion for its 'Joga Bonito' website, which is the highest-level internet advertising award given during the Cannes International Festival of Advertising.

Zidane's gone mad, Nike's created an ad

Nike went even further in communication innovation in its efforts to differentiate itself from Adidas. The campaign began after French star Zinedine Zidane head-butted Materazzi during the World Cup 2006 final and was subsequently sent off. Nike launched a commercial targeting the Italian market that was quickly available on the internet. One could see Materazzi avoiding different kinds of projectiles (e.g. bowling balls, an American football player, a jeep). Some weeks later, in October, Nike developed another campaign in the same vein, aimed at supporting the launch of new football shoes in Italy. Posters and TV ads (also found on the internet) showed Italian players promoting the quality and durability of local products, systematically emphasized by a French-language sentence, 'Produit en Italie' ('Made in Italy'). Materazzi even appeared as a stylized cupboard with the slogan: 'World durability, tested even with head butts'. The reactions in France to this campaign were less than positive.

From pure sportsmen to fashion victims

Originally, both Adidas and Nike were aimed purely at practitioners of sports. But this situation has progressively evolved, as more and more young people have adopted their products as everyday fashion clothing. If we take the football example, Nike's Total 90, launched at the end of 2001, is a shoe adapted for 'street soccer'. Initially considered as sports gear, it has become a fashion accessory for people who may never get closer to a football field than the spectator stands. More than 500,000 pairs have been sold in France, which represents about 20 per cent of the total market for the football segment there. Breaking down boundaries between sports and fashion has

Nike's T 90 football range in action

dramatically changed Nike's market of potential customers: the company has now become the European leader in the football shoe market, with a 34 per cent market share, as against 32 per cent for Adidas. This led the Adidas CEO to protest, 'Nike is selling a lot of the Total 90 street shoes and is including them in the soccer category. It is trying to turn the business model into a lifestyle-oriented one.' Nonetheless Nike's strategy is so profitable that competitors like Adidas and Puma are following suit.

Questions

1. Discuss the positioning strategies being employed by Adidas and Nike. Are they different?
2. How have these firms redefined the sports goods business?
3. Compare and contrast the promotional campaigns used by both firms to target the lucrative soccer market. Evaluate the promotional objectives, budget, creative treatment and media used in both cases.
4. Evaluate the strengths and weaknesses of both firms' promotional activity.

This case was prepared by Loïc Plé and Jacques Angot, IESEG School of Management, France, as a basis for classroom discussion rather than to show effective or ineffective management.

Bibliography

Adidas Group website: http://www.adidas-group.com/en/overview/strategy/default.asp, http://www.adidas-group.com/en/overview/history/default.asp, http://www.adidas-group.com/en/overview/values/default.asp.

Anonymous (2005) 'Nike-Adidas, le match est relancé', *Capital*, 170, November, 52–72.

Anonymous (2006) 'Adidas et Nike refont le match', *Challenges*, 37, 24 May, 72–4.

Anonymous, 'Nike l'italien joue avec les supporters français?', http://www.marketing-etudiant.fr/actualites/nike-materazzi-communication.php.

Anonymous, 'Nike-Adidas: le choc des grosses pointures', http://www.nouvo.ch/86-1.

Business Week Online (2004) 'The New Nike', 20 September, http://www.businessweek.com/magazine/toc/04_38/B3900magazine.htm.

Business Week Online (2006) 'Adidas' World Cup Shutout', 3 April, http://www.businessweek.com/magazine/content/06_14/b3978079.htm.

Business Week Online (2006) 'Nike: It's Not A Shoe, It's A Community', 24 July, http://www.businessweek.com/magazine/content/06_30/b3994068.htm.

Journal du Net, 'Cyber Lions 2006: la vidéo virale à l'honneur du palmarès', http://www.journaldunet.com/0606/060623-palmarescyberlion.shtml.

L'Expansion.com, 'Nike se paie la tête de la France . . . en Italie', http://www.lexpansion.com/art/17.0.147065.0.html.

La Tribune.fr (2005) 'Les équipementiers sportifs champions du marketing', 4 August, http://www.latribune.fr/Dossiers/sportbusiness.nsf/DocsWeb/IDC1256EE40033EA55C1257052006BCA85?OpenDocument.

Le Soir (2006) 'José, 10 ans, n'a pas hésité: il a renvoyé Kaka sur le banc!', 22 June, http://www.lesoir.be/sports/football_mondial_2006/focus/article_447359.shtml.

Les Echos (2006) 'Le pré-Mondial des équipementiers', 7 June, 13.

Les Echos (2006) 'Nike veut damer le pion à Adidas dans le football', 15 February, 17.

Les Echos (2007) 'L'intégration de Reebok reste délicate', 12 February, 30.

Nike website: www.nikebiz.com.

Stratégies (2006) 'Adidas adopte une stratégie offensive pour le Mondial', 6 April, 16, http://www.strategies.fr/archives/1408/page_33713/marques_en_vue_adidas_adopte_une_strategie_offensive_pour_le_mondial.html.

Stratégies.fr, 'Le coup de boule de Nike', http://www.strategies.fr/archives/1427/page_37331/buzz_le_coup_de_boule_de_nike.html.

Videos (streaming): http://www.youtube.com/watch?v=7_ydC-t2JM8, http://www.youtube.com/watch?v=cBr534DFZ0g, http://www.youtube.com/watch?v=Jkm86AfI48I, http://www.youtube.com/watch?v=z3hmYkJBUpU&NR, http://www.youtube.com/watch?v=YD8FTzUkf5A.

ZDNet.fr, 'États-Unis: les internautes appelés à la rescousse de la création publicitaire', http://www.zdnet.fr/actualites/internet/0,39020774,39351518,00.htm.

Note

[1] On 22 February 2008, Nike became the official sponsor of the French football team, with a €42 million per year contract, running from 2011 to 2018.

Chapter 10

Integrated Marketing Communications 2: Direct Communications Techniques

Chapter Outline

Database marketing

Customer relationship management

Direct marketing

Internet marketing

Buzz marketing

Personal selling

Sales management

Learning Outcomes

By the end of this chapter you will understand:

1 the importance of database management as the foundation for direct marketing activities
2 the reasons for the growth in customer relationship management (CRM)
3 the meaning of direct marketing and how to manage a direct marketing campaign
4 the marketing opportunities presented by the developments in internet technologies, and the role of the internet as a direct marketing medium
5 the emergence of buzz marketing as a popular and innovative promotional technique
6 the role of personal selling in the promotional mix, and the key issues involved in selling and sales management.

United reaches out to its fans

The relationship between football clubs and their supporters is a unique one. Unlike companies and brands that can quickly lose their customers if they fail to perform, a unique feature of many football supporters is their very high levels of loyalty to their team even though its performances on the field may be poor for years. Football clubs are now increasingly recognizing the value that can be had from interacting with these supporters, and direct marketing techniques are becoming a popular way to do so. For big clubs like Manchester United, which has a support base of over 50 million fans scattered all over the world, direct marketing is a very effective way of connecting with them.

Manchester United has come from humble origins. The club was formed by workers at the Lancashire and Yorkshire Railway Company in 1878 but, today, is one of the biggest and most recognized sports brands in the world. It is a powerful brand standing for flair, passion, camaraderie and working together, and these brand values are reflected by the players and the way they play each week. Sponsors have been quick to recognize the value of this association and Manchester United has

agreed sponsorship deals with leading companies such as Nike, AIG, Audi, Betfred and Anheuser-Busch. The success of its marketing and brand-building efforts has led to United becoming one of the biggest and most profitable clubs in the world, with profits of £50 million in 2006. Over three-quarters of its revenues now come from its merchandising and commercial activities.

Driving this growth has been its retailing and direct marketing activities. Merchandise sales are a key source of income, and products like replica shirts and other items are retailed through its megastore at Old Trafford and a chain of Manchester United shops in leading cities around the world. A newer retailing venture is the Reds Café restaurants in the Asia Pacific region. The first cafés were opened on a franchise basis in Beijing and Singapore in 2002 and there are plans to develop up to 90 in the region by 2012. Manchester United Television (MUTV) was launched in 1998. It operates five channels and offers subscribers the opportunity to watch all Premiership matches, archive footage, interviews and highlights of games. Similarly, its website allows fans access to merchandise, information, news and updates, and a recent link-up with Viatel means fans can have a Manchester United email address. Its relationship with Vodafone has also enabled it to explore the possibilities provided by mobile marketing. For example, fans are able to get access to information and action from games via their mobile phones. Overall revenues from MU Interactive were worth £1.5 million in 2003.

The power of direct marketing can be seen in the 'One United' approach. Though Old Trafford can hold only 76,000 fans, the objective of 'One United' is to convert all its other armchair fans into paying customers for merchandise, television, updates and other products, thus generating greater revenues for the club. For example, MU Finance already has 57,000 subscribers availing themselves of everything from mortgages to credit cards, and generating sales of £1.2 million for the club.

The next stage of development for the club will be expanding its customer relationship management (CRM) capabilities. Its fan base can be segmented in a variety of ways: by age, sex, region, ethnic background, level of loyalty, etc. Data mining will enable the company to analyse its customers and tailor offerings based on specific preferences. It currently has 1 million fans on its database, including 100,000 supporters from China who have registered since it launched a Chinese version of its website in 2002. It particularly wants to target children as team allegiance is usually decided very young and remains unswerving throughout adult life.[1]

For many decades, mass communications techniques were favoured by marketers, and the promotional mix was heavily weighted towards tools like advertising and sales promotion. But in recent times, direct communications techniques have become very popular. There are a number of reasons for this. As we saw in the previous chapter, both the audience and the media have begun to fragment significantly, making it very difficult for companies to reach the mass market through the classic 30-second television advertisement, for example. In its place, the emergence of some new technologically based solutions, such as customer relationship management (CRM) and online marketing, promise a much more direct and interactive relationship with the customer base. Also, one of the perennial challenges for marketers has been to justify promotional budgets, and demonstrate the impact of expenditure on awareness and sales. Direct communication techniques such as direct response advertising allow marketers to demonstrate more precisely the impact of marketing investments.

This chapter will examine the growing area of direct marketing communications. Many direct marketing communications techniques rely on the availability of a database of customers, which is the foundation upon which campaigns can be built. We shall first examine database marketing, which has evolved into one of the biggest growth areas in marketing, namely customer relationship management (CRM). We shall then go on to look at the field of direct marketing itself, which has grown out of the old mail-order business. Then we will examine internet marketing. At the turn of the century, the internet promised to revolutionize marketing and there were some spectacular successes as well as many failures. However, despite this shaky start, e-commerce has become a mainstream means of doing business. Finally, we shall examine one of the core elements of marketing namely, personal selling and sales management.

Database marketing

A marketing database is an 'electronic filing cabinet' containing a list of names, addresses, telephone numbers, and lifestyle and transactional data on customers and potential customers (see Exhibit 10.1). Information such as types of purchase, frequency of purchase, purchase value and responsiveness to promotional offers may be held.

Database marketing is defined as:[2] an interactive approach to marketing that uses individually addressable marketing media and channels (such as mail, telephone and the salesforce) to:

We'll help your clients lick their competitors

Data Ireland, a subsidiary of An Post is the market leader in consumer and business data.

Providing Direct Marketing mailing lists for over 80 business sectors from a pool of over 200,000 updated Irish business contacts, we output mailing lists to your specifications (based on location, size, sector and named contact).

With over 2 million consumer records and our Ogham geodemographic analysis model, mapping tools, software solutions, online applications and more, we'll help you target your customers.

Data Ireland offers a full range of database management services, including data profiling, data hygiene, data capture and address validation and correction. We also design bespoke data software solutions and offer a consultancy service on maximising profit from your database.

Call Data Ireland now at 01 8584800
www.dataireland.ie

Data Ireland

Exhibit 10.1 Many organizations outsource their customer data management to specialist companies like Kompass which have expertise in handling large quantities of data

- provide information to a target audience
- stimulate demand, and
- stay close to customers by recording and storing an electronic database of customers, prospects and all communication and transactional data.

Database marketing has some key characteristics. The first of these is that it allows direct communication with customers through a variety of media including **direct mail, telemarketing** and **direct response advertising**. Second, it usually requires the customer to respond in a way that allows the company to take action (such as contact by telephone, sending out literature or arranging sales visits). Third, it must be possible to trace the response back to the original communication. The potential of database marketing is enormous. For example, one supermarket analysed its sales and found that it was making a loss on a certain brand of cheese. Before cutting the line altogether, it correlated information about the people who were buying the product and found that they bought other high-ticket items and spent more on average on luxury goods. The supermarket concluded that it would make sense to continue selling the cheese in order to please these high-value customers.[3]

Computer technology provides the capability of storing and analysing large quantities of data from diverse sources, and presenting information in a convenient, accessible and useful format. The creation of a database relies on the collection of information on customers, which can be sourced from:

- company records
- responses to sales promotions
- warranty and guarantee cards
- offering samples that require the consumer to give name, address, telephone number, etc.
- enquiries
- exchanging data with other companies
- salesforce records
- application forms (e.g. to join a credit or loyalty scheme)
- complaints
- responses to previous direct marketing activities
- organized events (e.g. wine tastings).

However a key challenge for companies now is how to handle information overload due to the size and complexity of the data available. Winter Corporation's survey of databases found that over 90 per cent of those that it studied contained over 1 terabyte (1000 gigabytes) of data compared with just 25 per cent in 2001. Kmart had 12.6 terabytes of data covering stocks, sales, customers and suppliers, but this was not enough to save it from bankruptcy.[4]

Collecting information is easiest for companies that have direct contact with customers, such as those in financial services or retailing. However, even for those where the sales contact is indirect, building a database is often possible. For example, Seagram, the drinks company, built up a European database through telephone and written enquiries from customers, sales promotional returns, tastings in store, visits to company premises, exhibitions and promotions that encouraged consumers to name like-minded friends and colleagues.[5]

Figure 10.1 shows the sort of information that is recorded on a database. Customer and prospect information typically includes names, addresses, telephone numbers, names of key decision-makers within DMUs and general behavioural information. Transactional information refers to past transactions that contacts have had with the company. Transactional data must be sufficiently detailed to allow FRAC (frequency, recency, amount and category) information to be extracted for each customer. Frequency refers to how often a customer buys. Recency measures when the customer last bought; if customers are waiting longer before they rebuy (i.e. recency is

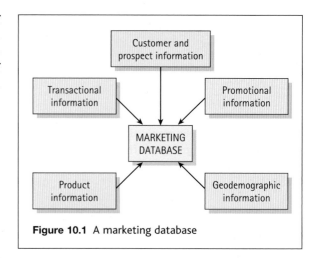

Figure 10.1 A marketing database

decreasing) the reasons for this (e.g. less attractive offers or service problems) need to be explored. Amount measures how much a customer has bought and is usually recorded in value terms. Finally, category defines the type of product being bought.

Promotional information covers what promotion campaigns have been run, who has responded to them, and what the overall results were in terms of contacts, sales and profits. Product information would include which products have been promoted, who responded, when and from where. Finally, geodemographics includes information about the geographic location of customers and prospects, and the social, lifestyle and business category to which they belong. Cross-tabulating these details with transactional information can reveal the customer profile most likely to buy a particular product. Because of the amount of information held about consumers, data privacy is becoming a major issue, as discussed in Technology Focus 10.1.

The main applications of database marketing are as follows.

- *Direct mail*: a database can be used to select customers for mailings.
- *Telemarketing*: a database can store telephone numbers so that customers and prospects can be contacted.
- *Distributor management systems*: a database can be the foundation on which information is provided to distributors and their performance monitored.
- *Loyalty marketing*: loyal customers can be selected from the database for special treatment as a reward for their loyalty
- *Target marketing*: groups of individuals or businesses can be targeted as a result of analysing the database.

Technology Focus 10.1: Data privacy

The advances in data tracking and storage technology mean that the amount of information that corporations and the state hold about us has never been greater. As we increase our usage of technology we leave more and more information trails behind us. Every mobile phone call that we make, and the texts and emails that we send are recorded, and some governments are now requiring that operators store all this information for periods of up to three years for security purposes. As we surf the web, click-stream analysis keeps track of where we go and what we view. Software being pioneered intercepts web page requests to build up a profile of user interests, which can then be used to target advertising. And every time we use a store loyalty card, we enable stores to build up a picture of the kind of customer we are. The key questions that arise are how well do organizations know us, what are they doing with this information and how safe is it.

In answer to the first question, they increasingly know us very well. Database information allows organizations to build up profiles of customers. When organizations share information as, for example, members of the Nectar Card scheme can do, then consumer profiles have the potential to be very accurate because details about grocery shopping (Sainsbury's), online shopping (Amazon.com) and banking (Barclaycard) can all be cross-tabulated and compared. Entry into a loyalty card scheme usually requires the submission of very valuable information like employment status, number of children, number of cars you have, and so on. When all these data are mined, very accurate profiles emerge. The 2008 takeover of DoubleClick by Google also raised significant privacy issues. DoubleClick, is one of the biggest users of 'cookies', small digital files that sit on computers and track the websites visited by users. When this information is combined with Google's search records, it can present a very accurate picture of a surfer's interests.

To maximize company profits, this kind of information can be used in different ways. For example, bonus points can be offered to consumers who switch purchases to high-profit items. Second, when consumers are identified as having preferences for particular kinds of products, such as organic ethnic foods, this range can be expanded and these particular consumers targeted directly. Third, products that offer low margins can be discontinued, which sometimes means that cost-conscious shoppers find their preferred brands are deleted and they may have to shop elsewhere, which is in effect a form of discriminatory pricing. Fourth, price changes can be tested to see how consumers react. For example, the price of a range of products might be increased for a short period and, if consumers do not react adversely, then these higher price levels might remain. Over time, a greater proportion of the store can be dedicated to higher-price items. In intensely competitive markets this is not always possible, but in sectors like grocery retailing the market is becoming dominated by a small number of very large players. Finally, in some industries like insurance, data can be used to identify and weed out high-risk customers.

In many instances, consumers are not aware of the extent to which information is shared between companies. For example, many users willingly put up a great deal of information about themselves on social networking sites like Bebo, Facebook and MySpace. Facebook, in particular, received very negative reactions to its decision to use Beacon technology on its site, which broadcast details of the purchases a user was making to all of the user's friends and allowed third parties access to members' data. In response, Facebook introduced a new set of privacy controls that allows users far greater control of who sees what within their profiles.

Once consumer profiles get very accurate, the security of this information is paramount. For example, in the USA, loyalty card data has been presented in legal cases such as divorces to show that one side has the facility to pay more alimony. In November 2007, the UK Government was seriously embarrassed when two computer disks containing the personal details, including bank account information, of 25 million people in receipt of child benefit payments went missing. HSBC, Britain's biggest bank, lost the personal details of 370,000 customers in the post while, in February 2008, a Home Office disk with encrypted information was found in a laptop sold on eBay.

All this adds up to a situation where consumers need to be very aware of what information they give organizations and what permissions they give these organizations with respect to that information. Consumer rights are protected through data protection legislation. Consumers have a right to know what information organizations hold about them and who this information can be passed on to. They also have the right to opt out of marketing databases. But, in an information society, it has effectively become impossible to live a truly private life!

Suggested reading: Turow (2008)[6]

Databases can also be used to try to build or strengthen relationships with customers. For example, Highland Distillers switched all of its promotional budget for its Macallan whisky brand from advertising to direct marketing. It built a database of 100,000 of its most frequent drinkers (those who consume at least five bottles a year), mailing them every few months with interesting facts about the brand, whisky memorabilia and offers.[7] It is these kinds of efforts to improve customer relationships that have caused the evolution of database marketing into what is now known as customer relationship management (CRM).

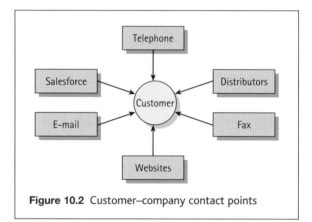

Figure 10.2 Customer–company contact points

Customer relationship management

Customer relationship management (CRM) is a term for the methodologies, technologies and e-commerce capabilities used by firms to manage customer relationships.[8] In particular, CRM software packages aid the interaction between the customer and the company, enabling the company to co-ordinate all of its communications efforts so that the customer is presented with a unified message and image. CRM companies offer a range of information technology-based services, such as call centres, data analysis and **website** management. The basic principle behind CRM is that company staff have a single-customer point of view for each client. Customers are now using multiple channels more frequently. They may buy one product from a salesperson but another from the company website. Interactions between the customer and the company may take place in a variety of ways—through the salesforce, call centres, email, distributors, websites, and so on (see Figure 10.2). For example, Heineken Ireland distributes its products through 8000 pubs/restaurants and over 1300 shops and off-licences in Ireland. Presenting a single, up-to-date view on all these customers to all organizational staff, including a field salesforce, is what a good CRM system should do.

Therefore, it is crucial that, no matter how a customer contacts a company, frontline staff have instant access to the same, up-to-date data about the customer, such as his/her details and past purchases. This usually means the consolidation of many databases held by individual departments in a company into one centralized database that can be accessed by all relevant staff on a computer screen. However. CRM is much more than the technology. To be effective, CRM must be integrated into the overall marketing strategy of the company. Staff must be trained on how to use the system, and accurate usage must be continually encouraged and monitored. The key customer management activities include the following:

- targeting customer and prospect groups with clearly defined propositions
- enquiry management—this starts as soon as an individual expresses an interest and continues through qualification, lead handling and outcome reporting
- welcoming—this covers new customers and those upgrading their relationship; it covers simple 'thank you' messages to sophisticated contact strategies
- getting to know—customers need to be persuaded to give information about themselves; this information needs to be stored, updated and used; useful

- information includes attitude and satisfaction information and relationship 'healthchecks'
- customer development—decisions need to be made regarding which customers to develop through higher levels of relationship management activity, and which to maintain or drop
- managing problems—this involves early problem identification, complaint handling and 'root cause' analysis to spot general issues that have the potential to cause problems for many customers
- win-back—activities include understanding reasons for loss, deciding which customers to try to win back, and developing win-back programmes that offer customers the chance to come back and a good reason to do so.

Measuring performance against a plan enables the refinement of future plans to continually improve the CRM programme; measurement may cover people, processes, campaigns, proposition delivery and channel performance.

To date, CRM initiatives have had a very mixed success rate. Some of the factors that have been associated with success are:[9]

- having a customer orientation and organizing the CRM system around customers
- taking a single view of the customer across departments, and designing an integrated system so that all customer-facing staff can draw information from a common database
- having the ability to manage cultural change issues that arise as a result of system development and implementation
- involving users in the CRM design process
- designing the system in such a way that it can readily be changed to meet future requirements
- having a board-level champion of the CRM project, and commitment within each of the affected departments to the benefits of taking a single view of the customer
- creating 'quick wins' to provide positive feedback on the project programmes.

Direct marketing

Direct marketing attempts to acquire and retain customers by contacting them without the use of an intermediary. Whereas mass advertising reaches a broad spectrum of people, some of whom may not be in the target audience and may only buy at some later unspecified date, direct marketing uses media that can more precisely target consumers and request an immediate direct response. The origins of direct marketing lie in direct mail and mail-order catalogues and, as a result, direct marketing is sometimes seen as synonymous with 'junk mail'. However, today's direct marketers use a wide range of media, such as telemarketing, direct response advertising and email to interact with people. Also, unlike many other forms of communication, direct marketing usually requires an immediate response, which means that the effectiveness of most direct marketing campaigns can be assessed quantitatively.

A definition of direct marketing is: 'the distribution of products, information and promotional benefits to target consumers through interactive communication in a way that allows response to be measured'.

A direct marketing campaign is not necessarily a short-term response-driven activity. More and more companies are using direct marketing to develop ongoing direct relationships with customers (see Marketing in Action 10.1). Some estimates consider that the cost of attracting a new customer is five times that of retaining existing customers. Direct marketing activity can be one tool in the armoury of marketers in their attempt to keep current customers satisfied and spending money. Once a customer has been acquired, there is the opportunity to sell that customer other products marketed by the company. Direct Line, a UK insurance company, became market leader in motor insurance by bypassing the insurance broker to reach the consumer directly through direct response television advertisements using a free-fone number and financial appeals to encourage car drivers to contact them. Once they have sold customers motor insurance, trained telesales people offer substantial discounts on other insurance products including buildings and contents insurance. In this way, Direct Line has built a major business through using a combination of direct marketing methods.

Direct marketing covers a wide array of methods, including:

- direct mail
- telemarketing (both in-bound and out-bound)
- direct response advertising (coupon response or 'phone now')
- catalogue marketing
- electronic media (internet, email, interactive cable TV)
- inserts (leaflets in magazines)
- door-to-door leafleting.

A survey of large consumer goods companies across Europe by the International Direct Marketing Network measured the use of these techniques (excluding catalogue marketing and online channels).[10] It found that 84 per cent of companies used some form of direct marketing, but there was a wide variation between countries. For example, 40 per cent used outbound telemarketing in Germany whereas none did in France. Overall, direct mail was the most commonly used technique (52 per cent) followed by coupon advertisements in the press (41 per cent). Telemarketing was not widely employed, although its use is more often associated with business-to-business marketing. In the UK, the proportion of the promotional budget being devoted to direct marketing has been increasing steadily, with one study finding companies planning to increase their spend on it by over 20 per cent.[11] The potential for growth in the area is reflected by the fact that per capita spend on direct marketing in the UK is US$71 compared with US$152 in the Netherlands and US$428 in the United States.[12]

The significant growth in direct marketing activity over the past 10 years has been explained by five factors. The first is the growing fragmentation of media and markets. The growth of specialist magazines and television channels means that traditional mass advertising is less effective. Similarly, mass markets are disappearing as more and more companies seek to customize their offerings to target groups (see Chapter 5). Second, developments in technology, such as databases, and software that generates personalized letters, have eased the task for direct marketers. Recent developments like variable data printing (VDP) have enabled different elements within direct mail documents, including text, pricing, offers, images and graphics, to be uniquely personalized. Third, there is a significantly increased supply of mailing lists available. List brokers act as an intermediary in the supply of lists from list owners (often either companies that have built lists through transactions with their customers, or organizations that have compiled lists specifically for the purpose of renting them). List brokers thus aid the process of finding a suitable list for targeting purposes. Fourth, more sophisticated analytical techniques such as geodemographic analysis (see Chapter 5) can be used to pinpoint targets for mailing purposes. Finally, the high costs of other techniques, such as **personal selling**, have led an increasing number of companies to take advantage of direct marketing techniques, such as direct response advertising and telemarketing, to make salesforces more cost-effective. This is particularly important where firms have limited promotional budgets, as shown in Marketing in Action 10.1.

Direct marketing activity, including direct mail, telemarketing and telephone banking, is regulated by a European Commission Directive that came into force at the end of 1994. Its main provisions are that:

- suppliers cannot insist on pre-payments
- customers must be told the identity of the supplier, the price and quality of the product and any transport charges, the payment and delivery methods, and the period over which the solicitation remains valid
- orders must be met within 30 days unless otherwise indicated
- a cooling-off period of 30 days is mandatory and cold calling by telephone, fax or electronic mail is restricted unless the receiver has given prior consent.

Managing a direct marketing campaign

Direct marketing as with all promotional campaigns, should be fully integrated with all marketing mix elements to provide a coherent marketing strategy. Direct marketers need to understand how the product is being positioned in the marketplace as it is crucial that messages, sent out as part of a direct marketing campaign, do not conflict with those communicated by other channels such as advertising or the salesforce.

The stages involved in conducting a direct mail campaign are similar to those for mass communications techniques described in the previous chapter (see Figure 10.3). The first step is the identification of the target audience, and one of the advantages of direct mail is that audience targeting can be very precise.

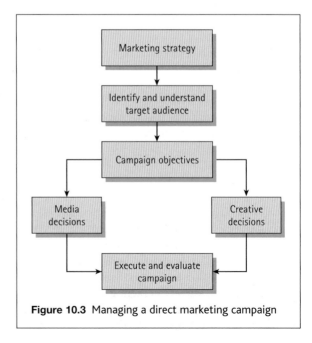

Figure 10.3 Managing a direct marketing campaign

Marketing in Action 10.1: Direct marketing at Perlico

> **Study guide:** Below is a review of a direct marketing campaign by a telecommunications company. Read it and think of other examples of direct marketing campaigns with which you are familiar.

The telecommunications industry has been undergoing rapid changes due to deregulation and the emergence of new technologies, and is also dominated by very large global players like Vodafone, Telefonica and BT. Therefore new entrants to the industry face major challenges in creating customer awareness, building brands and generating revenues. Because of their limited promotional budgets, many are turning to direct marketing techniques in order to develop their customer bases. One such company is Ireland's Perlico.

Perlico was founded in 2002; the word 'perlico' is a loose derivation from the Latin words for 'strength and longevity'. It was set up to provide fixed-line telecommunications and broadband access in the Irish market in competition with Ireland's legacy provider, Eircom. From the outset, it sought to build a brand that was more personal than existing operators and stood for good-quality service. However, it found that some of its early brand-building efforts, which used traditional advertising approaches and media, were relatively unsuccessful in generating new business. Having observed the success of direct sales businesses like Dell, the company switched its marketing efforts to direct marketing and even recruited some of Dell's Irish-based marketing team.

One of the key differences in Perlico's new marketing approach was its switch to direct response advertising using freefone numbers. This enabled it to be able to measure precisely the effects of adverts in different media. Having pursued this strategy for a number of years, the company claims that it can predict to within 5 per cent the level of new business that can be generated by a campaign. This focus on effectiveness has also led it to challenge media to carry its adverts free of charge. Based on consumer response to these trial campaigns it will decide whether or not it run a full campaign on these media. It also introduced humour into its marketing through viral campaigns. For example, in 2007, it parodied the extensive use of call screening by businesses by offering a menu option where callers could simply listen to a duck quack. In just over three days, it received 70,000 calls and the campaign generated additional publicity in the mass media.

Having built a user base of over 62,000 customers, Perlico was acquired by Vodafone in November 2007 for €80 million. The move gave Vodafone access to fixed-line and broadband telephony in Ireland, while Perlico became an additional marketing channel for Vodafone's mobile operations in Ireland.

Based on: Brown (2006);[13] Hancock (2007)[14]

For example, it may be possible to target only existing customers or lapsed customers provided that mailing lists of these groups are available.

The objectives of direct marketing campaigns can be the same as those of other forms of promotion: to improve sales and profits, to acquire or retain customers or to create awareness. However, one of the benefits of direct marketing is that it usually has clearly defined short-term objectives against which performance can be measured, which makes the evaluation of effectiveness relatively easy. For example, objectives can be set in terms of response rate (proportion of contacts responding), total sales, number of enquiries, and so on.

The next major decision involves the media to be used for conducting the direct marketing campaign. Each of the major alternatives available to the marketer is discussed below. Once the media have been selected, the creative decisions must be made. The creative brief usually contains details of the communications objectives, the product benefits, the target market analysis, the offer being made, the communication of the message and the action plan (i.e. how the campaign will be run). As direct marketing is more orientated to immediate action than advertising, recipients will need to see a clear benefit before responding. For example, Direct Line's success in the motor insurance business was built on a clear consumer benefit, namely substantial cost savings.

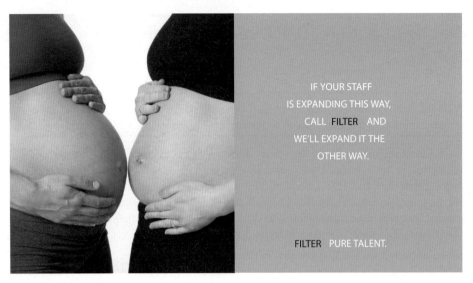

IF YOUR STAFF
IS EXPANDING THIS WAY,
CALL FILTER AND
WE'LL EXPAND IT THE
OTHER WAY.

FILTER PURE TALENT.

Exhibit 10.2 Because there is so much direct mail and it has such a limited opportunity to catch the potential viewer's attention, the visuals used must be very strong; Filter is a creative talent sourcing company

Finally, the campaign needs to be executed and evaluated. Execution can be in-house or through the use of a specialist agency. As we noted earlier, direct marketing does lend itself to quantitative measurement. Some of the most frequently used measures are response rate (the proportion of contacts responding), total sales, sales rate (percentage of contacts purchasing), enquiry rate, cost per contact or enquiry or sale, and repeat purchase rate.

Direct mail

Material sent through the postal service to the recipient's home or business address, with the purpose of promoting a product and/or maintaining an ongoing relationship, is known as direct mail (see Exhibit 10.2). For example, Heinz employs direct mail to target its customers and prospects. By creating a database based on responses to promotions, lifestyle questionnaires and rented lists, Heinz has built a file of 4.6 million households. Each one now receives a quarterly 'At Home' mailpack, which has been further segmented to reflect loyalty and frequency of purchase. Product and nutritional information is combined with coupons to achieve product trial.[15] A major advantage of direct mail is its cost. For example, in business-to-business marketing, it might cost £50 to visit potential customers, £5 to telephone them but less than £1 to send out a mailing.[16]

A key factor in the effectiveness of a direct mail campaign is the quality of the mailing list. Mailing lists are variable in quality. For example, in one year in the UK, 100 million items were sent back marked 'return to sender'. So the effectiveness of direct mail relies heavily on the quality of the list being used to target potential customers. Poor lists raise costs and can contribute to the growing negative perception of 'junk mail' since recipients are not interested in the contents of the mailing (see Ethical Debate 10.1). As a result, it is often preferable to rent lists from list houses rather than purchase them.

Direct mail facilitates specific targeting to named individuals. For example, by hiring lists of subscribers to gardening catalogues, a manufacturer of gardening equipment could target a specific group of people who would be more likely to be interested in a promotional offer than the public in general. Elaborate personalization is possible and the results directly measurable. Since the objective of direct mail is immediate—usually a sale or an enquiry—success can be measured easily. Some organizations, such as *Reader's Digest*, spend money researching alternative creative approaches before embarking on a large-scale mailing. Factors such as type of promotional offer, headlines, visuals and copy can be varied in a systematic manner and, by using code numbers on reply coupons, response can be tied to the associated creative approach.

Telemarketing

When trained specialists use telecommunications and information technologies to conduct marketing and sales activities, this marketing communications system is known as telemarketing. Telemarketing can be a most cost-efficient, flexible and accountable

Ethical Debate 10.1: Convenient or annoying?

Direct marketing has been criticized for being intrusive and for invading people's privacy. Receiving unsolicited calls from telemarketing companies can be annoying, while many consumers fear that every time they subscribe to a club, society or magazine their names, addresses and other information will be entered on a database and that this will guarantee a flood of mail from suppliers (see Technology Focus 11.1). Many consumers are registering with suppression files indicating that they do not want to be recipients of direct marketing activities.

Another form of invasion of privacy is the sending of unsolicited emails (spam). Most recipients find spam intrusive and annoying. One remedy is for internet service providers to install protection against spam on behalf of their customers. The EU's Electronic Data Protection Directive states that marketers must not send emails to consumers who have not expressly stated their wish to receive them.

Similarly, some of those people using the internet are extremely wary of online shopping because of the use of cookies, and the information they store and provide about consumers. Cookies serve many useful functions: they remember users' passwords so they do not have to log on each time they revisit a site; they remember users' preferences so they can be provided with the right pages or data; and they remember the contents of consumers' shopping baskets from one visit to the next. From a marketer's point of view, cookies allow customized and personalized content for online shoppers. However, many internet users probably do not know this information is being collected and would object if they did. Some people fear that companies will use this information to build psychographic profiles; others simply object to information about them being held without their express permission. Although users are identified by a code number rather than a name and address (and this, therefore, does not violate EU data protection regulations), the fear is that direct marketing databases will be combined with information on online shopping behaviour to create a major new way of peering into people's private lives.

The convenience afforded by direct marketing would, it appears, have several downsides for its recipients.

medium.[17] The telephone permits two-way dialogue that is instantaneous, personal and flexible, albeit not face to face.

Technological advances have significantly assisted the growth of telemarketing. For example, integrated telephony systems allow for callers to be identified even before the agent has answered the call. The caller's telephone number is relayed into the computer database and his/her details and account information appear on the screen even before the call is picked up. Technology has also greatly improved the effectiveness and efficiency of outbound telemarketing. For example, predictive dialling enables multiple outbound calls to be made from a call centre. Calls are only delivered to agents when the customer answers, cutting out wasted calls to answering machines, engaged signals, fax machines and unanswered calls. In addition, scripts can be created and stored on the computer so that operators have ready and convenient access to them on-screen.

Telemarketing can be used in a number of roles, and this versatility has also assisted in its growth. It can be used for direct selling when the sales potential of a customer does not justify a face-to-face call or, alternatively, an incoming telephone call may be the means of placing an order in response to a direct mail or television advertising campaign (see Marketing in Action 10.2). Second, it can be used to support the field salesforce, for example, in situations where salespeople may find contacting their customers difficult given the nature of their job. Third, telemarketing can be used to generate leads through establishing contact with prospective customers and arranging a sales visit. Finally, an additional role of telemarketing is to maintain and update the firm's marketing database.

Telemarketing has a number of advantages. First, it has lower costs per contact than a face-to-face salesperson visit. But such has been the success of telemarketing that calls to businesses are growing significantly, with many companies moving call centre operations to low-cost countries. To further save costs, Vodafone Australia has created a new 'character' called Lara, which is a computer-generated response system that sounds lifelike and uses everyday expressions like 'great' and 'let's get started'.[18] Second, it is less time consuming than personal visits. Third, the growth in telephone ownership has increased access to households, and the use of toll-free lines (800 or 0800 numbers) has reduced the cost of responding by telephone. Next, the increasing sophistication of new telecommunications technology has encouraged companies to employ telemarketing techniques. For example, digital networks allow the seamless transfer of calls between organizations. The software company Microsoft and its telemarketing agency can smoothly transfer calls between their respective offices. If the caller then asks for complex technical information, this can be transferred back to the relevant Microsoft department.[19] Finally, despite the reduced costs, compared to a personal visit, the telephone retains the advantage of two-way communication. On the other hand, telephone selling is often considered intrusive, leading to consumers objecting to receiving unsolicited telephone calls. For example, legislation introduced in the UK in 2004 bans marketing companies from cold calling businesses, with fines of up to £5000 for violations of the law, although this applies only to call centres located in Britain. Also, although cost per contact is cheaper than a personal sales call, it is more expensive than direct mail or media advertising.

Mobile marketing

Mobile marketing, which is the sending of short text messages direct to mobile phones, is becoming extremely popular with the rapid penetration of mobile phones in society. Every month in the UK over a billion chargeable text messages are sent, and estimates are that the global mobile advertising market will be worth somewhere between US$10 billion and US$20 billion by 2011.[20] Marketers have been quick to spot the opportunities of this medium to communicate, particularly to a youth audience. Marketers now send out messages to potential customers via their mobile phones to promote such products as fast food, movies, banks, alcoholic drinks, magazines and books. The acronym SMS (short messaging service) has appeared to describe this medium, while MMS (multimedia messaging service) is used to describe the sending of messages incorporating features like music, video, graphic, and so on.

Mobile marketing has several advantages. First, it is very cost effective. The cost per message is between 15p and 25p, compared with 50p to 75p per direct mail shot, including print production and postage. Second, it can be targeted and personalized. For example, operators like Vodafone, Virgin Mobile and Blyk offer free texts and voice calls to customers if they sign up to receive some advertising. In signing up, customers have to fill out questionnaires on their hobbies and interests. Third, it is interactive: the receiver can respond to the text message, setting up the opportunity for two-way dialogue and relationship development. Fourth, it is a time-flexible medium. Text messages can be sent at any time, giving greater flexibility when trying to reach the recipient. Fifth, it can allow marketers to engage in what is becoming known as **proximity marketing**. Messages can be sent to mobile users at nightclubs, shopping centres, festivals and universities, where recipients can immediately avail themselves of special offers, for example. Finally, like other direct marketing techniques, it is immediate and measurable, and can assist in database development. For example, Cadbury Ireland ran an ad campaign on O$_2$'s i-mode online service, offering participants a chance to win €10,000 as an enticement to click on a banner ad. The four-week campaign generated 24,446 clicks from 250,000 impressions, giving a click-through rate of close to 10 per cent. Of that number, 15 per cent entered their details on the site.[21]

Mobile marketing does have certain limitations, however. First, the number of words in a text message is limited to 160 characters, though technological advances are likely to remove this restriction. Second, text messages are visually unexciting, though again advances in multimedia messaging are likely to overcome this. Finally, as with other aspects of direct mail, poor targeting, giving rise to 'junk texts', leads to customer annoyance and poor response rates.

However, at present, mobile marketing is very popular. The arrival on to the market of powerful and aesthetically appealing new phones is likely to increase both mobile phone usage and mobile marketing.

Direct response advertising

Although direct response advertising appears in prime media, such as television, newspapers and magazines, it differs from standard advertising in that it is designed to elicit a direct response such as an order, enquiry or a request for a visit. Often, a freefone telephone number is included in the advertisement or, for the print media, a coupon response mechanism is used. This combines the ability of broadcast media to reach large sections of the population with direct marketing techniques that allow a swift response on behalf of both prospect and company. The acceptability and accessibility of a freefone number was proven during the launch of Daewoo cars in the UK. All Daewoo advertising and literature contained its freefone number when its cars were launched in April 1995. Daewoo hoped that the campaign would attract about 3500 enquiries in the first month following launch. The actual response was over 43,000, rising to over 190,000 four months after launch for a previously unknown product. Direct response advertising had played its part in the successful introduction of a car brand in a new overseas market.[22]

Direct response television has experienced fast growth. It is an industry worth £3 billion globally and comes in many formats, but is not without its controversies, as shown in Marketing in Action 10.2. The most basic is the standard advertisement with telephone number; 60-, 90- or 120-second advertisements are sometimes used to provide the necessary information to persuade viewers to use the freefone number for ordering. Other variants are the 25-minute product demonstration (these are generally referred to as 'infomercials') and live home shopping programmes broadcast by companies such as QVC. Home shopping has a very loyal customer base. For example, Shoppingtelly.com, a website that offers home shoppers news and information on home shopping products, receives between 20,000 and 35,000 hits per day and some of the leading home shopping presenters, such as Paul Lavers and Julia Roberts, have their own very popular websites.[23] A popular misconception regarding direct response television (DRTV) is that it is suitable only for products such as music compilations and cut-price jewellery. In Europe, a wide range of products, such as leisure and fitness products, motoring and household goods, books

Marketing in Action 10.2: Expensive phone calls

Study guide: Below are some examples of problems surrounding competitions on popular TV shows. Read it and examine the cost of competing in some of your favourite interactive shows.

In a bid to increase levels of consumer retention, television has become increasingly interactive and is always seeking novel ways of engaging with potential viewers. One of the most popular techniques in recent times is the screening of programmes that invite viewers to enter competitions, or to vote for participants in a competition such as a reality TV show. Participating in such competitions or votes usually involves making a phone call. What viewers are often unaware of is how much they are being charged for the call, though regulations increasingly require that this is made clear. What has been much more problematic are instances where consumers pay to enter competitions that they have no chance of winning, as happened with the popular breakfast TV show, *GMTV*.

GMTV's phone-in competitions were managed by a telecommunications company, Opera Interactive Technology. However, a *Panorama* investigation discovered that this company frequently chose competition winners before the phone lines were closed and continued to charge callers premium rate prices to enter the competitions. It was estimated that, between 2003 and 2007, 18 million callers had spent £20 million entering competitions that they had no chance of winning. Ofcom, the television regulator, fined Opera Interactive £250,000 for picking potential winners early. Though *GMTV* argued that is was not aware of the practice, it received a record fine of £2 million for what was described by the regulator as the 'widespread and systematic deception of viewers'. Two *GMTV* executives were forced to resign, it terminated its contract with Opera and offered refunds to disenfranchised entrants.

This is not the first time that TV stations have been in trouble over phone-in competitions. For example, the BBC was fined £50,000 for persuading a child to pose as the winner of a *Blue Peter* competition after a technical problem meant that callers could not get through. The company behind the Channel 4, *Richard and Judy* 'You Say, We Pay' competition were fined £150,000 after callers were encouraged to phone in on a premium line after the winners had been chosen. Tens of thousands of text votes for ITV competitions like *Dancing on Ice* and *Gameshow Marathon* were not counted due to technical problems.

Based on: Anonymous (2007);[24] Martin (2007)[25]

and beauty care products, are marketed in this way through pan-European channels such as Eurosport, Super Channel and NBC.

A growing form of direct response advertising is inter-active television (iTV). iTV invites viewers to respond to advertising, competitions and surveys using their remote controls. The advantage of this approach from a customer's point of view is convenience. Consumers can simply respond by pressing a button rather than having to log on to a website or make a phone call. As with many other forms of direct marketing, the effectiveness of campaigns is highly measurable, which is attractive to advertisers, who are also able to avail themselves of the multiplicity of digital channels in order to target adverts more carefully.

Catalogue marketing

The sale of products through catalogues distributed to agents and customers, usually by mail or at stores if the catalogue marketer is a store owner, is known as **catalogue marketing** (see Exhibit 10.3). This method is popular in Europe with such organizations as Germany's Otto-Versand, the Next Directory in the UK, La Redoute in France and IKEA in Sweden. Many of these companies operate in a number of

Exhibit 10.3 French company La Redoute is one of the world's biggest catalogue marketers

countries; La Redoute, for instance, has operations in France, Belgium, Norway, Spain and Portugal. Catalogue marketing is popular in some countries where, for example, legislation restricts retail opening hours. A common form of catalogue marketing is mail order, where catalogues are distributed and, tradi-tionally, orders received by mail. Some enterprising companies, notably Next, saw catalogue marketing as an opportunity to reach a new target market: busy, affluent, middle-class people who valued the convenience of choosing products at home.

Used effectively, catalogue marketing to consumers offers a convenient way of selecting products that allows discussion between family members in a relaxed atmosphere away from crowded shops and the high street. Often, credit facilities are available, too. For remote rural locations this method provides a valuable service, obviating the need to travel long distances to town-based shopping centres. For cata-logue marketers, the expense of high-street locations is removed and there is an opportunity to display a wider range of products than could feasibly be achieved in a shop. Distribution can be centralized, lowering costs. Nevertheless, catalogues are expens-ive to produce (hence the need for some retailers to charge for them) and they require regular updating, particularly when selling fashion items. They do not allow goods to be tried (e.g. a vacuum cleaner) or tried on (e.g. clothing) before purchase. Although products can be seen in a catalogue, variations in colour printing can mean that the curtains or suite that are delivered do not have exactly the same colour tones as those appearing on the printed page.

Catalogue marketing is big business. IKEA dis-tributes 46 versions of its catalogue in 36 countries and in 28 languages, accounting for 50 per cent of its total promotional budget. Increasingly, catalogues are being made available online, which reduces the costs of production and distribution, and means that they can easily be updated; 45 per cent of Next Directory's business is now conducted online.

Internet marketing

Internet marketing has been discussed throughout the book but here we shall look at it in some more detail. The impact of the **internet** on society has been described as being as significant as some of the greatest technological innovations in history, such as the telephone and the motor car. The internet is a global web of over 50,000 computer networks con-taining millions of web pages, which users can access once they connect to a server.

Electronic commerce or **e-commerce** has been defined as 'a wide range of technologies used to facilitate business interactions such as the internet, **electronic data interchange** (EDI), email, electronic payment systems, advanced telephone systems, hand-held digital devices, interactive television, self-service kiosks and smart cards'.

Therefore, e-commerce—or e-business, as it is also described—is a broad term and represents an evolution in the process of using the currently available technology to improve business processes or the delivery of service to customers. For example, prior to the advent of the internet, many companies had EDI systems (and some still do), which linked computers in and between organizations to enable the rapid exchange of information, such as that between suppliers and customers.

Internet marketing has been defined as, 'the achievement of marketing objectives through the utilization of the internet and web-based technologies'.

Though sometimes the terms are used interchangeably, e-marketing is broader than internet marketing in that it refers to the achievement of marketing objectives via a wider range of communications technologies such as mobile phones and digital television. Pepper and Rodgers identify the key features of e-marketing as the '5-Is'.[26]

1 *Identification*: customer specifics.
2 *Individualization*: tailored for lifetime purchases.
3 *Interaction*: dialogue to learn about customers' needs.
4 *Integration*: of knowledge of customers throughout the company.
5 *Integrity*: develop trust through non-intrusive marketing such as **permission marketing**.

Internet marketing opportunities

The extent of e-commerce is borne out by the fact that all possible combinations of exchange between consumers and business organizations take place (see Figure 10.4). Business-to-business exchanges may take many forms. As we saw in Chapter 3, corporations and government agencies manage their procurement electronically through vertical and horizontal exchanges such as covisint.com, which is a horizontal marketplace for a variety of industries. They also manage their sales to corporate clients through dedicated intranet sites. The most apparent form of e-commerce is that from business to consumer (B2C), with established retailers such as Tesco setting up home shopping facilities, and a variety of internet-

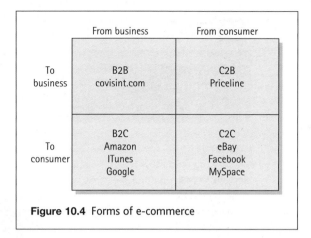

Figure 10.4 Forms of e-commerce

based companies, like Amazon, iTunes and Google, dominating their markets.

E-commerce from consumer to business (C2B) is less common, but demonstrates the versatility of the internet. An example is the facility provided by Priceline.com whereby would-be travellers can bid for airline tickets, hotels and car hire, leaving the sellers to decide whether or not to accept these offers. The internet also permits consumers to trade with other consumers via auctions: consumer to consumer (C2C). Would-be sellers can offer products through such sites as eBay, Portero and QXL to potential customers. C2C has been one of the biggest growth areas on the internet in recent years (see Marketing in Action 10.3). Though not specifically created for the purpose of trading goods, online communities and social networks such as MySpace, Facebook, Flickr and Bebo have become globally recognized brands, providing forums for people to communicate with each other and share interests (see Exhibit 10.4). Because of their size—for example, MySpace has 80 million unique visits per month—marketers are very interested in their commercial possibilities.

Once a company has decided to adopt e-commerce as a way to exploit new, entrepreneurial opportunities, one immediate outcome is that the organization's knowledge platform becomes much more closely linked with other knowledge sources, such as suppliers and customers, elsewhere within the market system. The reason for this is that once buyers and sellers become electronically linked, volumes of data interchange increase dramatically as trading activities begin to occur in real time. The outcome is the emergence of very dynamic, rapid responses by both customers and suppliers to changing circumstances within their market systems. For example, when a customer places an order with Dell, this order also automatically goes to Dell's suppliers so that product components can immediately begin their journey to a Dell assembly plant.

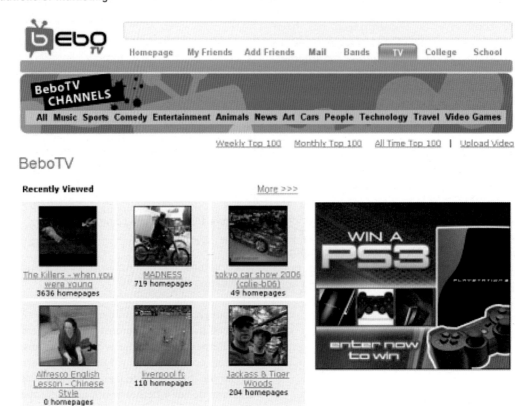

Exhibit 10.4 Social networking sites like Bebo, MySpace and Facebook have been among the biggest internet marketing success stories in recent years

Marketing in Action 10.3: Internet marketing—we're all marketers now!

> **Study guide:** Below is a review of some of the new pastimes and businesses that are being facilitated by developments in internet technology. Read it and examine the marketing strategies of your top three favourite websites.

One of the most fascinating features of the internet has been its ability to link up consumers from all over the world. Anybody with an interest in anything is likely to be able to find someone, somewhere that has a similar interest. The internet becomes the platform through which these shared interests can be developed, and technological developments have made it easy for users to upload text, pictures, videos, and so on. As a result, user-generated content on the internet has soared. Wikipedia is an online repository that anyone can contribute to; it has supplanted businesses like *Encyclopaedia Britannica*. Video-sharing sites like YouTube and photo-sharing sites like Flickr rely heavily on user-generated content. Social networking sites like Facebook and MySpace consist of primarily user-generated material. People trade with each other on eBay and some generate a living through full-time trading. Others make a living playing poker online. The internet has been a great democratizing tool. Consumers are no longer just the recipients of what businesses have to offer. Innovation is not restricted to the organizations that choose to invest in new product and service development. Anyone with a business idea, a profitable pastime or just something to say now has a forum for doing it.

One of the most obvious manifestations of this development is blogging, which is revolutionizing the world of public relations. Blogs are online diaries that provide comment, opinion and unfiltered, uncensored information on any subject area. They also facilitate interactions because they enable people to post replies and comments or link to other blogs. Private individuals use blogs as a way of staying in touch with families and friends when working abroad or travelling. They can use them to provide information and comment about business or political issues. The business of journalism is particularly challenged by blogging as any one journalist is never likely to be able to match the collective specialist knowledge of the masses. For example, CBS's famous news anchor, Dan Rather, lost his job when he ran a story about George W. Bush shirking National Guard duty, based on documents that bloggers quickly exposed as forgeries.

The biggest single challenge with user-generated content is that there is so much of it, that sorting the good from the dross becomes a real challenge. This has created a business opportunity for content aggregators. For example, Monitor110 is an information aggregator for the financial services industry. It filters information from hundreds of thousands of blogs and other sources to provide analysts with the key information that they need. Speedy, accurate information is critical for the investment community as delays in making decisions have the potential to cost investors a great deal of money. For the general public, sites like Blogbridge and Digg allow for content aggregation and news rankings. The world of user-generated content enables each one of us to become a marketer.

Furthermore, the internet helps to create business opportunities through the inherent benefits it offers to customers. The first of these is convenience. Access to a website is available 24 hours a day, seven days a week, and is significantly more convenient than offline distribution channels, which may involve driving, queuing, and so on. Second, the internet is a global medium. Consumers can get easier access to products/information from different parts of the world than is possible through other channels. Third, it can provide excellent value. Price-comparison technologies allow consumers to search for the cheapest brands and to do immediate, real-time comparisons of the prices being charged by different vendors. For example, the internet brought price transparency to the car rental market with the result that Avis, one of the market leaders and a premium-priced competitor, was forced to reduce its prices and saw its profits fall from £111 million in 1999 to around £20 million in 2005.[27] Finally, as the internet is an information resource, it assists with the buying decision process by enabling consumers to evaluate alternative brands or service providers. Trading information is one of the biggest business opportunities on the internet. The potential benefits and limitations of the internet to consumers are summarized in Table 10.1.

The potential benefits and limitations of the internet to businesses are summarized in Table 10.2. Some of these are described in more detail below.

Lower costs and prices

Communicating with customers online is significantly cheaper than serving them via telephone or person to person. Therefore, organizations like banks are encouraging their customers to carry out basic financial transactions such as account enquiries and bill payments online rather than at bank branches. Online banks typically offer better interest rates on savings and cheaper loans than their offline counterparts. The internet also permits suppliers to make contact with customers without using an intermediary, further reducing their costs. The savings generated by the removal of the intermediary from the transaction can be passed on to the customer in the form of lower prices. An example of this form of competitive advantage is provided by low-fares airlines such as easyJet. The advent of the internet allowed these companies to create automated, online flight enquiry and booking services, and ticket assurance systems. The process of bypassing traditional intermediaries such as travel agents is known as 'disintermediation'. Similarly, consumers are now able to book holidays directly and often can do so at prices lower than those advertised by tour operators.

Improved service quality

It is almost impossible—in most service markets—to offer a product proposition that is very different from that of the competition. As a result one of the few ways of gaining a competitive advantage is through

Table 10.1 Potential benefits and limitations of internet technologies to consumers

Benefits	Limitations
Convenience in terms of being able to provide access 24 hours a day, 365 days a year from a shopper's desk, and increasingly anywhere via mobile internet.	*Delivery times* are not quite so flexible. The logistical complexities of getting physical goods the last mile to the customer's home can mean that the customer must stay in and wait until the goods arrive.
As an *information resource*, the internet enables the end user to acquire detailed, real-time information about products, pricing and availability.	*Information overload*: the amount of information that can be accessed via the internet by an end user can be overwhelming.
Multimedia: through exploitation of the latest technology, customers can gain a better understanding of their needs by, for example, examining 3D displays of car interiors or hotel accommodation.	*Access to technology*: the greater the capacity to incorporate multimedia content into e-commerce operations, the higher the required specifications of the computer to download such content. Many consumers do not have access to even the most basic means of accessing the internet.
Products and services: digital products can be downloaded instantly, while online retailers typically offer vast ranges so that rare products can be bought.	*Security*: many consumers are concerned about using credit and/or debit cards to purchase goods online for fear that their details will be captured by hackers.
Lower prices: it is possible to search for the lowest price available for brands. Specific sites (e.g. Kelkoo and shopping.yahoo.com) allow consumers to find the best available prices.	*Cost implications*: the consumer has to make an initial investment in suitable equipment.

Table 10.2 Potential benefits and limitations of internet technologies to organizations

Benefits	Limitations
Investment reduction such as replacing retail outlets with an online shopping mall and reduced selling costs through online catalogues and SMS messaging.	*Operational costs*: significant investment and expertise can be required to achieve interoperability across networks and digital platforms.
Reduced order costs: e-procurement systems significantly reduce the costs associated with purchasing.	*Set-up costs*: moving from a paper-based system to a fully integrated e-procurement system, for example, can have high cost implications.
Relationship building: acquiring data on a customer's purchasing behaviour can be used to develop higher levels of customer service.	*High cost content*: end users have high expectations of the 'up-to-dateness' of online content. Not only does content have to be updated regularly, but also there are high cost implications for content creation.
Customized promotion: unlike television or print, promotion can be targeted to small niche audiences.	*Over-specialization*: while it is technically possible to target a segment of one, the organization should always question the profitability of such a strategy.
Marketing research opportunities: the internet is a rich source of secondary information, and email and internet surveys are relatively low-cost.	*Authenticity*: not all internet users respond to surveys by providing factual data, which may give rise to misleading results.

being able to deliver a superior level of customer service. A key influencer of service quality is the speed of information interchange between the supplier and the customer. Clearly, therefore, the information interchange capability of the internet offers some interesting opportunities to be perceived as superior to other firms in the same market. For many years, Federal Express has been a global leader in the application of IT, providing a superior level of customized delivery services to customers. The firm has enhanced its original customer-service software system, COSMOS, by providing major clients with terminals and software that use the internet to take them into the Federal logistics management system. In effect, Federal Express now offers customers the ability to create a state-of-the-art distribution system without having to make any investment in self-development of shipping expertise inside their own firms.

Greater product variety

In terms of the amount of space available to display goods, the average high-street retail shop is physically restricted. Hence its customers, who may already have faced the inconvenience of having to travel to the retailer's location, may encounter the frustration of finding that the shop does not carry the item they wish to purchase. Online retailers do not face the same space restrictions their 'bricks and mortar' competitors do. As a result, they can use their website to offer a much greater variety of goods to potential customers. Possibly one of the best-known examples of a firm that has exploited this source of competitive advantage is online bookseller Amazon.com. This phenomenon is sometimes described as the 'long tail of e-commerce'. About one-third of Amazon's sales come from outside its 130,000 top-selling book titles, while Rhapsody, a streaming music service, streams more tracks from outside than inside its top 10,000 tunes (see Technology Focus 11.1).[28]

Product customization

Dell Computer Corporation's extensive experience of computer direct marketing permitted it to be a 'first mover' in exploiting the internet as part of its strategy to offer customized products. Customers who visit the Dell website are offered assistance in selecting the type of technology most suited to their needs. These data provide the inputs to an online help system, which guides the customer through the process of evolving the most appropriate specification from a range of choices. Once a final selection has been made, the customer receives an instant quote on both the price of their purchase and the date on which it will be delivered. Several online marketers are attempting to gain competitive advantage through this idea of mass customizing products and services to customers (see Chapter 5).

The internet as a direct marketing medium

Because of the benefits and the advantages it confers, as described above, the internet is a powerful marketing medium. It presents novel ways of configuring the marketing mix, as shown in Figure 10.5.

Product

There are several ways that the internet offers an opportunity for product enhancement, as described below.

- *Individual*: personal specifications can lead to highly individual products being created.

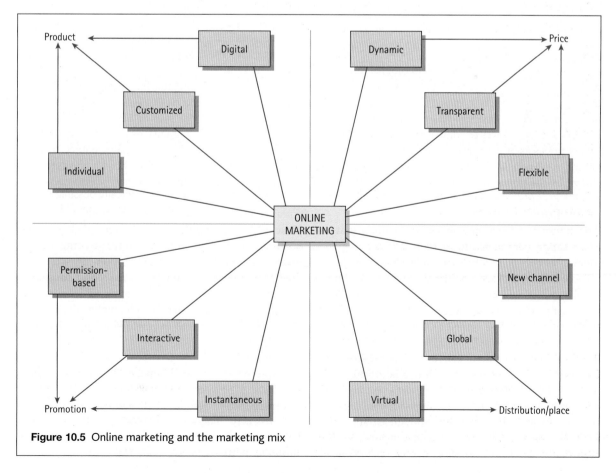

Figure 10.5 Online marketing and the marketing mix

- *Customized*: Tesco's online shopping website captures details of shopper's regular purchase choices and then provides a customized list of favourites; the main benefit for the customer is speedier online shopping. MySpace delivers advertisements that are targeted to users based upon the information that they submit about themselves.
- *Digital*: the emergence of the internet has facilitated the growth and distribution of bit-based products; bit-based products are digital goods and services that can be delivered via the internet straight to an online customer's desktop—for example, information, music, software upgrades, computer games, flight bookings and hotel reservations. Wikipedia is a classic example of a bit-based product that has grown to include over 9 million articles in 250 languages. The BBC now has 525 websites, providing information and entertainment on everything from current affairs to culture to science and nature. In doing so it has significantly expanded the reach of its business. Gorillaz is a virtual band that exists only online and in animation. An emerging online product category is audio and video podcasts, which can be used to distribute TV and radio shows as well as company information; for example, Cisco makes available audio and video podcasts on technology subjects.

Price

A major impact of internet technologies on economics is that they potentially reduce the search costs that buyers incur when looking for information about new products and services. The net effect is a reduction in suppliers' power to control and therefore charge higher prices as pricing strategies become more transparent. Additionally prices become more dynamic, as shown by the popularity of the auction site eBay.

Promotion

The internet is becoming increasingly important as a marketing communications tool. When using the internet as part of a marketing communications strategy, a company can send permission-based emailings, regular bulletins containing information about, say, the latest product features and any promotional offers that the customer has agreed to accept.

This kind of agreement can enable a company to begin to build a longer-term online relationship with the customer. Furthermore, the internet enables the customer to respond by interacting with communications message, unlike traditional broadcast and print media where a two-way dialogue is not possible on a large scale. Interactive features can be incorporated into online promotions in a number of different forms, such as surveys, competitions, links to other websites and tags, which are one-word descriptions that are used to classify and categorize content.

Another innovative characteristic of communications via the internet is that they can be instantaneous, and provide opportunities for immediate responses to enquiring customers. A particular example of this is what has become known as **viral marketing**. Most commonly associated with email, viral marketing is essentially electronic word-of-mouth promotion where jokes are shared among friends, or calls for action such as those in support of the Live8 concerts for poverty relief are publicized. Companies attempt to harness this viral effect by building messages that are suitably engaging and promote an aspect of their company with content that customers want to read and send on. This requires some creativity and a good understanding of the customer base. For example, as part of its 'Campaign for Real Beauty', Dove created a short film entitled *Evolution*, which was viewed over 10 million times on YouTube.[29]

'Giving something for nothing' is another effective means of increasing the viral effect. Hotmail grew its subscriber base from zero to 18 million in just 12 months by including the message 'Get your FREE email account at www.hotmail.com' at the end of each email. In this way, users of Hotmail became marketers for the company through every email they sent. The same strategy has been employed by Skype, whose software for making free telephone calls over the internet has been downloaded millions of times since the company was founded in 2003. Companies like 5pm.co.uk send emails promoting specific off-peak restaurant deals, only redeemable through unique links noted on the email, with the intention that these will be passed on to 'new' customers.[30]

Finally, a key consideration for companies is getting their websites identified by search engines. This requires marketing their websites to the search engines so that they can easily be found by web users (see Marketing in Action 10.4). A second consideration is trying to improve the placing of a website on search engine page rankings. The higher the placing, the more likely the web user will visit the website.

Distribution

The internet has created opportunities for companies to utilize a new channel to market. It has distinct advantages over traditional channels in reducing barriers to entry. The location issue, considered to be a key determinant of retail patronage in the physical sense, is reduced, along with the enormous capital investment in stores. Trading exchanges take place in a virtual market space, and these networks are global.

The commonest distribution model in the majority of offline consumer goods markets is to delegate both transaction and logistics processes (e.g. major brands such as Coca-Cola being marketed via supermarket chains). This can be contrasted with the online world where absolute delegation of all processes is a somewhat rarer event. The reason for this situation is that many firms, having decided that e-commerce offers an opportunity for revising distribution management practices, perceive cyberspace as offering a way to regain control over transactions by cutting out intermediaries and selling direct to their end-user customers. This process, in which traditional intermediaries may be squeezed out of channels is, as we have already seen, usually referred to as disintermediation. Hence, for those firms engaged in assessing the e-commerce distribution aspects of their marketing mix, there is a need to recognize that the technology has the following implications.

Marketing in Action 10.4: Search advertising

> **Study guide:** Below is a review of the growth of search advertising. Read it and consider the advantages and disadvantages of search advertising as a promotional tool.

The first port of call for most internet users is the search engine or portal, where leading companies like Google, Yahoo! and MSN help browsers to find the sites that they are looking for. One of the fastest-growing sources of revenue for these companies is word sponsorship. This is the practice whereby the search engine sells key words such as 'holiday' or 'hotel' to the highest-bidding advertiser in an online auction. The buyer then 'owns' the key word, so that when an internet user searches for that subject, the advertiser's site appears at the top of the list of websites turned up by the search. On sites like Google, sponsored search results are clearly distinguished from general search results, though this is not always the case on other search websites.

'Paid search' advertising is big business. The total market for online advertising is estimated to be worth US$40 billion, with search accounting for approximately 40 per cent of this and the remainder devoted to online display advertising such as banner ads and pop-ups, classified advertising and others. It is estimated that the search business alone will be worth US$65 billion by 2010. Therefore, though web users typically spend only 5 per cent of their time online engaged in search activities, this sector has captured 40 per cent of the advertising revenues. People using search engines are usually looking for something specific and click-through rates are much higher on sponsored searches than on ordinary banner ads. It is also a relatively efficient form of promotion as advertisers pay on the basis of 'price per click'. Every time the user clicks through on a sponsored search link, the advertiser pays a small sum, which can be a few pence, although it can rise depending on the value of the product being sold.

However, it not necessary to buy key words in order to have your site returned in a search. Prominent use of key words on your website can also ensure that it is picked up while web pages that use lots of Flash animation score poorly on search listings. Companies like Hitwise show all the websites that are returned when particular key words are used to assist companies in designing their sites effectively. Currently Google is the market leader in search advertising with a market share of 70 per cent, while Microsoft and Yahoo! are dominant in online display advertising. Google has been trying to keep its lead by increasing the 'quality' of its adverts. It does this by offering fewer ads on its search results page and sometimes none at all. This reduces visual clutter and should please both users and advertisers. This is also good for Google in that having fewer ads means that advertisers have to bid higher to get these slots. In turn, if having fewer ads leads to more click-throughs and then sales, this again should boost Google's revenues as the value of search advertising becomes evident. It would appear that revenue/click will ultimately become a more important metric than overall click rate.

Based on: Anonymous (2008);[31] Gapper (2006);[32] Smith (2007);[33] Thompson (2004);[34] Waters (2004)[35]

- Distance ceases to be a cost influencer because online delivery of information is substantially the same no matter what the destination of the delivery.
- Business location becomes irrelevant because the e-commerce corporation can be based anywhere in the world.
- The technology permits continuous trading, 24 hours a day, 365 days a year.

Finally, a characteristic of offline distribution channels is the difficulty that smaller firms face in persuading intermediaries (e.g. supermarket chains) to stock their goods. This scenario is less applicable in the world of e-commerce. Firms of any size face a relatively easy task in establishing an online presence. Market coverage can then be extended by developing trading alliances based on offering to pay commission to other online traders who attract customers to the company's website. This ease of entry reduces the occurrence of firms' marketing efforts being frustrated because they are unable to gain the support of intermediaries in traditional distribution channels. Eventually e-commerce may lead to a major increase in the total number of firms offering goods and services across world markets.

Buzz marketing

The most recent form of direct marketing to emerge is what has become known as **buzz marketing**, which is defined as the passing of information about products and services by verbal or electronic means in an informal, person-to-person manner (see Exhibit 10.5). For example, in the USA, Nintendo recruited suburban mothers to spread the word among their friends that the Wii was a gaming console that the whole family could enjoy together. Buzz marketing is similar to word-of-mouth marketing, long recognized as one of the most powerful forms of marketing, but it has enjoyed a renaissance due to advances in technology such as email, websites and mobile phones.

The first step in a buzz marketing campaign involves identifying and targeting 'alphas'—that is, the trendsetters that adopt new ideas and technologies early on—and the 'bees', who are the early adopters. Brand awareness then passes from these customers to others, who seek to emulate the trendsetters. In many instances, the alphas are celebrities who either directly or indirectly push certain brands. For example, the Australian footwear and accessories brand UGG became popular in the US and European markets when photographs of actresses like Sienna Miller and Cameron Diaz appeared in the media wearing these products. Celebrities may be paid to endorse products or simply popularize products through their own choices.

Critical to the success of buzz marketing is that every social group, whether it is online or offline, has trendsetters. The record company Universal successfully promoted its boy bands Busted and McFly by targeting these trendsetters. It recruited a 'school chairman' who was given the task of spreading the word

Exhibit 10.5 The energy drink brand Red Bull is a leading user of buzz marketing

Exhibit 10.6 Some industries, such as pharmaceuticals, are extensive users of personal selling

about a particular band in their school. This involved giving out flyers, putting up posters on school notice-boards and then sending back evidence that this had been done. In return, the 'chairman'—who was typically a 12–15-year-old schoolgirl—was rewarded with free merchandise and a chance to meet members of the band.

Developments in technology have allowed the 'buzz' to spread very quickly. As we saw earlier, viral marketing is popular because of the speed with which advertising gets passed on via email. The launch of Apple's iPhone is a classic example of the power of buzz marketing. According to Nielsen's Buzz Metrics, which tracks English-language blogs, the product had more mentions than even the President of the USA around the time of its launch in January 2007, and had an entry on Wikipedia within minutes of it going on show.[36]

Once the target audience has been identified, the next key decisions, like those for all forms of promotion, are the message and the medium. The message may take many forms, such as a funny video clip or email attachment, a blog or story, an event such as a one-off concert, and so on. For example, Diageo launched Smirnoff Raw Tea in the USA with a video clip featuring a spoof hip hop song. The clip, entitled 'Smirnoff Tea Partay', has been one of the most popular on YouTube, with over 3.5 million views. The medium used for carrying the message is frequently online but could also be through offline means such as posters or flyers. But, as with all aspects of buzz marketing, the only limitation is the imagination. For example, many individuals have used parts of their bodies or their private cars to carry commercial messages.

Finally, given its novelty, evaluating the effectiveness of buzz marketing is difficult. Numbers are available regarding how many times a video clip is viewed but marketers will not be able to determine by whom.

Personal selling

The final major element of the promotional mix is personal selling. This involves face-to-face contact with a customer and, unlike advertising, promotion and other forms of non-personal communication, personal selling permits a direct interaction between buyer and seller (see Exhibit 10.6). This two-way communication means that the seller can identify the specific needs and problems of the buyer and tailor the sales presentation in the light of this knowledge. The particular concerns of the buyer can also be dealt with on a one-to-one basis.

Such flexibility comes at a price, however. The cost of a car, travel expenses and sales office overheads can mean that the total annual bill for a field salesperson is often twice the level of a salary. In industrial marketing, over 70 per cent of the marketing budget is usually spent on the salesforce. This is because of the technical nature of the products being sold, and the need to maintain close personal relationships between the selling and buying organizations.

The make-up of the personal selling function is changing, however. Organizations are reducing the size of their salesforces in the face of greater buyer concentration, moves towards centralized buying, and recognition of the high costs of maintaining a field sales team. For example, Pfizer is cutting its

38,000-strong global sales force due to falling margins and greater competition from generic drugs. The concentration of buying power into fewer hands has also fuelled the move towards relationship management, often through key account selling. This involves the use of a small number of dedicated sales teams, which service the accounts of major buyers as opposed to having a large number of salespeople. Instead of sending salespeople out on the road, many companies now collect a large proportion of their sales through direct marketing techniques such as the telephone or the internet.

The three main types of salespeople are order-takers, order-creators and order-getters. Order-takers respond to already committed customers such as a sales assistant in a convenience store or a delivery salesperson. Order-creators have traditionally been found in industries like healthcare, where the sales task is not to close the sale but to persuade the medical representative to prescribe or specify the seller's products. Order-getters are those in selling jobs where the major objective is to persuade the customer to make a direct purchase. They include consumer salespeople such as those selling double glazing or insurance, through to organizational salespeople, who often work in teams where products may be highly technical and negotiations complex.

Personal selling skills

While the primary responsibility of a salesperson is to increase sales, there are a number of additional enabling activities carried out by many salespeople, including **prospecting**, maintaining customer records, providing service, handling complaints, relationship management and self-management. Prospecting involves searching for and calling on potential customers. Prospects can be identified from several sources including talking to existing customers, and searching trade directories and the business press. Customer record-keeping is an important activity for all repeat-call salespeople because customer information is one of the keys to improving service and generating loyalty. Salespeople should be encouraged and rewarded for sending customer and market information back to head office. Providing service to customers —including, for example, advice on ways of improving productivity and handling customer complaints —can also be a key salesforce activity. This is particularly true in cases where the selling situation is not a one-off activity. In general, there has been a rise in the number of salespeople involved in relationship management roles with large organizational customers. Trust is an important part of relationship development and is achieved through a high frequency of contact, ensuring promises are kept, and reacting

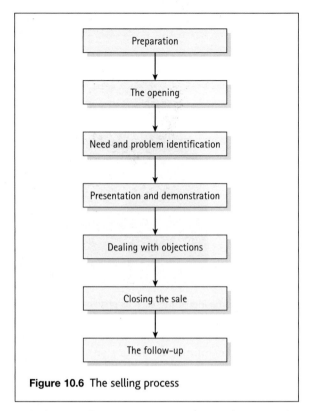

Figure 10.6 The selling process

quickly and effectively to problems. Finally, given the flexibility of the salesperson's job, many are required to practise self-management, including decisions on call frequencies and journey routing, for example.

Many people's perception of a salesperson is of a slick, fast-talking confidence trickster devoted to forcing unwanted products on gullible customers. In reality, success in selling comes from implementing the marketing concept when face to face with customers, not denying it at the very point when the seller and buyer come into contact. The sales interview offers an unparalleled opportunity to identify individual customer needs and match behaviour to the specific customer that is encountered.[37] In order to develop personal selling skills it is useful to distinguish six phases of the selling process (see Figure 10.6). We will now discuss each of these in turn.

Preparation

The preparation carried out prior to a sales visit can reap dividends by enhancing confidence and performance when the salesperson is face to face with the customer. Some situations cannot be prepared for: the unexpected question or unusual objection, for example. But many customers face similar situations, and certain questions and objections will be raised repeatedly. Preparation can help the salesperson respond to these recurring situations. Salespeople will benefit from gaining knowledge of their own and competitors' products, by understanding buyer behaviour, by having clear sales call objectives and by having planned their sales presentation. This is because the success of the sales interview is customer-dependent. The aim is to convince the customer; what the salesperson does is simply a means to that end.

The opening

It is important for salespeople to consider how to create a favourable initial impression with customers as this can often affect later perceptions. Good first impressions can be gained by adopting a businesslike approach, being friendly but not overly familiar, being attentive to detail, observing common courtesies like waiting to be asked to sit down and by showing the customer appreciation for having taken the time to see you.

Need and problem identification

Consumers will buy a product because they have a 'problem' that gives rise to a 'need'. Therefore the first task is to identify the needs and problems of each customer. Only by doing this can a salesperson connect with each customer's situation. Effective need and problem identification requires the development of questioning and listening skills. The hallmark of inexperienced salespeople is that they do all the talking; successful salespeople know how to get the *customer* to do most of the talking.

Presentation and demonstration

It is the presentation and demonstration that offers the opportunity for the salesperson to convince customers that they can supply the solution to their problem. It should focus on **customer benefits** rather than **product features**. The salesperson should continue to ask questions during the presentation to ensure that the customer has understood what he or she has said, and to check that what the salesperson has talked about really is of importance to the customer. This can be achieved by asking questions like 'Is that the kind of thing you are looking for?'

Dealing with objections

Salespeople rarely close a sale without first having to overcome customer objections. Although objections can cause problems, they should not be regarded negatively since they highlight issues that are important to the buyer. The secret of dealing with objections is to handle both the substantive and emotional aspects. The substantive part is to do with the objection itself. If the customer objects to the product's price the salesperson needs to use convincing arguments to show that the price is not too high. But it is a fact of human personality that the argument that is supported by the greater weight of evidence does not always win since people resent being proven wrong. Therefore, salespeople need to recognize the emotional

aspects of objection handling. Under no circumstances should the buyer be caused to lose face or be antagonized during this process. Two ways of minimizing this risk are to listen to the objection without interruption and to employ the 'agree and counter' technique, where the salesperson agrees with the buyer but then puts forward an alternative point of view.

Closing the sale

The inexperienced salesperson will sometimes imagine that an effective presentation followed by the convincing handling of any objections should guarantee that the buyer will ask for the product without the seller needing to work to close the sale. This does occasionally happen but, more often, it is necessary for the salesperson to take the initiative. This is because many buyers still have doubts in their minds that may cause them to wish to delay the decision to purchase. Closing techniques include simply asking for the order, summarizing the key points and asking for the order, or offering a special deal to close the sale (the concession close).

The follow-up

Once an order has been placed there may be a temptation for the salesperson to move on to other customers, neglecting the follow-up visit. However, this can be a great mistake since most companies rely on repeat business. If problems arise, customers have every right to believe that the salesperson was interested only in the order, and not their complete satisfaction. By checking that there are no problems with delivery, installation, product use and training (where applicable), the follow-up can show that the salesperson really does care about the customer.

Sales management

Because of the unique nature of the selling job, sales management is a challenging activity. For example, many salespeople spend a great deal of their time in the field, separated from their managers, while others may suffer repeated rejections in trying to close sales, causing them to lose confidence. Therefore, the two main aspects of the sales manager's job are designing the salesforce and managing the salesforce.

Designing the salesforce

The critical design decisions are determining salesforce size and organizing the salesforce. The most practical method for deciding the number of salespeople required is called the 'workload approach'. It is based on the calculation of the total annual calls required per year divided by the average calls per year that can be expected from one salesperson.[38]

There are three alternative approaches to organizing the salesforce. A *geographic* structure is where the sales area is broken down into territories based on workload and potential, and a salesperson is assigned to each one to sell all of the product range. This provides a simple, unambiguous definition of each salesperson's sales territory, and the proximity to customers encourages the development of personal relationships. A *product* structure might be effective where a company has a diverse product range selling to different customers (or at least different people within a given organization). A *customer-based* structure is where salesforces are organized on the basis of market segments, account sizes or new versus existing account lines. This structure enables salespeople to acquire in-depth knowledge of particular customer groups.

A growing form of customer-based salesforce organization is **key account management**, which reflects the increasing concentration of buying power into fewer but larger customers. These are serviced by a key account salesforce comprising senior salespeople who develop close personal relationships with customers, can handle sophisticated sales arguments and are skilled in the art of negotiation. A number of advantages are claimed for a key account structure, including that it enables close working relationships with customers, improved communication and co-ordination, better follow-up on sales and service, more in-depth penetration of the DMU, higher sales and the provision of an opportunity for advancement for career salespeople. The importance of effective salesforce management is illustrated in Marketing in Action 10.5.

Marketing in Action 10.5: Turnaround at HP

> **Study guide:** Below is a review of changes in the sales structure at Hewlett-Packard. Read it and identify the reasons why the new structure proved to be successful.

When Mark Hurd was appointed as chief executive officer of Hewlett-Packard (HP) in 2005, the giant technology company was floundering and suffering from problems caused by its takeover of the Compaq Computer Corporation. Its share price had been stagnating around the US$20 mark and it was facing intense competition from firms like Dell, who had pioneered the sale of low-price PCs. Coming from a sales background, Hurd believed that the future of the company was going to be determined by how effective the salesforce was, and he set about changing the sales operations at HP. His predecessor, Carly Fiorina, had set up a centralized sales structure with the goal of having just one salesperson or team handle each key account—a sort of one-stop shop. But HP sells the widest range of products to the widest range of customers in the information technology business so it became very difficult for one individual to represent the whole catalogue. And, because the salesforce was centralized, each product division had relatively little control over the sales process or the budget involved.

HP had a 17,000-strong salesforce. Hurd broke up this centralized sales team and dispersed it across HP's three main divisions: PCs, laptops and handheld devices; printers and printing; and IT solutions for large enterprises. Prior to the break-up, there were 11 administrative layers between order and fulfilment, meaning that responsiveness to customer queries was very slow. This has been reduced to six. Resources for sales training were increased through a programme called Sales Excellence, and new sales-enablement packages were introduced, aimed at reducing the desk work of each salesperson. Hurd had long been a believer that the salesperson's job is to sell and not be burdened by administrative duties. And HP introduced a new Total Customer experience programme, which measured promise fulfilment, adequate follow-up and customer support. The new sales structure also allowed for much clearer lines of responsibility, with division heads fully autonomous but also directly responsible for sales performance.

Within one year of Hurd's appointment, HP's profits were up by almost 30 per cent and its share price had risen to US$33. The quick turnaround in the company's fortunes was largely attributed to these changes in the sales structure.

Based on: Hosford (2006);[39] Lashinsky (2006)[40]

Managing the salesforce

The following elements are involved in salesforce management: setting specific salesperson objectives; recruitment and selection; training; **salesforce motivation** and compensation; and **salesforce evaluation**. These activities have been shown to improve salesperson performance, indicating the key role that sales managers play as facilitators, helping salespeople to perform better. Sales objectives are usually set in sales terms (sales quotas) but, increasingly, profit targets are being used, reflecting the need to guard against sales being bought cheaply by excessive discounting. The importance of recruiting high-calibre salespeople cannot be overestimated. A study into salesforce practice asked sales managers the following question: 'If you were to put your most successful salesperson into the territory of one of your average salespeople and made no other changes, what increase in sales would you expect after, say, two years?'[41] The most commonly stated increase was 16–20 per cent, and one-fifth of all sales managers said they would expect an increase of over 30 per cent. Based on extensive research, Mayer and Greenberg reduced the number of qualities believed to be important for effective selling to empathy and ego drive.[42] These are the kinds of qualities that need to be looked for in new salespeople.

It is believed by many sales managers that their salespeople can best train themselves by just doing the job. This approach ignores the benefits of a training programme, which can provide a frame of reference in which learning takes place. Training should include not only product knowledge, but also skills development. Success at selling comes when the skills are performed automatically, without consciously thinking about them, just as a tennis player or footballer succeeds.

A deep understanding of salespeople as individuals, their personalities and value systems, is the basis for effective motivation. Managers can motivate their sales staff by getting to know what each salesperson values and what they are striving for, increasing the responsibility given to salespeople in mundane jobs, providing targets that are attainable and challenging, and recognizing that rewards can be both financial and non-financial (e.g. praise). In terms of financial rewards, sales staff can be paid either a fixed salary, commission only, or on a salary-plus commission basis. Salaries provide security while commissions are an incentive to sell more as they are directly tied to sales levels. Great care must be taken in designing commission and bonus structures. For example, a Chrysler car dealership in the USA found that monthly sales for April were significantly down because salespeople who knew that they would not hit their targets for that month were encouraging customers to delay sales until May in hope of getting the May bonus.[43]

Salesforce evaluation gathers the information required to check whether targets are being achieved and provides raw information that will help guide training and motivation. By identifying the strengths and weakness of individual salespeople, training can be focused on the areas in need of development, and incentives can be aimed at weak spots such as poor prospecting performance. Often, performance will be measured on the basis of quantitative criteria such as sales revenues, profits generated or number of calls. However, it is also important to use qualitative criteria such as sales skills acquired, customer relationships, product knowledge and self-management.

Summary

This chapter has provided an overview of the direct communications techniques available to the marketer. In particular, the following issues were addressed.

1. The marketing database is the foundation upon which direct marketing campaigns are built. Databases can contain customer and prospect information, transactional information, product information, promotional information and geodemographic information. Technological developments have greatly assisted with database development.

2. Customer relationship management (CRM) is an outgrowth of database marketing and describes the use of technologies to build and foster relationships with customers. CRM aims to provide an up-to-date single point of view for each customer.

3. Direct marketing is a growing area where consumers are precisely targeted through a variety of different techniques including direct mail, telemarketing, mobile marketing, direct response

advertising and catalogue marketing. Direct marketing provides many advantages to companies, such as the ability to target customers directly, to run cost-effective campaigns and to allow the effectiveness of campaigns to be easily measurable.

4. The growth of the internet has facilitated the growth of novel business possibilities such as C2C enterprises. Internet-based businesses have four potential advantages over their offline rivals, namely lower costs and prices, superior customer service, greater product variety, and product customization.

5. Internet technologies allow for some very innovative ways of adapting the marketing mix to business problems such as customized products, permission and viral marketing, and user-generated content.

6. Buzz marketing is an emerging marketing tool that capitalizes on the importance of word-of-mouth promotion. Greater global electronic connectivity has fostered the rise of buzz marketing.

7. Personal selling plays an important role in the promotional mix and salespeople are required to develop a range of selling skills including preparing for the sale, opening the sale, identifying customer needs and problems, presenting and demonstrating, dealing with objections, closing the sale and following up. Sales management involves designing and managing a sales team.

Key terms

buzz marketing the passing of information about products or services by verbal or electronic means in an informal person-to-person manner

catalogue marketing the sale of products through catalogues distributed to agents and customers, usually by mail or at stores

customer benefits those things that a customer values in a product; customer benefits derive from product features (see separate entry)

customer relationship management (CRM) the methodologies, technologies and e-commerce capabilities used by firms to manage customer relationships

database marketing an interactive approach to marketing, which uses individually addressable marketing media and channels to provide information to a target audience, stimulate demand and stay close to customers

direct mail material sent through the postal service to the recipient's house or business address, promoting a product and/or maintaining an ongoing relationship

direct response advertising the use of the prime advertising media, such as television, newspapers and magazines, to elicit an order, enquiry or a request for a visit

e-commerce the use of technologies such as the internet, electronic data interchange (EDI), email and electronic payment systems to streamline business transactions

electronic data interchange (EDI) a pre-internet technology, which was developed to permit organizations to use linked computers for the rapid exchange of information

internet a vast global computer network that permits instant communication, such as the gathering and sharing of information, and that offers the facility for users to communicate with one another

internet marketing the achievement of marketing objectives through the utilization of the internet and web-based technologies

key account management an approach to selling that focuses resources on major customers and uses a team selling approach

mobile marketing the sending of text messages to mobile phones to promote products and build relationships with customers

permission marketing marketers ask permission before sending advertisements or promotional material to potential customers; in this way customers 'opt in' to the promotion rather than having to 'opt out'

personal selling oral communication with prospective purchasers with the intention of making a sale

product features the characteristics of a product that may or may not convey a customer benefit

prospecting searching for and calling upon potential customers

proximity marketing the localized wireless distribution of advertising content associated with a particular place

salesforce evaluation the measurement of salesperson performance so that strengths and weaknesses can be identified

salesforce motivation the motivation of salespeople by a process that involves needs, which set encouraging drives in motion to accomplish goals

telemarketing a marketing communications system whereby trained specialists use telecommunications and information technologies to conduct marketing and sales activities

viral marketing electronic word of mouth, where promotional messages are spread using email from person to person

website a collection of various files including text, graphics, video and audio content created by organizations and individuals

Study questions

1. Customer relationship management (CRM) is currently one of the 'hot topics' in marketing. What is meant by CRM and what role does it play in the organization?
2. Companies now have a variety of direct marketing media that they can consider when planning a direct marketing campaign. Compare and contrast any two direct marketing media. In your answer, give examples of the kinds of markets in which the media you have chosen might be useful.
3. Discuss the kinds of advantages an internet-based business might have over one that does not have an online presence.
4. Discuss the impact of the internet on each aspect of the marketing mix.
5. Salespeople are born, not made. Discuss.
6. Visit www.amazon.com and www.iTunes.com. Review these websites, and compare and contrast the marketing strategies employed by these global internet leaders.

Suggested reading

Economist (2005) Crowned At Last: A Survey of Consumer Power, 2 April, 3–16.

Jobber, D. and **G. Lancaster** (2009) *Selling and Sales Management*, 8th edn, Harlow: Pearson Education.

Godin, S. (2000) *Unleashing the Ideavirus*, New York: Do You Zoom Inc.

Kaikati, A.M. and **J.G. Kaikati** (2004) Stealth Marketing: How to Reach Customers Surreptitiously, *California Management Review*, **46** (4), 6–23.

Naissanoff, D. (2006) *Futureshop: How the New Auction Culture will Revolutionise the Way We Buy, Sell and Get The Things We Really Want*, London: Penguin Press.

Pepper, D. and **M. Rodgers** (2005) *Return on Customer*, New York: Random House.

Rigby, D.K. and **D. Ledingham** (2004) CRM done right, *Harvard Business Review*, **82** (11), 118–28.

Sargeant, A. and **D. West** (2001) *Direct and Interactive Marketing*, Oxford: Oxford University Press.

References

1. **Anonymous** (2004) Manchester United Aims to Expand New Media Use, *New Media Age*, 30 September, 4; **McCosker, P.** (2004) Manchester United: The Transformation of a Football Club into a Global Brand, European Case Clearing House, 304-178-1; **Mortimer, R.** (2003) Footie we Play, United we Brand, *Brand Strategy*, January, 18–20.
2. **Stone, M., D. Davies** and **A. Bond** (1995) *Direct Hit: Direct Marketing with a Winning Edge*, London: Pitman.
3. **Harvey, F.** (2003) They Know What You Like, *Financial Times*, Creative Business, 6 May, 4.

4. **London, S.** (2004) Choked by a Data Surfeit, *Financial Times*, 29 January, 17.

5. **Nancarrow, C., L.T. Wright** and **J. Page** (1997) Seagram Europe and Africa: The Development of a Consumer Database Marketing Capability, *Proceedings of the Academy of Marketing*, July, Manchester, 1119–30.

6. **Turow, J.** (2008) *Niche Envy: Marketing Discrimination in the Digital Age*, Boston MA: MIT.

7. **Murphy, C.** (2002) Catching up with its Glitzier Cousin, *Financial Times*, 24 July, 13.

8. **Foss, B.** and **M. Stone** (2001) *Successful Customer Relationship Marketing*, London: Kogan Page.

9. See **Ryals, L., S. Knox,** and **S. Maklan** (2002) *Customer Relationship Management: Building the Business Case*, London: FT Prentice-Hall; **H. Wilson, E. Daniel** and **M. McDonald** (2002) Factors for Success in Customer Relationship Management Systems, *Journal of Marketing Management*, **18** (1/2), 193–200.

10. **North, B.** (1995) Consumer Companies Take Direct Stance, *Marketing*, 20 May, 24–5.

11. **Curtis, J.** (2003) Down, But a Bit Up, *Financial Times*, Creative Business, 15 April, 4–5.

12. **Elgie, D.** (2003) A is for Ad Agency Angst . . . , *Financial Times*, Creative Business, 6 May, 11.

13. **Brown, J.M.** (2006) Pinpoint Aim Brings Success for Perlico, *Financial Times*, 24 November, 10.

14. **Hancock, C.** (2007) Vodafone to Acquire Perlico, *Irish Times*, 14 November, 18.

15. **Clegg, A.** (2000) Hit or Miss, *Marketing Week*, 13 January, 45–9.

16. **Benady, D.** (2001) If Undelivered, *Marketing Week*, 20 December, 31–3.

17. **McHatton, N.R.** (1988) *Total Telemarketing*, New York: Wiley, 269.

18. **Carter, M.** (2007) Hey! It's Your Virtual Call Operator, *Financial Times*, 19 January, 10.

19. **Stevens, M.** (1993) A Telephony Revolution, *Marketing*, 16 September, 38.

20. **Anonymous** (2007) Mobile Advertising: The Next Big Thing, *Economist*, 6 October, 67.

21. **Smith, G.** (2008) Upwardly Mobile, *Marketing Age*, January/February, 20–6.

22. **Starkey, M.** (1997) Telemarketing, in D. Jobber (ed.) *The CIM Handbook of Selling and Sales Strategy*, Oxford: Butterworth-Heinemann, 130.

23. **McCann, G.** (2003) Just Like Members of the Family, *Financial Times*, 15 January, 13.

24. **Anonymous** (2007) GMTV Hit with £2m Phone-in Fine, *bbc.co.uk*, 26 September.

25. **Martin, N.** (2007) Ofcom Fines GMTV £2m in Phone-in Row, *Telegraph.co.uk*, 27 September.

26. **Pepper, D.** and **M. Rogers** (1997) *The One to One Future: Building Relationships One Customer at a Time*, New York: Doubleday.

27. **Davoudi, S.** (2005) From Brand Leader to Struggler in Eight Years, *Financial Times*, 17 June, 24.

28. **Anonymous** (2005) Profiting from Obscurity, *Economist*, 7 May, 73.

29. **Smith, G.** and **A. O'Dea** (2007) Word of Mouse, *Marketing Age*, Autumn, 20–6.

30. **Anonymous** (2003) EU Rules to Outlaw Spam, *Marketing Business*, May.

31. **Anonymous** (2008) The Case of the Missing Clicks, *Economist*, April 5, 65.

32. **Gapper, J.** (2006) Search Engines are Not the Only Sites, *Financial Times*, 6 March, 19.

33. **Smith, G.** (2007) The Search is On, *Marketing Age*, Summer, 30–32.

34. **Thompson, C.** (2004) Search Engines Invite New Problems, *Marketing Management*, **13** (2), 52–3.

35. **Waters, R.** (2004) Billboards on the Superhighway, *Financial Times*, 3 December, 17.

36. **Grande, C.** (2007) iPhone Presents a Test Case for Media Buyers, *Financial Times*, 30 January, 22.

37. **Weitz, B.A.** (1981) Effectiveness in Sales Interactions: A Contingency Framework, *Journal of Marketing*, 45, 85–103.

38. **Talley, W.J.** (1961) How to Design Sales Territories, *Journal of Marketing*, **25** (3), 16–28.

39. **Hosford, C.** (2006) Rebooting Hewlett-Packard, *Sales & Marketing Management*, **58** (6), 32–6.

40. **Lashinsky, A.** (2006) The Hurd Way: How a Sales-obsessed CEO Rebooted HP, *Fortune*, **153** (7), 91–6.

41. **PA Consultants** (1979) *Sales Force Practice Today: A Basis for Improving Performance*, Cookham: Institute of Marketing.

42. **Mayer, M.** and **G. Greenberg** (1964) What Makes a Good Salesman, *Harvard Business Review*, **42** (July/August), 119–25.

43. **Griffith, V.** (2001) Targets that Distort a Company's Aim, *Financial Times*, 21 November, 18.

When you have read this chapter, log on to the Online Learning Centre for *Foundations of Marketing* at **www.mcgraw-hill.co.uk/textbooks/jobber**, where you'll find multiple-choice test questions, links and extra online study tools for marketing.

Case 10 Red Bull's innovative marketing: transforming a humdrum product into a happening brand

The energy drink brand Red Bull was launched in Austria in 1987. In just 20 years it has gone on to become a global best-selling beverage brand, recording sales in excess of US$2 billion. It is sold in over 100 countries, and the company, headquartered in Salzburg, Austria, employs over 1800 people. Much of the success of Red Bull is down to its unique marketing and promotional strategies.

Background

Dietrich Mateschitz was born in 1944 in Austria, and after graduating with a degree from the University of Commerce in Vienna, he took up marketing jobs at Unilever and Jacobs Coffee before becoming the international director for marketing at Blendax, a German company that dealt in fmcg products like toothpaste, skin creams and shampoos. His job involved a lot of travel around the world, and during one of his trips to Thailand, he discovered an 'energy drink' called Krating Daeng, which was very popular among blue-collar workers in the country. When he sampled it, Mateschitz reportedly discovered that the drink was good at combating jetlag. The idea for marketing an energy drink in Western markets came when he realized that energy drinks had a huge market in Asia and that there was no such product available in Europe.

He approached Chaleo Yoovidhya, the owner of TC Pharmaceuticals, which made Krating Daeng, with a proposal to market the beverage in Europe. Yoovidhya agreed to give Mateschitz the foreign licensing rights to the drink in return for a partnership in the venture. In 1984, Mateschitz resigned from his job to pursue his new business and changed the beverage's name to 'Red Bull' to make it more suitable for Western markets. He also modified the beverage but retained its core ingredients of caffeine, glucuronolactone and taurine, and packaged it in a slim, blue-and-silver can instead of the bottles that were used in Thailand. Before the launch in Europe, a marketing research firm was hired to test the market for energy drinks. The results showed that consumers neither liked the taste nor the name but Mateschitz chose to ignore the findings and launch the product anyway. One of his friends coined the slogan 'Red Bull gives you wings', which became the theme of the company's promotional campaigns.

A major obstacle to the launch of Red Bull was regulatory approval. Red Bull contained several ingredients that had not been used in European markets before. Austria was the first to grant approval, in 1987, and this was followed by launches in Hungary, the United Kingdom (UK), Slovenia, Germany and Switzerland in the early 1990s. Its main target market was young urban professionals, who often put in long hours at work, and weekend revellers who wished to party all night. By 1990, almost four million cans of Red Bull had been sold in Austria.

Elements of Red Bull's marketing strategy

Red Bull was generally acknowledged by marketing experts to be a good example of an ordinary product of uncertain worth that was transformed into a powerful brand through innovative marketing. The emphasis Red Bull placed on marketing was evident from the fact that the company spent around 30 per cent of its annual turnover on marketing—much higher than most other beverage manufacturers, which spent approximately 10 per cent.

Red Bull was positioned as an energy drink that 'invigorated mind and body' and 'improved endurance levels'. The beverage was targeted at people who sought increased endurance, speed, concentration and alertness. However, despite the company's claims, nutritional experts declared that the product had no ingredients that could confer actual benefits, other than providing an instant 'kick' after consumption. This is because the quantities of caffeine and sugar in Red Bull are almost twice those found in other soft drinks, such as Coca-Cola.

According to scientists, sugar and caffeine are absorbed by the human body immediately, and this is what gives a sudden surge of energy. A similar effect could be obtained by drinking extra-strong sweetened coffee. According to the American Dietetic Association (ADA), there was no evidence that Red Bull, or any other energy drink, could have a restorative effect on a tired mind and body.

From the start, Red Bull's marketing strategy was unconventional. When the drink was first launched in

Austria, Mateschitz understood that its target market in Europe would have to be different from its blue-collar market in Asia. In Europe, coffee was the preferred 'pick-me-up' used by all classes of people. However, Mateschitz was confident that he would be able to create a market around hip, young urban professionals and students who would be open to a new 'cool' alternative to coffee. Red Bull dispensed with traditional modes of advertising to make effective use of buzz marketing in promoting the beverage to the target market.

When Red Bull first entered a new market, the company's salespeople provided free cases of the drink to influential, trend-setting college students, and encouraged them to throw a party for their classmates and friends. The idea was that once the product had been tried out by the target group, it would be easier to establish in the market. This strategy allowed Red Bull to gain immediate acceptance among the college-going crowd as a cool and happening beverage. It also built its reputation as a party drink for people who needed the energy to party all night.

According to marketing experts, 'Generation Y' (people born after 1981) was generally sceptical of traditional marketing and, consequently, traditional modes of advertising have little impact on them. Red Bull's grassroots marketing helped it cut through the clutter effectively. The company was able to get its message across to the target market without being too 'obvious' about it. Using students to market the product to other young people gave it instant credibility in that consumer age group. Cool college students became Red Bull's best ambassadors because they carried the most credibility with cynical consumers.

The company also ensured that it chose people who were young, athletic and stylish to be its brand ambassadors, to enhance its image in the market. In addition to sponsoring student parties, Red Bull employed 'consumer educators' to get its message across to the general public. Consumer educators were the company's sales representatives, who frequented public places like beaches, exhibitions and meetings where young people congregated, and gave away free samples of the beverage. Additionally, they distributed promotional material about the product, and answered any questions people might have about Red Bull.

Red Bull also developed the Mobile Energy Team (MET) programme, where students drove around in cars and pick-up trucks, and distributed free cans of the beverage 'where energy was needed'. These vehicles were painted blue and silver—the colours of Red Bull—and had an oversize Red Bull can strapped on the back or top. These 'Racers', as they were called, created tremendous visibility for the company, and helped underscore Red Bull's image as a youthful and hip brand.

Red Bull was also widely available near gyms and colleges, and was aggressively marketed to bartenders and bar owners. If it was not possible to retail through convenience stores in the selected region, the sales reps opened kiosks to sell the drink. The company also advertised in *Wipeout 2*, a game on the Sony PlayStation, by putting the name of the drink on virtual billboards that flashed by as a player drove around on the virtual racetracks in the game. 'We don't bring the product to the people. We bring people to the product. We make it available and those who love our style come to us,' said Mateschitz about Red Bull's promotions.

When Red Bull first entered a market, the company's sales reps tied up with distributors in key locations (near colleges, gyms, etc.). Initially, the company paid for the distributors' promotional and advertising costs, and also bore the cost of the samples distributed, for a period of around three months. Once Red Bull established its presence in the region, the company gradually phased out this support. Red Bull usually attempted to establish an 'exclusive' network of distributors in each of its markets. After it gained a foothold in a new market, the company generally insisted that the distributors carry only Red Bull and no other beverage, even if the other beverages were not direct competitors.

Once Red Bull gained a foothold in the market and the distribution network was established, the company embarked on the promotional activities that were to supplement the grassroots marketing efforts. Sports sponsorships formed the core of Red Bull's marketing strategy. The company primarily associated itself with extreme alternative sports, and sponsored and organized sporting activities like kayaking, hang-gliding, rough-terrain biking, cliff diving and skateboarding. However, it also sponsored mainstream sports and owned several sporting teams, such as the Austrian football team, SV Austria Salzburg, which it renamed Red Bull Salzburg.

One of the sports with which the brand was most closely associated was motor racing. The company sponsored several racing events as well as teams around the world. Some of the motoring events sponsored by Red Bull were the Champ Car World Series, and World Rally Championship. Red Bull was also closely associated with F1 racing. The company entered the F1 arena through its sponsorship of the Sauber team in 1995, when it bought a 64 per cent stake in the holding company that owned the team. In November 2004, when Ford announced its decision to exit F1 after a major restructuring programme, Red Bull bought the company's Jaguar Racing F1 team for an undisclosed amount. Soon after the purchase, Jaguar was renamed Red Bull Racing.

By early 2006, Red Bull was estimated to have captured a market share of roughly 70 per cent in the global energy drinks market. It also commanded a 47 per cent market share in the USA, one of its major markets in early 2006, and sales had been growing at a rate of 40 per cent every year from the time it was launched in the country in 1997. Despite its premium pricing strategy, Red Bull sales were higher than those for other drinks like beer, water and soda in certain convenience stores. A unique feature of Red Bull's marketing was that the company sold the beverage in only one size: the 250 ml (8.3 oz) can. The exterior of the can was silver and blue and carried a picture of two charging red bulls. The can's smaller-than-normal size also reinforced the feeling that the beverage was a 'concentrated experience'.

Red Bull used conventional advertising media like print and television only when the market was thought to have matured. Traditional advertisements were used to reinforce the brand rather than to introduce it to a target market. Red Bull created two television advertisements a year for its mature global markets. The advertisements were usually animated and had quirky themes. Most of the advertisements featured people sprouting wings and flying after drinking Red Bull.

New challenges

However, despite its success with Red Bull, the company was unable to successfully extend its product line. The Red Bull beverage continued to be the main product sold, although a sugar-free version was introduced in 2003 with limited success. It is a brand that has also been mired in many controversies. Because of the lack of research on the impact of its ingredients, it is banned in France and Denmark, and sold only in pharmacies in Norway. Its use as a mixer with alcohol and its availability for consumption by children in some countries have also been sources of controversy.

In addition, there are several threats to the brand's long-term prospects. It has spawned a range of imitators, all wanting to cash in on the booming energy

drinks market. Some of the knock-offs even have names that evoke the Red Bull brand—Red Tiger and American Bull being notable examples. Major beverage companies like Coke, Pepsi and the beer company Anheuser-Busch have also come out with new energy drinks: Coke and Pepsi launched KMX and AMP respectively, while Anheuser-Busch launched 180 in the early 2000s. Overall, it was estimated that, by 2005, there were 125 players in the energy drinks market in the USA.

Many of Red Bull's competitors had introduced energy drinks in multiple flavours like cranberry, orange, lime and cola, among others. The reasoning was that energy drinks would find more buyers if they were offered in a variety of familiar tastes. Considering that Red Bull did not taste very good, this was a major threat to the company. Another limiting factor in Red Bull's long-term success was the nature of the company's target market. Red Bull's main market consisted of college students and young urban professionals. It was not clear whether the company would be able to retain these customers as they grew older.

By the early 2000s, Red Bull had become as ubiquitous as Coke and Pepsi in convenience stores and other retail outlets. With this ubiquity, Red Bull also faced the danger of diluting its 'coolness' factor, by losing its exclusivity and its identification with a specific group of customers. Growing health-consciousness among consumers was another factor that could potentially affect the brand's fate.

Subtlety was the key to a successful buzz marketing strategy, and Red Bull was one of the few companies that managed to execute such a strategy successfully. It was thought that a major part of Red Bull's success came about because, as a private company, Red Bull GmbH had the flexibility to take risks and market its product in ways that many publicly held companies could not. This had helped Red Bull create a successful brand around a rather pedestrian product of questionable merit. However, it remained to be seen whether Red Bull was a fad that would soon disappear.

Questions

1. Evaluate the elements of buzz marketing used in the successful launch of the Red Bull brand. Why were they effective?

2. Evaluate the role of the company's salespeople in building the brand.

3. Compare and contrast the roles played by direct communications techniques and mass communications techniques in the brand's marketing strategy.

4. Advise the company on the promotional strategies it should use to meet the new competitive challenges that it faces in the market.

This case was written by Shirisha Regani, under the direction of S.S. George, ICFAI Center for Management Research (ICMR). It was compiled from published sources and is intended to be used as a basis for class discussion rather than to illustrate either effective or ineffective handling of a management situation. © 2006, The ICFAI Center for Management Research.

Chapter 11
Distribution Management

Learning Outcomes

By the end of this chapter you will understand:

1. the different types of distribution channel for consumer goods, industrial products and services
2. the three components of channel strategy—channel selection, intensity and integration
3. the five key channel management issues—member selection, motivation, training, evaluation and conflict management
4. the key retailing management decisions
5. the components of a physical distribution system—customer service, order processing, inventory control, warehousing, transportation and materials handling.

Multichannel marketing

Video games have been one of the major growth industries in consumer electronics in the past two decades, and a well publicized hardware battle has been fought out between Sony, Microsoft and Nintendo. But the marketing of computer game software also highlights some interesting challenges. Top-of-the-range games can be expensive to produce, costing anything up to €15 million euro. Then, once they are launched on the market, they have a relatively short timeframe of a few months to prove their popularity before their place is taken by new competing games.

A key question for game developers, then, is what is the best way to distribute their products from the array of possibilities open to them in order to maximize the return on their investment? To date, most games are sold in consumer electronics retail chains, music shops and specialist game stores, but these outlets are limited in the titles they can carry and need to constantly refresh this stock in order to maximize their own profitability. Shelf space is precious and slow-selling items are quickly deleted. Games may disappear before they have had a chance to recoup their producers' investment. However, digital distribution offers publishers the opportunity to overcome many of these problems. Games can be made available on either a direct, pay-per-download service or on the basis of a subscription service. The advantage of digital distribution is that publishers can make available a much wider back catalogue of games, and specialist segments of the market, like AO (adult only) games, can be catered for.

When companies choose to employ multiple channels of distribution (multichannel marketing), some fundamental challenges arise. Can they employ digital channels without alienating their existing 'bricks and mortar' retailers? Video games are much cheaper to distribute online so should they sell for a lower price on the internet? Because of the short life span of most games these are important questions for publishers and retailers. Offline games retailers need only to look at the problems suffered by music stores like HMV to see the damage that can be done when consumers switch to digital consumption of products.

In the short term, the distribution of video games is likely to be similar to that for movies. Most games will be sold in physical stores first and then through digital channels, in the same way that movies move from cinema, to physical DVD sales, to digital download. But, over time, this model may be unsustainable as consumers shift a greater portion of their spending to the convenience offered by digital consumption. Video games buyers are primarily young males who are comfortable with technology. Retailers will have to examine how they can get part of that business by offering consumers the opportunity to download games in-store. They may even learn from the experience of coffee chains like Starbucks, which offers digital downloading of music as part of its 'customer experience'. The distribution channel for video games, like that for many products, is in a state of flux, driven by technological and consumer changes.[1]

Necessary, but not sufficient, conditions for customer satisfaction are: producing products that customers want, pricing them correctly and developing well-designed promotional plans. The final part of the jigsaw is distribution, the 'place' element of the marketing mix. Products need to be available in adequate quantities, in convenient locations and at times when customers want to buy them. In this chapter we will examine the functions and types of distribution channel, the key decisions that determine channel strategy, how to manage channels, the nature of retailing and issues relating to the physical flow of goods through distribution channels (physical distribution management).

Producers need to consider the requirements of **channel intermediaries**—those organizations that facilitate the distribution of products to customers—as well as the needs of their ultimate customers. For example, success for Müller yoghurt in the UK was dependent on convincing a powerful retail group (Tesco) to stock the brand. The high margins that the brand supported were a key influence in Tesco's decision. Without retailer support, Müller would have found it uneconomic to supply consumers with its brand. Clearly, establishing a supply chain that is efficient and meets customers' needs is vital to marketing success. This supply chain is termed a **channel of distribution**, and is the means by which products are moved from the producer to the ultimate customer. Gaining access to distribution outlets is not necessarily easy. For example, in the consumer food products sector, many brands vie with each other for prime positions on supermarket shelves.

An important aspect of marketing strategy is choosing the most effective channel of distribution. The development of supermarkets effectively shortened the distribution channel between producer and consumer by eliminating the wholesaler. Prior to their introduction, the typical distribution channel for products like food, drink, tobacco and toiletries was producer to wholesaler to retailer. The wholesaler would buy in bulk from the producer and sell smaller quantities to the retailer (typically a small grocery shop). By building up buying power, supermarkets could shorten this chain by buying direct from producers. This meant lower costs to the supermarket chain and lower prices to the consumer. The competitive effect of this was to drastically reduce the numbers of small grocers and wholesalers in this market. By being more efficient and better at meeting customers' needs, supermarkets had created a competitive advantage for themselves. In the same way, the more recent success of online music distribution companies is presenting a major challenge to leading retail chains like Tower Records and HMV.

We will now explore the different types of channel that manufacturers use to supply their products to customers, and the types of function provided by these channel intermediaries.

Types of distribution channel

Whether they be consumer goods, business-to-business goods or services, all products require a channel of distribution. Industrial channels tend to be shorter than consumer channels because of the small number of ultimate customers, the greater geographic concentration of industrial customers and the greater complexity of the products that require close producer/customer liaison. Service channels also tend to be short because of the inseparability of the production and consumption of many services.

Consumer channels

Figure 11.1 shows four alternative consumer channels. We will now look briefly at each one in turn.

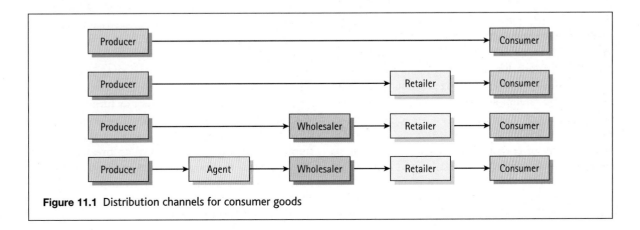

Figure 11.1 Distribution channels for consumer goods

Exhibit 11.1 The most traditional form of marketing, the farmers' market, is making a comeback due to concerns about food quality and the environment

Producer direct to consumer

This option may be attractive to producers because it cuts out distributors' profit margins. Direct selling between producer and consumer has long been a feature of the marketing of many products, ranging from the sale of fruit in local markets to the sale of Avon Cosmetics and Tupperware plastic containers. It is a form of distribution that is starting to grow rapidly again. Concerns over food quality in supermarkets and a growing market for organic foods have seen a rapid rise in farmers' markets in Europe (see Exhibit 11.1). And of course, in the past decade or so, the internet has been the great new direct distribution medium for products ranging from books and music to DVDs to air travel, and so on. This has had huge implications for traditional retailers like book shops, music shops and travel agents, many of whom have suffered falling sales or have ceased trading.

Producer to retailer to consumer

For a variety of reasons, a producer may choose to distribute products via a retailer to consumers. Retailers provide the basic service of enabling consumers to view a wide assortment of products under one roof, while manufacturers continue to gain eco-

nomies of scale from the bulk production of a limited number of items. For many people, retailing is the public face of marketing, and large out-of-town shopping centres have become popular venues for consumers to spend their leisure time. As we shall see later in the chapter, retailers have become increasingly sophisticated in their operations and dominate many distribution channels. For example, supermarket chains exercise considerable power over manufacturers because of their enormous buying capabilities, and have been expanding into other areas of retailing like financial services, music distribution, and so on.

Producer to wholesaler to retailer to consumer

The use of wholesalers makes economic sense for small retailers (e.g. small grocery or furniture shops) with limited order quantities. Wholesalers can buy in bulk from producers, and sell smaller quantities to numerous retailers (this is known as 'breaking bulk'). The danger is that large retailers in the same market have the power to buy directly from producers and thus cut out the wholesaler. In certain cases, the buying power of large retailers has meant that they can sell products to their customers more cheaply than a small retailer can buy from the wholesaler. Longer channels like this tend to occur where retail oligopolies do not dominate the distribution system. In some Asian countries, like Japan, distribution channels can involve up to two and three tiers of wholesalers who supply the myriad small shops and outlets that serve Japanese customers.[2]

Producer to agent to wholesaler to retailer to consumer

This is a long channel, sometimes used by companies entering foreign markets, which may delegate the task of selling the product to an agent (who does not take title to the goods). The agent contacts local wholesalers (or retailers) and receives a commission on sales. Companies entering new export markets often organize their distribution systems in this way.

Business-to-business channels

Common business-to-business distribution channels are illustrated in Figure 11.2. A maximum of one channel intermediary is used under normal circumstances.

Producer to industrial customer

Supplying business customers direct is common practice for expensive business-to-business products such as gas turbines, diesel locomotives, and aero-engines. There needs to be close liaison between supplier and customer to solve technical problems, and the size of the order makes direct selling and distribution economic.

Producer to agent to business customer

Instead of selling to business customers using their own salesforce, a business-to-business goods company could employ the services of an agent who may sell a range of goods from several suppliers (on a commission basis). This spreads selling costs and may be attractive to those companies that lack the reserves to set up their own sales operations. The disadvantage is that there is little control over the agent, who is unlikely to devote the same amount of time selling these products as a dedicated sales team.

Producer to distributor to business customer

For less expensive, more frequently bought business-to-business products, distributors are used; these may have both internal and field sales staff.[3] Internal staff deal with customer-generated enquiries and order placing, order follow-up (often using the telephone) and checking inventory levels. Outside sales staff are more proactive; their practical responsibilities are to find new customers, get products specified, distribute catalogues and gather market information. The advantage to customers of using distributors is that they can buy small quantities locally.

Producer to agent to distributor to business customer

Where business customers prefer to call upon distributors, the agent's job will require selling into these intermediaries. The reason why a producer may employ an agent rather than a dedicated salesforce is usually cost-based (as previously discussed).

Services channels

Distribution channels for services are usually short, either direct or via an agent (see Figure 11.3). Since stocks are not held, the role of the wholesaler, retailer or industrial distributor does not apply.

Service provider to consumer or business customer

The close personal relationships between service providers and customers often means that service supply is direct. Examples include healthcare, office cleaning, accountancy, marketing research and law.

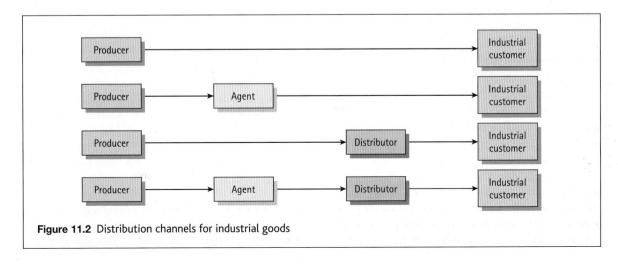

Figure 11.2 Distribution channels for industrial goods

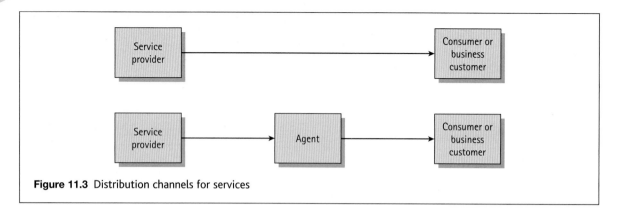

Figure 11.3 Distribution channels for services

Service provider to agent to consumer or business customer

A channel intermediary for a service company usually takes the form of an agent. Agents are used when the service provider is geographically distant from customers, and where it is not economical for the provider to establish their own local sales team. Examples include insurance, travel, secretarial and theatrical agents.

Channel strategy and management

The design of the distribution channel is an important strategic decision that needs to be integrated with other marketing mix decisions. For example, products that are being positioned as upmarket, premium items are usually only available in a select number of stores. **Channel strategy** decisions involve the selection of the most effective distribution channel, the most appropriate level of distribution intensity and the degree of channel integration. Once the key channel strategy decisions have been made, effective implementation is required. Channel management decisions involve the selection, motivation, training and evaluation of channel members, and managing conflict between producers and channel members.

Channel selection

Ask yourself why Procter & Gamble sells its brands through supermarkets rather than selling direct. Why does General Motors sell its locomotives direct to train operating companies rather than use a distributor? The answers are to be found by examining the following factors that influence channel selection. These influences can be grouped under the headings of market, producer, product and competitive factors.

Market factors

Buyer behaviour is an important market factor; buyer expectations may dictate that a product be sold in a certain way. Buyers may prefer to buy locally and in a particular type of shop. Failure to match these expectations can have catastrophic consequences, as illustrated by the experience of music retailers, who continue to struggle as more and more consumers switch to digital downloading.

The geographical concentration and location of customers also affects channel selection. The more local and clustered the customer base, the more likely it is that direct distribution will be feasible. Direct distribution is also more prevalent when buyers are few in number and buy large quantities such as in many industrial markets. A large number of small customers may mean that using channel intermediaries is the only economical way of reaching them (hence supermarkets). Buyers' needs regarding product information, installation and technical assistance also have to be considered. For example, products that require facilities for local servicing, such as cars, often use intermediaries to carry out the task.

Producer factors

When a producer lacks adequate resources to perform the functions of the channel, this places a constraint on the channel decision. Producers may lack the financial and managerial resources to take on channel operations. Lack of financial resources may mean that a salesforce cannot be recruited and sales agents and/or distributors are used instead. Producers may feel that they do not possess the customer-based skills to distribute their products, and prefer to rely on intermediaries instead.

The desired degree of control of channel operations also influences the selection of channel members. The use of independent channel intermediaries reduces producer control. For example, by distributing their products through supermarkets, manufacturers lose total control of the price charged to consumers. Furthermore, there is no guarantee that new products will be stocked. Direct distribution gives producers control over such issues.

Finally, an important decision for producers is whether they want to push their product through the channel or rather market to the end consumer, who then 'pulls' the product through the channel. The former requires investing heavily in trade support to ensure that products are carried and given desired shelf space. The latter means that marketing is targeted at the end user, who through their demand for the product, ensures that it is carried by middlemen. This has raised important ethical issues in the medical profession because of the increased consumer advertising of products by pharmaceutical companies. By building well-known brands like Viagra, Prozac and Vioxx, pharmaceutical companies have been accused of driving consumers to demand products that are not always necessary, in effect pulling them through the channel despite possible objections by medical practitioners. For example, the US drug firms Merck and Schering-Plough have been embroiled in controversy since a study concluded that their joint cholesterol drug, Vytorin, is no more effective than generic versions costing a third of its price. The drug had been aggressively marketed by these two companies.[4]

Product factors

Large and/or complex products are often supplied direct to the customer. The need for close personal contact between producer and customer, and the high prices charged, mean that direct distribution and selling is both necessary and feasible. Perishable products, such as frozen food, meat and bread, require relatively short channels to supply the customer with fresh stock. Bulky or difficult to handle products may require direct distribution because distributors may refuse to carry them if storage or display problems arise.[5] Finally, as noted in the previous chapter, where a product can be digitized this facilitates its direct distribution.

Competitive factors

An innovative approach to distribution may be required if competitors control traditional channels of distribution—for example, through franchise or exclusive dealing arrangements. Two available alternatives are to recruit a salesforce to sell direct or to set up a producer-owned distribution network (see the information about administered vertical marketing systems, a topic discussed later in this chapter under the heading 'Conventional marketing channels'). Producers should not accept that the channels of distribution used by competitors are the only ways to reach target customers. Direct marketing provides opportunities to supply products in new ways, as many online companies have shown. For example, traditional channels of distribution for personal computers through high-street retailers were circumvented by direct marketers such as Dell, which used direct-response advertising to reach buyers. The emergence of the more computer-aware and experienced buyer, and the higher reliability of these products as the market reached maturity meant that a local source of supply (and advice) was less important. However, by pursuing this strategy, Dell was not as effective in reaching corporate customers as some of its major competitors, which continued to use computer resellers. In a break with tradition, Dell announced in 2007 that it was broadening its business model to include computer resellers for the business market as well as Wal-Mart to reach the consumer market in the USA.

Distribution intensity

The choice of distribution intensity is the second channel strategy decision. The three broad options are intensive, selective and exclusive distribution. We will look at each of these now.

Intensive distribution

By using all available outlets, **intensive distribution** aims to provide saturation coverage of the market. With many mass-market products, such as snacks, foods, toiletries, beer and newspapers, sales are a direct function of the number of outlets penetrated. This is because consumers have a range of acceptable brands from which they choose and, very often, the decision to purchase is made on impulse. If a brand is not available in an outlet, an alternative is bought. The convenience aspect of purchase is paramount. New outlets may be sought that hitherto had not stocked the products, such as the sale of alcoholic drinks and grocery items at petrol stations.

Selective distribution

Selective distribution also enables market coverage to be achieved. In this case, a producer uses a limited number of outlets in a geographical area to sell its products (see Marketing in Action 11.1). The advantages to the producer are: the opportunity to select only the best outlets to focus its efforts on building close working relationships, to train distributor staff on fewer outlets than with intensive distribution, and, if selling and distribution is direct, to reduce costs. Upmarket aspirational brands like Hugo Boss and Raymond

Weil are often sold in carefully selected outlets (see Exhibit 11.2). Retail outlets and industrial distributors like this arrangement since it reduces competition. Selective distribution is more likely to be used when buyers are willing to shop around when choosing products. This means that it is not necessary for a company to have its products available in all outlets. Products such as audio and video equipment, cameras, clothing and cosmetics may be sold in this way.

Problems can arise when a retailer demands distribution rights but is refused by producers. This happened in the case of Superdrug, a UK discount store chain that requested the right to sell expensive perfume but was denied by manufacturers, which claimed that its stores did not have the right ambience for the sale of luxury products. Superdrug maintained that its application was refused solely because it wanted to sell perfumes for less than their recommended prices. A Monopolies and Mergers Commission investigation supported current practice. European rules allow perfume companies to confine distribution to retailers who measure up in terms of décor and staff training. Manufacturers are not permitted to refuse distribution rights on the grounds that the retailer will sell for less than the list price.[6]

Marketing in Action 11.1: Tyrell's takes a different route to market

Study guide: Below is a review of the distribution strategy used by Tyrell's Potato Chips. Read it and consider the role of distribution in the successful launch of this new brand.

Tyrell's Potato Chips is an example of a company whose distribution choices have helped it on the road to success. It was founded in 2002 by William Chase and born out of his frustration in supplying large supermarkets with the produce from his family farm. In dealing with the supermarkets, he had found that they were constantly pressing him for discounts and better deals, and that he was essentially selling commodity products with little differentiation from other suppliers. To reduce his dependence on this channel, he developed the Tyrell's crisps range, to be sold as a premium product. Products are made from home-grown potatoes and the diverse range include niche crisps like those that are gluten-free, and Halal and Kosher-compliant.

A decision was made from the beginning to sell directly to specialist retailers where possible. Exclusive shops such as Harrods, Fortnum & Mason and Harvey Nichols were targeted first, which also helped to give the brand a premium image. Distribution was then rolled out to community-based stores such as Budgens and local co-operatives. The only major supermarket that carries the range is Waitrose; an approach by Sainsbury's to distribute the brand nationally was rejected. The majority of Tyrell's customers are independent caterers such as delicatessens, sandwich shops and some chains, such as Costa Coffee and Pret A Manger. A fleet of Tyrell's vehicles is used to deliver products to outlets within a 90-mile radius of the Tyrell's factory and third-party carriers are used for longer deliveries. By using this selective distribution strategy, Tyrell's crisps are not as widely available as they could be but the brand has a premium image and profit margins in the region of 35 per cent are relatively high for this type of business.

To grow the company without resorting to mass distribution in the UK, Tyrell's has focused on the international market, with about 20 per cent of its sales coming from exports predominantly to France, where the brand is sold in top food halls such as La Grande Epicerie de Paris. However, this international expansion means that Tyrell's must deal with distributors, which introduces an additional player into the distribution channel and does not allow it to build up the kind of relationship with customers abroad that it has been able to achieve in the UK. Though Tyrell's was a latecomer to the crisps business that has entrenched competitors like Walkers, it has been successful because it carefully differentiated its product range and was selective in how it distributed its products.

Based on: Clegg (2005)[7]

Exhibit 11.2 Leading brands like Patek Philippe are selectively distributed

Exclusive distribution

Exclusive distribution is an extreme form of selective distribution in which only one wholesaler, retailer or business-to-business distributor is used in a particular geographic area. Cars are often sold on this basis, with only one dealer operating in each town or city. This reduces a purchaser's power to negotiate prices for the same model between dealers, since to buy in a neighbouring town may be inconvenient when servicing or repairs are required. It also allows very close co-operation between producer and retailer over servicing, pricing and promotion. The right to **exclusive distribution** may be demanded by distributors as a condition for stocking a manufacturer's product line. Similarly, producers may wish for exclusive dealing where the distributor agrees not to stock competing lines.

Exclusive distribution arrangements can restrict competition in a way that may be detrimental to consumer interests. The European Court of Justice rejected an appeal by Unilever over the issue of exclusive outlets in Germany. By supplying freezer cabinets, Unilever maintained exclusivity by refusing to allow competing ice creams into its cabinets.[8] How-ever, the European Court rejected an appeal by the French Leclerc supermarket group over the issue of the selective distribution system used by Yves Saint Laurent perfumes. The judges found that the use of selective distribution for luxury cosmetic products increased competition and that it was in the consumer's and manufacturer's interests to preserve the image of such luxury products.

Channel integration

Channel integration can range from conventional marketing channels—comprising an independent producer and channel intermediaries—through a franchise operation to channel ownership by a producer. Producers need to consider the strengths and weaknesses of each system when selecting a channel strategy.

Conventional marketing channels

The producer has little or no control over channel intermediaries because of their independence. Arrangements such as exclusive dealing may provide a degree of control, but separation of ownership means that each party will look after its own interests. Conventional marketing channels are characterized by hard bargaining and, occasionally, conflict. For example, a retailer may believe that cutting the price of a brand is necessary to move stock, even though the producer objects because of brand image considerations.

A manufacturer that, through its size and strong brands, dominates a market may exercise considerable power over intermediaries even though they are independent. This power may result in an **administered vertical marketing system** where the manufacturer can command considerable co-operation from wholesalers and retailers. For example, the big Hollywood studios carefully manage the distribution of movies through a sequence of cinema, video/DVD sale, video/DVD rental to pay-per-view television and finally free television to maximize their returns. Pfizer created some controversy when it sought to change its drug distribution arrangements in the UK, which would see all its products distributed through one company, UniChem. Other wholesalers sought to have the action deemed anti-competitive, while retailers were also concerned about the possible emergence of a single, powerful wholesaler.[9] Retailers, too, can control an administered vertical marketing system. For example, when the retail entrepreneur Philip Green bought the Arcadia group in 2002, he wrote to all suppliers setting out new terms and conditions, imposing a retrospective 1.25 per cent discount and lengthening the number of days taken to pay suppliers from 28 to 30. He then consolidated the number of suppliers completely, delisting some and increasing the work given to others.[10] Many Asian distributors who have profited from the growth of markets like India and China are now acquiring the brands that they previously distributed, such as the sale of the Swiss watch brand Milus to Peace Mark, Asia's biggest watch retailer.

Franchising

A legal contract in which a producer and channel intermediaries agree each member's rights and obligations is called a **franchise**. Usually, the intermediary receives marketing, managerial, technical and financial services in return for a fee. Franchise organizations such as McDonald's, Benetton, Hertz, the Body Shop and Starbucks combine the strengths of a large sophisticated marketing-orientated organization with the energy and motivation of a locally owned outlet, and hence have been highly successful in building global businesses. Although a franchise operation gives a degree of producer control there are still areas of potential conflict. For example, the producer may be dissatisfied with the standards of service provided by the outlet, or the franchisee may believe that the franchising organization provides inadequate promotional support. Goal conflict can also arise. For example, some McDonald's and Starbucks franchisees are displeased with the company's rapid expansion programme, which has meant that new restaurants have opened within a mile of existing outlets. This has led to complaints about lower profits and falling franchise resale values.[11] A franchise agreement provides a **contractual vertical marketing system** through the formal co-ordination and integration of marketing and distribution activities.

Three economic explanations have been proposed to explain why a producer might choose franchising as a means of distribution.[12] Franchising may be a means of overcoming resource constraints whereby the cost of distribution is shared with the franchisee. It may also be an efficient system for overcoming producer/distributor management problems, because producers may value the notion of the owner-manager who has a vested interest in the success of the business. Finally, franchising may be a way for a producer to access the local knowledge of the franchisee. Franchising may therefore be attractive when a producer is expanding into new international markets. The biggest franchises operating in Europe are listed in Table 11.1.

Franchising can occur at four levels of the distribution chain.

1   *Manufacturer and retailer*: the car industry is dominated by this arrangement. The manufacturer gains retail outlets for its cars and repair facilities without the capital outlay required with ownership (see Marketing in Action 11.3).

2   *Manufacturer and wholesaler*: this is commonly used in the soft drinks industry. Manufacturers such as Schweppes, Coca-Cola and Pepsi grant wholesalers the right to make up and bottle their concentrate in line with their instructions, and to distribute the products within a defined geographic area.

3   *Wholesaler and retailer*: this is not as common as other franchising arrangements, but is found with car products and hardware stores. It allows wholesalers to secure distribution of their product to consumers.

4   *Retailer and retailer*: an often used method that frequently has its roots in a successful retailing operation seeking to expand geographically by means of a franchise operation, often with great success. Examples include McDonald's, Benetton, Pizza Hut and Kentucky Fried Chicken (see Exhibit 11.3).

Table 11.1 Europe's top franchises, 2008

Rank	Franchise	Business	Country
1	McDonald's	Restaurants	USA
2	Tecnocasa	Real estate	Italy
3	Fornetti	Food distribution	Hungary
4	Burger King	Restaurants	USA
5	Jean Louis David	Health and beauty	France
6	Point S	Automotive services	France
7	Photo Quelle	Photo, frame, art	Germany
8	Remax	Real estate	USA
9	Pro et Cie	Retail: appliances	France
10	Glassinter	Automotive services	Spain

Source: www.franchiseeurope.com

Exhibit 11.3 Benetton is a leading retail fashion franchise

Channel ownership

Channel ownership brings with it total control over distributor activities. This establishes a **corporate vertical marketing system**. By purchasing retail outlets, producers control their purchasing, production and marketing activities. In particular, control over purchasing means a captive outlet for the manufacturer's products. For example, the purchase of Pizza Hut and Kentucky Fried Chicken by Pepsi has tied these outlets to the company's soft drinks brands.

The benefits of control have to be balanced against the high price of acquisition and the danger that the move into retailing will spread managerial activities too widely. Nevertheless, corporate vertical marketing systems have operated successfully for many years in the oil industry where companies such as Shell, Texaco and Statoil own not only considerable numbers of petrol stations but also the means of production.

Channel management

Channels need to be managed on an ongoing basis once the key channel strategy decisions have been made. This involves the selection, motivation, training and evaluation of channel members, and the resolution of any channel conflict that arises.

Selection

The selection of channel members involves two main activities: first, the identification of potential channel members and, second, development of selection criteria. A variety of potential sources can be used to identify candidates, including trade sources such as trade associations and participation at exhibitions, talking to existing customers and/or to the field salesforce, and taking enquiries from interested resellers.[13] Common selection criteria include market, product and customer knowledge, market coverage, quality and size of salesforce (if applicable), reputation among customers, financial standing, the extent to which competitive and complementary products are carried, managerial competence and hunger for success, and the degree of enthusiasm for handling the producer's lines. In practice, selection may be complex because large, well-established distributors may carry many competing lines and lack enthusiasm for more. Smaller distributors, on the other hand, may be less financially secure and have a smaller salesforce, but be more enthusiastic and hungry for success.

Motivation

Once they have been chosen, channel members need to be motivated to agree to act as a distributor, and allocate adequate commitment and resources to the producer's lines. The key to effective motivation is to understand the needs and problems of distributors, since needs and motivators are linked. For example, a distributor who values financial incentives may respond more readily to high commission than one who is more concerned with having an exclusive territory. Possible motivators include financial rewards, territorial exclusivity, providing resource support (e.g. sales training, field sales assistance, provision of marketing research information, advertising and promotion support, financial assistance and management training) and developing strong work relationships (e.g. joint planning, assurance of long-term commitment, appreciation of effort and success, frequent interchange of views and arranging distributor conferences). In short, management of independent distributors is best conducted in the context of informal partnerships.[14]

Training

Channel members' training requirements obviously depend on their internal competences. Large supermarket chains, for example, may regard an invitation by a manufacturer to provide marketing training as an insult. However, many smaller distributors have been found to be weak on sales management, marketing, financial management, stock control and personnel management, and may welcome producer initiatives on training.[15] From the producer's perspective, training can provide the necessary technical knowledge about a supplier company and its products, and help to build a spirit of partnership and commitment.

Evaluation

Channel member evaluation has an important impact on distributor retention, training and motivation decisions. Evaluation provides the information necessary to decide which channel members to retain and which to drop. Shortfalls in distributor skills and competences may be identified through evaluation, and appropriate training programmes organized by producers. Where a lack of motivation is recognized as a problem, producers can implement plans designed to deal with the root causes of demotivation (e.g. financial incentives and/or fostering a partnership approach to business).[16] It needs to be understood, however, that the scope and frequency of evaluation may be limited where power lies with the channel member. If producers have relatively little power because they are more dependent on channel members for distribution, then in-depth evaluation and remedial action will be restricted. Where manufacturer power is high through having strong brands, and many distributors from which to choose, evaluation may be more frequent and wider in scope. Evaluation criteria include sales volume and value, profitability, level of stocks, quality and position of display, new accounts opened, selling and marketing capabilities, quality of service provided to customers, market information feedback, ability and willingness to keep commitments, attitudes and personal capability.

Managing conflict

Finally, given that producers and channel members are independent, conflict will inevitably occur from time to time (see Marketing in Action 11.2). First, such discord may arise because of differences in goals—for example, an increase in the proportion of profits allocated to retailers means a reduction in the amount going to manufacturers. For example, when Irish tour operator Budget Travel cut the commissions its pays to travel agents for selling its holidays from 10 to 5 per cent, its subsequent research found that many agents were omitting Budget from the list of choices being presented to customers. Its response was to reach out directly to the end consumer through a €1 million multimedia campaign urging consumers to consider Budget as one of their potential travel choices.[17]

Second, in seeking to expand their businesses many resellers add additional product lines. For example, UK retailer WHSmith originally specialized in books, magazines and newspapers but has grown by adding new product lines such as computer disks, DVDs and software supplies. This can cause resentment among its primary suppliers, who perceive the reseller as devoting too much effort to selling secondary lines. This problem can also work in reverse. Small newsagents in Ireland asked the Competition

Marketing in Action 11.2: Trouble in the soft drink channel!

Study guide: Below is a review of some changes that are taking place in the distribution channel for soft drinks. Read it and consider the longer-term implications for Coca-Cola, Cola-Cola bottlers and Wal-Mart.

A well-established distribution channel is used to bring popular soft drinks to the marketplace. Leading firms like Coca-Cola and Pepsi Cola manufacture cola concentrate, which is then sold to independent licensed bottling companies, which hold exclusive contracts for particular geographic territories. They in turn manufacture the finished products, which are packaged in bottles and cans, and distributed directly to retail outlets such as shops, supermarkets and vending machines. Over time, bottlers have built up an expertise in serving retailers and many pride themselves on the relationships they have developed with the trade. Some bottlers are extremely large companies and the biggest, Coca-Cola Enterprises, is a publicly quoted company with a market capitalization in excess of US$12 billion.

However, the structure of this supply chain has been threatened by the growth in retailer power and the different systems powerful retailers use to manage supply. For economic reasons, retailers prefer distribution to be managed from large distribution centres rather than having direct delivery to shops by suppliers. Distribution centres are more efficient (see the section on physical distribution later in this chapter) and enable retailers to offer lower prices to consumers. As a result, major global retailers do not need, or favour, the kinds of local supply that Coca-Cola bottlers offer.

Consequently, when Wal-Mart asked that Coca-Cola distribute its Powerade brand to Wal-Mart warehouses rather than to individual stores, bottlers in the USA reacted angrily. Sixty independent bottlers filed a lawsuit against Coca-Cola and Cola-Cola Enterprises, fearing that the move would be the first in a shift away from the direct delivery model and would ultimately threaten their future. Coca-Cola had initially accepted Wal-Mart's proposal as it feared that not doing so would mean that the giant retailer would begin selling an own-label version of the drink. After some disruption to the supply chain, the bottlers settled with Coca-Cola, and agreed to develop and test new distribution and customer service systems.

Based on: Ward (2007)[18]

Authority to review the system whereby wholesalers insisted that they carry a full range of magazine titles, with the result that many were left unsold, increasing the costs to the retailer.[19]

Third, in trying to grow their business, producers can use multiple distribution channels, such as selling directly to key accounts or other distributors, which may irritate existing dealers. For example, Alanis Morissette's record company, Maverick Records, created a significant amount of channel conflict in North America when it gave exclusive rights for the sale of her *Jagged Little Pill* album to Starbucks, which was allowed to sell the album for six weeks in its then 4800 stores before it became available elsewhere. HMV reacted by removing all the artist's music from the shelves of its Canadian stores.[20]

Finally, an obvious source of conflict is when parties in the supply chain do not perform to expectations. For example DSG International, the owner of the PC World and Currys retail chains, claimed that its poor financial performance in 2007 was partly attributable to a lack of promotional support by Microsoft for its new Vista operating system, which left it with thousands of unsold computers that had to be heavily discounted.

There are several ways of managing conflict. Developing a partnership approach calls for frequent interaction between producer and resellers to develop a spirit of mutual understanding and co-operation. First, sales targets can be mutually agreed, and training and promotional support provided. Second, staff may need some training in conflict handling to ensure that situations are handled calmly and that possibilities for win/win outcomes are identified. Third, where the conflict arises from multiple distribution channels, producers can try to partition markets. For example, Hallmark sells its premium greetings cards under its Hallmark brand name to upmarket department stores, and its standard cards under the Ambassador name to discount retailers.[21] Fourth, where poor performance is the problem, the most effective solution is to improve performance so that the source of conflict disappears. Finally, in some cases, the conflict might be eliminated through the purchase of the other party or through coercion, where one party gains compliance through the use of force such as where a large retailer threatens to delist a manufacturer. The recent merger between Proctor & Gamble and Gillette was seen by many as a move to put these two manufacturers on an equal footing with giant retailers like Wal-Mart.

Retailing

Most retailing is conducted in stores such as supermarkets, catalogue shops and departmental stores, but non-store retailing, such as online, mail order and automatic vending, also accounts for a large proportion of sales. Many large retailers exert enormous power in the distribution chain because of the vast quantities of goods they buy from manufacturers. This power is reflected in their ability to extract 'guarantee of margins' from manufacturers. This is a clause inserted in a contract that ensures a certain profit margin for the retailer, irrespective of the retail price being charged to the customer. One manufacturer is played against another, and own-label brands are used to extract more profit.[22]

Major store and non-store types

Supermarkets

Supermarkets are large self-service stores, which traditionally sell food, drinks and toiletries, but the broadening of their ranges by some supermarket chains means that such items as non-prescription pharmaceuticals, cosmetics and clothing are also being sold. While one attraction of supermarkets is their lower prices compared with small independent grocery shops, the extent to which price is a key competitive weapon depends on the supermarket's positioning strategy. For example, in the UK, Sainsbury's, Waitrose and Tesco are less reliant on price than KwikSave, Aldi or Netto. Tesco is now the undisputed UK market leader, with a market share of over 30 per cent compared to 16–17 per cent for Sainsbury's and Asda. It is estimated that 60 per cent of the British public now enter a Tesco store at least once a month and that it takes £1 of every £8 spent in the UK. Its brand range stretches from its Value range to the Tesco Finest range to Organics and Healthy Eating, and means that it appeals to all segments.[23]

Department stores

Department stores are titled thus because related product lines are sold in separate departments, such as men's and women's clothing, jewellery, cosmetics, toys and home furnishings. In recent years such stores have been under increasing pressure from discount houses, speciality stores and the move to out-of-town shopping. Nevertheless, many continue to perform well in this competitive arena through a strategy of becoming one-stop shops for a variety of leading manufacturer brands, which are allocated significant store space.

Speciality shops

As their name suggests, these outlets specialize in a narrow product line. Many town centres, for example, have shops selling confectionery, cigarettes and newspapers in the same outlet. Many speciality outlets, such as Tie Rack and Sock Shop, sell only one product line. Specialization allows a deep product line to be sold in restricted shop space. Some speciality shops, such as butchers and greengrocers, focus on quality and personal service. Speciality shops can, however, be vulnerable when tastes change or competition increases. For example, speciality sports retailers such as JJB Sports and John David Group have been reporting disappointing results as the blending of sportswear and fashion, driven by cultural icons such as David Beckham, has opened up the market to a host of other retailers such as fashion shops and supermarkets.[24]

Discount houses

Discount houses sell products at low prices by accepting low margins, selling high volumes and bulk buying. For example, 'pound shops' sell a wide range of items such as fashion accessories, toys, stationery and tools for £1, and operate on low margins of 2–3 per cent. Good location and rapid product turnover are the keys to success. Low prices, sometimes promoted as sale prices, are offered throughout the year. Many discounters operate from out-of-town retail warehouses with the capacity to stock a wide range of merchandise.

Category killers

These retail outlets have a narrow product focus, but an unusually large width and depth to that product range. Category killers emerged in the USA in the early 1980s as a challenge to discount houses. They are distinct from speciality shops in that they are bigger, and carry a wider and deeper range of products within their chosen product category; they are distinct from discount houses in their focus on only one product category. Examples of category killers are Toys 'R' Us (toys), Nevada Bob's Discount Golf Warehouses (golf equipment), Woodies (DIY) and Halfords (bicycles and auto accessories).

Convenience stores

Convenience stores, true to their name, offer customers the convenience of a close location and long opening hours every day of the week. Because they are small they may pay higher prices for their merchandise than supermarkets, and therefore have to charge higher prices to their customers. Some of these stores, such as Spar, join buying groups to gain some purchasing power and lower prices. The main customer need they fulfil is that for top-up buying—for example, when a customer is short of a carton of milk or loaf of bread, say. Societal changes, such as rising divorce rates, decreasing family sizes, long commuting times and time-poor consumers, have all combined to help revitalize the convenience store sector. Consumers are once again favouring quick, convenient purchases, as offered by convenience stores, over a big weekly shop at a supermarket. Consequently, major retailers like Tesco and Sainsbury's have been aggressively buying into this sector.

Catalogue stores

This type of retail outlet promotes its products through catalogues, which are either mailed to customers or available in-store or online for customers to view on-site (see Chapter 10). Purchase is in city-centre outlets where customers fill in order forms, pay for the goods and then collect them from a designated place in the store. In the UK, Argos is a successful catalogue retailer selling a wide range of discounted products such as electrical goods, jewellery, gardening tools, furniture, toys, car accessories, sports goods, luggage and cutlery.

Mail order

This non-store form of retailing may also employ catalogues as a promotional vehicle, but the purchase transaction is conducted via the mail (see Chapter 10). Alternatively, outward communication may be by direct mail, television, magazine or newspaper advertising. Increasingly, orders are being placed by telephone or over the internet, a process that is facilitated by the use of credit cards as a means of payment. Goods are then sent by mail. Otto-Versand, the German mail-order company, owns Grattan, a UK mail-order retailer, and has leading positions in Austria, Belgium, Italy, the Netherlands and Spain. Its French rival, La Redoute, has expanded into Belgium, Italy and Portugal. Mail order offers the prospect of pan-European catalogues, central warehousing and processing of cross-border orders.

Automatic vending

Offering such products as drinks, confectionery, soup and newspapers in convenient locations, 24 hours a day, vending machines are particularly popular in some countries, such as Japan. No sales staff are required although restocking, servicing and repair costs can be high. Cash dispensers at banks have improved customer service by permitting round-the-clock financial services. However, machine breakdowns and out-of-stock situations can annoy customers.

Online retailing

Online retailing is one of the fastest-growing forms of distribution, and is proving particularly popular for products like electrical goods, groceries, clothing/footwear and music/video. It can take any of three major forms. First, in pure online retailing scenarios, the product is ordered, paid for and received online in a completely electronic transaction. Any product that can be digitized, such as a piece of music, computer software or a book, can be retailed in this way. Second, products can be ordered online and then distributed either through the postal system or through the use of local distribution companies in the case of groceries or wine, for example. Finally, most leading retailers have an online presence. For example, the top UK retailers that have a significant presence both online and offline include Tesco, Marks & Spencer, Argos, Next and Comet. These retailers work hard to link both channels. For example, Argos customers can select products from the Argos catalogue, order online and pick them up from a local outlet. M&S is looking at setting up internet kiosks in its stores, so that consumers can place online orders for products that are out of stock. Some of the strengths of online retailers are discussed in Technology Focus 11.1.

Key retail marketing decisions

A retail outlet needs to be thought of as a brand involving the same set of decisions we discussed when we looked at branding in Chapter 6. Retailers need to anticipate and adapt to changing environmental circumstances, such as the growing role of information technology and changing customer tastes. However, there are a number of specific issues that relate to retailing, and are worthy of separate discussion.

Technology Focus 11.1: The long tail of internet retailing

What is it that differentiates online retailers from the traditional retail shop? Online retailers offer you the convenience of shopping from your desk or the comfort of your own home—yes. Because it is easy to shop around and compare prices online you may be able to get yourself a better price—yes. But the key unique feature of internet shopping is captured in something that has become known as the 'long tail' of retailing.

If you take businesses like books and music, the focus for many years has been on the idea of the hit—that is, the best-selling book or the best-selling record. Each week, the UK pop music show *Top of the Pops* presented a countdown of the top-selling singles in the UK. The top 30 records would account for the vast majority of record sales for that week and, outside the top 30, there was a 'long tail' of other records that would only sell in ever decreasing amounts until it got down to sales of one or two copies. If you were a music store or a book retailer, making sure you carried the top-selling titles was critical to your profitability. In fact, because of your limited shelf space, your profitability was directly related to how efficiently you used it—in other words, your ability to identify and stock items that were likely to sell quickly and in large volumes, and not stock slow-selling or niche items.

In the world of online retailing, no such space restrictions apply. Because online retailers do not have to maintain expensive retail outlets, they can carry as many titles as they like, tucked away in a warehouse or through access to a title held by an affiliate. Because the cost of inventory and distribution is practically zero, whether an item is a big seller or a small seller its contribution to profitability is relatively similar. What online retailers quickly began to discover was that a large proportion of their sales was accounted for by titles outside the best-seller list. In the USA, in 2004, books selling more than 250,000 copies sold 53 million copies in total, but those selling under 1000 copies sold 84 million in total. The collective demand for thousands of niche items began to outweigh the mass demand for a small number of best-sellers. What the long tail does is shatter the 80/20 rule, whereby 20 per cent of products account for 80 per cent of sales. Instead a 98 per cent rule has been suggested, which means that 98 per cent of all items offered will sell at least once in a defined period of time.

So what are the implications of the long tail? First, it gives online retailers a distinct competitive advantage over physical retailers. The world's largest physical bookstore, Barnes & Noble, carries an average of about 130,000 titles. Amazon has a total inventory of 3.7 million titles. It is estimated that, for example, half of Amazon's sales come from outside its first 130,000 titles. What this means is that the market for books that are not sold in the average physical bookstore is the same size as those that are. Physical bookstores are unable to reach a massive market. The same rule applies to music, movies and video games. The average US cinema chain carries only about 100 films per year but an average of 13,000 new films are made in the USA each year.

The long tail also has significant implications for consumers and for content creation. Consumers now have the possibility to find almost any item they want, however obscure. The biggest challenge they face is finding these niche items. Companies like Amazon track purchases and offer a recommendation service to help consumers find what they want. Blogging, tagging and social networking are other emerging ways in which consumers can source material. But, ultimately, this leads to ever growing niche audiences pursuing their particular interests. From a content creation point of view, this means that the obsession with finding the next hit (and often using market research to help do it) may become less important. What will matter more is creating the content and making sure consumers hear about it in a world of myriad choice.

Suggested reading: Anderson (2006);[25] Jennings (2007)[26]

These are **retail positioning**, store location, product assortment and services, price and store atmosphere.

Retail positioning

Retail positioning—as with all marketing decisions—involves the choice of target market and differential advantage. Targeting allows retailers to tailor their marketing mix (which includes product assortment, service levels, store location, prices and promotion) to the needs of their chosen customer segment (see Marketing in Action 11.3). Differentiation provides a reason to shop at one store rather than another. A useful framework for creating a differential advantage has been proposed by Davies, who suggests that innovation in retailing can come only from novelty in

the process offered to the shopper, or from novelty in the product or product assortment offered to the shopper.[27] The catalogue shop Argos in the UK has offered innovation in the process of shopping, whereas Next achieved success through product innovation (stylish clothes at affordable prices). Hard discounters like Aldi and Lidl stock primarily own-label products, which are sold at competitive prices (product innovation). This is the dominant retail form in Germany, where discounters have a 40 per cent market share, and is beginning to grow rapidly in other European countries. Toys 'R' Us is an example of both product and process innovation through providing the widest range of toys at one location (product innovation) and thereby offering convenient, one-stop shopping (process innovation).

Marketing in Action 11.3: New standards at Lexus

> **Study guide:** Below are some examples of how luxury car showrooms seek to differentiate themselves in the marketplace. Read the text and consider how such design features contribute to the market positioning of brands like Lexus.

As we saw earlier in the chapter, cars are sold through franchise arrangements with dealers, who are given exclusive rights to particular territories. The public face of car marketing is the dealer showroom, and the quality and standards of these retail outlets have been rising dramatically in recent years. This is particularly true for top-of-the-range models such as Lexus, Mercedes and the Nissan Infiniti.

As Lexus continues to build its brand in the USA, its franchisees have continued to push the boundaries of what consumers have come to expect from a car dealer. One dealership in Orange County, California, cost US$75 million to build and resembles a luxury hotel. It is accessed through a palm tree-lined walkway and its landscaping includes a US$75,000 Senegal date palm tree. On entering the showrooms, customers are greeted with a glassed-in fireplace that crackles with flame on a cool day. The premises includes a reading room, a putting green, a café and a menswear boutique. The nearby Mercedes dealership in Orange also has a putting green, as well as a shoeshine attendant, a nail salon and a customer shuttle service to the nearby John Wayne Airport. In 2005, Nissan launched a global design for its Infiniti showrooms that featured glass walls leading to airy spaces adorned with natural materials such as marble, stone and slate.

While these luxury showrooms support the positioning of the brand and make the process of shopping for a new car more pleasurable, they also come at a significant cost to the franchisee. And the very small margins that dealers at all levels in the market operate within make it ever harder to recoup this type of investment. Consequently, despite high sales of new cars in major economies in recent years, many car dealers are struggling. For example, in Ireland's booming car market, the largest dealer, Motor Services, made a loss of €716,000 on sales of €221 million in 2005. This again illustrates the different levels of power that players can have in the distribution channel. Car dealers are critical to the marketing of new cars in terms of positioning, sales and service, yet their terms of business mean that they recoup a relatively small share of the value created.

Based on: Reed (2007);[28] Suiter (2005)[29]

Store location

Conventional wisdom has it that the three factors critical to the success of a retailer are location, location and location. Convenience is an important issue for many shoppers, and so store location can have a major bearing on sales performance. Retailers have to decide on regional coverage, the towns and cities to target within regions, and the precise location to select within a given town or city. The choice of town or city will depend on such factors as correspondence with the retailer's chosen target market, the level of disposable income in the catchment area, the availability of suitable sites and the level of competition. The choice of a particular site may depend on the level of existing traffic (pedestrian and/or vehicular) passing the site, parking provision, access to the outlet for delivery vehicles, the presence of competition, planning restrictions and whether there is an opportunity to form new retailing centres with other outlets. For example, Starbucks has sought to locate its coffee shops on the side of the street most favoured by commuters going to work, based on the notion that consumers would not cross a busy street for a coffee. Also, two or more non-competing retailers (e.g. Sainsbury's and Boots) may agree to locate outlets together in an out-of-town centre to generate more pulling power than each could achieve individually. Having made that decision, the partners will look for suitable sites near their chosen town or city.

Product assortment

Retailers have to make a decision on the breadth and depth of their product assortment (see Exhibit 11.4). A supermarket, for example, may decide to widen its product assortment from food, drink and toiletries to include clothes and toys: this is called 'scrambled merchandising'. For example, Tesco offers consumers books, video games, music downloads, insurance, credit cards, savings accounts, mobile phones, and travel, optical and legal services, as well as groceries. Currently in the UK, supermarkets sell 24 per cent of all CDs, 8 per cent of books and 40 per cent of all newly released DVDs, which has implications for specialist CD/DVD and book retailers.[30] Scrambled merchandising becomes a basis through which retailers can differentiate themselves. Therefore, we see companies like McDonald's offering DVD rentals, Gap selling CD mixes, Starbucks selling music and Tesco selling Starbucks coffee!

Within each product line, a retailer can choose to stock a deep or shallow product range. Some retailers, like Tie Rack, Sock Shop and Toys 'R' Us, stock one deep product line. Department stores, however, offer a much broader range of products, including toys, cosmetics, jewellery, clothes, electrical goods and household accessories. Some retailers begin with one product line and gradually broaden their product assortment to maximize revenue per customer. For example, petrol stations broadened their product range to include motor accessories and, more recently, confectionery, drinks, flowers and newspapers. Services like hot food and car washes offer much greater profit margins than the sale of petrol. A by-product of this may be to reduce customers' price sensitivity since selection of petrol station may be based on the availability of other products there rather than the fact that it offers the lowest price.

Own-label branding gives rise to another product decision. Major retailers may decide to sell a range of own-label products to complement national brands. Often the purchasing power of these large retail chains means that prices can be lower and yet profit margins higher than for competing national brands. This makes the activity an attractive proposition for many retailers. Supermarkets have moved into this area, as have UK electrical giants such as Dixons, which uses the Chinon brand name for cameras and Saisho for brown goods such as hi-fi and televisions, and Currys, which has adopted the Matsui brand

2 FOR 1 DESIGNER GLASSES for £125

Specsavers

Exhibit 11.4 Specsavers is a dominant optical products chain due to its wide product range and intensive marketing

name. In both cases the use of a Japanese-sounding name (even though some of the products were sourced in Europe) was believed to enhance the products' customer appeal.

Price

Price is a key factor in store choice for some market segments. Consequently some retailers major on price as their differential advantage. This requires vigilant cost control and massive buying power. A recent trend is towards the 'everyday low prices' favoured by retailers, rather than the higher prices supplemented by promotions that are supported by manufacturers. Retailers such as B&Q the do-it-yourself discounter, maintain that customers prefer predictable low prices rather than occasional money-off deals, three-for-the-price-of-two offers and free gifts. Supermarket chains are also pressurizing suppliers to provide consistently low prices rather than temporary promotions. This action is consistent with the desire to position themselves on a low price platform. For example, in France, Carrefour has introduced a system whereby the bonuses of store managers are linked to whether prices are lower than those of comparable retailers. The importance of price competitiveness is reflected in the alliance of European food retailers called Associated Marketing Services. Retailers such as WM Morrison (UK), Ahold (the Netherlands), ICA (a federation of Swedish food retailers) Migros (Finland), Superquinn (Ireland) and others have joined forces to foster co-operation in the areas of purchasing and marketing of brands. Their range of activities includes own branding, joint buying, the development of joint brands and services, and the exchange of information and skills. A key aim is to reduce cost price since this accounts for 75 per cent of the sales price to customers.[31]

Store atmosphere

Atmosphere is created by a combination of the design, colour and layout of a store (see Exhibit 11.5). Both exterior and interior design affect atmosphere. External factors include architectural design, signs, window displays and use of colour, which create an identity for a retailer and attract customers. The Body Shop, for example, projects its environmentally caring image through the green exterior of its shops, and through window displays that focus on environmental issues. Interior design also has a major impact on atmosphere. Store lighting, fixtures and fittings, and layout are important considerations. Colour, sound and smell can affect mood. Department stores often place perfume counters near the entrance, and supermarkets may use the smell of baking bread to attract customers and upmarket shirt

Exhibit 11.5 Retail outlets like Nike Town aim to create a customer experience

companies like Thomas Pink even pump the smell of freshly laundered linen around their stores. In addition, supermarkets often use music to create a relaxed atmosphere, whereas some boutiques use pop music to draw in their target customers.

The rise of experiential marketing has placed a significant focus on store atmospherics as retailers strive to create a shopping experience for consumers. Shoppers are considered to have three attention zones.[32] The first zone operates at a distance of 30 feet from the shopper, and requires the retailer to use a combination of sound, colour, scent and motion to attract potential buyers. At 10 feet what is important is placement on a shelf and an ability to stand out from competitors, placing a premium on how well manufacturers influence the distribution process. And, at 3 feet, the consumer is already holding a potential choice or reaching out for it, so it is the look and feel of the product or its packaging that is important.

Physical distribution

Earlier in this chapter we examined channel strategy and management decisions, which concern the choice of the correct outlets to provide product availability to customers in a cost-effective manner. Physical distribution decisions focus on the efficient movement of goods from producer to intermediaries and the consumer. Clearly, channel and physical distribution decisions are interrelated, although channel decisions tend to be made earlier. Physical distribution is defined as a set of activities concerned with the physical flows of materials, components and finished goods from producer to channel intermediaries and consumers. It is a business that has become increasingly complex as customers such as Wal-Mart, Tesco and others extend their global reach. This has given rise to mergers between logistics companies such as that involving Exel and Tibbet & Britten, as companies seek to provide integrated solutions for their clients ranging from warehouse management to home delivery.[33]

Distribution aims to provide intermediaries and customers with the right products, in the right quantities, in the right locations, at the right time. Distribution problems caused by, for example, a move to a new warehouse frequently impact on corporate performance. Physical distribution activities have been the subject of managerial attention for some time because of the potential for cost savings and improving customer service levels. Cost savings can be achieved by reducing inventory levels, using cheaper forms of transport and shipping in bulk rather than small quantities. For example, Benetton's blueprint for reviving its fortunes has been predicated on getting clothes from the factory to the shop rail faster to enable it to compete with fast fashion retailers like Zara and H&M.[34] Customer service levels can be improved by fast and reliable delivery, including just-in-time (JIT) delivery, holding high inventory levels so that customers have a wide choice and the chances of stock-outs are reduced, fast order processing, and ensuring that products arrive in the right quantities and quality. Physical distribution management concerns the balance between cost reduction and meeting customer service requirements. Trade-offs are often necessary. For example, low inventory and slow, cheaper transportation methods reduce costs but lower customer service levels and satisfaction.

As well as the trade-offs between physical distribution costs and customer service levels, there is the potential for conflict between elements of the physical distribution system itself. For example, low-cost containers may lower packaging costs but raise the cost of goods damaged in transit. This fact, and the need to co-ordinate order processing, inventory and transportation decisions, means that physical distribution needs to be managed as a system, with a manager overseeing the whole process. It can be a very challenging task, as demonstrated by the problems suffered by Sainsbury's, one of the leading British supermarkets. It invested £3 billion in its supply chain focused around four regional distribution centres. But the changeover led to several problems: suppliers were not packing orders to suit the new centres, deliveries were arriving at the wrong time, labour was often in the wrong place and stocks were frequently in the store room or delivery yard rather than on the shelves. The system was designed to generate savings of £600 million per year but, in 2004, Sainsbury's chief executive, Justin King, admitted that it had been a failure.[35]

The key elements of the physical distribution system are customer service, order processing, inventory control, warehousing, transportation and materials handling.

Customer service

It is essential to set customer service standards. For example, a customer service standard might be that 90 per cent of orders are delivered within 48 hours of receipt and 100 per cent are delivered within 72 hours. Higher customer service standards normally mean higher costs as inventory levels need to be higher. In some cases, customers value consistency in delivery time rather than speed. For example, a customer service standard of guaranteed delivery within five working days may be valued more than 60 per cent within two and 100 per cent within seven days. Customer service standards should be given considerable attention for they may be the differentiating factor between suppliers: they may be used as a key customer choice criterion. Methods of improving customer service standards include improving product availability, improving order cycle time, raising information levels and improving flexibility. An example of raising information levels is the kind of service now being provided online by courier companies like Federal Express and UPS, which offer their customers a facility whereby they can log on and get immediate updates on delivery status (see Exhibit 11.6). However, in modern global supply chains, the outsourcing of activities means a lack of control, which can impact on customer service. For example, a small disruption in its material supplies from Southeast Asia affected Zara's service levels and sales in 2005.

Order processing

This relates to the question of how orders are handled. Reducing time between a customer placing an order and receiving the goods may be achieved through careful analysis of the components that make up order processing time. A computer link between the salesperson and the order department may be effective. Electronic data interchange can also speed order processing time by checking the customer's credit rating, and whether the goods are in stock, issuing an order to the warehouse, invoicing the customer and updating the inventory records.

Exhibit 11.6 Delivery companies like DHL, UPS and FedEx provide a critical marketing service

Inventory control

Inventory control deals with the question of how much inventory should be held. A balance has to be found between the need to have products in stock to meet customer demand and the costs incurred in holding large inventories. Having in stock every conceivable item a customer might order would normally be prohibitively expensive for companies marketing many items. Decisions also need to be taken about when to order new stocks. These order points are normally before stock levels reach zero because of the lead time between ordering and receiving inventory. The JIT inventory system is designed to reduce lead times so that the order point (the stock level at which re-ordering takes place), and overall inventory levels for production items, are low. The more variable the lead time between ordering and receiving stocks, and the greater the fluctuation in customer demand, the higher the order point. This is because of the uncertainty caused by the variability leading to the need for **safety (buffer) stocks** in case lead times are unpredictably long or customer demand unusually high. How much to order depends on the cost of holding stock and order-processing cost. Orders can be small and frequent, or large and infrequent. Small, frequent orders raise order-processing costs but reduce inventory carrying costs; large, infrequent orders raise inventory costs but lower order-processing expenditure.

Warehousing

This part of the distribution chain involves all the activities required in the storing of goods between the time they are produced and the time they are transported to the customer. These activities include breaking bulk, making up product assortments for delivery to customers, storage and loading. Storage warehouses hold goods for moderate or long time periods, whereas distribution centres operate as central locations for the fast movement of goods. Retailing organizations use regional distribution centres where suppliers deliver products in bulk. These shipments are broken down into loads that are then quickly transported to retail outlets. Distribution centres are usually highly automated, with computer-controlled machinery facilitating the movement of goods. A computer reads orders and controls the fork-lift trucks that gather goods and move them to loading bays. Further technological advances are likely to have a significant impact on warehousing and the movement of goods through the supply chain (see Marketing in Action 11.4). Warehousing strategy involves the determination of the location and the number of warehouses or distribution centres to be used. The trend is towards a smaller number of ever larger warehouses. For example, the UK electrical retailer Dixons is aiming to cut its distribution centres from 17 to 2. Boots is closing its 17 regional distribution centres in favour of a £70 million automated warehouse in Nottingham. In 2007, MFI opened a huge national distribution centre in Yorkshire that is capable of holding £60 million worth of stock. At the extreme, some retailers are seeking single distribution centres for the whole of Europe, with locations such as Moissy-Cramayel in France measuring the size of 350 football pitches.[36]

Transportation

This refers to the means by which products will be transported; the five major modes are rail, road, air, water and pipeline. Railways are efficient at transporting large, bulky freight on land over long distances and are often used to transport coal, chemicals, oil, aggregates and nuclear flasks. Rail is more environmentally friendly than road, but the major problem with it is lack of flexibility. Motorized transport by road has the advantage of flexibility because of direct access to companies and warehouses. This means that lorries can transport goods from supplier to receiver without unloading en route. However, the growth of road transport in Europe, and particularly

Marketing in Action 11.4: How RFID technology will impact on the supply chain

> **Study guide:** Below is a review of the application of RFID technology in distribution. Read it and consider three advantages of this technology for the management of the physical distribution system.

Radio frequency identification (RFID) technology has been in use for about 13 years, most commonly in the easy-pass systems that allow drivers to speed through toll booths on highways around the world. But the technology now looks set to also revolutionize the movement of goods through the supply chain. Containers, palettes and even products are fitted with a tiny silicon chip and antenna, about the size of a pinhead, which contains a unique serial number and extensive information about each item. These chips are read by a 'reader' that sends out a high-frequency radio signal, which beams back the information and points to a web page containing detailed specifications for the product. The tag reader can scan dozens of items simultaneously and does not need a direct line of sight. Tags can be read from a distance of up to 20 metres, even through walls, and are read automatically once they come within range of the receiver.

RFID technology promises to improve the efficiency of warehouse operations by lowering error rates and requiring less time and labour. For example, the contents of palettes can be read without being opened, and fewer staff members will be needed to track and reconcile shipments and inventory. Estimates are that total labour warehouse costs could be cut by 3 per cent. The technology has already been used at marine terminals in California where cargos are transferred from international to domestic containers for delivery to regional distribution centres. By switching from manual operations to RFID tags, NYK Logistics reduced trucker turnaround times by more 50 per cent to an average of 14 minutes, and was able to increase the number of trucks it could handle at its facility from 70,000 to 120,000 without any increase in space. Similarly, speedier information on inventory levels will enable manufacturers to reduce stock-out costs in the channel. Another potential application is the removal of long queues at checkouts as traditional scanners are replaced with an RFID-type system.

A variety of major corporations around the world are experimenting with the technology. For example, Wal-Mart has required that its top 100 suppliers begin using it. In 2004, Delta Airlines announced that it would invest US$25 million to deploy disposable radio tags to track and locate lost luggage, which costs the airline US$100 million annually. IBM has suggested that banks should issue their best customers with cards containing the tags, allowing them to get special treatment, and Gillette ordered 500 million tags in 2003 in its first large-scale test of the technology.

Based on: Anonymous (2004);[37] Gilligan (2004);[38] Kelly (2003);[39] Niemeyer, Pat and Ramaswamy (2003)[40]

the UK, has received considerable criticism because of increased traffic congestion, damage done to roads by heavy juggernauts and the impact on the environment. The key advantages of air freight are its speed and long distance capabilities. Its speed means that it is often used to transport perishable goods and emergency deliveries. Its major disadvantages are high cost, and the need to transport goods by road to and from air terminals. Water transportation is slow but inexpensive. Inland transportation is usually associated with bulky, low-value, non-perishable goods such as coal, ore, grain, steel and petroleum. Ocean-going ships carry a wider range of products. When the cost benefits of international sea transportation outweigh the speed advantage of air freight, water shipments may be chosen. But some industries, such as fashion retailing, have seen production move from low-cost countries like China to Eastern Europe and Turkey because it takes 22 days by water to reach the UK from China compared with 5 days from Turkey. So, though the cost of production is lower in China, the fast turnaround of fashion items makes sea transportation unappealing. Finally, pipelines are a dependable and low-maintenance form of transportation for liquids and gases such as crude petroleum, water and natural gas.

Materials handling

Materials handling involves the activities related to the movement of products in the producer's plant, warehouses and transportation depots. Modern storage facilities tend to be of just one storey, allowing a high level of automation. In some cases robots are used to conduct materials-handling tasks. Lowering the human element in locating inventory and assembling orders has reduced error and increased the speed of these operations. For example, the pharmaceuticals distributor Cahill May Roberts has replaced a paper-based system with Vocollect voice technology whereby material handlers speak to computers to confirm the products that they have collected rather than making paper records. It distributes in the region of 180,000 product units per day to pharmacies in Ireland and accurate records are critical because of the nature of the products being dealt with.[41] Two key developments in materials handling are unit handling and containerization. Unit handling achieves efficiency by combining multiple packages on pallets that can be moved by fork-lift trucks. Containerization involves the combination of large quantities of goods (e.g. car components) in a single large container. Once sealed, such containers can easily be transferred from one form of transport to another.

Summary

In this chapter we have examined the final key element of the marketing mix, namely that of delivering products and services to customers. In particular, the following issues were addressed.

1. There are important differences in the structure of consumer, industrial and service channels. Consumer channels tend to be longer and involve more channel partners, while many industrial and service channels are direct to the customer.

2. Channel strategy involves three key decisions, namely channel selection, distribution intensity and channel integration. These decisions must be made in line with the firm's overall marketing strategy. For example, positioning decisions may drive the number and type of channel members selected to distribute a product and the extent to which they are controlled.

3. The key channel management issues are the selection and motivation of middlemen, providing them with training, evaluating their performance and resolving any channel conflict issues that may arise. Effective support for channel members is often necessary to achieve marketing objectives.

4. There is a diverse range of retail types, including supermarkets, department stores, speciality shops, discount houses, category killers, convenience stores, catalogue stores, mail order, vending machines and online retailing.

5. The key retail marketing decisions include retail positioning, store location, product assortment, price and store atmosphere. Many retailers are strong brands in their own right and need to be managed as such. Technology has enabled some internet retailers to achieve major competitive advantages in their markets.

6. Physical distribution concerns decisions relating to customer service, order processing, inventory control, warehousing, transportation and materials handling, which impact on the efficiency and effectiveness of the supply chain. Cost and customer service are two conflicting pressures that impact upon the structure and management of the physical distribution system.

Key terms

administered vertical marketing system a channel situation where a manufacturer that dominates a market through its size and strong brands may exercise considerable power over intermediaries even though they are independent

channel integration the way in which the players in the channel are linked

channel intermediaries organizations that facilitate the distribution of products to customers

channel of distribution the means by which products are moved from the producer to the ultimate consumer

channel strategy the selection of the most effective distribution channel, the most appropriate level of distribution intensity and the degree of channel integration

contractual vertical marketing system a franchise arrangement (e.g. a franchise) tying producers and resellers together

corporate vertical marketing system a channel situation where an organization gains control of distribution through ownership

exclusive distribution an extreme form of selective distribution where only one wholesaler, retailer or industrial distributor is used in a geographical area to sell the products of a particular supplier

franchise a legal contract in which a producer and channel intermediaries agree each other's rights and obligations; the intermediary usually receives marketing, managerial, technical and financial services in return for a fee

intensive distribution the aim of intensive distribution is to provide saturation coverage of the market by using all available outlets

multichannel marketing the distribution of products through a number of different channels to reach the consumer

retail positioning the choice of target market and differential advantage for a retail outlet

safety (buffer) stocks stocks or inventory held to cover against uncertainty about resupply lead times

selective distribution the use of a limited number of outlets in a geographical area to sell the products of a particular supplier

Study questions

1. A tour operator has just established a business in the UK selling short-break package holidays throughout Europe. Advise the founder on her options for distributing the company's products.

2. Distribution intensity decisions should be integrated with all other marketing mix decisions. Discuss.

3. Describe situations that can lead to conflict between channel members. What can be done to avoid and resolve conflict?

4. Discuss the impact of the growth of online retailing on other retail formats.

5. Discuss the reasons why more and more distribution channels are being characterized by a small number of large central distribution centres rather than by a large number of relatively small outlets.

6. Visit www.starbucks.com and www.costa.co.uk. Compare and contrast these two coffee chains in terms of the major retail marketing decisions such as retail positioning, product assortment, store location and store atmospherics.

Suggested reading

Corstjens, J. and **M. Corstjens** (1995) *Store Wars: The Battle for Mindspace and Shelfspace*, New York: John Wiley & Sons.

Ferdows, K., M.A. Lewis and **J. Machuca** (2004) Rapid-fire Fulfillment, *Harvard Business Review*, **82** (11), 104–11.

Maltz, E. and **V. Chiappetta** (2002) Maximising Value in the Digital World, *Sloan Management Review*, **43** (3) 77–84.

Moore, C.M., G. Birtwistle and **S. Burt** (2004) Channel Power, Conflict and Conflict Resolution in International Fashion Retailing, *European Journal of Marketing*, **38** (7), 749–70.

Myers, J.B., A.D. Pickersgill and **E.S. Van Metre** (2004) Steering Customers to the Right Channels, *McKinsey Quarterly*, **4**, 36–48.

Underhill, P. (2004) *The Call of the Mall: How We Shop*, New York: Profile Books.

References

1. **Anonymous** (2005) Starbucks Hits the Right Note with Music Sales, *Irish Times Business*, 2 September, 6; **Garrahan, M.** (2007) Too Slow a Roll-Out: Why Hollywood Needs Fresh Formats in Order to Shine, *Financial Times*, 23 February, 15; **High, K.** (2005) A Digital Distribution Revolution Gathers Pace, *Financial Times*, 21 June, 14.

2. **Fahy, J.** and **F. Taguchi** (1995) Reassessing the Japanese Distribution System, *Sloan Management Review*, Winter.

3. **Narus, J.A.** and **J.C. Anderson** (1986) Industrial Distributor Selling: The Roles of Outside and Inside Sales, *Industrial Marketing Management*, **15**, 55–62.

4. **Anonymous** (2008) Shock to the System, *Economist*, 2 February, 67–8.

5. **Rosenbloom, B.** (1987) *Marketing Channels: A Management View*, Hinsdale, IL: Dryden, 160.

6. **Laurance, B.** (1993) MMC in Bad Odour Over Superdrug Ruling, *Guardian*, 12 November, 18.

7. **Clegg, A.** (2005) Crisp Profits at the Potato Farm, *Financial Times*, 12 October, 14.

8. **Anonymous** (1993) EC Rejects Unilever Appeal on Cabinets, *Marketing*, 25 February, 6.

9. **Jack, A.** (2007) Wholesalers to Seek Injunction on Pfizer's Drug Distribution Plan, *Financial Times*, 1 March, 4.

10. **Voyle, S.** (2003) Supply Chain Feels Fresh Pressure, *Financial Times*, 28 April, 23.

11. **Helmore, E.** (1997) Restaurant Kings or Just Silly Burgers, *Observer*, 8 June, 5.

12. **Hopkinson, G.C.** and **S. Hogarth Scott** (1999) Franchise Relationship Quality: Microeconomic Explanations, *European Journal of Marketing*, **33** (9/10), 827–43.

13. **Rosenbloom, B.** (1987) *Marketing Channels: A Management View*, Hinsdale, IL: Dryden, 160.

14. **Shipley, D.D., D. Cook** and **E. Barnett** (1989) Recruitment, Motivation, Training and Evaluation of Overseas Distributors, *European Journal of Marketing*, **23** (2), 79–93.

15. See **Shipley, D.D.** and **S. Prinja** (1988) The Services and Supplier Choice Influences of Industrial Distributors, *Service Industries Journal*, **8** (2), 176–87; **Webster, F.E.** (1976) The Role of the Industrial Distributor in Marketing Strategy, *Journal of Marketing*, **40**, 10–16.

16. See **Pegram, R.** (1965) *Selecting and Evaluating Distributors*, New York: National Industrial Conference Board, 109–25; **Shipley, D.D., D. Cook** and **E. Barnett** (1989) Recruitment, Motivation, Training and Evaluation of Overseas Distributors, *European Journal of Marketing*, **23** (2), 79–93.

17. **Coyle, D.** (2004) Budget Travel Accuses Agents of Blacklisting, *Irish Times*, 16 November, 16; **Coyle, D.** (2005) Challenges Circle Overhead for Tour Operator, *Irish Times Business*, 7 January, 22.

18. **Ward, A.** (2007) Coca-Cola's Bottlers Settle Dispute Over Distribution, *Financial Times*, 13 February, 2.

19. **Slattery, L.** (2007) Concern at Merger Plan for Distributor Eason, *Irish Times*, 29 January, 18.

20. **Sexton, P.** (2005) A Music Sales Storm is Brewing in a Coffee Shop, *Financial Times*, 21 June, 14.

21. **Hardy, K.G.** and **A.J. Magrath** (1988) Ten Ways for Manufacturers to Improve Distribution Management, *Business Horizons*, November–December, 68.

22. **Krishnan, T.V.** and **H. Soni** (1997) Guaranteed Profit Margins: A Demonstration of Retailer Power, *International Journal of Research in Marketing*, **14**, 35–56.

23. **Tricks, H.** and **E. Rigby** (2005) Tesco's Juggernaut Shows no Sign of Stalling, *Financial Times*, 2 June, 22.

24. **Rigby, E.** (2004) Sports Specialists Lose Their Way in Quest to be Followers of Fashion, *Financial Times*, 20 August, 21.

25. **Anderson, C.** (2006) *The Long Tail: How Endless Choice is Creating Unlimited Demand*, London: Random House.

26. **Jennings, D.** (2007) *Net, Blogs and Rock'n'Roll*, London: Nicholas Brealey.

27. **Davies, G.** (1992) Innovation in Retailing, *Creativity and Innovation Management*, **1** (4), 230.

28. **Reed, J.** (2007) Showrooms That Put on a Show, *Financial Times*, 29 November, 16.

29. **Suiter, J.** (2005) Tiny Margins for Dealers, Huge Profits for Importers, *Irish Times Motors Supplement*, 10 August, 2.

30. **Rigby, E.** (2006) Supermarkets Prepare to Beef Up Non-Food Ranges, *Financial Times*, 21 February, 5.

31. **Elg, U.** and **U. Johansson** (1996) Networking When National Boundaries Dissolve: The Swedish Food Sector, *European Journal of Marketing*, **30** (2), 62–74.

32. **Roberts, K.** (2006) *The Lovemarks Effect: Winning in the Consumer Revolution*, New York: Powerhouse Books.

33. **Felsted, A.** and **S. Goff** (2004) Going Global is Crucial to Deliver Goods, *Financial Times*, 17 June, 27.

34. **Anonymous** (2003) Benetton Starts 'Dring' Drive, *Financial Times*, 10 December, 33.

35. **Rigby, E.** (2005) The Tricky Task of Moving From the Warehouse to the Shelves, *Financial Times*, 5 May, 21.

36. **Pickard, J.** (2005) Growing Trend sees Warehouses Swell, *Financial Times*, 17 August, 25.

37. **Anonymous** (2004) Tagging Toothpaste and Toddlers, *Information Management Journal*, September–October, 22.

38. **Gilligan, E.** (2004) How RFID Will Affect Warehousing, *The Journal of Commerce*, 3–9 May, 31.

39. **Kelly, S.** (2003) Mini-Revolution for Supply Chains, *Treasury & Risk Management*, July–August, 15.

40. **Niemeyer, A., M.H. Pak** and **S. Ramaswamy** (2003) Smart Tags for Your Supply Chain, *McKinsey Quarterly*, 4, 22–3.

41. **Lillington, K.** (2008) Giving Voice to New Technology, *Irish Times Health Supplement*, 29 January, 4.

Online **LearningCentre**

When you have read this chapter, log on to the Online Learning Centre for *Foundations of Marketing* at **www.mcgraw-hill.co.uk/textbooks/jobber**, where you'll find multiple-choice test questions, links and extra online study tools for marketing.

Case 11 IKEA

Introduction

The Sweden-based Inter IKEA Systems BV (IKEA) was ranked 42 by *BusinessWeek* magazine in its list of top 100 global brands for 2005. According to the BrandChannel rankings, IKEA was the number one brand in Europe and Africa. IKEA was the world's largest furniture retailer that specialized in stylish but inexpensive Scandinavian-designed furniture. Its success was attributed to its vast experience in the furniture retail market, its product differentiation and cost leadership. The company sold its furniture in kits, to be assembled by customers at home. In addition to furniture, IKEA also sold utility items such as utensils, hooks, clips and stands. IKEA's founder, Ingvar Kamprad, had built an international furniture chain of 226 stores in Europe, Africa, Asia and the USA. For fiscal year 2004–05, the company generated revenues of US$17.9 billion, a 15 per cent increase over the previous fiscal year.

IKEA held a market share of not more than 10 per cent in the markets in which it operated. In spite of this, it had been successful in almost all countries, because of public awareness of the IKEA brand. According to Anders Dahlvig, Chief Executive Officer (CEO) of IKEA, 'Awareness of our brand is much bigger than the size of our company. That's because IKEA is far more than a furniture merchant. It sells a lifestyle that customers around the world embrace as a signal that they've arrived, that they have good taste and recognize value.' The British design magazine *Icon* said, 'If it wasn't for IKEA, most people would have no access to affordable contemporary design.' The magazine also voted Kamprad the most influential tastemaker in the world.

About IKEA

Kamprad established IKEA in 1943 at the age of 17. He came up with the name IKEA by combining the first letters of his name (Ingvar Kamprad), followed by the first letters of the farm and village he grew up in (Elmtaryd and Agunnaryd). Kamprad started his business by buying pens, Christmas cards, matches, cigarette lighters, nylon stockings and other items in bulk. Furniture was introduced to IKEA's product portfolio in 1947 and, by 1951, furniture sales had increased so much that Kamprad decided to discontinue all other products and concentrate solely on

selling furniture that was classy and low priced at the same time. In the same year, the first IKEA furniture catalogue was issued, and the first IKEA furniture shop was opened in 1953 at Almhult in Sweden.

In 1956, IKEA launched its most successful product: flat-pack furniture. It was invented by accident when an IKEA employee, Gillis Lundgren, realized that a bulky wooden table could fit into a car only when its legs were removed. This technology brought IKEA two distinct advantages: it made furniture easy to carry (for both the buyer and the company), and it also reduced overall costs as buyers could assemble the products at home using instructions provided by the company. These savings were passed on to the customers. Over the years, many more innovative products came from IKEA. Prominent among these was the 'Olga' chair, 'Tore' home storage systems and 'Privat' sofas. IKEA followed the practice of giving a name to each of its products. It named its products after Nordic towns, rivers, islands and counties.

IKEA did not have its own manufacturing facilities. Instead, it used subcontracted manufacturers all over the world for supplies. All research and development activities, however, were centralized in Sweden. No matter how beautiful a design, it was not put up for sale if it could not be made affordable. To achieve this level of affordability, IKEA engaged 12 designers at Almhult in Sweden, along with 80 freelancers to work in tandem with the production teams to identify materials and suppliers. This was a trial-and-error process that could take as long as three years. IKEA usually phased out a third of its product line every year.

In 1997, IKEA introduced 'Children's IKEA'. The company realized that the play areas, children's room settings, baby areas and special meals in the IKEA restaurant made the company's showroom a place kids loved to visit. This prompted it to work with two groups of experts to develop products for children. These included child psychologists and professors, who helped to develop products that were good for children's motor skills, social development and creativity. IKEA also worked with children to understand what they were interested in. Based on the results of this study, IKEA launched its kids' range of products. By 2005, IKEA had grown into a US$17.9 billion company, with over 84,000 co-workers spanning 44 countries across four continents.

Complete shopping experience

IKEA stores were usually located outside urban areas, isolated from other shops. This was done intentionally so that IKEA could create a complete shopping experience for customers. The IKEA products were themselves beautifully crafted and appealing, and even its stores were constructed so as to enthral shoppers. The visual appearance of the stores was the same the world over. The blue-and-yellow buildings were generally 300,000 square feet in size and each store stocked about 7000 items, from kitchen cabinets to candlesticks. IKEA targeted middle-class customers worldwide. IKEA made shopping easy for customers. For example, right at the entrance of the store, customers could drop their kids at the playroom, which had many types of safe play equipment, and then shop on their own in a leisurely manner.

The stores were constructed in the form of a circle, to allow shoppers to view all sections of the store. They had wide passageways that let the customers examine the furniture, which was aesthetically arranged as it would look in a home, with accessories like lamps, bed sheets, etc. The beautiful arrangements enticed shoppers to buy the products, as they could see how they would be used in a home.

Most IKEA products were competitively priced. Kamprad believed that, 'To design a desk that may cost US$1000 is easy for a furniture designer, but to design a functional and good desk which will cost US$50 can only be done by the very best. Expensive solutions to all kinds of problems are often signs of mediocrity.' Kamprad ensured that IKEA not only brought out the best products, but also that many people could buy them. There were even things shoppers would never put on their shopping list, which when displayed in IKEA stores and priced at under US$2 seemed to be worth having. Thus IKEA seemed to have a knack for creating a need for totally new products. A case in point was the 'Mallen' clip, used to hang magazines in the bathroom. This was one of IKEA's hottest-selling accessories. Researchers said people would never have thought of hanging up magazines in the bathroom. However, IKEA felt that a Mallen clip was a must in every home. Once people had seen a row of magazines hanging up, neatly suspended from a Mallen clip, in the bathroom section of an IKEA showroom, most of them latched on to the usefulness of the item and snapped it up. The Mallen clip cost only 90 pence for three. It was so affordable that one did not have to think twice before buying it. IKEA insiders called such items 'hot dogs'.

IKEA realized that hunger could keep customers away from its stores. Hence, it had a cafeteria located in the centre of the vast building to give shoppers a breather and allowed them to refresh themselves at the store itself instead of winding up their shopping in a hurry. The final destination for a customer was the warehouse, where all the big items were flat-packed, enabling shoppers to take their furniture home comfortably.

The IKEA supply chain

To achieve cost cutting, IKEA ensured that suppliers were located in low-cost nations, with close proximity to raw materials and reliable access to distribution channels. Not only did IKEA have globally integrated operations, it had also found an effective combination of low-cost, standardization of products, technology and quality. For instance, in addition to having stores in many countries, IKEA also had a global web of 2000 suppliers operating in 55 countries, which allowed the company to design items and have them produced in countries where materials and labour costs were low. IKEA bought most of its raw materials from China and Poland. These two markets were strategically placed to cater to the European and Asian markets respectively. Labour was also cheap in these countries. Furniture designs were imported from Sweden and the items were manufactured in these countries. The suppliers and designers had to customize some of the IKEA products to make them sell better in local markets.

The IKEA buzz

The buzz around IKEA had been a healthy contributor to the company's popularity. Since its inception, IKEA store openings witnessed huge crowds the world over. In April 2000, when IKEA opened a store in Emeryville, in Berkeley, California, a huge crowd gathered in the hope of collecting gift vouchers and US$149 chairs for the first 100 in queue. People had started queuing as early as a day before the opening of the store. IKEA was such a reputed brand that one customer, Bethany Cue, came all the way from Albany in New York to claim her vouchers.

Similarly, in early 2005, IKEA announced that it would be introducing 'Boklok' homes in the UK. The Boklok was a flat-pack house. It offered hope to hundreds of thousands of people in UK who were unable to buy a house of their own. Boklok homes were made from timber frames and could be either one- or two-bedroom homes. These homes were targeted at lower-income families. Providing affordable houses had been an issue of concern for the UK Government for over a decade. Hence, it welcomed IKEA's Boklok venture. The Boklok home had been very popular in Denmark, Norway, Finland and Sweden, where more than 2000 Bokloks occupied 45 sites. IKEA offered the Bokloks at 13 stores across the UK. The British showed great enthusiasm for IKEA's Bokloks on the day they were launched, with over 6000 customers coming to the opening at a north London IKEA store.

The challenges

In spite of its success all over the world, IKEA has been criticized for traffic jams and overcrowding at its outlets, particularly at store openings, which brought in frenzied crowds. In September 2004, three people were crushed to death and sixteen seriously injured in a stampede that broke out at IKEA's store opening in Jeddah, Saudi Arabia. More than 8000 people had gathered near the store for the US$150 gift vouchers, some of them having camped overnight. Immediately after the incident, IKEA released a statement that read, 'The management of IKEA Saudi Arabia expresses deep sorrow over the tragic incident that occurred at the opening hours of Jeddah's new showroom and conveys its sympathies and condolences to the families of the dead.'

Again, in February 2005, five people were hospitalized after hundreds were crushed at the opening of England's biggest IKEA store in Edmonton, London. More than 6000 people flocked to the store, tempted by advertisements that guaranteed big discounts, including £45 sofas and £30 bed frames, to those who bought before 3 am. Hence when the main doors were opened, the 40 security guards were besieged and crowds pushed through, leaving people pinned to the wall. Similar incidents happened at other store openings as well. It was beginning to look like IKEA had not done much to curb the pandemonium it was causing.

IKEA was also criticized for quality of service provided at its stores, particularly the long queues at the checkout. Customers have reported that people had abandoned their carts due to the long wait involved: 'People just walk out. If you've got an hour or maybe two hours in [during the trip], and it's taking you 45 minutes to get to the cash register, some people just say, "The heck with it, it's not worth it."' Justine Forsythe, a law student in the State of Minnesota, USA, took over two hours to get her billing done. She said, 'I think they were incredibly understaffed. I don't know if they didn't hire as many people as they could [have], maybe they just weren't prepared for the deluge of Minnesotans who would arrive.' On her second visit to the store to return a defective dresser, she received no help from IKEA staff to unload the piece of furniture. She also had a bitter experience with rude employees. She added, 'I couldn't find an employee to help me lift the dresser out of my car to get into the store to return it, so I asked several employees, and they're, like, "That's not my job." Finally, another customer helped me get it into the store.'

Notwithstanding all these issues, analysts recognized that IKEA had managed to build a brand identity of a company offering good designs at low prices. Kamprad had clearly played a major role in creating this IKEA image. However, maintaining this image and success may be even more difficult as the retailer grows in size throughout the world.

Questions

1. Analyse IKEA's positioning in the market. Why has it succeeded in achieving global appeal?
2. What are the key features of IKEA's store atmosphere? What role has atmosphere played in enabling the company to gain a competitive advantage?
3. What role does its physical distribution system play in IKEA's global success?
4. To what extent has IKEA become a victim of its own success?

This case was prepared by Komal Chary, under the direction of Vivek Gupta, ICFAI Center for Management Research (ICMR), from various published sources as a basis for class discussion rather than to illustrate effective or ineffective management. © 2006, ICFAI Center for Management Research.

Chapter 12
Marketing Planning and Strategy

Chapter Outline

The process of marketing planning

Marketing audit

Marketing objectives

Core strategy

Competitive strategies

Marketing mix decisions

Organization and implementation

Control

The rewards of marketing planning

Problems in making planning work

Learning Outcomes

By the end of this chapter you will understand:

1 the role of marketing planning within businesses
2 the process of marketing planning
3 the rewards and problems associated with marketing planning
4 the roles of industry analysis and internal analysis in planning and strategy
5 the different competitive strategies, and the sources of competitive advantage.

Google: good planning or not?

Google Checkout is a service for users, advertisers and participating merchants. Google Mobile is a product line for users to search and view the mobile web, while applications like Google Labs are a test bed for engineers, and Google Enterprise provides solutions for small to medium-sized enterprises (SMEs).

Online advertising revenues are Google's primary income stream. Internet advertising is the fastest-growing sector of the advertising business and, as we saw in Chapter 10, Google claims the lion's share of it. Its primary competitor is Yahoo!, but the latter's failure to agree a deal with Microsoft in 2008 meant that it failed to secure access to the resources needed to truly challenge Google on a global basis. Other competitors include Microsoft's MSN, AOL and a variety of smaller players.

Google is arguably the biggest business success story of the past decade. The company was founded by two Stanford University students, Larry Page and Sergey Brin, in 1998. Since then it has undergone phenomenal growth to become a globally recognized brand, and the use of the term 'to google' has become commonplace in everyday language. The company is headquartered in Mountain View, California, and for the financial year 2007 it generated revenues of US$16.5 billion and profits of over US$4 billion. With a market capitalization of almost US$180 billion, it has come a very long way in a short space of time.

Google is best known for its search technology, for which it is the market leader and the first port of call for many students completing marketing assignments! But its product range is much broader than just search. Google.com provides search solutions and personalization, and contains products like Google Web Search, Google Image Search, Google Scholar, Google News, Google Finance, Personalized Homepage and Search, as well as Google Video and YouTube. But it also offers products like Google Calendar, Gmail, Google Reader and Blogger. In addition, it provides various downloadable applications such as Google Desktop, Google Toolbar, and the Google GEO product line, including Google Earth, Google Maps and Google Sketchup.

Google's rapid rise raises interesting questions regarding marketing planning and strategy. It has largely eschewed the traditionally accepted models whereby plans are carefully crafted by top management and pushed down through the organization. Indeed, it could be argued that had the company adopted this command-and-control model, it may not have grown nearly as quickly. It has a much more democratic and flexible organizational culture. Employees can spend up to 20 per cent of their time on projects of their own choosing, and innovations are encouraged. Google is trying to harness the imagination and creativity of all its employees, which helps to explain the speed with which it has come up with many of the new products listed above. It does not have a detailed mission statement but rather two open-to-interpretation phases, namely 'don't be evil' and 'organize and make accessible the world's information'. It has raced ahead of its competitors and its acquisition of other businesses, like YouTube and Doubleclick, indicates that it is showing no sign of slowing down.[1]

In Chapter 1 we introduced the notion of marketing planning. Then, throughout the book, we have examined the nature of customers and markets, and the environmental context within which organizations operate. We have also examined the variety of decisions that need to be taken by marketers. Given the challenging competitive environment in which firms operate, it is important that these decisions are not taken in an ad hoc way but rather in a systematic and rational manner. The process by which businesses analyse the environment and their capabilities, decide upon courses of marketing action and implement those decisions is called **marketing planning**, and it is this that will be the focus of this chapter. Equally, it is important to remember that there must be a strategic element to marketing plans—that is, they must map out a direction for the company over the medium to long term. In this chapter we will also examine some of the popular frameworks used by companies to help them answer key strategic questions, such as where and how to compete, and how to grow. Answers to these questions will be central aspects of any marketing plan.

Marketing planning forms part of the broader concept known as 'strategic planning'; this involves not only marketing but also the fit between production, finance and personnel strategies, and the environment. The aim of strategic planning is to shape and reshape a company so that its business and products continue to meet corporate objectives (e.g. profit or sales growth). Because marketing management is charged with the responsibility of managing the interface between the company and its environment, it has a key role to play in strategic planning.

The achievement of an understanding of the role of marketing planning in strategy development is hampered somewhat by the nature of companies. At the simplest level a company may market only one product in one market. The role of marketing planning would be to ensure that the marketing mix for the product matches (changing) customer needs, as well as seeking opportunities to use the companies' strengths to market other products in new markets. Many companies, however, market a range of products in numerous markets. The contribution that marketing planning can make in this situation is similar to that in the first case; however, there is an additional function: that of the determination of the allocation of resources to each product (see Chapter 6). Inasmuch as resource allocation should be dependent, in part, on the attractiveness of the market for each product, marketing is inevitably involved in this decision.

A firm may be composed of a number of businesses (often equating to divisions), each of which serves distinct groups of customers and has a distinct set of competitors. Each business may be strategically autonomous and thus form a **strategic business unit** (SBU). A major component of a corporate plan will be the allocation of resources to each SBU. Strategic decisions at the corporate level are normally concerned with acquisition, divestment and diversification. Here, too, marketing can play a role through the identification of opportunities and threats in the environment as they relate to current and prospective businesses.

Despite these complications, the following essential questions need to be asked in each situation.

- Where are we now?
- How did we get there?
- Where are we heading?
- Where would we like to be?
- How do we get there?
- Are we on course?

While these may seem relatively simple questions, they can be difficult to answer in practice. Businesses comprise individuals who may have very different views on the answers to these questions. Furthermore, the outcome of the planning process may have fundamental implications for their jobs. Planning is, therefore, a political activity, and those with a vested interest may view it from a narrow departmental, rather than business-wide, perspective. A key issue in getting planning systems to work is tackling such behavioural problems.[2] However, at this point in this chapter it is important to understand the process of marketing planning. A common approach to the analysis of the marketing planning process is at the business unit level (see, for example, Day)[3] and this is the level adopted here.

The process of marketing planning

The process of marketing planning is outlined in Figure 12.1. The process provides a well-defined path from generating a **business mission** to implementing and controlling the resultant plans. It provides a framework that shows how all the key elements of marketing discussed so far relate to each other. In real life, planning is rarely so straightforward and logical. Different people may be involved at various stages of the planning process, and the degrees to

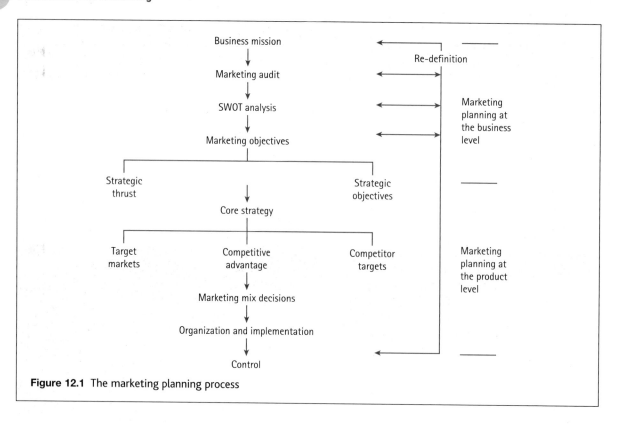

Figure 12.1 The marketing planning process

which they accept and are influenced by the outcomes of earlier planning stages are variable.

Business mission

Ackoff defined the business mission as:

> '. . . a broadly defined, enduring statement of purpose that distinguishes a business from others of its type.'[4]

This definition captures two essential ingredients in mission statements: they are enduring and specific to the individual organization.[5] Two fundamental questions that need to be addressed are: 'What business are we in?' and 'What business do we want to be in?' The answers define the scope and activities of the company, and will be determined by an assessment of the needs of the market, the competences of the firm and background of the company plus the personalities of its senior management.

Including the market and needs factors ensures that the business definition is market-focused rather than product-based (see Exhibit 12.1). Thus the purpose of a company such as Nokia is not to manufacture telephones but to allow people to communicate with each other as is exemplified by its slogan 'connecting people'. The reason for ensuring that a business definition is market-focused is that products are tran-

sient, but basic needs such as transportation, entertainment and eating are lasting. Thus, Levitt argued that a business should be viewed as a customer-satisfying process not a goods-producing process.[6] By adopting a customer perspective, new opportunities are more likely to be seen.

Management must be wary of a definition that is too wide, although this advice has merit in advocating the avoidance of a narrow business definition. Levitt suggested that railroad companies would have survived had they defined their business as transportation and moved into the airline business. However, this ignores the limits of business competence of the railroads. Did they possess the necessary skills and resources to run an airline? Clearly a key constraint on a business definition can be the competences (both actual and potential) of management, and the resources at their disposal. Conversely, competences can act as the motivator for widening a business mission. Asda (Associated Dairies) redefined its business mission as a producer and distributor of milk to a retailer of fast-moving consumer goods (fmcg) partly on the basis of its distribution skills, which it rightly believed could be extended to products beyond milk.

The background of the company and the personalities of its senior management are the final determinants

Exhibit 12.1 The vision of the legendary guitar-making company Gibson is to reflect the spirit and emotion of the people who use its products

of the business mission. Businesses that have established themselves in the marketplace over many years and have a clear position in the minds of the customer may ignore opportunities that are at variance with that position. The personalities and beliefs of the people who run businesses also shape the business mission. This last factor emphasizes the judgemental nature of business definition. There is no right or wrong business mission in abstract. The mission should be based on the vision that top management and their subordinates have of the future of the business. This vision is a coherent and powerful statement of what the business should aim to become.[7] The business mission will serve as an overriding influence on the nature of the marketing plan and should also serve to motivate all staff to attain the targets set out in the plan.

Marketing audit

A **marketing audit** is a systematic examination of a firm's marketing environment, objectives, strategies and activities, which aims to identify key strategic issues, problem areas and opportunities. The marketing audit is, therefore, the basis on which a plan of

action to improve marketing performance can be built. The marketing audit provides answers to the following questions.

- Where are we now?
- How did we get there?
- Where are we heading?

The answers to these questions depend on an analysis of the internal and external environments of a business. This analysis benefits from a clear mission statement since the latter defines the boundaries of the environmental scan and aids decisions regarding which strategic issues and opportunities are important.

An internal audit concentrates on those areas that are under the control of marketing management, whereas an external audit focuses on those forces over which management has no control. The results of the marketing audit are a key determinant of the future direction of the business and may give rise to a redefined business mission statement. Alongside the marketing audit, a business may conduct audits of other functional areas such as production, finance and personnel. The co-ordination and integration of these audits produces a composite business plan in which

Table 12.1 External marketing audit checklist

Macroenvironment (see Chapter 2)
Economic: inflation, interest rates, unemployment
Social/cultural: age distribution, lifestyle changes, values, attitudes
Technological: new product and process technologies, materials
Political/legal: monopoly control, new laws, regulations
Ecological: conservation, pollution, energy

The market
Market size, growth rates, trends and developments
Customers: who are they, their choice criteria, how, when, where do they buy, how do they rate us vis-à-vis competition on product, promotion, price, distribution
Market segmentation: how do customers group, what benefits does each group seek
Distribution: power changes, channel attractiveness, growth potential, physical distribution methods, decision-makers and influencers
Suppliers: who and where they are, their competences and shortcomings, trends affecting them, future outlook

Competition
Who are the major competitors: actual and potential
What are their objectives and strategies
What are their strengths (distinctive competences) and weaknesses (vulnerability analysis)
Market shares and size of competitors
Profitability analysis
Entry barriers

marketing issues play a central role since they concern decisions about which products to manufacture for which markets. These decisions clearly have production, financial and personnel implications, and successful implementation depends on each functional area acting in concert. A checklist of those areas that are likely to be examined in a marketing audit is given in Tables 12.1 and 12.2.

External analysis

External analysis covers the macroenvironment, the market and competition. The macroenvironment consists of broad environmental issues that may impinge on the business. These include the economy, social/cultural issues, technological changes, political/legal factors and ecological concerns (as we saw in Chapter 2).

The market consists of statistical analyses of market size, growth rates and trends, and **customer analysis** (including who they are, what choice criteria they use, how they rate competitive offerings and market segmentation bases); next, **distribution analysis** covers significant movements in power bases, channel attractiveness studies, an identification of physical distribution methods, and understanding the role and interests of decision-makers, and influences within distributors.

Table 12.2 Internal marketing audit checklist

Operating results (by product, customer, geographic region)
Sales
Market share
Profit margins
Costs

Strategic issues analysis
Marketing objectives
Market segmentation
Competitive advantage
Core competences
Positioning
Portfolio analysis

Marketing mix effectiveness
Product
Price
Promotion
Distribution

Marketing structures
Marketing organization
Marketing training
Intra- and interdepartmental communication

Marketing systems
Marketing information systems
Marketing planning system
Marketing control system

Competitor analysis examines the nature of actual and potential competitors, and their objectives and strategies. It would also seek to identify their strengths (distinctive competences), weaknesses (vulnerability analysis), market shares and size. For example, the downloading of movies over the internet presents a significant threat to sales of DVDs, one of the biggest revenue earners for movie-makers. Profitability analysis examines **industry** profitability and the comparative performance of competitors. Finally, entry barrier analysis identifies the key financial and non-financial barriers that protect the industry from competitor attack.

A very popular external analysis framework is Porter's 'five forces' model. Porter was interested in why some industries appeared to be inherently more profitable than others, and concluded that industry attractiveness was a function of five forces: the threat of entry of new competitors; the threat of substitutes; the bargaining power of suppliers; the bargaining power of buyers; and the rivalry between existing competitors. Each of these five forces, in turn, comprises a number of elements that combine to determine the strength of each force, as shown in Figure 12.2. So, for example, industries that have high barriers to entry but relatively low levels of buyer/supplier power, low threat of

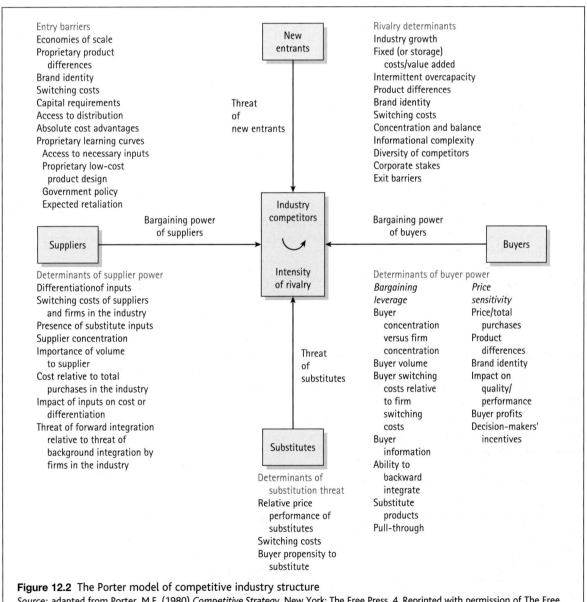

Figure 12.2 The Porter model of competitive industry structure
Source: adapted from Porter, M.E. (1980) *Competitive Strategy*, New York: The Free Press, 4. Reprinted with permission of The Free Press, an imprint of Simon & Schuster. Copyright © 1980 by The Free Press.

Marketing in Action 12.1: Airbus vs Boeing

> **Study guide:** Below is a review of the competition between Airbus and Boeing. Read it and examine the drivers of profitability in aircraft manufacturing. Is it or is it not a profitable industry, and why?

Few industries are as concentrated as the aircraft manufacturing business. Here two titans, one in Europe (Airbus) and the other in the United States (Boeing), slug it out for dominance of a business worth over US$40 billion annually. So why are there only two competitors in such a big industry?

First, it is a sector with significant barriers to entry. The manufacture of an aeroplane involves huge technical risks, particularly in terms of safety. So a new-model aircraft requires an upfront R&D spending in the region of US$10 billion even before its first test flight. (By way of comparison, for example, the Channel Tunnel between Britain and France cost US$11 billion.) Once production starts, the learning curve is steep and difficult. Each doubling of production generally yields a cut of one-fifth off the unit cost per plane. Consequently it takes production of about 500–600 aircraft before a model starts to earn a profit. This typically amounts to around 10 years of production as industry demand varies between 700 and 800 planes covering all segments such as short-haul, single-aisle, long-range and jumbo aircraft. Both major airlines receive significant state subsidies and access to such financial support represents another significant barrier to entry.

Modern planes sell for between US$50 million and US$250 million, depending on whether they are 120 seaters or jumbos. In general, the bargaining power of buyers is relatively limited as the industry is more concentrated than the buyers, volumes are small, switching costs are high and there is little threat of backward integration. Occasionally, in times of slack demand in the industry generally, buyers are able to extract good deals from the manufacturers. Similarly, the bargaining power of suppliers is relatively limited and the threat of substitutes is not an issue in this business.

The core of the battle between Boeing and Airbus lies in product development. Airbus launched its super-jumbo A380 in 2005 but technical and production problems delayed the delivery of the first aircraft by two years. Despite the fact that it has almost 200 orders for the jet, it will be 2010 before it can deliver at least 45 per year. All the added costs of the delays and extra work have pushed the A380's development costs from the original US$10 billion to US$17 billion. Its break-even point has now jumped from 250 units in 2000 to 420.

Based on: Anonymous (2005);[8] Done (2007);[9] Marlowe (2005)[10]

substitutes and relatively benign competition will be more attractive than industries with the opposite set of forces. For an example of the forces affecting profitability in an industry see Marketing in Action 12.1. We shall now look briefly at each of the forces in turn, and see how this framework can assist firms in answering the first three key planning questions identified earlier:

- Where are we now?
- How did we get there?
- Where are we heading?

The threat of new entrants

Because new entrants can raise the level of competition in an industry, they have the potential to reduce its attractiveness. The threat of new entrants depends on the barriers to entry. High entry barriers exist in some industries (e.g. pharmaceuticals), whereas other industries are much easier to enter (e.g. restaurants). Key entry barriers include:

- economies of scale
- capital requirements
- switching costs
- access to distribution
- expected retaliation.

If you enjoy flying first class with our competitors
may we recommend our business class cabin?

FIRST
BRITISH AIRWAYS

Exhibit 12.2 This British Airways advertisement makes comparisons with its competitors' offerings; to ensure that the advert stood out from others, it appeared as a bound insert printed on specially imported Italian paper; the premium look and feel was further established through the stylish, minimalist art direction, featuring silver embossed text

The bargaining power of suppliers

The cost of raw materials and components can have a major bearing on a firm's profitability. The higher the bargaining power of suppliers, the higher these costs. The bargaining power of suppliers will be high when:

- there are many buyers and few dominant suppliers
- there are differentiated, highly valued products
- suppliers threaten to integrate forward into the industry
- buyers do not threaten to integrate backward into supply
- the industry is not a key customer group to the suppliers.

A firm can reduce the bargaining power of suppliers by seeking new sources of supply, threatening to integrate backward into supply and designing standardized components so that many suppliers are able to produce them.

The bargaining power of buyers

As we saw in Chapter 11, the concentration of European retailing has raised buyers' bargaining power relative to that of manufacturers. The bargaining power of buyers is greater when:

- there are few dominant buyers and many sellers
- products are standardized
- buyers threaten to integrate backward into the industry
- suppliers do not threaten to integrate forward into the buyer's industry
- the industry is not a key supplying group for buyers.

The influence of buyers on an industry is demonstrated in Marketing in Action 12.2.

The threat of substitutes

The presence of substitute products can lower industry attractiveness and profitability because they put a constraint on price levels. For example, tea and coffee are fairly close substitutes in most European countries. Raising the price of coffee, therefore, would make tea more attractive. The threat of substitute products depends on:

- buyers' willingness to substitute
- the relative price and performance of substitutes
- the costs of switching to substitutes.

The threat of substitute products can be lowered by building up switching costs, which may be psychological—for example, by creating strong distinctive brand personalities and maintaining a price differential commensurate with perceived customer values.

Industry competitors

The intensity of rivalry between competitors in an industry depends on the following factors.

- *Structure of competition*: there is more intense rivalry when there are a large number of small competitors or a few equally balanced competitors; there is less rivalry when a clear leader (at least 50 per cent larger than the second) exists with a large cost advantage.
- *Structure of costs*: high fixed costs encourage price cutting to fill capacity.
- *Degree of differentiation*: commodity products encourage rivalry, while highly differentiated products that are hard to copy are associated with less intense rivalry.
- *Switching costs*: when switching costs are high because a product is specialized, the customer has invested a lot of resources in learning how to

Marketing in Action 12.2: Chilly time for convenience foods

> **Study guide:** Below is a review of competitive conditions in the chilled foods business. Use Porter's 'five forces' framework to explain why the manufacturing of chilled foods is a low-profit business.

As we saw in Chapter 3, on consumer behaviour, people's lifestyles have changed dramatically. They are working longer hours, commuting greater distances to work, and family unit sizes are getting smaller due to increases in divorce levels and decisions to defer having children. All these factors have combined to create a boom for chilled foods that meet the consumer's demand for convenience. Chilled foods like ready meals, desserts and dressed salads were deemed to be fresher and healthier than their predecessor, frozen foods. The market in the UK has doubled in a period of 10 years to over £2 billion and continued growth is being predicted. But, despite these promising market conditions, the industry is not as profitable as it might appear.

The primary reason for this is the bargaining power of buyers. Chilled foods are one of the most buoyant sectors for sales of own-label or retailer brands, which dominate the industry. There are a variety of manufacturers of these products, such as Northern Foods, Hazlewood and Uniq, but they have struggled to effectively build their own brands in the marketplace. As a result, consumers buy retailer brands like Marks & Spencer or Tesco, which in turn means that they can be more demanding of their suppliers. They expect rapid service and product innovation, and regularly switch contracts between suppliers as a way of driving prices down. Prices for some products are actually falling and this presents major challenges for manufacturers as chilled foods is a heavily capital-intensive industry. Approximately £1 of investment is required for every £2 to £3 of sales.

The effect of all this has been to reduce the profitability in the industry for chilled food manufacturers. They have responded to the pressure from own-labels by dropping the prices of their own brands, with the result that this sector is the one with the smallest differentials between the price of own-label and manufacturer brands. So, despite its strong top-line growth, the forces of competition have eroded profitability for many of the industry players.

Based on: Urry (2005);[11] Wiggins (2005)[12]

---

use a product or has made tailor-made investments that are worthless with other products and suppliers, rivalry is reduced.

- *Strategic objectives*: when competitors are pursuing build strategies, competition is likely to be more intense than when playing hold or harvest strategies.
- *Exit barriers*: when barriers to leaving an industry are high due to such factors as lack of opportunities elsewhere, high vertical integration, emotional barriers or the high cost of closing down plant, rivalry will be more intense than when exit barriers are low.

Internal analysis

An internal audit permits the performance and activities of a business to be assessed in the light of envir-onmental developments. Operating results form the basis of assessment through analysis of sales, market share, profit margins and costs. **Strategic issues analysis** examines the suitability of marketing objectives and segmentation bases in the light of changes in the marketplace. Competitive advantages and the core competences on which they are based would be reassessed and the positioning of products in the market critically reviewed. Finally, product portfolios should be analysed to determine future strategic objectives.

Each aspect of the marketing mix is reviewed in the light of changing customer requirements and competitor activity. The **marketing structures** on which marketing activities are based should be analysed. Marketing structure consists of the marketing organization, training, and the intra- and interdepartmental communication that takes place within an organization. Marketing organization is reviewed to determine fit with strategy and the market, and marketing training requirements are examined. Finally, communications and relationships within the marketing, department, and between marketing and other functions (e.g. R&D, engineering, production) need to be appraised.

Marketing systems are audited to check their effectiveness. This covers the marketing information, planning and **control** systems that support marketing activities. Shortfalls in information provision are analysed; the marketing planning system is critically appraised for cost effectiveness, and the marketing control system is assessed in the light of accuracy, timeliness (whether it provides evaluations when managers require them) and coverage (whether the system evaluates the key variables affecting company performance).

The checklists in Tables 12.1 and 12.2 provide the basis for deciding on the topics to be included in the marketing audit. However, to give the same amount of attention and detailed analysis to every item would cause the audit to grind to a halt under the weight of data and issues. In practice, the judgement of those conducting the audit is critical in deciding the key items to focus upon. Those factors that are considered of crucial importance to the company's performance will merit most attention. One by-product of the marketing audit may be a realization that information about key environmental issues is lacking.

All assumptions should be made explicit as an ongoing part of the marketing audit. For example, key assumptions might be:

- inflation will average 5 per cent during the planning period
- VAT levels will not be changed
- worldwide overcapacity will remain at 150 per cent
- no new entrants into the market will emerge.

The marketing audit should not be a desperate attempt to turn around an ailing business, but an ongoing activity. Some companies conduct an annual audit as part of their annual planning system; others, operating in less turbulent environments, may consider two or three years an adequate period between audits. Some companies may feel that the use of an outside consultant to co-ordinate activities and provide an objective, outside view is beneficial while others may believe that their own managers are best

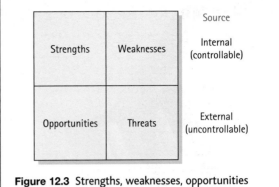

Figure 12.3 Strengths, weaknesses, opportunities and threats (SWOT) analysis

equipped to conduct such analyses. Clearly there is no set formula for deciding when and by whom the audit is conducted. The decision ultimately rests on the preferences and situation facing the management team.

SWOT analysis

A structured approach to evaluating the strategic position of a business by identifying its strengths, weaknesses, opportunities and threats is known as a **SWOT analysis**. It provides a simple method of synthesizing the results of the marketing audit. Internal strengths and weaknesses are summarized as they relate to external opportunities and threats (see Figure 12.3).

For a SWOT analysis to be useful a number of guidelines must be followed. First, not only absolute, but also relative strengths and weakness should be identified. Relative strengths focus on strengths and weaknesses as compared to the competition. Thus, if everyone produces quality products this is not identified as a relative strength. Two lists should be drawn up based on absolute and relative strengths and weaknesses. Strengths that can be exploited can be both absolute and relative, but how they are exploited and the degree to which they can be used depends on whether the competition also possesses them. Relative strengths provide the distinctive competences of a business (see Exhibit 12.3). But strengths need to be looked at objectively as they can sometimes turn into weaknesses. A case in point is Sony, one of whose strengths has been its product innovation capabilities. Such was the success of its products, like the Walkman, that it seems to have taken its eye off the market and technological trends. For example, the Walkman has been supplanted by the Apple iPod in the portable audio business and similarly its dominance of cathode ray tube TV

Exhibit 12.3 Jo Malone has used its strengths in putting together unique combinations of ingredients to build a distinctive position in the competitive cosmetics industry

technology has caused it to miss the trend towards flat-screen televisions.[13]

An absolute weakness that competitors also possess should be identified because it can clearly become a source of relative strength if overcome. If all businesses in an industry are poor at after-sales service, this should be noted as a weakness, as it provides the potential for gaining competitive advantage. Relative weaknesses should also be listed because these may be the sources of competitive disadvantage to which managerial attention should be focused. For example, internal analysis by the DSG group, which owns Dixons, PC World and Currys, found that customer service, the internal layout of stores and product presentation were significant weaknesses.[14]

Second, only those resources or capabilities that would be valued by the customer should be included when evaluating strengths and weaknesses. Thus, strengths such as 'We are an old established firm', 'We are a large supplier', and 'We are technologically advanced' should be questioned for their impact on customer satisfaction. It is conceivable that such bland generalizations confer as many weaknesses as strengths.

Third, opportunities and threats should be listed as anticipated events or trends *outside* the business that have implications for performance. They should not be couched in terms of strategies. For example, 'To enter market segment X' is not an opportunity but a strategic objective that may result from a perceived opportunity arising from the emergence of market segment X as attractive because of its growth potential and lack of competition. The ability to spot and exploit an opportunity can lead to success that dramatically exceeds expectations, as demonstrated by the rapid growth of companies like Amazon and Google. It also requires the kind of foresight described in Marketing in Action 12.3.

Marketing objectives

The definition of **marketing objectives** may be derived from the results of the marketing audit and the SWOT analysis. Two types of objective need to be considered: strategic thrust and strategic objectives.

Strategic thrust

Objectives should be set in terms of which products to sell in which markets. This describes the **strategic thrust** of the business. The strategic thrust defines the future direction of the business, and the basic alternatives are summarized in the Ansoff Growth Matrix, as shown in Figure 12.4. These are:

- existing products in existing markets (market penetration or expansion)
- new products for existing markets (product development)

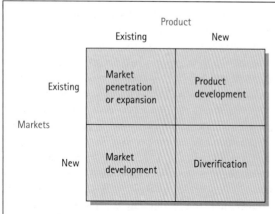

Figure 12.4 Product growth strategies: the Ansoff Matrix

Marketing in Action 12.3: Time to Think

Study guide: Below is a review of the development and marketing of the Think electric car. Electric cars have been in development for some time. Why is it that the market opportunity for these cars seems to be appearing only now?

The motor car is one of the most celebrated product innovations, but is it sustainable in a world of depleting oil stocks and climate change caused by carbon emissions? Not according to a small Norwegian company called Think Nordic ASA, which has pioneered the development of small, electric city cars. Having been part of the Ford Group until 2003, Think has been developing and refining its prototype for some time. It anticipates launching the first version of its car in 2008 and aims to be selling over 10,000 in Norway, Denmark, Switzerland and the UK by 2009. The brand, which will be known as the Think City, is a small two-seater car, about two feet shorter than a Mini Cooper. Its current battery is speed-limited to 62 miles per hour and it can travel for about 112 miles on a single charge.

Aside from being very different in appearance, the car is also manufactured differently. Essentially, it is assembled from prefabricated parts, which means that it can be made quickly, flexibly and close to its market rather than the assemble-and-export model used by current manufacturers, which also leaves a significant carbon footprint. Think also aims to dispense with car showrooms, inviting customers to buy the product online and to design their own Thinks in brand stores like those run by Apple. In a manner similar to global leaders like Dell, Think aims to build a car only after it has been sold to a customer. Mainstream advertising will also be avoided, with the company preferring to use buzz marketing instead. And, in a novel innovation, the car will be internet-ready so that a user can send it a text message to check its battery charge, for example.

Think is aiming to capitalize on an emerging market opportunity for more environmentally friendly cars. The Toyota Prius hybrid car has been a best-seller and several other companies are developing prototypes of electric cars. These new cars have been in development for many years, but it appears that increasing concern for the environment means that their time has finally come.

Based on: Reed (2007);[15] Woody (2007)[16]

- existing products in new markets (market development)
- new products for new markets (diversification).

We will now look at each of these in turn.

- *Market penetration*: this strategy involves taking the existing product in the existing market and attempting to increase penetration. Existing customers may become more brand loyal (i.e. brand switch less often) and/or new customers in the same market may begin to buy the brand. Other tactics to increase penetration include getting existing customers to use the brand more often (e.g. eat breakfast cereals as daytime snacks) and to use a greater quantity when they use it (e.g. two teaspoons of coffee instead of one). The latter tactic would also have the effect of expanding the market. Market penetration is usually achieved by more effective use of promotion or distribution, or by cutting prices.

- *Product development*: this strategy involves increasing sales by improving current products or developing new products for current markets. For example, many companies provide additional services to their customers. Faced with pressure on their margins for product sales, drugstores in the USA have started providing walk-in clinics where patients are examined by nurse practitioners who conduct basic procedures such as vaccinations for lower prices than doctors. Global accounting firms like KPMG and Deloitte provide management consulting services to clients.

- *Market development*: this strategy is used when current products are sold in new markets. This may involve moving into new international markets or moving into new market segments. For example, two-thirds of Americans live within three miles of a Pizza Hut, Taco Bell or KFC, therefore Yum! Brands, the owner of these franchises, has concentrated on China for its future growth, where it has established a clear lead over McDonald's, its main rival.[17]
- *Diversification*: this strategy occurs when new products are developed for new markets. This is the most risky strategy but may be necessary when a company's current products and markets offer few prospects of future growth. When there is synergy between the existing and new products this strategy is more likely to work. For example, by developing an online library, Google is aiming to become a content provider rather than just a search engine. It has signed deals with a number of leading libraries around the world, where it will scan thousands of volumes and make them available online.[18]

Strategic objectives

Alongside objectives for product/market direction, **strategic objectives** for each product also need to be agreed. This begins the process of planning at the product level. There are four alternatives:

1. build
2. hold
3. harvest
4. divest.

For new products, the strategic objective will inevitably be to build sales and market share. For existing products the appropriate strategic objective will depend on the particular situation associated with the product. This will be determined in the market audit, SWOT analysis and evaluation of the strategic options outlined earlier. In particular, product portfolio planning tools such as the Boston Consulting Group's Growth-Share Matrix (as outlined in Chapter 6) may be used to aid this analysis.

The important point to remember at this stage is that *building* sales and market share is not the only sensible strategic objective for a product. As we shall see, *holding* sales and market share may make commercial sense under certain conditions; *harvesting*, where sales and market share are allowed to fall but profit margins are maximized, may also be preferable to building; finally, *divestment*, where the product is dropped or sold, can be the logical outcome of the situation analysis.

Together, strategic thrust and strategic objectives define where the business and its products intend to go in the future.

Core strategy

When objectives have been set, a way to achieve them must be decided upon. **Core strategy** focuses on how objectives can be accomplished, and consists of three key elements: target markets, competitor targets and establishing a competitive advantage. We shall now examine each of these elements in turn and discuss the relationship between them.

Target markets

The choice of **target market**(s) is a central plank of core strategy. As we saw in Chapter 5, marketing is not about chasing any customer at any price. A decision has to be made regarding those groups of customers (segments) that are attractive to the business, and that match its supply capabilities. To varying degrees, the choice of target market to serve will be considered during SWOT analysis and the setting of marketing objectives. For example, when considering the strategic thrust of the business, decisions regarding which markets to serve must be made. However, this may be defined in broad terms—for example, 'Enter the business personal computer market'. Within that market there will be a number of segments (customer groups) of varying attractiveness and a choice has to be made regarding which segments to serve.

In Chapter 5, we identified a variety of bases for segmenting markets. Information regarding size, growth potential, level of competitor activity, customer requirements and key factors for success is needed to facilitate the assessment of the attractiveness of each segment. This may have been compiled during the marketing audit and should be considered in light of the capabilities of the business to compete effectively in each specific target market. The marketing audit and SWOT analysis will provide the basis for judging the business's capabilities.

Competitor targets

In tandem with decisions regarding markets are judgements about **competitor targets**. These are the organizations against which a company chooses to compete directly, and sometimes the competition is head-on. Weak competitors may be viewed as easy prey and resources channelled to attack them. For example, major airlines are accused from time to time of aggressively targeting the routes used by their smaller competitors, either through heavy promotion or price discounting.

Competitive advantage

The key to superior performance is to gain and hold a competitive advantage. Firms can gain a competitive advantage through differentiation of their product offering, which provides superior customer value, or by managing for lowest delivered cost. Evidence for this proposition was provided by Hall,[19] who examined the competitive strategies pursued by the two leading firms (in terms of return on investment) in eight mature industries characterized by slow growth and intense competition. In each industry, the two leading firms offered either high product differentiation or the lowest delivered cost. In most cases, an industry's return-on-investment leader opted for one of the strategies, while the second-place firm pursued the other.

Competitive strategies

When combined with the competitive scope of activities (broad vs narrow) these two means of competitive advantage result in four generic strategies: differentiation, cost leadership, differentiation focus and cost focus. The differentiation and cost leadership strategies seek competitive advantage in a broad range of market or industry segments, whereas differentiation focus and cost focus strategies are confined to a narrow segment (see Marketing in Action 12.4). Seeking one of these positions of advantage is critical to survival. For example, the only players remaining in the fashion business are either megabrands with a billion dollars in sales, such as Gucci, Louis Vuitton, Burberry, Prada and others, or niche brands with sales of between US$1 million and US$100 million, such as Rochas and Balenciaga.

Differentiation

Differentiation strategy involves the choice of one or more choice criteria that are used by many buyers in an industry. A firm then uniquely positions itself to meet these criteria. For example, firms might seek to be better (i.e. have superior quality), be faster (i.e. respond more quickly) or be closer (i.e. build better relationships with customers).[20] The aim is to differentiate in a way that leads to a price premium in excess of the cost of differentiating. Differentiation gives customers a reason to prefer one product over another and thus is central to strategic marketing thinking. But it can also be a risky strategy, as demonstrated by the case of Volkswagen. In an effort to develop high-quality cars, it has the highest capital

spending of any car manufacturer at 8.2 per cent of sales.[21] This level of investment has not resulted in differentiated brands in the marketplace.

Cost leadership

The cost leadership approach involves the achievement of the lowest cost position in an industry. Many segments in an industry are served and great importance is placed on minimizing costs on all fronts. So long as the price achievable for its products is around the industry average, cost leadership should result in superior performance. Thus, cost leaders often market standard products that are believed to be acceptable to customers. Ryanair is a cost leader in aviation and Dell a cost leader in personal computers. They market acceptable products at reasonable prices, which means that their low costs result in above-average profits. Toyota is working on a new approach to car design, development and manufacturing in a bid to come up with an ultra-low-cost car. Some cost leaders need to discount prices in order to achieve high sales levels. The aim here is to achieve superior performance by ensuring that the cost advantage over the competition is not offset by the price discount. No-frills supermarket discounters like Costco, KwikSave and Aldi fall into this category.

Differentiation focus

By taking a differentiation focus approach, a firm aims to differentiate within one or a small number of target market segments (see Exhibit 12.4). The special needs of the segment mean that there is an

Exhibit 12.4 The unique designs of Spain's Camper shoes give them a competitive advantage in the marketplace

opportunity to differentiate the product offering from competitors who may be targeting a broader group of customers. For example, some small speciality chemical companies thrive on taking orders that are too small or specialized to be of interest to their larger competitors. Similarly, Domino's Pizza has built the world's biggest home-delivery pizza company on the back of a strategy of fast service and consistent quality. The company now delivers a million pizzas a night from 7300 outlets in 50 countries.[22] Micro-breweries have been on the rise around the world to meet niche tastes not catered for by the big brewers. Those firms adopting a differentiation focus must be clear that the needs of their target group differ from those of the broader market (otherwise there will be no basis for differentiation) and that existing competitors are underperforming.

Cost focus

By adopting a cost focus strategy, a firm seeks a cost advantage with one or a small number of target market segments. By dedicating itself to a segment, the cost focuser can seek economies that may be ignored or missed by broadly targeted competitors. In some instances, competition, by trying to achieve wide market acceptance, may be overperforming (for example, by providing unwanted services) to one segment of customers. By providing a basic product offering, a cost advantage will be gained that may exceed the price discount necessary to sell it. For example, Kiwibank is a low-cost domestic bank that was set up by the New Zealand Government as an alternative to the foreign-owned banks dominating the market. It has proven particularly attractive to low-income customers because of its low fee structure.[23]

Marketing in Action 12.4: Competitive strategy in semiconductors

Study guide: Below is a review of competition between Intel and AMD in the semiconductor business. Read it and describe the competitive strategies being pursued by both companies.

Though we may not even know what they look like, semiconductors play a very important part in our everyday lives. They are the tiny electronic devices that are central to the operation of a variety of modern products like personal computers, mobile phones and music players. There are two main manufacturers in this industry, both based in America. Intel is the best known, thanks to its pioneering use of the 'Intel Inside' slogan, which was made famous in the advertising used by computer manufacturers. Its rival is AMD (Advanced Micro Devices); the two companies have been locked in a struggle for industry leadership over the years.

The battle between Intel and AMD illustrates the different approaches that are taken to competitive strategy. Between them, they sell the chips for four out of every five computers sold and the main weapon of competition is differentiation based on semiconductor performance. For example, AMD has traditionally been seen as the maker of cheap processors for consumer desktops, so, in 2003, it released its Opteron processor to run company servers, and built a reputation for quality and reliability. It also led with innovations such as the 'dual core' processor—that is, a processor with two 'brains' that could handle multiple programs running at the same time. These innovations enabled it to grow its share of the market to almost 25 per cent and challenge Intel's dominance.

But its larger competitor was able to use its scale and resources to respond aggressively. In June 2006, Intel launched its 'dual core' chips and also moved to the next level of miniaturization, making chips with circuit widths of 65-billionths of a metre, down from 90 nanometres. These new chips are 30 per cent smaller, and size matters because they are cheaper to produce and use less energy in operation. Price competition and relationships with leading customers are also important weapons in this competitive battle. Intel has frequently dropped the prices of its chips to clear old stocks when new products come along, and AMD has also filed lawsuits against it, alleging that it has engaged in exclusive deals with leading customers and/or offered them incentives not to purchase AMD chips.

Based on: Anonymous (2006);[24] Nuttall (2006);[25] Nuttall (2007)[26]

Choosing a competitive strategy

So it seems that the essence of corporate success is to choose a generic strategy and pursue it enthusiastically. Below-average performance is associated with failure to achieve any of these generic strategies. The result is no competitive advantage: a stuck-in-the-middle position that results in lower performance than that of the cost leaders, differentiators or focusers in any market segment. An example of a company that made the mistake of moving to a stuck-in-the-middle position was General Motors with its Oldsmobile car. The original car (the Oldsmobile Rocket V8) was highly differentiated with a 6-litre V8 engine, which was virtually indestructible, very fast and highly reliable. In order to cut costs this engine was replaced with the same engine that went into the 5-litre Chevrolet V8. This had less power and was less reliable. The result was catastrophic: sales plummeted.

Firms need to understand the generic basis for their success and resist the temptation to blur strategy by making inconsistent moves. For example, a no-frills cost leader or focuser should beware of the pitfalls of moving to a higher cost base (perhaps by adding on expensive services). A focus strategy involves limiting sales volume. Once domination of the target segment has been achieved there may be a temptation to move into other segments in order to achieve growth with the same competitive advantage. This can be a mistake if the new segments do not value the firm's competitive advantage in the same way.

Differentiation and cost leadership strategies are incompatible in most situations: differentiation is achieved through higher costs. However, there are circumstances when both can be achieved simultaneously. For example, a differentiation strategy may lead to market share domination that lowers costs through economies of scale and learning effects; or a highly differentiated firm pioneers a major process innovation that significantly reduces manufacturing costs, leading to a cost leadership position. When differentiation and cost leadership coincide, performance is exceptional since a premium price can be charged for a low-cost product. This is akin to achieving the dual position of high effectiveness and high efficiency discussed in Chapter 1.

Sources of competitive advantage

In order to create a differentiated or lowest cost position, a firm needs to understand the nature and location of the potential sources of competitive advantage. The nature of these sources are the superior skills and resources of a firm. Management benefit by analysing the superior skills and resources that offer, or could contribute to, competitive advantage (i.e. differentiation or lowest cost position). Their identification can be aided by **value chain** analysis (see Figure 12.5). A value chain comprises the discrete activities a firm carries out in order to perform its business.

Superior skills

These are the distinctive capabilities of key personnel, which set them apart from the personnel of competing firms. The benefit of superior skills is the resulting ability to perform functions more effectively than other firms. For example, superior selling skills may result in closer relationships with customers than competing firms can achieve. Superior quality assurance skills can result in improved and more consistent product quality.

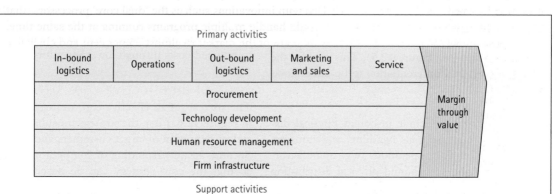

Figure 12.5 The value chain
Source: Porter M.E. (1985) *Competitive Advantage*, New York: The Free Press, 37. Reprinted with the permission of The Free Press, an imprint of Simon & Schuster. Copyright © 1985 by Michael E. Porter.

Exhibit 12.5 The marketing resources involved in the creation of the distinct M&M's characters has enabled the brand to appeal to both children and adults, and to prosper in a very competitive market

Superior resources

The tangible requirements for advantage that enable a firm to exercise its skills are known as superior resources (see Exhibit 12.5). Superior resources include:

- the number of salespeople in a market
- expenditure on advertising and sales promotion
- distribution coverage (the number of retailers who stock the product)
- expenditure on R&D
- scale of and type of production facilities
- financial resources
- brand equity
- knowledge.

Value chain

The value chain provides a useful method for locating superior skills and resources. All firms consist of a set of activities that are conducted to design, manufacture, market, distribute and service its products. The value chain categorizes these into primary and support activities (see Figure 12.5). This enables the sources of costs and differentiation to be understood and located.

- *Primary activities* include in-bound physical distribution (e.g. materials handling, warehousing, inventory control), operations (e.g. manufacturing, packaging), out-bound physical distribution (e.g. delivery, order processing), marketing (e.g. advertising, selling, channel management) and service (e.g. installation, repair, customer training).
- *Support activities* are found within all of these primary activities and consist of purchased inputs,

technology, human resource management and the firm's infrastructure. These are not defined within a given primary activity because they can be found in all of them. Purchasing can take place within each primary activity, not just in the purchasing department; technology is relevant to all primary activities, as is human resource management; and the firm's infrastructure—which consists of general management, planning, finance, accounting and quality management—supports the entire value chain.

If management examines each value-creating activity, it can pinpoint the skills and resources that may form the basis of low cost or differentiated positions (see Marketing in Action 12.5). To the extent that skills and resources exceed or could be developed to exceed the competition, they form the key sources of competitive advantage. Not only should the skills and resources within value-creating activities be examined but the *linkages* between them should also be examined. For example, greater co-ordination between operations and in-bound physical distribution may give rise to reduced costs through lower inventory levels.

Tests of an effective core strategy

The six tests of an effective core strategy are detailed in Figure 12.6. First, the strategy must be based upon a clear definition of target customers and their needs. Second, an understanding of competitors is required so that the core strategy can be based on a competitive advantage. Third, the strategy must incur acceptable risk. Challenging a strong competitor with a weak competitive advantage and a low resource base would not incur acceptable risk. Fourth, the strategy should be resource and managerially supportable. It

Marketing in Action 12.5: Luxottica redefines the value chain

Study guide: Below is a review of the growth of Luxottica in the eyewear business. Using the value chain framework, identify its sources of competitive advantage.

Luxottica Group, which was founded in Italy in 1967, is the world's biggest eyewear company. The eyewear business is a complex one with a variety of segments, ranging from prescription glasses to top-of-the range designer sunglasses. Luxottica began manufacturing prescription frames but quickly branched into sunglasses capitalizing on the growth of that part of the business. Its best-known brand is RayBan but it also manufactures a variety of other labels, including Persol, Vogue, Luxottica and Revo. In 1988, it signed its first licensing deal, with Armani. This aspect of its business has grown rapidly and it now supplies glasses under a wide variety of brands, including Chanel, Prada, Dolce & Gabbana, Versace, Polo, Ralph Lauren and many others.

But while most of its competitors in the Italian eyewear industry chose to focus on manufacturing, Luxottica decided to integrate further aspects of the value chain into its business. In 1995, it branched into retail with the takeover of LensCrafters, the biggest optical retailer in America. This was followed in 2001 by the acquisition of Sunglass Hut, the world's leading retailer of sunglasses, and in 2004 it also purchased Cole National, another big US retailer. This integration of manufacturing and retailing was a revolution for the industry and retail now accounts for over two-thirds of Luxottica's revenues. It also represents a major difference between it and its major rival, Safilo, in Italy. Both are roughly equal in size in terms of manufacturing but Safilo only has 50 retail outlets compared with Luxottica's 5700 stores.

Luxottica's focus is the mid-priced and premium segments of the market. But in controlling both production and retailing, it has been able to capture the value added at different stages of the supply chain. Combined with production efficiencies, Luxottica is the world's lowest-cost producer of eyewear, while at the same time being able to charge premium prices for designer frames. Careful management of the value chain has enabled the company to reap significant profits.

Based on: Anonymous (2007);[27] Owen (2007)[28]

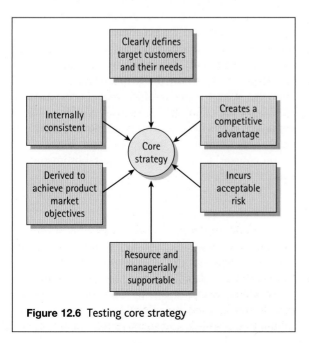

Figure 12.6 Testing core strategy

should match the resource capabilities and managerial competences of the business. Fifth, core strategy should be derived from the product and marketing objectives established as part of the planning process. A strategy (e.g. heavy promotion), which makes commercial logic following a build objective may make no sense when a harvesting objective has been decided. Finally, the strategy should be internally consistent. The elements should blend to form a coherent whole.

Marketing mix decisions

Decisions regarding each of the elements of the marketing mix make up the next stage of the planning process. As we have seen, these decisions consist of judgements about price levels, the blend of promotional techniques to employ, the distribution channels and service levels to use, and the types of products to manufacture. Where promotional, distribution and product standards surpass those of the competition, a competitive advantage may be gained. Alternatively, a judgement may be made only to match or even undershoot the competition on some elements of the marketing mix. To outgun the competition on everything is not normally feasible. Choices have to be made about how the marketing mix can be manipulated to provide a superior offering to the customer at reasonable cost.

Organization and implementation

It is said that no marketing plan will succeed unless it 'degenerates into work'.[29] Consequently, the business must design an organization that has the capabilities necessary to implement the plan. Indeed, organizational weaknesses discovered as part of the SWOT analysis may restrict the feasible range of strategic options. Reorganization could mean the establishment of a marketing organization or department in the business. A study of manufacturing organizations by Piercy[30] found that 55 per cent did not have a marketing department. In some cases, marketing was carried out by the chief executive, in others the sales department dealt with customers and no need for other marketing inputs was perceived. In other situations, environmental change may cause strategic change, and this may imply reorganization of marketing and sales. The growth of large corporate customers with enormous buying power has resulted in businesses focusing their resources more firmly on meeting their needs (strategy change), which has led in turn to dedicated marketing and sales teams being organized to service these accounts (reorganization).

Control

Control is the final stage in the marketing planning process. The aim of control systems is to evaluate the results of the marketing plan so that corrective action can be taken if performance does not match objectives. Short-term control systems can plot results against objectives on a weekly, monthly, quarterly and/or annual basis. Measures include sales profits, costs and cash flow. Strategic control systems are more long term. Managers need to stand back from week-by-week and month-by-month results to critically reassess whether their plans are in line with their capabilities and the environment.

Where this kind of long-term control perspective is lacking this may result in the pursuit of plans that

Table 12.3 Key questions and the process of marketing planning

Key questions planning	Stages in marketing
Where are we now and how did we get there?	Business mission Marketing audit SWOT analysis
Where are we heading?	Marketing audit SWOT analysis
Where would we like to be?	Marketing objectives
How do we get there?	Core strategy Marketing mix decisions Organization Implementation
Are we on course?	Control

have lost strategic credibility. New competition, changes in technology and moving customer requirements may have rendered old plans obsolete. This, of course, returns the planning process to the beginning since this kind of fundamental review is conducted in the marketing audit. It is the activity of assessing internal capabilities and external opportunities and threats that results in a SWOT analysis. This outcome may mean a redefinition of the business mission, and, as we have seen, changes in marketing objectives and strategies to realign the business with its environment.

How, though, do the stages in marketing planning we have looked at relate to the fundamental planning questions stated earlier in this chapter? Table 12.3 shows this relationship. The questions 'Where are we now?' and 'How did we get there?' are answered by the business mission definition, the marketing audit and SWOT analysis. 'Where are we heading?' is forecast by reference to the marketing audit and SWOT analysis. 'Where would we like to be?' is determined by the setting of marketing objectives. 'How do we get there?' refers to core strategy, marketing mix decisions, organization and implementation. Finally 'Are we on course?' is answered by the establishment of a control system.

Marketing metrics

A key emerging area of control is that of marketing metrics. The marketing discipline has traditionally been criticized for the quality of its metrics. For example, sales revenues are an important metric but many of the factors influencing sales levels are outside the control of marketers, such as economic conditions or competitor activity. And because marketers

Table 12.4 The use of marketing metrics in UK firms

Rank	Metric	% using measure	% rating it as important
1	Profit/profitability	92	80
2	Sales, value and/or volume	91	71
3	Gross margin	81	66
4	Awareness	78	28
5	Market share (value/volume)	78	37
6	Number of new products	73	18
7	Relative price	70	36
8	Customer dissatisfaction	69	45
9	Customer satisfaction	68	48
10	Distribution/availability	66	18

Source: Ambler, Kokkinaki and Puntoni (2004)[31]

are not good at measuring what they do, they are often poorly represented in corporate boardrooms compared with disciplines such as production and finance. In addition, marketing budgets are often the first to be cut when companies need to make cost savings.

As a result, more attention than ever is being paid to the metrics used to measure marketing activity. A vast array of potential metrics can be identified.[32] In short, there are two key elements of marketing measurement, namely the effectiveness of operational marketing activity and the impact of marketing on the bottom line. Measuring the former is contingent on the type of marketing activity undertaken. For example, distribution activity can be measured by inventory levels, markdowns, facings and out-of-stock levels. But, ultimately, marketing decisions must contribute to increasing profits by increasing sales volumes, increasing prices or reducing unit costs.[33] The most common metrics in use in UK firms are shown in Table 12.4.

The rewards of marketing planning

Various authors[34,35,36] have attributed the following benefits to marketing planning.

- *Consistency*: the plan provides a focal point for decisions and actions. By reference to a common plan, decisions by the same manager over time, and by different managers, should be more consistent and actions co-ordinated more effectively.
- *Encourages the monitoring of change*: the planning process forces managers to step away from day-

to-day problems and review the impact of change on the business from a strategic perspective.

- *Encourages organizational adaptation*: the underlying premise of planning is that the organization should adapt to match its environment. Marketing planning, therefore, promotes the necessity to accept the inevitability of change. This is an important consideration since adaptive capability has been shown to be linked to superior performance.[37]
- *Stimulates achievement*: the planning process focuses on objectives, strategies and results. It encourages people to ask 'What can we achieve given our capabilities?' As such, it motivates people, who otherwise might be content to accept much lower standards of performance, to set new horizons for objectives.
- *Resource allocation*: the planning process asks fundamental questions about resource allocation. For example, which products and services should receive high investment (build), which should be maintained (hold), which should have resources withdrawn slowly (harvest), and which should have resources withdrawn immediately (divest).
- *Competitive advantage*: planning promotes the search for sources of competitive advantage.

However, it should be borne in mind that this logical planning process, sometimes referred to as synoptic, may be at variance with the culture of the business, which may plan effectively using an *incremental* approach.[38] The style of planning must match business culture.[39] Saker and Speed argue that the considerable demands on managers in terms of time and effort implied by the synoptic marketing planning process may mean that alternative planning schemes are more appropriate, particularly for small companies.[40]

An incremental planning approach is more focused on problems, in that the process begins with the realization of a problem (for example, a fall-off in orders) and continues with an attempt to identify a solution. As solutions to problems form, so strategy emerges. However, little attempt is made to integrate consciously the individual decisions that could possibly affect one another. Strategy is viewed as a loosely linked group of decisions that are handled individually. Nevertheless, its effect may be to attune the business to its environment through its problem-solving nature. Its drawback is that the lack of a broad situation analysis and strategy option generation renders the incremental approach less comprehensive. For some companies, however, its inherent practicality, rather than its rationality, may support its use.[41]

Problems in making planning work

Research into the marketing planning approaches of commercial firms has discovered that most companies did not practise the kinds of systematic planning procedure described in this chapter and, of those that did, many did not enjoy the rewards described above.[42] However, others have shown that there is a relationship between planning and commercial success (e.g. Armstrong and McDonald).[43,44] The problem is that the 'contextual difficulties' associated with the process of marketing planning are substantial and need to be understood. In as much as forewarned is forearmed, the following paragraphs offer a checklist of potential problems that have to be faced by those charged with making marketing planning work.

Political

Marketing planning is a process of resource allocation. The outcome of the process is an allocation of more funds to some products and departments, and the same or less to others. Since power bases, career opportunities and salaries are often tied to whether an area is fast or slow growing, it is not surprising that managers view planning as a highly political activity. An example is a European bank, whose planning process resulted in the decision to insist that its retail branch managers divert certain types of loan application to the industrial/merchant banking arm of the group where the return was greater. This was required because the plan was designed to optimize the return to the group as a whole. However, the consequence of this was considerable friction between the divisions concerned because the decision lowered the performance of the retail branch.

Opportunity cost

Some busy managers take the view that marketing planning is a time-wasting process that interferes with the need to deal with day-to-day problems. They view the opportunity cost of spending two or three days away at a hotel thrashing out long-term plans as too high. This difficulty may be compounded by the fact that people who are attracted to the hectic pace of managerial life may be the type who prefer to live that way. Hence, they may be ill at ease with the thought of a long period of sedate contemplation.

Reward systems

In business, reward systems are increasingly being geared to the short term. More and more incentives and bonuses are linked, not just to annual but to quarterly results. Managers may thus overemphasize short-term issues and underemphasize medium- and long-term concerns if there is a conflict of time. Marketing planning, then, may be viewed as of secondary importance.

Information

A systematic marketing planning system needs informational inputs in order to function effectively. Market share, size and growth rates are basic inputs into the marketing audit, but may be unavailable. More perversely, information may wilfully be withheld by those with vested interests who, recognizing that knowledge is power, distort the true situation to protect their position in the planning process.

Culture

Efforts to establish a systematic marketing planning process may be at odds with the culture of an organization. As we have already seen, businesses may 'plan' by making incremental decisions. Hence, the strategic planning system may challenge the status quo and be seen as a threat. In other cases, the values and beliefs of some managers may be altogether hostile to a planning system.

How to handle marketing planning problems

Various authors[45,46] have proposed the following recommendations for minimizing the impact of these problems.

- *Senior management support*: top management must be committed to planning and be seen by middle management to give it total support. This should be ongoing support, not a short-term fad.
- *Match the planning system to the culture of the business*: how the marketing planning process is

managed should be consistent with the culture of the organization. For example, in some organizations the top-down/bottom-up balance will move towards top-down; in other less directive cultures the balance will move towards a more bottom-up planning style.

- *The reward system*: this should reward the achievement of longer-term objectives rather than focus exclusively on short-term results.
- *Depoliticize outcomes*: less emphasis should be placed on rewarding managers associated with build (growth) strategies. Recognition of the skills involved in defending share and harvesting products should be made. At General Electric managers are classified as growers, caretakers and

undertakers, and matched to products that are being built, defended or harvested in recognition of the fact that the skills involved differ according to the strategic objective. No stigma is attached to caretaking or undertaking; each is acknowledged as contributing to the success of the organization.

- *Clear communication*: plans should be communicated to those charged with implementation.
- *Training*: marketing personnel should be trained in the necessary marketing knowledge and skills to perform the planning job. Ideally, the management team should attend the same training course so that they each share a common understanding of the concepts and tools involved, and can communicate using the same terminology.

Summary

In this chapter we have examined the important issues of marketing planning and marketing strategy. The following key issues were addressed.

1. The role of marketing planning is to give direction to the organization's marketing effort and to co-ordinate its activities. It helps to answer core questions like, where are we now, where would we like to be and how do we get there.

2. The various stages of the marketing planning process include developing or adjusting the business mission, conducting a marketing audit, conducting a SWOT analysis, setting marketing objectives, deciding the core strategy, making marketing mix decisions, and organizing, implementing and controlling the marketing effort.

3. The marketing audit is divided into an external audit, which examines environmental and competitive conditions, and an internal audit, which reviews marketing decisions and operating results. The information generated by a marketing audit should guide managerial choices regarding future directions for the organization.

4. Marketing objectives need to be decided at two levels, namely strategic thrusts and strategic objectives. Strategic thrusts deal with the ways in which the organization can grow; there are four core choices, namely market penetration, product development, market development and diversification. Strategic objectives are decided for each product and again there are four choices, namely build, hold, harvest and divest.

5. As well as decisions regarding how to grow, organizations also need to make choices regarding how to compete. Four strategies are available, namely differentiation, cost leadership, differentiation focus and cost focus. Value chain analysis can assist companies to identify the skills and resources necessary to implement effective competitive strategies.

6. There are a number of rewards to be gained for pursuing careful planning, including consistency, encouraging the monitoring of change, encouraging organizational adaptation, stimulating achievement, resource allocation and competitive advantage.

7. Making planning work is difficult because of office politics, perceived opportunity costs, pressures for short-term results, availability of the necessary information and cultural issues. However, top management leadership, matching planning to organizational culture, reward systems, and communication and training can all help to overcome these problems.

Key terms

business mission the organization's purpose, usually setting out its competitive domain, which distinguishes the business from others of its type

competitor analysis an examination of the nature of actual and potential competitors, their objectives and strategies

competitor targets the organizations against which a company chooses to compete directly

control the stage in the marketing planning process or cycle when the performance against plan is monitored so that corrective action can be taken, if necessary

core strategy the means of achieving marketing objectives, including target markets, competitor targets and competitive advantage

customer analysis a survey of who the customers are, what choice criteria they use, how they rate competitive offerings and on what variables they can be segmented

differentiation strategy the selection of one or more customer choice criteria, and positioning the offering accordingly to achieve superior customer value

distribution analysis an examination of movements in power bases, channel attractiveness, physical distribution and distribution behaviour

industry a group of companies that market products that are close substitutes for each other

marketing audit a systematic examination of a business's marketing environment, objectives, strategies and activities, with a view to identifying key strategic issues, problem areas and opportunities

marketing objectives there are two types of marketing objective—strategic thrust, which dictates which products should be sold in which

markets, and strategic objectives, which are product-level objectives, such as build, hold, harvest and divest

marketing planning the process by which businesses analyse the environment and their capabilities, decide upon courses of marketing action and implement those decisions

marketing structures the marketing frameworks (organization, training and internal communications) on which marketing activities are based

marketing systems sets of connected parts (information, planning and control) that support the marketing function

strategic business unit a business or company division serving a distinct group of customers and with a distinct set of competitors, usually strategically autonomous

strategic issues analysis an examination of the suitability of marketing objectives and segmentation bases in the light of changes in the marketplace

strategic objectives product-level objectives relating to the decision to build, hold, harvest or divest products

strategic thrust the decision concerning which products to sell in which markets

SWOT analysis a structured approach to evaluating the strategic position of a business by identifying its strengths, weaknesses, opportunities and threats

target market a segment that has been selected as a focus for the company's offering or communications

value chain the set of the firm's activities that are conducted to design, manufacture, market, distribute and service its products

Study questions

1. Discuss some of the difficulties that can be encountered in making marketing planning work in an organization. How can these difficulties be overcome?

2. Discuss the role and limitations of the external analysis phase of marketing planning.

3. Under what circumstances may incremental planning be preferable to synoptic marketing planning, and vice versa?

4. Compare and contrast a cost leadership strategy

with a differentiation strategy. Is it possible to pursue both strategies simultaneously?

5. Discuss why it is important for marketers to be able to measure and justify the effectiveness of marketing activities.

6. Visit www.bplans.com, www.knowthis.com/general/marketplan.htm and www.howstuffworks.com/marketing-plan.htm. Review some of the sample marketing plans available on these sites.

Suggested reading

Day, G.S. (1999) *Market Driven Strategy: Processes for Creating Value*, New York: Free Press.

Gulati, R. and **J.B. Oldroyd** (2005) The Quest For Customer Focus, *Harvard Business Review*, **83** (4), 92–102

McDonald, M.H.B. (2008) *Marketing Plans*, 4th edn, Oxford: Heinemann.

Porter, M.E. (1980) *Competitive Strategy: Techniques for Analysing Industries and Competitors*, New York: Free Press.

Shaw, R. and **D. Merrick** (2005) *Marketing Payback: Is Your Marketing Profitable?* London: Pearson Education.

Sidhu, J. (2003) Mission Statements: Is it Time To Shelve Them?, *European Management Journal*, **21** (4), 439–47.

References

1. **London, S.** (2006) Google's Random Genius is no Accidental Strategy, Can it Last?, *Financial Times*, 1 February, 13; **Waters, R.** (2008) Google Triumphant, *Financial Times*, 13 May, 11.

2. **Piercy, N.** (2002) *Market-led Strategic Change: Transforming the Process of Going to Market*, Oxford: Heinemann.

3. **Day, G.S.** (1984) *Strategic Marketing Planning: The Pursuit of Competitive Advantage*, St Paul, MN: West, 41.

4. **Ackoff, R.I.** (1987) Mission statements, *Planning Review*, **15** (4), 30–2.

5. **Hooley, G.J., A.J. Cox** and **A. Adams** (1992) Our Five Year Mission: To Boldly Go Where No Man Has Been Before . . . , *Journal of Marketing Management*, **8** (1), 35–48.

6. **Wilson, T.** (1992) Realizing the Power of Strategic Vision, *Long Range Planning*, **25** (5), 18–28.

7. **Porter, M.E.** (1980) *Competitive Strategy: Techniques for Analyzing Industries and Competitors*, New York: Free Press.

8. **Anonymous** (2005) Nose to Nose, *Economist*, 25 June, 77–9.

9. **Done, K.** (2007) Airbus Hopes its Troubles Will Finally Take Flight, *Financial Times*, 15 October, 23.

10. **Marlowe, L.** (2005) New Jet Could Carry Up to 800 Passengers, *Irish Times*, 18 January, 10.

11. **Urry, M.** (2005) Chilled Food Gets a Frosty Reception, *Financial Times*, 8 August, 23.

12. **Wiggins, J.** (2005) Food Groups See the Benefits of Chilling Out, *Financial Times*, 25 October, 29.

13. **Nakamoto, M.** (2005) Caught in its Own Trap: Sony Battles to Make Headway in a Networked World, *Financial Times*, 27 January, 17.

14. **Rigby, E.** (2008) DSG Contracts With a View to Improved Service, *Financial Times*, 16 May, 17.

15. **Reed, J.** (2007) Jump-start in the Race to go Electric, *Financial Times*, 11 December, 18.

16. **Woody, T.** (2007) Have You Driven a Fjord Lately, *CNNMoney.com*, 31 July.

17. **Anonymous** (2005) Fast Food's Yummy Secret, *Economist*, 27 August, 53–5.

18. **Nuttall, C.** (2004) Google Writes its Place in the World's History Books, *Financial Times*, 16 December, 24.

19. **Hall, W.K.** (1980) Survival Strategies in a Hostile Environment, *Harvard Business Review*, **58** (Sept/Oct), 75–85.

20. **Day, G.S.** (1999) *Market Driven Strategy: Processes for Creating Value*, New York: Free Press.

21. **Mackintosh, J.** (2004) Volkswagen Misfires: The Carmaker Counts the Cost of its High Spending and its Faltering Search for Luxury, *Financial Times*, 9 March, 19.

22. **Buckley, N.** (2003) Domino's Returns to Fast Food's Fast Lane, *Financial Times*, 26 November, 14.

23. **Fifield, A.** (2003) Kiwibank Can Afford to Hold Critics to Account, *Financial Times*, 24 April, 11.

24. **Anonymous** (2006) Not Paranoid Enough, *Economist*, 27 May, 58–9.

25. **Nuttall, C.** (2006) AMD Tempts Fortune with $5.4 billion ATI Buy, *Financial Times*, 25 July, 25.

26. **Nuttall, C.** (2007) Intel Eats Away at AMD's Share of Chips, *Financial Times*, 3 May, 25.

27. **Anonymous** (2007) Looking East, *Economist*, 8 October, 69.

28. **Owen R.** (2007) Oakley Goes to Luxottica in $2bn Deal, www.timesonline.co.uk, 22 June.

29. **Drucker, P.F.** (1993) *Management Tasks, Responsibilities, Practices*, New York: Harper & Row, 128.

30. **Piercy, N.** (1986) The Role and Function of the Chief Marketing Executive and the Marketing Department, *Journal of Marketing Management*, **1** (3), 265–90.

31. **Ambler, T., F. Kokkinaki** and **S. Puntoni** (2004) Assessing Marketing Performance: Reasons for Metrics Selection, *Journal of Marketing Management*, **20**, 475–98.

32. **Farris, P.W., N.T. Bendle, P.E. Pfeifer** and **D.J. Reibstein** (2006) *Marketing Metrics*, New Jersey: Wharton Publishing Company.

33. **Shaw, R.** and **D. Merrick** (2005) *Marketing Payback: Is Your Marketing Profitable?* London: Pearson Education.

34. **Leppard, J.W.** and **M.H.B. McDonald** (1991) Marketing Planning and Corporate Culture: A Conceptual Framework which Examines Management Attitudes in the Context of Marketing Planning, *Journal of Marketing Management*, **7** (3), 213–36.

35. **Greenley, G.E.** (1986) *The Strategic and Operational Planning of Marketing*, Maidenhead: McGraw-Hill, 185–7.

36. **Terpstra, V.** and **R. Sarathy** (1991) *International Marketing*, Orlando, FL: Dryden, Ch. 17.

37. **Oktemgil, M.** and **G. Greenley** (1997) Consequences of High and Low Adaptive Capability in UK Companies, *European Journal of Marketing*, **31** (7), 445–66.

38. **Raimond, P.** and **C. Eden** (1990) Making Strategy Work, *Long Range Planning*, **23** (5), 97–105.

39. **Driver, J.C.** (1990) Marketing Planning in Style, *Quarterly Review of Marketing*, **15** (4), 16–21.

40. **Saker, J.** and **R. Speed** (1992) Corporate Culture: Is it Really a Barrier to Marketing Planning?, *Journal of Marketing Management*, **8** (2),
177–82. For information on marketing and planning in small and medium-sized firms, see **Carson, D.** (1990) Some Exploratory Models for Assessing Small Firms' Marketing Performance: A Qualitative Approach, *European Journal of Marketing*, **24** (11), 8–51; and **Fuller, P.B.** (1994) Assessing Marketing in Small and Medium-sized Enterprises, *European Journal of Marketing*, **28** (12), 34–9.

41. **O'Shaughnessy, J.** (1995) *Competitive Marketing*, Boston, MA: Allen & Unwin.

42. **Greenley, G.** (1987) An Exposition into Empirical Research into Marketing Planning, *Journal of Marketing Management*, **3** (1), 83–102.

43. **Armstrong, J.S.** (1982) The Value of Formal Planning for Strategic Decisions: Review of Empirical Research, *Strategic Management Journal*, **3** (3), 197–213.

44. **McDonald, M.H.B.** (1984) *The Theory and Practice of Marketing Planning for Industrial Goods in International Markets*, Cranfield Institute of Technology, PhD thesis.

45. **McDonald, M.H.B.** (1984) *The Theory and Practice of Marketing Planning for Industrial Goods in International Markets*, Cranfield Institute of Technology, PhD thesis.

46. **Abell, D.F.** and **J.S. Hammond** (1979) *Strategic Market Planning*, Englewood Cliffs, NJ: Prentice-Hall.

Case 12 The turnaround at LEGO

LEGO, the iconic Danish toy maker, is best known for its LEGO brick, which was voted 'Toy of the 20th Century' and was a must-have for generations of children. However, after years of uninterrupted growth, the company began to experience its first losses in the early part of this decade. The toy market had changed, with young consumers increasingly attracted to technologically based products like computer games and MP3 players. Competition had also increased, with toys made in low-cost countries eroding margins. LEGO made the biggest loss in its history in 2003 and its very survival was threatened. However, some tough management decisions have brought the company back on track, though it still faces several challenges in a rapidly changing industry.

History

In 1932 Ole Kirk Christiansen, a Danish carpenter, established a business making wooden toys. He named the company 'LEGO' in 1934, which comes from the Danish words 'leg godt', meaning 'play well'. Later, coincidentally, it was discovered that in Latin it means, 'I put together'. The LEGO name was chosen to represent company philosophy, where play is seen as integral to a child's successful growth and development. In 1947 the company began to make plastic products and in 1949 it launched its world-famous automatic building brick. Ole Kirk Christiansen was succeeded by his son Godtfred in 1950, and under this new leadership the LEGO group introduced the revolutionary 'LEGO System of Play', which focused on the importance of learning through play. The company began exporting in 1953 and soon developed a strong international reputation.

The LEGO brick, with its new interlocking system, was launched in 1958. During the 1960s LEGO began to use wheels, small motors and gears to give its products the power of motion. LEGOLAND was established in Billund in 1968, as a symbol of LEGO creativity and imagination. Later, in the 1990s, two new parks were opened in Britain and California. LEGO figures were introduced in 1974, giving the LEGO brand a personality. The 1980s saw the beginning of digital development, with LEGO forming a partnership with Media Laboratory at the Massachusetts Institute of Technology in the USA. This resulted in the launch of LEGO TECHNIC Computer Control and paved the way for LEGO

robots. LEGO introduced a constant flow of new products in the 1990s, and placed greater focus on intelligence and behaviour. The new millennium saw LEGO crowned the 'Toy of the Century' by *Fortune* magazine and the British Association of Toy Retailers, and everyone on earth has an average of 52 of them. LEGO is currently the fifth largest toy manufacturer in the world after Mattel, Hasbro, Bandai and MGA Entertainment, with a presence in over 130 countries.

Challenges for the toy market

A number of environmental shifts have been affecting the toy market over the past decade. Some of these are described below.

- *Kids getting older younger.* By the time most kids reach the age of eight they have outgrown the offerings of the traditional toy market. A central factor in children abandoning toys earlier is their lack of free time to play. Children today have a lot more scheduled activities and, with greater emphasis on academic achievement, a lot more time is spent studying. Faced with more media and entertainment choices these sophisticated and technologically savvy consumers are favouring electronic, fashion, make-up and lifestyle products. The most susceptible group to this age compression are 'tweens'—children between the ages of 8 and 12—a US$5 billion market, accounting for 20 per cent of the US$20.7 billion toy industry.
- *Intensifying competition from the electronic and games market.* Today's young consumer is far more likely to be seen surfing the web, texting on their mobile phone, listening to their MP3 player or playing on their Game Boy than enjoying a LEGO set. A survey by NPD Funworld, in 2003, found that tween boys who played video games spent approximately 40 per cent less time playing with action figures when compared with the previous year. Handheld toys with a video and gaming element suit the mobile lifestyle of today's tween. As demand for these more sophisticated toys increases, traditional toy makers are facing more direct competition with the electronic and video games market.
- *Fickleness of young consumers.* The toy market today is very fashion-driven, leading to shorter product life cycles. Toy manufacturers are facing increasing pressure to develop a competency in

forecasting market changes and improving their speed of response to those changes. In an effort to get a share of the huge revenues generated by the latest hot toy, many toy manufacturers have left themselves more vulnerable to greater earnings volatility.

- *Power of the retail sector.* Consolidation in the retail sector and the expansion of many retail chains has placed enormous pressure on the profit margins of toy makers. Major retailers can exert tremendous power over their suppliers because of the vast quantities they buy. Many retailers insert a clause in their supplier contracts that gives them a certain percentage of profit regardless of the retail price.

What went wrong for LEGO?

According to Kjeld Kirk Kristiansen, owner of the business and grandson of its founder, following many years of success the LEGO culture had become 'inward looking' and 'complacent' and had failed to keep pace with the changes taking place in the toy market. This lack of environmental sensitivity was evident in the US market in 2003, where LEGO failed to predict demand for its Bionicle figures, resulting in two of its best-selling products from this range being out of stock in the run-up to Christmas. It appeared nothing had been learned from the previous year, when also in the run-up to Christmas the much sought-after Hogwarts Castle sets were out of stock across the UK.

LEGO had also become over-dependent on licences in the 1990s, for products such as Star Wars and Harry Potter, as its main source of growth. This left LEGO vulnerable to the faddishness of these products: the years in which the Star Wars and Harry Potter films were released coincided with profitable years for LEGO, while losses were reported in the intervening years.

The diversification of the brand into the manufacture of items such as clothing, bags and accessories was another mistake for LEGO. The company over-complicated its product portfolio and it ran close to over-stretching the LEGO brand.

The phasing-out of its long-established pre-school Duplo brand, to be replaced by LEGO Explore, was another error. Parents were left confused, with many believing the larger-size Duplo brick had been discontinued. This error resulted in a loss of revenues from the pre-school market in 2003. Adult fans of LEGO (AFOLs) were also left disgruntled when LEGO changed the colour of its new building bricks so that they no longer matched the colour of the old bricks.

The turnaround

LEGO hit rock bottom in 2003 when it made a DKr1.6 billion loss and had debts of over DKr5 billion. Rumours abounded that the world's largest toy maker, Mattel, would attempt a takeover and the company was also seen as a prime target for takeover by private equity groups given that it was a medium-sized firm, still in the hands of the Kristiansen family.

But, instead, the family decided to stand by their business. They injected DKr800 million of their own funds into it and appointed Jorgen Vig Knudstorp, a former McKinsey management consultant, to get the company back on track. To do so LEGO has developed a number of new marketing and business strategies. These included the following.

- A back-to-basics strategy saw LEGO refocus on its core brick-based product range and place more emphasis on its key target group—boys aged five to nine. Classic ranges such as the Duplo brand have been reinstated and LEGO also introduced the Quarto brand, which consists of larger bricks for children under two. While the traditional audience for LEGO has always been young boys it has introduced a new range, 'Clikits', a social toy developed specifically for a female audience. Clikits consists of pretty pastel-coloured bricks, which provide numerous options to create jewellery and fashion accessories.
- LEGO has sought huge efficiencies in its business including, laying off about 3500 of its 8000 workforce, and factories in Switzerland and the USA have been closed down, with production moved to Eastern Europe and Mexico. Specialized and skills-related production has been retained at the group's headquarters in Billund. A more simplified management structure and performance-based pay systems have also been introduced.
- LEGO has admitted to over-diversifying its brand. In response to this, a majority stake in its four LEGOLAND theme parks was sold to the Blackstone Group in 2005 and several of its brand extensions in sectors like clothing have been deleted from its range.
- As part of its diversification, the company had also engaged in a range of licensing deals with other brands. Many of these have been trimmed but the Bionicle range, which was launched in 2001, continues to be key. The Bionicles combine physical snap-together kits with an online virtual world. This toy brand has also been

Table C12.1 LEGO financial information

LEGO financial information (mDKK)	2006	2005	2004	2003	2002
Income statement					
Revenue	7,823	7,050	6,704	7,196	10,116
Expenses	(6,475)	(6,582)	(6,601)	(8,257)	(9,248)
Profit/(loss) before special items, financial income and expenses and tax	1,348	468	103	(1,061)	868
Impairment of fixed assets	292	95	(723)	(172)	–
Restructuring expenses	(112)	(104)	(502)	(283)	–
Operating profit/(loss)	1,528	459	(1,122)	(1,516)	868
Financial income and expenses	34	(3)	(115)	18	(251)
Profit/(loss) before tax	1,562	456	(1,237)	(1,498)	617
Profit/(loss) on continuing activities	1,430	331	(1,473)	(953)	348
Profit/(loss) on discontinuing activities	–	174	(458)	18	(22)
Net profit/(loss) for the year	1,430	505	(1,931)	(935)	326
Employees: Average number of employees (full-time), continuing activities	4,922	531	5,569	6,542	6,659

extended into entertainment in the form of comics, books and a Miramax movie: *Bionicle: Mask of Light*.

- Sub-brands that LEGO has neglected, including Mindstorms and LEGO TECHNIC, both aimed at older children and enjoyed by some adults, are being given more attention. With so many adult fans of LEGO, efforts are also being made to further engage with this market.

- LEGO has overhauled its packaging, and the style and tone of its advertising. The emphasis is now being placed on the LEGO play and educational experience as opposed to product detail. The strap-line 'play on' was introduced in January 2003 to accompany the change. The slogan draws its inspiration from the company's five core values: creativity, imagination, learning, fun and quality. LEGO is also making greater use of more interactive communication tools to promote its products, which it is believed will encourage consumers to interact more with the brand. 2005 has seen LEGO invite fans on a tour of the company. Here they are given the opportunity to meet new product developers, designers and toolmakers, and learn about the company's history, culture and values.

- The company established the LEGO Vision Lab in 2002 to examine how the future will look to children and their families. A variety of sources are being used to make assessments of future worldwide family patterns, including anthropology, architecture, consumer patterns and awareness, culture, philosophy, sociology and technology. Its creative core of about 120 designers from 15 different countries will be critical to its future success.

These strategies have combined to bring LEGO back to profitability through increased revenues and reduced cost levels (see Table C12.1).

Alpha Rex from the Lego Mindstorm Range

Conclusion

LEGO has made a remarkable turnaround in a short space of time. But the rapid competitive, economic and market-based changes taking place in the industry will continue to present many challenges. The company has returned to its core ethos of supplying products that enable good play. This vision has helped LEGO to become a global company, and it has also got it through the most challenging period in its history. But it will also have to continue to develop its product range to meet the educational and play needs of future generations of children and their parents. As an example of this, it launched legofactory.com, where customers can build models before having the pieces sent to them, and can upload them on to websites such as Flickr and YouTube.

Questions

1. Why did LEGO encounter serious financial difficulties in the early part of the decade?
2. Conduct a SWOT analysis of LEGO and identify the company's main sources of advantage.
3. Critically evaluate the LEGO's competitive strategy.

This case was prepared by Sinéad Moloney and Professor John Fahy, University of Limerick, as a basis for classroom discussion rather than to show effective or ineffective management.

Bibliography

The material in this case was drawn from the following sources.

Anonymous (2006) LEGO's Turnaround: Picking up the Pieces, *Economist*, 28 October, 80.

Brown-Humes, C. (2004) After the Crash: LEGO Picks up the Pieces, *Financial Times*, 2 April, 10.

Carter, M. (2003) LEGO's Bid to Rebuild and Keep its Balance, *Financial Times*, 28 October, 8–9.

Foster, L. (2004) Toys are Child's Play No More, *Financial Times*, 10 June, 12.

Goodman, M. (2004) LEGO's Rescue Brick by Brick, *The Sunday Times*, Business Section 1, 14 November.

Mortimer, R. (2003) Building a Brand out of Bricks, *Brand Strategy*, April, 16–19.

Sibun, J. (2008) LEGO Renaissance Builds on Key Strengths, 28 January, www.telegraph.co.uk.

Widdicombe, R. (2004) Online: Building Blocks for the Future, *Guardian*, 29 April, 19.

www.lego.com.

Glossary

ad hoc research a research project that focuses on a specific problem, collecting data at one point in time with one sample of respondents

administered vertical marketing system a channel situation where a manufacturer that dominates a market through its size and strong brands may exercise considerable power over intermediaries even though they are independent

advertising any paid form of non-personal communication of ideas or products in the prime media (i.e. television, the press, posters, cinema and radio, the internet and direct marketing)

advertising agency an organization that specializes in providing services such as media selection, creative work, production and campaign planning to clients

advertising message the use of words, symbols and illustrations to communicate to a target audience using prime media

advertising platform the aspect of the seller's product that is most persuasive and relevant to the target consumer

ambush marketing any activity where a company tries to associate itself or its products with an event without paying any fee to the event owner

attitude the degree to which a customer or prospect likes or dislikes a brand

awareness set the set of brands that the consumer is aware may provide a solution to a problem

beliefs descriptive thoughts that a person holds about something

benefit segmentation the grouping of people based on the different benefits they seek from a product

bonus pack pack giving the customer extra quantity at no additional cost

brainstorming the technique whereby a group of people generate ideas without initial evaluation; only when the list of ideas is complete is each one then evaluated

brand a distinctive product offering created by the use of a name, symbol, design, packaging, or some combination of these, intended to differentiate it from its competitors

brand equity the goodwill associated with a brand name, which adds tangible value to a company through the resulting higher sales and profits

brand extension the use of an established brand name on a new brand within the same broad market

brand stretching the use of an established brand name for brands in unrelated markets

brand values the core values and characteristics of a brand

business analysis a review of the projected sales, costs and profits for a new product to establish whether these factors satisfy company objectives

business mission the organization's purpose, usually setting out its competitive domain, which distinguishes the business from others of its type

buying centre a group that is involved in the buying decision; also known as a decision-making unit (DMU) in industrial buying situations

buzz marketing the passing of information about products or services by verbal or electronic means in an informal person-to-person manner

catalogue marketing the sale of products through catalogues distributed to agents and customers, usually by mail or at stores

cause-related marketing the commercial activity by which businesses and charities or causes form a partnership with each other to market an image, product or service for mutual benefit

channel integration the way in which the players in the channel are linked

channel intermediaries organizations that facilitate the distribution of products to customers

channel of distribution the means by which products are moved from the producer to the ultimate consumer

channel strategy the selection of the most effective distribution channel, the most appropriate level of distribution intensity and the degree of channel integration

choice criteria the various attributes (and benefits) people use when evaluating products and services

classical conditioning the process of using an established relationship between a stimulus and a response to cause the learning of the same response to a different stimulus

cognitive dissonance post-purchase concerns of a consumer arising from uncertainty as to whether a decision to purchase was the correct one

cognitive learning the learning of knowledge, and development of beliefs and attitudes without direct reinforcement

communications-based co-branding the linking of two or more existing brands from different companies or business units for the purposes of joint communication

competitive advantage a clear performance differential over the competition on factors that are important to target customers

competitive bidding drawing up detailed specifications for a product and putting the contract out to tender

competitor analysis an examination of the nature of actual and potential competitors, their objectives and strategies

competitor targets the organizations against which a company chooses to compete directly

concept testing testing new product ideas with potential customers

consumer movement an organized collection of groups and organizations whose objective it is to protect the rights of consumers

consumer panel household consumers who provide information on their purchases over time

consumer pull the targeting of consumers with communications (e.g. promotions) designed to create demand that will *pull* the product into the distribution chain

continuous research repeated interviewing of the same sample of people

contractual vertical marketing system a franchise arrangement (e.g. a franchise) tying producers and resellers together

control the stage in the marketing planning process or cycle when the performance against plan is monitored so that corrective action can be taken, if necessary

core strategy the means of achieving marketing objectives, including target markets, competitor targets and competitive advantage

corporate vertical marketing system a channel situation where an organization gains control of distribution through ownership

culture the traditions, taboos, values and basic attitudes of the whole society in which an individual lives

customer analysis a survey of who the customers are, what choice criteria they use, how they rate competitive offerings and on what variables they can be segmented

customer benefits those things that a customer values in a product; customer benefits derive from product features (see separate entry)

customer relationship management (CRM) the methodologies, technologies and e-commerce capabilities used by firms to manage customer relationships

customer satisfaction the fulfilment of customers' requirements or needs

customer value perceived benefits minus perceived sacrifice

customized marketing a market coverage strategy where a company decides to target individual customers and to develop separate marketing mixes for each

database marketing an interactive approach to marketing, which uses individually addressable marketing media and channels to provide information to a target audience, stimulate demand and stay close to customers

decision-making process the stages that organizations and people pass through when purchasing a physical product or service

depth interviews the interviewing of consumers individually for perhaps one or two hours with the aim of understanding their attitudes, values, behaviour and/or beliefs

differential advantage a clear performance differential over competition on factors that are important to target customers

differentiated marketing a market coverage strategy where a company decides to target several market segments and to develop separate marketing mixes for each

differentiation strategy the selection of one or more customer choice criteria, and positioning the offering accordingly to achieve superior customer value

diffusion of innovation process the process by which a new product spreads throughout a market over time

direct mail material sent through the postal service to the recipient's house or business address, promoting a product and/or maintaining an ongoing relationship

direct marketing (1) acquiring and retaining customers without the use of an intermediary; (2) the distribution of products, information and promotional benefits to target consumers through interactive communication in a way that allows response to be measured

direct response advertising the use of the prime advertising media, such as television, newspapers and magazines, to elicit an order, enquiry or a request for a visit

distribution analysis an examination of movements in power bases, channel attractiveness, physical distribution and distribution behaviour

distribution push the targeting of channel intermediaries with communications (e.g. promotions) to *push* the product into the distribution chain

e-commerce the use of technologies such as the internet, electronic data interchange (EDI), email and electronic payment systems to streamline business transactions

economic value to the customer (EVC) the amount a customer would have to pay to make the total life cycle costs of a new and a reference product the same

effectiveness doing the right thing, making the correct strategic choice

efficiency a way of managing business processes to a high standard, usually concerned with cost reduction; also called 'doing things right'

electronic data interchange (EDI) a pre-internet technology, which was developed to permit organizations to use linked computers for the rapid exchange of information

environmental scanning the process of monitoring and analysing the marketing environment of a company

ethics the moral principles and values that govern the actions and decisions of an individual or group

event sponsorship sponsorship of a sporting or other event

evoked set the set of brands that the consumer seriously evaluates before making a purchase

exaggerated promises barrier a barrier to the matching of expected and perceived service levels caused by the unwarranted building up of expectations by exaggerated promises

exclusive distribution an extreme form of selective distribution where only one wholesaler, retailer or industrial distributor is used in a geographical area to sell the products of a particular supplier

exhibition an event that brings buyers and sellers together in a commercial setting

experiental marketing the term used to describe marketing activities that involve the creation of experiences for consumers

experimentation the application of stimuli (e.g. two price levels) to different matched groups under controlled conditions for the purpose of measuring their effect on a variable (e.g. sales)

exploratory research the preliminary exploration of a research area prior to the main data collection stage

family brand name a brand name used for all products in a range

focus group a group, normally of six to eight consumers, brought together for a discussion focusing on an aspect of a company's marketing

focused marketing a market coverage strategy where a company decides to target one market segment with a single marketing mix

franchise a legal contract in which a producer and channel intermediaries agree each other's rights and obligations; the intermediary usually receives marketing, managerial, technical and financial services in return for a fee

full cost pricing pricing so as to include all costs, and based on certain sales volume assumptions

generic brands brand names that have become so popular that product categories actually become known by the brand name

geodemographics the process of grouping households into geographic clusters based on such information as type of accommodation, occupation, number and age of children, and ethnic background

global branding achievement of brand penetration worldwide

going-rate prices prices at the rate generally applicable in the market, focusing on competitors' offerings rather than on company costs

group discussion a group, usually of six to eight consumers, brought together for a discussion focusing on an aspect of a company's marketing strategy

hall tests bringing a sample of target consumers to a room that has been hired so that alternative marketing ideas (e.g. promotions) can be tested

horizontal electronic marketplaces online procurement sites that cross several industries and are typically used to source low-cost supplies such as MRO items

inadequate delivery barrier a barrier to the matching of expected and perceived service levels caused by the failure of the service provider to select, train and reward staff adequately, resulting in poor or inconsistent delivery of service

inadequate resources barrier a barrier to the matching of expected and perceived service levels caused by the unwillingness of service providers to provide the necessary resources

individual brand name a brand name that does not identify a brand with a particular company

industry a group of companies that market products that are close substitutes for each other

information framing the way in which information is presented to people

information processing the process by which a stimulus is received, interpreted, stored in memory and later retrieved

information search the identification of alternative ways of problem solving

ingredient co-branding the explicit positioning of a supplier's brand as an ingredient of a product

inseparability a characteristic of services, namely that their production cannot be separated from their consumption

intangibility a characteristic of services, namely that they cannot be touched, seen, tasted or smelled

integrated marketing communications the concept that companies co-ordinate their marketing communications tools to deliver a clear, consistent, credible and competitive message about the organization and its products

intensive distribution the aim of intensive distribution is to provide saturation coverage of the market by using all available outlets

internet a vast global computer network that permits instant communication, such as the gathering and sharing of information, and that offers the facility for users to communicate with one another

internet marketing the achievement of marketing objectives through the utilization of the internet and web-based technologies

just-in-time (JIT) the JIT concept aims to minimize stocks by organizing a supply system that provides materials and components as they are required

key account management an approach to selling that focuses resources on major customers and uses a team selling approach

lifestyle the pattern of living as expressed in a person's activities, interests and opinions

lifestyle segmentation the grouping of people according to their pattern of living as expressed in their activities, interests and opinions

macroenvironment a number of broader forces that affect not only the company but the other actors in the environment, e.g. social, political, technological and economic

manufacturer brands brands that are created by producers and bear their chosen brand name

marginal cost pricing the calculation of only those costs that are likely to rise as output increases

market segmentation the process of identifying individuals or organizations with similar characteristics that have significant implications for the determination of marketing strategy

market testing the limited launch of a new product to test sales potential

marketing audit a systematic examination of a business's marketing environment, objectives, strategies and activities, with a view to identifying key strategic issues, problem areas and opportunities

marketing concept the achievement of corporate goals through meeting and exceeding customer needs better than the competition

marketing environment the actors and forces that affect a company's capability to operate effectively in providing products and services to its customers

marketing ethnography the study of consumer behaviour in its naturally occurring context, through observation and/or discussion

marketing information system a system in which marketing information is formally gathered, stored, analysed and distributed to managers in accordance with their informational needs on a regular, planned basis

marketing mix a framework for the tactical management of the customer relationship, including product, place, price, promotion (the 4-Ps); in the case of services, three other elements to be taken into account are process, people and physical evidence

marketing objectives there are two types of marketing objective—strategic thrust, which dictates which products should be sold in which markets, and strategic objectives, which are product-level objectives, such as build, hold, harvest and divest

marketing orientation companies with a marketing orientation focus on customer needs as the primary drivers of organizational performance

marketing planning the process by which businesses analyse the environment and their capabilities, decide upon courses of marketing action and implement those decisions

marketing research the gathering of data and information on the market

marketing structures the marketing frameworks (organization, training and internal communications) on which marketing activities are based

marketing systems sets of connected parts (information, planning and control) that support the marketing function

mass customization the opposite to mass production, which means that all products produced are customized to the predetermined needs of a specific customer

media class decision the choice of prime media (i.e. the press, cinema, television, posters, radio) or some combination of these

media vehicle decision the choice of the particular newspaper, magazine, television spot, poster site, etc.

microenvironment the actors in the firm's immediate environment that affect its capability to operate effectively in its chosen markets— namely, suppliers, distributors, customers and competitors

misconceptions barrier a failure by marketers to understand what customers really value about their service

mobile marketing the sending of text messages to mobile phones to promote products and build relationships with customers

modified rebuy where a regular requirement for the type of product exists and the buying alternatives are known but sufficient (e.g. a delivery problem has occurred) to require some alteration to the normal supply procedure

money-off promotions sales promotions that discount the normal price

motivation the process involving needs that set drives in motion to accomplish goals

multichannel marketing the distribution of products through a number of different channels to reach the consumer

new task refers to the first-time purchase of a product or input by an organization

omnibus survey a regular survey, usually operated by a market research specialist company, which asks questions of respondents

operant conditioning the use of rewards to generate reinforcement of response

own-label brands brands created and owned by distributors or retailers

parallel co-branding the joining of two or more independent brands to produce a combined brand

parallel importing when importers buy products from distributors in one country and sell them in another to distributors who are not part of the manufacturer's normal distribution; caused by significant price differences for the same product between different countries

perception the process by which people select, organize and interpret sensory stimulation into a meaningful picture of the world

perishability a characteristic of services, namely that the capacity of a service business, such as a hotel room, cannot be stored—if it is not occupied, there is lost income that cannot be recovered

permission marketing marketers ask permission before sending advertisements or promotional material to potential customers; in this way customers 'opt in' to the promotion rather than having to 'opt out'

personal selling oral communication with prospective purchasers with the intention of making a sale

personality the inner psychological characteristics of individuals that lead to consistent responses to their environment

place the distribution channels to be used, outlet locations, methods of transportation

portfolio planning managing groups of brands and product lines

positioning the choice of target market (*where* the company wishes to compete) and differential advantage (*how* the company wishes to compete)

premiums any merchandise offered free or at low cost as an incentive to purchase

price (1) the amount of money paid for a product; (2) the agreed value placed on the exchange by a buyer and seller

price escalation the additional costs incurred in taking products to an international market, including transportation costs, distribution costs, taxes and tariffs, exchange rates and inflation rates

price unbundling pricing each element in the offering so that the price of the total product package is raised

product a good or service offered or performed by an organization or individual, which is capable of satisfying customer needs

product features the characteristics of a product that may or may not convey a customer benefit

product life cycle a four-stage cycle in the life of a product, illustrated as a curve representing the demand; the four stages being introduction, growth, maturity and decline

product line a group of brands that are closely related in terms of the functions and benefits they provide

product mix the total set of products marketed by a company

product placement the deliberate placing of products and/or their logos in movies and television programmes, usually in return for money

product-based co-branding the linking of two or more existing brands from different companies or business units to form a product in which the brand names are visible to the consumer

production orientation a business approach that is inwardly focused either on costs or on a definition of a company in terms of its production facilities

profile segmentation the grouping of people in terms of profile variables such as age and socio-economic group so that marketers can communicate to them

promotional mix advertising, personal selling, sales promotion, public relations and direct marketing

prospecting searching for and calling upon potential customers

proximity marketing the localized wireless distribution of advertising content associated with a particular place

psychographic segmentation the grouping of people according to their lifestyle and personality characteristics

psychological pricing taking into consideration the psychological impact of the price level that is being set

public relations the management of communications and relationships to establish goodwill and mutual understanding between an organization and its public

publicity the communication of a product or business by placing information about it in the media without paying for time or space directly

qualitative research exploratory research that aims to understand consumers' attitudes, values, behaviour and beliefs

reasoning a more complex form of cognitive learning where conclusions are reached by connected thought

reference group a group of people that influences an individual's attitude or behaviour

relationship marketing the process of creating, maintaining and enhancing strong relationships with customers and other stakeholders

repositioning changing the target market or differential advantage, or both

research brief written document stating the client's requirements

research proposal a document defining what the marketing research agency promises to do for its client and how much it will cost

retail audit a type of continuous research tracking the sales of products through retail outlets

retail positioning the choice of target market and differential advantage for a retail outlet

reverse marketing the process whereby the buyer attempts to persuade the supplier to provide exactly what the organization wants

rote learning the learning of two or more concepts without conditioning

safety (buffer) stocks stocks or inventory held to cover against uncertainty about resupply lead times

sales promotion incentives to customers or the trade that are designed to stimulate purchase

salesforce evaluation the measurement of salesperson performance so that strengths and weaknesses can be identified

salesforce motivation the motivation of salespeople by a process that involves needs, which set encouraging drives in motion to accomplish goals

sampling process a term used in research to denote the selection of a subset of the total population in order to interview them

secondary research data that has already been collected by another researcher for another purpose

selective attention the process by which people screen out those stimuli that are neither meaningful to them nor consistent with their experiences and beliefs

selective distortion the distortion of information received by people according to their existing beliefs and attitudes

selective distribution the use of a limited number of outlets in a geographical area to sell the products of a particular supplier

selective retention the process by which people retain only a selection of messages in memory

service any deed, performance or effort carried out for the customer

services marketing mix product, place, price, promotion, people, process and physical evidence

shareholder value the returns to a company's shareholders, which grow when the company increases its dividends or its share price rises

social responsibility the ethical principle that a person or an organization should be accountable for how its actions might affect the physical environment and the general public

sponsorship a business relationship between a provider of funds, resources or services and an individual, event or organization that offers in return some rights and association that may be used for commercial advantage

straight rebuy refers to a purchase by an organization from a previously approved supplier of a previously purchased item

strategic business unit a business or company division serving a distinct group of customers and with a distinct set of competitors, usually strategically autonomous

strategic issues analysis an examination of the suitability of marketing objectives and segmentation bases in the light of changes in the marketplace

strategic objectives product-level objectives relating to the decision to build, hold, harvest or divest products

strategic thrust the decision concerning which products to sell in which markets

SWOT analysis a structured approach to evaluating the strategic position of a business by identifying its strengths, weaknesses, opportunities and threats

target audience the group of people at which an advertisement or message is aimed

target market a segment that has been selected as a focus for the company's offering or communications

target marketing selecting a segment as the focus for a company's offering or communications

telemarketing a marketing communications system whereby trained specialists use telecommunications and information technologies to conduct marketing and sales activities

test marketing the launch of a new product in one or a few geographic areas chosen to be representative of the intended market

trade-off analysis a measure of the trade-off customers make between price and other product features, so that their effects on product preference can be established

undifferentiated marketing a market coverage strategy where a company decides to ignore market segment differences and to develop a single marketing mix for the whole market

value chain the set of the firm's activities that are conducted to design, manufacture, market, distribute and service its products

value-based marketing a perspective on marketing which emphasizes how a marketing philosophy and marketing activities contribute to the maximization of shareholder value

variability a characteristic of services, namely that being delivered by people the standard of their performance is open to variation

vertical electronic marketplaces online procurement sites that are dedicated to sourcing supplies for producers in one particular industry

vicarious learning learning from others without direct experience or reward

viral marketing electronic word of mouth, where promotional messages are spread using email from person to person

website a collection of various files including text, graphics, video and audio content created by organizations and individuals

Author Index

Companies and Brands Index

Page locators in **bold** refer to main entries and those in *italics* refer to illustrations

Subject Index